CONSTITUTIONS AND THE CLASSICS

Constitutions and the Classics

Patterns of Constitutional Thought from Fortescue to Bentham

Edited by
D. J. GALLIGAN

OXFORD
UNIVERSITY PRESS

OXFORD
UNIVERSITY PRESS

Great Clarendon Street, Oxford, OX2 6DP,
United Kingdom

Oxford University Press is a department of the University of Oxford. It furthers the University's objective of excellence in research, scholarship, and education by publishing worldwide. Oxford is a registered trade mark of Oxford University Press in the UK and in certain other countries

First Edition published in 2014

Published in the United States of America by Oxford University Press
198 Madison Avenue, New York, NY 10016, United States of America

British Library Cataloguing in Publication Data
Data available

Library of Congress Control Number: 2014942351

ISBN 978–0–19–871498–9

Preface

This collection of essays is the product of a programme of workshops that took place at Oxford University between 2008 and 2012. The aim of the programme was to examine from a constitutional perspective the writings of a selection of authors who may justly be considered to have provided the classics of legal and political theory in the British, French, and American contexts. The emphasis is on the British, beginning with John Fortescue in the fifteenth century and ending with Jeremy Bentham in the nineteenth. In light of the constitutional ferment in the United States and France in the late eighteenth century, the interconnections with the British system, and the enduring influence of the ideas that emerged, a selection of French and American writers from that time has been included. Some of the authors were deliberately constitutional theorists, while for others whose aims were different it is a matter of drawing out the constitutional aspects.

Both the programme of workshops and this volume were made possible by the support of two institutions, the *Foundation for Law, Justice and Society* (FLJS) and the *Centre for Socio-Legal Studies* (CSLS). The FLJS conceived, organized, and funded the programme, while the CSLS contributed through its academic support and the involvement of many of its academic staff and research students. I wish to thank the Chairman of the FLJS, Mr John W. Adams, lawyer, businessman, and philanthropist, for his very generous intellectual and financial support over many years. The contributors join me in acknowledging with appreciation and gratitude the outstanding support of the FLJS, its Chairman, and the Board of Trustees.

The CSLS is a long-established research institute within Oxford University dedicated to the study of law in society and the training of research students. The FLJS is an independent institute, affiliated with the CSLS and hence Oxford University, which was created in 2005 by John Adams and myself to provide a forum for discussion of the role of law in society. Central to our mission is the bringing together of academic researchers and scholars, and practitioners and professionals, to share and discuss ideas and interests. Our intention is to make academic research relating to the role of law in society more accessible to practitioners and professionals, whether these are lawyers, government officials, businesses, or the institutions of civil and international society.

If this volume of essays seems at first sight to be relentlessly academic, on closer inspection it will become plain that the issues with which the classic authors grappled at different times and in different societies are still at the foundation of contemporary issues. I have no doubt that constitution-makers, practitioners, and interpreters would derive considerable benefit from close attention to the ideas discussed, the problems confronted, and the solutions offered. One does not have to look far to see that, far from constitutional history having reached its apogee somewhere in the twentieth century, constitutions remain a site of contention, a focus of conflict, and a domain of ignorance and misunderstanding.

On behalf of all the contributors, I wish to thank members of the FLJS Ms Judy Niner and Ms Amy Richards, who organized the workshops, arranged travel and accommodation, and handled the many aspects of an international programme of this kind. Mr Phil Dines is thanked as Communications Director and for creating and maintaining an excellent website displaying the work of the FLJS: <http://www.fljs.org>.

I would like to thank Dr Tanya Baldwin for applying her literary and editorial expertise to the essays, with support from Ms Claire Palmer, who is joint author with me of the introductory essay. The Law Faculty of Oxford University and Wolfson College are thanked for making funds available for editing.

I offer special thanks to Dr Christopher Brooke of Bristol University whose counsel was invaluable in the selection of the classic authors and the scholars best suited to write about them. Professor Mark Philp of Warwick University also gave advice on various matters and for that he is warmly thanked. Our final thanks go to Oxford University Press for publishing the collection, and the editors Mr Alex Flach, Ms Natasha Flemming, Dr Elissa Hansen, and Ms Briony Ryles.

D. J. Galligan

Oxford
September 2014

Contents

List of Contributors ix

1. Patterns of Constitutional Thought from Fortescue to Bentham 1
   D. J. Galligan and C. Palmer
2. Sir John Fortescue and the Political Dominium: The People, the Common Weal, and the King 51
   M. R. L. L. Kelly
3. Edward Coke 86
   Ian Williams
4. Constitutions in Hobbes's Science of Politics 108
   Tom Sorell
5. The Levellers, the People, and the Constitution 122
   D. J. Galligan
6. Locke's Contribution to the Intellectual Foundations of Modern Constitutionalism 152
   Jean-Fabien Spitz
7. Narrative Constitutionalism and the Kinetics of James Harrington's *Oceana* 169
   J. C. Davis
8. David Hume: Constitution by Convention 191
   John W. Adams
9. William Blackstone and the 'free Constitution of Britain' 210
   Wilfrid Prest
10. Jeremy Bentham 231
    Philip Schofield
11. Montesquieu 250
    Giovanni Grottanelli de'Santi
12. The General Will Constitution: Rousseau as a Constitutionalist 265
    Ruzha Smilova
13. L'Abbé de Sieyès: Champion of National Representation, Father of Constitutions 290
    Raymond Kubben

14. 'Perfection in Imperfection': Joseph de Maistre and the Limitations of Constitutional Design 312
Mila Versteeg

15. James Madison's Republican Constitutionalism 327
Mark A. Graber

16. The Constitutional Thought of Alexander Hamilton 354
M. N. S. Sellers

17. Jefferson's Constitutions 369
Gerald Leonard

18. John Adams, Constitution Monger 389
David Thomas Konig

19. Thomas Paine 414
Richard Whatmore

Index 439

List of Contributors

John W. Adams is President of the Board of Trustees at the Foundation for Law, Justice and Society in Oxford and an Adjunct Professor of Political Science at Rutgers University. From 1984 to 2004, he served as president of Smith Management Company, an investment firm in New York City. He holds degrees from Rutgers University (BA, History), Seton Hall University (JD), and New York University (LLM).

J. C. Davis, Emeritus Professor of History at the University of East Anglia, has written extensively on utopian thought and the political and religious thought of the mid-seventeenth century English Revolution. In particular, he has published five substantial essays on the thought of James Harrington. A revised edition of his book *Oliver Cromwell* (Bloomsbury, 2001), which assesses Cromwell and his reputation, is in preparation and due to be published in 2017.

Denis J. Galligan is Professor of Socio-Legal Studies at the University of Oxford. He is also a Professorial Fellow of Wolfson College, Jean Monnet Professor of European Public Law at the Università degli Studi di Siena, and a Visiting Professor at the Woodrow Wilson School of Public and International Affairs at Princeton University. His works include *Law in Modern Society* (Oxford University Press, 2005), *Due Process and Fair Procedures* (Clarendon, Oxford, 1997) and *Discretionary Powers* (Clarendon, Oxford, 1987).

Mark A. Graber is a Professor of Law at the University of Maryland Carey School of Law. He is the author of *A New Introduction to American Constitutionalism* (Oxford University Press, 2013) and three other books, as well as a co-editor of the *American Constitutionalism* series.

Giovanni Grottanelli de'Santi read law at the University of Siena and was a postgraduate at the Yale Law School. In the course of his academic life spent at the Universities of Siena and Florence he has published an extensive number of books, essays, and book reviews, mainly in the field of judicial control of legislative and administrative action, decentralization and self government, and civil liberties. He has lectured often in various European and American universities. In Great Britain he has been a visiting fellow in Cambridge (Wolfson; Trinity) and Oxford (Lincoln; Wolfson).

M. R. L. L. Kelly holds degrees in English Literature (University of Queensland) and Law (Australian National University) and a doctorate in Constitutional History and Constitutional Law (Macquarie University). She is a senior lecturer at Macquarie Law School, Sydney, where she teaches Administrative Law, and Politics and the Constitution.

David Thomas Konig earned his PhD in History at Harvard University. He is Professor of History and Professor of Law at Washington University in St. Louis, where he teaches courses on the American Founding, Anglo-American Legal History, and Property Law. He has published on constitutional law and the Bill of Rights, the development of the rule of law in colonial and early national America, and the law of slavery and freedom. His current projects include a monograph on the legal thought and practice of Thomas Jefferson and an annotated edition of Jefferson's legal commonplace book.

Raymond Kubben is a legal historian. In 2009, he obtained his PhD at Tilburg University (the Netherlands) with a thesis on legal relations between the French and Batavian Republics from 1795 to 1803 (*Regeneration and Hegemony*, Leiden: Brill, 2011). Up to

July 2014 he worked as Assistant Professor at Tilburg Law School teaching International Legal History, Research Methods, Early Modern Political History, and History of Dutch Public Administration. He presently serves as legal and policy adviser to the Education Council of the Netherlands. His contribution to this volume was written *à titre personnel.*

Gerald Leonard is Professor of Law and Law Alumni Scholar at Boston University School of Law. He is the author of *The Invention of Party Politics* (University of North Carolina Press, 2002) and numerous articles on American constitutional and political history. He co-edits the pamphlet series New Essays on American Constitutional History for the American Historical Association and writes on the history and theory of American criminal law.

Claire Palmer graduated with Bachelor of Laws and Bachelor of Commerce from the University of Sydney in 2005 after receiving the Henry S. Albinski Prize for Best Undergraduate Thesis in Australian Foreign and Defence Policy. She is the recipient of a Clarendon Scholarship to study the MPhil/DPhil (International Relations) at the University of Oxford, and has taught International Relations in several Oxford colleges. Her research interests include international law, business and human rights, and constitution-writing and institution-building in post-conflict countries.

Wilfrid Prest has long been interested in law, lawyers, and legal institutions, although his degrees from the universities of Melbourne and Oxford are in Modern History, and he has taught History, mainly at the University of Adelaide, since 1966. Besides the outline survey *Albion Ascendant: English History 1660–1815* (1998), Prest has written *The Rise of the Barristers: A Social History of the English Bar 1590–1640* (1986) and most recently *William Blackstone: Law and Letters in the Eighteenth Century* (2008, 2012), all published by Oxford University Press. He has also edited Blackstone's correspondence for the Selden Society.

Philip Schofield is Professor of the History of Legal and Political Thought in the Faculty of Laws and Director of the Bentham Project, University College London. He is General Editor of the new authoritative edition of *The Collected Works of Jeremy Bentham*, and has edited or co-edited ten volumes in the series. He has published *Utility and Democracy: the Political Thought of Jeremy Bentham* (Oxford University Press, 2006), winner of the W. J. M. Mackenzie Book Prize awarded by the Political Studies Association, and *Bentham: A Guide for the Perplexed* (Continuum, 2009).

Mortimer Newlin Stead Sellers is Regents Professor of the University System of Maryland and Director of the University of Baltimore Center for International Law. Among his books are: *American Republicanism: Roman Ideology in the United States Constitution* (1994); *The Sacred Fire of Liberty: Republicanism, Liberalism and the Law* (1998); and *Republican Legal Theory: The History, Constitution and Purposes of Law in a Free State* (2003). Prof. Sellers is editor of the book series *Studies in the History of Law and Justice* and of *ASIL Studies in International Legal Theory.* He was educated at Harvard University (AB, JD) and as a Rhodes Scholar and Frank Knox Fellow at University College, Oxford (BCL, DPhil).

Ruzha Smilova is a senior assistant professor at the Political Science Department of Sofia University, where she teaches History of Political Ideas and Contemporary Political Philosophy. Her academic research is focused on such issues as the authority of democracy, normative and positive theories of democracy, and the relation of media to democracy. She is also a programme director at the Centre for Liberal Strategies, an independent think-tank in Sofia, where she participates in research and policy-related projects on voting behaviour, participation in politics, and the quality of representative institutions, among others. Dr Smilova holds a doctorate from the Central European University in Budapest. Her dissertation, 'A reason-based justification for liberal-democratic authority', received a CEU award in 2006.

Tom Sorell is Professor of Politics and Philosophy at the University of Warwick. He is the author of *Hobbes* (Routledge, 1986), editor of *The Cambridge Companion to Hobbes* (Cambridge University Press, 1994), and co-editor (with John Rogers) of *Hobbes and History* (Routledge, 2000), (with Luc Foisneau) of Leviathan *After 350 Years* (Oxford University Press, 2004), and (with Luc Foisneau and Jean-Christophe Merle) of Leviathan *Between the Wars* (Peter Lang, 2005).

Jean-Fabien Spitz teaches Political Philosophy and the History of Political Thought in the University of Paris 1 Panthéon-Sorbonne. He is the author of several books, including *La liberté politique* (Presses universitaires de France, 1995); *John Locke et les fondements de la liberté moderne* (Presses universitaires de France, 2001); *Le moment républicain en France* (Gallimard, 2005); and *Le Mythe de l'impartialité* (Presses universitaires de France, 2014).

Mila Versteeg is an Associate Professor of Law at the University of Virginia School of Law. She holds a DPhil from the Oxford Centre for Socio-Legal Studies, an LLM from Harvard Law School, and first law degree from Tilburg University. Her research is mainly in the area of constitutions.

Richard Whatmore is Professor of Modern History at the University of St Andrews, where he directs the St Andrews Institute of Intellectual History. He is the author of *Republicanism and the French Revolution* (Oxford University Press, 2000) and *Against War and Empire* (Yale University Press, 2012).

Ian Williams is a lecturer in the Faculty of Laws at University College London, specializing in Early Modern Legal History. His work on the royal prerogative and equity was awarded the David Yale prize by the Selden Society in 2014.

1

Patterns of Constitutional Thought from Fortescue to Bentham

*D. J. Galligan and C. Palmer**

I. Aims and Authors

The main question in reflecting on constitutions is how a community, a people, a nation is to govern itself or be governed. This raises issues about the nature of society, the role of government, and relations between government and the people. Any community, people, or nation from the least advanced to the most modern has to confront and resolve these issues. They have long preoccupied the minds of lawyers, philosophers, and statesmen, and although much has changed in the social, economic, political, and technological spheres—so that the society of Aristotle bears faint resemblance to that of seventeenth-century England, eighteenth-century France, or twenty-first-century central Europe—the fundamental questions remain the same and the answers fall into familiar patterns.

Questions about constitutions are also practical. They concern the creation of institutions responsible for governing, the definition of their powers and responsibilities, and the formulation of rules for their exercise. We live in an age of unprecedented activity in constitution-making. Although there is always some traffic in creating, amending, and abandoning constitutions, no earlier period rivals the years since the Second World War, a period marked by constitutional activity in Europe, post-colonial Africa, post-communist central and eastern Europe, and post-dictatorships in South America. The constitution-making that has followed the Arab Spring in North Africa and the Middle East continues this trend.

Each nation is now expected to have a constitution set out in a single document, partly as a symbol of nationhood and a sign of membership of the international community, and partly in hope that it will provide the foundations for internal peace, stability, and the protection of rights, as well as effective government. A text containing all the right provisions is often a necessary condition of aid and support for development from external sources. Constitution-making is a complex and exacting process, where several aims and purposes compete and sectional interests

* We wish to thank several colleagues who have offered comments on this essay: G. Grottanelli de'Santi, B. Hass, D. Konig, W. Prest, P. Schofield, M. Sellers, and R. Smilova.

are prone to conflict. One aim is to resolve past problems and make provisions for the future; another is the creation of a system of government and institutions that will be effective and reasonably permanent in coordinating society and politics; a third is to meet international expectations. Constitutions include a statement of values and aspirations; they often project a sense of national identity and may become an instrument of social cohesion.[1]

Constitutions owe much to the accumulation of ideas over time so that each nation has to address issues in a setting made and moderated by its history and culture.[2] Yet contemporary constitutions, especially those towards the democratic end of the scale, have a common heritage, conform to common conventions, and pursue common aims and purposes. All this occurs within a shared tradition of ideas and ideals, and draws on a history of practical experience in governing and being governed. Among the approaches that contribute to contemporary ideas, the British tradition merits a special place for the constitutional legacy it has left. Despite the absence of a single text, British history and experience have been a formative influence on constitutional thought. Our aim in compiling this collection of essays is to give an account of that legacy by examining the ideas on constitutions of a selection of authors from the fifteenth century to the early nineteenth century. These ideas have earlier origins but, in confronting fuller forms of nationhood from which emerged the modern state, this period is critical to the character of modern constitutions. The English constitution was transformed from being one of monarchical rule, subject to limited constraints imposed by law and by duties to consult and obtain consent of aristocracy and commons, to a system of representative parliamentary government. Changes at the practical constitutional level were accompanied by a wealth of literature on constitutions, written from different and often competing perspectives. They include such names as Hobbes, Locke, Harrington, Hume, and Bentham, as well as a host of others, including Coke, the Levellers, and Blackstone, and many lesser figures. All were engaged in the constitutional affairs of the day, by which they were often provoked into setting out their ideas. Whether or not they influenced the issues of the time, all retain an interest as more than local writers embroiled in local matters, for the themes they treat are timeless in understanding constitutions.

By historical coincidence, as the self-assured English Parliament of the late eighteenth century was laying claim to sovereignty and the balanced constitution was being celebrated, major constitutional change and upheaval were taking place in America and France. The inclusion of a selection of authors from the revolutionary era in both nations—an era of intense discussion, reflection, and practical action—adds to the attraction of this collection. The American constitutionalists and the colonists before them inherited the conventions, understandings, and

[1] For a fuller analysis of the social foundations of constitutions, see D. J. Galligan and M. Versteeg, 'Theoretical Perspectives on the Social and Political Foundations of Constitutions', in D. J. Galligan and M. Versteeg (eds), *The Social and Political Foundations of Constitutions* (Oxford: Oxford University Press, 2013).

[2] See further G. Vico, *New Science Principles of the New Science Concerning the Common Nature of Nations* (1744) (London: Penguin Books, 1999).

outlook of the English constitution, and looked to authors such as Locke, Harrington, Hume, and Sydney for guidance. In their search for a new republicanism as an alternative to the monarchy but one capable of sustaining effective government in a modern nation, American writers added to the canon of constitutional thought and practice in a manner that still repays study. This is clearly demonstrated in the writings of the four American authors within this collection, comprising James Madison, Alexander Hamilton, Thomas Jefferson, and John Adams.

Events in France ran more or less parallel to those in America, although triggered by different causes, conducted with different aims in mind, and resulting in strikingly different outcomes. The writings of Jean-Jacques Rousseau, who preceded the revolution, and had earlier offered advice on the constitutions of Poland and Corsica, loomed large over constitutional debates and constitution-drafting, particularly in relation to popular sovereignty and the general will of the nation. Emmanuel Sieyès was an active participant in, and perhaps the dominant presence over, the discussion and design of the revolutionary constitution. Sieyès advanced a theory of representation, which despite being at odds with direct self-government has become the foundation of modern constitutional thought, practice, and texts. Both Montesquieu who preceded the revolution, and de Maistre who survived it, reflected on the nature of constitutions and constitutional government. Their approaches differ but their understandings of society and the limits of rational planning in human affairs are similar. The extent to which the French writers, in the course of creating their own canon of constitutional ideas, drew on, engaged with, and challenged the British and the American writers, deserves more attention than it has received.[3] The relationship among the authors of the three nations—the British, the French (although bearing in mind that Rousseau was Swiss), and the Americans—brings into sharp focus the similarities and differences in their approaches. Despite the fact that each group could support a volume of its own, and although the focus here is mainly British, we gain a sense of the traffic and tension amongst the three groups by including a selection of the leading figures from France and America.

Other periods, other nationalities, and other authors could have been chosen, and each reader is likely to be disappointed that a preferred name does not appear. Some not included are mentioned briefly, such as Thomas Smith, Richard Hooker, Algernon Sydney, and Edmund Burke, each of whom added to the stock of constitutional thought but not, in our opinion, to the extent sufficient to earn a place in a limited collection. The experience of a different set of nations could have been the focus of attention—the Greek city states, the medieval Italian republics, renaissance Europe, the Polish–Lithuanian kingdom—to name but a few of the landmarks of constitutional history. Without wishing to detract from other places and traditions, we have chosen a period that marks the formation and growth of the modern constitutional state in England, which in turn has stimulated a richness of constitutional ideas and approaches. When to that is added the tumultuous events

[3] For a detailed study: K. M. Baker, *Inventing the French Revolution* (Cambridge: Cambridge University Press, 1990).

in America and France, and the interlacing of the three experiences is considered, a cogent case is made for the approach taken and the authors chosen.

The contributors to this volume come from a variety of academic backgrounds: law, history, and political theory. The essays reflect the different disciplinary perspectives, and, whilst that presents a challenge in achieving consistency of approach from one essay to another, it adds to the interest of the volume. Each of the contributors has been commissioned to provide an outline of the constitutional ideas of a particular author and in doing so has been allowed, within guidelines, the customary freedom to judge what most matters. We hope that the diverse disciplines of the authors will be matched by a similarly diverse readership. Lawyers and students of law who are accustomed to concentrating on constitutional texts may wish to acquire a better understanding of their foundations. Students of politics are likely to be familiar with the authors, or most of them, but may not have considered fully the constitutional aspects of their political thought. Historians may find value in seeing familiar threads of thought woven into a larger tapestry. If by chance the collection should fall into the hands of the general reader, it will surely be an accessible initiation into the mysteries of matters that much concern them.

II. Ruling and Being Ruled

The main theme running through the essays is the relationship between rulers and ruled, between government and the people.[4] Questions considered include: Why do the people form a nation? Once formed, how is the nation to be governed and for what ends? Are the people able to govern themselves? If not, who is to govern and on what terms? These are the threads woven into the tapestry of constitutional thought in the British, French, and American traditions. From the same threads every nation has to weave its own constitutional pattern. 'Constitution' at its most elemental means the rules, conventions, and understandings for the formation and discharge of political authority.[5] To compress them into a text, as is now the case for most nations, they have to be distilled and simplified; but much has to be left unsaid so that the text is dependent on history and context. A written document can never capture the full spirit of the constitution, can never be a complete account of relations between the people and government. Here we focus on the British experience, one of the few without a text, and consider how over several centuries a selection of authors has answered constitutional questions of the first order. The issues they confront and the solutions they offer are at one level local and particular; at another they are common to all nations and raise questions that each must answer. The French and American experiences of the eighteenth century add

[4] The ruler–ruled relationship as a lens through which to view the place of the people I question elsewhere: D. J. Galligan, 'Keepers of the Common Weale: the Constitution of Populism' (Workshop Paper: Foundation for Law, Justice and Society, 2013) (forthcoming).

[5] On the background to 'constitution', see G. Stourzh, '*Constitution*: Changing Meanings of the Term from the Early Seventeenth to the Late Eighteenth Century', in T. Ball and J. G. A. Pocock (eds), *Conceptual Change and the Constitution* (Lawrence: University Press of Kansas, 1988).

further interest. The turbulent events of the time forced reflection on the nature of government and the foundations of constitutions. The case of Britain and the wealth of ideas it yielded loomed large and could not be ignored, even by persons intent on rejecting them. The authors collected here have been chosen in the main for their contribution to these first-order constitutional questions. There is a second order of issues that relate to institutional arrangements, the division of powers, measures of accountability, and scrutiny of government. Although the two orders overlap and the essays touch on both, it is the first—the relationship between the people and government—that tends to dominate.

In order to understand how Western constitutional thought deals with the relationship between the people and government, we need to consider why the people associate to form a nation, what they expect from it, and how they succeed in constructing it. Although there are as many answers as there are theorists, two main approaches emerge.[6] One may be designated idealist; the other pragmatic. In the idealist approach, association has its own virtue. It finds early expression in Aristotle and has been a constant theme in constitutional history.[7] A state or nation consists of 'a self-sufficient community containing everything necessary for its citizens to live a good life; and the common realization of a good life for all its citizens is the end and object of the state'.[8] Since men and women are naturally sociable, they gain satisfaction and virtue from being engaged in the life of society as citizens. The common good consists then in the people associating and in that association deciding practical matters. Means and ends are inseparable since association is both a means to the common good and itself constitutes the common good.

Active engagement of the people in practical decision-making is the central idea and the imperative for constitutional design. The Roman law definition of citizenship renders the idea more concrete: to be a citizen is to be self-governing, which requires all citizens to participate in governing, not through representatives but directly and personally. To be self-governing is to be free, the corollary being that not to be self-governing is to fall under the will of another and, like the slave, to be unfree. To these ideas modern notions of popular sovereignty and democracy owe their origins. The idealist approach requires a certain kind of constitutional order; it should value and foster the community of active citizens and provide institutions and mechanisms of self-government. Since the common good is their good, citizens are naturally best able to decide what this means and how best to achieve it, for there is no sense of the common good other than that chosen by citizens engaged in communal life. Among the authors under consideration, the idea that to associate is good in itself and that active citizenship is the core of constitutionalism attracts only limited support. Rousseau comes closest to this view, considering the emphasis he places on active citizenship, whilst Adam Ferguson's aim of restoring *virtù*—the

[6] 'Nation' is not used in a technical or legal sense, but to denote the coming together of the people.
[7] Aristotle, *Politics* (London: Everyman, 1959).
[8] A. H. Armstrong, *Introduction to Ancient Philosophy* 2nd ed. (London: Methuen, 1965), 109.

will to advance the common good—has its roots in the inherent good of community. Hobbes scorned this approach. He denounced the idealist position for distorting the true nature of government and constitution, whose advocates he called the 'Democratical Gentlemen', a term reeking with contempt. Hobbes blamed this group for the English Civil War and other great evils. However, Hobbes's opinion has not prevailed. As the essays here show, the idealist position has enjoyed continuing influence on constitutional thought, and in the minds of many has triumphed as the democratic basis of modern constitutions. The truth is more nuanced: idealist and pragmatic principles are thrown together, sometimes offering mutual support, more often competition, and their contours are carved by shifts and changes in ideas and circumstances.

The pragmatic approach is orientated towards outcomes, towards constitutional order as a means to achieving social goods and stated goals. For the pragmatists, the motive for association and hence for a constitution is to provide the basic social goods of security, liberty, and protection of person and property. The common good is still the ruling concept, but its meaning and logic change. They call for a different constitutional order, one whose central plank is to provide institutions and mechanisms capable of producing desired outcomes. In place of community, active citizenship, and self-government, the standard is effective government. Citizens as sociable persons are ousted from the core of the constitution and left in a state of uncertainty. Since the pragmatic approach revolves around effective government, the people have a place only to the extent that they can contribute to that end. It might be thought that the people still decide what constitutes the common good, for the common good is their good. However, even that is not certain, for the common good might best be determined not by the people but by a few of their number who know better. They might also know better how to achieve the common good.

The people cannot be excluded from the calculus, for they must at least acquiesce in or tacitly accept the constitutional order and the outcomes of government. But their role is determined by pragmatism—that is, whether and how the people can contribute to the successful securing of desired social goods and goals. Successful outcomes depend on effective government, and the people may be useful in ensuring effective government by exerting influence, subjecting government to scrutiny, and censuring poor government. Exactly what their roles and responsibilities are, or should be, is a matter of argument and opinion as the following essays demonstrate. Notice that, according to the pragmatic approach, stronger forms of direct popular self-government are not ruled out, since, in some conditions, that might be the most effective constitutional arrangement. But in practice such forms are likely to fail the test of providing effective government in which the people acquiesce. That the people are not capable of good and wise government, that direct popular government is bound to be riven by faction and division, and that it will end in anarchy or levelling or both, are attitudes commonly encountered in constitutional thought. Madison is precise in summing up: 'the public voice, pronounced by the representatives of the people, will be more consonant to the public good than if pronounced by the people themselves.'[9] Whether such claims are empirically sound is another matter.

The classic authors considered here on the whole take a pragmatic approach to constitutions, tempered by variable touches of idealism. Each begins with a few salient truths about the nature of society drawn from history and experience. Giambattista Vico, observing the world from eighteenth-century Naples, identified necessity and utility as the two sources of 'the natural law of nations', by which he meant the sociological foundations.[10] We need not here enter into Vico's account except to note in passing its current neglect. The essential idea is the need in studying constitutions to distil from the complexities of nations the critical social features on which to erect a constitutional order. For the English and Scottish authors, the first truth is that people associate as a practical means for achieving social goods, goods which could not otherwise be effectively or permanently achieved. Thomas Hobbes imagines the state of nature in all its brutishness, the conquering of which is necessary for security of person and property.[11] Whilst few doubt the need for and utility of association, for many Hobbes's prescription is too severe and holds little appeal. Adam Smith paints a calmer picture of the birth of constitutions in the bucolic setting of shepherds, who once they own their own flocks need someone to guard them.[12] Here in the notion of property we get an inkling of the origins of constitutional authority, a relationship that, once cemented into Western consciousness through Roman law, pervades constitutional thought.[13] John Locke's people are not shepherds but the protection of property remains high in their expectations: '... the comfortable safe and peaceable living one amongst another, in a secure enjoyment of their properties, and a greater security against any that are not of it'.[14] The demands of utility and necessity led David Hume to single out coordination of politics and society as the aim of association, a purpose best achieved by a constitutional order of authoritative institutions committed to liberty in which the people acquiesce.[15] Jeremy Bentham fastens on utility as the bedrock of association,[16] whilst for Thomas Paine the point is to propound and protect an agenda of rights.[17] These ideas are typical of the authors under consideration and the common foundation on which they build accounts of the nature and purpose of constitutions. Once the aims of association

[9] A. Hamilton, J. Madison, and J. Jay, *The Federalist or The New Constitution* (London: Everyman, 1970), 45. See further Mark Graber's essay herein.

[10] G. Vico, *New Science: Principles of the New Science Concerning the Common Nature of Nations* 3rd ed. (London: Penguin, 1974, originally published 1744), 79.

[11] T. Hobbes, *Leviathan*, ed. R. Tuck (Cambridge: Cambridge University Press, 1991), ch. XVII ff.

[12] A. Smith, *Lectures on Jurisprudence* (1762–3) (Indianapolis: Liberty Fund, 1978).

[13] A. Schiavone, *The Invention of Law in the West* (Cambridge, MA: Harvard University Press, 2012).

[14] J. Locke, *An Essay Concerning the True Original, Extent, and End of Civil Government*, ed. P. Laslett (Cambridge: Cambridge University Press, 1960, first published 1689 presumed), Book II: Chapter VIII: 96, 331.

[15] D. Hume, A *Treatise on Human Nature* (first published 1739–40), ed. L. A. Selby-Bigge, 2nd edition revised by P. H. Nidditch (Oxford: Oxford University Press, 1978). The leading exponent of Hume is: R. Hardin, *David Hume: Moral and Political Theorist* (New York: Oxford University Press, 2008); see also: Galligan and Versteeg, 'Theoretical Perspectives on the Social and Political Foundations of Constitutions'.

[16] See the essay herein by Philip Schofield.

[17] See the essay herein by Richard Whatmore.

are defined, the next question is how to achieve them. What are the best means and devices, institutions and standards, relations and alliances, in other words, the best constitutional arrangements, for pursuing these goals? Is the constitution, including the rules and institutions it creates, simply an instrument serving utility and necessity? Does it matter who governs and by what means, provided the people are protected and their interests advanced?

Having sketched the pragmatic approach, we can now return to consider further how the people fit within it. Another sociological fact is that the people have a special kind of interest in the constitutional order, which cannot be denied or ignored even by the most ardent pragmatist. They are not mere units of account in the calculus of utility; nor are they passive beneficiaries of the efforts of others to govern well, even though they have been thought of traditionally in this way. That they are unfit to govern was and probably still is widely believed; but they have to be engaged in some way and allowed some influence over those who do. In practice, the two modes of constitutionalism—the idealist and the pragmatic—become entangled, each exerting influence on constitutional attitudes whilst leaving open to opinion the optimum balance between the two. The many attempts to find the right balance—one aimed at outcomes, the other at self-government—can be plotted along a scale with the highly pragmatic at one end, the resolutely idealist at the other, and many points in between. For one, the objective is to find the form of government most capable of delivering certain social goods; for the other, self-government moves to centre position.

The authors resolve these tensions in different ways. Hobbes's answer is an all-powerful sovereign who, once appointed, has no need of the people. Locke opts for a legislature on which the people impose limits and constraints. Hume trusted in the mixed and balanced constitution that made room for the people. Bentham, however, thought representative government optimal in securing utilitarian outcomes.[18] In each case the role of the people depends on how they can contribute to making effective the general aim. The early modern English constitution, in allowing the people a limited role through the elected House of Commons in moderating the monarch and aristocracy, is a good example. Charles Stuart described the role of the people, the democratic element, as useful in guarding liberty in the face of a potentially over-zealous monarch,[19] an idea often repeated and which Hume, Blackstone, and many parliamentarians of the eighteenth century celebrated. Bentham found the mixed constitution defective and argued for more control in the hands of the people through a fuller sense of representative democracy, the point being that the people are good at getting their representatives to govern well by censuring poor government, keeping governors honest, and rooting out corruption. On the assumption that governments and officials naturally veer towards self-interest, incompetence, and corruption, the best protection is to let the people elect the rulers and

[18] John Fortescue as an earlier voice from the 15th century may be seen from the same perspective; see Margaret Kelly's essay herein.

[19] *His Majestie's Answer to the Nineteen Propositions* (1642) in *Divine Right and Democracy: An Anthology of Political Writing in Stuart England*, ed. D. Wootton (London: Penguin, 1987).

then give them powers of scrutiny and control over them.[20] The case rests neither on representative government being a good thing in itself nor on its being an expression of self-government; it rests on the presumed utility of representative government in securing good government, a presumption open to empirical investigation.

Constitutions, however, are never just about providing effective government, and the place of the people is never entirely instrumental to that end. That the people have a central and irreducible place finds expression in modern constitutions in the sovereignty of the people. Since the people are the source of constitutional authority, they are entitled to put in place whatever form of government they wish. They may decide on a high degree of self-government, but in practice prefer to delegate authority to representatives and officials on the grounds of effective government. This is, in part, the legacy of the idealist tradition, mediated via republican Rome and medieval Italy by a notion of liberty. Since liberty is one of the essential social goods in English constitutionalism, its affinity with republican notions comes naturally. It is generally assumed that in modern constitutions popular sovereignty and self-government have emerged triumphant and have become the foundation of both modern constitutionalism and contemporary texts. 'We the People' are the opening words of around one-quarter of the constitutions of broadly democratic nations. However, in expressing the foundation of modern constitutionalism, these words could be considered symbolic of today's constitutions more generally. Yet behind such confident assertion of popular hegemony hides a different social reality.

In the first place, the concept of sovereignty is divided and elusive, and in constitutional texts does not have the meaning or force attributed to it.[21] Some accept the people as the source of sovereignty but vest sovereignty itself in representatives and officials. Those constitutions that proclaim the sovereignty of the people insist that it be exercised by representatives and officials, some of whom are subject to election but many of whom are not. None provides the systematic accountability that a sovereign people might reasonably expect from representatives and officials. Some constitutions open up avenues of direct expression of sovereignty, but in practice they remain marginal to the main course of government. The second point is that we have to look behind the text and assertions of popular sovereignty to understand how authority is allocated, who exercises it, and under what conditions. Only then will we know how the differences in aim and logic of the two approaches—the idealist and the pragmatic—are reconciled to form a constitutional order. The essays here show the variety of views available. Rigorous pragmatists, amongst whom Hobbes is notable, allow that authority derives from the people, but then construct constitutions as means to practical ends in which the people hand over sovereignty to representatives and leave the constitutional stage. For more moderate pragmatists, including Locke, Madison, Sieyès, Bentham, Paine, and others, authority derives from the people but in order to have effective government must be exercised by representatives and officials. The people do not

[20] Discussed in Philip Schofield's essay herein.

[21] For a detailed analysis of sovereignty in constitutions, see D. J. Galligan, 'The Sovereignty Deficit of Modern Constitutions' *Oxford Journal of Legal Studies* 33(4) (2013), 703–32.

govern in any direct sense, but they watch over government and help to keep it honest and effective. In this way modern constitutions marry the two: government as a means to social goals and elements of self-government, the fruit of whose union is representative government, which is hailed as the culmination of constitutional history. The true position is more complex and solutions more contingent on history and circumstance, but it is enough to note that how the two are reconciled in theory and how they work out in practice are central to contemporary constitutional thought and design. This is not new and the reader will see in the following essays how, from its origins in early accounts of the ruler–ruled relationship, through the mixed constitution and republican democracy, to experiments in direct self-government, this theme has woven itself into the great unfinished narrative of constitutional history.

III. The British Tradition of Constitutional Writers

Why begin in the mid-fifteenth century with John Fortescue (*c.*1394–1476)? The centuries before had found in Roman law concepts suited to emerging nations across Europe and produced a literature on the nature of ruling and what makes a virtuous ruler. Among many who contributed, John of Salisbury and Gratian of Bologna stand out in the twelfth century, Thomas Aquinas and John of Paris in the thirteenth, and Marsilius of Padua and William of Ockham in the fourteenth.[22] Writing in the fifteenth century, Fortescue would have known the works of these writers; he certainly knew those of Aquinas on whom he relies and whose ideas he applies and develops. In his two main writings, *In Praise of the Laws of England* and *The Governance of England*, Fortescue's intentions are partly to describe the English constitution as he saw it and partly to formulate an ideal of what a constitution should be.[23] The concept of *dominium politicum et regale* is well known in constitutional thought: that government is political and royal means that the power to rule is vested in the king but derives from the people and must be used for their welfare. Similar ideas were circulating in Europe long before Fortescue composed his account. John of Salisbury almost three centuries before had described in detail the organs of the body politic at whose head sat the king, but whose authority was based on advancing the common good—the common weal as it was known.[24] In advising on good rule, John urged care of the feet, the common people, without whom the body would have to crawl on its belly. Aquinas refrained from such vivid bodily images, but in setting out the duties of a good and virtuous king laid the foundations on which Fortescue and others drew.[25]

22 For analysis of the writings of each, see A. P. Monahan, *Consent, Coercion, and Limit: The Medieval Origins of Parliamentary Democracy* (Montreal/Kingston: McGill-Queen's University Press, 1987).

23 J. Fortescue, *In Praise of the Laws of England* and *The Governance of England: Otherwise Called the Difference Between an Absolute and a Limited Monarchy* (published 1471), in *Sir John Fortescue: On the Laws and Governance of England*, ed. S. Lockwood (Cambridge: Cambridge University Press, 1997).

24 John of Salisbury, *Policraticus*, ed. C. J. Nederman (ed) (Cambridge: Cambridge University Press, 2000).

25 Discussed in: Monahan, *Consent, Coercion, and Limit*, 150 ff.

In her essay on Fortescue in this volume, Margaret Kelly writes in reference to his account of the regal and political kingdom: 'This was a new and significant departure in both political and constitutional thinking, and reveals the significance which Fortescue attached to the involvement of the people through their representatives.' Such an idea of kingship was already present, though perhaps less developed, in English constitutional thought.[26] Medieval constitutionalism and English law both acknowledged the people as the ultimate source of authority and insisted that the king rule with counsel and consent.[27] Fortescue advanced constitutional thought by positioning kingly rule firmly within the relationship between the ruler and the ruled. He relied on the ancient idea of consent of the people through their representatives, an idea at first of limited practical effects, but later to become essential to constitutionalism. In rendering clear and concrete the relationship between ruler and ruled, Fortescue set the scene for later advances whereby the strength and influence of the people within the relationship has grown, culminating in contemporary worship of representative democracy as the sacred doctrine of civilized nations and the apex of constitutionalism.

The other reason why Fortescue has earned a seat in constitutional thought is his application of the ruler–ruled relationship to the English system of governance. England was ruled, he wrote, according to *dominium politicum et regale,* unlike France and other nations whose kings ruled royally but not politically. England's happiness, strength, and prosperity are 'the fruit of "the political and royal law", under which we live'.[28] We need not here enquire into the empirical basis of this claim, since its value depends less on the causal reality than on the idea of a particular relationship of constitutional dimension between king and people. In construing the English constitution as a combination of royal authority and political accountability, Fortescue confers on a notion already embedded in the English constitution a firmer foundation, whose development and refinement provided the constitutional contours of the early modern state. For these reasons, Fortescue warrants a place in this collection and serves as a good starting point. His ideas do not mark, in our opinion, a turning point or paradigm shift in constitutional thought, but the two main ideas together are a milestone along the way, so that looking back it may justly be said that here, at this point, early notions of rule based on the virtue of the ruler matured to embrace the notion that ruling takes place in a relationship with the ruled, that it involves mutual cooperation, and that within the relationship the conventions and understandings can change and shift,

[26] For an account of kingship and the place of the people, see J. Watts, *Henry VI and the Politics of Kingship* (Cambridge: Cambridge University Press, 1996). Watts' analysis shows that earlier understandings of kingship were somewhat different from that of Fortescue: 1–79.

[27] The need for consent is stated in many sources, including both Glanvill and Bracton: *The Treatise on the Laws and Customs of the Realm of England Commonly Called Glanvill*, ed. G. D. G. Hall (Nelson and Selden Society, 1965); and *Bracton on the Laws and Customs of England* (Harvard University Press, 1968); although the meaning of consent and what constituted consent has to be analysed in the context of medieval thought and the legacy of Roman law, see further: G. Post, 'A Roman Legal Theory of Consent, *Quod Omnes Tangit*, in Medieval Representation', *Wisconsin Law Review* 1 (1950), 66.

[28] J. Fortescue, *The Governance of England*, in *Sir John Fortescue*, ed. S. Lockwood (Cambridge: Cambridge University Press, 1987), 90.

and from time to time be re-balanced and re-geared, without abandoning the paradigm.

After Fortescue there is an interlude until the explosion of constitutional ideas in the seventeenth century. This does not mean writing about constitutions came to a standstill between the mid-fifteenth and the mid-seventeenth centuries, but there is no one who, in our view, stands out for the originality or lasting interest of their writings sufficient to justify a place in the collection. Christopher St Germain began a long line of publications in 1528 with *Dialogues de fundamentis legume Anglie et de conscientia,* which became known as *Doctor and Student.*[29] He defended the actions of the King in enforcing the English Reformation and appears to have been more interested in relations between church and state than matters constitutional. Where in later works he does touch on such matters, St Germain adopts Fortescue's distinction between *jus regale* and *jus politicum* without attribution, analysis, or further insight.[30] If there is a contribution to constitutional ideas, it was his praise of the supremacy of parliament in the sense of the king-in-parliament, a doctrine that suited the King's purposes in enlisting the services of Parliament in imposing the Reformation.[31] Thomas More's *Utopia*, published in 1516, describes the perfect republic, but to the extent it engages with the constitutional issues of the day it does so through satire and makes only a modest addition to familiar notions.[32]

Two figures of the sixteenth century who are not included are Thomas Smith (1513–77) and Richard Hooker (1554–1600). Smith's principal work is *De Republica Anglorum: the Manner of Government or Policie of the Realme of England* (published in 1583 but written between 1562 and 1565).[33] It is a finely written treatise covering many topics, including the nature of commonwealths, the various forms of government based on the division of monarchy, aristocracy, and democracy, and the character of the government of England. Whilst the treatise is on the whole an elegant and unadorned account of the conventions of the time, which had not changed significantly since Fortescue, two matters retain our attention. One is an endorsement of parliament as 'the most high power of the realme of England', where the monarch, lords, and commons become 'the force and power of England'. The other is that parliament 'represents and hath the power of the whole realme'; but it does more: 'For everie Englishman is intended to bee there present, either in person or by procuration and attornies... and the consent of the Parliament is taken to bee everie man's consent.'[34] That parliament embodies the people of the

[29] See for a brief account of St Germain: J. H. Baker, 'St Germain, Christopher (*c*.1460–1540/41)' in H. C. G. Matthew and B. Harrison (eds), *Oxford Dictionary of National Biography* (Oxford: Oxford University Press, 2004).

[30] St Germain never refers to Fortescue by name.

[31] See for further discussion: F. L. Baumer, 'Christopher St Germain: The Political Philosophy of a Tudor Lawyer', *The American Historical Review* XLII (1937), 631.

[32] T. More, *Utopia*, ed. G. M. Logan and R. M. Adams (Cambridge: Cambridge University Press, 2002). More was a contemporary of St Germain with whom he conducted a long and acrimonious debate over relations between church and state: see Baumer, n. 31 above.

[33] T. Smith, *De Republica Anglorum: the Manner of Government or Policie of the Realme of England* (London, 1583).

[34] Smith, *De Republica Anglorum*, The Second Book: Chapter 1.

realm later became foundational in constructing the doctrine of parliamentary sovereignty, as we shall see later in this essay.

Turning now to Richard Hooker, in the course of his principal work, *Of the Laws of Ecclesiastical Polity,* published in 1594,[35] in which the main subject is governance of the church, Hooker devotes some thought to secular constitutionalism and to the two pillars on which it rests. One pillar concerns the reasons why men enter into society, essentially because they desire 'a sociable life and fellowship'; the other 'touching the manner of their union in living together', which is the law of the commonwealth. The law is the 'very soul of the body politic, the parts whereof are by law animated, held together and set on work in such actions as the common good requireth'. Laws will succeed in their aims only if the lawmakers presume 'the will of man to be inwardly obstinate, rebellious, and averse from all obedience unto the sacred laws of his nature'.[36] With this bleak but pragmatic view of human nature, a view reminiscent of Machiavelli and Vico, Hooker goes on to enquire which laws will serve the purpose of uniting men in a commonwealth.

IV. The Seventeenth-Century Explosion

The explosion of ideas in seventeenth-century England, before, during, and after the Civil War, in fields as diverse as science, philosophy, and literature, raised fundamental questions about the nature of government and the constitution. The legitimacy of royal authority, the notion of the people as sovereign and self-governing, and relations between the people and parliament were discussed and debated as never before, prompted by events and facilitated by a fleeting easing of censorship. The issues were not new, but tensions concealed in the reign of James I became, in the reign of his son Charles I, uncontainable, with terrible consequences: breakdown of government, civil war, execution of the King, Cromwell's dictatorship, and restoration of monarchy. The crisis brought royal authority into question and cultivated a new confidence among parliamentarians in holding the king to account and claiming more say in government.[37] The ancient and balanced constitution, which Thomas Smith had celebrated and Charles Stuart praised in *His Majesties Answers to the Nineteen Propositions of Both Houses of Parliament,* was overturned, leaving in its wake an uncertain future. The debates in Putney Church in 1647 among officers and men of the New Model Army and civilians, a unique event in English constitutional history where issues were discussed in the manner of a constitutional convention, show just how uncertain the future was.[38] Questions about the constitution, about kingship, ruling, and the place of parliament and the people, were torn from the realm of ideas and thrust into the cauldron of practical

[35] R. Hooker, *Of the Laws of Ecclesiastical Polity* (1594).

[36] Hooker, *Of the Laws of Ecclesiastical Polity,* Book 1: Chapter 10.

[37] Well-analysed in: M. Judson, *The Crisis of the Constitution* (New Brunswick: Rutgers University Press, 1988).

[38] On the Putney Debates, see M. Mandle (ed.), *The Putney Debates of 1647: The Army, The Levellers, and the English State* (Cambridge: Cambridge University Press, 2001).

action. The rest of the century was hardly more settled, with Cromwell's Commonwealth following in the wake of civil war, the restoration of the monarchy under Charles II, the destruction of trust under James II, and finally the Glorious Revolution in 1689. This last event is often considered the turning point—the moment when the position of parliament in relation to royal authority was secured. Although that may be true, this moment was also the culmination of what had gone before.[39]

This was the age of Thomas Hobbes and John Locke, the upheavals of the century the social setting in which they wrote. Both are leading figures in the Western canon, not only in the history of political thought but in political thought itself. If the implications of their ideas for constitutions are less well known, the essays by Tom Sorell and Jean-Fabien Spitz in this volume will do much to remedy the oversight. The seventeenth century produced a legion of lesser figures, some of whom have quietly passed into history, others still deserving study. From a populous field, we have selected Edward Coke, James Harrington, and the Levellers. If the collection were devoted to just the seventeenth century, others such as Henry Parker, Robert Filmer, Matthew Hale, Philip Hunton, John Milton, Marchmont Nedham, and Algernon Sydney (considered briefly later) would all have a case for inclusion. Each added to the ferment of ideas, policies, and practices of the day. Some such as Sydney were known and respected in the American colonies, yet none stands out as the source of constitutional ideas that are new, of more than local interest, and lasting.

Thomas Hobbes (1588–1679) is linked inescapably to the English Civil War. His *Elements of Law* was in circulation in 1640 as civil war loomed; *De Cive* appeared in 1642, the year the war broke out, and *Leviathan* in 1651 as Cromwell was settling into the seat of power. As Tom Sorell points out, Hobbes was doing much more than responding to the disorder of civil war; his principal contention and perhaps why he remains so prominent is his claim to have invented the science of politics.[40] This might strike the reader as reminiscent of Bentham's later assertion that it was a waste of time to read anything written before him, and it neglects the claims of others, such as John of Salisbury and Nicolò Machiavelli, to have sown the seeds of social science much earlier. Although traces of the moralist and the political philosopher appear in his writings, Hobbes considered both 'pre-scientific', whilst Aristotle, who held such sway in the epistles of earlier writers, is singled out for singular criticism. Whether it is deserved is not straightforward, and it could be argued that Aristotle, too, tried to locate his views within social reality, although one very different from Hobbes's.

To be a social scientist is to search for precepts of interpretation and understanding rooted in reality rather than the imagination. The two precepts of social life for Hobbes are: first, that people do not naturally live in cooperative harmony; and second, that they want to be secure and for that purpose enter into political

[39] See further: M. Knights, *Representation and Misrepresentation in Later Stuart Britain* (Oxford: Oxford University Press, 2005), Chapter 1.

[40] T. Sorell, 'Constitutions in Hobbes's Science of Politics' (herein).

society. This can be achieved only by the people covenanting with each other to create a state represented by a sovereign who 'is supposed to be unlimited, permanent, and unitary'.[41] The unity of the state is the crucial factor and that is achieved best by a constitution based on a powerful sovereign. The argument is instrumental and prudential in claiming that, of the possible constitutional systems a people might adopt, one based on a sovereign who may do whatever is necessary for security offers the best prospect of success. As to the forms this sovereignty might take, and whether it should be vested in one or several persons, the evidence points to monarchy as the most reliable. The constitutional consequences are then plain: there is no place for a separation of powers, for limits on sovereign power, or for a judiciary with authority to review the sovereign's acts. The duties of the sovereign are to be found not in a prescriptive constitutional theory but in 'civil science', that is to say, in the realities of society and the needs of the people. Contrary to the impression often conveyed by Hobbes's commentators, it does not follow from the sovereign's being unrestrained by fundamental law that there are no restraints on how government is conducted. Hobbes accepted the utility of a settled legal system, where rights were protected and responsibilities stated. But all are contingent on the governing precept of providing for the safety and security of the people, which according to Hobbes is the supreme law.[42]

We may wonder what Hobbes would have made of modern constitutions, especially those of democratic nations, which combine restrictions on government with firm and effective government to produce a society secure and stable. Hobbes said little specifically about constitutions, but his analysis of political power remains influential on such notions as: the people being the source of political power but being incapable of governing well; the need for the people to covenant among themselves to create a sovereign state and surrender their power to it for a secure and effective civil society; and the people exercising power through representatives, whilst accepting the actions of the representatives as their own.[43] In supplying the link between the people and government, representation is the first and foremost concept of modern constitutions, and although Hobbes was not the first to reflect on the nature of representation, nor the first philosopher 'to define a concept of representation' within a theory of government, his account lays bare an analysis of the concept that has shaped constitutional thought, texts, and practices.[44]

That John Locke (1632–1704) be so often mentioned in the same breath as Hobbes is understandable because one of his aims, despite admiration for Hobbes, was to remove the obstacles the latter erected to a sovereign government's being

[41] Sorell, 'Constitutions in Hobbes's Science of Politics', herein.

[42] For the route by which Hobbes arrived at this supreme law, and the influences on his thinking, see P. Rahe, *Against Throne and Altar: Machiavelli and Political Theory under the English Republic* (Cambridge: Cambridge University Press, 2008).

[43] For further discussion: J. Plamenatz, *Man and Society*, Volume 1 (London: Longman, 1963); Q. Skinner, *Visions of Politics: Hobbes and Civil Science Volume III* (Cambridge: Cambridge University Press, 2002).

[44] Hobbes's notion of representation is examined in: H. Pitkin, *Representation* (University of California Press, 1967), and Q. Skinner, 'Hobbes on Representation', *European Journal of Philosophy* 13 (2005), 155.

limited by law, where the purpose of limitation is to protect the rights and liberties of the people. Locke's ideas on constitutions are set out in *The Second Treatise on Government: An Essay Concerning the True Original, Extent, and End of Civil Government,* published in 1688.[45] Jean-Fabien Spitz in his essay on Locke argues that herein is to be found the kernel of constitutionalism as a means less to foster democracy than to preserve freedom. Although the full thrust of that distinction would become plain only much later, Locke contributed to constitutional thought by asking as the central question how government could be prevented from becoming tyrannical and a threat to liberty. There are some similarities with Hobbes in that men and women, in order to gain the benefits of security, supposedly or notionally enter into a contract to create civil society. In Locke's account the people are not content with security; they want to enjoy their rights and liberties and be protected from government's natural tendency towards autocracy and even tyranny. Government must be subject, therefore, to the scrutiny and judgement of the people, for which each person has a moral capacity—indeed duty—to monitor government, to assess whether it is being conducted in accordance with the principles of right, and in pursuit of the ends for which it was created. The people as a moral community, made up of free and equal citizens, create government, monitor its actions, and where necessary resist and dissolve government. The people as a community of individual citizens cannot divest themselves of these capacities, for they are immanent in their creation by God as free moral beings.[46]

In highlighting in Locke's writing the priority of liberty over democracy, Spitz touches on a distinction within pragmatic approaches between two positions. In the first, which is Locke's, the people delegate constitutional authority to government in order to achieve certain ends, in this case liberty and property, the protection of which is the reason for entering civil society and creating government. There is no pretence of the people governing themselves; they plainly are governed by a few of their number, but it is up to them to make sure by scrutiny and vigilance that they are governed well. The second approach deploys different concepts: the people surrender their natural liberty to others, who then represent the people and govern in their name. This is the position of Hobbes and Harrington and many others; it is seminal to English constitutional doctrine and practice and its legacy appears in contemporary constitutions. Hobbes's people want security of a kind similar to that sought by the people in Locke, and in both cases government is a means to that end. But the Hobbesian government, the sovereign, is a representative of each person and its acts are the acts of each person. The people are subsumed in the sovereign to whom they surrender their political life, for the sovereign is 'entire and absolute'. The one and only political act of the people is to agree among themselves

[45] J. Locke, *Two Treatises of Government*, ed. P. Laslett (Cambridge: Cambridge University Press, 1960).

[46] Further on Locke, see D. A. Lloyd Thomas, *Locke on Government* (London: Routledge, 1995), and L. Marshall, *John Locke: Resistance, Religion, and Responsibility* (Cambridge: Cambridge University Press, 1994).

to create a sovereign authority and surrender their natural power to a government, which then embodies them.

English parliamentarians of the seventeenth and eighteenth centuries raised the notion to new heights in speaking proudly and brazenly of parliament being the embodiment of the people, the only body that could express the will of the people, with the consequence that no space was left for political action outside parliament.[47] 'The people' becomes a corporate concept that acts only through representatives, whilst the real people are excluded from the constitutional arena. 'This House', declared Welbore Ellis in a commons debate on 25 March 1771, 'in its legislative capacity, constitutes the only people of England which the law acknowledges'.[48] Harrington, distant from Hobbes on most matters, advocated a similar vacating or neutering of the political sphere, although for different reasons. Harrington's republic of Oceana is 'tongue-ty'd', by which is meant that once the people consent to the constitution and government, they have no further role to play, since Harrington in company with Hobbes could think of 'nothing more dangerous' than 'debate in a crowd'.[49] Harrington's republic has no room for those discords or tumults that Machiavelli thought essential to the well-being of a republic.[50] Madison and his fellow founders suffered a milder form of the same fear, which has rebounded throughout the course of constitutional history, left its influence on the texts of modern constitutions, and is the basis for contemporary notions of representative government. Locke accepts that the people are governed and that to be governed well depends on many factors, including a vigorous political sphere, within which representation is one instrument amongst several for controlling government. That his solution is one of good common sense, based on the social reality of constitutional orders and aimed at locating the most effective way to achieve the goals of political association, whilst eschewing gilded theories of self-government and fanciful images of representation, has passed largely unnoticed.[51]

There is still some distance between Locke and the constitutions of modern liberal democracies, and anyhow Locke's ideas about authority originating in the people and rulers being limited by law have their roots in earlier constitutional history. Nevertheless, in seventeenth- and eighteenth-century England and elsewhere, it was fairly novel and very dangerous to contend that the sovereign body could be limited by a constitution, that the people could have their natural rights acknowledged and protected, and that they retained final control over the constitution. Locke's ideas are another milestone along the road to modern constitutionalism

[47] An early expression of this concept is found in Smith, *De Republica Anglorum*, The Second Book: Chapter 1; slightly later and fuller is H. Parker, *Observations upon Some of his Majesties Late Answers and Expresses* (London, 1642); for extensive analysis of the idea in eighteenth-century House of Commons debates: P. Ihalainen, *Agents of the People: Democracy and Popular Sovereignty in British and Swedish Affairs 1734–1800* (Leiden and Boston: Brill, 2010), 142, 144, 148 ff., 243.

[48] Ihalainen, *Agents of the People*, 148.

[49] Quoted by Rahe whose analysis is illuminating: Rahe, *Against Throne and Altar*, 332.

[50] N. Machiavelli, *The Discourses*, ed. B. Crick (London: Penguin Books, 1970), Book 1:4.

[51] As have the similarities between Locke and Machiavelli, especially the Machiavelli of *The Discourses*—both, in their understanding of society and constitutions, display an unrelenting realism.

and struck the right note a century later in the minds of American constitutionalists, Hamilton, Madison, and Jefferson in particular. The *Declaration of Independence* contains a direct quote from the *Second Treatise on Government* and Locke had a part in the drafting of the *Fundamental Constitution of the Carolinas.* We should not overstate the claim: Locke's writings are principally about liberty and on that his reputation rests. By close attention to Locke's writings, Jean-Fabien Spitz shows how salient they are to the formation of constitutional thought in liberal societies.[52]

A name often associated with Locke for having put forward similar ideas is that of Algernon Sydney (1622–83). Although we have not included his writings amongst the constitutional classics, his *Treatise on Government*,[53] completed shortly before his execution for treason in 1683, deserves mention for expressing two main ideas, which although not novel, were considered dangerous when written and, like Locke's, proved to be of utility to the American colonists almost a century later. One idea was the illegitimacy of absolute monarchs, the other that all authority has its source in the people, who are entitled to choose their own form of government, set limits on it, and resist or dismiss it. Sydney was provoked to the first position by Robert Filmer's defence of monarchy, even absolute monarchy, as the gift of God, a notion to which, in Sydney's view, James II subscribed.[54] The alternative to God as the source of the authority is the people, who in the exercise of their natural liberty are free to form governments and dictate their powers. This idea naturally appealed to the American colonists as they confronted a later king in whom they saw if not absolutism at least autocracy. Sydney has been proclaimed an early reviver of republicanism, although the term he used was popular government, by which he rather curiously meant the mixed monarchy, aristocracy, and democracy of the English constitution.[55]

Since Hobbes and Locke are regarded as the two leading figures of the century, with Harrington close behind, the case for their inclusion is easily made. Neither Coke nor the Levellers have the same stature, but there are good reasons for selecting them as shall appear in the following account. In his essay on Edward Coke (1552–1634), Ian Williams challenges the reader to look beyond the standard constitutional narrative associated with Coke's dismissal as chief justice of the King's Bench by James I in 1616. The clash between Coke and James I is often held up by authors from S. Gardiner and A. V. Dicey to the present as the epiphany of judicial independence and the separation of powers. As Williams shows, however, Coke's views were more nuanced and less conclusive than commonly presented. There is a side to him that portrays the judges, at least those of the King's Bench, as independent of the crown; but this rests as much on practical reasons, such as their

[52] For further discussion see P. Laslett, 'Introduction: Locke and Hobbes' in Locke, *Two Treatises of Government;* J. Dunn, *The Political Thought of John Locke* (Cambridge: Cambridge University Press, 1969); S. A. Lloyd Thomas, *Locke on Government* (London: Routledge, 1995).

[53] A. Sydney, *Discourses concerning government by Algernon Sydney with his letters trial apology and some memoirs of his life* (London: Printed for Mr A. Miller, 1763).

[54] R. Filmer, *The Anarchy of a Limited or Mixed Monarchy* (London, 1648).

[55] See further: A. Charles, *The Life and Times of the Hon. Algernon Sydney* (London, 1873).

expertise and training to decide certain matters, as on constitutional theory. The judges of the seventeenth century were after all appointed by the king, charged to do the king's justice and often to advise the king as members of the Privy Council, and dismissible at his pleasure. This is not to deny that in the early seventeenth century there were signs of judges asserting independence, as any institution of government ancient or modern is likely to do when the very doing of its job unavoidably involves interaction with other institutions.

To see Coke's words and actions as a benchmark and to draw from them a theory of judicial independence, or even to interpret his claims and experiences as a turning point in the genesis of the principle, as judges and lawyers have for centuries, is to attribute to one set of events a certainty and significance beyond its deserts.[56] If Coke's writings have fallen victim to the temptation to interpret historical events through a lens of modern concepts, Ian Williams's essay does much to restore him to his relatively modest place in constitutional thought. The essay unearths and illuminates the legal and constitutional rules, conventions, and understandings of the time, which were complex, in some matters inconclusive, and very different from those of today. To take an example, Coke saw all institutions of government, other than the crown, as courts exercising judicial functions, each with specific areas of expertise. Unless we enter into Coke's frame of mind and accept that premise, his account of the constitution, and the place and powers of the King's Bench within it, will be elusive.

The first step towards restoration is to see Coke as a figure prominent in English public life, as lawyer, Attorney-General, judge, and parliamentarian during a period of constitutional change and impending upheaval. As Attorney-General, he served Elizabeth I and her court, whilst as judge he confronted in James I a king who not only inherited the absolutist views of the Tudors, but had wit enough to invest them with the language of the sacred and the will of the divine. Charles, his son, if less gifted in rhetoric, was his equal in autocratic leanings and more steadfast in stubbornness to the point of civil war. Upon this stage Edward Coke played several roles, each different, each dangerous, and each demanding its own perspective on matters of government and constitution. He was not a legal or political theorist reflecting on the nature of constitutions. His interests were in the English legal system and its constitution, which, in common with John Fortescue almost two centuries earlier and many others later, Coke esteemed as practically perfect. Considering these two background factors, we may ask: what was Coke's contribution to better understanding of the English constitution, and how does that remain of interest to the contemporary reader?

It is not easy, as Maitland pointed out, 'to pin Coke to a theory', but there are issues, besides relations between king and courts, on which Coke commented in his case reports and in the *Institutes of the Lawes of England*,[57] and which merit study of the kind presented in Williams's essay. One issue central to seventeenth-century

[56] See further: M. R. L. L. Kelly, 'King and Crown' (Doctoral Thesis, Macquarie University, Sydney, 1998), 15 ff.

[57] E. Coke, *Institutes of the Laws of England* 4 vols (London, 1640s).

thought and practice was the common-law foundations of the English constitution. The 'ancient constitution', it was thought, had origins in and was inseparable from the common law. It constituted fundamental law in settling relations between the people and government, and between the institutions of government, especially between king and parliament.[58] The common lawyers were its keepers and authentic interpreters, but it could be invoked in wider constitutional disputes, as it was by groups as diverse as King Charles II and the Levellers. Vagueness as to its origins and uncertainty of its content should not obscure the constitution's function in binding together the body politic and embracing all its members. Body imagery was common currency in the seventeenth century, as it had been since the eleventh, and long before, as a way of depicting the nation and demonstrating its organic unity—a unity in which all sectors of society, from the king to the peasant, had a proper place. Laws 'are things of constitution', as an anonymous writer expressed it; they are the basis of social unity, the ties binding the body politic.[59] The notion of a fundamental law applying to all, and protecting the rights of all, central to Fortescue and made plain in Coke, was of great moment in later events in the seventeenth century, a point of reference in the eighteenth and nineteenth, and is now a foundation stone of modern constitutions.

Other matters of interest and debate for men of affairs of the early seventeenth century were the nature of parliament, its powers, whether it was subject to legal limits, and relations between king and parliament. Coke wrote about each in terms standard for the time and not always consistently. That parliament consisted of the three elements of king, lords, and commons, that statutes were made by parliament, and that parliament represented the whole realm, were taken for granted and raised no resistance. That the king governed and had extensive prerogative power to do so was unquestioned, although the limits of this power were unclear, as was its relationship with common law and statute, which was contentious, contested, and ultimately an issue in the growing divide between king and commons. Whether parliament was unlimited in its law-making powers was not yet settled and a matter on which Coke offered not wholly consistent views. The doctrine of parliamentary sovereignty lay in the future, an invention of the eighteenth century, the child of the 1689 revolution and the pen of William Blackstone. These then are the issues in which Coke involved himself. His observations on them allow the modern reader an insight from a legal point of view into the constitutional universe of early seventeenth-century England, much of which is now a foreign land, although early signs of what was to come can be detected. As an entry into the complex legal and constitutional order of that period, an order soon to undergo major change, Coke is of lasting interest.

[58] Amongst a large literature, see J. G. A. Pocock, *The Ancient Constitution and the Feudal Law* (Cambridge: Cambridge University Press, 1957); for more recent treatment: A. Cromartie, *The Constitutionalist Revolution: An Essay on the History of England, 1450–1642* (Cambridge: Cambridge University Press, 2006).

[59] Unnamed author, *Touching the Fundamental Laws, or Politique Constitution of this Kingdom* (London, 1643).

In one of his numerous trials, as depicted on the cover of this book, John Lilburne cited the *Institutes of the Laws of England*, whose author Coke he saluted as 'that most excellent of English lawyers'.[60] What united two such unlikely companions caught up in the turmoil of seventeenth-century England was a common belief in both the law of the land and its foundation in reason. The Levellers stand out from the other authors included here in being not one person but several, among whom the leading names are John Lilburne, Richard Sexby, Richard Overton, and to a lesser extent William Walwyn and John Wildman.[61] A fragmented and undefined group, the Levellers came to public notice in the early 1640s, were active during and immediately after the Civil Wars, then, with the rise of Cromwell and the death of Lilburne, quietly dissolved. During this period they produced a flow of pamphlets, petitions, and letters, which taken as a whole expresses ideas about the English constitution of a novel and provocative character. They and their supporters had the leading parts in the Putney Debates, where, as noted earlier, fundamental issues of constitution were under review. Pamphlet-writing they combined with engagement in political events and in defending themselves in numerous trials in the courts and impeachments before the Houses of Parliament. But they were more than political activists. Their pamphlets and petitions contain views about the constitution, which, although framed as the restoration of ancient notions and settled standards, in fact, by pushing those notions and standards beyond their conventional bounds, advances vision quite out of step with the constitution of the seventeenth century. Their ideas had hardly any practical impact on the course of constitutional events in England and their writings were soon forgotten, ignored, and later lost from sight, even in the more welcoming soil of the American colonies.

Yet, Leveller literature contains ideas that to the contemporary mind seem strikingly modern. The people as the source of authority, relations between the people and government, the singling out of arbitrary power as the curse of government, and the notion of a written constitution to which all eligible citizens would subscribe—all resonate with modern ideas of liberty, democracy, and the protection of rights. That ideas, now so central to constitutional thought, should have been so live in the mid-seventeenth century is intriguing and reason enough to include them here. Amid the streams, often more reminiscent of a flow of consciousness than the measured prose of Hobbes or Locke, appear two reasonably coherent sets of ideas. One concerns arbitrary power and the role of law in its prevention. Arbitrariness is an unruly notion, but at its most basic means either an absence of law or, where there is law, its violation.[62] In constituting relations between rulers and the ruled, law defines the health of the body politic. Arbitrary power, whether by king, parliament, or other government entity, is an abuse of law

[60] J. Lilburne, 'London's Liberty in Chains' in T. C. Pease, *The Leveller Movement: A Study in the History and Political Theory of the English Civil War* (Milton Keynes: General Books, 2009, originally published in 1916), 74–5.

[61] See further: G. E. Aylmer, *The Levellers in the English Revolution* (London: Thames and Hudson, 1975).

[62] For analysis of arbitrariness, see D. J. Galligan, *Discretionary Powers: A Legal Analysis of Official Discretion* (Oxford: Clarendon, 1987).

and a sign of sickness. The cure is to restore respect for law. In seeking a solution to the problem of arbitrary power, the Levellers are forced to reflect on relations between the people and the institutions of government. Since the House of Commons, the only part of government genuinely representative of the people and the only part to be trusted, commits the same acts of oppression as the king and the institutions serving him, the Levellers have to find ways of controlling parliament, making sure it works for the good of the people, and holding it to account. This means lifting the veil on the conventional constitution to rediscover the original purposes of civic association and return the constitution to its roots. It is not a question of direct or popular rule, since the Levellers accept that authority has to be delegated to institutions of government. The difference is that the institutions are the creation of the people by way of a constitution to which each person positively consents. If the people's own parliament cannot be trusted, then the people must assert their authority over it. Parliament must be made accountable to them through elections and other mechanisms and its powers limited. These matters are to be set out in a document—an agreement of the people—stating the terms on which parliament governs and which all eligible citizens will sign. This will serve as the basis for preparing a full constitutional text. The Levellers are pragmatists whose concern is government for the common good where the people are the best judges of the common good and government no more than an instrument for its achievement.

> After Thomas Hobbes's *Leviathan* and John Locke's *Two Treatises on Government*, James Harrington's *Oceana* has been perhaps the most discussed political text from that most fertile period in the history of English political thought, the seventeenth century.

So writes C. J. Davis in introducing his essay on Harrington herein. He goes on to say that whilst Hobbes and Locke were concerned with the principles of government, in particular rights and obligations and the limits of authority, Harrington concentrates on the 'detailed workings and machinery of government'. To these two reasons, which would be enough to earn a place in the collection, a third should be added: in explaining the causes of the civil war, the failure of monarchical government, and ruin of the old order, Harrington sought an alternative in republican government. By republican government he meant, to quote from Davis's essay, that:

> [T]he perfect and immortal commonwealth would contain the historical movement of the balance of property in land, maintain and embody its current popular balance, give full expression to the interest of the many and ensure that whilst options might be identified by the wisdom of the few, final decisions would remain in the hands of the many from whom all power now emanated.

Older traditions of political thought served as a foundation on which to build a republican government suitable to the contours of seventeenth-century England.[63]

[63] See further: J. G. A. Pocock, 'Introduction: Harrington's Life and Writings' in *Harrington: The Commonwealth of Oceana and A System of Politics*, ed. J. G. A. Pocock (Cambridge: Cambridge University Press, 1992).

His efforts to bring together strands of republicanism, to design a stable system of government based on the people's ruling themselves, and to apply it to a disordered England, all contribute to the lasting interest of Harrington's writings. His revival of republicanism in a form fit for emerging nations ensured his writings were known to American constitutionalists, who a century later found themselves engaged in a similar search. The utopian side of Harrington's ideas should be neither overlooked nor exaggerated, because, unlike the utopias of More and Bacon, Harrington's is based on the social, political, and even psychological attributes of a constitutional order. An essential attribute, he claims, is a shift in the balance of ownership in land from the one to the few to the many. The 'democratization' of land ownership was not matched by a shift in the structures of government. The Stuart regime remained essentially ruled by king and aristocracy, hence maintaining an imbalance, an asymmetry, between the distribution of property and the structure of government. Unless a balance were retrieved by acknowledging the people as both the source of authority and self-governing in practice, it would be unstable.

At this point we encounter Harrington as constitutional theorist for whom the key to social stability is a political architecture, or as we would now say constitutional order, the rules and institutions of which are in balance with social and political reality. Much of *Oceana* is directed to that end, to the design of a constitutional order 'from the bottom up', an expression of Colin Davis rather than James Harrington, the main features of which would be a structured system of participatory government, from the parish, the hundred, and the county to the senate and the popular assembly. The design is complex and detailed and would confound the over-simplified and standardized templates of modern constitution-makers. Constitutions for Harrington are practical solutions to complex problems of social order, so that loose or lazy design is unlikely to serve that purpose. The constitutions of modern democratic nations, supposedly founded on the sovereignty and self-government of the people, far from learning from the Harringtonian design or grasping the occasion to test and apply it, take refuge in an orthodox and unreflective notion of representative government, top down rather than bottom up, with the glaring but predictable outcome that the sovereign people are largely absent from their own constitution.

V. Eighteenth-Century Britain

The two authors selected are David Hume (1711–76) and William Blackstone (1723–80). Hume's ideas on constitutions are spread throughout his writings, which include his *History of England*,[64] *A Treatise of Human Nature*,[65] and

[64] D. Hume, *History of England: From the Invasion of Julius Caesar to the Revolution of 1689*, 6 vols (published 1778) (current edition: Indianapolis: Liberty Fund).

[65] D. Hume, *A Treatise of Human Nature* (Published 1739), ed. D. F. Norton and M. J. Norton (Oxford: Oxford University Press, 2007).

Enquiries Concerning Human Understanding and Concerning the Principles of Morals,[66] as well as shorter essays such as *The Idea of a Perfect Commonwealth*.[67] Reflecting on the seventeenth century, which he considered 'the most curious, interesting, & instructive Part of our History', Hume found flaws in both Hobbes and Harrington, the one for being 'positive and dogmatic' and blinded by dogged faith in human reason, the other for proposing 'a perfect and immortal commonwealth' which will always be 'as chimerical as that of the perfect and immortal man'.[68] The alternative to blind faith in reason and false belief in perfection is to cast one's gaze at the system of government in which we find ourselves, and in this case the 'we' are those fortunate enough to find themselves in England, Scotland, or Wales. We will then find, according to Hume, a constitutional order 'if not the best . . . at least the most entire system of justice, that ever was best known amongst mankind'.[69] Its virtues lie in being mixed, with a division of powers between the legislative and executive branches, an independent judiciary, and freedom of the press. If we enquire further as to how this order came about, the answer is by neither reason nor idealism, but convention. Conventions are central to Hume's account of constitutions and society. They are binding standards that arise in response to social, economic, and political needs. They are not decreed by a superior authority, nor are they based on a social contract. As John Adams points out in his essay herein, Hume's 'study of government and his political philosophy in general is the product of, and derived from, his insight into human nature', from which we learn that political institutions, and we might add constitutions, 'are dependent on human nature and human experience'. From the enquiry into human nature, Hume identifies the centrality of reciprocity and mutual advantage in social relations, which find expression in conventions. Conventions guide reason and action; they are standards promoting 'the common interest' both in public and private.

Constitutions are best understood as social conventions native to a society. The eighteenth-century constitution of England and Scotland emerged from a history scarred by disorder and rebellion, which rose to a crescendo in the seventeenth century before finding resolution in the Glorious Revolution, the Act of Settlement, and the rise in power and status of the House of Commons. The conventions that emerged ensured reasonably effective and stable government, which the people tacitly accepted. The system was not perfect, but then social institutions composed of imperfect human beings are not likely to be perfect. It succeeded in coordinating politics and society, and that according to Hume is the purpose of a constitution. Whether a constitution succeeds as a coordinating device, that is to say, provides successful government in which the people acquiesce, depends on the history, culture, and expectations of the society, and these will vary from one to another.

[66] D. Hume, *Enquiries Concerning Human Understanding and Concerning the Principles of Morals*, ed. L. A. Selby-Bigge, 3rd edition by F. H. Nidditch (Oxford: Clarendon, 1985).

[67] D. Hume, *Political Essays*, ed. K. Haakonssen (Cambridge: Cambridge University Press, 2006).

[68] D. Hume, *History of England*, Volume 6: 153. Needless to say Hume had no truck with the notion of a social contract.

[69] Hume, *History of England*, quoted in John Adams' essay herein.

In providing stable and effective institutions, a developed legal system, and respect for liberty and property, the English constitution satisfied both conditions. Hume's understanding of human nature, society, and the purposes of government has long been regarded as foundational to modern social science, although the impact on constitutional ideas and practice is less certain. The drafters of the Constitution of the United States knew and were influenced by Hume's works. Madison's pen being guided by the hidden hand of Hume is easily imagined and reassuring. However, as the modern age of constitutions unfolds, with constitution-making a major industry, Hume's realism has been forgotten. Constitutions are now seen as statements of ideals, mission statements even, of how a particular society sees itself and its aspirations for the future.[70] Whether a constitution will work, whether it will provide effective government and popular acquiescence, are questions rarely asked, whilst the consequences of failing to ask are all too plain. Hume's legacy is not the idealized scheme outlined in his *Idea of a Perfect Commonwealth*, interesting as it is. His legacy is more elemental: the recognition of what constitutions are and the conditions necessary for their success; the simple truth that unless constitutions succeed in coordination all else they try to do will be in vain.[71]

William Blackstone (1723–80), the first Vinerian Professor of English Law at Oxford University, and lawyer, judge, and parliamentarian, merits a place among the classics of constitutional writings on the basis of his *Commentaries on the Laws of England,* published in four volumes between 1765 and 1769.[72] As a systematic analysis of English law, the *Commentaries* became the standard authority in both Britain and the Anglo-American common-law world on the institutions and practices of the Westminster government. The *Commentaries* were known and influential in eighteenth- and early nineteenth-century England as a consolidation of the constitution and an authoritative statement of the core elements. The mixed and balanced constitution was celebrated. Sovereignty was placed firmly in parliament, whilst the source of sovereignty was the community as a whole, a distinction that reappears in numerous eighteenth-century constitutions and serves a crucial purpose.[73] It was not a democracy, although a 'democratical part' was essential and integral to the mixed constitution. That part was discharged by the people, or rather a section of the people, voting at elections.[74] In revealing 'the elegant proportion of the whole,' Blackstone portrays the English constitution as exceptional, a rare case

70 For fuller discussion of these issues, see Galligan and Versteeg, 'Theoretical Perspectives on the Social and Political Foundations of Constitutions'.

71 The leading expert on Hume and coordination is Russell Hardin; see his 'Constitutions as Coordination' in Galligan and Versteeg, *Social and Political Foundations of Constitutions*; see also a development of Hardin's analysis in: Galligan and Versteeg, 'Theoretical Perspectives on the Social and Political Foundations of Constitutions'. See also: R. Hardin, *Hume: Moral and Political Theorist* (Oxford: Oxford University Press, 2007).

72 W. Blackstone, *Commentaries on the Laws of England,* 4 vols (Oxford, 1765–9).

73 See Galligan, 'The Sovereignty Deficit of Modern Constitutions'. Blackstone's distinction between the source of sovereignty and the vesting of sovereignty, and thus the separation of sovereignty from the people, was anathema to notions of popular sovereignty, especially in the context of the French Revolution.

74 See further: Ihalainen, *Agents of the People*, 130 ff.

in which the three ancient types of government—democracy, aristocracy, and monarchy—are mixed and balanced with unrivalled success.

The force of the *Commentaries* was felt far beyond England. They have been described as 'the most influential law book in Anglo-American history';[75] they were widely read and referred to around the time of the American Revolution and in the design and adoption of the Federal Constitution. The Declaration of Independence, the Constitution, the *Federalist Papers*, and seminal decisions of the Supreme Court under John Marshall, it has been suggested, 'were drafted by attorneys steeped in Sir William Blackstone's *Commentaries on the Laws of England*'.[76] Thomas Jefferson apparently knew Blackstone's writing well enough to deplore the defence of a constitutional system which he, Jefferson, detested.[77] Other notables, such as John Adams, John Jay, John Marshall, and Abraham Lincoln, were influenced by and more favourably disposed towards Blackstone's account.

Wilfrid Prest in his essay on Blackstone herein invites us to move beyond his common image as 'a spokesman for the Tory country squires of Hanoverian England' and to consider his contribution to the consolidation and dissemination of modern constitutional ideas, including the protection of rights, the separation of powers, judicial independence, and the state's duties to its citizens. In *An Analysis of the Laws of England* (1758),[78] adopting an approach familiar from the writings of David Hume and Adam Smith, Blackstone writes that '[s]ociety is formed for the Protection of Individuals; and States, or Government, for the Preservation of Society'. The primary purpose of society is to protect the rights of its members, and allow political and civil liberty to flourish. The 'spirit of liberty' is 'deeply implanted in our constitution'; of ancient lineage, it is achieved and sustained by law. As to the origins of a constitutional order, Blackstone considered it 'too wild to be seriously admitted' the notion of an original contract formed by mutual agreement between a body of persons living in a state of nature; rather men are unified by their weakness and imperfection, by their wants and fears. Government and law are the means, and no more than the means, to the cultivation of liberty and the protection of rights. Without the submission of all, it is 'impossible that protection could be extended to any'. A political union is necessary because political communities are comprised of persons whose wills cannot be merged together. For these reasons, the consent of the governed can be taken for granted, and supreme and absolute authority vested in the sovereign. The sovereign is not Hobbes's *Leviathan* but the already settled institutions composed of the three classical elements—monarchy, aristocracy, and democracy—mixed, balanced, and mutually checked.

Blackstone included in his account the new notion of the separation of powers, most likely derived from Montesquieu's *The Spirit of the Laws*. The British

[75] A. A. Alschuler, 'Rediscovering Blackstone', *University of Pennsylvania Law Review* 145 (1996), 2.

[76] W. D. Bader, 'Some Thoughts on Blackstone, Precedent and Originalism', *Vermont Law Review* 19 (1995), 5.

[77] G. Bailey, 'Blackstone in America: Lectures by An English Lawyer Become the Blueprint for a Nation's Law and Leaders', *Early America Review* 1 (4) (Spring 1997).

[78] W. Blackstone, *An Analysis of the Laws of England*, (Oxford, 1756).

constitution is depicted by Blackstone in the imagery of architecture, its various components interacting 'through a complex system of checks and balances so that every branch supports and is supported by the rest'. The separation of powers requires the rigorous separation of parliament's legislative power from the executive power of the crown. The mixed constitution of parliament, comprising king, lords, and commons, is justified on the basis that the royal veto prevents the legislature assuming the rights of the executive power. The separate upper house is needed to prevent the nobility from being overwhelmed by the 'popular torrent' of the common man. The nobility are 'pillars', reared and educated to protect the throne. The protection of rights is compatible with a hierarchical, ordered, and unequal society with which Blackstone was at ease. Rank and the distribution of honours are necessary in any well-governed state. The judiciary has a vital voice in mediating between the executive and legislative bodies, whilst a final brake on judicial and legislative ambition is the natural law.

Two authors whose ideas were well known at the time they wrote and after, but who are not included in this selection, are Adam Ferguson (1723–1816) and Edmund Burke (1719–97).[79] Both addressed issues of constitutional interest, but not enough to warrant a place in the first rank. Ferguson is known for his *An Essay on the History of Civil Society,* published in 1767 and widely read in Britain, continental Europe, Russia, and beyond, in which he made 'a bid to reclaim the idea of civic virtue on behalf of the modern, commercial state'.[80] Although Adam Smith and David Hume saw and praised the connections among Britain's growing economic prosperity, the protection of liberty under the law, and the mixed and balanced constitution, Ferguson sought continuity and revival of the republican tradition of civic virtue and active citizenship, the *virtù* of Nicolò Machiavelli.[81] Ferguson admired the constitution of Great Britain and enjoyed its benefits, but believed it arose from and depended upon active and vigilant citizens. One brief but telling case is enough to illustrate his position: in referring to the remedy of *habeas corpus,* 'which forces the secrets of every prison to be revealed, the cause of every commitment to be declared, and the person of the accused to be produced, that he may claim his enlargement, or his trial, within a limited time', Ferguson describes it as the wisest form 'ever opposed to the abuses of power'; yet 'it requires a fabric no less than the whole political constitution of Great Britain, a spirit no less than the refractory and turbulent zeal of this fortunate people, to secure its effects'.[82]

[79] A third figure who was prominent in the later part of the eighteenth century is Richard Price, whose *Observations on the Nature of Civil Liberties,* published in 1776, was relied on by the more radical elements for the notion that the people must have a share in governing and control over their representatives, a notion squarely at odds with parliamentary sovereignty at least in its Blackstonian–Burkean form.

[80] F. Oz-Salzberger, introduction in *An Essay on the History of Civil Society* (Cambridge: Cambridge University Press, 1995), xvii.

[81] J. G. A. Pocock thought Ferguson the most Machiavellian of the Scottish writers.

[82] Ferguson, *An Essay on the History of Civil Society*, 160.

Edmund Burke is a major figure of the eighteenth century as philosopher, historian, man of letters, parliamentarian, and dogged scourge of Warren Hastings.[83] His writings range widely from the philosophy of the mind to political theory and current events, notably the two revolutions of his age: the American and the French. His writings and his speeches in the House of Commons deal with constitutional affairs, especially the nature and virtue of the British system and the ideas and understandings on which it is based.[84] Having spent his earlier years working out a system of philosophy based on the combination of reason and experience, Burke's method was to view the issues of the day through that prism, with reference to which he stated: 'my Principles are all settled and arranged.'[85] He had much in common with his Neapolitan contemporary, Giambattista Vico, who would have agreed with Burke's belief that 'every age has its own manners and its politicks dependent upon them'.[86] In common with Hume and Blackstone, and the vast majority of men of affairs, Burke celebrated the constitution of Great Britain for its moderate and incremental nature. He recognized that from the experience and events of centuries, a mixed and balanced constitution had emerged from which sprang firm government and strength as a nation.

Parliamentary sovereignty was by then sealed in the minds of parliamentarians as the core of the constitution. It formed a firm base for resisting overweening monarchs and for turning a deaf ear to the clamours of the people. The Houses of Parliament provide the setting in which matters of law and policy are aired, proposals debated, and diverse interests represented, all according to the conventions of decorum and moderation. The French Revolution was condemned for its lack of moderation, for moving inexorably towards 'anarchical democracy', which Burke believed must result in despotism.[87] He conceded the value of the democratic element of the mixed constitution, but had firm ideas on what that meant. It certainly did not mean popular sovereignty, which he described as 'the most pernicious element of the French Revolution'.[88] His version of parliamentary sovereignty was comprehensive and uncompromising: parliament and only parliament may speak for and represent the people, or as it became in later speeches, 'the nation'. Burke went further, reviving an idea of long provenance and well stated by Thomas Hooker, that 'the Commons and the people are virtually the same'.[89] Parliamentarians are elected by the people, but they are not delegates of the people, and once elected exercise independent judgement as to the good of the people.

Both Blackstone and Hume were contemporaries of Jeremy Bentham (1748–1832) and influenced his ideas in sharply different ways. Blackstone's

[83] For Burke's life, see F. P. Lock, *Edmund Burke* (Oxford: Clarendon, 1999), and I. Crowe, *An Imaginative Whig: Reassessing the Life and Thought of Edmund Burke* (Colombia and London: University of Missouri Press, 2005).

[84] On Burke's contribution to debate in the commons: Ihalainen, *Agents of the People*, 282 ff.

[85] Quoted in the *Stanford Encyclopaedia of Philosophy* (2004, revised 2010), <http://plato.stanford.edu/entries/burke>.

[86] *Stanford Encyclopaedia of Philosophy*, 13; on Vico: G. Vico, *Principles of the New Science Concerning the Common Nature of Nations* (London: Penguin, 1999, first published 1744).

[87] Ihalainen, *Agents of the People*, 353.

[88] Ihalainen, *Agents of the People*, 391.

[89] Ihalainen, *Agents of the People*, 138.

views on the common law and its virtues, advanced in his lectures as Vinerian Professor at Oxford, which Bentham attended as a student, were a point of critical reference throughout his life. He attacked Blackstone's 'antipathy to reformation . . . [his] universal inaccuracy and confusion'.[90] As Blackstone was anathema, Hume was inspiration.[91] Referring to Hume's *Treatise,* Bentham wrote: 'That the foundations of all *virtue* are laid in *utility*, is there demonstrated.'[92] As Philip Schofield shows in his essay herein, utility is the cornerstone of Bentham's views on constitutions and the basis for his embracing representative democracy as their foundation. Application of the greatest-happiness principle means that 'the best disposition that could be made of the sovereign power was to give it to the people'.

Bentham's project was to demonstrate how utility ought to be the governing standard in designing and judging a legal system. He sought to demonstrate the power of utility by drafting civil and penal codes, which he initially believed could be introduced into any constitutional order but later realized that only under a system of representative democracy could they be made effective. This led to his promoting a constitutional code based on representative democracy on the grounds that no other system would be as committed to promoting the greatest happiness of the greatest number, or would be capable of restraining the 'sinister interests' of selfish rulers. This is in itself enough to justify Bentham's place as a major figure in the development of constitutional thought. Representation was an old idea long since integrated into the English constitution; democracy had its place but only as an element of the mixed constitution. As only one element it had to compete with the interests of the monarchy and the aristocracy. Bentham proposed a full representative democracy as the only way to achieve a constitutional system to the benefit of all. He supposed the election of representatives by the people, and their accountability to the people, to be the only practical ways of ensuring the utility of the constitutional order.

The people would exercise their constitutive power through the election of representatives, whom they would then judge, harshly if necessary, in the tribunal of public opinion. The appeal of representative democracy is not as an ideal of overriding merit but instead a means to ensure that the constitutional order maximizes utility. Bentham would be pleased to see that representative democracy has become the standard constitutional form in more than half the nations of the world.[93] This is unlikely to be due in any direct way to the force of his views, the appeal of which has waned. Even if, improbably, constitution-makers know of such views, they are not accustomed to invoking them, and utility anyhow is out of

[90] J. Bentham, *A Fragment on Government*, ed. J. H. Burn and H. L. A. Hart (Cambridge: Cambridge University Press, 1988), 4, quoted in Wilfrid Prest's essay on Blackstone, herein.

[91] D. Hume, *A Treatise on Human Nature* (first published 1739–40), ed. L. A. Selby-Bigge, 2nd edition revised by P. H. Nidditch (Oxford: Oxford University Press, 1978). See the discussion by P. Schofield, *Utility and Democracy: The Political Thought of Jeremy Bentham* (Oxford: Oxford University Press, 2006), 3, and G. J. Postema, *Bentham and the Common Law Tradition* (Oxford: Clarendon, 1986).

[92] Quoted in Schofield, *Utility and Democracy*, 3.

[93] Galligan, 'The Sovereignty Deficit of Modern Constitutions'.

fashion. Representative democracy is more likely to be justified as a necessary and pragmatic modification of fuller forms of democracy and therefore of value in its own right. If, however, we dig deeper into the history of constitutions, we will find in the writings of Machiavelli, Harrington, Locke, and many others a vein of pragmatism according to which the constitutional role of the people is not to govern themselves but to make sure that they are governed well. Bentham's account of representative democracy as a means of restraining those 'sinister interests' fits firmly within that pragmatic approach.

If in his pragmatic approach to constitutions Bentham's ideas have a modern tone, the same cannot be said of his assault on the notion of constitutions being permanent and hard to change, although we should note that in practice constitutions are often fairly easy to change and many have a shorter life than might be expected.[94] Bentham rejected the idea of 'a constitution' as simply a set of articles established to limit government activity and regulate the relations between the organs of government. He imagined by contrast a constitution as embodying all principles of constitutional law. Constitutions should not be considered fixed and permanent texts, nor should they be more difficult to change than other legislation. As Schofield writes: 'Bentham found it was absurd that the assembly of twelve-hundred persons who had passed the constitution, and who, from the time of their election, had been "doubting, disputing, changing, struggling, wrangling, sometimes one man's notions prevailing, sometimes another", should suddenly have "worked itself up into infallibility".' To confer infallibility and immutability on constitutions, or even to give special protection to a constitution, is inexpedient, which is to say offends utilitarian principles. The utilitarian position, however, is surely more subtle and compatible with some degree of constitutional stability and permanence.

The purpose of Bentham's constitution, according to Schofield, is to 'replace the natural opposition of interests which existed between the ruler and subjects with an artificial identification of interests'. Bentham introduces a principle—the 'junction of interests' principle—to bring the selfish interests of rulers in line with the general interests of all. Rulers should be punished with dishonour and removal from office if the public decide that their actions are contrary to the general interest. It follows that the purpose of constitutional law is or ought to be to ensure the best people—those with moral, intellectual, and 'active' aptitude—hold office. This leads Bentham to profess ideas that today sound surprising. That each candidate for an official post should make a sealed bid for the pay associated with the office is one, the idea being that applicants would accept a smaller sum than the offered salary or even pay for the appointment. The more the applicant is willing to pay, the greater the pleasure anticipated from holding office; the greater the pleasure expected, the more likely the applicant will be to exercise his functions with superior skill. Bentham's views on the division of powers are similarly challenging. He rejected the theory of the separation of powers amongst legislative, executive, and judicial

[94] For analysis: Z. Elkins, T. Ginsburg, and J. Melton, *The Endurance of National Constitutions* (Oxford: Oxford University Press, 2010).

bodies. Assuming that all parts of government work to promote the greatest happiness of the greatest number, it follows that checks and balances are 'not only pointless but pernicious'. If the legislature were constituted so that its interest aligned with the general interest, any check received from the executive or judicial bodies would be by definition counter to the general interest. The better course is to ensure that the executive, administrative, and judicial branches are made subordinate to the legislature.

VI. French and American Dimensions

Ideas on constitutions sown in seventeenth-century England came to maturity in the eighteenth. The balance within the mixed constitution celebrated by Charles Stuart in 1642 shifted after 1689 in favour of the Houses of Parliament, especially the House of Commons. Monarchs still governed but their ministers became progressively more answerable to parliament for their actions and policies. Blackstone, Hume, and others among whom Burke is prominent, could praise the constitution for its balance, its moderation, and its effectiveness in providing sound government and protecting liberty.[95] And yet change was in the air. Bentham, a younger contemporary who straddled the second half of the eighteenth century and much of the first half of the nineteenth, having unearthed the roots of utilitarianism in Hume, was ambitious to create a new and different constitutional order. The balanced constitution was set on a long slow progress that would eventually, but much later, give way to a representative democracy, although one subject to limitations from the lingering powers of monarch and peers. By the time of Bentham's death in 1832, the year of the first major statutory reform of the electoral system, the British constitutional order was edging towards that goal, although its full attainment is still in the twenty-first century unrealized.

But that is to leap ahead, for quite apart from Bentham's emerging ideas on the future constitution, two episodes of constitutional moment were unfolding abroad: one the American Revolution and later adoption of a federal constitution by the newly independent American colonies, the other the French Revolution. Both episodes not only collided with and challenged British constitutional ideas and practices, but gave birth to new constitutional horizons that were inspiring, to some degree frightening, and for the future providential. We have selected for inclusion in this collection four authors from each of France and the United States. Since each country would easily support a whole volume of its own, we have included those whom we judge to have stood out at the time, whose writings are of enduring interest, and who represent a range of contrasting views: in the case of France, Montesquieu (1689–1755), Rousseau (1712–78), Sieyès (1748–1836), and de Maistre (1753–1821); for the United States, Madison (1751–1836), Jefferson

[95] Among the more prominent of Burke's many works are: E. Burke, *Speech to the Electors of Bristol at the Conclusion of the Poll* (1774), and *Reflections on the Revolution in France* (1790); his speeches in the House of Commons are analysed in Ihalainen, *Agents of the People*.

(1743–1826), Hamilton (1755/7–1804), and Adams (1735–1826). We conclude with Thomas Paine (1737–1809), whose reach touched all three nations—Britain, France, and the United States.

During the revolutionary upheaval in France, the fundamental principles of government and constitution were being contested; old ideas were rejected while new ideas conflicted. Writing at the dawn of a new constitutional era, the French authors in some cases invested old concepts and ideas with a new fluidity and a new energy, whilst in other cases they were replaced by radical innovation. The first to consider, Charles-Louis de Secondat, Baron de la Brede et de Montesquieu, known as Montesquieu (1689–1755), did not live to witness the revolution, and his ideas are in no way radical, for he preferred to build on and refine notions already established in constitutional thought and practice. He would have felt at home in the company of David Hume, but put forward no complete and cogent theory of constitutions in the manner of Hobbes, Harrington, and Locke. Nevertheless, his writings on the subject were influential across Europe and the Americas, especially in British North America and later among the founders of the Federal Constitution, particularly Madison, Jefferson, Hamilton, and Jay.[96] His writings have endured beyond the turbulent times of the eighteenth century, and his major work, *The Spirit of the Laws,* published in 1748, is considered to be central to the canon of constitutional thought and a point of reference on the path to modern constitutions.[97]

Montesquieu's ideas about constitutions come from his dissection of societies as they are, not as he or we would like them to be. He sees no need to invent contracts or covenants or founding moments as a way of understanding and limiting power relations. Men and women are naturally located in society with its web of customs, laws, traditions, and habits of mind, from which emerge constitutions and governments. Once having emerged, they become part of the social web that they in turn help to weave. The social goods and the goals of constitutions are achieved through accommodation and compromise amongst competing and overlapping elements of society. Constitutions are more likely to be effective and enduring if they are rooted in the *moeurs et manières* that 'could not be legislated into existence by law'.[98] The incline is towards Humean conventions and the people's acquiescence, rather than the Hobbesian sovereign issuing commands. 'Mankind is influenced by various causes: by climate, by religion, by laws, by maxims of government, by precedents, morals, and customs; whence is formed a general spirit of nations.'[99] The method of study, for which some have claimed Montesquieu as both an early anthropologist[100] and

[96] On Montesquieu's influence in British North America, see D. Lutz, 'The Relative Influence of European Writers on Late Eighteenth Century American Political Thought', *American Political Science Review* 78 (1984), 189.

[97] C. L. de Secondat, Baron de Montesquieu, *The Spirit of the Laws*, (first published as *De L'Espirit des Lois*, Paris, 1748).

[98] S. S. Wolin, *Tocqueville Between Two Worlds: The Making of a Political and Theoretical Life* (Princeton: Princeton University Press, 2001), 40.

[99] *Spirit of the Laws,* Book XIX: 4.

[100] See further: G. Baladier, *Political Anthropology* (New York: Random House, 1970), and D. Pocock, *Social Anthropology* (Sheed and Ward, 1961).

sociologist,[101] is to examine relations between forms of thought and feelings, that is to say, ideas, loyalties, opinions, perceptions, notions of right and wrong, and social institutions, in particular, laws, customs, and governments.[102] Constitutions and governments can then be classified according to their social elements.

Giovanni Grottanelli in his essay in this volume reveals the origin of Montesquieu's reflections on government in the ancient classical categories: government by the people (democracy), government by the aristocracy (oligarchy), or government by one person (monarchy). These are the ideal types of constitutional orders, each of which depends for its application on a corresponding social order. Montesquieu did not recommend government by either the people or the aristocracy alone, preferring instead government along the English lines, which combined the three forms and offered the best guarantee of freedom. He could not countenance the demise of the aristocracy (or for that matter the monarchy), but believed the preservation of their privileges would encourage them to serve more usefully in government. In creating a republic, virtue and education in virtue are essential. As Grottanelli writes of Montesquieu:

> [V]irtue is love of country and its laws, a love that requires preference for public interest as opposed to private interest... [c]onsequently the most important mission in a republican government is to inspire the young with this love... civic education and love of laws and country cannot be separated from the idea of consensus and the exercise of sovereignty.

In a large nation, virtue is unlikely to be in sufficient supply to sustain a constitutional order. Montesquieu is not so much advocating a republic but isolating the social qualities necessary if a republic is to function effectively. Liberty might be just as well secured in other systems, such as that of the mixed constitution of eighteenth-century Britain, which is for Montesquieu a kind of case study of how a society divided by class and interest can yet be free, harmonious, and stable.

The guarantee of freedom is the main purpose of government, where freedom means the ability to act as one chooses and to be free to do whatever is not prohibited by law. To protect freedom from despotic monarchs, Montesquieu relied on the rule of law, which means at its simplest that government should be conducted according to the fundamental laws. The will of the monarchy should be filtered through intermediary bodies, such as the nobility, the church, and local government. By observing the pattern of distribution of powers and the system of checks and balances in operation in France, Montesquieu identified the best ways to foster freedom, which he thought had been well achieved in the constitution of Great Britain. The three main elements of government—legislature, executive, and judiciary—correspond more or less to the form of modern government. If executive power is vested in the monarch, the legislature should be entrusted to the aristocracy

[101] R. Aron, *Main Currents in Sociological Thought* (London: Penguin, 1965) Volume II, 17. Aron writes: 'if sociology is defined by the peculiar aims I have suggested, then Montesquieu is more of a sociologist than Comte... I do not consider Montesquieu a precursor of sociology, but rather one of its great theorists' (17).

[102] This approach is described lucidly in J. Plamenatz, *Man and Society* (London: Longman, 1963) Volume I, 257–74.

and the people, who would meet separately to ensure that the less populous aristocracy would not be overrun by the commons and could have a voice of its own. The distribution of power amongst government bodies would be a brake on the natural tendencies of institutions to exceed their powers. Other ideas and concepts, such as due process and independence of the judiciary, should be woven together to produce a full and well-functioning constitutional order.

Jean-Jacques Rousseau's (1712–78) standing in the canon of political thought needs neither definition nor defence. His contribution to constitutional affairs whilst perhaps not so evident is of equal interest, for it is Rousseau who faces head-on the question of how a free and equal people can be subject to government yet remain free and equal. Few have made the case so robustly: to be free and equal, to be truly sovereign, the people must govern themselves. The accustomed answer—the answer implicit in Bentham, the champion of representative democracy—is that the people govern themselves through their representatives. This answer will not do for Rousseau, according to whom representative government is a surrender of the people's freedom and equality to a select few.[103] Whether Rousseau manages to convey a convincing account of self-government is debatable. He fails in our view because the idea of people governing themselves directly and genuinely is incompatible with the social and political reality of modern nations. It is more realistic to accept that in practice the people are governed by a few and then set about finding ways of making sure they are governed well and in the interests of all. This is the approach of Machiavelli and Locke, as well as many other pragmatists. Yet, despite the disappointments of the past, the lesson has not yet been learnt and theorists to the present day yearn for a solution to the 'paradox' of popular sovereignty and the delegation of government to others.[104] Rousseau's writings live on among the constitutional classics, partly because the question he asks about constitutional authority is one to be confronted by every nation and each generation, and partly because the sovereignty of the people is a concept constantly invoked in modern constitutions. To fathom fully the question and Rousseau's answer, we need to sketch the context from which his ideas came.

Central to both constitutional theory and constitutional practice, as we suggested earlier, is the relationship between the people and government, between ruled and rulers. Even in autocratic orders, where rulers rule as they choose and the people are expected to obey, the relationship is present in rudimentary form, for even autocratic rulers need the cooperation or at least acquiescence of the people on whom the functioning and survival of any order depends. Popular acquiescence, as Hume contends, is necessary for effective government and a viable constitution. John of Salisbury earlier had warned that there is nothing worse than a barefoot republic, for when the feet stop working, the body politic collapses and must scrape

[103] Representative democracy is usually seen by its advocates as a form of self-government, whilst those of a Lockean disposition make no such pretence and accept that the people are governed. See the discussion of Locke earlier in this chapter.

[104] Consider the essays in: M. Loughlin and N. Walker, *The Paradox of Constitutionalism* (Oxford: Oxford University Press, 2008).

along on its belly.[105] This brutal truth tends to coax the haughtiest ruler into some relationship of reciprocity with the people, whilst in the constitutions of democratic nations the relationship is essential, taken for granted, and applauded. But exactly what the relationship is, or should be, has long been the preoccupation of constitutional thought, whilst around it constitutional orders have risen and fallen. A salient sign of modern constitutions, allowing for some exceptions, is that within the relationship the people are the principals and government their agents, an idea associated with the sovereignty of the people, the social contract, and the notion of trust. Political authority derives from the people and is held on trust for the people, whilst the duty of constitutions is to render the relationship into a system of practical government.

Within that ideological setting, the constitutional flow divides into two streams. One is associated with the pragmatic tradition outlined earlier, for which David Hume could justly claim fatherhood, William Blackstone kinship, and Russell Hardin inheritance.[106] The quest is not for a perfect justification according to principles of political theory; it is the practical project of creating and sustaining firm and effective government in which the people acquiesce, conceding to the different groups and orders some role, and striking a rough-and-ready balance amongst competing ends and goals, some for the collective good, some for the benefit of groups, others for the good of individual persons. Little wonder Hume was one of many to admire and praise the mixed and balanced constitution of Great Britain, which in providing liberty, protecting rights, and ensuring security was the near-perfect realization of that aim. The other stream flows from theoretical purity, imagining how the constitutional order should be, or the system in place could be, justified according to a higher theory. Its advocates face a dilemma: if the people are the source of political authority, if they are naturally free and self-governing, then how can a constitutional order be created and government established without destroying the people's freedom and self-government? The obvious answer is to design a system in which the people truly govern themselves, as the republican tradition in its purer forms insists. Quite apart from 'self-government' being open to several meanings, the obvious answer is ruled out in advance for a medley of reasons buried in constitutional thought and history: it would be unworkable in a modern nation for the people actually to govern themselves, and anyway they lack the ability to do so. Furthermore, even if the people had the ability, the inevitable divisions and factions would make government impossible. Even if those obstacles could be overcome, the people should not be trusted to respect (rather than level) a social order of glaring inequality. The upshot is that although on one hand the support of the people is essential to constitutional authority, on the other, the people must be kept

[105] John of Salisbury, *Polycraticus* (first published between 1153 and 1159), ed. C. J. Nederman (Cambridge: Cambridge University Press, 1990).

[106] R. Hardin: *Liberalism, Constitutionalism, and Democracy* (Oxford: Oxford University Press, 1999) and *David Hume: Moral and Political Theorist* (Oxford: Oxford University Press, 2007).

away from government for practical reasons. How to synthesize these two supposed truths is the riddle of the constitution.[107]

The English solution was to collapse the divide between the people and government by adopting a corporate concept of the people and deeming representatives in parliament to be its embodiment.[108] Acts of the king-in-parliament are then, by definition, the acts of the people. By the late eighteenth century, the corporate approach had led to the division, made concrete by Blackstone, between the people as the source of sovereignty, and parliament as the holder and wielder of sovereignty. Both Hobbes and Locke, the two leading theorists of the seventeenth century, begin with the people as the source of political authority and then bridge the gap between them and their rulers by having the people enter into a fictitious social contract, under which they agree to delegate their natural power to government, in the first case on a fairly unlimited and irrevocable basis,[109] in the second to a supreme but limited legislature.[110] The people are the source of sovereignty, of political authority, but they have practically no place in the conduct of government. The American constitutionalists of the eighteenth century, intent on reviving the republican tradition, dispensed with the monarch easily enough, even trimmed the aristocracy, but struggled to find a form of republicanism suitable for a modern nation, where the people could in some realistic sense be free and self-governing and yet have effective government. The solution was representative government bearing the hallmark of the English system as it was evolving at the time. The Americans subscribed to the doctrine of popular sovereignty, perhaps under the influence of Rousseau, whilst in practice, in vesting government in representatives, adopted a variation on the English theme. The question common to all such approaches is how to smooth the tensions between the people as the source of authority and the realities of government; the answers to the question are commonly debatable.

Rousseau was one of the last great theorists who tried to answer the leading question: how can the people be self-governing? In her essay on Rousseau, herein, Ruzha Smilova notes that 'popular sovereignty has become a defining mark of modern constitutions', from which follows, according to Rousseau, the conclusion that: 'No one has a right to rule over the rest. Rather, the people as a collective body rule themselves, fully preserving each member's freedom and equality.' Starting from that foundation, Rousseau argues that sovereignty must be absolute and unlimited, for otherwise the people would be under the control of someone else and not be self-governing. He argues that the people as the sovereign body can have a general will, by which he means that the private wills of self-interested private persons can be transformed into the general will of citizens who are concerned only with the common good. The success of the project depends on a distinction

[107] An expression borrowed from S. Marks, *The Riddle of All Constitutions* (Oxford: Oxford University Press, 2003).

[108] For discussion of the corporate notion, see D. J. Galligan, 'The People, Representation, and Modern Constitutions', in *The Social and Political Foundations of Constitutions*.

[109] T. Hobbes, *Leviathan*.

[110] J. Locke, *Second Treatise on Government*, in *Two Treatises on Government*.

between the general will and the aggregate will of all, a distinction to which Rousseau devotes much effort to establish.

Once the concept of the general will is understood, Rousseau explains how it can be expressed and known, and cultivated in the people, and how it forms the foundations of a constitutional order. The notion of a 'god-like Legislator' is introduced to determine what the general will is, to design a constitution, and to draft laws giving effect to the constitution. But just how the Legislator relates to the people, how someone can embody the supreme legislature and yet not have power over the people, is one of the puzzles Rousseau has to solve. In expressing the general will, the Legislator is not the government, which is separate and distinct and whose task it is to implement the general will. Government in the sense of the executive body is the agent of the people; it is limited by the general will as expressed in law and the constitution; it is also representative in character. The success of the constitutional system depends on an active citizenry in shaping the general will and scrutinizing the actions of the executive. The relationship between political action and formation of the general will is not wholly clear; nor is it clear whether there are limits on the power of the sovereign body acting through the Legislator. The sovereign expresses the general will through laws, which, being the will of all, preserve freedom. When it comes to practical constitution-making, Rousseau admits that in larger modern states, legislative power may need to be exercised by representatives rather than directly. However, representation is open to corruption and endangers the freedom of citizens. Whether Rousseau solves the ultimate theoretical constitutional puzzle of how free people can govern themselves in a modern nation remains questionable. In practice, modern constitutions, in adopting representative legislatures and executives with only moderate participation or control by the people, are distinctly un-Rousseauan.

Ideas associated with Rousseau have seeped into constitutional consciousness. The sovereignty of the people as the foundation of constitutional authority we have already considered, although a close reading of modern constitutions, especially those of democratic nations, shows that issues of sovereignty are complex and variable as to what it means, who has it, and the effects of having it. In some cases, sovereignty is vested in the people, in others the people are the source whilst sovereignty is vested elsewhere, and in yet others sovereignty is replaced by supremacy or not mentioned at all.[111] Another notion that resonates in modern constitutions is Rousseau's claim that the sovereign people cannot be limited in the use of their sovereignty. Many have been troubled by this idea, including Benjamin Constant (1767–1830), who wrote at the time of the French Revolution and was struck by the barbarity of actions taken in the name of the sovereign people.[112] He feared that unlimited power in anyone's hands, whether monarch, aristocracy, or the people, is dangerous, as was amply testified by the Terror. Constant

[111] For discussion: Galligan, 'The Sovereignty Deficit of Modern Constitutions'.

[112] B. Constant, *De la Force du Gouvernment Actuel et de la Necéssité de S'y Rallier* (1796), and *Des Reflections du Terreur* (1797), discussed in detail in S. Holmes, *Benjamin Constant and the Making of Modern Liberalism* (New Haven: Yale University Press, 1984).

distinguished between two forms of liberty: liberty as understood by the ancient *polis* was popular self-government, whilst modern liberty consists in private independence.[113] Rousseau's liberty was that of the ancients, whilst private independence is the liberty of modern constitutions. Far from following Rousseau, the path of modern constitutions leads in the opposite direction by limiting the constitutional role of the people and expanding the spheres of protected private interests. The effect is to reduce the scope for political action and the role of popular sovereignty in favour of a rights-based juridical constitution.[114]

A more positive legacy of Rousseau, and one that might still hold lessons for modern nations, is the emphasis placed on active citizenship. There is, wrote Rousseau, a key quality 'in the hearts of the citizens; a law which creates the *real constitution* of the State'.[115] The real constitution is sustained by public deliberation, civic education, participation in rituals and games, and the distribution of public honours. Active citizenship is essential to forming the general will; it is also essential in scrutinizing the actions of government, so that even in the face of scepticism of a general will, the value of active citizenship remains. It is the basis for understanding constitutional history and the role of the people in influencing government;[116] it can be linked to contemporary ideas of deliberative democracy,[117] and may have potential in rescuing the political side of modern constitutions from the creeping shadow of the juridical.[118]

Emmanuel Joseph Sieyès (*c.*1748–1836) was a French Roman Catholic *abbé*, philosopher, pamphleteer, and politician who influenced constitutional developments through his writings and his active involvement in the events of the French Revolution. *Qu'est-ce que le tiers état?*, published in January 1789,[119] is one of the classic documents of the time. Sieyès was engaged in drafting the 1791 Constitution, which established a constitutional monarchy; he contributed to the post-coup 1795 Constitution through speeches at the National Convention; and he took part in the 1799 coup that brought Napoleon Bonaparte to power.[120] Such was his part in political events that Raymond Kubben writes in his essay that 'Sieyès made the Revolution as much as the Revolution made him'. He is much more, however, than

[113] Holmes, 19.

[114] R. Bellamy, *The Political Constitution* (Oxford: Oxford University Press, 2009); D. J. Galligan, 'The Indirect Origins of the Juridical Constitution', *Annual Lecture in Law and Society* (Oxford University, 2011) (forthcoming).

[115] That the real constitution is written in the heart of citizens is an old idea: discussed in Galligan, 'The Levellers, the People, and the Constitution'.

[116] Discussed in D. J. Galligan, 'The Keepers of the Common Good: the People and the Constitution of Populism' (paper delivered at the Foundation for Law Justice and Society Workshop, Jay Heritage Centre, Rye, New York, September 2013).

[117] For a recent account, see J. Dryzeck, *Deliberative Democracy* (Oxford: Oxford University Press, 2012).

[118] See further: Galligan, 'Indirect Origins of the Juridical Constitution'.

[119] E. J. Sieyès, *Political Writings*, ed. M. Sonenscher (Cambridge: Cambridge University Press, 2003).

[120] On Sieyès' role in these events, see the detailed account in: Baker, *Inventing the French Revolution,* Part III.

a man of the French Revolution. His ideas were forged from the need to design a constitutional order for a new France that had wider appeal and could provide practical guidance in constitution-making. They stem from the nature of society, from isolating the social dynamics of a nation that is successful in serving the interests of all its members. Conclusions then are drawn as to the most suitable constitutional order, which must be true to the social order and provide good government.[121] Sieyès is not advancing a normative political theory or an idealized vision of society: his natural place is among social theorists from John of Salisbury, through Hobbes, Hume, and Bentham in Britain, and Montesquieu and de Maistre in France, whose constitutional ideas originate in social relations rather than from an ideal to which social relations should be moulded.[122] As Michael Sonenscher notes, 'much of this restless intelligence was applied to the creation of a new conceptual vocabulary for analysing and describing political society.'[123]

The main concepts considered are the nation and representation. A nation is 'a body of associates living under a *common law,* represented by the same *legislature,* etc.'[124] A nation comes about through three epochs: first, an association of individual persons wishing to unite; second, the association forms a common will by coming together and agreeing on specific issues; third, as the community becomes numerous and dispersed, it transpires that its members can no longer form a common will by the agreement of all so instead entrust to a few the task of forming and exercising the common will. Ultimate power stays with the community but is exercised by representatives. The common will is no longer the real will of the members of the nation, but a representative common will. The need for a constitution and its contents are now apparent: since the people, as the *constitutive* power, delegate the authority to govern to representatives, the *constituted* power, their powers and the terms of the delegation have to be stated in a constitutional text.[125] The main objective of the constitution is to ensure good government, which Sieyès thought could not be achieved whilst privileged orders were sustained and the Third Estate—the totality of citizens—was excluded from full constitutive power. The criterion of good government is its success in fostering private employment and providing public services, whilst at the same time protecting personal liberty and natural rights. The source of wealth in society is labour, not land,

[121] See further: D. J. Galligan, 'Constitutional Paradox or the Promise of Constitutional Theory', *Oxford Journal of Legal Studies* 28 (2008), 343.

[122] See further discussion by Sonenscher: 'Emmanuel Joseph Sieyès and the Idea of Representative Government' in *Political Writings.*

[123] Sonenscher, *Political Writings*, ix.

[124] Sieyès, *What Is the Third Estate?*, 97.

[125] Sieyès, *What Is the Third Estate?*, ch. 5. Sieyès' threefold distinction between the constituent power, the constituted power, and the constitution has been resurrected in recent years and features in contemporary constitutional theory; see for instance: M. Loughlin and N. Walker (eds), *The Paradox of Constitutionalism* (Oxford: Oxford University Press, 2010), although ironically Sieyès' ideas are used at a high level of theory, both descriptive and normative, rather than as an analysis of society. How much practical influence Sieyès has had on modern constitution-making remains to be studied, but certainly the Constitution of the Republic of Turkey, whether deliberately or not, is a model of the Sieyèsian approach; see Galligan, 'The Sovereignty Deficit of Modern Constitutions'.

and society achieves greater complexity through the processes of exchange and specialization.

Representation is the other foundation stone of Sieyès's account of society and constitutions. Representation works at many levels in a society, and is indeed necessary for its effective organization, including the system of government. Not only is representation pragmatically and morally desirable, it is consistent with Sieyès's belief in the value of the division of labour in a developed society. As each person depends on others to produce the necessities of life, each individual who works is representative of and is represented by others. By means of representative government established according to a constitution, the will of the nation is determined by representatives. Notice the similarities with Sieyès's near contemporary Bentham: both arrive at representative government as the only practical instrument for ensuring actions are taken for the common good. Nevertheless, there are differences, too. For Bentham, the emphasis is on government being in the hands of democratically elected representatives, whereas for Sieyès, the various forms of representative government potentially serve the ends of good government, his own preference being a limited monarchy.

Sieyès's ideas are directly relevant to constitutions and constitution-making. As Raymond Kubben outlines in his essay in this volume, for Sieyès, constitutions are made by the people through their representatives. In designing the constitution, the nation's representatives create government and set the terms of its exercise including limits. Constitutions cannot be changed by governments; they are made by representatives of the nation and can be changed only by such representatives. Although the creation of a political community calls for each person's consent, the constitution originates from a decision of the nation as a whole rather than individual wills. It follows that the nation acting through representatives can change the constitution freely. In this way, Sieyès 'opened the door for radical constitutional reform' whilst keeping the constitution as a 'beacon of order and stability'. He hoped that if a constitution were to contain the means of its own modification, it would act as a 'living document' and be able to adjust as political conditions change.

To the contemporary reader, Sieyès's language and the concepts he advances seem strange and artificial, despite their popularity amongst contemporary constitutionalists. The idea of a nation having a will, a notion Sieyès shares with Rousseau, is alien to modern constitutional thought. Where the will of the nation is invoked, it means only what a group of representatives declare it to mean. Some contemporary constitutions, such as that of the Republic of Turkey, follow the Sieyèsian approach and speak of sovereignty having its source in the people but being vested in the nation, whose will is determined by the organs of government.[126] Some say Sieyès illuminates, others that he has cast a shadow over, modern constitutions in another way. In confronting the central question of the relationship between the people and government, Sieyès's solution is representation: the people are the source of political authority, but the exercise of that

[126] Discussed in: Galligan, 'The Sovereignty Deficit of Modern Constitutions'.

authority is for representatives and it does not matter much how the representatives are selected. What matters is that the representatives of the people or the nation make the constitution, create government, and monitor its actions. The people, the real people, in whose name such steps are taken are kept on the sidelines.[127]

Joseph-Marie, Comte de Maistre, (1753–1821) represents a rather different approach from that of his contemporaries Montesquieu, Rousseau, and Sieyès, and for that reason has been included in this collection. Whereas each of the other three encouraged reform and progress towards a more enlightened constitutional system in France, de Maistre poured scorn on the idea that constitutions and systems of government could be designed according to reason and be effective. Constitutions must grow out of and respond to the needs of the social order—an old idea in the more conservative strands of constitutional thought, of which Edmund Burke is often depicted as the main spokesman, although Giambattista Vico, his Neapolitan contemporary, is arguably the true source and indisputably the more profound exponent of this approach.[128] De Maistre's conclusions, however, clash with the moderate conservatism of Burke and Vico. He shared with Hobbes the idea that a powerful sovereign is needed to ensure effective government, but there the similarities end, for it is hard to find in de Maistre the concern Hobbes had for law and liberty. In common with Montesquieu and others we have considered, de Maistre based his views on an analysis of society and has been described as an early sociologist. His writings include an undercurrent of intolerance, reaction, and even violence, as many have pointed out, but whether he deserves to be described, as he was by Isaiah Berlin, as 'the last despairing effort of feudalism . . . to resist the march of progress'[129] may need to be reconsidered.

De Maistre's writings must be seen in the social context of France at the end of the eighteenth century. Disturbed by the escalating violence, including the 1789 Revolution, the Reign of Terror, and the 'legislative fury' of a new Republic that adopted three new constitutions in less than five years, de Maistre moved abroad. In her essay herein, Mila Versteeg reminds us that de Maistre is more than merely an 'outspoken' French counter-revolutionary. His works offer a particular perspective on constitutions and a critique of the prevailing ideas of the Enlightenment. Constitutions in his account are indigenous, irrational, and symbolic. Whereas the *philosophes* sought to reveal natural rights and universal constitutional rules, de Maistre instead looked to a nation's history, culture, and traditions to determine the origins of constitutions, and in this he has much in common with British thinkers besides Burke, including Adam Smith, David Hume, and William Blackstone. He did not believe constitutions could transform society, quite the opposite. If they tried they would fall on barren soil. This was certainly against the current of enlightened thought and contrary to the belief among political and social theorists

[127] See further discussion of Sieyès in Richard Whatmore's essay herein on Thomas Paine, a contemporary and protagonist of Sieyès.

[128] Vico, *New Science: Principles of the New Science Concerning the Common Nature of Nations*; on the signal significance of Vico, see I. Berlin, *Vico and Herder* (London: Hogarth Press, 1976).

[129] I. Berlin, *Freedom and Its Betrayal: Six Enemies of Human Liberty*, ed. H. Hardy (London: Pimlico, 2001).

that there exists a reciprocal relationship between a society and its constitution, by which constitutions emerge from society but have the capacity in turn to change society. In advancing such ideas, de Maistre denies the basic tenet of Enlightenment thought. He considered it unrealistic to design a constitution from scratch and expect it to change the course of history. Constitutions must be evolutionary, not revolutionary, and a written constitution is merely a reflection of the true constitution, which 'lives in the hearts of all Frenchmen'.

The focus of the Enlightenment on the rational design of constitutions was another target of de Maistre's attack. He saw 'perfection in imperfection' and believed in the random and even irrational nature of constitutional evolution. Successful political arrangements that withstand the test of time, such as monarchies, survive not because they are rational, but because they have deep historical foundations with 'neither author nor date'. The constitutional instability of the new French Republic, which produced three constitutions in five years, offers some support for de Maistre's argument. The trust in reason as the basis for constitutional design appeared to be misconceived, and led to constitutions less stable and permanent than those growing organically over time and in context. His scepticism of written constitutions fed on the belief that a constitution should come from an almost mystical source, from which it derives its authority. This is the ultimate constraint on government, for 'the essence of a fundamental law is that no one has the right to abolish it'. These are provocative ideas and spurn many of the truths now taken for granted. They challenge the conviction that constitution-making can and ought to be a rational process, that if a constitution is to succeed it must address and deal with certain core social and political issues, and in addition meet international standards. It would be overly optimistic to claim a science of constitutions, but experience of constitutions produces its own wisdom, which is now more easily shared than ever before, and the knowledge gained from social science research is accumulating.[130] There is still place for de Maistre, Burke, and others of like mind, for the best-designed constitution can still fail, and although the causes of failure are many, one of obvious moment is a lack of regard for context, culture, and custom.

Like the French authors of the eighteenth century, the Americans included here—Madison, Hamilton, Jefferson, and Adams—were engaged in a great constitutional experiment. The British legacy of a mixed constitution, and the legal protection of rights and liberties as applied in the colonies, were thought to have let them down. A new constitutional order had to be created that would revive and redefine the republican tradition according to enlightened and rational principles. As Mortimer Sellers writes:

> the innovation of the American revolutionaries was not in their principles, which they borrowed from the English commonwealth and from republican Rome, but in their attention to the details of constitutional reform, and their willingness to attempt republican government on a continental scale, something not considered possible in Europe.

[130] For evidence of how much progress has been made in advancing a social science of constitutions, see Galligan and Versteeg, *The Social and Political Foundations of Constitutions.*

The design of a new constitutional order based on enlightened and republican ideals, and fit for a large modern nation, was a major endeavour without precedent. It gradually took shape within the framework of several main documents, including the Declaration of Independence, the Constitution of the United States, the Bill of Rights, and various State constitutions.

This would be enough to justify inclusion of the protagonists in this collection and to revisit their ideas. Although they are often grouped together, there are differences in their views on the nature of constitutions. They shared a commitment to a system of republican government, whose elements would include the separation of powers, an elected executive and legislature, an independent judiciary, and the protection of political and property rights. However, they differed on many points connected to the form and substance of a federal constitution. The wealth of ideas expressed by numerous writers before, during, and after the creation of the Federal Constitution has again forced hard choices to be made. The four we have settled on are James Madison (1751–1836), Thomas Jefferson (1743–1826), Alexander Hamilton (1755/7–1804), and John Adams (1735–1826). The selection has been made on three main grounds. The first is the role of each in the constitutional events of the second half of the eighteenth century in America, whether in writing the texts of constitutions or influencing the ideas and understandings on which they are based. Another reason is the diversity of the views expressed among them, whilst a third is that taken together the four authors have imagined, designed, and argued for a version of republicanism suitable for modern nations. This was not full democracy but republicanism with democratic elements, which became to some degree a benchmark for constitution-making, and which retains its power in the contemporary world. The selection ends, fittingly, with Thomas Paine (1737–1809), who straddles all three nations—Britain, France, and the United States—and who has exerted unexpected influence on the course of modern constitutions.

Madison's place in the constitutional culture of the United States is plain and permanent.[131] As a delegate for the state of Virginia at the Philadelphia Convention, he is said to have dominated the debate due to his knowledge of history and a clear vision of the new republican order. His influence on the text of the Federal Constitution and the Bill of Rights is well known. Beyond the United States, Madison's fame rests more on his role as a leading author, in company with Hamilton and Jay, of *The Federalist*, a set of newspaper articles written to persuade wavering states to ratify the constitution.[132] Drawing on the British legacy, historical studies, and social and political theory, Madison arrived at a form of republican government suitable for the new federation. The deadliest threat to a republic, he thought, is factions, a threat most likely to arise when too much power is vested in

[131] For details of Madison's life and career, the biography by Jack Rakove is a valuable source: J. Rakove, *James Madison and the Creation of the American Republic* 3rd ed. (New York: Pearson/Longman, 2007).

[132] A. Hamilton, J. Madison, and J. Jay, *The Federalist or The New Constitution* (London: Dent, Everyman's Library, 1971).

popular assemblies. Government by popular assemblies is prone to place private rights and the public interest at the mercy of factions.[133] Yet the extension of the franchise at the state level could not be reversed, and a democratic element had to be built into the republican model. The result is a system of representative government, where the representatives are elected, but once elected have the wisdom 'to discern the true interest of their country'.[134]

Madison's republicanism, how it differs from democracy, and its consequences for a constitutional order, form the focus of Mark Graber's essay herein. After noting how easy it is to lose sight of the distinction between republicanism and democracy, Graber draws our attention to the prominence in Madison's republicanism of civic virtue and the public good. Madison was not a democrat in the modern sense of the word; he did not believe that all should have an equal share of political power, or that all interests were equal or deserving of equal concern and respect. The idea of democratic equality has become, Graber argues, the standard for evaluating political processes and the outcomes they produce. According to the contemporary conception of the public good, people have equal rights to influence government policy and to equal treatment by government. Madison, by contrast, contends for a conception of 'the good' that is steeped in Christian virtue and directed at public service. Electoral systems should be designed to promote the most able and virtuous men, rather than the most popular, since the representatives so chosen would be the best protectors of the common good, which of course includes the protection of rights to liberty and property. To illustrate this approach, Graber recounts how in the early 1790s, Madison objected to treating bonds purchased by speculators as equal to those purchased by soldiers during the Revolutionary War. It emerged that a proportion of loan certificates, originally bought by soldiers and patriotic citizens, was later purchased by speculators for far less than the original price. Madison advocated a discriminatory scheme that would pay original holders full value and speculators less, meaning that the value of one's property rights varied depending on whether the bonds had been acquired for 'patriotic or pecuniary' reasons. The same preoccupation with virtue appears in Madison's support for the right of religious freedom, which he held to be essential because religious duties are owed to God, not government. Free speech should be promoted less on grounds of individual liberty and more to protect the common good. This is because free speech, in enabling the scrutiny of public figures and their policies, is the guardian of the common good. Graber's analysis brings into sharp focus how much the foundational principles of constitutions have changed since the adoption of the United States Constitution in the eighteenth century. The notion that the primary purpose of a constitution is to promote virtuous behaviour and a vision of the common good has little appeal in contemporary societies. And just as liberty was the ruling good in older traditions of republicanism, it now has been displaced by equality.

[133] See especially *The Federalist No. 10.*

[134] *The Federalist No. 10*, 45.

Next to Madison, Alexander Hamilton (1755/7–1804) holds high rank among American constitutionalists.[135] Having long been dissatisfied with the Articles of Confederation, Hamilton appears to have influenced Congress's call for the Philadelphia Convention, from which emerged the draft constitution. As Mortimer Sellers writes: 'the nation's constitutional project was his too, from the beginning.' Hamilton was chosen as a delegate for the state of New York. His lasting contribution, however, is not so much his influence within the constitutional convention, which appears to have been moderate, but in defending the draft and persuading wavering states of its merits.[136] That would be enough from an American standpoint to ensure his place in the constitutional pantheon but not necessarily to commend him to a wider readership two centuries later. The wider appeal is similar to that of Madison: together with John Jay they proposed and defended in *The Federalist* a republican constitution suitable for a modern nation, drawing on ideas and experience stretching back to Rome and Greece in addition to the British model, whose mixed constitution succeeded in combining liberty and firm government.

Hamilton's advocacy of the federal cause is tied to his conception of republicanism.[137] He believed in a 'noble and magnificent' vision of a great Republic, 'tranquil and prosperous at home, respectable abroad'. This is to be contrasted with 'something proportionally diminutive and contemptible in the prospect of a number of petty states, with the appearance only of union, jarring, jealous and perverse, without any determined direction'. Acknowledging the strength and stability of the British constitution, Hamilton argued those same qualities could be achieved in America only by a federal republic. Republicanism was associated at the time with small states and considered to be of doubtful utility for large nations. Hamilton challenged this approach. He imagined a large nation founded on republicanism but capable of uniting a continent. The English constitution showed how a polity could unite 'public strength' with 'individual security' and how checks on government could temper the enthusiasm, even potential violence, of the 'democratic spirit'.[138]

The text produced by the convention was not the constitution Hamilton had hoped for. Yet he promoted its ratification, commending robust federal powers in matters of taxation, commerce, and foreign affairs. He wrote 51 of the 85 instalments of *The Federalist*, in which he recommended direct federal authority over the people and the promotion of free trade among the states, which he expected would enhance wealth, taxation, and international prestige. As Sellers notes, even

[135] For biographical details, see D. Ambrose and R. W. T. Martin (eds), *The Many Faces of Alexander Hamilton: The Life and Legacy of America's Most Elusive Founding Father* (New York: New York University Press, 2006).

[136] See further: M. Meyerson, *Liberty's Blueprint: How Madison and Hamilton Wrote the Federalist Papers, Defined the Constitution, and Made Democracy Safe for the World* (New York: Basic Books, 2008).

[137] See further: S. M. Elkins and E. McKitrick, *The Age of Federalism: The Early American Republic, 1788–1800* (Oxford: Oxford University Press, 1993).

[138] A good selection of Hamilton's writings are found in: A. Hamilton, *Writings*, ed. J. B. Freeman (Washington: Library of America, 2001).

Jefferson, who was Hamilton's rival and a supporter of states' rights, would declare *The Federalist* to be 'the best commentary on the principles of government which was ever written'. Despite their differences over the proper scope of federal power, Hamilton and Jefferson were united on other matters, including the rule of law, judicial review to ensure impartial administration of the laws, and the permanent tenure of judges to protect the constitution from legislative excess.

Thomas Jefferson (1743–1826) was the third President of the United States and principal author of the Declaration of Independence of 1776. In listing the colonists' grievances against the British Crown, the declaration states that 'all men are created equal, that they are endowed by their Creator with certain unalienable Rights, that amongst these are Life, Liberty and the pursuit of Happiness'. The influence of Locke and the Enlightenment *philosophes* is visible, although the exact sources and their influence on Jefferson are still under debate. In order to protect those rights, Jefferson envisaged a government based on the consent of the people. As Gerald Leonard recounts in his essay herein, Jefferson saw the new constitution as an opportunity to create an 'empire of liberty' in which a national government would oversee and 'hold the balance' among a growing number of republics. 'He adhered', writes Leonard, 'to a radical states' rights position from the earliest days of his life to the last.' The role of the national government was to remain strictly limited: it would not be permitted to interfere in the internal affairs of the republics and could not assume any power not expressly granted to it by the states. The scope of such powers would be confined to maintaining peace, commerce, and equal justice within the federation. Jefferson doubted that state republics would survive in the long term without a federal structure: 'Freedom and prosperity of each political community depended on the existence of a central authority empowered to preserve peace and commerce among otherwise independent states.'[139] In Jefferson's view, a limited form of federalism would serve that purpose.

Of all the problems and dilemmas Jefferson faced throughout his political career, none surpassed slavery. A prosperous slave-owner, who is said to have owned six-hundred slaves during his life, Jefferson knew that slavery was a negation of liberty and the spirit of the law; he proclaimed it to be a 'degeneracy' that would 'eat to the heart of a republic's laws and constitutions'. Yet he remained a slave-owner and argued that slavery was a matter for each state republic to settle. He advanced a similar case when he and Madison turned to the state legislatures to resist the *Alien and Sedition Acts* of 1798, on the basis that the constitution had not authorized the national government to criminalize speech.

The reasons for his inclusion in this collection relate to his perhaps less-well-known ideas on constitutions. These are set out in his two main published writings, *A Summary View of the Rights of British America* (1774) and *Notes on the State of Virginia* (1781 and 1784). In the first, which discusses at length the relations between the British government and the colonies, Jefferson sets out his idea of a republic and its function in preserving liberty. The second, although mainly about

[139] G. Leonard's essay, herein.

issues local to the state, contains general prescriptions for the constitution of a republic. On the role of the people in a republic, Jefferson's ideas are neither wholly coherent nor wholly convincing. In stating the common good to be the goal of government, and the constitution the practical means for bringing it about, he treads familiar territory. Public education is critical in cultivating a public vigilance in the scrutiny of government, since lapse from civic virtue is a natural law of governments. Public education would nurture talent in both the poor and the rich, from which would emerge a meritocracy qualified to govern. In order to govern well, the members of the meritocracy must have virtue in the sense of concern for the common good.[140] There is little room in this scheme of things for the wider public to get involved in affairs of government. Pure democracy in the sense of direct popular government is the purest form of republicanism, but is 'impracticable beyond the limits of a town'. A practical, working republic has to be a representative democracy, where government is conducted by elected representatives.[141] As Leonard explains, the role of the people is to vote from time to time for representatives and occasionally rebel when threatened with tyranny; between the two they have no place. To settle on representative government as the new republicanism is hardly original or imaginative, and differs only in emphasis from that proposed by Madison, Hamilton, Adams, and others. It was an advance on the British system where the elected representatives were just one component of the mixed constitution of monarch, aristocracy, and commons. At a time when the British parliament was declaring itself the embodiment of the people, Jefferson was arguing for an educated people as a necessary watchdog over government, an idea whose utility has come to be acknowledged in contemporary theories of constitutional democracy.[142]

As his ideas matured and his political career progressed, Jefferson came to see that even an educated elite might be tempted by tyranny. The solution, when virtue wavers, is a settled constitution: a statement of legal standards that would include a separation of powers. Law becomes the foundation of the republic, its task to 'hem in the legislature' and 'guide and structure the people's will'. In relying on law in this way, Jefferson aligned himself, whether intentionally or not, with a long tradition of English constitutionalism and a host of earlier writers, including Fortescue, the Levellers, and Locke. He warned against concentrating legislative, executive, and judicial power in the legislative body, and advocated a strong judiciary and judicial review. He argued against political parties, but learnt how effective they could be in organizing the people in elections and in providing organized opposition to government once in power. It was not until the next generation, which had no such qualms, that the party system prospered and became the vehicle for expressions of popular opinion.

140 J. G. A. Pocock, *The Machiavellian Moment: Florentine Political Thought and the Atlantic Republican Tradition* (Princeton: Princeton University Press, 1975).

141 See further: *The Papers of Thomas Jefferson* (Princeton: Princeton University Press, 1950).

142 D. E. Green, *The Eyes of the People* (Oxford: Oxford University Press, 2010); D. Keane, *The Life and Death of Democracy* (London: Pocket Books, 2009).

John Adams (1735–1826) shared the same commitment as his three countrymen to republican government and joined in the search for a form suitable for a modern nation. Adams's active political life culminated in his election in 1796 as the second President of the United States. He was engaged in constitutional affairs during the American Revolution, contributed to the Continental Congress, and took part in drafting the Declaration of Independence. The decisive episode in making his name was the part he played in drafting the Constitution of the Commonwealth of Massachusetts in 1779. The task of designing a system of government based on republican ideals, and drafting a document giving it practical effect, forced Adams to distil from the many ideas floating around the essence of republicanism and to formulate an enlightened and moderate version. Since the Constitution of Massachusetts is still in force and largely intact, Adams's ideas on republicanism merit study and deserve a place in constitutional thought.

The main question is by now familiar: how to reconcile popular sovereignty of the people with good, strong, and practical government. Adams advanced an account broadly similar to that of his contemporaries but with its own variations. The basis of republicanism was for Adams clear enough: it is, as David Konig writes in this volume, a system 'bound by fixed laws, which the people have a voice in making, and a right to defend'.[143] The problem lay in reconciling the principle with social reality, a necessary process as Adams saw it, if the constitution is to be of practical use. Two aspects of social reality weighed on him. One was the fear that the people may become the mob, a fear felt throughout constitutional history and which Adams saw for himself in the streets of Boston. The other was the tendency in any association for elites to emerge and, as Adams saw it, the obstinate truth that they were better suited to government than the people as a whole.[144] The principle of popular sovereignty implicit in republicanism must then be interpreted so that the people can respect the government even if it is in the hands of others. The people as a whole have to consent to government by a few. The British tradition of strong and effective government, with its protection of liberty and respect for law, was for Adams an admirable basis from which to work. As Konig in his essay writes, as 'a conservative seeking continuity with . . . the English government, he moved—reluctantly though forcefully—to accept and incorporate emerging principles of popular sovereignty into a constitution.'

The English system had a democratic element in the House of Commons, but since constitutional power was shared with a monarch and an aristocratic chamber, it was not republican or not republican enough to meet the needs of the new nation. Republicanism is not democracy, since democracy means popular government or at least popular control over government, and that for Adams was foreclosed from serious consideration. The version of republicanism that resulted, as it appears in the Constitution of Massachusetts and is defended by Adams, is

[143] J. Adams, 'Thoughts on Government', in *The Works of John Adams, Second President of the United States; with a life of the author, notes, and illustrations* 10 vols (Boston, 1850–6), 4:106–7.

[144] An idea developed much later by Max Weber, *Economy and Society*, ed. G. Roth and C. Wittich (Berkeley: UCLA Press, 1963).

based on the separation of powers, elected legislative and executive bodies, and an independent judiciary. The demands of popular sovereignty are met by elections, whilst power is in the hands of those who by election or appointment are best qualified to govern. The realities of social life as understood at the time are respected: the people should have a place in the selection of government, for government must be by consent, but they are denied a role in governing because that would be unattainable and unworkable.

Thomas Paine (1737–1809) was a truly transatlantic figure. Born an Englishman, he became a citizen of the United States where he spent the years 1774–87 and 1797–1801. He passed the 1790s in Paris before and during the revolution and became a French citizen. His writings are influenced by life in late eighteenth-century England, and the revolutions in both France and America. In several publications, including *Common Sense* (1776), *The American Crisis* (1776), and *Rights of Man* (completed in 1791),[145] Paine gave vent to his hatred of the English constitutional order, declared his support for the American Revolution, and advocated representative government as the best form of constitution to protect the rights of man. Among the many issues that caught his imagination, the two of most interest constitutionally are: first, his strictures on the English system of mixed government, and, second, his championing of representative government as the form of republicanism most suited to a society of equals. Richard Whatmore in his essay herein confirms the point made earlier that, by the late eighteenth century, 'republican doctrines were seen to be backward and largely irrelevant' to European nations. The reasons are worth repeating: republicanism was associated with small states rather than modern nations, and was considered of dubious value even in small states, which after brief moments of glory would be riven by factions and fall into decline and collapse. If the monarchies of European nations, even the mixed monarchies of nations such as Great Britain, were corrupt, run by 'fools, madmen, knaves, and tyrants', as Paine believed, then an alternative had to be found. The republican approach, although apparently obsolete, offered most promise and the new America was the most likely place for that promise to be realized.[146] Being the only land of true liberty, according to Paine, America was the nation of the future and needed a constitution fit for liberty. He later revised his views and conceded that even Great Britain was capable of transforming itself into a republic; but to do so old biases against republicanism had to be overthrown and a new vision defended.

Since these are familiar claims, what is Paine's contribution to constitutional thought? The answer is not straightforward but seems to consist of several parts, none of which were original to Paine, but which when combined amount to a reasonably coherent conception of the new republicanism. Liberty is the foundation stone, but to liberty must be added equality, for once rank was abolished all men

[145] T. Paine: *Common Sense* (Philadelphia: R. Bell, 1776); *The American Crisis* (London: R. Carlile, 1819); *Rights of Man* (London: J. S. Jordan, 1791).

[146] Paine appears later on to have modified his views and conceded that even Great Britain could reform itself and transform itself into a republic: Whatmore, herein.

would have equal rights. The constitution must be based on popular sovereignty, but popular sovereignty is compatible with different forms of constitutions. When Paine argues that the proper constitutional expression of the sovereignty of the people is representative government in the election of which all men should share equally, he is on a well-worn path.[147] In common with the American authors, he did not advocate democracy in the sense of government by the people, since that would lead to endless division and revive the unhappy spectre of medieval republics. Government should be by representatives who, unlike monarchs and aristocrats, would govern only for the good of the nation. Why representatives should be immune from division and faction, and trusted to govern in this way is not considered; nor is their relationship with the people made clear. The republicanism of Greek states and Italian cities might be unsuited to the modern nation, but its ideal of an active citizenship, men reared in a culture of *virtù* was to live on in the modern state. The French Revolution at first held great promise and showed encouraging signs of how active citizenship might secure a republic founded on liberty and equality; but as promise gave way to terror, even Paine had doubts, just as he later came to doubt the republican experiment in America.[148]

Once Paine's ideas are explained, they unfold with a certain logic. The old regimes of monarchy and aristocracy are condemned, rank is destroyed, equality and liberty are to be the birthright of all: then arises the constitutional question, to which Paine's answer is republicanism based on representation. Its virtues are twofold: on one hand, government will be conducted by representatives in the interests of all and will be answerable to the people at elections; on the other hand, the people will have no hand in government, for which they are unqualified and unsuited, and which anyhow would be dangerous and impracticable. What is missing, however, is a firm social foundation—an understanding of the realities of social and political life, of the problems that power poses whether in the hands of monarchs, tyrants, or representatives of the common good. Paine detested Adams's conservative republicanism, his sense that elites will form unavoidably, that republics are as prone to special interests and special pleading as any other political order, and that a balanced constitution might be of utility in curbing the passions of popular movements. Yet, whatever the merits of his constitutional conclusions, Adams at least had the intuition that if a constitution is to work it has to be grounded in those realities. Nevertheless, and this is surely a suitable note on which to end, it is Paine's vision that has largely come to pass, for the constitutions of modern nations, especially those considered democratic, are based on a notion of representative government although one severely confined by what Paine held to be the natural rights of man.[149]

[147] For further discussion, see M. Philp, 'Revolutions in Paris: Paine, Jefferson, and Democracy', in his *Reforming Ideas in Britain: Politics and Language in the Shadow of the French Revolution* (Cambridge: Cambridge University Press, 2013).

[148] Whatmore, herein.

[149] For an analysis of such constitutions, see Galligan, 'The Sovereignty Deficit of Modern Constitutions'.

2

Sir John Fortescue and the Political Dominium

The People, the Common Weal, and the King

*M. R. L. L. Kelly**

Arma virumque cano . . .

Virgil, *The Aeneid*, I.1

Imperatorium maiestatem non solum armis decoratum, sed etiam legibus opertet esse aramtam, ut utrumque tempus et bellorum et pacis recte possit gubernari.

Imperial majesty should not only be graced with arms but also armed with laws, so that good government may prevail in time of war and peace alike.

Justinian, *Institutes*, Proemium (Birks & McLeod translation, 1987)

I. Introduction

Sir John Fortescue is one of the unacknowledged architects of the Westminster system of governance and of the common law. He was a politician, a lawyer and a Chief Justice, a Lord Chancellor in exile, a patriot or a traitor but certainly a 'partial man',[1] a soldier, a propagandist, and a pragmatist. He was also the author of two of

* This chapter is derived from a paper presented to the Centre for Socio-Legal Studies and the Foundation for Law, Justice, and Society at Wolfson College, Oxford, in December 2008, at the Colloquium on *Constitutions and the Classics*. The author wishes to thank CSLS and FLJS, and all participants at the Colloquium, for their support, criticism, and collegiality.

[1] From Fortescue's recantation before Edward IV, *Declaracion upon Certayn Wrytinges sent oute of Scotteland ayenst the Kinges Title to the Roialme of Englond* (1471–3): 'and ye no Judge, but a partial man, servant to him for whose favour ye made the arguments, and his cause is now expired, and he dead, ye may now honestly and commendably, without any note of blame, argue to the contrary intent of that ye have done before this time, if ye find reasons and grounds to do so.'

the seminal works on English governance—*De Laudibus Legum Angliae*[2] (*In Praise of the Laws of England*) and *The Governance of England.*[3]

His times were turbulent. He lived through a civil war between Lancaster and York, Henry VI and Edward IV, each of whom claimed to be and was recognized by the people as king while the other lived. Henry VI, a prisoner, was prevailed upon to ratify an agreement reached after the House of Lords finally settled the *Duke of York's case*[4] in York's favour in 1460. Henry would keep the 'crowns and his estate and royal dignity during his life' with Richard of York and his heirs succeeding him.[5] But the king remained captive, hostilities continued, York was killed, and his son Edward Earl of March seized the crown proclaiming himself Edward IV, dating his reign from that day, 4 March 1461.[6] Civil war continued; Henry was restored to the throne on 3 October 1470[7] (the Readeption); the war went on; in 1471 at the battle of Tewkesbury, Edward son of Henry VI and pupil of Fortescue, was killed;[8] Edward IV reclaimed London; Fortescue was declared a traitor then pardoned; and Henry VI was murdered in the Tower of London.

Fortescue lived in the eye of the storm; he was a political player. Yet at the same time he was a pragmatist, with a keen eye both for past flaws and the future prospects of the governance of England. *De Laudibus* and *Governance* are both directed towards maximizing the common weal; to correcting past faults while laying the foundations for a new construction. His vision would have lasting impact, grounded as it was in the will of the English people, constraints upon the king, and power to parliament.

[2] S. B. Chrimes, *Sir John Fortescue: De Laudibus Legum Anglie* (Cambridge: Cambridge University Press, 1949); this together *De Laudibus Legum Angliae by Sir John Fortescue . . . illustrated with the Notes of Mr. Selden*, ed. F. Gregor (London: T. Evans, 1775, new edition), are the versions of *De Laudibus* referred to throughout.

[3] Sir John Fortescue, *The Governance of England: Otherwise Called The Difference between an Absolute and a Limited Monarchy*, (*c.*1471) ed. C. Plummer, (London: Oxford University Press, 1885; 2nd impression Muston Company, London, 1926; text also reprinted by The Lawbook Exchange, 1999). The text is sometimes referred to as *De dominio regale et politico* (*The Difference between an Absolute and a Limited Monarchy*), see E. W. Ives, 'Sir John Fortescue', in the *Oxford Dictionary of National Biography*. Also see Sir John Fortescue, *The Governance of England*, in *Sir John Fortescue On the Laws and Governance of England*, ed. S. Lockwood (Cambridge: Cambridge University Press, 1997, 2002).

[4] *The Duke of York's case*, 1460, *Rot. Parl.*, v, 376–9, extracted in *English Historical Documents 1327–1485*, ed. A. R. Myers (London: Eyre & Spottiswoode, 1969), 415–19; see also S. B. Chrimes, *English Constitutional Ideas in the Fifteenth Century* (Cambridge: Cambridge University Press, 1936), 22–32. And see discussion of the case below in text accompanying nn. 32–3.

[5] See W. Stubbs, *The Constitutional History of England*, 3 vols (Oxford: Clarendon Press, 1883) vol. III, 192.

[6] See F. W. Maitland, *The Constitutional History of England: A Course of Lectures delivered by F. W. Maitland* (Cambridge: Cambridge University Press, 1st ed., 1908; reprinted 1950), 194, and Stubbs, *The Constitutional History of England* vol. III, 195.

[7] See R. A. Griffiths, *The Reign of King Henry VI* (Ernest Benn, 1981; 2nd ed., Thrupp: Sutton Publishing, 1998), 891.

[8] Note here though, that Chrimes, in his notes to his translation of *De Laudibus* says 'accounts differ as to how he met his death. According to one version he was killed in battle, and to another and more circumstantial but later version, he was captured and then murdered by several Yorkist nobles in the presence of Edward IV': 14.3.

Fortescue is impossible to categorize, as his was such a rounded and interesting life. The dilemma posed by Sir John Fortescue is a multifaceted one—was he 'first and foremost a lawyer' as McFarlane dismissed him?[9] Pocock's amateur philosopher?[10] Or was he, as Holdsworth speculated, rather like Bentham,[11] sharing with him 'the fame of being at once a lawyer and a practical political philosopher'?[12] Or was he Coke's mentor on the jury whose chapters are worthy of being 'written in letters of gold'?[13] Or Sir Walter Raleigh's 'notable bulwark of our laws'?[14] Was he the author of 'the earliest constitutional treatise written in the English language [*The Governance of England*]'?[15] Or rather a fantasist as Pollard apostrophized him,[16] or a mere 'propagandist . . . propping up successive fragile political regimes of his own day'?[17]

Scholars have referred to Fortescue's 'genial intellect'.[18] and noted that '[o]ne has, indeed, at times the uneasy feeling that he is in some odd way more than the sum of his parts'.[19] Others have suggested that Fortescue was an 'amateur of philosophy' who 'wrote philosophy like a Lord Chief Justice' and whose argument exhibited 'naivety'.[20] Fortescue's writings have been described as a 'constitutional ideal' which 'had little more relevance to the practice of his day than More's Utopia had to the government of Cardinal Wolsey'.[21]

Chrimes, the most considered analyst of Fortescue's *De Laudibus* since Selden, said in connection with that work:

[9] See K. B. McFarlane's damning with faint praise review of S. B. Chrimes's *English Constitutional Ideas in the Fifteenth Century* (Cambridge: Cambridge University Press, 1936), in *English Historical Review* 53 (1938), 707–10, 708.

[10] See J. G. A. Pocock, *The Machiavellian Moment: Florentine Thought and the Atlantic Republican Tradition* (Princeton: Princeton University Press, 2003), 9.

[11] This comparison was made first by H. J. Randall, in 'Sir John Fortescue' *Journal of the Society of Comparative Legislation*, 16 (2) (1916), 248–64, 248. The appellation was reproduced in his 'The Beginnings of English Constitutional Law,' in *Celebration Legal Essays: To Mark the Twenty-fifth Year of Service of John H. Wigmore as Professor of Law in Northwestern University* (Chicago: Northwestern University Press, 1919; republished by Wm. S. Hein Publishing, 1987), 287–323, 292).

[12] Sir William Holdsworth, *The History of English Law*, vol. II, 569, as quoted by Chrimes, *De Laudibus*, n. 2 above, cv, n. 1.

[13] Sir Edward Coke, Preface to the Eighth Part of the *Reports*, 1611; 8 Co. Rep., f. xiv; text available in *The Selected Writings and Speeches of Sir Edward Coke*, ed. S Sheppard, 3 vols (Indianapolis: Liberty Fund, 2003), vol. I, 250, see <http://files.libertyfund.org/files/911/0462-01_LFeBk.pdf> accessed 8 November 2008.

[14] Sir Walter Raleigh, *The Works of Sir Walter Ralegh, Kt*, ed. W. Oldys and T. Birch, 8 vols (Oxford: Oxford University Press, 1829), vol. III (*The History of the World*, Book 2): Ch 4, § XVI: 147.

[15] John Fortescue-Aland, preface to *The Difference Between an Absolute and Limited Monarchy; As it more particularly regards the English Constitution* (White Fryars, London: E. Parker, 1724).

[16] A. F. Pollard, *The Evolution of Parliament* (London: Longmans, Green and Co., 1934), 133.

[17] J. R. Lander, preface to A. Gross, *The Dissolution of the Lancastrian Kingship* (Stamford Lincolnshire: Paul Watkins, 1996), xviii.

[18] A. B. Ferguson, 'Fortescue and the Renaissance: A Study in Transition', *Studies in the Renaissance* 6 (1959), 175–94, 175.

[19] Ferguson, 'Fortescue and the Renaissance', 176.

[20] Pocock, *The Machiavellian Moment*, nn. 10, 9 and 15 respectively.

[21] See Pollard, *Evolution of Parliament*, 133.

We cannot but stand amazed at the robust vitality of this old man, more than seventy years of age, who composed this work after a life of such enormous exertion and such tribulation... this work above all the rest has a freshness, an alertness of mind, a sprightliness, a dry humour, a humanity, an enthusiasm, and an almost boyish zest that are astounding in the circumstances, and are highly suggestive of what may have been the true character of the period within which it was written.[22]

This indeed is the key to Fortescue: he is reflective of his era, symptomatic of as well as an exemplar of his age. It is easy to underestimate the complexity, ebullience, and creativity of the fifteenth century. His work mirrors the temper of his time. While his writings certainly reflect partisan propaganda, they also stand as a very real attempt to marry politics with the law to establish a sound basis for governance in England, both during and after a time of civil war.

1. Who was John Fortescue?

John Fortescue[23] was born *c.*1385[24] in the reign of Richard II; he was admitted as a member of Lincoln's Inn before 1420, becoming Governor of the Inn three times between 1424 and 1429. He was elected eight times to the House of Commons between 1421 and 1436 during the reigns of Henry V and Henry VI;[25] was appointed a Justice of the Peace on 33 occasions;[26] became a King's Serjeant at Law in 1441; and was appointed Chief Justice of King's Bench in 1442 by Henry VI.

As both lawyer and judge, he led numerous commissions into offences, and sat as Justice of Assize on many occasions. He was knighted in 1443, attending meetings of Henry's council in Star Chamber. He came under threat of attack during and after Cade's Rebellion from 1450–1.[27] He was consulted by the lords and arbitrators in a number of significant cases.[28] But it was only after his appointment to the Alchemic Commission in 1457 that he became intimately acquainted with issues relating to governance from the inside, as opposed to merely seeing their effects through judicial peregrinations. After the birth of Prince Edward to Henry VI in 1453 and Henry's second documented illness in 1455, three Alchemical Commissions were appointed to search for the 'philosopher's stone' and alchemic means of transmutation. In part this was designed to redress the king's ill health, but also to discover a source of finance to settle the king's debts; Sir John

[22] Chrimes, n. 2 above, cvii–cviii.

[23] I use Chrimes's 'Introduction', *De Laudibus Legem Anglie*, n. 2 above, as the basis for the following biographical details.

[24] Chrimes, 'Introduction', *De Laudibus*; but note *contra* Ives, 'Sir John Fortescue', n. 3 above, who gives 1397 as the birthdate.

[25] That is, during the reigns of Henry V (March 1413) and Henry VI (September 1422)—1421 (twice), 1423, 1425, Tavistock; 1426, 1432, Totnes; 1429, Plympton; 1436, Wiltshire; Chrimes, 'Introduction', *De Laudibus*, lix–lx.

[26] See Chrimes, *De Laudibus*, n. 2 above, lx.

[27] *Paston Letters*, vol. II, 205, as cited in Gross, *The Dissolution of the Lancastrian Kingship*, n. 17 above, 71; see also Fortescue, *Governance of England*, ed. Plummer, n. 3 above, 49–51.

[28] *Thorpe's case*, 1454, *Rot. Parl.* v, 239; disputes between Wentworth and Fastolf, 1456, *Paston Letters*, vol. I, no. 275; *Petyt and Feld v Lynham, Cat. Anc. Deeds*, I, C. 1242.

Fortescue was appointed commissioner to the third commission in November 1455.[29] Perhaps due to this work on the Alchemical Commission, or by virtue of observation, Fortescue became a proponent of the capacity of anointed lawful kings to touch to cure the King's Evil (scrofula).[30] As part of his polemic to discredit the Yorkist title to the crown, he later maintained that Yorkists could not touch for the King's Evil, and that no woman, even were she queen, could exercise the power.[31]

In 1460, Richard Duke of York made overt physical claims to the throne but, more significantly, made judicial application to the lords in Parliament for recognition of his claim to the throne on the basis of indefeasible hereditary right.[32] This case (*The Duke of York's case*) is the first and only legal decision concerning succession to the English crown. Fortescue was Chief Justice of King's Bench during this case, in which the judges refused to advise the lords, the King's high estate being 'above the law and passed their learning', and the matter pertaining to the Lords of the King's blood and 'the peerage of this his land' [th'apparage of this lond'].[33] Fortescue's name does not appear in the Year Books after Easter Term 1460, and his last certificate as Chief Justice was dated earlier than 29 January 1461.

About Candlemass[34] in 1461, he made provision for his wife, joined the Lancastrian forces and was present at their defeat by Edward IV at the battle of Towton, later joining Henry VI's party in exile in Scotland. He was attainted by Edward's Parliament in November 1461.[35] While in Scotland, if not before, he was named Chancellor to Henry VI;[36] he advised on propaganda, composed tracts on the succession and wrote *De Natura Legis Nature*.[37]

In July 1463, Fortescue went with Queen Margaret and Prince Edward to the castle of Koer near St Mihiel at Bar, France. While there, he undertook a number of diplomatic missions for Henry VI. Between 1468 and 1471, he wrote *De Laudibus Legum Anglie*[38] and in 1471 wrote *The Governance of England*.[39] That year he arrived back in England and was proclaimed traitor. Fortescue was present at the Battle of Tewkesbury where Prince Edward was slain; he was taken prisoner, and Margaret captured. Within days of Tewkesbury, Henry VI was murdered in the Tower of London. Edward IV granted Fortescue a general pardon, subject to his

[29] See Gross, n. 17 above, 20–1, 60, 71–2; and see Chrimes, *De Laudibus*, n. 2 above, lxv.

[30] See Sir John Fortescue, *De Titulo Edwardi Comitis Marchiæ*, C. x, in *The Works of Sir John Fortescue . . .*, ed. Thomas Lord Clermont, I: 70; *Defensio Juris Domus Lancastriæ*, in Clermont, *Works*, 508; *Of the Title of the House of York*, in Clermont, *Works*, 698, as quoted by Marc Bloch in his *The Royal Touch: Monarchy and Miracles in France and England*, trans. J. E. Anderson (New York: Dorset Press, 1989), 65; see also Bloch, *The Royal Touch*, 103–4, 313 n. 46, and 331–2 n. 37.

[31] Note here, however, that Bloch records that Mary Tudor undertook similar healing tasks through the blessing of rings, and suggests that princesses succeeding by hereditary right like Elizabeth, Mary II, Anne, and Victoria, could also have undertaken similar tasks: *Royal Touch*, 103–7, 331 n. 36.

[32] *The Duke of York's case*, 1460, *Rot. Parl.*, v, 376–9: see Myers n. 4 above, 415–19; see also Chrimes, *English Constitutional Ideas*, n. 9 above, 22–32.

[33] See Myers, *English Historical Documents*.

[34] 2 February.

[35] Chrimes, *De Laudibus*, n. 2 above, lxvi, lxxii.

[36] Chrimes, *De Laudibus*, lxxii–lxxiii; see also Gross, n. 17 above, 75.

[37] Chrimes, *De Laudibus*, lxvi, lxxii.

[38] Chrimes, *De Laudibus*, lxvi.

[39] Chrimes, *De Laudibus*, lxvi.

retraction of his Lancastrian propaganda.[40] This Fortescue did in *Declaracion upon Certayn Wrytinges sent oute of Scotteland ayenst the Kinges Title to the Roialme of Englond.*[41] From October 1471, he was a member of Edward's council and sat in Star Chamber.[42] His attainder was reversed in February 1475.[43]

He died some time after May 1479, at the age, if Chrimes's calculations as to his birth are correct, of 94.

2. Fifteenth-Century Background

The 1400s received a bad press in subsequent centuries. Tudor propaganda deliberately portrayed it in terms of 'widespread ruin and destruction', primarily to distinguish Tudor grasp on the crown from earlier attempts.[44] The fifteenth century was reviled by Victorian Whig-oriented historians; Plummer referred to the character of 'futility' which Bishop Stubbs had 'so justly ascribed' to it.[45]

Later scholars repeated this appraisal,[46] but work of C. L. Kingsford, then later K. B. McFarlane, J. R. Lander, Charles Ross, R. A. Griffiths, and John Gillingham revised the traditional approach to the century in the sense that the emphasis was less on its previously perceived bloodiness, and more on its economic, political, cultural, and social ethos.[47] More recently still, Christine Carpenter has noted the disjunction between the study of fifteenth-century politics and constitutional history,[48] calling for a new examination of the 'public face of governance' and of the 'constitution of the body politic'.[49] It is here that Fortescue's work shines like a beacon.

Often overlooked as well is the century's notability both for the flowering and the demise of chivalry—witness *Knyghthode and Bataile*,[50] *Livre des fais d'armes et*

[40] Chrimes, *De Laudibus*, lxvi–lxvii.

[41] *Declaration upon Certain Writings*, written between 1471–3, see Chrimes, lxvii (relying on *Cal. Pat. R.* Edward IV, ii, 296); lxxv, lxvii.

[42] Chrimes, *De Laudibus*, lxvii.

[43] Chrimes, *De Laudibus*, lxvii, n. 8.

[44] Gross, n. 17 above, 5.

[45] Plummer, introduction to his revised 1885 edition of the *Governance of England*, n. 3 above, 2. See also Stubbs, n. 5 above, vol. II, 652.

[46] See, e.g., Randall, 'The Beginnings of English Constitutional Law', n. 11 above, 289: 'The period of the Wars of the Roses is almost the least interesting in English history . . . Stubbs struck the right note . . . The 15th century was a century of continuous war, but war of a sordid character, ennobled by no great object of policy.'

[47] For a discussion of the contribution of various scholars, see A. J. Pollard, *The Wars of the Roses*, 2nd ed. (Basingstoke: Palgrave, 2001), 8–16; and see C. Carpenter, *The Wars of the Roses: Politics and the Constitution in England, c.1437–1509* (Cambridge: Cambridge University Press, 2007), ch. 1 and *passim.*

[48] C. Carpenter, 'Political and Constitutional History: Before and After McFarlane', in R. H. Britnell and A. J. Pollard (eds), *The McFarlane Legacy: Studies in Late Medieval Politics and Society* (New York: St Martin's Press, 1995), 175–206, 192–8.

[49] Carpenter, *Wars of the Roses*, n. 47 above, 25.

[50] John of Burgundy engaged Christine de Pizan to make a French translation of Flavius Vegetius Renatus' *De re militari*, which same text would later be translated into English verse in the late 1450s as *Knyghthode and Bataile*—text available as *Knyghthode and Bataile* (Early English Text Society Original Series), ed. R. Dyboski and Z. M. Arend (Early English Text Society, 2007).

de chevalerie (*The Book of Deeds of Arms and of Chivalry*),[51] and Malory's *Le Morte d'Arthur.*[52] Earlier works concerning politics and governance also received considerable attention,[53] such as Giles of Rome's *De Regimine Principum*, William of Moerbeke's translation of Aristotle's *Politics*, *The Libelle of Englyshe Polycye*,[54] and Chapter 7 of John Gower's *Confessio Amantis* concerning *policie.*[55] Such works were, as McFarlane himself noted, 'meant to influence men's actions'.[56] This resurgence of interest in the concepts associated with good governance is indicated also in the various Mirrors for Princes,[57] of which Fortescue's *De Laudibus Legum Angliae* is but the most notable indisputably English example.

Here it should be remembered that Sir John Fortescue, like John Lydgate,[58] was a rhetorician.[59] As J. Allan Mitchell has argued, 'practitioners of secular rhetoric' had

> a sense of obligation and even entitlement . . . participating as they [did] in forms of rhetorical culture that gave occasion to invent, improve, provoke, enable, and judge the social order. In theory they join a tradition of public oratory deriving from Aristotle and

[51] Christine de Pizan, *Livre des fais d'armes et de chevaleri*, *c.*1410, published by Caxton in 1489 as *The Book of Fayttes of Armes and of Chivalrye*. See also *The Book of the Deeds of Arms and Chivalry by Christine de Pizan*, ed. Charity Cannon Willard and trans. Sumner Willard (Sumner Park: Pennsylvania State University Press, 1999); and see Rosemarie McGerr, 'A Statute Book and Lancastrian Mirror for Princes: The Yale Law School Manuscript of the *Nova Statuta Angliae*', in *Textual Cultures: Text, Contexts, Interpretation* 2 (2006), 6–59, 19.

[52] Sir Thomas Malory, *Le Morte d'Arthur (The hoole booke of kyng Arthur & of his noble knyghtes of the rounde table)* written 1450–70, published by Caxton in 1485.

[53] Generally here see P. Strohm, *Politique: Languages of Statecraft between Chaucer and Shakespeare* (The Conway Lectures in Medieval Studies 2003), (Indiana: University of Notre Dame, 2005), 'Introduction', 17–18.

[54] Written *c.*1435–6, *The Libelle of Englyshe Polycye: A Poem on the Use of Sea-Power 1436*, ed. Sir George Warner (Oxford: Clarendon Press, 1926).

[55] *c.*1390–3, originally dedicated to Richard II, rededicated to Henry of Lancaster. Gower, together with Lydgate and Chaucer, were referred to as 'the first rhetoricians' by Osborn Bokenham in *Life of St Anne*, line 1403 (38), in *Legendys of Hooly Wummen*, ed. M. S. Serjeantson, EETS os 206 (1938), as referred to by J. A. Mitchell in 'John Gower and John Lydgate: Forms and Norms of Rhetorical Culture', from P. Brown (ed.), *A Companion to Medieval English Literature and Culture c.1350–c.1500* (Blackwell Publishing, 2007): Blackwell Reference Online, <http://www.blackwellreference.com/subscriber/tocnode?id=g9780631219736_chunk_g978063121973639>, accessed 28 November 2008.

[56] K. B. McFarlane, 'Bastard Feudalism', and 'William Worcester, a Preliminary Survey', *Fifteenth Century England*, 23, 216, as referred to and cited in Gross, n. 17 above, 62 n. 66.

[57] See also John Lydgate (*c.*1370–1450), *The Fall of Princes*; George Ashby, *On the Active Policy of a Prince*, in *George Ashby's Poems*, ed. M. Bateson, EETS, Extra Series, 76 (1899), as discussed in Gross, n. 17 above, 37 and *passim*; St Thomas Aquinas, *On Kingship: to the King of Cyprus* (*De Regno, ad regem Cypri*); Ptolemy (Tolomeo or Bartholomew) of Lucca, *De Regimine Principum* (On the Governance of Princes/Rulers). See also McGerr, 'Lancastrian Mirror' n. 51 above, *passim.*

[58] John Lydgate was a Benedictine religious and Lancastrian supporter; *The Fall of Princes* (written 1431–9) is 'a translation of Giovanni Boccaccio's *De casibus virorum illustrium* (1355–60) via an intermediary French prose version by Laurent de Premierfait, the *Des Cas des nobles hommes et femmes* (1409): see N. Mortimer, *John Lydgate's Fall of Princes* (Clarendon Press, Oxford English Monographs, 2005), abstract at <http://www.oxfordscholarship.com/view/10.1093/acprof:oso/9780199275014.001.0001/acprof-9780199275014>.

[59] This view is largely supported by P. Raffield in his interesting examination of rhetoric, masques, and lawyers, drawing upon Fortescue's *De Laudibus*—'The Elizabethan Rhetoric of Signs: Representations of *Res Publica* at the Early Modern Inns of Court', *Law Culture and the Humanities*, 7 (2) (2011), 244–63. Raffield notes that rhetoric's effectiveness was concerned with 'supplanting falsehood with truth, and inequity with justice' (263).

Cicero, expressing venerable notions of rhetoric and *res publica* familiar to medieval writers. Rhetoric here has first of all to be understood as a pragmatic activity and attitude, a disposition towards words as much as a manner of disposing words. Gower and Lydgate[60] both begin with the assumption that rhetoric is improving, humanizing, civilizing—not (or not just) artful embellishment. Such ideas survived in the handbooks of the ancients, but were also transmitted in thirteenth-century works of rhetorical and regiminal instruction such as Giles of Rome's *De regimine principum* and Brunetto Latini's *Livres dou trésor*.[61]

and he quotes Brunetto's concept of rhetoric, as a 'species of practical politics':

that noble science which teaches us to compose and organize and say good and beautiful words, full of meaning, in keeping with the nature of the utterance... Without doubt we need it every day, and many things we can achieve merely by saying well the proper words, things we could not do through force of arms or any other means.[62]

This is as good a summation of Fortescue's work as any: a species of 'practical politics' informed by the common law. Bertie Wilkinson observed in 1964 that '[the fifteenth century] witnessed the firm foundation of a national state in which the essential link was between the monarch and all the commonality'.[63] Or, to put it another way, the law and the constitution are inextricably linked to the people, all three are interconnected as Fortescue saw, and all three are also, as Matthew Hale recognized later in the seventeenth century, organic.[64]

3. Background: Summary

Over Fortescue's lifetime, England had been engaged in the Hundred Years War (1337–1453). Henry V had been successful at Agincourt (1415);[65] under Henry VI France had been lost.

The Black Death had decimated England during the fourteenth and fifteenth centuries,[66] the population falling from 4.5–6 million in 1348[67] to 2–2.5 million

60 And, the author argues, Fortescue.

61 See J. A. Mitchell, *Forms and Norms of Rhetorical Culture,* n. 55 above.

62 Brunetto Latini, *The Book of the Treasure* (*Li Livres dou Tresor*), trans. Paul Barrette and Spurgeon Baldwin (New York: Garland, 1993), 5, quoted by Mitchell, *Forms and Norms.*

63 Bertie Wilkinson, *Constitutional History of England in the Fifteenth Century* (1399–1485), (London: Longmans Green & Co. Ltd, 1964), 398.

64 (Sir Matthew Hale), 'Touching the Original of the Common Law of England', in *The History and Analysis of the Common Law of England, written by a Learned Hand* (In the Savoy, printed by J. Nutt, 1713, The Legal Classics Library facsimile, Alabama, 1987), ch. IV, 58–9, 59–60.

65 But see A. Curry, *The Battle of Agincourt: Sources and Interpretations: Warfare in History* (Woodbridge: Boydell & Brewer, 2000), and A. Curry, *Agincourt: A New History* (Stroud: Tempus Publishing, 2005, paperback ed., 2006).

66 The Black Death arrived in England in 1348, and later outbreaks occurred in 1361–4, 1368, 1371, 1373–5, 1390, 1405, and also in 1471, 1479–80, and 1498, with later recurrences in the sixteenth and seventeenth centuries—see Mike Ibeji, *The Black Death* (BBC History, 2011), <http://www.bbc.co.uk/history/british/middle_ages/black_01.shtml#nine>; see also J. Munro, *Review* of S. J. Borsch, *The Black Death in Egypt and England: A Comparative Study*, (Austin: University of Texas Press, 2005), Economic History Service, EH. Net, <http://web.archive.org/web/20080504134636/http://eh.net/bookreviews/library/1053>.

67 Alastair Dunn, http://www.st-andrews.ac.uk/~histweb/medhist/dunn/04.pdf, gives the figure of 5–6 million. John Hatcher gives the figure of 4.5–6 million—see J. Hatcher, 'Plague, Population and

in 1450.[68] This figure is endorsed by later research, where John Aberth suggests that the mortality rate in England was between 40 per cent and 70 per cent,[69] with an average of a 50 per cent mortality rate generally according with medieval chroniclers' reports.[70] In addition, the worship of God in England was relatively homogeneous, all people being Catholic, other than some few who still held to the doctrines of Wycliffe or the Lollards. So there was a relatively small number of people in England in the mid-fifteenth century, all engaged in some fashion in assessing, reappraising, and using the instruments of governance.

The fifteenth century may be seen then as:

- an intensely political century where political factions developed in a loose fashion; Maitland says of the 'Wars of the Roses' that it was 'a great faction fight in which the whole nation takes sides'.[71]
- a time where the settlement of political disputes gradually moved from settlement by passage of arms to settlement through political accommodation and the application of law.
- part of a long revolution dating from the deposition of Edward II in 1327 to the establishment of the Tudor regime under Henry VII in 1485, where the preoccupation of the people and the active participants was to establish good governance
- a time when the question of the succession to the crown was but one of the issues that fell for determination by the people.

Indeed, drawing upon Aberth's percipient conclusions,[72] the fifteenth century should no longer be seen as a time of decline, decay, and stultification interrupted by outbreaks of barbarity, but rather as a time of innovation, reinvigoration, and rebirth following upon the devastation of the Black Death.

II. Analysis and Impact of Fortescue's Work

1. Fortescue's Ideas

Fortescue's three great works are *De Natura*, *De Laudibus*, and *The Governance of England*.[73] *De Natura* was a polemic designed to show that by the laws of nature and God, title to the crown could not descend through the female line—in essence

the English Economy, 1348–1530, Conclusion', in M. Anderson (ed.), *British Population History: From the Black Death to the present day* (Cambridge: Cambridge University Press, 1996), 74.

[68] See Dunn, n. 67 above; and see Hatcher, n. 67 above, graphs at 77.

[69] J. Aberth, *The Black Death: The Great Mortality of 1348–1350, A Brief History with Documents* (Boston: Bedford/St Martins, 2005), 3, 95; see also J. Aberth, *From the Brink of the Apocalypse: Confronting Famine, War, Plague and Death in the Later Middle Ages* (New York: Routledge, 2000), 127.

[70] Aberth, *Black Death*, n. 69 above, 3.

[71] Maitland, n. 6 above, 194.

[72] Aberth, *Black Death*, n. 69 above, 4.

[73] See Annex at end of chapter for complete list.

a rebuttal of the Yorkist claim, which was through the granddaughter of Edward III.[74] It will not be examined here.

The following analysis is heavily indebted to S. B. Chrimes's examination of Fortescue in *De Laudibus Legum Anglie*,[75] and in *English Constitutional Ideas in the Fifteenth Century*,[76] and also to other scholars as represented in the footnotes. In addition, John Selden's translation of *De Laudibus* (1616) and his comments are discussed at some points, because of the use made of Fortescue's work, especially *De Laudibus* and *Governance*, by the actors in seventeenth-century constitutional politics.

The most famous of these books is *De Laudibus*. It is in the form of a dialogue between a 'certain grave old knight',[77] the Chancellor (Fortescue), and a prince (Prince Edward). Fortescue was Edward's tutor, and his book begins with urging the Prince to recall Justinian's words that 'Imperial Majesty ought to be not only adorned with arms but also armed with laws, so that it can govern aright in both times of peace and war'.[78] The remainder of the dialogue progresses Socratic-fashion to discuss the best means of governing and law-making for the common weal. *Governance*, on the other hand, adopts a more straightforward, less rhetorical analysis of the same issue. Fortescue's major ideas are discussed, necessarily briefly, below.

i. The Four Dominiums

J. H. Burns[79] notes that *dominium*, the word Fortescue associates with the various types of governance, is susceptible to differing interpretations or translations in English, depending on its context. At the beginning of *Governance*, Fortescue uses the words 'Ther bith ij kyndes off kyngdomes, of the wich that on is a lordship callid in laten *dominium regale*, and that other is callid *dommium politicum et regale*.' Here Fortescue is concerned with *dominiums* that are *kingdoms*.[80] However, this does not mean that these are the only types of kingdoms, nor that only kingdoms are *dominiums*.

In *De Laudibus*, Fortescue refers to the institution of both *regna tantum regaliter* or *dominatus tantum regalis*[81] (entirely regal kingdom [Chrimes], Kingdoms ruled

[74] Richard of York was descended from Lionel, Duke of Clarence, Edward III's second surviving son, through his mother and grandmother; Henry VI was descended from Edward III's third surviving son, John of Gaunt, Duke of Lancaster, in the male line; after the deaths of Bedford and Gloucester, it was arguable that Richard was next in line to the throne, if one did not hold to strictly male primogeniture.

[75] See Chrimes, n. 2 above. [76] See Chrimes, n. 9 above.

[77] *De Laudibus*, Introduction; Chrimes's translation is 'certain aged knight'; 3.

[78] *De Laudibus*, c. 1; Justinian, *Institutes*, Prooemium—*Imperatoriam maiestatem non solum armis decoratam, sed et legibus oportet esse armatam, ut utrumque tempus bellorum et pacis recte possit gubernare.*

[79] J. H. Burns, 'Fortescue and the Political Theory of Dominion', *The Historical Journal* 28 (1985), 777–97.

[80] See Burns, 'Fortescue and the Political Theory of Dominion', 784–5.

[81] *De Laudibus*, Chapter XII, Chrimes, n. 2 above, 28, 29.

by Regal Government [Selden])[82] and *regni politici* (political kingdom: Selden,[83] Chrimes, and Lockwood[84] all use these words).[85] However there is a third kind of kingdom—the *regimine politico et regale in regno Anglie* (the political and regal government in the kingdom of England)[86]—but here Selden uses the words 'The Comparative Advantages in England, where Government is of a mixed nature.'[87] Because in England the king cannot impose taxes or change the laws nor make new ones *sine concessione vel assensu tocius regni sui in parliamento suo expresso* (without the concession or assent of his whole realm expressed in his parliament),[88] therefore all the inhabitants are rich in the necessities of life (*Unde inhabitants terre illius locupletes sunt . . . et cunctis necessaries vite*)[89] and receive the protection of the laws of the land.[90] Fortescue's glowing description of the English had earlier been described as mere wishful thinking;[91] however, the diminution of the population had ensured that living conditions had improved for all surviving English people.[92] This, Fortescue argues, is the fruit of *regimen politicum*[93] *et regale*[94] (Chrimes—'political and regal government;'[95] Selden—'political mixed government'[96]).

There are however, other kinds of *dominium* of which Fortescue writes. In *De Natura*, he refers to *socialis dominii*[97] shaken off impatiently by Julius Caesar; Burns refers to this as *domimium sociale* in which 'a number of people are associated together in government';[98] Lockwood translates this as 'shared dominion'[99] but it seems more likely that this represents what in Fortescue's mind was a republic.[100] In addition, Burns notes that Fortescue makes it clear in *De Natura* II: iv that *dominium politicum* 'allows for (or even requires) a number of rulers, which a *dominium regale* never does.'[101] The point here is that for Fortescue, *dominium* was

[82] John Selden translated *De Laudibus* from Latin to English in 1616; this translation was used by Francis Gregor in his 1737 and 1775 editions: see Chrimes, n. 2 above, lxxx; and see Selden/Gregor, n. 2 above, 29.

[83] Selden/Gregor, *De Laudibus*, 34.

[84] Lockwood, *Governance*, n. 3 above, 21.

[85] *De Laudibus*, Chapter XIII, Chrimes, n. 2 above, 32, 33.

[86] *De Laudibus*, Chapter XXXVI, Chrimes, n. 2 above, 86, 87; Lockwood, *Governance*, n. 3 above, 51.

[87] Selden/Gregor, n. 2 above, 127.

[88] *De Laudibus*, Chapter XXXVI, Chrimes, n. 2 above, 86, 87. Selden—'He can't . . . without the express consent of the whole kingdom in Parliament assembled' (Selden/Gregor, n. 2 above, 128).

[89] Chrimes, n. 2 above, 86, 87.

[90] . . . *leges terre illius et coram iudicibus antedictis*. (XXXVI, 10).

[91] Cf. Pollard, *Evolution of Parliament*, n. 16 above.

[92] See Dunn, n. 67 above; see also Hatcher, n. 67 above, graphs at 77, which show that real wage rates for craftsmen hit a peak between 1450 and 1475, at exactly the same time that the population of England fell to its lowest (the range of time is from 1250 to 1750).

[93] Note a most interesting interpretation from J. R. Maddicott, *The Origins of the English Parliament 924–1327* (Oxford: Oxford University Press, 2010), 377, n. 2, where he argues the case for translating '*politicum*' to mean 'public', noting that this would appear to be in accord with D. R. Howlett, *Dictionary of Medieval Latin from British Sources* (Oxford: Oxford University Press for the British Academy, 2007), 2332–3.

[94] *De Laudibus*, Chapter XXXVI, Chrimes, n. 2 above, 88, 89; Selden/Gregor, n. 2 above, 129.

[95] Chrimes, n. 2 above, 87, 89.

[96] Selden/Gregor, n. 2 above, 129.

[97] *De Natura*, C. xvi, reproduced in Chrimes, n. 2 above, 152.

[98] Burns, 'Fortescue and the Political Theory of Dominion', 781.

[99] Lockwood, *Governance*, n. 3 above, 129.

[100] Cf. see Burns, 'Fortescue and the Political Theory of Dominion', 784–5.

[101] Burns, 'Fortescue and the Political Theory of Dominion', 784.

not necessarily co-extensive with kingship. And yet again, a *dominium* may be regal, in the sense that the ruler makes laws which please him, but may still be *politicum*, in that the laws are designed for common weal, or the good of many or the 'plurality'—*sed quia ad plurium usum videlicet Romanorum regebant rempublicam.*[102]

Again, Fortescue refers to *dominium despoticum* making a connection between conquest and despotic power, whereby the society is incorporated by the ruler[103] rather than by the will of the people as is the case in his preferred model. Fortescue associates *dominium despoticum* with tyranny[104] and sometimes with *dominium regale tantum.*[105] Consequently, for Fortescue a *dominium despoticum* may be either that of a dictator, or a tyrant, or sometimes a benevolent dictator—though this last may well turn out in fact to be a *dominium regale et politicum*, in that laws are made for the benefit of the people.

However, Fortescue's writings were concerned with kingship—in *De Natura* justifying the Lancastrian claim and demolishing that of York; in *De Laudibus* both delineating and praising the lineaments of English monarchical government; and in *Governance*, setting out parameters for better monarchical governance. But this means that for Fortescue there were *four*, not three, types of *dominium*—*regna tantum regaliter, regni politici, regimine politico et regale* (the monarchical *dominiums*), and a fourth general class, encompassing other types of *dominium* that do not fit into these three categories, which would include a republic.

ii. The English Dominium

a. The English people incorporated

How exactly did Fortescue describe English governance as coming into being? He begins with a 'people' as defined by Augustine, meaning *a body of men united by consent of law and by community of interest.*[106] But that body of people cannot really be called a 'body' since it is acephalous; a body politic[107] needs a head—therefore a people (*populum*) wishing to make itself a kingdom or other body politic (*in regnum aliudve corpus politicam*) must set up one person for the government of all of that body,[108]

[102] For text see Chrimes, n. 2 above, 153; for translation, see Lockwood, *Governance*, n. 3 above, 130; see also Burns, 'Fortescue and the Political Theory of Dominion', 781.

[103] *De Natura*, II: xlvi; *Declaracion on certaine Wrytinges*, in Clermont, *Works*, I:533, as cited in Burns, 'Fortescue and the Political Theory of Dominion', 786; see also Burns, 791.

[104] See *De Natura*, I: xlvi; Burns 'Fortescue and the Political Theory of Dominion', 785–6.

[105] Burns, 'Fortescue and the Political Theory of Dominion', 786.

[106] St Augustine, *De Civitate Dei*, lib. xix, 24; see *De Laudibus*, XIII, Chrimes, n. 2 above, 31. Augustine also wrote a treatise *On Kingship*, but it has been lost.

[107] Selden also uses these words, 'body politic'—see Selden/Gregor, n. 2 above, 32; Lockwood, 'in political things', *Governance*, n. 3 above, 20.

[108] *De Laudibus*, XIII, Chrimes, n. 2 above, 30, 31; Selden: 'some one should preside as the governing Principle' in Selden/Gregor, n. 2 above, 33.

known as a king. Using the anthropomorphic image of a physical body (foreshadowing Hobbes's *Leviathan*[109]), Fortescue says that

the kingdom issues from the people . . . as a mystical body . . . (*ex polulo erumpit regnum, quod corpus extat misticum*) . . . in the body politic the will of the people (*in corpore politico intencio populi primum vivens est*) is the source of life, having in it the blood, namely political forethought for the interest of the people (*provisionem politicam utilitatis populi illius*), which it transmits to the head and all the members of the body, by which the body is maintained and quickened. (Chrimes)

(From a confused Multitude is formed a regular kingdom . . . in the Body Politic, the first Thing which lives and moves is the Intention of the People, having in it the Blood, that is, the prudential Care and Provision for the Public good, which it transmits and communicates to the Head, as the principle Part; and to all the rest of the Members of the said Body politic. [Selden]).[110]

In summary, for Fortescue, the 'body politic' grows as does a physical body from an embryo to be regulated by one head, with the kingdom growing from the embryo of 'the people', and existing as a mystical body governed by one person, the king, as head, with 'the will of the people' being the heart and source of life of the body politic, and the law being the nerves and nourishment of it.[111] Such a body politic is a 'political kingdom', where the king is 'obliged to protect the law, the subjects, and their bodies and goods, and he has power to this end issuing from the people, so that it is not permissible for him to rule his people with any other power'.[112]

England is of this latter kind, because, while the law of nature is the same everywhere,[113] and while English customs are 'the best',[114] with regard to the third arm of the law—statutes—English statutes are made 'not only by the prince's will, but also with the assent of the whole realm, so they cannot be injurious to people nor fail to secure their advantage'.[115]

But it is Law that truly makes a 'group of men' 'into a people' (Chrimes) [Selden: 'The Law, under which the People is incorporated'—*Lex, Vero, sub qua cestus hominum populus efficitur*].[116] The mystical body is bound (or, the body is bound mystically) together and united in one by the law (*sic per legem que ligando dicitur, corpus huiusmodi misticum ligatur et servatur in unum*), which in turn sustains the community by a solid basis of truth (*que veritas qua communitas illa sustenatur, soliditatem denotant per legem*).[117] Just as, then, the head of a body cannot change the sinews that bind it together, neither can a king who is head of a body politic so created (*nec rex qui caput corporis politici est*) change the laws, nor deprive

109 Thomas Hobbes, *Leviathan, or the Matter, Form and Power of a Commonwealth Ecclesiastical and Civil*, 1651, edited and abridged by John Plamenatz (London: Collins, The Fontana Library, 1962, 3rd impression, 1967), 59. Fortescue in *De Laudibus* refers to Leviathan twice in XXXII, Chrimes, 78, 79.

110 *De Laudibus*, Chrimes, n. 2 above, XIII, 30, 31; Selden/Gregor, n. 2 above, 33.

111 *De Laudibus*, Chrimes, n. 2 above, 31.

112 *De Laudibus*, Chrimes, n. 2, 33.

113 *De Laudibus*, Chrimes, n. 2, 39.

114 *De Laudibus*, Chrimes, n. 2, 41.

115 *De Laudibus*, Chrimes, n. 2, 41. Fortescue himself had been elected as a member of parliament on 8 occasions, which may account for his touching faith in the probity and altruism of the 'more than three hundred chosen men'—see Chrimes, n. 2.

116 *De Laudibus*, Chrimes; Selden, n. 2.

117 Chrimes, n. 2.

the people of their own substance (what is theirs by Right: Selden) against their will (*nec eiusdem populi substancias proprias subtrahere reclamantibus eis aut invites*). This is the institution of the *political kingdom—institucionis regni politici.*

The king's power issues from the people (*potestam a populo effluxam ipse habet*[118]). He has no other power but this. The purpose of the power is to protect the law, the subjects, their bodies, and their goods (Selden: protect his Subjects in their Lives, properties and Laws).[119]

But the regal kingdom is far different.

b. The regal kingdom

For Fortescue, purely regal kingdoms began through subjugation or conquest and the imposition of laws upon the subjugated people; but the people eventually acquiesced in the subjugation for the purpose of being protected.[120] Such kingdoms were characterized by the application of the maxim *Quod principi placuit legis habet vigorem—What pleases the Prince has the force of law.*[121] In the civilian European law, this maxim applied in a 'detestable and damnable fashion, by no colour of law' but the maxim itself,[122] with devastating results for the populace (and he used France as an exemplar). Such a king levied taxes without approval, billeted soldiers without consent, set high prices on necessities such as salt, approved guilt solely on the basis of his conscience without trial, and impoverished his people to the extent that they wore only canvas, ate little meat and drank only water.[123] The English kingdom compared favourably on all fronts to such regal kingdoms, especially France.

However, Fortescue acknowledged that a king ruling solely regally may also provide the same goods to his subjects as does a political and regal ruler, provided he did not degenerate into tyranny. The best man may in fact be the better option to the best laws,[124] drawing upon Aristotle (*regi viro optimo quam lege optima*); but this clearly does not always happen.[125]

118 Chrimes, 32, 33; Selden/Gregor, n. 2 above, 34, interprets this as 'he has the Delegation of power from the People'.

119 Chrimes; Selden/Gregor. 120 *De Laudibus*, Chapter XII, Chrimes, 28, 29.

121 *De Laudibus*, Chapter XXXIV, Chrimes, 78, 79; Justinian, *Institutes*, I:2, vi. The entire quotation (as noted by Selden—Selden/Gregor, n. 2 above, 116–17, n. 22) is: '*Sed et quod principi placuit legis habet vigorem, cum lege regia, quae de imperio eius lata est, populus ei et in eum omne suum imperium et potestatem concessit*—That which seems good to the emperor has also the force of law; for the people, by the *Lex Regia,* which is passed to confer on him his power, make over to him their whole power and authority.'

122 *De Laudibus*, Chapter XXXV, Chrimes, n. 2 above, 84, 85: *non alio quam legis colore, detestabiliter damnabiliterque perpetrate . . .*

123 *De Laudibus*, Chrimes, 80–5.

124 Bracton *c.*1250–60 had earlier suggested that by taking the coronation oath, the king became 'the just man'—*Homo enim iustas habet voluntatem tribuendi unicuique ius suum, et ita ella voluntas dicitur iusta. Et dicitur voluntas tribuere ius suum, non quantum ad actum sed quantum ad affectionem*—see Bracton, *De Legibus et Consuetudinibus Angliae*, ed. G. E. Woodbine (Yale University Press, 1922), reproduced with translation by S. E. Thorne, Selden Society and Harvard University Press, Cambridge MA, 1968: *Bracton on the Laws and Customs of England*, trans. S. E. Thorne; Latin text copyright 1922 Yale University Press; translation copyright 1968 Harvard), 23, 2b; see also 22, folio 2.

125 *De Laudibus*, Chapter IX, Chrimes, 24–7.

c. The political and regal kingdom—England?

In England, none of the faults of a purely regal kingdom like France occur, the people being rich and prosperous[126] and treated justly according to the law of the land. The king is bound by his own laws and cannot impose taxes or any other burdens on his subjects or change the laws or make new ones (*aut leges eorum mutat, vel novas conduit*) without the concession or consent of his whole realm as expressed in his parliament[127] (Selden: 'He can't alter the Laws or make new ones without the Express consent of the whole Kingdom in Parliament assembled').[128] This is a government political and regal (*regimine politico et regale*).[129] Earlier, Fortescue had said that the regal and political king is unable to change the laws without the 'assent of his subjects' (*sine subditorum assensu*) so that they are ruled by 'laws they themselves desire' (*bonis suis legibus quas cupit regulatus*).[130] While acknowledging the possible benefits of the rule of the just man, Fortescue was boldly making the case, as was much later to be made by James Harrington,[131] John Adams,[132] and John Marshall,[133] for 'an empire of laws, and not of men'; but for Fortescue, as always, the laws themselves emanated from the men.

However, an analysis of the development of Fortescue's thinking through *De Natura* and *De Laudibus* to *Governance* raises, as Burns points out, some serious questions about the nature of this political and regal kingdom, asking whether it is really all that far removed from the purely regal kingdom, and to what extent the assent of the people is really required to make new laws:

- Each of Fortescue's three types of kingdom has a ruler who rules according to law (*De Natura*, I: xvi).[134]
- The power of both regal and political kings is the same (*De Laudibus*, XIV, XXXVII),
  - but the regal king can fall into impotency or 'non-power' by doing wrong which diminishes his power (*De Laudibus*, XIV; *Governance*, Chapter 6),[135]
  - and the political and regal king can in times of emergency rule purely 'regally' when necessary to suppress rebellion, or for reasons of equity (*De Natura*, I: xxxv and xxiv respectively).[136]

126 See Hatcher, n. 92 above.

127 *De Laudibus*, Chapter XXXVI, Chrimes, 86, 87.

128 Selden/Gregor, n. 2 above, 128.

129 *De Laudibus*, heading to Chapter XXXVI; see also Chapter IX, Chrimes, 24, 25.

130 *De Laudibus*, Chapter IX, Chrimes, 24, 25.

131 James Harrington, *The Commonwealth of Oceana* (1656), ed. J. G. A. Pocock (Cambridge: Cambridge University Press, 1977), 171: 'The main question seems to be, how a commonwealth comes to be an empire of laws, and not of men?'

132 John Adams, *Thoughts on Government*, 1775—'the very definition of a republic is "an empire of laws, and not of men."' (Adams sourced the phrase to Harrington, see David McCullough, *John Adams* (New York: Simon & Schuster, 2001), 102, see note at 664). See also the 1780 Massachusetts Constitution drafted by Adams, Pt. 1, Art. XXX.

133 *Marbury v Madison*, (1803) 1 Cranch 137, 163, Marshall CJ.

134 Burns, n. 79 above, 778.

135 See also *De Natura* in Lockwood, n. 3 above, 133–5.

136 See Lockwood, n. 3 above, xxiii.

  - Furthermore, relying on *De Natura*, Burns argues that Fortescue's 'political king' does not necessarily have to make laws with the consent of the people, but rather must act for their benefit and/or as a result of counsel,[137] thus severely reducing the 'political' element of a 'political' kingship.
- However, the need for the assent of the people to laws, especially to taxing laws, is made emphatically by Fortescue in both *De Laudibus* and in *Governance*.[138]
  - Chrimes notes that any ordinances that the king could make without the assent of the lords and commons were not regarded in the fifteenth century as either making new law, or changing the law.[139]

Notwithstanding Burns's argument, it seems inarguable that Fortescue saw the congregation of the representatives of the people in the commons, together with the lords, as being fundamental to good governance and the making of the law, especially in regard to any laws imposing taxes. That is, the people's representatives in the Houses of Parliament *must assent* to the levying of any taxes. He saw the English governance as implementing the advice of St Thomas Aquinas in what Fortescue refers to as *De Regimine Principum*[140] that the regal power is restrained by *political* power.[141]

This was a new and noteworthy departure in both political and constitutional thinking, and reveals the significance which Fortescue attached to the involvement of the people through their representatives.

The role of the people through the Houses of Parliament in contributing to law-making is fundamental to Fortescue's thought. He was a former parliamentarian himself. He was Chancellor to the exiled Henry VI. He was a 'doughty champion of monarchy and common law' to whom a law-making parliament representative of the people was as necessary and as inevitable as the common law and the monarchy themselves, because 'the *principle* of it had become firmly rooted'.[142]

iii. Conclusion on the English dominium

In both *De Laudibus* and *Governance* Fortescue was constructing a norm of what good governance in England should be, as opposed to that of France (a purely regal kingdom) or certain of the Prince's predecessors who had attempted 'to introduce the civil laws into the government of England, and tried to repudiate the laws of the land'.[143] These references are very likely to Edward IV, for whom there is no

[137] Burns, n. 79 above, 781, relying on *De Natura*—see n. 102 above.

[138] See *De Laudibus*, XVIII, XXXVI; *The Governance of England*, in Lockwood, *Governance*, n. 3 above, 83, 86.

[139] Chrimes, n. 2 above, 185.

[140] This is a reference to St Thomas Aquinas (1225–74), *On Kingship: to the King of Cyprus* (*De Regno, ad regem Cypri*).

[141] *De Laudibus*, IX, Chrimes, n. 2 above, 26, 27.

[142] Chrimes, n. 2 above, cii.

[143] *De Laudibus*, XXXIII, XXXIV, Chrimes, n. 2 above, 79.

record of a coronation oath,[144] the sources also being strangely silent on his coronation.[145] The possibilities arising from these lacunae are discussed below.[146]

Fortescue's work re-emphasised that the whole purpose of governance and the law is to provide peace and protection for the people, and that the best means of achieving this end is through involvement of the people themselves. Selden called this a 'political mixed government'[147] in which the people through their representatives were a vital part. For Fortescue, governance was synonymous with the *res publica* and the common weal.

2. The law

Underlying Fortescue's analysis of good governance is always the law.[148] Firstly, it is 'the law' which incorporates a group of humans into a people[149] or a body politic, and the will of the people gives life to the body politic through laws.[150] Thus, a body politic grows as does a physical body from an embryo to be regulated by one head, with the kingdom growing from the embryo of 'the people', and existing as a mystical body governed by one man; the king, as head, with 'the will of the people' being the heart and source of life of the body politic, and the law being the nerves and nourishment of it.[151] Such a body politic is a 'political kingdom', where the king is 'obliged to protect the law, the subjects, and their bodies and goods, and he has power to this end issuing from the people, so that it is not permissible for him to rule his people with any other power'.[152]

Why England had (and should have) such good governance, is because the civilian maxim *What pleases the Prince has the force of law* has no place in English law. Fortescue said:

[144] Percy E. Schramm's *A History of the English Coronation*, translated from the German by L. G. Wickham Legg (Oxford: Clarendon Press, 1937) has no reference at all to either Edward IV's coronation or his oath, nor is there one in the index or Appendix. It is possible that Edward IV did not take the coronation oath at all, which could account for the elliptical reference by Sir John Fortescue in his *De Laudibus*, to kings who endeavoured to 'throw off ' the 'political yoke' of the coronation oath—see Chrimes's translation of *de Laudibus*, n. 2 above, Chapter XXXII, 79 and 80. Indeed, given Edward IV's cavalier attitude towards his responsibilities concerning his marriage, and Maitland's animadversions on his cruelty, illegality and autocracy (see Maitland, n. 3 above, 195, 221, and 266–7) it would not be surprising if Edward IV did not take the coronation oath at all. If he did not, this could account for Richard III's subsequent almost over-conscientious following of all the common law forms.

[145] Stubbs, n. 5 above, III: 192, says that 'it was said that [Edward] had chosen 1 November 1460 as the date for his coronation, in case the lords had accepted him as king'. *And* Michael St John Parker, *Britain's Kings and Queens* (London: Pitkin Pictorials Ltd, first published 1974; further edition 1990, reprinted 1992), 17, says Edward IV was crowned at Westminster. J. Cannon and R. Griffiths (eds), *The Oxford Illustrated History of the British Monarchy* (New York: Oxford University Press, 1988, reprinted with corrections, 1989, 1992), makes no mention of Edward IV's coronation.

[146] See discussion later in this chapter under the heading 'King-making and the people', 74, and at 75 ff.

[147] See n. 96 above.

[148] See also discussion later in this chapter under the heading 'Mirrors for princes and the law', at 71.

[149] See text accompanying nn. 116–17 above.

[150] See text accompanying nn. 106–10 above.

[151] *De Laudibus*, Chrimes, 31.

[152] *De Laudibus*, Chrimes, 33.

The laws of England do not sanction any such maxim, since the king of that land rules his people not only regally but also politically [Selden: 'in a mixed political capacity'[153]], and so he is bound by his oath at his coronation to the observance of his law.[154]

Indeed, he saw English law as complying with the precepts of St Thomas Aquinas set out in *De Regimine Principum*, that a king should govern his people with his 'regal power . . . restrained by *political law* . . . *potestas regia lege politica cohibitur*'.[155] Such a king has no less power than one who rules purely regally, but 'their authority over their subjects is different.'[156]

Exactly what is the 'political' yoke placed about the neck of the English king that renders him confined in his use of power? Clearly this peculiarity of English governance is to be found in the coronation oath, or the oath of governance, which places restraints upon an English monarch.[157]

But not only is a king bound by the law. The study of law itself is the prime directive that Fortescue (the Chancellor) gives to the Prince at the beginning of *De Laudibus*; referring to Justinian's precepts, he urges the Prince to spend more time in the study of the law, at least equivalent to his chivalric and knightly duties. He quotes I Kings 8: 20, 'For the office of a king is to fight the battles of his people and to judge them rightfully', noting that 'as battles are determined by arms, so judgements are by laws'.[158] On the Prince's mind, as on a *tabula rasa*, is law to be impressed to ensure that he is imbued with 'the habit of justice' and 'enjoy happiness through the law'.[159] The whole argument in *De Laudibus* and also in *Governance* is built upon the foundation of the law as it exists in England—that is, the law of nature, custom, and statutes made by both king and people all together amount to the common law of the English.[160] As opposed to the civilian governance, which is founded upon violence and oppression, English governance is grounded in law, justice being the object of all royal administration.[161]

All human law consists of three kinds: the law of nature, the law of customs, and that of statutes (the last also being called constitutions). But, Fortescue notes, if the laws of nature and customs are reduced to writing, and promulgated by the authority of the Prince and commanded to be observed, then they become accepted as constitutions or statutes, and must be obeyed due to a stricter penalty by virtue of the Prince's command.[162]

[153] Selden/Gregor, n. 2 above, 118. [154] *De Laudibus*, XXXIV, Chrimes, 78, 79.

[155] *De Laudibus*, IX, Chrimes, 27, 26, emphasis added.

[156] *De Laudibus*, Chrimes, 28–9.

[157] *De Laudibus*, 79, 80—'*Qualiter non sancciunt leges Anglie, dum nedum regaliter sed et politice rex eiusdem dominatur in populum suum, quo ipse in coronacione sua ad legis sue observanciam astringitur sacremento*'. See also discussion later in this chapter under the heading 'King-making and the people', at 74 ff.

[158] *De Laudibus*, I, Chrimes, 3–5. [159] *De Laudibus*, VI, Chrimes, 16–19.

[160] For a discussion of the common law in this context, see M. R. L. L. Kelly, 'Common Law Constitutionalism and the Oath of Governance: "An Hieroglyphic of the Laws"', 28 *Miss. C. L. Rev.*, 121–80, 131 ff., 'The Nature of the Common Law'.

[161] *De Laudibus*, IV, Chrimes, 10–15; VI, Chrimes, 16–19 respectively; see also discussion later in this chapter under the heading, 'Mirrors for princes and the law', at 71 ff.

[162] *De Laudibus*, XV, Chrimes, 36–7.

i. English customs and the 'ancient constitution'

While the law of nature is the same everywhere, insofar as English laws enjoin observance of it, they are no better or worse than the laws of other nations. But, Fortescue argued, English customs are the best, because they have been endorsed by successive monarchs over the centuries, including those who conquered England.[163] Fortescue had earlier alluded to England having its original form from 'Brutus and his band of Trojans'[164] and later compared the antiquity of English laws favourably with those of Rome and Venice. John Selden noted that Fortescue's assertions depend upon the veracity of the Brute story,[165] and 'with no disparagement to our Common Laws' he says (like Fortescue) that all laws are derived from natural law and thus all laws are 'originally equally ancient' and '[t]hose which best fit the State wherein they are, clearly deserve the name of best laws'. He considers questions as to the antiquity of the 'Common Laws' to be 'trivial', but asks why the Roman law was neglected some 600 years if it were so excellent.[166]

Selden defended Fortescue's assertion that the customs have remained the same, and while noting the admixture in early times of British, Danish, Saxon, and Norman laws, also noted that William I had undertaken to continue 'St Edward's laws' which were still so called 'to this day'.[167] Further, he compares the English laws to a 'ship that by often mending had no Piece of the first Materials, or as the house that's so often repaired *ut nihil ex pristine material supersit*', a comment analogous to that later made by Sir Matthew Hale, that the laws are the same over hundreds of years, just as the body of Titus remains the same though all parts of it have been renewed.[168]

This idea of an ancient lineage for the 'common laws' grew into a rubric of 'the ancient constitution', formed the basis of much polemic in the seventeenth century, and has been a preoccupation of scholars ever since.[169] The idea that both customs and the law of nature could become akin to statutes if promulgated by the king was not new, and indeed much of the law as decided by the courts was based upon this notion.

Fortescue, having been a serjeant and then judge and Chief Justice, was well aware of, and loved (it can be said) the law that the courts used. He wrote of 'customs, statutes, and the law of nature, from which *all the laws of the realm*

[163] *De Laudibus*, XVII, Chrimes, 38–41. [164] *De Laudibus*, XIII, Chrimes, 32–3.

[165] For a recent examination of the *Brute* by Laȝamon (Man of Law) *c.*1215 [Brute or Brutus was said to be a descendant of Aeneas], see C. Cannon, 'Laȝamon and the Laws of Men', *ELH* 67 (2000), 337–63.

[166] Selden/Gregor, n. 2 above, footnote to 50–3. [167] Selden, n. 2 above, 47.

[168] Cf. Hale, n. 64 above.

[169] See C. H. McIlwain, *Constitutionalism, Ancient and Modern*, (Ithaca: Cornell University Press, 1940); J. G. A. Pocock, *The Ancient Constitution and the Feudal Law: A Study of English Historical Thought in the Seventeenth Century* (Cambridge: Cambridge University Press, 1957, 1987); Pocock, *The Machiavellian Moment*, n. 10 above; G. Burgess, *The Politics of the Ancient Constitution: An Introduction to English Political Thought, 1603–1642* (Pennsylvania State University Press, 1993); A. Cromartie, *The Constitutionalist Revolution* (Cambridge: Cambridge University Press, 2006).

proceed as natural things do out of matter and form'.[170] All three, then, form the common law of the realm. Fortescue went on to refer to 'certain universals which those learned in the laws of England and mathematicians alike call maxims, just as rhetoricians speak of paradoxes, and civilians of rules of law'.[171] These maxims[172] or 'precise points of the law' are to be discovered by the judges and advocates,[173] in a fashion described by Fortescue in Chapters XLVIII–LIV through an Academy (*studium*—a 'third University') which is constituted by the Inns of Chancery and the Inns of Court.[174] That is, the courts, responding to controversies relating to customs, statutes, or in rare cases, the law of nature or of God,[175] propounded maxims based on legal analysis. Inevitably, the interplay of custom, statute, and judicial pronouncements came to form a body of law—this had been the case in England since the time of Cnut—[176] all of which came to be known generically as the common laws of England.

Thus in the 1475 case of *R v Bishop of Ely*,[177] Littleton J and Choke J both held that the *Prerogativa Regis*[178] could not be held as a true statute, but only as 'an affirmance of the common law (*del comon ley*)'.[179] Littleton J did not see the king's prerogative (at least in that case) as dependent on, derived from, or derivable from, a statute. That view coheres with those of Fortescue, in that the king's powers and the restraints upon them emanate from the coronation oath and his binding to the people.

De Laudibus certainly had a profound effect on a number of subsequent legal scholars. While it was not printed until *c.*1545–6,[180] manuscript copies of it were many; and again while *The Governance of England* was not published until 1714 by Sir John Fortescue-Aland, again the manuscript was well copied in legal circles.[181] John Rastell, a lawyer and printer to the legal trade and perhaps the first English

[170] *De Laudibus*, VIII, 21, emphasis added. [171] *De Laudibus*, VIII, 21.

[172] On maxims generally, note Sir Francis Bacon, *Maxims* and *De Augmentis*, as referred to by H. D. Hazeltine, General preface to Chrimes's *De Laudibus*, n. 2 above, xxxiv.

[173] *De Laudibus*, VIII, Chrimes, n. 2 above, 20–5.

[174] *De Laudibus*, XLVIII–IX, Chrimes, 116, 117.

[175] For a later seventeenth-century reference, see *Calvin's case*, 7 Co. Rep., 11 a; 77 ER (KB) 377, 391–2—'the *lex æterna*, the moral law, called also the law of nature'.

[176] See Kelly, n. 160 above, 140–1, 152–3.

[177] 1475, *Y.B.* 15 Edward IV, *Mich.* pl. 17; and see the discussion in Chrimes, *Constitutional Ideas*, n. 9 above, 44, and the text reproduced in his Appendix, 373.

[178] Cited as 17 Edw. II, statute declaratory of the common law; see O. Ruffhead (ed.), *The Statutes at Large, Magna Charta to the Twenty-fifth year of the reign of George III inclusive* (London: Charles Eyre and Andrew Strahan, 1786), I: 180; and see also *Statutes in Force*, Official Revised Edition, *Prerogativa Regis. Of the King's Prerogative* (temp. incert.), revised to 1 February 1978 (London: Her Majesty's Stationery Office, 1978) Cc. 13, 17. See also for the current version *Prerogativa Regis. Of the King's Prerogative* (temp. incert.) (1322) (*c.* 13), <*http://www.legislation.gov.uk/aep/Edw2cc1317/15/13/contents*>, accessed 14 July 2014.

[179] See Chrimes, *Constitutional Ideas*, n. 10 above, 44; per Littleton J, '*mes come un affirmance del comon ley*', Chrimes, *Constitutional Ideas*, 373; and *Y.B.* 15 Edw. IV, *Mich.* pl. 17, 44, 254, 256.

[180] The Edward Whitechurch edition: see Chrimes, *Constitutional Ideas*, lxxix.

[181] See P. C. Herman, 'Rastell's *Pastyme of People*: Monarchy and the Law in Early Modern Historiography', *Journal of Medieval and Early Modern Studies* 30.2 (2000), 276–308, n. 46 at 307.

constitutional historian,[182] wrote *The Pastyme of the People*, clearly influenced by Fortescue amongst others, as a means of educating the people about England's legal traditions;[183] in his introduction to *The Book of Assizes*, he says:

the laws of this realm of England been ordained and made to the great commonweal and ease of the people of the same as much as the laws of any other realm, nation, or country as by the book that is compiled, *De Laudibus Legum Angliae* by the right honorable Master Fortescu, sometime Judge in this realm, more plainly is showed and by reason approbate, argued, and well declared.[184]

Christopher St Germain also drew upon Fortescue's form and philosophy in his *Dialogue between a Doctor of Divinity and a Student of the Laws of England*,[185] which refers to Fortescue's work,[186] though much of St Germain's work is reminiscent of moot topics aired in the Inns of Court.

ii. Statutes and the people

The most significant of the laws were statutes. These emanate from the will of the whole realm and with its assent, and therefore are bound to be for the benefit of the people.[187] They are replete with wisdom, as they result from the counsel of more than '300 chosen men'[188]—this was the number of representatives in the commons.[189] Since Fortescue himself had been returned to the commons eight times, the role of the members was both familiar to him and of great significance in representing the ideas of the people as to how they were to be governed. While it is true that kings continued to impose taxes without the consent of the houses[190] in contradistinction to Fortescue's assertion that this could not happen in England,[191] *De Laudibus* in its function as a *Speculum Regis* or Mirror for Princes (sometimes referred to as a *Fürstenspiegel*) was propounding a new norm for governance in the interests of the people.

iii. Mirrors for princes and the law

It has been said that Fortescue was the 'first of medieval writers to bring "political philosophy from the clouds to earth by basing his theoretical analysis upon

[182] Herman, 'Rastell's *Pastyme of People*', 277. [183] Herman, 'Rastell's *Pastyme of People*'.

[184] J. Rastell, *Liber Assissarum* (1513) fo. 3, quoted in Chrimes, n. 2 above, lxxv, Chrimes's n. 3; also quoted in Herman, n. 181 above, 'Rastell's *Pastyme of People*', from E. M. Nugent, 'John Rastell', in *The Thought and Culture of the English Renaissance: An Anthology of Tudor Prose, 1481–1555* (Cambridge: Cambridge University Press, 1956), 170.

[185] Christopher St Germain's *Dialogue between a Doctor of Divinity and a Student of the Laws of England*, published 1523 in Latin and by St Germain in English in 1530; see *St Germain's Doctor and Student*, T. F. T. Plucknett and J. L. Barton, (eds), Selden Society, Vol. XCI (London: Selden Society, 1974).

[186] See St Germain, *Dialogue*, ii, *c.*46, 'but after such manner as Mr Fortescue in his book that he entituleth the book *De Laudibus legum Angliae*'.

[187] *De Laudibus*, XVIII, Chrimes, 41. [188] *De Laudibus*, XVIII, Chrimes, 41.

[189] Chrimes, n. 2 above, 161—in 1439–61 the number of representatives in the commons probably was between 264 and 290.

[190] Cromartie, *Constitutionalist Revolution*, n. 169 above, 31–2.

[191] See text accompanying nn. 87–90 127–31, 139–43.

observation of existing conditions";[192] he thus in a measure anticipates the work of Machiavelli'.[193] Machiavelli's *The Prince*[194] is the best known of all the Mirrors for Princes; but it is clear that Machiavelli was writing from a point of view far removed from that of Fortescue. Machiavelli wrote:

We said above that a prince must build on sound foundations; otherwise he is bound to come to grief. The main foundations of every state, new states as well as ancient or composite ones, are good laws and good arms; and because you cannot have good laws without good arms, and where there are good arms, good laws inevitably follow, I shall not discuss laws but give my attention to arms.[195]

Fortescue, like all his predecessor legal English writers on the needs of the prince ('arms and the law'[196]) concentrated on the law; Machiavelli after observing the same needs of arms and the law, concentrated on arms.

Strohm has argued that the fifteenth century itself saw a 'pre-Machiavellian moment' in that it saw a burgeoning of 'practical statecraft and political calculation' in a:

. . . broad contemporary confluence of shrewdly informed, unsentimental writings, keenly concerned with political practice in the world. When compared with these canny precursors, Machiavelli, for all his brilliance, looks less like an inaugurator and more like a participant in a general tendency.[197]

In additional support, he points to an early 1460s British Library MS. Harley 7353 which shows Edward IV sitting on top of Fortune's Wheel, but with the wheel spiked by *Ratio* (reason) and flanked on the right and left by the parliamentary classes; he notes also that the notion that a prince could resist Fortune by 'foresight and qualities of *vertue*' had been articulated earlier by John Lydgate in his *The Fall of Princes*.[198]

[192] *Governance*, Plummer, n. 3 above, 82.

[193] C. A. J. Skeel, 'The Influence of the Writings of Sir John Fortescue', *Transactions of the Royal Historical Society* 10 (1916), 77–114; Chrimes concurs in Fortescue's anticipation of Machiavelli—see note 22 above, ci.

[194] Niccolò Machiavelli, *The Prince*, written 1513–14, dedicated to the 'Magnificent Lorenzo de' Medici', trans. G. Bull (London: Penguin Books, 1961, reprinted (with revisions, 1981), 1988).

[195] Machiavelli, *The Prince*, 77.

[196] See Glanvill *c.*1187 *Tractatus de legibus et consuetudinibus regni Anglie qui Glanvilla vocatur, The Treatise on the laws and customs of the realm of England, commonly called Glanvill*, ed. G. D. G. Hall (London: Nelson in association with the Selden Society, 1965), Prologue, 1; and Bracton *c.*1250–60 *De Legibus et Consuetudinibus Angliae*, f. 1.

[197] See Strohm, *Politique*, note 53 above, 1.

[198] See Strohm, *Politique*, note 53 above, 2; see also *Oxford Dictionary of National Biography*. Lydgate's *The Fall of Princes* was written *c.*1431–38 and published in print by Caxton, London, 1494, ed. Richard Pynson (see Daniel Wakelin, 'Writing the Words', in A. Gillespie and D. Wakelin, (eds), *The Production of Books in England 1350–1500* (Cambridge: Cambridge University Press, 2011), 34–58, 56). The text is conveniently available online through the University of Virginia Library at <http://xtf.lib.virginia.edu/xtf/view?docId=chadwyck_ep/uvaGenText/tei/chep_1.0297.xml;chunk.id=d3;toc.depth=1;toc.id=d3;brand=default>; however, this edited version by Dr Henry Bergen dates from 1924–7—see H. Bergen, *Lydgate's Fall of Princes* (4 Vols., Oxford University Press, London, EETS ES, 121, 122, 123, 124).

For Fortescue, however, neither virtue nor Fortune is key, but rather law, it being the prime mover in incorporating humans into a people, from which the people's will in turn prescribes the law by which a king is to be bound.[199] To this end, the *De Laudibus* is the template by which the prince ought to govern. That this is so can be seen from the rhetorical nature of the work, and its focus on the utility and comparative felicity of English laws. Moreover, McGerr makes a convincing argument that the richly illustrated codex Yale Law School Goldman Library MS G. St. 11.1 of the *Nova Statuta Angliae* was in fact a statute book commissioned to serve the purpose of Prince Edward's personal copy of the laws which he should read daily in accordance with Moses' directive for kings, as Fortescue stated in *De Laudibus*.[200] McGerr points out important parallels between this *Nova Statuta* and *De Laudibus*, and argues that through the 'visual and verbal traditions' into which the Yale MS sets the *Nova Statuta*, it 'transforms a record of English statutes into a mirror for princes that comments on England's mid-fifteenth century political crisis from a Lancastrian perspective'.[201]

It needs to be said that Fortescue's *De Laudibus* was the first indisputably and idiosyncratically *English* Mirror of Princes.

Lurie,[202] analysing primarily Fortescue's *Governance*, suggests that he offered nothing new, merely rehearsing what earlier Mirror writers had said, relying on Genet's edited version of four political tracts[203] from the 'later middle ages'.[204] But informed criticism of Genet[205] notes that for Genet to describe the tracts as 'English' is 'a bit misleading' because one is 'an English translation of an original French work' (*c.*1347) and the other three having 'only minimally greater claims to be "English"' being 'very much more European or Mediterranean in origin and content'.[206]

Moreover, English poets who are frequently referred to as writers of *Fürstenspiegel* were merely rehashing what other earlier continental writers had said. John Lydgate's *Fall of Princes* was 'a translation of Giovanni Boccaccio's *De casibus virorum illustrium* (1355–60) via an intermediary French prose version by Laurent

[199] See text accompanying nn. 116–117.

[200] *De Laudibus*, I, Chrimes, 5; see McGerr, 'Lancastrian Mirror' n. 51 above, 7, 21–2.

[201] McGerr, n. 51 above, 7.

[202] See G. Lurie, 'Sir John Fortescue's Political Expertise', *History of Political Thought* 32 (Summer) (2011), 293–315, 295, n. 17. Lurie does however make an interesting suggestion concerning the use by Fortescue in *Governance* of the words 'due consideration', (at 307) referring to Lockwood's edition, n. 3 above, 112.

[203] See *Four English Political Tracts of the Later Middle Ages*, ed. Jean-Philippe Genet (London: Offices of the Royal Historical Society, 1977), as referred to in Laurie, 'Sir John Fortescue's Political Expertise', 295, n. 17. There Lurie also refers to Judith Ferster, *Fictions of Advice: The Literature and Politics of Counsel in Late Medieval England* (Philadelphia: University of Pennsylvania Press, 1996), a book written from the English literature perspective. Gent's editing was severely criticized by William Chester Jordan in his review of the book: see *Speculum* 54 (4) (1979), 801–2.

[204] Genet, *Four English Political Tracts of the Later Middle Ages.*

[205] See W. C. Jordan (Princeton), 'Review: Jean-Phillipe Genet, (ed.), *Four English Political Tracts of the Later Middle Ages*' (Camden Fourth Series, 18, London: Royal Historical Society, University College London, 1977), *Speculum* 54 (1979), 801–2.

[206] Jordan, 'Review: Jean-Phillipe Genet, (ed.)', 801.

de Premierfait'.[207] George Ashby (*c.*1385–1475)[208] penned *The Active Policy of the Prince* (1463),[209] which is 'little more than a metrical translation of *the Liber de dictis philosophorum antiquorum*', which in turn 'was a collection of aphorisms and anecdotes compiled, by the Arab Mubassir ibn Fatik, in the eleventh century.'[210] He borrowed[211] also from Benedict Burgh's translation of the *Distichs* of Cato (1460),[212] and from *The Court of Sapience* (possibly written by Lydgate).[213] Thomas Hoccleve (1368–1450?) wrote *The Regement of Princes* (*De regimine principum*) (1411),[214] which is 'a tedious homily on the virtues and vices, imitated from Aegidius de Colonna's work of the same name, from the suppositious epistle of Aristotle, known as the *Secreta Secretorum*, and the work of Jacques de Cessoles (*fl.* 1300)'.[215]

By comparison, Fortescue's *De Laudibus* and *Governance* are all his own work, and while Fortescue was no poet, there is no doubt his writing is far superior to anything the aforementioned authors could muster, penned with vibrancy and enthusiasm, and more to the point, with real practical knowledge of both English law and English politics.

3. The king

i. King-making and the people

On kingship, Fortescue concluded in *De Natura* that the 'law of nature' was 'the only law in the light of which the succession to kingdoms can be decided'.[216] He said that it was 'indupitable that a king reigns duly by God, if he is duly anointed,

[207] See Mortimer, *John Lydgate's Fall of Princes*, n. 58 above; and see nn. 55, 57, 58, and 198, and accompanying text.

[208] See U. Graßnick, 'Mirrors for Princes, Literary Strategies, and the set of Values and Norms in Late Medieval England', in R. Suntrup and J. R. Veenstra (eds), *Konstruktion Der Gegenwart Und Zukunft;Kultureller Wandel vom Mittelalter zur frühen Neuzeit* (Shaping the Present and the Future: Medieval to Early Modern Culture) (Frankfurt am Main: Peter Lang, 2008, bilingual ed.), 25–50, 38–9. Neither this article, nor Graßnick's earlier publication, *Ratgeber des Königs: Fürstenspiegel und Herrscher ideal im spätmittelalterlichen England*, Europäische Kulturstudien: Literatur–Musik–Kunst im historischen Kontext (Cologne: Böhlau, 2004), a study of seven late medieval vernacular English mirrors of princes, which included Ashby and Hoccleve, mentions Fortescue's *Governance of England*.

[209] Graßnick, 'Mirrors', 39.

[210] M. Kekewich, 'George Ashby's *The Active Policy of a Prince*: An Additional Source' *The Review of English Studies* 41 (1990), 533–5, 533.

[211] Kekewich, 'George Ashby's *The Active Policy of a Prince*', 535, 533.

[212] M. M. Sauer, *The Facts on File Companion to British Poetry Before 1600* (New York: Facts on File, Inc., 2008) 118.

[213] Kekewich, 'George Ashby's *The Active Policy of a Prince*', 533.

[214] *Encyclopaedia Britannica*, Thomas Hoccleve, <http://www.britannica.com/EBchecked/topic/268521/Thomas-Hoccleve>.

[215] *Luminarium: Anthology of English Literature*, 'Thomas Hoccleve', extracted from *Encyclopaedia Britannica*, 11th Ed. Vol XIX. (Cambridge: Cambridge University Press, 1910), 967, <http://www.luminarium.org/medlit/hocclevebio.htm>.

[216] Fortescue, *De Natura Legibus Naturae*; all this discussion is heavily indebted to Chrimes's explication of Fortescue and his works in Chrimes's introduction and notes to *De Laudibus*.

crowned, and sceptred *according to the law and custom of the realm*, in conformity with the law of God and of the Church'.[217] He concluded that because the House of Lancaster had enjoyed all the stipulations of just kingship set out by Saint Augustine—divine and ecclesiastical approval, the consent of the people, and possession through a long period[218]—any right that the Yorkists may have had was defeated by sixty years' prescription, had been renounced and adjured, and was barred by matters of record. Henry IV had been anointed and crowned king of England by the whole assent and will of the land, no man objecting, 'after the common law used in all the world'.[219]

Fortescue admits of a number of avenues by which a man could become king:[220] by the law of nature; by hereditary right (the Yorkist claim); and by prescription (the Lancaster claim). But there is one common denominator to all three: the person had to be accepted by the consent of the people, anointed and crowned according to the law and custom of the land, in accordance with God's law and that of the church. The law and custom of England demanded that before a king could be crowned in the sight of God and the people, he had to be accepted by the people and to take the coronation oath.

But it is only when Fortescue has the Prince question why some earlier kings were so little pleased with these excellent English laws that they tried to introduce the civil continental laws to England,[221] that he adverts to the coronation oath:

[217] Italics added; quotation from *De Titulo Edwardi Marchiae*, in Clermont, *Works*, 86; quoted by Chrimes, *English Constitutional Ideas*, n. 9 above, 64–5. Fortescue immediately went on to say that 'Neither the inhabitants of England nor of any other kingdom were allowed to transfer the realm from a duly constituted king reigning according to law and custom, to another'.

[218] Fortescue, *De Titulo*, 84; *Defensio Juris Domus Lancastriae*, 501–2 in Clermont, *Works*. St Augustine's treatise *On Kingship* has been lost.

[219] Fortescue, *Defensio*, 500.

[220] Fortescue would not however, have seen the crown passing to any female of the blood royal, and the succession of Mary and Elizabeth would have filled him with dread, as would also the anointing of Anne, Richard III's queen. Fortescue was opposed to women succeeding to the crown, because it 'is uncustomary, inconvenient, and unlawful'... 'That no woman could be anointed on the hands and thus could not exercise the thaumaturgical powers of a king [though all female English monarchs up to Anne would do so]; nor could she bear a sword, [though Eleanor of Aquitaine had done so] nor be fitted to act as a judge in criminal cause. Besides it was unlawful for women to rule over men; God had made a law that women should not have power directly from him over man, and so be without a sovereign on Earth. God's word to females was: *Eris sub potestate viri et ipse dominabitur tui.*'—quoted by Chrimes, *English Constitutional Ideas*, n. 9 above, 62–3, from *De Titulo*, 78, 80–1; *Defensio*, 511, 513; *Of the Title of the House of York*, 498.

[221] Neither Chrimes (181) nor Selden could imagine any such king, other than possibly Richard II; but I hypothesize that he is animadverting subtly upon Edward IV. This hypothesis is strengthened by Fortescue's referring in the paragraph following hard upon the mention of the coronation oath that 'certain kings of England bore hardly' the taking of the coronation oath, 'thinking themselves therefore not free to rule over their subjects as the kings ruling merely regally do', and hence they 'endeavoured to throw off this political yoke', i.e. the coronation oath—see *De Laudibus*, 79, 81 and see text accompanying notes 224–228 below. It seems clear that when Edward first asserted his right to the crown before and after the Battle of Towton in 1461, he had not at that time taken the coronation oath—Stubbs, *Constitutional History*, n. 3 above, vol. III, 192.

The laws of England do not sanction any such maxim [*What pleased the prince has the force of law*], since the king of that land rules his people not only regally but also politically, and so he is bound by oath at his coronation to the observance of his law.[222]

Fortescue then proceeds to make a biting comparison between the king who takes his coronation oath and thus rules his people according to law (politically), and the king who does not (who rules purely regally):

This [taking the coronation oath] certain kings of England bore hardly, thinking themselves therefore not free to rule over their subjects as the kings ruling merely regally do, who rule their people by the civil law, and especially by the aforesaid maxim of that law, so that they change laws at their pleasure, make new ones, inflict punishments, and impose burdens on their subjects, and also determine suits of parties at their own will and when they wish. Hence those ancestors[223] of yours endeavoured to throw off this political yoke, in order thus to rule merely regally over their subject people, or rather to rage unchecked, not heeding that the power of the two kings is equal, as is shown in the aforesaid Treatise on the Nature of the Law of Nature, nor heeding that it is not a yoke but a liberty to rule a people politically, and the greatest security not only to the people but to the king himself, and no small alleviation of his care.[224]

This passionate discussion of a king who refused to take the coronation oath, who has contempt for the law, comes immediately after Fortescue had written at length and with vehemence about someone contracting a clandestine marriage, afterwards betrothing himself to another woman, and as a result how *Leviathan's testicles are perplexed*.[225] Edward IV was a notorious libertine. His alleged betrothal to Lady Eleanor Butler before his clandestine marriage was the *cause célèbre* of 1464.[226] He had married Elizabeth Woodville, an English-born commoner, in secret, with only a few members of her family present, and by a local priest, in the forest of Wychwood, after stealing away during the night of 30 April/1 May 1464,

[222] *De Laudibus*, 79, 80—*Qualitee non sancciunt leges Anglie, dum nedum regaliter sed et politice rex eiusdem dominatur in populum suum, quo ipse in coronacione sua ad legis sue observanciam astringitur sacremento.*

[223] Fortescue's Latin here is *progenitores tui*, (folio 17v, *De Laudibus*, Chrimes, 80), referring back to the prince's question (at folio 17r) as to why 'his ancestors the kings of England' tried to 'repudiate the law of the land'—*tamen progenitorum meorum Anglie regum quosdam audivimus, in legibus suis minime delectatos, satagentes proinde leges civiles ad Anglie regimen inducere, et patrias leges repudiare fuisse conatos.* Chrimes has translated this as 'ancestors'; but it may also be possible that in context Fortescue means not merely the prince's ancestors by blood, but his predecessors in the crown, thus allowing of a subtle condemnation of Edward IV as discussed in the text immediately below.

[224] *De Laudibus*, Chrimes, 79–80, folios 17r and 17v.

[225] *De Laudibus*, 79, folio 17r, ostensibly quoting Job, *Perplexi sunt testiculi Leviatan.* Job Chapter 3, verse 8 says: 'Let those curse it who curse the day, who are skilled to rouse up Leviathan'.

[226] For the strongest arguments as to the existence and consequences of such a pre-contract, see P. M. Kendall, *Richard III* (London: George Allen & Unwin, 1955; reprinted 1973; published in paperback by Unwin Paperbacks, London, 1987), 215–23, and nn. 4–20 to 474–7. For a statement that 'there is no truth in the pre-contract story', see A. Weir, *The Princes in the Tower* (London: The Bodley Head, 1992; Pimlico edition, London, 1993), 121 [no sources given by Weir]. For details of the possibility of other pre-contracts, see the discussion in Sir George Buck, Master of the Revels, *The History of King Richard the Third*, 1619, edited and with an introduction and notes by A. N. Kincaid (London: Alan Sutton Publishing, 1982), 175–87.

Walpurgis night,[227] and whilst Warwick's negotiations of a marriage contract for a French union had almost reached finality. This same Edward was castigated by Maitland for his contempt for the law.[228] It may well be that there is no record of Edward IV's coronation oath, because on all the evidence to date, there is no record of his ever having taken one.[229]

Clearly Fortescue saw the coronation oath as the mechanism whereby the king's regal *dominium* becomes a political one *as well*, that it is the oath he swears at his coronation that binds him to political rule, and to the observance of 'his law'. Because the king receives his kingship as a result of the will of the people, and as the law is the nervous system of the body politic, binding all parts of it together, the king is obliged to maintain and protect the laws, and not to change the laws himself without the assent of his subjects. The major significant difference between the authority of a king under the civil law who rules entirely regally and that of the political and regal English king is that the source of the English king's authority in the body politic comes from the people, and the nature of this distinction is made clear in his coronation oath, where the king's obligations are clearly stated, and by which he enters into his office of king.

ii. Binding the king and people to the law—the oath

Henry VI had been crowned king of England on 6 November 1429, and as king of France at Nôtre Dame on 16 December 1431,[230] after the capture of Joan the Maid of Orléon in 1430.[231] (Joan had earlier inspired the French, leading to the coronation of Charles VII at Rheims on 17 July 1429 as king of France.)[232] Henry had been recognized as king by the people of both realms,[233] and proceeded to take the oath of governance or coronation oath, known in France as the 'oath of the kingdom'.[234]

[227] See J. Potter, *Good King Richard?: An Account of Richard III and his Reputation 1483–1983* (London: Constable and Company, 1983), 43; R. Fabyan, *The New Chronicles of England and France*, ed. H. Ellis (London, 1811), 654; Sir George Buck, *The History of King Richard the Third*, 177–8; Edward Hall, *Chronicle*, ed. Henry Ellis (London, 1809), 264.

[228] See Maitland, n. 3 above.

[229] See, e.g., Potter, *Good King Richard?*, 43; see also Fabyan, *The New Chronicles of England and France*, 654; and see Sir George Buck, *The History of King Richard the Third*, 177–8; and see Hall, *Chronicle*, 264; and see M. R. L. L. Kelly, 'King and Crown: An Examination of the Legal Foundations of the British Kingship' (Macquarie University, unpublished PhD thesis, 1998), ch. 3, 107.

[230] R. A. Griffiths, *The Reign of King Henry VI The Exercise of Royal Authority 1442–1461* (Berkeley and Los Angeles: University of California Press, 1981), 2; and R. A. Griffiths, *The Reign of King Henry VI* (1981; 2nd ed., Stroud: Sutton Publishing, 1998), 190, 193, 220–1.

[231] Griffiths, 1998, *The Reign of King Henry VI*, 191.

[232] Griffiths, 1998, *The Reign of King Henry VI*, 189–91.

[233] Griffiths, 1998, *The Reign of King Henry VI*, 190–3.

[234] R. A. Jackson, *Ordines Coronationis Franciae* (Philadelphia: University of Pennsylvania Press, 1995, 2000), 2 Vols., I: 171–2.

The exact terms of the oath[235] taken by the eight-year-old king are not known, but scholars have argued that it was similar to that of the *Forma et Modus*[236] and the *Liber Regie Capelle.*[237] Those texts are very similar to the *Liber Regalis* of 1308.[238] Unlike the French oath of Charles VII that replicated the terms of the early ninth-century English Anglo-Saxon oath,[239] the 1429 English oath likely to have been taken by Henry VI incorporated a number of controls upon the king, while confirming his powers, thus:

Will you grant and keep, and by your oath Confirm, to the people of England, the Laws and Customs to them granted, by the Kings of England your lawfull and religious predecessors; and namely the Laws Customs and franchises granted to the Cleargy [and to the people] by the glorious King St. Edward your predecessor?

I grant and promise to keep them.

And when the king says that he will grant and keep all these things the metropolitan shall set forth to him what he shall swear, saying:
Will you keep peace and godly agreement, entirely according to your power, both to God, the holy Church, your [the] Cleargy and your [the] People?

Response: I will keep it.

Will you to your power cause Lawe Justice and Discretion, in Mercy and truth, to be executed in all your Judgements?

Response: I will.

Will you grant to hold and keep, the Laws and rightful Customs, which the Commonalty of this your Kingdom have: and will you defend, and uphold them to the honour of God, so much as in you lieth?

I grant and promise so to do.

235 The oath itself was always written on a separate piece of paper, and, thought to be kept by the Archbishop of Canterbury, frequently became lost ephemera—see H. G. Richardson, *Speculum* 24 (1949), 46, and *Traditio* 16 (1960), 111–202, 162, 165, 171. The *Ordines*, or the liturgical form of the order of proceedings, frequently attempted to replicate the previously taken vernacular oath in Latin. For a discussion of the Oaths of Governance, see Kelly, 'King and Crown'; see also C. Condren, *Argument and Authority in Early Modern England: The Presupposition of Oaths and Offices* (Cambridge: Cambridge University Press, 2006), ch. 12, 'Coronation oaths', *passim.*

236 See R. Strong, *Coronation: From the 8th to the 21st Century* (London: Harper Perennial, 2006), 146, relying in part on L. G. Wickham Legg, *English Coronation Records* (Westminster: Archibald Constable & Company Limited, 1901), 172–90.

237 *Liber Regie Capelle*, ed. W. Ullmann, manuscript in the *Biblioteca Publica*, Evora (Cambridge: University of Cambridge Press for the Henry Bradshaw Society, Vol. XCII, 1961); that text was copied *c.*1449 from *Liber Regalis* of Abbot Lytlington (1362–8), as recorded in the *Missal of Westminster*—see 6, 22.

238 For text, see Legg, *Coronation Records*, n. 236 above, 81–130.

239 See Jackson, n. 234 above, I: 24, 171–2, and II: 368; see also J. L. Nelson, *Politics and Ritual in Early Medieval Europe* (London: Hambledon Press, 1986), 341–60. The text of the French oath for Charles VII is from the *Last Capetian Ordo*, and replicates exactly the *Promissio Regis* of the Anglo-Saxon kings—for text see Jackson, n. 234 above, II: 383–4. The Latin of the early Anglo-Saxon oaths can be found in *Two Anglo-Saxon Pontificals*, ed. H. M. J. Banting (London: Boydell Press for the Henry Bradshaw Society, 1989), 1 ff.; the Anglo-Saxon may be found in F. Liebermann, *Die Gesetze der Angelsachsen, Text und Übersetzung, Unveränderter Neudruck der Ausgrabe 1903–1916* (Sindelfingen: Scientia Aalen, Germany, 1960), 3 v, I:214. All texts are discussed in detail by Kelly, n. 235 above.

Then shall follow the admonition of the Bishops to the king, to be read by one of the Bishops before all in a loud voice saying:

Our Lord and King : We beseech you to pardon and to grant, and to preserve unto us and your [the] Churches committed to our Charge, all Canonical privileges, and due Law and Justice; And that you would protect and defend us, as every good King in his Kingdom, ought to be Protector, and Defendor of the Bishops, and the Churches under their government.

He shall answer:

With a willing and devout heart, I grant My Pardon; and promise that I will preserve, and maintain to you, and the Churches committed to your Charge, all Canonical Privileges, and due Law, and Justice; and that I will be your protector and defendor to my power, by the assistance of God, as every good King in his Kingdom, in right ought to protect and defend the Bishops and Churches under their government.

Then shall be added to the aforesaid questions what is just ; when all the above have been put, then the prince shall confirm them by swearing upon the altar in sight of all that he shall keep all the above.[240]

This oath represents:

- The king's guarantee to keep the laws, customs, and franchises (liberties) previously endorsed by his predecessors to the people and the clergy, especially those of Edward the Confessor.[241]
  - That is, it stands for continuity from one reign to the next, acknowledging that king and people are in a continual symbiotic relationship.
- The king's obligation to maintain the peace, to the people, the clergy, and the church, so far as he can.
  - This is a recognition of the obligation of the King's Peace, in force from the Anglo-Saxon time to the present day.[242]
- The king's obligation to ensure that law, justice, and discretion, in mercy and truth, was present and taken into account in all judicial judgements.
  - This is the obligation to hold not just to any rule of law, but to consider equity and mercy, for which there is always a discretion.
- The king's obligation to uphold, keep, and defend the laws and just customs, which the community of the realm, the common people of the kingdom, already have, so long as they accord with the laws of God.[243]
  - This was seen, in particular by later generations, to refer to the people's involvement in law-making; though in Fortescue's thinking, this would have been merely a recognition of the proper and lawful method of law-making—the king, with the ideas of the people's representatives in

240 Ullmann, n. 237 above, 82–3.

241 See here Selden's comment at text accompanying n. 167 above.

242 See here Kelly, 'King and Crown', n. 235 above, ch. 2, 'The King and His Peace'; see also Kelly, 'Hieroglyphic of the Laws', n. 160 above, 'The folcriht, The King's Peace and the Common law', 152 ff.

243 This later became a cause of much agitation; but not so in Fortecue's time.

the commons and the lords, and more particularly in his new foundation, of those people on the council.[244]

- The king's obligation to uphold, protect, and defend canonical privileges within law and justice.

* * *

The most often used quotation from *The Governance of England* is that referring to Fortescue's distinction between a *dominium regale* and a *dominium politicum et regale*,[245] which invariably is used to support some idea of parliamentary sovereignty. But I argue that what Fortescue had in mind in making such a distinction was the difference between a king bound by his coronation oath to observe the laws, and one who was not.

Moreover, Fortescue in fact says in the *Governance of England* when discussing an ordinance for the king's routine charges:

> ... so is the kynges power more, in that he may not put ffrom him possesciones necessaries for his own sustenance, than yff he myght put ham ffrom hym, and aliene the same to his owne hurte and harme. Nor this is ayen the kynges prerogatiffe, be wich he is exaltid above his subgettes; but rather this is to hym a prerogatiff. Ffor no man saue he mey haue ayen the land þat he hath onis aliened.[246]

Later in *Governance*, after his oft-quoted statements about *dominium politicum et regale,* he advocates a monarchy greater than any of its parts, where the king is so endowed financially as to obviate the necessity of asking the Houses of Parliament for much money, and where the king's income over and above the revenues assigned to the ordinary expenses of government be 'greater than the livelihood of the greatest lord in England'. He says that the king's council should be composed of the wisest of the kingdom's men, not factious noblemen, and have power to amend the laws, and thus guide parliament by presenting bills 'ripened to their hands'.[247] Clearly, these views were heavily influenced by Fortescue's own observations and experiences of the lawlessness and confusion during the civil wars. He was, however, nothing if not a pragmatist; his experience of justice and the executive, not to mention politics, warfare, exile, return, and recantation, meant that he had a realistic grasp of the necessities for good and effective government. In no fashion could he be said, overall, to have been an advocate of the supremacy of parliament—rather was he a supporter of the welfare of the people through effective kingship which involved the use of parliament. H. B. Hazeltine noted that:

> First in *De Laudibus Legum Angliae* and then later in the *Governance of England*, he not only advocated a strong executive based on the prerogative, but advanced the view that the executive, in legislation and taxation, must be limited by parliament. This duality in his constitutional policy, which favoured both the kingship and the parliament, resulted in a twofold influence of his books on later constitutional development. His books anticipate

[244] See section headed 'The involvement of the people', 82 below, and also the section headed 'The council', 82.

[245] See Plummer, *Governance*, n. 3 above, 109.

[246] *Governance of England*, vi; quoted in Chrimes, *English Constitutional Ideas*, n. 9 above, 42.

[247] See *Governance*, Lockwood, n. 3 above, XV, 116.

some of the reformative measures which in fact led to the establishment of the Tudor kingship in the sixteenth century as the strongest English monarchy since the time of the Normans and the Angevins; they also furnished the arguments that were effectively used in the seventeenth century by the parliamentary opponents of arbitrary rule.[248]

But the prime consideration in relation to the Fortescuean kingship was the people and the common weal.

4. The people, counsel, and council

i. A political people

The 'people' for Fortescue was that group of persons present in England who at some time in the past through law had self-incorporated into a people or a body politic the life-blood of which was the people's will.[249] The English people in the fifteenth century were no mere ciphers. Chrimes noted that at that time there existed a:

> currency of a conception of the *respublica*, common-weal, or state, which transcends theory of a purely monarchical derivation. Talk of the body politic, elaborate anthropomorphic conceits, concern or the *respublica Angliae* and the 'whole weal publique,' and questions of 'politic governance' are all characteristic of the period, and all are significant commonplaces of everyday political thought.[250]

Strohm noted the use of the term *commen welthe* particularly in *Somnium Vigilantis* as an 'emergent term of political art so common in the 1450s'.[251] And Gill[252] noted the use of propaganda by the major factions to court the support of the 'people', He referred[253] to numerous Yorkist manifestos[254] whereby the Yorkists 'came to be recognized as offering a clear alternative, based on recognizable political ideas, to a debased Lancastrian rule'[255] primarily because the commons 'loved the duke of York because York loved the communes and preserved the common profit of the land'.[256] He referred to the success of the original Lancastrian revolution of 1399 as depending upon the support of the 'people',[257] and noted the significance of Fortescue's polemical and propagandist works supporting the Lancastrian succession in combating the

248 H. D. Hazeltine, General Preface to Chrimes's *De Laudibus*, n. 2 above, l (50).

249 See text accompanying nn. 106–19.

250 S. B. Chrimes, 'Sir John Fortescue and His Theory of Dominion', *Transactions of the Royal Historical Society* 17 (1934), 117–47, 119.

251 Strohm, *Politique*, n. 53 above, 13.

252 P. E. Gill, 'Politics and Propaganda in Fifteenth-Century England: The Polemical Writings of Sir John Fortescue', *Speculum* 46 (1971), 333–47.

253 Gill, 'Politics and Propaganda', 337.

254 e.g. *William Gregory's Chronicle of London*, ed. J. Gairdner (Westminster: Camden Society, 1880,) 206; *Three Fifteenth Century Chronicles*, ed. J. Gairdner (Westminster: Camden Society, 1880), 74; J. Stow, *Annales* (London: R. Newbury, 1592), 407–8.

255 Wilkinson, *Constitutional History of England in the Fifteenth Century*, n. 63 above, 104.

256 *An English Chronicle from Richard II to Henry VI*, ed. J. S. Davies (Westminster: Camden Society, 1856), 71.

257 Gill, note 252 above, 335–7, relying on G. Lapsley, 'The Parliamentary Title of Henry IV', *English Historical Review* 49 (1934), 586, and Bertie Wilkinson, 'The Deposition of Richard II and the Accession of Henry IV', *English Historical Review* 54 (1939), 215–39.

Yorkist propaganda, written as they were by a former Chief Justice. Obtaining, and keeping, popular support was fundamental to the stability of fifteenth-century governance.

These fifteenth-century political writings were clearly taken very seriously; that this was so is demonstrated by Edward IV's requirement that Fortescue specifically recant in writing his earlier Lancastrian writings—and here it is worthwhile noting that Fortescue explicitly confines his recantation in *Declaracion upon Certayn Wrytinges* only to those *sent oute of Scotteland*. This does not include *De Laudibus*, nor does it include *Governance*, the latter being written in France and amended to apply to Edward IV, to whom it had been submitted.

The fact that Edward IV, by no means a compassionate man, recruited Fortescue to his council and to his cause is arguably indicative of the effectiveness of Fortescue's political tracts, and of resonance they had with the populace at large. This may well be due not only to the 'propagandist' nature of the writing, to which both Hazeltine and Gill refer,[258] but also to the acquaintance of a literate population with rhetorical devices which had flowered during the century.[259] In turn, this is also indicative of a certain degree of political sophistication as well as political engagement in the populace, and that the views of the people with respect to governance were both an underlying bedrock to all reigns during the fifteenth century, and also the catalyst to constitutional and political change.

a. The involvement of the people

In addition to the people's being the prime mover in the establishment of a body politic, in Fortescue's political understanding of good governance they were central to law-making for the common weal in a number of ways.

First, the people were the basis of the implementation of the criminal law of the time through their presence on juries.[260] Second, the common people were involved in the meetings of parliament[261] without whose consent no new laws could be made, or old ones changed, and no taxes levied upon them.

ii. The council

But third, and most significantly, they were to play a pivotal role in Fortescue's conception of what he described in *Governance* XIX[262] as the 'new foundation' of the crown—in addition to the king's finances and lands being secured and incapable of alienation without parliament's (i.e. the people's) consent,[263] the king was to be advised by a new council.

This was no longer to be comprised of the greatest lords of the land who overlooked the common weal in pursuit of their own economic and patronage

[258] Hazeltine, n. 248 above; Gill, n. 252 above.
[259] See discussion accompanying nn. 55, and 58–71.
[260] *De Laudibus*, XXIV–XXXII. This very important aspect is not examined in detail in this article.
[261] See text accompanying nn. 189–190.
[262] *Governance*, XIX, Lockwood, n. 3 above, 121.
[263] *Governance*, XIX, Lockwood.

interests. Rather it was to be comprised of 12 spiritual men, and 12 temporal men 'from the wisest and best disposed men that can be found in all parts of this land' who shall be 'sworn to counsel the king' taking a fee from the king only for their work, one of whom shall be chosen by the king to head the council (*Capitalis consiliarius*). Each year, this council was to be supplemented by four lords spiritual and four lords temporal for that year, and they would also be sworn.[264]

The work of the council was to 'deliberate upon matters of difficulty that appertain to the king; and then upon the matters of the policy of the realm', economic matters like trade, monetary and fiscal policy, defence, and the need for reformation of the laws. In respect of this last matter, the council would propose matters to the houses in a form 'ripened to their hands' thus facilitating parliament's work and ensuring laws needing change are amended quickly.[265] Moreover the council could call the 'great officers of the land (the chancellor, the treasurer) and the judges and such others as the council thought appropriate to assist in its deliberations, as the council saw fit; but not otherwise would anyone other than the councillors themselves deliberate and advise.[266]

It is noteworthy that it is the common people, the 'wisest and best disposed of men' who are to form the bulk of the council, and that one of them should be the Chief Councillor, or 'president' as Fortescue later calls him.[267] In many ways this device suggested by Fortescue is reminiscent of the later development of the Cabinet, something that would not occur for over 200 years. It is not difficult to agree with Harry L. Stephen, who, though writing of *De Laudibus* and Fortescue's concept of the jury said:

> Legally [Fortescue] represented enlightenment and progress to an astonishing degree, and . . . the whole treatise is in many ways almost prophetical of the future.[268]

III. Conclusion: More than the Sum of His Parts

Fortescue's work has been characterized in numerous ways:

- He was 'the first Englishman, so far as we know, to perceive that the differences in legal and constitutional institutions must be sought in the underlying difference of economic and social conditions, and in so doing he anticipated the outlook of Bodin and Montesquieu.'[269]
- His was the first book about English law and the legal profession written by an English lawyer for the benefit of his 'unlearned brethren'.[270]

264 *Governance*, XV, Lockwood, 114–15.
265 *Governance*, XV, Lockwood, 116.
266 *Governance*, XV, Lockwood, 116–17.
267 *Governance*, XV, Lockwood, 116.
268 H. L. Stephen, 'The Trial of Sir Walter Raleigh: A Lecture Delivered in Connection with the Raleigh Tercentenary Commemoration' (1919) *Transactions of the Royal Historical Society*, Fourth Series, vol. 2, 172–87, 182.
269 Chrimes, *De Laudibus*, ciii; see also A. B. Ferguson, 'Fortescue and the Renaissance', note 18 above, 187.
270 Cf. Holdsworth, *History of English Law*, II: 570, and Chrimes, *De Laudibus*, c.

- *De Laudibus* was the first 'deliberate attempt at comparative jurisprudence'.[271]
- He anticipated 'something like Hobbes's idea of the social compact'.[272]
- *De Laudibus* anticipated the work of Machiavelli.[273]
- The effect of his work on both later lawyers and thinkers was profound, e.g. John Rastell, Christopher St Germain, Sir Thomas Smith, John Selden, Sir Matthew Hale.[274]
- It has been speculated that his fiscal and monetary policy as evinced in the *Governance* was deliberately pursued by Henry VII in order to secure the realm.[275]

That Fortescue loved the law is clear from his writings, especially in *De Laudibus*. That he saw the law as the vehicle for both instituting a state—a political and regal *dominium*—and for securing the welfare of the people within that *dominium* is also manifest.

But his greatest achievement was to marry politics with the constitution. All the parts constituting the body politic must play their proper roles, and of these the roles of the people and of the king in Fortescue's analysis were paramount. Without support and involvement of the people, the realm will dissolve into impotence; with it, it will flourish.

His templates in *De Laudibus* and *Governance* were for optimizing good governance. They were essentially political documents setting out the constitutional role of the people for the best body politic in accordance with the law. They were prescient in many ways. Many future generations of scholars, lawyers, and politicians were influenced by them.

Sir John should take his rightful role in the pantheon of political and constitutional thinkers of the English peoples. He was a far-sighted statesman, far more than a lawyer or judge, and no mere polemicist or propagandist. It was he who, in times of political upheaval, bloodshed, grave uncertainty, and disruption, firmly placed the development of the English constitution on the path of law, not arms, to the great benefit of the English-speaking peoples ever since.

[271] Cf. Levy-Ullman, *The English Legal Tradition*, xxxii, 160; Chrimes, *De Laudibus*.

[272] Chrimes, *English Constitutional Ideas*, n. 9 above, 319–20; Chrimes, *De Laudibus*, c.

[273] See the discussion earlier in this chapter under the heading 'Mirrors for princes and the law', at 71.

[274] See Hazeltine, n. 248 above, ix, xi, xxix.

[275] Chrimes, *De Laudibus*, n. 2 above, cv; see also S. B. Chrimes, *Henry VII* (London: Eyre Methuen, 1972, reprinted 1977).

Annex: Fortescue's Works

Works which are known (or on stylistic grounds, suspected) to be his are:

1459–60, in England:

- *Somnium Vigilantis (Dream of the Watchful [One])—Royal MS. 17 D. xv in the British Museum (? Fortescue?)*[276]

1461–3, while in Scotland:

- *De Titulo Edwardi Comitis Marchiæ (Latin. Complete.)*
- *Of the Title of the House of York (English. Fragmentary.)*
- *Defensio Juris Domus Lancastriæ (Latin. Fragmentary.)*
- *A Defence of the House of Lancaster: otherwise called, A replication to the claim of the Duke of York (English. Complete.)*
- *Opusculum de Natura Legis Naturæ et de ejus Censura in Successione Regnorum Supprema (de Natura)*

1468–71, while in France:

- *De Laudibus Legum Anglie (1468–71)*
- *Memoranda on the Political Situation for Louis XI (1470)*
- *Articles from Prince Edward to the Earl of Warwick (1470)*
- *The Governance of England (also sometimes called Monarchia, or The Difference between an Absolute and a Limited Monarchy* (*1471* [Chrimes's date, *De Laudibus,* lxvi])

1471–3, while in England:

- *Declaracion upon Certayn Wrytinges sent oute of Scotteland ayenst the Kinges Title to the Roialme of Englond (1471–3)*

276 See J. P. Gilson, 'A Defence of the Proscription of the Yorkists in 1459,' (1911) xxvi *EHR*, 512–25; the text of the *Somnium Vigilantis* is reproduced at 513–25; see also Gross, n. 17 above, 37, 58–60, and illustration at p. 103.

3

Edward Coke

Ian Williams

I. Introduction

Edward Coke makes regular appearances in works on English constitutional history and constitutional law.[1] Coke was born in 1552, and by 1572 was a student observing the courts in London.[2] In 1578 he was called to the bar. Over the next five decades, Coke was a private practitioner, an educator in the Inns of Court and Chancery, a crown law officer, author, chief justice, privy councillor, prisoner, and a member of parliament. In many respects Coke's career followed the same trajectory as other successful Elizabethan and Jacobean lawyers.

Some aspects of Coke's career and writings have not yet been investigated in detail. There is no scholarly biography of his whole life,[3] no study examining Coke's parliamentary careers,[4] and manuscript material remains relatively unused, at least in the accounts more concerned with the constitution.[5] Recently, historians

[1] S. R. Gardiner, *History of England from the Accession of James I to the Outbreak of the Civil War 1603–1642*, vols 1–3 (London: Longmans, Green, and Co., 1883); J. S. Hart Jr, *The Rule of Law 1603–1660: Crown, Courts and Judges* (Harlow: Pearson, 2003); A. Lyon, *Constitutional History of the United Kingdom* (London: Cavendish, 2003), 199–201; I. Loveland, *Constitutional Law, Administrative Law, and Human Rights: A critical introduction*, 5th ed. (Cambridge: Cambridge University Press, 2009), 58 and 87; C. Turpin and A. Tomkins, *British Government and the Constitution: Texts and Materials*, 7th ed. (Cambridge: Cambridge University Press, 2011), 86; A. W. Bradley and K. D. Ewing, *Constitutional and Administrative Law*, 15th ed. (Harlow: Longman, 2011), 50, 58, 247.

[2] Biographical details are taken from A. Boyer, 'Coke, Sir Edward', in H. C. G. Matthew and B. Harrison (eds), *Oxford Dictionary of National Biography*, vol. 12 (Oxford: Oxford University Press, 2004), 451.

[3] Existing biographical works include the seriously outdated C. Drinker Bowen, *The Lion and the Throne: the life and times of Sir Edward Coke, 1552–1634* (London: Hamiltons, 1957), and A. D. Boyer, *Sir Edward Coke and the Elizabethan Age* (Stanford: Stanford University Press, 2003) which does not cover Coke's life after 1603. Boyer, 'Coke, Sir Edward' (n. 2) is very full.

[4] Coke had been a member of the House of Commons on various occasions before he became a judge, serving as speaker in 1593, and was also a member after his dismissal from the bench, including in the Parliament of 1628, where he was heavily involved in the proceedings that led to the Petition of Right. Coke features frequently in C. Russell, *Parliaments and English Politics 1621–1629* (Oxford: Clarendon, 1979).

[5] Several of Coke's notebooks survive (see J. H. Baker, 'Coke's Note-Books and the Sources of His Reports', *Cambridge Law Journal* 30 (1972), 59). Coke appears regularly in manuscript law reports of the period. Scholars have made some use of this material with regard to particular cases of interest, but not in a systematic fashion. See, e.g., C. M. Gray, 'Bonham's Case Reviewed', *Proceedings of the American Philosophical Society* 116 (1972), 35, and J. I. Corré, 'The Argument, Decision, and Reports of *Darcy v Allen*', *Emory Law Journal* 45 (1996), 1261.

have been particularly interested in Coke's political thought and the idea of the 'ancient constitution', but these works have tended to focus on Coke's writings and relatively high-level theory, placing Coke into a wider intellectual context, rather than his actions and career. On some practical legal issues of the day which touched on constitutional matters (writs of habeas corpus and prohibition), legal historians have shown that Coke was neither the first nor the most active of the judges in those fields, which may raise doubts about Coke's contemporary constitutional importance.[6] No attempt has been made to examine whether Coke genuinely held a coherent view about English constitutional issues or whether his views on constitutional matters changed over time. Recent work examining Coke's historical thinking has shown both how he formed his early views on the history of the common law, and how his thinking developed in his later work. Given that Coke's political thought was related in some way to his view of the past, his constitutional ideas may also have changed.[7] Apparent contradictions in Coke's actions and statements can easily be perceived.[8] Whether these differences should simply be accepted as based upon Coke's changed roles, a genuine change of mind, or possibly even underlying consistency at a deeper level, has not been carefully investigated.

It is the abnormalities of Coke's career that have created the perception of Coke's constitutional importance. Coke's career was abnormal in two ways: first, his disagreements with James I and others, and second, his considerable writings. For lawyers and constitutional historians, Coke is probably best known for his seemingly antagonistic relationship with James I and the confrontations and arguments that resulted, ultimately leading to his dismissal from the bench in 1616. Historians of political thought make considerably more use of Coke's writings, but are less concerned with the relationship between Coke and James. These writings include considerable discussion of the history and quality of the English constitution in terms that were important in political discourse in pre-Civil War England.

II. Coke's Career

In many respects, Coke's constitutional significance depends upon his dismissal as chief justice of the King's Bench in 1616, three years after his apparent promotion from the post of chief justice of the Common Pleas to which he had been appointed in 1606. Coke's dismissal was perceived by some historians as a defining moment in

[6] P. D. Halliday, *Habeas Corpus: From England to Empire* (Cambridge, MA, Harvard University Press, 2010), 30, and C. M. Gray, *The Writ of Prohibition: Jurisdiction in Early-Modern English Law* vol. 1 (New York: Oceana Publications, 1994), xvii.

[7] I. Williams, 'The Tudor Genesis of Edward Coke's Immemorial Common Law', *Sixteenth Century Journal* 63 (2012), 103; A. Musson, 'Myth, Mistake, Invention? Excavating the Foundations of the English Legal Tradition', in A. Lewis and M. Lobban (eds), *Law and History* (Oxford: Oxford University Press, 2003). On the links between Coke's view of the past and his constitutional thought, see nn. 34–45 and text.

[8] Russell (n. 4), 57–8 and 128 and A. Cromartie, *The Constitutionalist Revolution: An Essay on the History of England, 1450–1642* (Cambridge: Cambridge University Press, 2006), 228.

seventeenth-century history. Samuel Gardiner's *History of England from the Accession of James I to the Outbreak of the Civil War*[9] incorporated a two-volume work entitled *History of England from the Accession of James I to the disgrace of Chief Justice Coke*.[10] Compared to previous judicial dismissals, Coke did not seem to have committed any misconduct; instead he was dismissed for disagreeing with the king.

Gardiner's *History of England* was the principal reference for Dicey when writing about the English constitution in the early seventeenth century. In this way, Gardiner's views on Coke have become part of the standard constitutional history presented in English works on constitutional law.[11] For Gardiner, Coke earned the 'approbation of posterity' in resisting demands from James I for the judges to submit to the crown.[12] The judges who bowed to James I's demands that they not derogate from his prerogative, or determine cases affecting the crown without first consulting him, were condemned by Gardiner for 'dereliction of duty'.[13] Such submission to the crown, and the potential for the crown to prevent cases being heard which affected its interests, reflected a principle 'equally bad' as that in 'so many French constitutions'.[14] Such a constitutional narrative elevates Coke as an example of the importance of judicial independence, often now linked with the separation of powers.[15] As we shall see in this chapter, while some of Coke's actions may look like those considered appropriate under the separation of powers, Coke's motivations and justifications for acting seem to be very different.

According to a contemporary, '[t]he common speech is that fowre Ps have overthrown and put him [Coke] down, that is Pride, Prohibitions, Premunire and Prerogative'.[16] Coke's personality was certainly a contributing factor in his dismissal; as Hart puts it, Coke 'may have been the most brilliant and learned jurist of his day, but he was also obstinate, opinionated, argumentative and willful[*sic*]. In fact he was, to an alarming degree, James's alter ego, and, given their respective positions, collision was almost inevitable'.[17] Opinionated and argumentative lawyers did not suddenly appear around 1600, or disappear later, so it took more than Coke's personality to bring matters to a head. The personalities of other participants in the various legal dramas were also important. Lord Chancellor Ellesmere was at least as proud, obstinate, and opinionated as Coke, while James himself had a strong conviction about the place and role of the monarch, convictions that were not always shared with Coke. Unlike Elizabeth, his predecessor, who also held

[9] London: Longmans, Green, and Co., 1883–4 (10 volumes).

[10] London: Hurst and Blackett, 1863.

[11] See J. W. F. Allison, *The English Historical Constitution: Continuity, Change and European Effects* (Cambridge: Cambridge University Press, 2007), 136.

[12] Gardiner, *History of England*, vol. 3 (n. 1), 24.

[13] Gardiner, *History of England*, vol. 3 (n. 1), 18.

[14] Gardiner, *History of England*, vol. 3 (n. 1), 7.

[15] This is not limited to works written by lawyers. Hart (n. 1), 102–9 similarly focuses on the idea of judicial independence as underlying the Jacobean disputes, especially at 107.

[16] *The Letters of John Chamberlain*, ed. N. E. McClure, vol. 2 (Philadelphia: American Philosophical Society, 1939), 34.

[17] Hart (n. 1), 45.

strong views, James sometimes sought to persuade those who disagreed with him, descending from his imperial majesty to debate with his political inferiors.

The references to prohibitions and praemunire encompass the various jurisdictional disputes in which Coke was engaged (especially the jurisdictional conflict with the Chancery just before Coke's dismissal), as well as the particular issues concerning writs of prohibition which were raised in the *Case of Prohibitions*, and the confrontation with James I that resulted. Finally, the mention of prerogative refers to the *Case of Commendams*, where the judges refused to delay a case despite the king claiming that it affected his prerogative. These two latter issues raised questions of political principle and theory, and Gardiner saw Coke's dismissal as due to his resistance to James I's views about the powers of the King.

Several of the issues with which Coke was associated were not new. Jurisdictional disputes existed during the reign of Elizabeth, but became more heated during James's reign; Elizabeth was also jealous of her prerogative, but largely avoided discussion of it. Some of the responsibility for this change seems to lie with James I. The Stuart regime made highly successful use of the courts to ascertain the legality of controversial policies. By doing so, James was able to levy extra-parliamentary taxation with judicial approval,[18] and to determine some of the legal consequences of his accession to the English throne when parliament had proved unwilling to reach James's desired conclusions.[19] Such an approach demonstrated respect for the importance of law in England, but risked giving the judges a degree of control or veto over royal policies. The idea of law as important to English political thought was not new, but the spheres into which the common law intruded did expand in the sixteenth century, and the use of the courts by James reflected and amplified that trend.[20] When disputes could not be resolved in the courts, or at least not resolved to James's satisfaction, James sought to resolve the issues himself through debate. This led to the enunciation of ideas and conclusions on all sides, revealing strong differences in opinion between James and his chief justice.

III. Coke's Writings

Coke was unusual in producing a large volume of writings. Eleven volumes of reports, each accompanied by a preface, appeared during Coke's lifetime, with two more posthumous volumes. After his enforced retirement from the bench, Coke published the first part of his *Institutes of the Laws of England*, the final three volumes being printed with parliamentary support in the 1640s. Coke's writings,

[18] *Bates's Case* (1606) 2 State Trials 371.

[19] *Calvin's Case* (*The Case of the Post-Nati*) (1608) 2 State Trials 559.

[20] Cromartie has argued that this trend was so pronounced that during the sixteenth century a view developed amongst common lawyers that the common law was omnicompetent and viewed by common lawyers as a complete 'science of the common weal' (Cromartie (n. 8)). This goes too far, but Cromartie is correct to observe that more facets of a wider range of activities were in some way encroached upon by the jurisdiction of the common-law courts.

and some of the constitutional ideas expressed there, have become the focus of renewed interest in recent years, especially with the (re)emergence of the idea of 'common law constitutionalism', and in particular in relation to questions concerning parliamentary sovereignty.[21]

There is a disjunction between the events in Coke's career that are considered important by lawyers and constitutional historians and Coke's writings. Though Coke made personal notes of controversial cases concerning constitutional and public law issues, he did not have those cases printed. The cases of *Prohibitions* and *Proclamations*, for example, were only included in the twelfth volume of Coke's *Reports*, printed posthumously. Other cases that are important for Coke's constitutional reputation were never reported by Coke at all, such as *Peacham's Case* and the *Case of Commendams*. For those cases, which Coke noted but did not print, the explanation probably lies in the conventions of early modern law reporting. Other early modern printed reports did not include cases on sensitive issues.[22] The omission of *Peacham's Case* and the *Case of Commendams* is more difficult to explain because Coke's notebooks for the relevant period have been lost after being used as a source for the twelfth part of the *Reports*.[23] It is therefore impossible to ascertain whether Coke made notes on these cases but the editor of the twelfth *Reports* did not think the cases sufficiently important to print, or whether Coke did not report the cases at all. Either of these explanations highlights differing views of matters of importance between writers in the seventeenth century and writers from the nineteenth century onwards.

Coke's *Reports* addressed many areas of development in the law that were not reflected in the earlier law reports. The sixteenth century was a period of rapid change in English law, and Coke's *Reports* provided guidance on new or developing legal issues. A good example that touched on constitutional matters is *Bagg's Case*, in which Coke made a sweeping statement about the powers of the King's Bench. *Bagg's Case* concerned the first use of the developed form of *mandamus* writ, and so Coke's *Reports* provided a valuable resource to practitioners in demonstrating the existence of the writ and some suggestions about its use.[24] Coke's *Reports* were particularly significant in this regard because they were printed, so capable of wider dissemination than manuscript collections, and Coke sometimes published quite quickly.

[21] E.g. T. R. S. Allan, 'The rule of law as the rule of reason: consent and constitutionalism', *Law Quarterly Review* 115 (1999), 221 and Allison (n. 11).

[22] Baker has observed that both such sensitive matters were omitted from the posthumous reports of Dyer too (J. H. Baker, 'Introduction', in *Reports from the Lost Notebooks of Sir James Dyer*, ed. J. H. Baker vol. 1 (London: Selden Society Publications, vol. 109, 1993), xlv).

[23] Baker, 'Coke's Note-Books' (n. 5), 66.

[24] (1615) 11 Rep 93b, 77 ER 1271. On the writ of mandamus and its development see E. G. Henderson, *Foundations of English administrative law: certiorari and mandamus in the seventeenth century* (Cambridge, MA: Harvard University Press, 1963), 46–82. Henderson shows that *Bagg's Case* was not the first mandamus writ to be issued (the first was in 1608), but was the first to lead to a judgment.

However, Coke's *Reports* are difficult texts for historians to use. As Francis Bacon put it when criticizing them in 1616, they contain too much '*de proprio*'.[25] Certainly Coke's style of reporting (or perhaps his memory) did not lead to reports that accurately reflected what was said or decided in cases. The *Reports* often treated Coke's own views as those of the court, and did not clearly separate Coke's commentary from the report itself.[26] The *Case of Prohibitions* is particularly problematic in this regard. Usher showed that the report of the case in Coke's *Reports* is not easily reconciled with the other surviving reports and may misrepresent which issues were considered most important by the parties in the debates.[27]

Coke's *Institutes* are used less frequently by historians and lawyers, and have been little studied.[28] As Coke seems to have regarded the English constitution as ideal, the descriptions of constitutional matters in the four volumes of the *Institutes* provide valuable material for understanding Coke's views on constitutions. Coke makes no references to the *Institutes* project during his judicial career, suggesting that he only began work on them after 1616. When the first part, the *Commentary on Littleton*, was printed in 1628, Coke claimed that the second and third parts were also completed, but that he had only begun to gather material for the fourth part.[29] If this is correct, then the *Fourth Part of the Institutes of the Laws of England*, which contains Coke's longest discussion of the legislature, was written only around the time of, or after, the parliament in which Coke was one of the members who complained about Charles I's use of the 'Forced Loan' and ultimately worked to create the Petition of Right.

Although they purport to be descriptions of the contemporary state of English law and legal institutions, there is good evidence that the *Institutes* should be treated with some caution. It appears that Coke used the opportunity provided by his *Institutes* to reiterate his own views. Coke had always reused earlier material in his printed publications,[30] but in the *Institutes* Coke seems to have done this to present his conclusions on disputed points as an accurate statement of the law. For example, in the *Third Part of the Institutes of the Laws of England*, Coke discussed the criminal offence of praemunire.[31] Coke's discussion included consideration of the illegitimacy of the Chancery interfering with judgments in common law courts and the possibility of using praemunire to punish those involved in doing so.

[25] F. Bacon, *A Memorial Touching the Review of Penal Laws and the Amendment of the Common Law*, in J. Spedding (ed.), *The Letters and the Life of Francis Bacon*, vol. 5 (London: Longmans, Green, Reader, and Dyer, 1869), 86.

[26] For various early modern criticisms in this vein, see J. W. Wallace, *The Reporters, chronologically arranged: with occasional remarks upon their respective merits*, 3rd ed. (Philadelphia: T & JW Johnson, 1855) 119–20, and T. Egerton, 'The Lord Chancellor Egertons Observacions upon ye Lord Cookes Reportes', in *Law and Politics in Jacobean England: The tracts of Lord Chancellor Ellesmere*, ed. L. A. Knafla (Cambridge: Cambridge University Press, 1977).

[27] R. G. Usher, 'James I and Sir Edward Coke', *English Historical Review* 18 (1903), 664.

[28] A notable exception is Musson (n. 7), who considers Coke's use of historical sources in the *Institutes*.

[29] Co Litt sig¶¶2a.

[30] See Williams, 'Tudor Genesis' (n. 7), 114, where Coke is shown to have reused material from a speech he gave in the Inns of Court in the preface to the third volume of the *Reports*.

[31] 3 Co Inst 119–27.

Praemunire had been used by Coke in a jurisdictional dispute with the Chancery on the issue of Chancery interference after judgment just before his dismissal, and Coke repeated the same arguments and authorities. However, in the *Institutes* Coke then added:

See a Privy Seal bearing *Teste 18 Julii*, Anno Domini 1616, to the contrary, obtained by the importunity of the then Lord Chancellor being vehemently affraid... And besides, the supposed Presidents (which we have seen) are not authenticall, being most of them in torn papers, and the rest of no credit.[32]

Without an understanding of Coke's earlier arguments, this passage makes little sense: it is a reference to a statement by the king that praemunire was not to be used against the Chancery. Coke never provides the 'supposed Presidents' against the use of praemunire, against which he inveighed here. The reference must be to the precedents that were used in the debates before Coke's dismissal, rather than any text in the *Institutes* themselves. As with the *Reports*, we should therefore consider the *Institutes* as works that purport to be descriptive but actually present Coke's own views.[33]

1. Coke's political thought

Coke's legal, historical, and political thought has been the subject of considerable interest since the publication of Pocock's *The Ancient Constitution and the Feudal Law* in 1957, in which Coke was one of the paradigm examples of the early modern 'common law mind'.[34] Broadly, Pocock presented Coke as representative of Jacobean common lawyers, lawyers who thought that the common law was a form of customary law that had existed since time immemorial. The common law had survived political upheaval and invasion more or less unchanged because it was the best law for England.[35] Related to this was a belief in the 'ancient

[32] 3 Co Inst 125.

[33] Other examples include: the jurisdiction of the court of Common Pleas to issue writs of prohibition in 4 Co Inst 100, which was one of the issues in dispute about prohibitions in the first decade of the seventeenth century (see e.g. Henry E. Huntington Library Ellesmere MS 2011, which includes arguments against the Common Pleas' jurisdiction); the discussion of monopolies considered below (nn. 90–3 and text) concerned a statute (21 Jac c 3) which Russell observes was Coke's 'pride and joy' as a legislator in the 1620s and for which Coke introduced the initial bill (Russell (n. 4) 110, 187 and 190).

[34] The outline here is based on Pocock's retrospect on his book (J. G. A. Pocock, *The Ancient Constitution and the Feudal Law: A Study of English Historical Thought in the Seventeenth Century. A Reissue with a Retrospect* (Cambridge: Cambridge University Press, 1987). It does not attempt to take account of all the nuances of the academic discussions on this topic. See, *inter alia*, G. Burgess, *The Politics of the Ancient Constitution: An Introduction to English Political Thought, 1603–1642* (Basingstoke: Macmillan, 1992); Cromartie (n. 8); and C. W. Brooks, *Law, Politics and Society in Early Modern England* (Cambridge: Cambridge University Press, 2008). Many of these works consider a much wider range of sources than Pocock.

[35] The possibility of change does not seem to have been disputed by early modern lawyers, although the advisability of such change clearly was. See Burgess (n. 37), 23, for an explanation of the Aristotelian basis of the idea that changing law was inadvisable and dangerous.

constitution', an English constitution that had similarly existed unchanged beyond the memory (and records) of man.

Within the English constitution and the common law, Coke recognized 'fundamental law'. This was often associated with Magna Carta, but Coke made it clear that Magna Carta was only declaratory of the older fundamental law contained within the common law.[36] The ancient constitution therefore linked the constitution and the common law, and early modern lawyers held a view that the common law could determine constitutional questions. This did not necessarily mean the common law was all encompassing. Early modern common lawyers clearly recognized spheres in which other laws (such as canon law in the ecclesiastical courts) were legitimate and many (perhaps even all, at least until some point in the reign of Charles I) recognized an 'absolute' royal prerogative which, within its sphere, was legally unrestricted.[37]

This outline does seem to reflect Coke's thinking, if not that of all other common lawyers. Aside from one or two isolated comparative remarks, Coke never considered 'constitutions' in his writing, only the English constitution. The English constitution with which Coke was concerned was that which he believed existed in his lifetime (probably, in fact, an idealized Elizabethan constitution)[38] and had always existed.

From the perspective of constitutionalism, the most important aspect of this constitutional model was its focus on law as determining the relationship between government and governed, and between different institutions of government. There is nothing especially novel about these particular points. Law had long been an important element in thinking about constitutional matters in Western Europe.[39] The novelty in the thinking of Coke and his contemporaries was not in the role of law, but the role of common law. Rather than any form of higher-order law, such as divine or natural law, the ancient constitution was determined by a temporal body of law.

For Coke, because the English constitution was an historical artefact, the content of the constitution could be proved. Because the old constitution was the best constitution, there was no clear distinction between the constitution as it was/is and what the constitution ought to be. Such a view had important constitutional effects, notably that the same techniques that were used to 'prove' the law in private law cases could also be used in cases concerned with the constitution.[40] By the time

36 2 Co Inst proheme (unpaginated).

37 See Burgess (n. 34), 139–78; Halliday (n. 6), 65–9; Cromartie (n. 8), 208 identifies material by Coke referring to the 'absolute' prerogative.

38 Brooks has described Coke as a 'long-lived Elizabethan' (Brooks (n. 34), 135), while Russell observes that in the parliaments of the 1620s, 'Coke was an old Elizabethan, constantly reminiscing about the days of his youth, when England had been glorious' (Russell (n. 4), 169).

39 E.g. M. P. Gilmore, *Argument from Roman Law in Political Thought, 1200–1600* (Cambridge, MA: Harvard University Press, 1941); B. Tierney, *Religion, Law and the Growth of Constitutional Thought, 1150–1650* (Cambridge: Cambridge University Press, 1982).

40 See I. Williams, 'English Legal Reasoning and Legal Culture, *c.*1528–*c.*1642' (PhD thesis, University of Cambridge, 2008) on legal argument in this period generally, 44–7 and 105–6 for the idea of the law being 'proved'.

Coke began to write about the English constitution, the onset of printing had led to English law being determined principally through textual means, especially through printed texts, rather than the medieval oral/manuscript tradition.[41] Coke's idea that the constitution was based on common law led to an assumption that the constitution could be determined through the examination and interpretation of texts, just as would be done in private-law cases, and this can clearly be seen in the *Institutes*.[42] This could privilege the common lawyers: they were a group who could claim training conducive to finding and interpreting the relevant material and consequently expertise in discerning the constitution from it. Coke never made this point explicitly, but it lay behind several of his views: his warning to law students to avoid chroniclers as not understanding legal matters (thereby excluding a potential source for identifying the historical constitution);[43] his criticism, in the preface to the *Sixth Reports*, that the Jesuit Robert Parsons' attempt to argue with Coke's recently printed views about English ecclesiastical history was flawed because it did not make reference to matters of record and common law sources;[44] and his denial of James I's capacity to judge because James did not possess the 'artificial reason' of those with 'long study and experience' in the law.[45]

2. Coke's view of the (ideal) English Constitution

According to Coke, England was a monarchy.[46] The relationship between the monarch, the constitution, and the law in Coke's thinking was complex. When Coke discussed the institutions of government in his *Fourth Part of the Institutes*, there was no specific discussion of the monarch. The monarch clearly existed, and was in many respects central to the constitution, but was not identified as a participant in government.[47]

One of Coke's views that remained consistent is that the English monarch had two capacities, a natural body and a politic body.[48] Coke was not the first common lawyer to make this point.[49] However, Coke integrated the idea of the king's two bodies into the existing common law and drew conclusions that related to issues

[41] I. Williams, '"He Creditted More the Printed Booke": Common Lawyers' Receptivity to Print, *c*.1550–1640' *Law and History Review* 28 (2010), 39.

[42] Another good example of this trend is the remark of the judge, Richard Hutton, upon the death of Charles I's Attorney General, William Noy, in 1634: 'in his time many novelties pretended to be grounded upon ancient records in olden times were introduced' (*The Diary of Sir Richard Hutton 1614–1639*, ed. W. R. Prest (London: Selden Society Supplementary Series, vol. 9, 1991), 98).

[43] Edward Coke, *Le Tierce Part des Reportes* (London, 1602), sig Ciii.

[44] Edward Coke, *La Size Part des Reports* (London, 1607), sig ¶v–vi. Ecclesiastical history was an important aspect of debates about the powers of the crown over the English church.

[45] *Prohibitions del Roy* (1610) 12 Co Rep 63, 65; 77 ER 1342, 1343.

[46] Edward Coke, *Le Quart Part des Reportes* (London, 1604), sig Bii.

[47] For example, the king was '*Caput, principium* & *finis*' (the head, the beginning, and the end) of parliament, but was not present (4 Co Inst 3). In the King's Bench, the king was always present, but never answered (4 Co Inst 73).

[48] *Calvin's Case* (1608) 7 Co Rep 1a, 10a; 77 ER 377, 388.

[49] See E. H. Kantorowicz, *The King's Two Bodies: A Study in Mediaeval Political Theology* (Princeton: Princeton University Press, 1957), 7–16 for discussion and references to its appearance in the *Commentaries* of Plowden in the 1570s.

beyond property law. The language of body politic was used for both the king and corporations, which were sometimes described as 'bodies politic' in medieval law reports.[50] Coke used material and ideas from the medieval discussions of corporations when considering the crown. For example, the king's politic body meant that the king 'cannot give or take but by matter of Record for the dignitie of his person'.[51] The same position was taken in the second part of the *Institutes*, '[t]he King being a body politique cannot command but by matter of Record'.[52] In this respect the king was like other corporate bodies, such as towns. The king as a natural person evidently could take property or issue instructions, but as a body politic these actions were not legally effective unless done by record. While Maitland thought that the theory of the king's two bodies 'stubbornly refuses to do any real work in the case of jurisprudence',[53] at the level of constitutional theory this view is misplaced. Coke's approach not only led to concrete conclusions on matters of law, but also suggested a broader idea: that the king was integrated into the legal system, rather than outside it.[54]

Coke's approach inevitably limited the powers of the monarch. As Coke made clear, even in the period when he was Attorney General, unlawful actions by the monarch could not be enforced through the courts. In the preface to the second volume of *Reports* (1602), Coke proclaimed that while in other countries 'the Lawes seeme to governe', in England the judges actually would not obey an unlawful command from the monarch.[55] Coke seems to have taken the same view in actual cases through his career. In *Darcy v Allen* (the '*Case of Monopolies*'), in which Coke appeared as counsel, Coke conceded that if the king granted a monopoly by letters patent, and the grant was unlawful, then the courts could not enforce it.[56] Coke was Attorney General at the time, but does not seem to have thought his concession would be problematic or controversial. Similarly, Coke explained how the king by charter could not abridge existing common-law rights in subjects, another example of the king not being able to act contrary to law.[57] To some extent, Coke's model of the constitution presupposed the supremacy of law: not even the king could act contrary to law, at least in the sense that unlawful actions would not be enforceable.[58]

[50] D. J. Seipp, 'Formalism and realism in fifteenth-century English law: Bodies corporate and bodies natural', in P. Brand and J. Getzler (eds), *Judges and Judging in the History of the Common Law and Civil Law: From Antiquity to Modern Times* (Cambridge: Cambridge University Press, 2012), 39–40.

[51] *Calvin's Case* (1608) 7 Co Rep 1a, 12a; 77 ER 377, 391.

[52] 2 Co Inst 186.

[53] F. W. Maitland, 'The Crown as Corporation', in H. D. Hazeltine, G. Lapsley and P. H. Winfield (eds), *Maitland: Selected Essays* (Cambridge: Cambridge University Press, 1936), 111.

[54] It is not clear to me whether Coke reached this view consciously or as a political theory, or it simply reflected his approach to interpreting legal sources, which was to integrate ideas into his existing understanding. For examples of this, which are shown to be linked to contemporary reading techniques, see Williams 'Tudor Genesis' (n. 7), 121–2.

[55] Edward Coke, *Le Second Part des Reportes* (London, 1602) 'To the learned reader' (unpaginated).

[56] See Corré (n. 5), 1297. Tanfield, then the solicitor general, agreed with this concession.

[57] *Case of the Tailors of Ipswich* (1615) 11 Co Rep 53b–54a; 77 ER 1218, 1219–20.

[58] An important qualification is the 'absolute' prerogative (n. 37 and text).

IV. The Institutions of Government and their Accountability

Coke referred to England as 'governed by law'.[59] His *Fourth Institutes* 'was a treatise on structural constitutional law and organs of government. Coke reviewed the powers of the various government bodies existing in England – legislative, administrative, fiscal, mercantile, ecclesiastical, collegiate, metropolitan, and baronial.'[60] However, the subtitle of this book was 'concerning the Jurisdiction of Courts'. For Coke, every governmental body was in some sense a court. Parliament was a court,[61] the King's council was a court; so were the 'Counting House of the King's Household', and 'Commissioners and others for the maintaining and erecting of Beacons, signes of the sea, or Light-houses'.[62] If a body had legal powers, it was a 'court'.

This position made sense in early modern England. The earliest institution of central government in Anglo-Norman England, the Exchequer, clearly was a court and its judicial jurisdiction was determined by its revenue function;[63] the most important figure in early modern local government, the Justice of the Peace, was a judge who also exercised important investigatory and administrative functions.[64]

This identification of all sorts of governmental institutions as courts is a salutary reminder that Coke could not have thought in anything like modern terms about government or the separation of powers. Coke did not classify governmental bodies based upon their functions: all governmental bodies were courts and their activity was 'judicial'. Moreover, it was this understanding of other institutions as courts which seems to have justified Coke's ideas about the accountability of these institutions. According to Coke in *Bagg's Case*:

> to this Court of King's Bench belongs authority not only to correct errors in judicial proceedings, but other errors and misdemeanors extra-judicial, tending to the breach of peace, or oppression of the subjects, or to the raising of faction, controversy, debate, or to any manner of misgovernment; so that no wrong or injury, either public or private, can be done but that it shall be (here) reformed or punished by due course of law.[65]

For Coke, errors were either 'judicial' or 'extra-judicial', an interpretation which presupposes an interpretation of government as itself curial. The jurisdiction of the King's Bench over 'judicial' errors was largely accepted at the time, and criticisms of

[59] Coke, *Second Part* (n. 55), 'To the learned reader' (unpaginated).

[60] Boyer, 'Coke, Sir Edward' (n. 2), 462.

[61] 4 Co Inst 1. In the preface to 2 Co Inst (unpaginated), Coke even states that parliament acts as a court when legislating, describing statutes as 'enacted by that court'.

[62] 4 Co Inst 131 and 148.

[63] See J. H. Baker, *An Introduction to English Legal History*, 4th ed. (London: Butterworths, 2002), 48–9. The fictitious writ of *quo minus*, which changed the Exchequer into a common-law court of general jurisdiction was not fully accepted until around 1649, see W. Hamilton Bryson, 'The court of Exchequer comes of age', in D. J. Guth and J. W. McKenna (eds), *Tudor Rule and Revolution: essays for G. R. Elton from his American friends* (Cambridge: Cambridge University Press, 1982).

[64] See e.g. Henderson (n. 24), 9–25.

[65] *Bagg's Case* (1615) 11 Co Rep 93b, 98a; 77 ER 1271, 1277–8.

Coke's remarks in *Bagg's Case* focused on the assertion of jurisdiction over 'extra-judicial' errors.

Halliday has recently drawn attention to a manuscript report that provides evidence as to how Coke justified the King's Bench jurisdiction over 'judicial' errors.[66] The passage suggests that by identifying governmental institutions as courts, Coke necessarily concluded that the King's Bench would have review of them. In 1605, Coke intervened in a habeas corpus application argued in the King's Bench concerning imprisonment on the orders of the Council of the Marches of Wales, despite not being counsel in the case. Coke asked the court's permission to 'plead a little for the prerogative of the king, the jurisdiction of the court, and the benefit of all the king's subjects'. Coke explained that

> [a]ll courts of justice within the dominions of the king are subordinate, this court alone excepted, in which the king is always by law intended to be present, and which is restrained to no place but extends to all his dominions. Thus only this court will have the examination of all other courts of justice, and when the king gives authority by his commissions, or the law by act of parliament, to any man to execute justice, still the examination of them shall be made by such authority that will remain in the absolute and supreme power of the king and in his bench, which is his proper seat of justice.[67]

Coke's remarks show an assumption that the review jurisdiction of the King's Bench, the king's prerogative, and the interests of the king's subjects could all be upheld simultaneously, something which is not apparent from many discussions of Coke's constitutional ideas. The jurisdiction of the King's Bench was an emanation of the royal prerogative.[68] Contempt of the King's Bench and its orders was therefore also contempt of the royal prerogative and the king.

From this perspective, habeas corpus and all resolutions of jurisdictional disputes could be described as protecting the king's prerogative. Prohibitions to ecclesiastical courts, and praemunire against the Chancery, were not mere assertions of power by the central common-law courts, but attempts to protect the king's judicial prerogative from illegitimate usurpation. Jurisdictional usurpation would also have dangerous effects for subjects seeking justice and the realm as a whole. Coke explained this using the metaphor of the realm as a body politic. He explained that if the hands or feet tried to exercise

> the office of the eie to see, these should assuredly produce disorder, and darknesse, and bring the whole body out of order, and in the end to distruction: So in the Commonwealth (Justice being the main preserver thereof) if one Court should usurp, or incroach upon another, it would introduce incertainty, subvert Justice, and bring all things in the end to confusion.[69]

[66] For what follows, see Halliday (n. 6), 11–13.

[67] *Whitherby v Wetherley* (1605) Harvard Law School MS 1180, fos 68^{v}–69. The same passage is quoted by Halliday, with a slightly different translation from the law-French. Similar ideas were expressed by Thomas Fleming when Elizabeth's solicitor general (see the material quoted in Halliday (n. 6), 64–5).

[68] Coke also made this point in the fourth part of the *Institutes*: the king had delegated his judicial powers to the King's Bench (4 Co Inst 70–1).

[69] 4 Co Inst sig B-B^{v}.

What Coke's explanation for the King's Bench's jurisdiction does not provide is clarification as to why the King's Bench had jurisdiction over 'extra-judicial' errors. The breadth of Coke's statement was criticized by some of his opponents. Lord Chancellor Ellesmere announced that Coke sought to subordinate the entire government of the realm to the King's Bench.[70] However, the substance of Ellesmere's criticism was subtler and can only be understood in the context of *Bagg's Case* as a whole. *Bagg's Case* was the first case initiated by a writ of mandamus to proceed to trial. The writ of mandamus emerged in the King's Bench in the early seventeenth century and, unlike its precursors or writs such as prohibition or habeas corpus, was not necessarily directed to a 'judicial' body. Nor was the writ of mandamus the main subject in *Bagg's Case* itself.[71] Coke's remark in *Bagg's Case* was directed to providing some justification for the writ of mandamus itself, rather than a wide theory of government by judiciary.[72] Ellesmere's criticism of Coke recognized this. The substance of his complaint was not that Coke was trying to run the country through the King's Bench, but that Coke was asserting a jurisdiction for the King's Bench which had previously been exercised by the king, the Privy Council, or the Court of Star Chamber.[73]

In *Bagg's Case,* Coke did not explain why the King's Bench had jurisdiction over extra-judicial errors. That explanation is found in the fourth part of the *Institutes*, where Coke expressly linked the King's Bench's jurisdiction to issue writs of mandamus with the jurisdiction to grant writs of habeas corpus or prohibition.[74] If Coke's justification for the jurisdiction of the King's Bench in matters of 'judicial' error was the presence of the king and his judicial prerogative, it seems that this justification was also to explain the jurisdiction over 'extra-judicial' error. In some sense, this jurisdiction had already been recognized as existing in the Star Chamber. All that Coke had done was move the jurisdiction to (or claim shared jurisdiction for) the King's Bench.

V. Legislature and Law-Making

Because Coke's ideal constitution was the English constitution, his discussion of the legislature was to a great extent descriptive of the English parliament. Most of Coke's writings about parliament are found in his *Institutes*, especially the *Fourth Part*. This poses an interpretative challenge. According to Coke he had not written the *Fourth Part* by 1628 (when the *First Part* was printed), but had begun to collect

[70] Egerton, 'The Lord Chancellor Egertons Observacions' (n. 26), 307.

[71] Henderson (n. 24), 62 makes this clear.

[72] There is no evidence that Coke influenced the development of the mandamus writ before *Bagg's Case*. The key developments in the form of the writ occurred under his two predecessors (Henderson (n. 24), 68–9). By the time of *Bagg's Case*, Coke may have felt that he had to find a justification for a writ which was by then established as part of his court's jurisdiction.

[73] Egerton, 'The Lord Chancellor Egertons Observacions' (n. 26), 307. Henderson provides some evidence that the type of dispute in *Bagg's Case* itself had previously been addressed by the Privy Council. In fact the dispute in *Bagg's Case* had itself gone to the Council (Henderson (n. 24), 72–6).

[74] 4 Co Inst 71.

material.[75] This means that the views Coke expressed in the *Fourth Part* may reflect Coke's experience in the tumultuous Parliament of 1628. Coke never directly refers to this parliament, but it may have coloured some of his views in ways that cannot easily be identified.

Parliament consisted of the king and the three estates of the realm: lords spiritual, lords temporal, and the commons. Those elected as members of the commons 'represent all the Commons of the whole Realme, and trusted for them'.[76] According to Coke, statute was consequently 'made by authoritie of the whole Realme', of which the king was a part.[77] Certain remarks by Coke present a view that parliament had a power greater than that of the monarch. According to Coke, 'the power and jurisdiction of the parliament, for making of laws in proceeding by Bill, it is so transcendent and absolute, as it cannot be confined either for causes or persons within any bounds',[78] and '[t]he highest and most binding Laws are the Statutes which are established by Parliament'.[79]

Coke explained the power of parliament through the metaphor of the body politic:

> [A]s in the naturall body when all the sinews being joyned in the head do join their forces together for the strengthning of the body, there is *ultimum Potentiae* [greatest power]: so in the politique body when the king and the Lords Spirituall and Temporall, knights, Citizens, and Burgesses, are all by the kings command assembled and joyned together under the head in consultation for the common good of the whole realm, there is *ultimum Sapientiae* [greatest wisdom].[80]

Like his justification for judicial independence, Coke's explanation as to parliament's unique power was based upon parliament's superior capacity to reach the correct decisions due to its greater wisdom than any other person or institution.

However, while in the *Institutes* Coke stressed parliament's pre-eminent wisdom and power, Coke is well known for remarks which present a very different view. Coke not only doubted parliament's wisdom, but may have propounded limitations on its power. For example, in the preface to his third volume of *Reports*, Coke described how parliament sometimes changed the common law, which was not a wise thing to do. For example:

> the wisedome of the Common Law, was that all estates of inheritance should bee Fee simple, so as one man might safely alien, demise, and contract, to and with an other: But the Statute of Westminster the second cap.1. created an estate taile, and made a Perpetuitie by Act of Parliament, restraining Tenant in taile from aliening or demising... which in process of time brought in such troubles and inconveniences, that after two hundred yeeres, necessitie found out a way by Law for a Tenant in taile to alien.[81]

[75] Co Litt sig¶¶2a. [76] 4 Co Inst 1.

[77] Co Litt 19b. Despite stating that statutes were made by the whole realm, Coke accepted that many were bound by statutes who were not parties to elections (4 Co Inst 4).

[78] 4 Co Inst 36. [79] 2 Co Inst proheme (unpaginated). [80] 4 Co Inst 3.

[81] Coke, *Tierce Part* (n. 43), sig Div^r.

Coke's changing views may reflect changing circumstances. In the 1628 parliament, Coke and others were trying to resolve the problems caused by the *Five Knights' Case*. That case seemed to show that the judges could not be relied upon to protect the liberties of the subject. If so, Coke needed to justify parliament having the final say. While Coke had earlier stressed the excellence, wisdom and reasoning of the judges,[82] in the fourth part of his *Institutes*, Coke instead stressed the wisdom of parliament. By doing so, Coke provided a justification for parliamentary intervention that did not upset his theory: if parliament was wiser than the judges, it was appropriate for parliament to be the final arbiter.

One of the statements for which Coke is most famous was made in *Dr Bonham's Case*, where Coke suggested that parliament's power was limited and that the courts had a role in controlling parliament's power. In his report of *Dr Bonham's Case*, Coke stated that:

> it appears in our books, that in many cases, the common law will controul Acts of Parliament, and sometimes adjudge them to be utterly void: for when an Act of Parliament is against common right and reason, or repugnant, or impossible to be performed, the common law will controul it, and adjudge such Act to be void.[83]

The meaning of this passage, and quite what Coke meant by 'common right and reason', has been much discussed. No consensus has been reached, although recent work has been more sceptical about the idea that Coke was claiming a genuine power in the courts to review legislation.[84] It may be significant that the early-seventeenth-century parliament acknowledged that it was not sovereign in all respects, and had itself recently complained about the practice of 'letting out of penalties to subjects', which was the issue in *Bonham's Case*.[85] Unless significant new evidence is identified, it seems unlikely that agreement is possible over such an ambiguous passage. Coke may have been referring to ideas of higher-order law, common-law norms, or maybe mere contradiction in the statute itself, and there are questions about whether the language of 'void' refers to declaratory judgments or mere non-application in particular cases.

A further complication in Coke's view of the power of the legislature related to dispensations, an aspect of the royal prerogative that enabled the king to dispense a particular person from the rules imposed by legislation. In the *Case of Non Obstante*, Coke clearly stated that the king had just such a dispensing power, even if parliament included a provision in its legislation denying the possibility of

[82] See nn. 101–3 and text.

[83] *Dr Bonham's Case* (1610) 8 Co Rep 107a, 118a; 77 ER 646, 652.

[84] The most recent contributions offering competing views are: I. S. Williams, '*Dr Bonham's Case* and "void" statutes', *Journal of Legal History* 27 (2006), 111; R. H. Helmholz, 'Bonham's Case, Judicial Review, and the Law of Nature' *Journal of Legal Analysis* 1 (2009), 325; and P. Hamburger, *Law and Judicial Duty* (Cambridge, MA: Harvard University Press, 2008), 622–30. See Allison (n. 11), 136–9 for further references.

[85] Conrad Russell, *King James VI & I and his English Parliaments* (Oxford: Oxford University Press, 2011), 31 and 60.

such a dispensation with regard to the statute.[86] In this respect, Coke seems to have regarded parliament's 'transcendent and absolute' legislative power as weaker than the royal prerogative.

Related to the legislature was Coke's view of non-parliamentary legislative powers. Notoriously, James I thought that the king had power to make law by issuing proclamations under the royal prerogative. Coke apparently rejected this position in the *Case of Proclamations*, proclaiming 'that the king cannot change any part of the Common Law, nor create any Offence by his Proclamation, which was not an Offence before, without Parliament'.[87] Modern readers tend to take the interpretation that Coke here established that the monarch could not alter the law.[88] As with many of Coke's quotes, the interpretation may not be as simple as it first appears, in this instance because of the early modern jurisprudential context. It is clear that some other common lawyers considered that a practice could be prohibited or regulated by proclamation if the practice was not punished by the common law or statute but was nonetheless 'unlawful'. For example, in the *Case of Monopolies*, Altham argued precisely this position with regard to the monarch having power to regulate monopolies through the prerogative.[89] In this context, unlawfulness must mean something other than contrary to common or statute law. Whether Coke agreed with this position is not entirely clear.

The views about monopolies expressed by Coke in the third part of his *Institutes* demonstrate the difficulty in understanding Coke's views on identifying what was an offence. According to Coke, '[t]hat offence which is contrary to the ancient and fundamentall laws is *malum in se*'.[90] To explain the characterization of monopolies as contrary to the ancient laws of the realm, Coke argued that

> the law of the Realm in this point is grounded upon the law of God, which saith . . . Thou shalt not take the nether or upper milstone to pledge, for he taketh a mans life to pledge: Whereby it appeareth that a mans trade is accounted his life, because it maintaineth his life and therefore the Monopolist that taketh away a mans trade, taketh away his life.[91]

However, Coke does not provide any evidence of the ancient law relating to monopolies, other than parliamentary materials from the reign of Edward III onwards. Coke's view would therefore seem to be that prohibition by divine law

[86] *Case of Non Obstante* 12 Co Rep 18; 77 ER 1300. See also *Penall Statutes* (1605) 7 Co Rep 36, where the dispensing power was affirmed.

[87] *Case of Proclamations* (1611) 12 Co Rep 74, 75; 77 ER 1352, 1353.

[88] Bradley and Ewing (n. 1), 50.

[89] Corré (n. 5), 1298. Coke was counsel in *Darcy v Allen*, and there is no evidence of him taking a contrary position.

[90] 3 Co Inst 181. In the *Case of Proclamations*, Coke said 'that which is against common law is *malum in se*' ((1611) 12 Co Rep 74, 76; 77 ER 1352, 1354).

[91] 3 Co Inst 181. It would be interesting to identify if the arguments from the law of God which Coke advances at various points had wider support among divines or other writers. For example, the bishop Lancelot Andrewes condemned unjust monopolies in his catechism, regarding them as contrary to the eighth commandment against theft (see N. Tadmor, *The Social Universe of the English Bible: scripture, society, and culture in early modern England* (Cambridge: Cambridge University Press, 2010), 157–8).

would also mean prohibition by the 'ancient and fundamentall laws'.[92] If that is correct, anything that could be identified as contrary to divine law[93] could be punished by proclamation, because in theory at least it was already contrary to existing law. While Coke's position stated a clear theoretical limitation on the monarch's power, one which modern authors can identify as related to a modern doctrine, in the early modern context this limitation may have been of much narrower effect.[94] What Coke's position would have achieved is the resolution he reported later in the *Case of Proclamations*: 'that the King hath no Prerogative, but that which the Law of the Land allows him'.[95] By stating that proclamations would not be enforced unless the offence was already recognized as an offence by the existing law, Coke effectively denied the king's potential to determine the scope of his own prerogative power to issue proclamations, a power that Coke described as a 'grand prerogative of the king'.[96]

VII. Judicial Independence

Coke is usually identified by writers on the constitution as an early champion for the idea of judicial independence from the crown. Medieval and early modern judges were not obviously independent of the crown. Even Coke described the judges as part of the 'King's Council'.[97] Nevertheless, *Peacham's Case* and the cases of *Prohibitions* and *Commendams* are taken as specific examples of the ideas of the separation of powers and judicial independence, while Coke's willingness to resist royal pressure itself demonstrated judicial independence.[98] The *Case of Prohibitions*, in particular, became well known following its inclusion in Coke's twelfth volume of *Reports*. This case is an excellent example of the difficulty in reconstructing Coke's views, while *Peacham's Case* is more problematic in its significance.

The *Case of Prohibitions* concerned a jurisdictional dispute between the common-law and ecclesiastical courts, centred on the use by the common-law courts of writs of prohibition that ordered ecclesiastical courts to cease hearing a case. Such jurisdictional disputes were not first encountered in Jacobean England, but what was new was James I's decision to attempt to resolve the dispute personally. Prohibitions issued to the ecclesiastical courts related to important matters of public

[92] Exactly the same position is taken with regard to brothel-keeping, for example (3 Co Inst 205).

[93] For modern readers it is important to observe the capacity of 'divine law' to be stretched. Coke considered monopolies to be addressed by divine law because monopolies deprived people of livelihoods and then life; Lancelot Andrewes extended the prohibition on theft to monopolies, which does not seem an obvious point to all modern readers.

[94] In addition to the potential breadth of offences which might be identified as part of the law, there is the fact that conciliar courts such as the Star Chamber clearly did punish either for breaches of proclamation in themselves or for contempt of the king in breaching his proclamation. See Frederic A. Youngs, *The Proclamations of the Tudor Queens* (Cambridge: Cambridge University Press, 1976) 70, 117–19, 153 and 237–40.

[95] *Case of Proclamations* (1611) 12 Co Rep 74, 76; 77 ER 1352, 1354.

[96] (1611) 12 Co Rep 74, 75; 77 ER 1352, 1353.

[97] Co Litt 110.

[98] Lyon (n. 1), 199–200; Loveland (n. 1), 58 and 87; Bradley and Ewing (n. 1), 247.

interest. Such prohibitions undermined the capacity of the church courts to enforce religious discipline, and made it more difficult for the church to raise revenue (especially in cases concerning tithes) and thereby fund its ministry.

Quite what happened on the two days of debate over which James presided is unclear; there are several reports, none of which entirely match. The only report of the debate that was printed was Coke's (printed in the *Interregnum*), which also happens to be the report that is most different to the others.[99] From the perspective of later influence, it was Coke's report which became well known and to which reference is still made in works on the English constitution. In comparison to the other reports, Coke's report focuses on an issue which seems to have been of less importance in the debates themselves: whether the king was permitted to resolve such a jurisdictional dispute.[100]

According to Coke, he explained to James that the king could not act as a judge because he lacked the 'artificial reason' of those trained in the law.[101] Coke's claim to a particular constitutional role and power, that of judging, was grounded upon a claim to expertise and particular skill.[102] Coke's argument denied the king any judicial role. The argument was unsuccessful, at least in the short term: James appeared as a judge in the court of Star Chamber in 1616, pronounced a resolution to another jurisdictional dispute, and explained that he was entitled to act in a judicial capacity. In the longer term, Coke effectively reiterated his conclusion in the *Second Institutes*, but in terms that would, perhaps, have been more palatable to James. There, Coke accepted that kings had a judicial power from their status as God's lieutenant. However, the king had delegated his judicial power to the judges of the various courts.[103]

Peacham's Case arose in rather different circumstances. After discovering a draft treatise by Peacham, which hinted at rebellion and regicide, the crown asked the judges for their views about whether Peacham could be regarded as having committed treason.[104] Unusually, the judges were consulted individually.[105] Three of

[99] Usher 'James I and Sir Edward Coke' (n. 27). [100] See n. 27.

[101] On 'artificial reason' see A. D. Boyer, '"Understanding, Authority, and Will": Sir Edward Coke and the Elizabethan Origins of Judicial Review', *Boston College Law Review* 39 (1998), 43 and A. D. Boyer, 'Sir Edward Coke, Ciceronianus: Classical rhetoric and the common law tradition', *International Journal for the Semiotics of Law* 10 (1997), 3, n. 12 which includes references to earlier discussions. Coke accepted the monarch being concerned about jurisdictional disputes and being involved in their resolution; he reports Elizabeth ordering just such a resolution (3 Co Inst 124), but Elizabeth referred the dispute to the judges and did not involve herself in the substance of the resolution.

[102] The same reliance upon expertise was made by James Morice in his reading in the Middle Temple in 1578. According to Morice, if the king appointed someone as a judge 'who never studyed the lawes of the Realme althouh otherwise he be profoundly learned, Authorising him thereby to be a Justice of the one Bench or thother, this man is no sufficient Judg lawfully ordeyned by the kings Prerogative' (British Library Egerton MS 3376 fo 30^{v}).

[103] 2 Co Inst 103; the same point is also made in 4 Co Inst 70–3.

[104] On the facts, see Gardiner, *History of England*, vol. 2 (n. 1), 272–83.

[105] The usual practice when asking the judges questions was to consult them as a group (see Bacon's letter to the king in Spedding (n. 25), 101). In the dispute over prohibitions, judges were consulted in small groups, but Usher observes that the judges seemed to have 'intended to disagree in private and invariably present a united front to their enemies' (R. G. Usher, *The Rise and Fall of the High*

the four justices of the King's Bench accepted this, but Coke initially refused to be party to the consultation, on the basis that individual consultation was 'new and dangerous'.[106] Eventually Coke did agree to be consulted alone, but the initial refusal can be interpreted as a demonstration of judicial independence. However, this view should not be taken too far. Coke did not object to the practice of consultation in itself,[107] merely the practice of consulting the judges as individuals. This rejection seems to have been based upon the quality of the advice that would be given as a result. Assessments of the authority of cases in early modern legal argument placed considerable weight on two factors: unanimity amongst the judges and the existence of argument and discussion. Cases that lacked either (or both) of these features were considered to be less authoritative because they were more likely to be mistaken.[108] Individual consultation of the judges did lack both of these features. From Coke's perspective, such individual consultations may therefore have been more likely to generate incorrect conclusions. If this is correct, then Coke's objection was not to providing advice, but that James's request for individual consultation risked providing the king with bad advice.

Interpreted in this way, *Peacham's Case* is a useful corrective to the view of Gardiner that 'Coke was clearly in the right in instinctively feeling that the true place for a judge was on the Bench, not in the council chamber of the King'.[109] Coke did not object to judges being in the king's council chamber, rather Coke objected to the judges not being able to exercise their role as councillors as well as they could. It was only in his *Institutes* that Coke expressed the view that consultation itself should not occur, even then limiting this solely to criminal cases.[110]

It is only in the *Case of Commendams* that we see something that looks like genuine judicial independence. The king as head of the church in England granted a bishop an additional living in the church. The plaintiffs in the case sued the bishop, claiming that they held the right to appoint to the living in question. Such rights of appointments were recognized as property rights, advowsons, by the common law. The case raised difficult questions about the king's prerogative as head of the church in England, especially in relation to private property rights. Once James learned of the case, he sent the judges an order by letter, instructing them not to hear final arguments, or give judgment, before consultation with him.

Commission (Oxford: Oxford University Press, 1913), 218), perhaps explaining James's desire for individual consultations.

106 Bacon's letter to the king in Spedding (n. 25), 107.

107 Unlike Hussey CJKB in (1486) YB Trin 1 Hen VII, fo 25a, pl 1 at 26a. Hussey's objection (which arose in the content of the possibility of judges giving advice in a case of treason and then having to try the case too) was generalized by Brooke in his *Graunde Abridgement*, a standard Elizabethan reference work (Brooke Abr, tit Judgement, pl 157). James Morice, in his 1578 reading in the Middle Temple, disagreed with Brooke's conclusion, stressing that 'it is not small part of the Justices allegiance expressed in their oath faithfully and lawfully to Councell and advise the king in his affaires', concluding that if any judge did refuse to advise the king, dismissal of the judge would be justified (Morice (n. 101) fo 36^{v}–37).

108 Williams, 'English Legal Reasoning' (n. 41), 72–3 and 101.

109 Gardiner, *History of England*, vol. 3 (n. 1), 24.

110 3 Co Inst 29. Coke relied upon Hussey's objection in 1486 (n. 106), but the restriction to criminal cases meant his position was narrower than that of Brooke.

The judges refused. The judges justified their refusal in a letter to James, and again in a conference with him in June 1616,[111] claiming that to obey the king's command would be unlawful and expressly forbidden by the judicial oath.[112] According to James Morice in 1578, the judicial oath required judges to swear that 'yee deny no man common Right by the kings Lettres nor non other meanes nor for none other cause, and in case any Lettres come to you Contrary to the Law that you doe noething by such Lettres but certifie the king thereof and goe forth to do the law'.[113] This is precisely what the judges did in the *Case of Commendams*.

The *Case of Commendams* therefore does not seem to reflect any new developments in either Coke's thought or wider constitutional thinking. Morice described the terms of the judicial oath as arising from statute in the reign of Edward III.[114] What is significant is that the *Case of Commendams* was the practical application of constitutional ideas, unlike earlier remarks by Coke or the terms of the oath itself. The *Case of Commendams* was the first occasion where the judges expressly stated that the instruction they had received was unlawful, and as Coke had said in the preface to his *Second Reports* in 1602, they refused to act on such an instruction.[115]

VI. Concluding Remarks

In some respects the *Case of Commendams* is a useful point at which to end consideration of Coke and constitutionalism. The fact that the concern is with a particular case is itself significant. Coke's constitutional thought (such as it was) was never expressed in a single document, or even a collection of documents, purporting to be a coherent or complete collection. Despite the importance of the *Case of Commendams* for Coke's reputation, Coke himself never reported it.

The events of the *Case of Commendams* were also closely linked to Coke's dismissal, a dismissal that some time later made Coke a martyr to the idea of judicial independence. For writers on English constitutional law, much of Coke's

[111] See *Acts of the Privy Council of England 1615–1616* (HMSO 1925), 595–609 for the letters and debates.

[112] This reliance upon the judicial oath was not new. In 1591 the judges delivered an opinion to the Lord Chancellor and Lord Treasurer that condemned certain aspects of imprisonment without cause. As such imprisonment was an aspect of the royal prerogative, there was the potential to cause offence to Elizabeth, and so the judges stressed that they were 'bound by office and oath to relieve and help' people who had been so imprisoned (see the two versions of the opinion in W. S. Holdsworth, *A History of English Law* vol. 5 (London: Methuen & Co, 1924) 495 and 497).

[113] Morice (n. 101) fo 29^{v}.

[114] Morice bases this oath on a statute of 18 Edward III. This must be a reference to 20 Edw III c 1. The oath of a judge in *The Book of Oaths, and The severall forms thereof, both Antient and Modern* (1649), 10 is in the same terms as Morice, but the relevant passage is printed simply as 'notwithstanding the Kings Lees [Lettres?], &c'.

[115] In an earlier case where a writ *non procedendo rege inconsulto* was brought on behalf of the crown, the judges declined to obey the writ but the case was settled (see Hart (n. 1), 104–5). This writ was a regular feature of medieval legal procedure (T. F. T. Plucknett, *A Concise History of the Common Law*, 5th ed. (London: Butterworths, 1956), 196). However, in the *Case of Commendams* the delay was instructed by a royal letter, not a recognized (if rarely used) writ. The instruction to delay could therefore be seen as unlawful in part because such a letter was not a regular form of legal process.

significance is linked to events in which Coke was involved, rather than Coke's actual ideas. In that sense, Coke provides a historical example of contemporary ideas, a useful figure in the narrative of the English constitution identified as important because of the significance of certain ideas to modern writers.

Coke was more than that. In the 1620s he was described as the 'father of the law'.[116] In 1631, when an order was given that Coke's books and papers be seized, Coke was described as 'too great an oracle amongst the people, and they may be misled by anything that carries such an authority as all things do that he either speaks or writes'.[117] Some of Coke's remarks and actions are as delphic as those from the original oracle. As Maitland observed over a century ago, '[i]t is always difficult to pin Coke to a theory', a difficulty which has not been solved despite considerable discussion in some contexts.[118] In the *Case of Commendams*, we have no real explanation of Coke's theory. There is a letter from all the judges to the king, which sets out their reasons for refusing to delay the case, but there is no explanation as to why the instruction given was considered unlawful. Much modern writing on Coke has been attempting to understand and explicate Coke's legal and political theory based around such isolated remarks and actions.

Despite his publications, Coke is silent on many of the issues which modern constitutionalists consider important. In some respects, this may explain Coke's appearance in later discussions of the constitution. Coke provides an example which can be interpreted to suit later theories, without expressing any theory which demonstrates quite how different his underlying ideas were or might have been. Where Coke does express theory, he rarely explains his underlying assumptions and the resulting expression is often ambiguous, providing plenty of scope for interpretation.[119] The various attempts to understand, and sometimes to rely upon, Coke's report of *Bonham's Case* are a good example of this. In the early eighteenth century, Coke's language of controlling statutes contrary to 'common right and reason' in *Bonham's Case* could be interpreted through the prism of social contract theory.[120] In Blackstone's *Commentaries* in the second half of the eighteenth century the same language is interpreted as a rule of construction.[121] In the late

[116] R. Zaller, *The Parliament of 1621: A study in constitutional conflict* (University of California Press, 1971), 69 and Cromartie (n. 8), 232.

[117] *Calendar of State Papers, Domestic Series, of the Reign of Charles I: 1629–1631*, ed. J. Bruce (London: Longman, Green, Longman, and Roberts, 1860), 490.

[118] F. W. Maitland, *The Constitutional History of England*, ed. H. A. L. Fisher (Cambridge: Cambridge University Press, 1961), 300.

[119] Cromartie regards some of Coke's expressions as 'craftily ambiguous' (Cromartie (n. 8), 214). Russell describes Coke as a 'great rambler' (Russell (n. 4), xix) whose parliamentary speeches lacked structure, which might suggest ambiguity was not deliberate.

[120] See P. A. Hamburger, 'Revolution and Judicial Review: Chief Justice Holt's Opinion in *City of London v. Wood*', *Columbia Law Review* 94 (1994), 2091.

[121] J. V. Orth, 'Blackstone's Rules on the Construction of Statutes' in Prest (ed), *Blackstone and his Commentaries: Biography, Law, History* (Oxford: Hart, 2009). Orth suggests that Blackstone was trying to interpret Coke's words in *Bonham's Case* so that they continued to have some validity in the eighteenth-century context, observing that Blackstone's interpretation seems to be 'wrung from him against his will' and that he 'salvaged what he could' from Coke's remarks (85 and 89).

twentieth century the words could be interpreted as related to the principle of legality and rule of law.[122]

Nevertheless, Coke clearly did think that theory was important as a justification for action. Coke's remarks about the jurisdiction of the King's Bench in relation to habeas corpus and other courts discussed above[123] were made when Coke thought it was worthwhile for him to raise such points for the benefit of the court, despite not being counsel in the case and simply present in court. In this case Coke did present a theory about ideas of legality and royal power. Unlike Coke's usual posthumous reputation, the theory was a prerogative theory, one that does not fit neatly with the view of Coke presented in works that stress Coke as an opponent of the prerogative.[124]

A recurring element in this chapter has been Coke's stress on the importance of expertise, which in his view justified power and allotted constitutional roles. Judges were to judge, not the king, because judges had greater skill. The same assumption can be seen in the refusal to consult with the king as an individual judge, rather than as the judicial collective: it was in a group, through a process of discussion and debate, that judges were able to exercise their expertise. To consult individually, before such discussions had occurred, would be to prevent the judges exercising their skill. Parliament was to legislate because of its greater wisdom; where the common law was already wise and parliament unwisely intervened, the law would ultimately correct the situation. In a very broad sense, this aspect of Coke's constitutional thought was aristocratic:[125] certain people or institutions were the best at certain functions and so were to perform them. Power and legitimacy were both premised on expertise. This perspective, however, was only taken so far: although the king could neither judge, nor create law of the same status as statute, because of his want of expertise, the question of expertise to be king was, unsurprisingly, never raised.

[122] Allan (n. 21). [123] Above nn. 65–8 and text.

[124] In this regard Coke demonstrates in microcosm the argument of Halliday concerning the writ of habeas corpus: that the writ was initially an emanation of prerogative power, which parliament in fact tended to restrict, rather than to expand in the cause of 'liberty' (see generally Halliday (n. 6)).

[125] Goldsworthy has raised the idea of common law constitutionalism as introducing an 'aristocratic' element into democratic constitutions (J. Goldsworthy, *Parliamentary Sovereignty, Contemporary Debates* (Cambridge: Cambridge University Press, 2010), 10–11), but in a very different sense to that raised here.

4

Constitutions in Hobbes's Science of Politics

Tom Sorell

I

Hobbes's philosophical remarks about the state are often read as veiled commentary on English parliamentary politics after the 1620s.[1] His lifelong service to the Cavendish family aligned him with Charles I before the Civil War, and copies of his first full-length political treatise, *The Elements of Law*, were circulated among parliamentarians in 1640 as a partisan briefing paper in defence of the absoluteness of that king's rule. Although the later *De Cive* (1642; 1647) and *Leviathan* (1651) introduced some changes to Hobbes's political doctrine, and shifted its areas of application, Hobbes remained committed to undivided and absolute sovereignty, limited only where obedience to it was life-threatening. If obedience did not seem fatal to whomever was being required to do something by the head of state, then it was owed no questions asked. The argument supported de facto sovereignty with or without royalty, and so it was adaptable to Stuart rule before and after the Civil War and also to the government that prevailed in between.

I do not wish to deny the relevance of Hobbes's politics to his circumstances, but I want to call attention to the way in which his views about the preferred constitution of the state are also directed against political philosophies he considered to be pre-scientific. Hobbes claimed to have invented the *science* of politics in the same way that Galileo had invented the science of mechanics or Copernicus a scientific celestial physics.[2] The scientific status of his civil philosophy is connected with the way in which all of the new sciences broke from the ancient authorities,

[1] See J. Sommerville, 'Lofty science and local politics' in T. Sorell (ed.), *Cambridge Companion to Hobbes* (Cambridge: Cambridge University Press, 1996), ch. 10. See more generally Sommerville's *Thomas Hobbes: Political Ideas in Historical Context* (London: Palgrave Macmillan, 1992). Quentin Skinner is of course the most famous exponent of contextualism as an approach to the intellectual history of political thought. See e.g. *Visions of Politics*, vol. 1 (Cambridge: Cambridge University Press, 2002). See also e.g. 'The Ideological Context of Hobbes's Political Thought', *Historical Journal* 9 (1966), 286–317 and 'Thomas Hobbes and His Disciples in France and England', *Comparative Studies in Society and History* 8 (1966), 153–67. Also relevant is Noel Malcolm's 'Summary Biography' in the *Cambridge Companion*, 13–44.

[2] See my 'The Science in Hobbes's Politics', in G. A. J. Rogers and A. Ryan (eds), *Perspectives on Thomas Hobbes* (Oxford: Clarendon Press, 1988). On the same topic, see N. Malcolm, 'Hobbes's Science of Politics and his Theory of Science', in N. Malcolm (ed.), *Aspects of Hobbes* (Oxford: Clarendon Press, 2002), 146–55.

particularly Aristotle.[3] The political treatise that, more than any other, associated Hobbes with the invention of a scientific politics was his *De Cive* (1642). That book begins with the openly revolutionary denial of one of Aristotle's most famous part-definitions of *man*, according to which man is by nature suited to life in the *polis.* Hobbes insists to the contrary that human beings are naturally antisocial, and that, when there is nothing to coerce them into civility, they find themselves in a kind of antagonism that results in premature death by mass slaughter.

His difference with Aristotle over this axiom of the latter's politics is reflected in further differences over the purpose of political association, the requirements of citizenship, the conditions under which acts can be attributed to a state as opposed to individuals, and the different ways in which political roles should ideally be distributed. In other words, there is a direct link between Hobbes's anti-Aristotelian theory of human nature and his anti-Aristotelian theory of the preferred form of political association or ideal constitution. The anti-Aristotelian character of his politics, while perhaps more explicit in *De Cive* and *Leviathan* than in the *Elements of Law,* is nevertheless present in all three of those texts.

After showing how Hobbes's preference for concentrated and unlimited sovereignty grows out of his view that man is by nature warlike, I trace the systematic opposition between Hobbes's views and those on citizenship and constitutions in Aristotle's *Politics.* I consider in what ways Hobbes can plausibly call the Aristotelianism that he repudiates 'pre-scientific'. I shall argue that Hobbes's radical reduction of Aristotelian constitutional forms, and his deflationary understanding of justice and citizenship, reduce the need for practical wisdom as an adjunct to political life. This helps us to understand what Hobbes meant by political science, even if we are not persuaded that it is the huge advance on all previous writers that Hobbes proclaims it to be.

II

Hobbes's theory of what human beings are like comes out in his description of the so-called 'state of nature'. This plays more than one role in his writings.[4] Perhaps its most important function, and the one that is least noticed in, for example, discussions of Hobbes and Locke, is that of repudiating some principles of Aristotle's ethics and politics. Man is *not* naturally suited to life in the polis, or more generally a society, according to Hobbes. We all know that people have many antisocial impulses. Not only can human beings sometimes be violent, but they are often proud, competitive, and greedy. When they are not trying to outdo or denigrate one another, they can shrink from one another in fear. And this is how

[3] *The Politics of Aristotle*, ed. and trans. E. Barker (New York: Oxford University Press, 1981).

[4] See Kinch Hoekstra, 'Hobbes on the Natural Condition of Mankind', in P. Springborg (ed.), *The Cambridge Companion to Hobbes's Leviathan* (Cambridge: Cambridge University Press, 2007), 109–27. See also F. Tricaud, 'Hobbes's Conception of the State of Nature from 1640 to 1651: evolution and ambiguities', in Rogers and Ryan, *Perspectives*, 107–24.

people can be seen behaving when there are laws and they are enforced. If people have nothing to fear from the state, they often behave even worse, as is shown by the lootings and assaults that occur during periods of crisis. In view of these widely observed facts about human behaviour—facts that Hobbes thinks can be confirmed by reasoning from the elements of a scientifically analysed human nature—societies do not exist naturally but artificially. They have to be made, and, once made, kept going by suppressing what is antisocial in human beings. Or, to put it another way, the state is only the artificial suppression of the state of nature, which is the warlike behaviour of people in groups.

Hobbes's so-called science of politics is a set of precepts for constructing societies whose primary purpose is the relatively uncontroversial one of collective security. He is not unaware that other purposes of the state are conceivable and that they have been proposed by earlier political philosophers; but he denies that they can command wide enough assent to motivate groups of human beings to come together into long-term unions. He is aware of the fact that people are mostly born into societies without recognizable overall purposes, and that some of these societies survive. But he thinks that when states do endure, it is because their governments have a reasonable number of strictly enforced, security-promoting, and prosperity-permitting laws. Permanently enduring states, he thinks, could be constructed if the things that actually make states last were systematized, and this system is what his political writings, with some variations, describe.

Government for Hobbes is a way in which people organize themselves to stifle permanently the causes of war in the state of nature. The key to this organization is each individual's laying down the right of self-government. Instead of each deciding for him*self* what ends to pursue in general, each agrees to act only within bounds determined by an agreed authority that decides how general contention is to be avoided. The means of avoiding general contention are communicated to each of the many in the government's binding laws. Citizenship consists of strict obedience to these laws.

The sovereign power is supposed to be unlimited, permanent, and unitary. Hobbes was no supporter of a separation of powers, still less of rolled-back government, and he thought it was folly for a government to transfer any powers or to cease to exercise any. He believed that a sovereign authority in the form of a body of men was open to a sort of divisiveness reminiscent of a war. So in his writings he seems to favour a one-man dictatorship, albeit an authorized dictatorship. That is the form sovereignty should take, according to Hobbes. His conceptions of citizenship and sovereignty are alien to those of us who are comfortable with liberal democracy,[5] except perhaps in periods of emergency. In emergencies,

[5] A recent trend in Hobbes scholarship is to emphasize liberal-seeming elements in the political writings, so as to defend him against charges of crude authoritarianism and legal positivism. See D. Dyzenhaus, 'Hobbes and the Legitimacy of Law', *Law and Philosophy* 20 (2001). For more in the same vein, see L. May, *Law and Equity in Hobbes* (Oxford: Oxford University Press, 2013). See also E. Fox-Decent, 'Hobbes's Relational Theory: Beneath Power and Consent', in D. Dyzenhaus and T. Poole (eds), *Hobbes and the Law* (Oxford: Clarendon Press, 2012), 118–44. My own view is that these interpreters go wrong by over-emphasizing the concept of equity in Hobbes (a point to

liberal democratic governments are given great latitude to act, while the great latitude to act of citizens is taken away. Freedom of movement, property rights, freedom from arbitrary arrest—all of these may be legitimately curtailed or suspended in periods of emergency, it is widely thought, so long as those with emergency powers assume more limited powers as soon as they can.

The liberal democratic conception assumes that emergency conditions prevail only exceptionally, and that, in these conditions, both citizenship and government are deformed. This brings us to the heart of the difference between a familiar conception of citizenship and government on one hand, and Hobbes's on the other. Hobbes claims that government and citizenship are centrally to do with the prevention and curtailment of an emergency waiting to happen, namely the violent conflict in which human beings are disposed to engage if nature is allowed to take its course. He thinks that authorized dictatorship, with its very great scope for limiting individual freedom, is far less dangerous than war, and justified by what makes war so necessary to avoid. In a sense, he agrees with the liberal democrat in thinking that only the prevention or curtailment of a major emergency justifies the concentration of power and the limitation of freedom, but he thinks this emergency is permanently waiting to happen, and therefore that the concentration of government power and the limitation of individual freedom are permanently justified. The measures necessary for the prevention of public emergency must be available to a sovereign—an authorized dictator—whenever s/he judges that s/he needs them, and, from the standpoint of Hobbes's civil science, the sovereign ought to judge that s/he needs these powers all of the time.

III

The main sources in Hobbes's writings for preferred constitutional arrangements are chapters 20 and 21 of *The Elements of Law* (*EL*), chapters 6 and 7 of *De Cive*,[6] and chapter 19 of *Leviathan*. The two earlier political treatises, *The Elements of Law* and *De Cive,* start from the point that a state or commonwealth is not the same as a group or crowd of human beings—something gives it unity, and a constitutional arrangement must either confer this unity or be consistent with unity. Aristotle also acknowledges (*Pols* III, iii, 1276a) that for an act to be attributable to a polity as opposed to individuals, there has to be an organized way of life to which individuals contribute, and the variety of this organization is the variety of constitutions. But in Aristotle this is one consideration among others in a relatively disorderly review of the characteristics of a state in chapter 3 of the *Politics*. In Hobbes's early political writings, the necessary unity of the commonwealth is pivotal, for *disunity* is the

which I return). Earlier interpreters of Hobbes, notably Leo Straus, have also aligned him with liberalism. For discussion, see L. Jaume, 'Hobbes and the Philosophical Sources of Liberalism', in Springborg, *Cambridge Companion*, 199–216.

[6] T. Hobbes, *On the Citizen*, ed. and trans. R. Tuck and M. Silverthorne (Cambridge: Cambridge University Press, 1998).

mark of the state of nature, or war, and the argument that a given constitutional arrangement will reawaken or maintain disunity is repeatedly deployed as decisive against that arrangement counting as a constitution of a state.

Not only is there supposed to be a kind of conceptual incoherence in a constitutional arrangement that invites or maintains disunity; there is something morally outrageous about it, according to Hobbes. For the leading moral obligation individuals are under is to seek peace—or 'concord' as Hobbes sometimes calls it—when it is not life-threatening to do so,[7] and achieving peace or concord is the same thing as achieving the unity that turns a multitude or a crowd into a commonwealth or state. *How* individuals in a group in a certain place and time make peace or achieve the unity required of a commonwealth is by most of them agreeing amongst themselves to carry out the will of an individual or council that decides for them all how each is to behave for the sake of peace. In other words, by a majority vote of a mass democratic gathering, each agrees with every other willing person to be ruled in their actions and omissions not by their own practical judgement but by that of an individual or body of individuals. In practice, this means abiding by the laws issued by the designated individual or body of individuals.

Can one agree to be ruled by a council, or a body of men and women, and still help to manufacture a *unitary* state, or commonwealth, or body politic? After all, the members of a ruling council do not necessarily agree amongst themselves, and they are subject to the passions that human beings are affected by before they submit to a sovereign. So is submission to a council a means of coordinating the practical judgement of the many and making it dispassionate? *EL*[8] answers this question by enlarging at length on the advantages of monarchy compared with sovereignty shared by a few or by many. *De Cive* is officially neutral between sovereignty vested in a council, either democratic or aristocratic, and sovereignty vested in a single person. Both an individual and a council can have the unity lacking in a people or a multitude, but councils can lack continuity if they do not have a fixed schedule of meetings, or if, even with a schedule, they do not meet very often. Between meetings, Hobbes suggests, states headed by councils disintegrate, and a people/multitude reappears.[9] Monarchy does not encounter the problem of disintegration, though Hobbes willingly concedes that it can change its mind or exhibit indecision in ways that correspond to differences of opinion between persons.

Leviathan also seems to conclude that monarchy is, on balance, the best constitutional form. But its argument makes less of the point that commonwealths are either unitary or else not commonwealths: the emphasis is instead on how powers should be distributed given the *purpose* of the commonwealth, that is, the maintenance of peace. Peace is a length of time in which there is no war, that is, no signs of a will to violence among a multitude that lives together. Whatever social arrangement best meets the requirements of making peace is seen as the best constitution. *Leviathan* chapter 19 acknowledges that the two main kinds of

[7] *EL* xiv, 1; *De Civ.* ii, 2; *Leviathan*, ch. 14. [8] Ch. xxiv. [9] Ch. vii, 10.

constitution—monarchy on one hand, and, on the other, sovereignty vested in a council of the few or the many—each have drawbacks, but judged by how far each neutralizes the ingredients of war, monarchy is strongly implied to be the better constitution. This is because councils, by distributing sovereignty, reproduce within themselves some of the conditions of war; in particular, passionate judgement and passionate oratory. Councils are also limited in whom they can get counsel from, and they more readily tolerate poverty and misery among subjects than a king may prudently allow.[10]

Hobbes says repeatedly that there is no important difference between democracy and aristocracy. Sometimes he seems to mean that, if sovereignty resides in more than one man, it doesn't matter how *many* more than one, because it is *any* distribution of sovereignty—a distribution among a few, or among a whole people—that matters to the unity and effective peace-keeping powers of a commonwealth.[11] At other times, he seems to imply that democracy is a special case of aristocracy, because when the people rule, it is not all of the people who are foremost, but only the most effective orators, and so these few are in fact sovereign, rather than the whole people.[12] At other times again, he seems to write as if aristocracies are self-appointed elites who do not owe their status to the consent of others.[13] In none of these cases is aristocracy or democracy written about approvingly.

In all three of his political treatises, Hobbes associates distributed sovereignty with the stage of political development of a people immediately *before* they assume the form of a state or commonwealth.[14] In this form, a people is a loose democratic assembly of individuals, that is, a large number of agents who live together in the state of nature and who now convene to consider laying down the right of self-government. If a majority of those present simultaneously promise one another to surrender this right to a willing third party, a commonwealth comes into existence, and the third party decides for all what the conditions of individual security and prosperity will be.[15] The vote cast by each in the majority decision to submit is the last act of each individual in matters of his own security, and the last result of using his own judgement. From then on, each draws his conclusions about what his safety requires from what the law laid down by the designated third party prescribes or prohibits for everyone. When the sovereign's judgement and will—expressed as the sovereign's law—governs the behaviour of each subject, each is ruled by a common judgement. And at that point democracy dissolves. It is the ladder that

[10] Tuck, ed., 131–3.

[11] J. C. A. Gaskin (ed.), *The Elements of Law Natural and Politic* (New York: Oxford University Press, 1994); *Leviathan*, ch. 19; Tuck, ed., 129.

[12] *EL*, ch. xxi, 5. [13] *EL*, ch. xxi, 6–7.

[14] Cf. esp. *EL*, ch. xxi; *De Cive*, ch. vii, 5; *Leviathan*, ch. 17.

[15] This agreement among the majority does not only bind them. It binds dissenting parties. They are either brought into the resulting union or become enemies of the union. Either way, the effect of majority agreement is for there to be no more dissenting minority. The minority submits with the rest, in which case it stops dissenting; or else it doesn't, in which case it is alienated from—cast out of—the union that has outvoted it. Not only are dissenters cast out, but they acquire the role of enemies—people who invite attack—because they repudiate or show contempt for the sovereign.

is kicked away to get to unified political judgement. The ladder is more thoroughly kicked away when the meeting of the many gives way immediately to monarchy, but even when the meeting of the many gives way to a council of the few, majority rule can deliver unequivocal pronouncements about what each citizen can do. Parliamentary law is no less law than decrees that a king makes solo. It is just that it may be less satisfactorily arrived at and less effective at maintaining the peace.

IV

Monarchy stands apart from democracy and aristocracy not only because it has the unity of an individual person, but, according to Hobbes, because it can suppress the causes of war better than other constitutions. This latter claim may seem implausible. Are not monarchs, precisely because they take all the power to themselves, likely to be tempted to use it selfishly? Won't they enrich themselves at the expense of their subjects, and rule arbitrarily because of the gratification of seeing their will done? Hobbes's answer to this question is complex. On one hand, he has a normative theory of monarchy. The monarch by institution, for example, receives a gift of submission, and is morally obliged—by the fourth law of nature—not to make the donors regret their decision.[16] This obligation counts against the selfish exploitation of office. Again, monarchs by institution consent to be the judge of the means to peace. If their decrees are unintelligible as means of promoting peace, seeming only to be directed at gilding their palaces or adding to the number of concubines, then the monarch will be neglecting the requirements of public prosperity and security and will weaken their defences against internal rebellion and foreign attack. Failure to see to defence is not only blameworthy but dangerous for a selfish king or queen. This is because subjects are only obliged to obey if doing so is compatible with survival. If the monarch's policies so impoverish the many that they are starving, or so expose them to attack that they are better off defending themselves, they regain the right of nature and the monarch is reduced to the status of a vulnerable single individual in the state of nature who has disappointed his fellows in their gift of submission. So it is in the interest of the sovereign not to reduce the subjects' standard of living to the depths that release them from submission. In short, both morality and prudence drive the sovereign away from putting the interests of his natural person before the nation his office is *supposed* to personify. Hobbes goes so far as to say in *Leviathan* that, uniquely in monarchy, as opposed to other constitutional forms, the monarch's interest and the public interest are identical.[17]

[16] *Leviathan*, ch. 15; Tuck, ed., 105.

[17] '. . . where the publique and private interest are most closely united, there is the publique most advanced. Now in Monarchy, the private interest is the same with the publique. The riches, power and honour of a Monarch arise onely from the riches, strength and reputation of its Subjects. For no King can be rich, nor glorious, nor secure; whose Subjects are either poore, or contemptible, or too weak, through want, or dissention, to maintain a war against their enemies: Whereas in a Democracy, or Aristocracy, the publique prosperity conferres not so much the private fortune of one that is corrupt, or

The monarch, though he has the passions of an individual, is detached from the passions of his subjects. These are the passions that, when acted upon by the right of nature, put individuals of a mix of temperaments onto a collision course. The monarch is able to impose legal prohibitions that, if respected, minimize violence and create enough security for people to have the hope of enjoying the fruits of their labour. Restrained from violence, occupied in productive work, and taxed on consumption rather than saving, citizens are kept from one another's throats but not straitjacketed. They are able to create modest wealth, enjoy family life, even form themselves into associations for the collective pursuit of lawful business or leisure activity. In *Leviathan*, Hobbes suggests that when sovereigns legislate well, and bring in only those laws that are 'necessary',[18] a considerable everyday latitude can be extended to individual citizens. This latitude, however, is compatible with perfect discretion on the part of a monarch in the appropriation of resources that really are necessary for preventing crime and conquest. No quantity of money that is sincerely thought by the sovereign to be necessary for collective defence, no item of real estate that can be used for necessary billeting of troops, is out of bounds to confiscation. Similarly, no restriction on outward behaviour that seems to the sovereign to be necessary for preventing violent crime or conquest is out of the question. It is not subject to the agreement of a parliament, a powerful aristocratic circle, or the church. For the sovereign's demands to be out of the question, some judgement other than the monarch's about what is necessary for peace would have to operate, and that would be a violation of the agreement that establishes the sovereign.

This is a large part of the line of thought that in all three political treatises accompanies Hobbes's insistence on undivided and unlimited sovereignty. The sovereign cannot be subject to law *and* be delegated to rule as he sees fit for security. The sovereign cannot be obliged to respect the property rights of subjects *and* be given perfect discretion in the means for protecting the many from foreign invasion: repelling the invader may require expenditure on such a scale that only mass confiscation of property can finance it—and only someone who can rise above the viewpoints of those whose wealth is taken may appreciate this fact. On the other hand, and just as the sovereign's actions cannot be judged from the blinkered perspective of the individual citizen, the monarch cannot create conditions for prosperity and security by thinking only of himself. He needs to identify with the needs and interests of a whole citizenry. Hobbes thinks it is easier for a single individual to achieve this identification than it is for a council, for a council has its own internal tensions and is probably more beholden to a class of people than to the people in general. Again, sovereignty cannot be hived off into separate compartments. Security and prosperity require a coordination of lawmaking, law enforcement, military action, money raising, and education; but these policies need to be, in Blairite parlance, 'joined up', and Hobbes's model for what joins up government

ambitious, as doth many times a perfidious advice, a treacherous action, or a Civill warre' (*Leviathan*, ch. 19; Tuck, ed., 131).

[18] Ch. 30, Tuck, ed., 240.

is the single, directing, practical intelligence of a living human body. This is not only the model in *Leviathan*, where the metaphor of the artificial man predominates; something like it is implicit in the earlier treatises, where the demand for joined-up government is reflected in the more austere concept of union.

Not only joined-up government, but power by government over other non-governmental bodies with popular influence, is required by Hobbes's theory. The sovereign cannot be answerable to a court of law, if law is defined as any rule or command that the *sovereign* thinks will promote peace. The sovereign cannot be in competition with a church or with a powerful aristocrat when conceiving and implementing public policy. For then the sovereign's power would be limited by someone or some body of people who unjustly go back on the promise of submission, or who refuse that promise, and who can be punished or attacked accordingly. Either that, or else the sovereign's power is challenged by someone—a warlord, say—who declares himself outside any contract. In the latter case, the challenger becomes an enemy of the state and can be killed. For the sovereign to tolerate the warlord would be to acknowledge and even be complicit in the limitation of power, contrary to the norm of not inviting war.

The concentration of legislative, judicial, and executive powers in an unchallengeable head of state may seem to belong to an anti-constitutionalist doctrine, in a modern sense of 'constitutionalist'. If a constitution is a higher law with which common-or-garden legislation must be consistent, then Hobbes is against a constitution. On the other hand, the space that might be occupied by a higher law is not entirely vacant in Hobbes's theory. It is occupied by the laws of nature, and the precepts for ruling well that come from Hobbes's civil science. The laws of nature are the laws to which all human beings, even sovereigns, are subject, in the sense that human beings do something wrong by giving them no weight in practical deliberation. The laws of nature present the need for peace as overriding, and the need to lay down rights for the sake of peace as the general form of pursuing peace. Hobbes's design of state institutions conforms first and foremost to these 'fundamental' laws of nature. But the sovereign is also subject to laws of nature that prohibit self-serving, vengeful, and greedy rule, not to mention the rule that outlaws ingratitude for the gift of submission.

Among the laws of nature that apply to the sovereign is the moral 'Law of Equity'. This is not a law of nature that attends all human activity. It applies to those who settle disputes. As the ultimate judge of right and wrong, the sovereign falls under what *Leviathan* counts as the eleventh law of nature:

> if *a man be trusted to be judge between man and man,* it is a precept of the Law of Nature, *that he deale Equally between them.* For without that, the Controversies of men cannot be determined but by Warre.[19]

Not that this is a precept that the sovereign is obliged to follow in practice, if he sincerely thinks that his, i.e. the public's, safety is imperilled by doing so; the laws of

[19] Tuck, ed., 108.

nature only oblige in the sense of having to be given weight *in foro interno*, that is, in deliberation before it issues in action. It may be overridden if, for example, the agent's life might be lost by abiding by it. The question is whether a breach of the law of equity *can* typically be sincerely thought to be overridden by considerations of public safety. Exceptionally, certainly. But typically?[20]

Apart from the laws of nature, there are the duties of sovereignty declared by Hobbes's civil science. Chapter 28 of *EL*, chapter 13 of *De Cive*, and chapter 30 of *Leviathan* all deduce duties of sovereigns from the sovereign's acceptance of responsibility for public safety. These chapters undo the impression that the rule for subjects is 'Do what you are told' and the rule for sovereigns, 'Do what you like'. For although, according to Hobbes's theory, no-one—certainly no subject—can accuse the sovereign of injustice when he rules arbitrarily or selfishly or cruelly, since the sovereign has not promised anything to the people he rules, this does not mean that there is no standpoint from which sovereign rule can be judged defective. Civil science provides such a standpoint, and the standard applied is whether an action or law of a sovereign promotes public safety. In *De Cive*, Hobbes goes so far as to adopt the formula that *the safety of the people is the supreme law*,[21] going on to instance the main types of neglect or violation of that law. Characteristic failures to abide by this standard include policies of self-enrichment on the part of kings; failure to fortify against attack and raise armies in anticipation of attempted conquest; failure to tax consumption; and failure to educate the people about the dangers of popular individuals, especially popular speakers. Since these characteristic failures were spelt out in a book that had a wider readership than kings or queens, it made available to the public a standard of judgement that was authoritative without being the monarch's.

V

Hobbes claimed that the science of politics began with *De Cive*, and that the works that preceded it, especially those of the ancients, belonged to the history of pre-scientific moral and political philosophy. The question of what distinguishes the

[20] This point notwithstanding, the commentators mentioned in footnote 3, who discern a liberal voice in Hobbes's political writings, overemphasize the concept of equity. Equity is clearly central to Hobbes's theory of the laws of nature, and it has an important place in his doctrine of the duties and exercise of sovereignty. It is also prominent in his general theory of law, especially as it is articulated in the later *Dialogue between a Philosopher and a Student of the Common Laws of England.* The concept of equity may well contribute to an apparent anti-authoritarianism in Hobbes, i.e. to the elements of his political philosophy that permit and even require the Leviathan to be limited. Still, equity is not *more* central to the understanding of Hobbes's ethics, politics, and legal philosophy than is his concept of justice, or even *as* central. On the contrary, his theory of justice is presupposed by his views about equity—in the sense that fidelity to a social contract is a condition of adjudication and definitive interpretation of law. It is the essence of justice to defer entirely to what the sovereign requires through law for safety and well-being, even if what is required is untypically against equity. For a full discussion, see my 'Law and Equity in Hobbes', forthcoming 2015.

[21] Ch. xiii, 2.

scientific from the pre-scientific in this area is directly addressed in the first chapter of the first book of Hobbes's trilogy, *The Elements of Philosophy*. Hobbes says there:

> But the utility of moral and civil philosophy is to be estimated, not so much by the commodities we have by knowing these sciences, as by the calamities we receive from not knowing them. Now, all such calamities as may be avoided by human industry, arise from war, but chiefly from civil war.... The cause... of civil war is that men know not the causes neither of war nor peace, there being but few in the world that have learned those duties that unite and keep men in peace, that is to say, that have learned the rules of civil life sufficiently. Now the knowledge of these rules is moral philosophy. But why have they not learned them, unless for this reason, that none hitherto have taught them in a clear and exact method.... Could the ancient masters of Greece, Egypt, Rome and others persuade the unskillful multitude to their innumerable opinions concerning the nature of their gods... and could they not persuade the same multitude to civil duty, if they had understood it?... Nevertheless, I deny not that but the reading of some of [their] books is very delightful.... Now that which is chiefly wanting in them, is a true and certain rule of our actions, by which we might know whether what we undertake be just or unjust.[22]

In other words, he is saying that the difference between a scientific and a pre-scientific moral and civil philosophy is that the former succeeds, and the latter does not succeed, in saying clearly to citizens how to do their duty. Hobbes claims that his own philosophy cannot be faulted on this score; and he is right, for it encapsulates the whole of citizenly duty in a three-word rule: 'obey the law'.

It is clear that Hobbes regarded Aristotle's ethics and politics as the leading specimen of pre-scientific politics, and the foremost object of contempt among the pre-scientific works of moral and civil philosophy. For Aristotle was worse than vague about duty. Aristotle's *Ethics* was 'ignorant', according to chapter 46 of *Leviathan*, and in the same place Hobbes says there is nothing in the whole history of philosophy 'more repugnant to government' than Aristotle's *Politics*.[23] He means that, far from telling people how to behave so as to avoid the calamity of war, the view of the state and citizenship that Aristotle develops is actually a recipe for conflict. How are we to understand this accusation?

To begin with, Aristotle's *Politics* stigmatizes tyranny as the worst deformation of the polity,[24] lending weight to the arguments of those who resisted Charles I on the grounds that *he* was a tyrant. In Aristotle, tyranny is rule by a king not in the public interest but in his own interest. Hobbes, as we have seen, has a theory according to which public and private interests coincide perfectly in monarchy. The king either sees to the security or prosperity of the many, or else in effect disempowers himself, taking away the conditions for the many to create the wealth and loyalty that is necessary for keeping the commonwealth together. It is true that even when the monarch rules for the sake of public safety in Hobbes's sense, his subjects may not like his taxation policy or his laws on public assembly, and may express this dislike by calling the king a tyrant. That does not mean that government actually *is* deformed. It may turn out instead that even onerous demands on citizens are

[22] *De Corpore*, ch. i, 7, reprinted in Gaskin, 183–93.
[23] Tuck, ed., 461.
[24] IV, ii, 1289b.

justified for the sake of peace, if peace is correctly valued as the supreme good. Hobbes's response to the Aristotelian category of tyranny, in short, is to deny that it is objectively a perversion of government. Instead, the term 'tyranny' refers to monarchy, which is a respectable form of government, perhaps even the best available to human beings. In addition to its referring function, the term 'tyranny' also has an emotivist expressive function, according to Hobbes: it is used by speakers to signify the dislike a speaker has for monarchy. So the content that 'tyranny' adds to 'monarchy' is feeling. It does not add scientific content.

Aristotle says that people band together into states not just for self-preservation, but for the collective pursuit of a life that is good for humans, and he thinks it is of the essence of this life that citizens play roles in which, at different times, they exercise, and submit to, power. They are to take turns at discharging legislative and judicial duties, and in these roles, as well as the private one of running a household, they are supposed to use their practical judgement, that is, their faculty of deciding which goods to pursue, and how they might do so. Hobbes turns this way of thinking on its head. There is no uncontroversial, stable, or shared conception among human beings of what is good for them, he says: the differences among individual physical constitutions and experiences see to that. What is more, relentless sensory bombardment and the constant influence of different appetites and aversions render people unable to achieve a flourishing state. The best that can be hoped for is the satisfaction of the endless succession of desires in life, not a settled flourishing; and it is Aristotle's ignorance of the workings of sense and appetite that makes him think that there is a settled good, for any member of the species, that politics promotes and that any clear-headed human being can recognize. Again, forming one's own judgements about what it is best to do, or what law is best, or what judicial verdict is best, is a recipe for the kind of opinionated frame of mind that second-guesses all authority, according to Hobbes. It is a recipe for war. The very essence of seeking peace is *abandoning* one's sense that one's own judgement about what is best is authoritative. This is what is called for by the second law of nature.

Another important point of disagreement is over whether two heads are better than one. Hobbes claims that there is no natural standard of right reason,[25] and that people are carried away by their passions even in the defence of their factual beliefs. What is more, he thinks it is rare for people to be acquainted with science, let alone to develop any. When people lack science they lack any insight into why observed facts are what they are. This means that people are likely to fall into error, and that they are likely to be stubborn in maintaining their views when others disagree with them. In these circumstances, two heads are rarely better than one, according to Hobbes. On the contrary, the more heads, the more natural sources of controversy, and the greater the need for enquirers to be willing to submit to the judgement of an arbitrator.[26] In relation to matters of security and well-being, as opposed to the proofs of mathematical theorems or the proposal of hypotheses in

[25] *Leviathan*, ch. 5; Tuck, ed., 33. [26] *Leviathan*, ch. 5; Tuck, ed., 33.

physics, individual judgements are likely to be even less authoritative. They are likely to be short-term, geared too much to pleasure rather than other sorts of well-being, and selfish. They will also lead people to go after things that cannot be shared, which will make them fight over them. The remedy for all of this is a better standard of practical guidance than that offered by the numerous conflicting and untutored practical judgements of the many. A better standard of judgement will be more dispassionate than natural practical judgements, and it will be employed by a judge that unites the individuals who make judgements in the state of nature. This is of course Hobbes's sovereign.

The line of thought just summarized could not be a more thorough repudiation of Aristotle. Chapter 11 of Book III of the *Politics* starts off with a passage that perfectly summarizes what Hobbes rejects:

> There is this to be said for the Many. Each of them by himself may not be of a good quality, but when they all come together it is possible that they may surpass—collectively and as a body, though not individually—the quality of the few best. Feasts to which many contribute may excel those provided at one man's expense. In the same way, when there are many [who contribute to the process of deliberation], each can bring his share of goodness and moral prudence; and when all meet together the people may thus become something in the nature of a single person who, as he has many feet, many hands, and many senses, may also have many qualities of character and intelligence.[27]

Against all of this, Hobbes's point—again a plausible one—is that when many contribute to judgement, *no* single person is formed. The people remain a multitude and not a state. What is more, far from pooling insight, the many combine their individual irrationality to produce either indecision or bad decisions.

The disagreement between Hobbes and Aristotle extends to constitutions and to the nature of justice in the state. Aristotle insists on the need for the rule of law, partly to counteract the intrusion of self-interest into offices of state. Hobbes, as we have seen, puts the sovereign above the law. Aristotle opposes absolute rule except in the rare case where someone of surpassing merit is in a position to rule. Hobbes does not make merit of any kind a condition of acquiring sovereignty, and he thinks that civil science can remedy deficiencies that would-be rulers might have. Above all, and here in opposition to Plato rather than Aristotle, he denies that rulers have to have intellects formed by exposure to esoteric sciences.

Justice for citizens in Aristotle is reward or status commensurate to their contribution through public office to a shared good life; but in Hobbes, justice is keeping the social contract so long as it is safe to do so. In Aristotle but not in Hobbes, the preferred form of constitution is a cross between democracy and oligarchy with a strongly participatory middle class.[28] The one form of constitution that seems to be excluded is Hobbes's preferred form: monarchy. It is true and relevant that in Hobbes monarchy is only supposed to see to public safety—freedom from violence plus the freedoms necessary for modest prosperity—while in Aristotle the preferred constitution is supposed to see to the transmission of

[27] 1281a–b. [28] IV, xi, 1295b.

virtue from those who cultivate it individually to the many, via legislation. Perhaps it is possible to codify avoidance of war and to concentrate responsibility for implementation of the code. Perhaps it is by deflating the purpose of the state that Hobbes is able to systematize so much more successfully than Aristotle the means of achieving that purpose. Aristotle's more expansive vision for society may require a less definite constitution and an ineliminable role for good judgement. Still, it is not nothing to show how a population can be organized for the purpose of a non-violent shared existence. This is the achievement of Hobbes's civil science.

5

The Levellers, the People, and the Constitution

D. J. Galligan

I. Introduction

In tracts, petitions, pamphlets, and letters circulated between 1644 and the early 1650s, a group of political activists, who came to be known as the Levellers, put forward ideas for righting the wrongs that had befallen England before, during, and after the Civil Wars. Prominent among such wrongs were abuses of power by king and parliament. The leaders of the movement, principally John Lilburne and to a lesser degree Richard Overton, suffered abuse at first hand, often imprisonment without charge or trial, usually for criticism of one or other of the organs of government. Other leading figures Richard Sexby and William Walwyn published tracts and pamphlets, often in defence of Lilburne, while a fifth, John Wildman, was prominent in arguing the Leveller case in the Army Council debates in Putney Church in late 1647. Out of direct and personal confrontation with the institutions of government grew the ideas of the Levellers.

Their punitive treatment at the hands first of king and Star Chamber, then of both Houses of Parliament, and finally of Cromwell's Council of State, which they claimed was imposed without certain legal authority and in the absence of due process, led the Levellers to the notion of arbitrary power. Arbitrary power was their key to the constitutional universe. It began as the basis for criticizing the actions of parliament, the House of Commons in particular; it then served to show that, despite the abuses, there was a real and living constitution in which arbitrary action had no place; and it ended by drawing out ideas immanent in the constitution that led to conclusions at variance with prevailing views and unacceptable to the times.[1]

The Levellers placed their faith in the House of Commons, as the only body truly capable of representing the people, to cure the alleged abuses of king,

[1] On arbitrary power: J. P. Reid, *Constitutional History of the American Revolution* (Madison: University of Wisconsin Press, 1995), xvii ff.

lords, and special courts. When the Commons, having assumed the powers of government, failed to live up to expectations, and continued the practices it had previously condemned, behaving in the manner of the institutions it had abolished, it became the target of the Levellers' criticisms and the spur to their constitutional ideas. How to curb those abuses, how to make the House of Commons serve the common good—the common weale—and be truly protective of the 'welfare and freedoms' of the people, was the issue that drew the Levellers beyond their own experiences to reflect on the nature of government and the constitution.[2] They were not scholars in the mould of near contemporaries Thomas Hobbes and John Locke, nor did they write treatises on government along the lines of James Harrington; they were men, and in some cases women,[3] who wrote from their own sometimes harrowing experiences. By 1647, the Levellers were a political force of moderate influence; they had made common cause with soldiers of the New Model Army, whose grievances over arrears of pay, indemnity for actions during the war, and the threat of being sent to Ireland, were further evidence of the nation's ills and parliament's evils.[4]

Between 1647 and 1649, with the king in captivity and parliament discredited, the future of English government and the constitution was in jeopardy. The Levellers held some sway with senior officers of the New Model Army, including Oliver Cromwell and Henry Ireton, in whose hands the future lay. In the army debates in Putney Church in late October 1647, presided over by Cromwell and one of the rare events in English history that could be considered a constitutional convention, the ideas of the Levellers and their army supporters, particularly those in the first *Agreement of the People,* dominated.[5] The debates were a defining moment in the fortunes of the Levellers. In a setting that began broadly sympathetic to their proposals, the mood soon changed as it became apparent just how deeply the Levellers' ideas went beyond current notions of government and constitution to become a challenge to the foundations of English society even in the minds of those who had just overturned the established order, and were poised to destroy the constitution by executing the king and abolishing the monarchy. It

[2] Sexby (possibly), *England's Miserie and Remedie in a Judicious Letter from an Utter Barrister to His Speciall Friend, Concerning Leiutenant Col. Lilburn's Imprisonment in Newgate* (14 September 1645) in *Divine Right and Democracy: An Anthology of Political Writing in Stuart England*, ed. D. Wootton (London: Penguin Classics, 1986), 276 ff.

[3] On the place of women in the debates of the time, see P. Crawford, '"The poorest she": women and citizenship in early modern England', in M. Mendle (ed.), *The Putney Debates of 1647: The Army, the Levellers, and the English State* (Cambridge: Cambridge University Press, 2001).

[4] Opinions differ as to how significant the Levellers were as a political force, although two of the leading historians of the movement describe them as follows: according to H. N. Brailsford, the Levellers were 'a modern political party run on democratic lines': *The Levellers and the English Revolution* (Nottingham: Spokesman University Paperback, 1976); while G. E. Aylmer calls them the 'first democratic political party in modern history': *The Levellers in the English Revolution* (London: Thames and Hudson, 1975), 9.

[5] There were three such agreements, the first appearing in September 1647, the last in 1649, to which should be added an 'Officers' Agreement' of June 1649. For an account of the agreements, see I. Gentles, 'The Agreements of the people and their political contexts' in M. Mendle (ed.), *The Putney Debates of 1647* (Cambridge: Cambridge University Press, 2001), 148.

was one thing to tamper with the institutions of government, even undermine the constitution, but quite another to threaten the foundations of society, which the claim for a wider constitutional role for the people seemed to Ireton and Cromwell to do.[6] Attempts to mount common cause of Levellers and army in curbing parliament and reforming the constitution were fragile and brief, and soon sank beneath the wave of disagreement.

As Cromwell gathered about him the reins of power, his vision of the future constitution changed and was at odds with that of the Levellers, who saw him repeating the same abuses and misuses that had earlier been condemned first in the king and later in the Long Parliament. There was no place in Cromwell's regime for the Levellers or for their views, and old allies became enemies. The Levellers' leaders were marginalized, then, as their condemnation of Cromwell escalated, were harassed, arrested, prosecuted, and imprisoned until, by the late 1650s, the movement and John Lilburne, its leader, were dead. Ideas similar to theirs surfaced and took root more than a century later in the colonies and later independent commonwealths of North America, but there is no evidence that their founders knew about or were influenced by the Levellers, who were largely forgotten even in their home country until the late nineteenth century.[7]

II. Why the Levellers?

In the light of this brief history, we might ask what is to be gained from studying the history and ideas of the Levellers. Modern commentators present them as visionaries, liberal and democratic before their time, harbingers of modern ideas of government and constitutions, from where it is a short step to seeing them as a link in the historical chain leading to modern constitutions. It is true that some of their ideas, particularly the tying of government and the constitution to the people, the wider suffrage, and legal limits on the powers of government, are familiar features of modern constitutions. It is also true that this band of activists, through engagement in the turbulence of the time and reflection on the travails of the English nation, settled on a constitutional structure that contains within it the seeds of modernity. Historical continuity is always pleasing to find and the idea is often current that modern constitutions have evolved slowly but surely from past events, each exerting its own small influence and nothing wasted. No harm is done in holding this view and there might be scraps of evidence to support it, but it is largely a distraction, a reading of the past through the lens of the present. In this essay I propose another way of viewing the Levellers. Equally misleading is the Levellers' claim to have been reviving an ancient constitution of Anglo-Saxon

[6] Their idea on a wider franchise was arguably just one of several main ideas; but it was the one seized on by Ireton during the debates and became the defining one. Other Leveller ideas are of more interest constitutionally, as I hope to show in this chapter.

[7] John Locke's ideas, which are similar to those of the Levellers in some respects, were know in the American colonies and Locke himself was engaged in their affairs; but there is no evidence that Locke knew of or was influenced by the Levellers.

England that had been buried under the heavy hand of the Normans. It is pleasingly romantic but only vaguely related to reality to find in pre-Norman England something approaching constitutional paradise.

To show that the Levellers were engaged in a movement more elemental and original than either of these accounts is the aim of this essay. They came to realize that the precepts and practices known and referred to as the constitution, although apparently distinct and established, were not the complete constitution. It slowly dawned on them, as they reeled from one outrage to another of practices not living up to the precepts and promises of the constitution, that it had become uncoupled from its social foundations and taken on a life of its own. Separated thus, it served in the hands of king, peers, and parliamentarians as an empty vessel into which, under cover of constitutionalism, they could pour private interests and personal ambitions. The losers were the people, the population at large, who had no adequate recourse against oppression, abuse, and malpractice. At first the king, his councils, and his special courts could be blamed for exceeding the proper uses and reaches of prerogative powers. But when parliament, the representative of the people in a way the other branches were not, and the champion of constitutional propriety and reform, turned out to be no better than the crown, there was nowhere to turn other than to the foundations of the constitution, to re-examination of its origins. This meant reconsidering the base of political society and from there rebuilding a constitutional order. The idea of constitution is expanded; working precepts and practices are necessary for effective government, but they must always be understood and interpreted as part of a larger whole. And from the whole they must not be allowed to break loose, for only in maintaining the whole is a true and complete sense of constitution achieved.

Herein lie the reasons the Levellers are still of interest. They approach the constitution as a social form comprised of ideas, concepts, and rules whose purpose is to serve the interests of all: the common good. It does so by establishing government that is capable of acting and deciding for the common good and is empowered to implement its actions and decisions. Government has no other purpose and has no justification for acting other than to serve the common good. They understood the natural tendency of a constitutional order so established to lose sight of its social foundations and its purposes, to appear complete and self-contained, and to be expropriated by special interests. They saw through the mode of thought, the language, the concepts, the practices—an upper register of constitutionalism—that encrusts and endorses the constitutional order. They grasped the consequences and saw what had to be done: processes and mechanisms have to be put in place to prevent these tendencies and to encourage a different mode of thought, different sets of concepts, language, and practices—a lower register of constitutionalism. To this, the people are central, since they are the best protectors of their own interests and hence the common good. This did not lead the Levellers to advocate direct rule by the people, nor do their proposals amount to direct rule or popular government. The aim was to secure a system of government in which the common good and hence the rights and liberties of the people were recognized and protected. The role of the people was to make sure that such a system was in place and once in place worked well for the interests of all.

The Levellers may have seen themselves as restorers of what had been or what was immanent in the English constitution. To others they were revolutionaries who threatened the social order of England in the 1640s;[8] so their chances of success were never high and their efforts finally came to nothing. But the Levellers were engaged in constitutional affairs of great moment for the English nation, with fundamental matters in issue and new avenues opening up. The way they excavated the foundations of government and the constitution, exposing them to scrutiny and reinvigorating them, with dramatic consequences; even the grounds for their defeat and failure—all provide ample reasons for studying their ideas and actions, and the social and political setting in which they took place.

III. Social and Political Context

The name of John Lilburne came to public notice in the summer of 1645 when questions were asked about his imprisonment for refusing to answer the charges of a parliamentary committee,[9] an event we may take to mark the beginning of the Leveller movement. Lilburne had been in trouble years before when he was brutally punished by Star Chamber for publishing criticisms of the role of the bishops in government and then refusing to recognize the legality of the court.[10] After fighting for the parliamentary side in the Civil War, he resigned his commission in 1644, probably under pressure to do so, and returned to civilian life. For the rest of the decade and most of the next, until his death in 1658, he was in and out of prison, often on the orders of the commons, sometimes the lords, and later on the Council of State, and usually without charge or trial in a court of law, although in 1649 he and others were tried for treason and acquitted. Whether in prison or out, Lilburne published pamphlets, organized petitions, and joined with Overton and others in forming a political movement, the aim of which was chiefly reform of government and parliament, but which included wider issues of social reform. Before considering the constitutional ideas of Lilburne and his associates, and how they rose and fell, it is useful to have before us a brief account of the social and political context of the time.

[8] To take the further step of establishing causal links between that set of historical events and the structure of modern constitutions is more problematical, for the connection between the two, if it exists, has not been established. Ideas do take on a life of their own and, after a brief lease of life may then seem lost to the world, only to return through uncharted passages to exert their influence on men and events. That cannot be ruled out in the case of the Levellers, but nor on present knowledge can it be established. Historians of constitutional thought may not have searched hard enough, and perhaps in the future those passages will be discovered.

[9] The circumstances are discussed in T. C. Pease, *The Leveller Movement: A Study in the History and Political Theory of the English Great Civil War* (first published 1916; republication 2009, General Books), 49 ff.

[10] The House of Commons later acknowledged the illegality of the action against Lilburne and granted him compensation.

In the years 1628 to 1640, Charles I governed without parliament. During the years of 'Personal Rule', he used his prerogative in ways which, especially in relation to taxation but also in curtailing liberties, appeared to violate the law—if not the positive law, constitutional understandings, including those concerning parliament. By 1640, having exhausted sources of funding, and facing war with Scotland, the king summoned parliament for supply, which was granted conditional on his agreeing to major reforms, including abolition of the prerogative courts. Disagreement between the king on the one side and parliament and powerful political forces backing it on the other as to the roles of each within the constitution persisted and deepened.[11] Constitutional issues became political and finally, in August 1642, the king raised his standard against parliament and civil war began. Negotiations towards a settlement continued throughout the war years and after, but came to nothing.

With the outbreak of war, the two Houses of Parliament became the effective government with the commons the dominant partner. Parliament at first relied on local militias, but soon formed a national army, which although under the authority of parliament quickly gained in power and prestige. After purging the House of Commons and reducing its numbers, the army became the centre of power with Cromwell at its head and Ireton his right-hand man. By 1647, the first war was over, the king captive, and the political and constitutional future uncertain. Relations between king, parliament, and the army were both complex and fluid, the assumption being until late 1648 that a settlement with the king would be reached. Relations within the army were another source of conflict and dissension, especially among the ranks, who, having fought for the parliamentary cause, were without pay and in fear for their future. Following the king's escape, a brief second civil war, and his recapture, hopes of settlement were gone and the mood changed. Parliament created a special commission to try the king for treason, for which he was convicted and then executed in January 1649. Cromwell was now in control of both army and parliament, and by 1650 had assumed the powers of a king in all but name, which he held until his death in 1659.

In the turmoil of the war years and after there was an outpouring of books, pamphlets, and early forms of newspapers on a breadth of subjects, from literature, philosophy, and science to government and the constitution.[12] Censorship laws were still in place but enforcement was less vigorous so that subjects such as criticism of the king or the bishops, previously forbidden, were now tolerated. There were still risks, especially if criticism touched the pride and privileges of the Houses of Parliament, of which each house was the sole judge and jealous guardian, as Lilburne and Overton learnt to their cost. The Levellers exploited the relative freedom to publish and to organize petitions, bringing to light the abuses of power

[11] For an account of events and the overthrow of Charles I, see J. Adamson, *The Noble Revolt: The Overthrow of Charles I* (London: Weidenfeld and Nicolson, 2007).

[12] For discussion of the rapid development of the press and other forms of publication at the time, see I. Atherton, 'The Press and Popular Political Opinion', in B. Coward (ed.), *A Companion to Stuart Britain* (Chichester: Wiley-Blackwell, 2009), 88 ff.

by the organs of state and seizing the moment to propound their ideas of government and the constitution.

IV. Constitutional Setting

By the time the Levellers appear on the scene, differences between king and parliament had been overtaken by civil war. The constitutional divisions were complex and shifting, and merit a more extensive treatment than is possible here, where it is enough to consider the two matters most relevant to the Levellers' movement. One is the relationship between the king's prerogative and the law, the other that between the king and parliament. As to the first, it was accepted that the king had the right to govern, to exercise executive authority, and in governing to be guided by the general welfare, the common good, the 'safety of the people'. It was expected, as the king at his coronation swore, that he would govern 'by the law, the constitution, and the consent of men'.[13] What that meant was a matter on which views differed since the exact nature of the law and the constitution was open to interpretation. Of more moment and just as contested was the extent to which the king could override the law and rights protected by law when he thought it necessary for the safety and welfare of the people. The *Petition of Right* of 1628, agreed by king and parliament, established that rights protected by law could not be traduced by prerogative but changed or reduced only by act of king-in-parliament.[14] Yet, during the years 1628 to 1640 with Personal Rule and no parliament, the king appeared to stretch the prerogative beyond its legitimate limits, notably in relation to questionable levies as seen in the Ship-Money saga, and in relation to personal liberty as witnessed in the actions of the Privy Council and the prerogative courts, of which Star Chamber and High Commission were notorious. Personal Rule became, in the eyes of opponents, Arbitrary Rule, and the king indelibly tainted.

The relationship between king and parliament was the second source of contention.[15] In *His Majesties Answer to the Nineteen Propositions of Both Houses of Parliament* of 1642, the king, through advisers Culpeper and Hyde, accepts that laws are made jointly by the king and the two Houses of Parliament.[16] He concedes that the House of Commons is 'an excellent conserver of liberty, *but* was never intended for any share in government or in choosing of them that should govern' [emphasis added].[17] Frank acceptance by the king, arguably for the first time, of the king-in-parliament as the supreme legislative body pleased parliamentarians, who nevertheless resisted his claim to exclusive authority in governing and the choice of

[13] M. A. Judson, *The Crisis of the Constitution: An Essay on Constitutional and Political Thought in England, 1603–1645* (New Brunswick: Rutgers University Press, 1949, reissued 1988), 20.

[14] *Petition of Right* 1628, Article 1 in Wootton, 168.

[15] For analysis: A. Cromartie, *The Constitutionalist Revolution: An Essay on the History of England, 1450–1642* (Cambridge: Cambridge University Press, 2006), 73–4.

[16] Wootton, 171. [17] Wootton, 171.

councillors.[18] It was not enough that Culpeper and Hyde probably were right on the constitutional position, for by now the issue was political rather than constitutional and parliamentarians were set on having a say in governing, choosing the king's councillors, and holding them and the king accountable for their actions. In looking beyond the constitution to make their case, parliamentarians hit on the novel idea that they, not the king, had first responsibility for the common good and the safety of the people and that they were best able to speak for the nation.

The ancient notion of governing in the name of the people is given a new meaning, a fresh lease of life, for now it turns on the fact that the House of Commons best speaks for the people because it is elected by the people. The language of representation remains the same but the concepts are different, and, as we shall see, in propounding these new ideas, parliamentarians supplied the foundations for the Levellers' constitutional case. Although not challenging the ancient bond between the monarch and the people, in claiming to be the true representative of the people, parliamentarians introduce a new concept of 'the people'. The corporate identity of the people, which had long been vital to the constitution, is replaced by the idea of real people with real, diverse, and individual interests, which they express through voting and which they expect their representatives to represent. That the parliamentarians' claim rests on shaky foundations, is badly argued, and riddled with ambiguity, is true, but not the point. The point is that it was a radical claim, for it challenged the accepted mode of constitutional thought; and it suited the Levellers, for they now had a constitutional basis for their attacks on parliament: if the people, the real people, are the foundation of the constitution, the source of parliamentary authority, it is natural to examine parliament's treatment of the people, and if parliament is misusing its powers and abusing the people, then the relationship between them must be open to scrutiny and revision.

V. Constitution as the Health of the Nation and Law as the Sign of Good Constitution

We now think of constitutions as written documents stating the rules of government. 'Certainly all those who have framed written constitutions contemplate them as forming the fundamental and paramount law of the nation',[19] wrote Chief Justice Marshall in 1803 in *Marbury* v. *Madison,* whose expression made concrete an idea until then imperfectly formed: the rules of government are to be found in the written constitution, and there is no sense of fundamental law outside the written document. 'Constitution' in the seventeenth century meant something quite different; it meant something both broader and deeper, something in which

[18] How far the king's concession on the legislative aspect really was a concession, a departure from established doctrine, is a matter of debate. Some see it as a change, others as merely stating what had by then been accepted by all parties.

[19] *Marbury* v. *Madison* 1 Cranch 137.

the rules of government are just part of an organic whole. One spoke candidly of the 'body politic' by analogy to the body natural and the 'constitution' as its state of health and well-being.[20] The constitution of the body politic, its well-being, comprises those features essential to its nature and well-functioning. Parliamentarians and Levellers were agreed that after years of Personal Rule the body politic was of poor constitution and needed to be restored to good constitution, to those qualities fundamental to well-being. In the House of Commons in 1641, Stephen Marshall spoke of parliament's aim in its contest with the king being: 'to restore the nation' to 'the fundamental and vital liberties, the propriety of our goods, and freedom of our persons'.[21] Both parliamentarians and Levellers were intent on restoring the nation to good constitution.

That nothing is more essential to good constitution than the fundamental law was agreed by all. In the *Petition of Right* of 1628, the king accepted the supremacy of law. When the Levellers emerge in the 1640s, they regard respect for the fundamental law as vital to restoration of good constitution, although parliament rather than the king is now the source of ill-health. In *England's Miserie and Remedie,* an early statement of Leveller ideas, Richard Overton exposes the symptoms of a poor constitution. He refers to the 'body of the commonwealth' consisting of the House of Commons as representative and the people as the represented.[22] The representatives are there to serve the people, and yet the representatives have three times imprisoned John Lilburne without his knowing the accuser or the accusations, without being able to 'speak one word in his own defence'. He goes on to ask how it could be that the people would entrust themselves, 'their lives, liberties and all' to the parliament. Government is necessary for the good of the nation, but 'this sovereign or legislative power is not lent them for the ruin and destruction of our laws and liberties, but for the edification and strengthening of the same, in particular, as well as general.'[23]

Law is then vital to good constitution, to the well-being of the nation. Law is used in two ways: as the opposite of arbitrariness and as a set of standards. As to the first, Overton states the merit of law with simplicity: 'it is better to live under a rigorous and unjust law, than an arbitrary government, though just. The reason is, because by the first he is at certainty and knows what he must trust to, the last leaves him uncertain and so in danger.'[24] Lilburne's treatment by parliament is a violation of that idea, an idea found in Magna Carta, the *Petition of Right,* even Scripture. Overton ends by asking how a parliament professing 'reformation and defence of our laws and liberties' could thrice imprison a man without charge or trial. Lilburne invokes the same notion in condemning action taken against five royalist peers: 'No man', he argued, 'could legally be accused, tried, and convicted, except by a legally

[20] For a good account of the use and development of the notion of 'constitution': G. Stourzh, 'Constitution: Changing Meanings of the Term', in T. Ball and J. G. A. Pocock (eds), *Conceptual Change and the Constitution* (Kansas: University Press of Kansas, 1988).

[21] Stephen Marshall, House of Commons, 17 November 1641, quoted in *Judson.*

[22] *England's Miserie and Remedie*, in Wootton, 276.

[23] *England's Miserie and Remedie*, in Wootton, 277.

[24] *England's Miserie and Remedie*, in Wootton, 278.

constituted court, for an offence against a known law enacted by a legally constituted legislative body'.[25]

Law is also substantive, setting standards essential to the well-being of the nation. Laws are 'things of constitution' wrote an anonymous author in 1643, which constitution 'in the very being of it is a Law held forth with more evidence, and written in the very heart of the Republique, far firmlier than can be by pen and paper'.[26] This law, 'written in the very heart of the Republique', constitutes the relationship between king and subjects similar to that between the 'Head and Members' of a body. So constitution means law, but law has a special and somewhat elusive sense. It is more than common law and statutes, although both could be part of it; it is law in the sense of the standards, conventions, and understandings that characterize the body politic, which in this case include the rights and duties of free-born Englishmen. Law, like constitution, can be defined narrowly as the stated rules, or it can be more broadly positioned as a constituent part of the full constitution. Constitution and government should not be confused. The rules of government, the modern sense of constitution, derive from that deeper sense of constitution as health of the nation. But rules of government are not themselves fundamental to constitution; they are a means for achieving the good health of the nation, and are liable to revision if they fail in their purposes. Both notions, constitution as the health of the nation and law as the content of constitution, are essential to Leveller thought.

In making law of such moment the Levellers were within the mainstream of seventeenth-century thought. But the idea of law, while powerful, is not sufficient. It is not sufficient in the Levellers' condemnation of the commons for the same reasons it was not sufficient in the commons' condemnation of the king. One reason is that, while law is a constraint on government, sets the boundaries of government authority, it does not control adequately what happens within the boundaries, does not guide the practical use of authority. The other reason is that what amounts to fundamental law is contentious. As to the first, the Levellers at first thought the problem of arbitrariness would be solved by sovereign power being vested in the House of Commons, which, being directly representative of the people, should be expected to act in the interest of the people. In that expectation the Levellers were disappointed. As to the second, we shall see that the more closely the Levellers examined the law, the more elusive the fundamental standards prove to be.

The Levellers never wavered in their belief in the House of Commons as the legitimate centre of government. Their complaint was that the commons was committing the same abuses as it had condemned in the king, ranging from arbitrary arrest and imprisonment to the imposition of tithes, the granting of monopolies, and pressing men into service. The commons should plainly be subject

[25] J. Lilburne, *The Legall Fundamental Liberties of the People of England* (8 June 1649), in *The Leveller Tracts 1647–1653*, ed. W. Haller and G. Davies (New York: Columbia University Press, 1944) 339 at 445.

[26] Unnamed author, *Touching the Fundamental Laws, or Politique Constitution of this Kingdome* (London, 1643), 3–4, quoted in Stourzh, 'Constitutions: Changing Meanings of the Term', 41.

to constitutional constraints, to some guiding standards, but what were these to be? Parliamentarians again supplied the necessary concept, for they invoked against the king the notion that the first duty of government is to act for the safety and protection of the people, the *salus populi.* The king pledged to rule for the *salus populi* but was judged to have failed, and in failing breached the bond of trust with the people. In resisting the king's attempt to override the law in the interests of public safety, John Pym declared in parliament that *salus populi* is 'the Element of all Laws, out of which they are derived, the End of all Laws, to which they are designed, and in which they are perfected'.[27] The safety and welfare of the people is then the foundation of government: the guiding standard in law and government. Laws are essential to good constitution, but laws must serve the safety and welfare of the people.

Again the Levellers have resort to a full and organic sense of constitution. That government and the laws and institutions through which it is conducted are founded on the safety and welfare of the people forms another of the foundation stones of Leveller thought and criticism of parliament.[28] As the case unfolds, the tempo quickens. The 'end and purpose' of the House of Commons, as Overton declared, is to govern for the people's 'welfare and freedoms'.[29] In *An Appeal from the Commons to the Free People,* Overton states that parliament is entrusted with power to look after the people's 'safety and weal',[30] the safety and weal of the people being the end of all government, the supreme law. Safety includes 'the enjoyment of liberty, peace, and tranquillity, civil and human'. In *England's Lamentable Slavery* of the same year, Walwyn writes that 'Parliament cannot justly do anything to make the people less safe and less free'.[31] The author (thought to be either Sexby or Wildman) of *The Case of the Army Truly Stated,* published late in 1647, goes further in claiming that all power is originally in the people and the 'reason and end' for which they appoint governors is for their 'safety and good'.[32]

We now have two of the three core elements of the Levellers' notion of the constitution. Law, in the double sense of fundamental standards and respect for law, is the first and perhaps most important. But laws can be unjust, and even fundamental law can take on a life of its own and be divided from social reality, and indeed the Levellers came to view English law, including common law and even

[27] Quoted in Pease, 25.

[28] In *An Appeale from the Commons to the Free People* (17 June 1647), Overton, after noting that the House of Commons had used the *salus populi* argument against the king, now turns it on the house: in *Puritanism and Liberty,* ed. A. S. P. Woodhouse (London: Dent, 1938), 323. See also Pease, 96 ff. and Judson, 364 ff.

[29] R. Overton, *England's Miserie and Remedie,* in Wootton, 277.

[30] R. Overton, *An Appeal from the Commons to the Free People* in Woodhouse, 323. Elsewhere Overton and Lilburne refer to parliament being chosen 'to provide for the people's weale but not for their wo': J. Lilburne, R. Overton, and T. Prince, *Picture of the Councel of State* and *The Fountain of Slaunder Discovered* (April 1649) in Haller, 197.

[31] W. Walwyn, *England's Lamentable Slavery* (1647), in *The Levellers in the English Revolution,* ed. G. E. Aylmer (London: Thames and Hudson, 1975) 65. Walwyn earlier made the same point in arguing that the sharing of government between church and state 'is contrary to the people's safety': W. Walwyn, *The Compassionate Samaritan* (5 January 1644) in Haller *III,* 21.

[32] R. Sexby or J. Wildman, *Case of the Army Truly Stated* (15 October 1647) in Woodhouse, 429.

such foundational laws as Magna Charta, in this way. Law must then be rooted in society, must have direction and purpose, which the safety and welfare of the people provides. Yet there is still a problem: everything depends on parliament, or more precisely on the House of Commons, and what if the House of Commons, as Pym's 'Physician', fails in its duties, fails to ensure the 'Patient' is properly cared for? That the Physician was failing in its duty is the Levellers' complaint. Who then is to watch over the Physician? If the House of Commons as the representative body fails to govern for the welfare of those it represents, there is nowhere to turn but to the people: the represented. Once again the ground is prepared: in claiming special legitimacy by dint of election, the commons, as we noticed before, invoke a new notion of the people and confer on it constitutional significance, the consequences of which at first went unnoticed. The 'people' then is the third element of good constitution, which becomes in the hands of the Levellers one of its foundations. But before considering the people, we should note further the two distinct senses of constitution.

1. Competing conceptions of constitutions

The Levellers did not intend, at least not at first, to create a new constitutional order, to discard the old for something bold and new. They worked instead within a settled constitutional discourse and adopted its words and concepts. The English are a free people, 'the sole origin of their own authority', managing their own affairs by 'their own elected Parliaments or Common Councils of England'. The Levellers disclaimed any intention 'to tear up these foundations, to innovate or introduce any new constitution or frame of government'. They wished instead to restore the foundations, 'to maintain, defend, and preserve the old',[33] but the old 'freed from the encroachments of king, lords, and priests'.[34] This is the crucial point: king, peers, priests—and, we should add, parliamentarians—have taken control of the constitution and exploited it for their own ends. If exploitation is to be countered, a new language and discourse is needed; but the concepts that would naturally be invoked have been expropriated by the upper register. The only opening is re-interpretation of the concepts—a paring back to their original state—and for that there is utility in appealing to history: to a view of history formed from the influence of natural rights, a reading of Coke's *Institutes*, and reliance on republican writings dating back to Roman law. The aim is to draw out that which is already there but concealed and lost sight of: to lift the veil of the upper register and lay bare the more elemental, essential, and socially grounded lower register of constitutional thought, where the health of the body politic depends on being in harmony with the common good. That requires interpretation

[33] J. W. Gough, *Fundamental Law in English Constitutional History* (Oxford: Clarendon Press, 1955), 123.

[34] *The Fundamental Laws and Liberties of England* (1653) quoted in Gough, *Fundamental Law*, 123.

and judgement with which others might not concur, as, in Putney, Cromwell and Ireton did not concur.

The constitution in the Levellers' view is the 'fundamental and vital liberties, the propriety of our goods, the freedom of our persons'. After abuse by king and parliament, the issue is how best to restore such features of good health. The existing institutions of government having failed, a new way must be found, the key to which is the people: since the good health of the nation is defined by the rights and liberties of the people and the fundamental law protecting them, it seems natural, almost necessary, to focus on the idea, already in place, of government being for and with the consent of the people. It is now a matter of re-interpreting what that means, and the new and perhaps obvious shift is to substitute, as the foundation of the constitution and its guardian, the real people rather than a fictional, corporate notion. The monarchy and the House of Lords, despite their antiquity, can then be swept away without harming the constitution of the nation because they concern merely the mechanics of government. A reformed House of Commons, elected by a wider franchise and accountable to the people, will be retained as the primary institution of government.

What to the Levellers is already in the old constitution, inherent in its structure and assumptions is, from another point of view, innovation of a dangerous kind. Constitutions based on that other view are compromises of principle, prudence, and private interest, and all three of these are present at Putney. Cromwell and Ireton understand the power of the case that the constitution is for the good of the people and that parliament's authority derives from the people. They understand the Levellers' case for wider voting rights; they concede that if parliament is to represent and serve the people then there is a case for the people being involved in its selection.[35] They grasp the link between the consent of the people as the foundation of government's legitimacy and the idea that each person counts in the giving of consent. They understand all this and yet balk at giving them constitutional meaning, accepting them as signs of good health. For the Levellers' case, however compelling at a profound and elemental level, would have uncertain social consequences, and neglects other signs of good health: social order, peace, prosperity, and stability. Social goods like these depend on tried-and-tested institutions, on government being in the hands of those able to govern with skills equivalent to those of the physician, who knows what is best for the patient and how to achieve it. The social order is not perfect, does not fully reflect political ideals, but it has grown and strengthened over time, is rooted in practice and reality, and supports a stable and prosperous social order. To build a new constitution from first principles, or even too rigorously to interrogate the existing one, puts all that at risk. Cromwell and Ireton reject the notion that the forms and institutions of

[35] Historically, representation did not depend on the representatives being elected; medieval and early modern thought had no difficulty with the notion that the capacity to represent others was separate from the manner by which the representative is appointed. The idea that representatives have to be elected emerged and evolved only much later. Election is linked to consent, not the capacity to represent.

government are incidental to the constitution, are mere means to ends; on the contrary, the forms and institutions of government are tied to and evolve in step with the nation's well-being, so to meddle with government is to meddle with the constitution.[36]

The tension between the two understandings of constitutions becomes plain during the debates at Putney. In *A Representation of the Army,* Henry Ireton had made the case for the pay and indemnity of the common soldiers, who, he states, 'were not a mere mercenary army, hired to serve any arbitrary power of a state, but called forth . . . to the defence of our people and the people's just rights and liberties'.[37] A few months later at Putney, when it comes to giving the same soldiers the right to vote, the mood and language change. From being brave soldiers and worthy citizens, they become commoners who have no status in the constitution, for they have no 'permanent interest' in the nation, and to allow them to vote would be a threat of anarchy; for Cromwell they are 'mere breathers'. The image of the men as soldiers will not do when it comes to devising a system of government, for the stakes are different and higher, and other factors come into play: social order and stability, good and wise government, even property itself would be at risk if those now common men were given the vote.

And so we see that within the bounds of a shared concept of constitution as the health of the nation, of the central place of law and liberty within it, and of the need for restoration, two strikingly different senses emerge as to the particular conception of the nation's constitution and the purpose of government. The Levellers begin with conventional ideas and enter into the prevailing discourse; but by focusing on one set of values and pursuing them to their logical conclusion, they end up with a sense of the constitution that appears idealistic and divorced from the social and political realities of the time. 'We are for Government and against popular confusion', write the Levellers, 'our aim being to reduce it [government] as near as might be to perfection.'[38] What begins as a campaign for restoring the basic elements of the nation's well-being by righting such plain wrongs as imprisonment without charge or trial, turns into a plan for transformation of the body politic, where the people are supreme, the government limited, and rights and liberties are guaranteed. That they reached this point by following the logic of conventional concepts, revealing the values at their foundation, and showing how the orthodox constitution is truly part of a more fundamental constitution from which it has become uncoupled, is true but not to the point. Society had shaped

[36] At the time, late 1647, Cromwell and Ireton were still working on the assumption that a settlement would be reached with the king and the usual institutions of government restored. It may be noted in passing that Edmund Burke held a strikingly similar view of the constitution: E. Burke, *Speech on Constitutional Government* 1775 reproduced in J. H. Fowler (ed.), *A Book of English Prose* (London: Macmillan, 1911). Note that when the Putney Debates took place no major institutional changes had yet been made and settlement with the king was still thought likely.

[37] *A Representation of the Army* (14 June 1647), in Woodhouse, 404.

[38] J. Lilburne, W. Walwyn, T. Prince, and R. Overton, *A Manifestation from lieutenant John Lilburne, Master William Walwyne, Master Thomas Prince, and Master Richard Overton (now prisoners in the Tower of London) and others, commonly (though unjustly) stiled Levellers* (April 1649), in Haller, 276 at 280.

itself around that upper register of constitutional thought, had arranged its affairs in the manner glimpsed in the account of Cromwell and Ireton, so that to be reminded of the foundations was unwelcome, in the same way that to the Grand Inquisitor the sudden reappearance of Jesus was unwelcome.[39]

VI. Arbitrary Power and Law as the Cure

In the disputes between king and parliamentarians, both parties agreed that the fundamental law was essential to the health of the nation—even agreed, as Francis Pym declared in the commons, that law, not the king, binds society together.[40] In a study of the constitutional crisis of the 1640s, Margaret Judson found that men of the seventeenth century held a 'profound belief in the importance of law': a belief shared by the Levellers. In *Killing Not Murder,* Edward Sexby presents the law as essential to social life, which we achieve only by subjection and submission to law.[41] 'Laws', he goes on, drawing on the imagery of a body and its health, 'are the nerves or sinews of every society or commonwealth, without which they must necessarily dissolve and fall asunder.'.Sexby was branded a dangerous radical, but the words could have come from king, lords, or commons.

Law's centrality to the social order was proclaimed rather than explained and a full account would take us deep into English history. It is enough to suggest that, in an age of high monarchy where the royal power, although not absolute if measured against that of the French, posed a threat of becoming so, law is one means of restraint and hence protection of liberty and property. By the start of the seventeenth century, parliament was beginning to assert a more independent voice than previously, but it was not until the crisis of the 1640s that it claimed a measure of control over royal authority. The courts were the king's courts and in contests over the scope of royal power generally could be relied on to support the king. The people lacked any constitutional role, beyond the myth of their being in some sense present in parliament, and had no legal means for checking or restraining royal authority. In the absence of checks and balances from parliament, courts, and the people, there was just the law—not law in a narrow sense, but law as the means and gauge of the nation's well-being, as a set of ideas of ancient provenance embedded in social consciousness and available to be invoked by all. The law to a seventeenth-century Englishman occupied a place in society similar to that of the written constitution in modern societies, and just as it is damaging to a president, prime minister, or other official to be accused of violating the constitution, a charge that the king was acting contrary to law had the same effect,[42] for, as the *Petition of Right*

[39] The Grand Inquisitor's reaction is displayed in F. Dostoyevsky, *The Brothers Karamazov* (Oxford: Oxford University Press, 2008).

[40] For analysis of fundamental law, the two authoritative texts are: Gough, *Fundamental Law in English Constitutional History*, and Judson, *The Crisis of the Constitution.*

[41] E. Sexby, *Killing Not Murder* (1657), in Wootton, 371.

[42] For further discussion of the role of law, see Judson, 44 ff.

states, it was by 'the good laws and statutes of this realm your subjects have inherited this freedom'.[43]

The Levellers shared the common esteem for law and found it useful in dealing with arbitrary treatment by king, lords, and commons. The curse of arbitrary action appears early on and becomes a rallying point in the Leveller cause, for arbitrary action is a mortal threat to the well-being of the nation. 'We must pray you to make a law against all kinds of arbitrary government', begged many thousand citizens, according to Overton and Walwyn, 'as the highest capital offence against the commonwealth.'[44] If this seems to be a wild overstatement, it is within the conventional frame of reference where arbitrariness on the part of officials threatens rights and liberties. The two go together: arbitrariness is condemned, law revered. They were embedded in constitutional discourse, and had already been made inseparable by parliamentarians in their condemnation of the king. They were the natural categories the Levellers should adopt to deal with their grievances. Lilburne's trial and punishment by Star Chamber and his arrest and imprisonment without trial by the Houses of Lords or Commons, widely considered outrageous and unjust, had all the hallmarks of arbitrariness and questionable legal authority. When others were treated in this way—notably at the summary execution of a mutinous soldier by Fairfax, and Cromwell's indictment of five royalist peers for treason—the Levellers came to their defence.[45] When the House of Commons seemed over-zealous in asserting and exerting its privileges, it was attacked for impinging on or acting outside the law and so arbitrarily. The Star Chamber, the House of Lords, and later the Council of State were all open to criticism for wrongly claiming the jurisdiction of a criminal court over common citizens and in denying them due process.

The use the Levellers made of law and arbitrariness illustrates their methods. They first display the inner tensions and contradictions which they then resolve by resorting to a deeper level of constitutional understandings. In framing a petition to the House of Commons against his imprisonment and that of his wife and brother by the House of Lords, Richard Overton writes of his 'indignation and detestation against the Arbytrary tyrannie and usurpation of the House of Lords over the Commoners natural and legal Freedoms and Rights'.[46] John Lilburne relates how he dedicated his life to exposing and attacking arbitrariness and illegality in whatever form it took. In *The Legal Fundamentall Liberties of the People of England*, addressed to the Speaker of the Commons, Lilburne, reflecting on his life's work, refers to himself as the 'Arbitrary and Aristocratical prisoner in the Tower of London'.[47] He charges the recently purged House of Commons as 'most fit . . . to destroy the old Laws Liberties and Customs of England, the badges of our

[43] *Petition of Right*, Article 1 in Wootton, 168.

[44] R. Overton and W. Walwyn, *A Remonstrance of Many Thousand Citizens* (7 July 1646), 4.

[45] Considered by Lilburne in *The Legall Fundamental Liberties of the People of England*, in Haller, 399.

[46] R. Overton, *The Commoners Complaints or, a Dreadful Warning from Newgate, to the Commons of England* (10 February 1646).

[47] J. Lilburne, *The Legall Fundamentall Liberties of the People of England*, in Haller, 399 ff.

freedom'.[48] He recites how he 'smarted under the king's irregular government, in the violating of the Laws of England'; he refers to parliament's resolve to 'secure the People's Laws and Liberties to them'.[49] He lists his encounters with the parliament, and those of others (some of whom were his enemies), and shows how its promises were betrayed. He condemns the trial and execution of the king as illegal, and explains how he refused an office in the Rump Parliament because: 'it is in his opinion an unjust and illegal body, exercising a tyranny similar to that formerly charged against the king and his ministers'.[50]

When the Levellers detect actions that appear unjust, they class them as arbitrary, from which it follows they are in breach of the law. They attribute the nation's poor constitution to arbitrariness and prescribe law as the cure. Arbitrariness is given a wide meaning to include such matters as arrest and imprisonment without trial, requiring citizens to answer questions before the bar of either house, oppression for religious non-conformity, usurpation of jurisdiction by the organs of government, and the House of Commons' claim to privileges, to name but some of the alleged abuses. Whether all these amount to arbitrariness—and if they do whether they would best be cured by law—is debatable; but not for the Levellers who had of it high hopes. If law is the remedy for an array of government abuses, what sense of law do the Levellers have in mind? Common law and statutes are candidates, but they soon come to be seen as part of the problem rather than the solution. The common law turns out to be the handiwork of corrupt and arbitrary judges and the cause of injustice rather than the remedy: 'a badge of slavery'.[51] It is part of an oppressive legal and political order that began centuries before with the Norman destruction of the old, authentic English legal order, which in Leveller thought takes on the appearance of social paradise lost. Statute law fares no better, for, according to Overton and Walwyn, 'the laws that have been made since by parliaments have in many particulars made our government much more oppressive and intolerable';[52] and anyhow parliament is unlikely to pass laws to curb its own abuses.

If common law and statute are tainted, a more fundamental sense of law is needed, and it is found in that anonymous writer's 'things of constitution', in Sexby's 'nerves and sinews'. In protesting against imprisonment for unspecified offences, Lilburne accuses parliament of acting 'directly contrary to fundamental principles',[53] committing the same arbitrary acts for which it had condemned the king. Known laws are 'Rules for all the Commons of England whereby to walk'; parliament is subject to law and has no authority to act where there is no law, and to do so is to act arbitrarily. Magna Carta, the *Petition of Right*, the Coronation Oath, and statutes passed in the early days of the new parliament, such as that abolishing

[48] *The Legall Fundamentall Liberties*, 400. [49] *The Legall Fundamentall Liberties*, 406.

[50] *The Legall Fundamentall Liberties*, 434.

[51] J. Lilburne, *The Just Man's Justification*, discussed in Pease, 72.

[52] *The Compassionate Samaritans: Liberty of Conscience Asserted and the Separatist Vindicated*, in Wootton, 247.

[53] *England's Birthright Justified Against all Arbitrary Usurpation* (October 1645), author uncertain, likely to be either Lilburne or Wildman; also *England's Lamentable Slavery*, in Haller *III*.

Star Chamber, are evidence of a fundamental law, which creates rights in the people and imposes restraints on authority. Magna Carta itself becomes suspect, for despite protecting against arbitrary rule, it is 'a beggarly thing containing many marks of intolerable bondage'.[54] It is 'a messe of pottage'[55] compatible with oppression and iniquity, for the system of which Magna Carta forms part is a legacy of 'Norman bondage whereof we now as well as our predecessors have felt the smart by these bloody wars'. Unless parliament takes the Levellers' advice and studies 'the common interest of this nation . . . we cannot expect to be delivered from the Norman bondage . . . or from all unreasonable laws made ever since that unhappy conquest'.[56] If the law is to be the main instrument of reform, the Levellers have to look beyond the positive legal order for 'its false principles concerning kings and governments and parliaments and freedoms', in favour of those happy principles that prevailed before 1066. At this point the two main ideas—restoring the health of the nation and law being the means for doing so—begin to lose their vigour, for one refers to a state of health not enjoyed for more than six centuries, and the other to a notion that is law only in a wide and diluted sense of the word.

Having found the legal order wanting, the Levellers look elsewhere for the foundations of fundamental law. One is pre-Conquest England where men were free rather than in bondage and lived in peace and happiness. But when it comes to defining the legal character of that society, the answers are not so clear. There is praise for local courts over the centralized judicial system of the Normans; praise for the absence of laws allowing imprisonment for debt or pressing men into service to fight wars. Other lessons were to be learnt from Anglo-Saxon society, but the main idea is that government should take 'care that all sorts of men find comfort and contentment' in it, and that, if it 'showed love for the people in the constitutions of the government', the conditions of liberty would be restored.[57]

Another source of fundamental law is religion, which had major influence on ideas of government and constitution in the seventeenth century, an influence the Levellers keenly felt. The Bible provides enlightenment: God made man lord over the earth, but man 'falling from his perfection of reason' became tyrannical, and the beastliness evident in the story of Cain and Abel entered 'the spirit of all mankind'.[58] To overcome this, God 'institutes a perpetual, morall, unchangeable, and everlasting LAW', which contains such imperatives as 'love thy neighbour' and 'do good unto all the sons of Adam'. The greatest good, after the love of God, is

> rationally to discern the privileges, that is, the Rights, Due, and Propriety of all the sons of Adam as men . . . to maintain those Rights and Privileges in any kingdom or nation . . . not Lord it, domineer over, and destroy [them] by their Prerogative-will and pleasure.[59]

[54] R. Overton and W. Walwyn, *A Remonstrance of Many Thousand Citizens* (7 July 1646), 9.
[55] *England's Lamentable Slavery,* in Haller *III,* 309 ff.
[56] *England's Lamentable Slavery,* in Haller *III,* 11.
[57] *England's Lamentable Slavery,* in Haller *III,* 15.
[58] J. Lilburne, *Postscript* to *London's Liberty* (1646) in Aylmer, 71.
[59] J. Lilburne, *Postscript,* 73.

From the precepts of law that God gives each man, rights and liberties follow, which should then be expressed in the law of the land. If the law of the land does not confer them, as the Levellers judged English law did not, then it should be condemned.[60]

A third source of fundamental law links law and reason. Against the background of divine precepts, the Levellers appeal to 'the law of reason', which exists 'by virtue of a perceptive power innate in every man, taught or untaught, enabling him to distinguish right and wrong, good and evil' and importantly 'what was just or unjust'.[61] Right reason is then the standard for positive law: 'Human government is just only if its laws accord with the principles of right reason and justice implanted in the hearts of men.' In making the connection between right reason and the laws of England, Lilburne relies on Edward Coke's *Institutes of the Lawes of England*, where Coke states maxims of law and establishes reason as the beacon of the common law. Lilburne looks to 'that most excellent of English lawyers' for the proposition that 'where reason ceaseth, there the law ceaseth; for seeing reason is the very life and spirit of the Law itself'.[62] The laws of England are extolled as 'the Perfection of Reason, consisting of Lawful and Reasonable Customes, received and approved of by the people: and of the old Constitutions'. Then comes the caveat: 'such only as are agreeable to the Law Eternal and Naturall . . . For whatsoever laws, usages, and customes, not thus qualified, are not the law of the land.'[63] Since natural reason is invested in the breast of all men, regardless of their position in society and 'however mean his intellect',[64] and not just in the breast of parliamentarians, and since law is for the welfare and safety of all men, then it follows that laws which do not reasonably advance that safety and welfare are not true laws. What is in accordance with reason is then the fundamental law and on this foundation the Levellers build the case for limitations on the law-making powers of parliament.

VII. The People

The Levellers believed the House of Commons, as the true representative of the 'Commons of England', to be the only part of government with authority to restore to health the constitution of the nation. When the Commons fails, it comes under scrutiny and its authority is questioned. The Levellers begin with the common view

[60] The Levellers' view of English law, and the extent to which it did or did not embody the precepts of God's law, changed over time. In *London's Liberties in Chains* (1646), Lilburne refers to English law as the 'perfection of reason' (quoted in Pease, 75). Yet at the same time, Overton and Walwyn are rejecting English law as part of the Norman bondage and a denial of God's law: *A Remonstrance of Many Thousand Citizens.*

[61] J. Lilburne, *Innocency and Truth Justified* (1645), 27. These words bear close similarity to a passage in C. Saint-Germain's *The Dialogue in English betweene a Doctor of Divinity and a Student in the Laws of Englande* (first published in English 1530/31; edition used 1623), 4.

[62] J. Lilburne, *The Legall Fundamantal Liberties of the People of England,* in Haller, 407.

[63] J. Lilburne, *London's Liberty in Chains,* quoted in Pease, 74–5.

[64] J. Lilburne, *London's Liberty in Chains,* 75.

that the authority of government derives from the people; a position accepted in the 1640s, which had been accepted for centuries before and continues to be to the present day. As is their way, the Levellers engage with common ideas to reach uncommon conclusions, which in this case are perhaps their main contribution to constitutional thought. In *England's Miserie and Remedie,* Richard Sexby, in attacking John Lilburne's imprisonment by the House of Commons, states the case:[65] (i) 'all lawful sovereign command has its basis on firm foundations in the consent, approbation, and good liking of the people'; (ii) the House of Commons is 'nothing but a representative body of the people' and has no authority other than that given to it by the people; it is 'the servant of the people';(iii) and its task is to 'hear and relieve the grievances of the people' and to 'reform what is amiss in the Commonwealth'; it is elected, in other words, to govern for the people's 'welfare and freedom'; (iv) if the House of Commons is presently governing not for their 'lives and liberties' but for their 'ruin and destruction', it does so without the consent of the people. Consent cannot be expected from those 'who daily see themselves abused in their liberties and ruined in their estates'. The multitude will 'shake off all bonds of obedience' for 'who but a madman will yield obedience unto those who are regardless of their laws and liberties, their subsistence livelihood and safety'?[66]

The case is strengthened in later tracts by proclaiming the natural equality of men in 'power, dignity, authority, and majesty'.[67] Each has a 'natural property' in his liberty and welfare. That natural property and the natural rights flowing from it are the basis of all political rights. People may give up some of that natural property to government, for government is a necessity in advancing the liberty and welfare of the people. But men part with only such of their natural property as is needed for their liberty and welfare, it being 'unnatural, irrational, . . . wicked and unjust' for them to surrender powers which will then be used to 'destroy and undo them'.[68] It is equally 'unnatural, irrational, sinful, wicked, and unjust' for any man to assume authority over another without the other's free consent. In short: government takes its authority from the consent of men and women, who confer authority for specified ends; government has no authority to use its power other than for those ends; and if it acts contrary to them, its authority is forfeit. A major shift has taken place, moving away from parliament as the centre of authority to the people; and these are not the people as an abstract entity, but the real people, who now will appoint parliament and expect it to act in their interests, and who, if it fails, may revoke its authority. The conventional constitution is returned to its foundations, to a deeper sense of constitution, on the basis of which the conventional must be re-interpreted and re-modelled.

[65] Sexby, *England's Miserie and Remedie*, in Wootton, 276.

[66] Sexby, *England's Miserie and Remedie*, Wootton, 276–8. Similar ideas are expressed in numerous tracts, the most important being: R. Overton, *An Appeale from the Commons to the Free People*; W. Walwyn, *England's Lamentable Slavery*; *Long Petition*; R. Sexby (or J. Wildman), *The Case of the Army Truly Stated*; J. Lilburne, *The Freeman's Freedom Vindicated.*

[67] J. Lilburne, *The Freeman's Freedom Vindicated* (1646) in Woodhouse, 317.

[68] J. Lilburne, *The Freeman's Freedom Vindicated*, in Woodhouse, 317.

1. Representation

These ideas look familiar to the modern eye and are hardly controversial, but to received wisdom of the seventeenth century they were seriously unsettling. It is true that parliamentarians, king, and aristocracy all accepted that government's authority in some sense comes from the people, that they must in some sense consent to government, and that the powers of government should be used for their safety and welfare. The Coronation Oath expresses the bond between people and king: 'the willingness of the people or peoples to accept the person about to take the oath as king'.[69] Once accepted by the people, the king has duties to them, to govern in their interests, for their safety and welfare. The people accept the king through their representatives, who are present at the coronation and who speak for them. Parliament, consisting of the king and the two houses as the supreme authority, represents and acts on behalf of the people. But notice the ambiguities: the people are the source of authority but do not exercise it; the institutions of government represent the people but the people have no control over them. The 'people as the source of authority' has been construed to allow a constitution to form in which the people have no practical place or status. A mode of constitutional thought has been nurtured in which the people are necessary but have only a notional role. In arguing for return of the constitution to its foundations, to a different mode of thought in which the fictions are dispelled and the people are restored to a real role, the Levellers appeared to be dangerously radical and as such were to be resisted.

As the dispute between king and commons deepens in the 1640s, the commons begins to claim that its being elected by the people gives it a special claim to represent them. Without denying the king's bond with the people or his position as head of the body politic, the commons contends that its authority in representing the people is superior because it is based on a direct and real mandate from them. This is a departure from the notion, essential to the upper register, of the people as a corporate body capable of acting only through representatives; in its place are the people as a collective of individual persons with a real and direct relationship to their representatives. The parliamentarians were abandoning accepted constitutional concepts for political gains, without it seems realizing the consequences for constitutional thought; for to bring into constitutional thought the people as real live individual persons is a paradigm shift. The Levellers sense the significance of the new discourse on representation and follow it through to logical but unexpected conclusions.

To enter into that discourse, we have to put aside two pillars of modern constitutional thought. According to the modern view, election by the people is the normal way of appointing government and the basis of its authority. Consent of the people means consent positively displayed through elections. In the seventeenth century, things were seen differently; popular election was neither the usual mode for selecting government, nor necessary for its authority. Consent of the people was

[69] M. R. L. L. Kelly, 'King and Crown' (Doctoral Thesis, Macquarie University, 1998), 165.

expressed through representatives whose authority to speak on their behalf was not dependent on election.[70] Since the aim of government is the welfare of the people, the main concern is to entrust government to those who know what that means and how to achieve it. Elections were feared because they might replace the natural leaders of the nation with popular figures incapable of governing for the welfare of the people. The commons was the elected branch but only by a small part at the upper end of the adult population.[71] The commons was mainly a source of advice to the king and as late as the 1640s was seen by Charles I in that light.[72] Advice from knights of the shires as to the state of the shires was useful in knowing how best to advance the welfare of the people of the shire, but the commons was not part of executive government. No special constitutional status was gained from being elected, and it would be as much a mistake to regard the fact of the commons' election as early recognition of the merits of governments being chosen by election, as it would be to see a steady progress from that base to modern democracy.

The other feature of seventeenth-century constitutional thought is that 'the people' constitute a corporation, an *universitas,* which has a legal identity separate and distinct from its members, in the same way that a modern company has legal identity and is distinct from its shareholders. The welfare of the people means the welfare of the corporate entity, so that the task of government is to act on behalf of the corporation and advance its welfare. For constitutional purposes the primary relationship is between the corporate entity and government. The welfare of individual members of the corporation is part of the overall welfare of the people, but it is not the only or primary part, and it has to be absorbed into the wider sense of the good of the corporation. The people (singular) as a corporate entity is distinguished from the people (plural) as a collective of individual persons. The modern tendency is to reject or at least reduce the sense of corporate identity and to place the welfare of individual persons at the centre of the constitution.[73] From that it follows that the primary constitutional relationship is between the government and the people as individual persons, whose rights have to be respected and diverse interests taken into account.

The sense of the people as a corporation, an *universitas*, is at the heart of the seventeenth-century English constitution. It was taken for granted rather than examined; it was the way men of affairs thought; it was the notion they had in

[70] The nature of consent and its history are complicated matters and a full account is beyond the scope of this essay; for a fuller account the leading authority is Gaines Post; see G. Post, *Studies in Medieval Legal Thought: Public Law and the State, 1100–1322* (Princeton: Princeton University Press, 1964).

[71] For discussion of the electoral system: M. A. Kishansky, *Parliamentary Selection: Social and Political Choice in Early Modern England* (Cambridge: Cambridge University Press, 1986).

[72] On the early origins and development of the English Parliament: J. R. Maddicott, *The Origins of the English Parliament 924–1327* (Oxford: Oxford University Press, 2010).

[73] Although traces of the corporate notion of the people are present in contemporary constitutional texts and still have influence on constitutional thought; see further: D. J. Galligan, 'The People, the Constitution, and the Idea of Representation', in D. J. Galligan and M. Versteeg (eds), *Social and Political Foundations of Constitutions* (New York: Cambridge University Press, 2013), 134.

mind when they spoke of the people, made claims on the people's behalf, or wielded power in their name. The idea has its origins in Roman law, was naturalized into medieval canon law in order to solve problems of government within the Roman Catholic Church, and from there found its way into secular constitutional thought.[74] Once 'the people' is understood in the corporate sense, some of the puzzles of seventeenth-century constitutional thought dissolve. It makes sense of the king's claim that his authority derives from the people and that he in turn represents them. The corporation according to Roman law is an entity distinct from its members and acts only through its appointed agents or representatives, the procedure of appointment being a matter for the corporation. Representatives have authority to speak for the corporation and act in its name. The king's Coronation Oath attests to the people's acceptance of the sovereign through their representatives, and affirms that he as their representative will govern for their welfare. Once accepted by the people, the king has authority to act as he thinks best for the welfare of the people, who are bound by his actions.

The 'people as a corporation' is necessary in understanding the authority of parliament. When parliament is assembled, the whole nation is there assembled. As early as the fourteenth century, an English judge wrote: 'Parliament represents the body of the whole realm', and 'Parliament of the King and Lords and Commons are a corporation.'[75] In the Ship Money case two centuries later, Justice Berkeley refers to the basic constitutional notion that 'Parliament is a most ancient and supreme court, where the King and Peers, as judges, are in person, and the whole body of the Commons representatively'.[76] Thomas Smith went further in declaring of parliament that 'everie Englishman is entitled to be there present' and that 'the consent of Parliament is taken to be everie man's consent'.[77] The idea of every man being represented in parliament takes on the added sense of every man being *present* in parliament, and the two become synonymous.

The corporate notion of the people serves several social ends. First, where the aim is to ensure that whoever represents the people knows what is best for their safety and welfare, the quality of representatives is what counts, not how they are appointed. Another is that what constitutes the safety and welfare of the people is considered to be a matter of good judgement and depends on neither popular nor majority vote. Monarchs and their councillors drawn from the upper reaches of society were thought best able to determine the right course of action, and the idea that each society has its natural rulers lingers on even today. A third consideration is that, once representatives are given full authority by the people in accordance with

[74] The origins and development of the corporate idea are traced and analysed in B. Tierney, *Religion, law and the growth of constitutional thought 1150–1650* (Cambridge: Cambridge University Press, 1982).

[75] Quoted in E. H. Kantorowicz, *The King's Two Bodies* (Princeton: Princeton University Press, 1957), 207–32.

[76] *State Trial* 1638, iii. Column 1090, quoted in *The Constitutional Documents of the Puritan Revolution*, ed. S. W. Gardiner (Oxford: Oxford University Press, 1889), 121.

[77] T. Smith, *De Republica Anglorum*, ed. L. Alston (Cambridge: Cambridge University Press, 1906).

the procedures for appointment, their actions and decisions are binding on the people both as a corporation and as individual persons. It was normal to confer on representatives plenary powers, although a corporation could impose limits as the people of England did in requiring that king and parliament act in accordance with fundamental law. Fourthly, consent to representatives is expressed through the process of appointment, the form of which the corporation decides. Consent of the people to one set of representatives is often expressed through another set, while acquiescence by the people rather than positive action is taken to be consent.[78] Finally, at some notional point in the history of a nation, the people as individual persons are deemed to have agreed to form themselves into a corporation, after which individual persons are bound by their representatives. The people have no authority within the constitution to dissent from representative actions; indeed the people as individual persons have no place in the constitution, have no constitutional standing, and no authority to change or revoke the constitution.[79] The only course open to them in extreme cases is to reject the constitutional order by direct action, and for that reason fear of popular rebellion haunts early constitutional thought.[80]

In place of the corporate sense of the people, the Levellers substitute the people as a collection of individual persons, each of whom has a direct interest in government, and in who governs and how they govern. They found the sense implicit in the conventional concepts and discourse which accepted that each person is a right-bearer, has a natural right to liberty, and gives up part of that liberty to government in order to advance individual and communal welfare. The Levellers concluded that each person has a direct relationship with government and a direct interest in how government is conducted. Each person has a claim to be involved in the selection of government, in setting the terms on which their representatives govern, in monitoring their performance, and in having the authority to change the government and dismiss their representatives. In this renewal of the relationship between the people and government, the fundamental constitution is restored and revived. But how did the Levellers manage to break the mould of constitutional thought by lifting the corporate veil and inserting a sense of the people as a collective of individual persons?

The answer is that the corporate entity of the people is unstable. As an abstraction from social reality and experience it is at risk of collapse when confronted with real people with real interests and a real sense of justice and injustice. The abstract idea is needed to sustain a constitutional order that depends on the

[78] The concept of *acquiescence* became central to David Hume's later analysis of constitutions and society; it is advanced as more accurately expressing the attitudes of the people; see R. Hardin, 'Why a Constitution?' in Galligan and Versteeg (eds), *Social and Political Foundations of Constitutions*, 51.

[79] For further discussion of these ideas, see H. Parker, *Jus Populi or a Discourse wherein clear satisfaction is given as well concerning the Right of Subjects, as the Right of Princes* (London, 1644), discussed at length in *Judson*, ch. X.

[80] Although these ideas and the fictions supporting them may seem relics of pre-modern societies, they are the basis for one of the most important attempts to formulate a modern social theory of constitutions; see E. Sieyès, *Qu'est-ce que le tiers état?* in *Sieyès: Political Writings*, ed. M. Sonenscher (Indianapolis and Cambridge: Hackett, 2003).

people and yet has to exclude them. But social reality and personal experience are liable to break through. It is one thing to assume the consent of the people to the system, another to ask whether they in fact consent; one thing to expound and praise the legal principles of the system, another to see how they apply in practice and wonder why individual persons—Lilburne, Overton, and others—can be savagely punished without reference to them. It is one thing to conceive of parliament as the coming together of the whole nation, where grievances may be aired and resolved, another to witness the contempt parliament has for the bearers of petitions of which it does not approve.[81] That there should be tension between the abstractions and fictions and social reality is understandable, but a constitution has to harness and guide social and political life—'coordination' is David Hume's term[82]—where people have experiences quite at odds with constitutional precepts. Constitutions survive when the abstractions and fictions, here the corporate sense of the people, take adequate account of, are in balance with, the needs and interests of real people. When the balance is upset, when the people as individuals suffer harm at the hands of government, it is to be expected that the veil will be lifted and social reality confronted.

The Levellers' case turns on just that: lifting the veil on the corporate notion of the people, seeing what happens in the real social world, and then proposing an alternative sense of the people. Two factors stand out. In the first place, as described earlier, the House of Commons paved the way by claiming authority in representing the people superior to that of the king. This was a challenge to the corporate notion, according to whose logic what matters is whether they govern for the welfare of the people not how they are appointed. The king and both houses held authority on that basis: each had a legitimate place in the constitution, in representing the people; each acquires authority by different means. When the House of Commons asserts superior authority on the basis of being elected, it changes the discourse, introduces new concepts, ruptures the corporate identity of the people, and threatens the constitutional order. That its members are elected is relevant only on the basis that between the people and their representatives a special relationship is created, one different from that between king and subjects. The parliamentary case was never clear, but seems to amount to the claim: first, that being directly elected by the people, members of the House of Commons can claim the real rather than notional consent of the people; second, being elected by local constituencies, the Commons are in a better position to represent the people's real and local interests. This was a challenge to the notion of representation at the heart of the English constitution, which depends on neither true representation nor election. In claiming the real consent of the people, parliamentarians invite scrutiny as to just how real it is. The Levellers, perhaps realizing the incoherence of the parliamentary position, seize the opportunity to show what real consent means and the institutions needed to achieve it.

[81] On petitions to parliament, see further discussion in C. S. Emden, *The People and the Constitution* (Oxford: Clarendon, 1956), ch. IV, and E. S. Morgan, *Inventing the People,* 223.

[82] Discussed and developed in Hardin.

The other factor is the direct experience of Lilburne, Overton, and Walwyn, their associates, and even old enemies, at the hands of king, council, Houses of Parliament, and the courts, direct experience of being summoned and punished without charge or trial. The focus falls on relations between the organs of government and individual persons, and to that the corporate idea of the people is irrelevant. It has nothing to offer individual persons in their encounters with such organs, for here the issue is different: how can individual persons be subjected to arbitrary and oppressive treatment by the very organs of government that are entrusted with their safety and welfare? Real people are suffering real oppression at the hands of government, so that the constitutional question is on what basis to condemn such action and how to protect individual persons against it. The solution lies in the law, for the law regulates relations between the individual person and the state; it creates rights and duties, it places constraints on state power, and it offers concrete remedies. If common law and statutes are lacking, recourse may be had to a more elemental sense of constitution whose precepts are grounded in reasons and a sense of justice and which has its origins in a social reality where authority is dependent on the people.

2. Agreement of the People

Having reached this constitutional bedrock, pared away the conventional constitution to reveal its foundations, and restored authentic precepts, the Levellers have to face the issue of how to make it work in practice. Implementation is the other main theme running through their writings. The House of Commons has sole authority to govern, since it is authorized by the people. But if abuses are to be avoided, the commons has to be controlled. Accountability to the people is one form of control, substantive limitations on its powers another. These two ideas appear early on in the Levellers' writings and become the basis for *An Agreement of the People*, which went through several versions, the first presented to the Army Council during the debates in Putney Church in October 1647, the last issued by Lilburne and others in June 1649, by which time the king was dead and Cromwell and Ireton were in control. The Levellers were not alone in concluding that government has to be limited; many shared the view that the constitution should be protected from being 'set aside by rivalry of king and parliament'.[83] According to Pease, 'The idea of limiting government by law was in the air'.[84] Since king and parliament could not be trusted to respect the limits of a largely unwritten fundamental law, a natural and practical step by those who had suffered at their hands was to impose on legislative and executive bodies restrictions that are clear, written, and unalterable. The New Model Army had the additional worry of being unpopular with the people and at risk of punitive action by future governments. Some form of written document would be needed, although different views were

[83] C. H. McIlwain, *Constitutionalism Ancient and Modern* (Ithaca: Cornell University Press, 1940).
[84] Pease, 103.

held as to what form it should take, what it should contain, and how it could be made binding.[85] In the first *Agreement of the People,* the Levellers, drawing on the common ground between the common people and the soldiers, take the first step towards giving constitutional status to ideas long-held.

The Levellers had earlier advocated that the rules of government should be set out in a document which all the people would sign. In *A Remonstrance of many thousand citizens* (1646), Overton and Walwyn call for the laws of the nation, which they declare to be 'unworthy [of] a free people', to be 'reduced to an agreement with common equity and right reason, which ought to be the form and life of every government'.[86] These ideas are developed a year or so later in *The Case of the Army Truly Stated,* where the author, probably Sexby or Wildman, after adverting to the grievances of both soldiers and commoners, and parliament's failure to address them, expresses three main ideas: that all power is 'originally and essentially in the whole body of the people'; that the people delegate that power to their representatives whom they must freely choose by free election every two years; and that a 'paramount law' be enacted which 'is unalterable by Parliament'.[87] The first *Agreement,* drawing on these ideas, has one principal theme: popular control of government, which has two main components. The first concerns the House of Commons, which would now constitute the parliament, and declares that the people are the source of government authority, which it delegates to the House of Commons, subject to such terms and conditions as the people decide. The practical application of this idea requires: (i) electoral redistribution of parliamentary seats according to the number of the inhabitants; (ii) the dissolution of the Long Parliament at a fixed date and parliamentary elections every two years; (iii) supremacy of the House of Commons, whose power is to be 'inferiour only to those who chuse them'.[88] The second component is to restrict the powers of the House of Commons with respect to several matters, including: religion to be for each person a matter of conscience; conscription and pressing of men into service to be abolished; immunity from acts done during the war; equality before the law; and all laws made by parliament must be for the safety and welfare of the people.

The history of the *Agreements of the People,* interesting and complex as it is, and the charged political atmosphere in which it took place, is beyond the scope of this essay, except for a few remarks. After the debate at Putney, the *Agreement* went through several stages of discussion between Levellers and army officers, until a second *Agreement,* accepted by both parties, was presented to the House of Commons on 20 January 1649. As the trial of the king and his execution were

[85] The army's ideas are set out in *Heads of Proposals* issued on 17 July 1647 and probably written by Ireton or under his supervision. For further discussion of the issues and the rush of writings dealing with them, see Pease, 103 ff.

[86] Overton and Walwyn, *A Remonstrance,* 9.

[87] J. Wildman or R. Sexby, *The Case of the Army Truly Stated* (15 October 1647) in Woodhouse, 429; see also a document accompanying the first *Agreement of the People,* entitled: *Address to the Free-Born People of England.*

[88] This summary is taken from I. Gentles, 'The *Agreements of the people* and their political contexts, 1647–1649' in M. Mendle, *The Putney Debates of 1647,* 150.

about to take place, this was poor timing. The commons never gave its attention to the *Agreement* and the army officers did not press the case.[89] The leading Levellers shortly after found themselves in the Tower from where they issued a third and final *Agreement.* But the moment had passed and it fell on deaf ears.

The *Agreement* in various versions merits fuller study than is possible here, where I offer just a few brief comments on its constitutional status, the voting proposals, and the limits on parliament. As to the first, it is often said that the *Agreement* is an early form of written constitution. There is some uncertainty about its status and the intentions of its framers, but the evidence shows that the *Agreement* was not intended to be a draft constitution and lacks many of the elements of a constitution. It was intended to be a real agreement, a genuine social contract, among the people as to the basic structure of government, the powers of parliament, and relations between parliament and the people. The Levellers promoted the *Agreement* as the foundation for a written constitution, which would be drafted by a constituent assembly drawn from the army and the 'well-affected' in each county, meaning those who had supported the parliamentary cause. The constitution would be in the form of an agreement between the people and their parliamentary representatives and would be signed by all 'well-affected' citizens.

As to the issue of voting, exactly where the Levellers stood on the scope of the franchise is not easy to determine and their ideas evolved and changed, with members holding varying views.[90] The first *Agreement* said nothing expressly about voting, although in the course of the debate at Putney, Ireton assumed an extension of the suffrage was implicit in the proposals. Exploiting this assumption in his main line of attack, Ireton argued that universal male suffrage would lead to the levelling of estates and the end of private property. Only property owners and merchants had a sufficiently 'permanent' interest in the affairs of the nation to entitle them to elect members of parliament. The extravagance of Ireton's argument prompted Colonel Thomas Rainsborough to make the most famous speech of the debate in which he spoke of the 'right of the poorest hee that is in England' to have a voice in choosing the government.[91] Later versions of the *Agreement* were more explicit in providing for an extension of voting rights, but they still fell far short of full adult male suffrage. The Levellers intended that the right to vote should be extended beyond the current electorate but different ideas emerged at different times, until the third *Agreement,* which describes the right to vote as a natural right belonging to all men of twenty-one years or more, except servants, recipients of alms, and those who had served the king.

The final matter for comment concerns limits on the law-making powers of parliament. The Levellers had to face the fact that, although parliament is elected by the people and is under a duty to govern for their safety and welfare, there is still the

[89] For a detailed account of the course of the agreements, see Gentles, 'The *Agreements of the people,* 1647–1649' in Mendle, *The Putney Debates of 1647.*

[90] The voting proposals are much debated; see for instance, the Levellers' documents in Woodhouse, 317–38.

[91] 'Debate in the General Council of the Army, Putney Church, 29 October 1647', in Aylmer, 99 ff.

risk that either the people or their representatives will act contrary to the common good and fundamental law, earlier expressed as the dictates of right reason and equally well viewed as the precepts implicit in the constitution. It would be a happy nation where the will of the people expressed in parliament and right reason coincided, but reality is not always so obliging. The Levellers' solution was to put certain matters beyond the powers of parliament. In the first *Agreement* the reserved issues are those listed above.[92] The second *Agreement* retained the limitations with some modification, but in addition attached a list of matters which would be left to the next parliament for consideration. The list is long and includes such matters as: a right not to incriminate oneself; freedom of trade; abolition of excise and tithes; trial by jury; no one to be barred from public office due to his religion; and the abolition of capital punishment except for murder and for attempting to destroy the *Agreement of the People.*[93] The matters reserved in the third and final version are broadly similar.

One matter that should be made plain, and a convenient note on which to end, is that the Levellers were not espousing a form of direct democracy, even if at that they sometimes hint. The constitutional foundation is for them the common good, the issue being how best to achieve it. The Levellers' solution is by a representative parliament that concerns itself with both the welfare of society as a whole and that of all its members. Good laws properly and fairly applied are essential in advancing the good of each member of society. Government is to be representative but it is a particular kind of representation: representatives are to be elected by the people to whom they were to be properly and systematically answerable. The people would truly be principals, the representatives their agents. There is no room for the fiction that parliament represents the people in the sense of embodying them. Nor is there room for the notion that once elected the bond between the people and parliamentarians is suspended, allowing the latter to do as they wish. Representatives have to act for the good of all, as well as their electors; between the two equilibrium has to be established. Accountability means more than answering for their actions at elections; the Levellers had in mind a scheme of systematic scrutiny and questioning, explanation, and justification quite unlike and much more exacting than the form of representative government now to be found in modern constitutions. The Levellers' scheme was neither direct popular rule nor the emaciated form of representative government now commonly accepted. Their scheme had a different pitch: it sought genuinely to ground constitutional authority in the people; it acknowledged the need for effective government in reaching and sustaining the common good; it concluded that government by elected representatives was the form most likely to serve the common good and respect the rights and interests of the people; and it insisted on an informed citizenry being vigorous in

[92] The *Agreement* includes, in addition, a declaration that the laws 'must be good and not evidently destructive to the safety and well-being of the people'.

[93] Discussed more fully in Gentles, 'The *Agreements of the people,* 1647–1649'. Gentles also points out that, at Lilburne's instigation, a second list of matters is attached to the second *Agreement*; they include ridding the nation of lawyers and returning the administration of justice and the court system to local districts.

scrutiny and supervision of government. The chance for the Levellers to test the strength of this structure was denied them. If later experience were to be our guide, we would conclude that the constitutional space between direct popular rule and abdication of authority to representatives and officials is perilously hard to occupy and tame.

VIII. Conclusion

My aim in this essay has been to explain the ideas of the Levellers concerning government, law, and constitution, and to show how their ideas began and developed and why they failed finally to influence events of the 1640s. In pursuing this aim, I propose an understanding of the Levellers which places them centrally in the constitutional and political events of the time, and, I hope, makes them more interesting. It may seem that contemporary societies have finally discovered the holy grail of constitutions, have finally settled on a form broadly suitable for all societies regardless of time or place or history, so that the constitutional crisis of 1640s England is too particular and remote to be of interest. That is not I think true and even if that were, it would still be instructive to know how one fairly small group of Englishmen and -women was forced to reflect on the nature of its constitution, on the place of the people within it, on how to reconcile the will of the people and the need for good government, on the exercise of power and how to control it. These are the issues that preoccupied the Levellers and which remain of central concern for any nation which wishes to have its rights and liberties respected and good government.

6

Locke's Contribution to the Intellectual Foundations of Modern Constitutionalism

Jean-Fabien Spitz

I. Aim and Approach

In order to assess Locke's possible contribution to modern constitutionalism, it might be judicious to start from what could be termed a fully fledged formulation of the very concept of a constitution. Such a definition can nowhere be more efficiently looked for than in Thomas Paine's *Rights of Man*:

> A constitution is a thing antecedent to a government, and a government is only the creature of a constitution. The constitution of a country is not the act of its government but of the people constituting its government. It is the body of elements to which you can refer and quote article by article, and which contains the principles on which the government shall be established, the manner in which it shall be organized, the powers it shall have, the mode of elections, the duration of parliaments, or by what other names such bodies may be called; the powers which the executive part of the government shall have, and in fine everything that relates to the complete organization of a civil government, and the principles on which it shall act and by which it shall be bound. A constitution therefore is to a government what the laws made afterwards by that government are to a court of judicature. The court of judicature does not make the laws, neither can it alter them; it only acts in conformity to the laws made, and the government is in like manner governed by the constitution.[1]

Despite being fully fledged, Paine's definition remains somewhat ambiguous because it contains two very distinct elements which can open the way to two different interpretations of what constitutionalism is today: the power of the people, and the idea that government is bound by principles.

The first interpretation of the definition emphasizes the fact that the constituent power of the people is superior to the constituted power of those who represent the people in government. This amounts to saying that, in a constitutional government, representatives cannot claim for themselves the kind of political supremacy or sovereignty that can belong only to the people as they act by themselves. This is, so to say, the democratic version of constitutionalism, in which the function of a

[1] Thomas Paine, *Rights of Man. Being an Answer to Mr Burke's Attack on the French Revolution*, 2nd ed. (London: 1791), 56–7.

constitution is to make sure that the power of the people is not confiscated by a governing representative group. Bruce Ackerman has recently presented a sophisticated version of this kind of constitutionalism, which defines a constitution as an efficient tool for the preservation of democracy, or for the preservation of the authenticity of the popular will from its possible erosion in the hands of the governing elites.[2]

According to the second interpretation of the definition, constitutionalism means that the government's actions should be bound by principles of the kind asserted in the ten amendments added to the Constitution of the United States in 1790, and that those should be seen as substantial moral principles to which the government's actions must be conformable in order to be legitimate, or, some would say, in order to deserve the democratic character they purport to possess. Since such principles claim that, under a constitutional government, a number of fundamental rights and liberties should always limit the government's actions, to say that government is bound by those principles is to stress constitutionalism less as a democracy-preserving tool than as a freedom-preserving tool. Accordingly, constitutional government is government that respects fundamental rights and sets free its citizens from undue interference in their private rights by collective or public authorities, including those which emanate from the democratic will of the people themselves. We may refer to Ronald Dworkin as a major exponent of this view, which defines constitutional government as a form of power which takes rights seriously and which thus respects the moral independence of each citizen considered as a person invested with equal moral worth. According to Dworkin, no government can be defined as democratic unless it respects rights, so that constitutionalism in the proper sense would necessarily include this second component. On the other hand, a government which would guarantee only that the people can enforce their own interpretation of fundamental rights against the interpretation of the governing elites could be considered neither as a constitutional nor as a free and democratic government. The reason is that the normative quality of democracy can be derived only from the fact that each citizen is treated with equal respect, not from the fact that the constitution ensures that the collective will of the people always prevails.[3] In my view (though I have no time to expand on this claim here) this second interpretation should be taken as the proper meaning of constitutionalism today, and this is the definition with which I would like to try to assess Locke's contribution.

These are relatively modern ideas of constitutionalism and we would not expect to find in Locke the two different views or a discussion of their merits. Locke contributed to the intellectual development of modern constitutionalism by asking how to prevent government, including democratic government, from becoming tyrannical, and how to preserve individual liberty under the government of the majority. He contributed in particular to removing the obstacles created by Hobbes

[2] B. Ackerman, *We The People, vol. 1 Foundations* (Cambridge, MA: Harvard University Press, 1991).

[3] R. Dworkin, *Law's Freedom* (Cambridge, MA: Harvard University Press, 1999).

and Filmer, which prevented the full development of a concept of constitutionalism in the seventeenth century.

II. Hobbes, and Locke's *Second Treatise*

The obstacles are easily formulated as the Hobbesian dilemma: how, Hobbes asked, could the government be bound or limited by moral principles? Moral principles need to be interpreted, since their consequences in particular cases are not obvious. If the government is the authorized interpreter of those principles, it is bound only as far as it wants to be, and any real limitation vanishes. If, on the other hand, the subjects are considered to be ultimate interpreters, two solutions are possible. First, the sovereign interpreter is the body of the people acting through its majority. In this case, the government is not supreme and the people become in turn the sovereign power, which is what we wanted to prevent by restricting political power by moral principles. In the second solution, the people are the ultimate interpreters, each person for himself. In this case, according to Hobbes, we are back to the state of nature where each man is at the disposal of his own reason and of his own strength in order to defend and preserve himself. Hobbes's conclusion is thus simple: there is no middle way between arbitrary sovereignty without moral bounds and anarchy. If we have a sovereign, the very concept implies that it cannot be bound unless it wants to be; and if we have no unbound sovereign, we have neither a political society nor common protection.

Why, one might ask, are we faced with this simple alternative between the people as a corporate sovereign and the people as a simple multitude in which each member is at the disposal of his own will? Why is it impossible for those who hold political power to be bound and limited by the people—a collective body which would not be a true sovereign without ceasing to be a collective body and without being susceptible to being assimilated to anarchy? Hobbes's answer to this question is straightforward and well known: no multitude of men has one will, or is able to act in any way to limit political power or to interpret moral standards, unless it is represented by a sovereign body, whether individual or collective, and unless it itself is a sovereign political power. According to Hobbes:

> By *multitude*, because, it is a collective word, we understand more than one; so as a multitude of men is the same with many men. The same word, because it is of a singular number, signifies one thing, namely one multitude. But in neither sense can a multitude be understood to have one will given to it by nature, but to each a several; and therefore, neither is any one action whatsoever be attributed to it. Wherefore a multitude cannot promise, contract, acquire right, convey right, act, have, possess and the like, unless it be every one apart, and man by man, so as there must be as many promises, compacts, rights and actions as men. Wherefore a multitude is no natural person. But if the same multitude do contract one with another, that the will of one man, or the agreeing wills of the major part of them, shall be received for the will of all, then it becomes one person. For it is endued with a will, and therefore can do voluntary actions such as commanding, making laws, acquiring and transferring of right and so forth; and it is oftener called the people than the multitude. We

must therefore distinguish thus. When we say the people or the multitude wills, commands or does anything, it is understood that the city which commands, wills and acts by the will of one, or the concurring will of more; which cannot be done but in an assembly. But as oft as anything is said to be done by a multitude of men, whether great or small, without the will of that man or assembly of men, that is understood to be done by a subjected people, that is, by many citizens together, and not proceeding from one will, but from diverse wills of diverse men; who are citizens and subjects, but not a city.[4]

If Hobbes is right, the people cannot exist as a collective entity outside the institutionalized form of a settled government, or independently of the representative person or persons who bear its unity. So, if the collective entity of people binds the government, either it is itself an unbound sovereign body, or it is unable to bind because it is unable to act. How can any political entity be able to bind without being itself unbound? Such is the question. Robert Filmer made a similar point in his attack on Philip Hunton in *The Anarchy of a Limited or Mixed Monarchy*, published in 1648.

Constitutionalism in the proper sense thus requires a third entity which pertains to neither the rulers nor the ruled: a body which is not a body; a corporate entity which is not incorporated so as to become an arbitrary sovereign; a bizarre institution able to state what rights require, while being constitutionally unable to make law in a sovereign and supreme way. No constitutional theory can be launched without the concept of a society or the idea of the people having a political existence and status outside and independent of the government itself, for how could the government be bound by a constitutional law without such a society being the guardian and interpreter of this higher law? Conversely, no constitutional theory can be prevented from merging into some idea of popular sovereignty and democracy-preserving devices if such a society is not conceived as something other than a corporate body in the full sense of the term, invested with a right to govern and make law whenever it wants to. But how could such a third entity exist if Hobbes is right and if, independently of the process of incorporation by representation which gives birth to the sovereign, there can be no collective body or entity but only discrete and separated individuals acting each under the direction of his own reason and by his own independent will?

Locke's *Second Treatise* is heavily influenced by the consequences of those dilemmas. He tries to formulate the concept of a political entity which would be able to limit any power without being itself an unlimited power. The text bears testimony to the difficulties inherent in formulating such a concept, and, though these difficulties are well known, it is worthwhile showing how, at some nodal points, Locke's thought gravitates towards certain Hobbesian themes, while at the same time being alert to the fact that, were he to submit to such themes, he would

[4] Hobbes, *De Cive*, VI, 1. A little further on in the same paragraph, Hobbes writes: 'Neither must we ascribe an action to the multitude as its own; but if all or more of them do agree, it will not be an action, but as many actions as men. For although in some great sedition, it is commonly said that the people of that city have taken up arms; yet it is true of those only who are in arms, or who consent to them. Whatsoever, therefore, is done by the multitude, must be understood to be done by every one of those by whom it is made up.'

not understand what it means for a citizen to be free and to have rights over public authorities.

The first question is: who shall be the judge in the case of conflict between an executive and a legislative that depends on the will of the executive for its assembling; or, more generally, in the case of conflict between the legislative or the executive and the people on whether the government has or has not betrayed its trust. In chapter XIV, Locke's answer is that, in such cases, there is no judge on earth and that appeal can only be to heaven; more precisely, Locke explicitly claims that the people in their collective capacity cannot be the judge in their contests with the government:

> The people cannot be judge, so as to have by the constitution of that society any superior power to determine and give effective sentence in the case.[5]

This answer parallels the one Locke gave in chapter III to the question: 'Who shall be judge' in the controversies between individuals in 'the state of nature'. In this case, Locke claims:

> In such controversies, where the question is put 'Who shall be judge?', it cannot be meant who shall decide the controversy, every one knows what Jephta here tells us, that the lord the Judge shall judge.[6]

So, the question is not who shall make the final decision, for it is self-evident that God is the only one to do that. Nor can it be: who shall decide that some other man 'has put himself in a state of war with me and whether I may appeal to heaven'. For the answer to that question cannot be doubted: 'Of that, I myself can only be judge in my own conscience, as I will answer it at the great day to the supreme judge of men.'

The two situations are similar: when I suspect that some person is trespassing on my rights in the state of nature, it is for me to decide whether he is violating the law of nature which gives me the right to resort to resistance and violence. Since I have to answer for this resort to violence before God, no one can take such a decision in my stead. In the same way, when I or we suspect that our governors are betraying their trust and putting themselves in a state of war with us, it is for each of us to decide whether to resort to violent resistance. We cannot entrust such a decision to a collective or a majoritarian decision without escaping our moral responsibilities.

But in chapter XIX, Locke's answer has a different ring.

> Who shall be judge whether the prince or legislative act contrary to their trust? . . . To this I reply: The people shall be judge . . . If a controversy arise betwixt a prince and some of the people, in a matter where the law is silent, or doubtful, and the thing of great consequence, I should think the proper umpire in such a case should be the body of the people. Or in cases where the prince has a trust reposed in him and is dispensed from the common ordinary rules of the law, there, if any men find themselves aggrieved and think the prince acts

[5] (§168). [6] (§21).

contrary to or beyond that trust, who so proper to judge as the body of the people (who at first lodged that trust in him) how far they meant it to be extended?[7]

Locke's answer is framed in the context of a conflict between the executive and the people, without mention of a possible conflict between the people and the legislative branch. Nevertheless, Locke's idea seems to be that the people, constituted as a political society and acting as a collective body by the voice of its majority, are the supreme judge of the government's behaviour, the main reason being that the one who gave the trust is naturally the only one qualified to judge whether it is betrayed or not.

However, in the very paragraph inserted between the two elements of the above quotation, Locke seems to have something different in mind and to revert to what he said in § 168: each man has to judge for himself, and not the collective body of the people:

Every man is judge for himself, as in all other cases, so in this, whether another man has put himself in a state of war with him and whether he should appeal to the supreme judge, as Jephta did.[8]

A second textual difficulty touches on the distinction between the dissolution of society and the dissolution of government. Sometimes, and in line with his claim that one should distinguish between the dissolution of government and the dissolution of society, Locke seems to say that political society continues under the form of a perfect democracy after the dissolution of the government as it was trusted in some specific hands. But, on other occasions, he seems to imply that no constituted society can subsist independently of the government, and that, if government is dissolved, men are back in the state of nature where every man is at the disposal of his own will. Since perfect democracy and the state of nature seem to be mutually exclusive, this is a very serious textual difficulty indeed.

Let's start with the texts where Locke clearly suggests this second interpretation. He writes:

He that has once, by actual agreement, and any express declaration, given his consent to be of any commonweal, is perpetually and indispensably obliged to be and to remain a subject to it, and can never be again in the liberty of the state of nature, unless by any calamity, the government he was under comes to be dissolved.[9]

The meaning of this text seems clear: when government is dissolved, whatever the manner of this dissolution ('any calamity'), subjects are no longer subjects since they are again 'in the liberty of the state of nature' where each of them can provide for himself as he sees fit.

Again in chapter XIX, Locke says that 'everyone is at the disposure of his own will when those who had, by the delegation of the society, the power to declare the public will are excluded from it, and others usurp the place who have no such authority or delegation'.[10] Locke is speaking here of usurpation, that is of one of the

[7] (§ 240 and 242). [8] (§ 241). [9] *Second Treatise*, ch. VIII. [10] ST § 212.

ways the government can be dissolved from within. Nevertheless, when he states the consequences of such a dissolution of government, he clearly resorts to an expression which is fit to describe the state of nature and which cannot refer to civil society: 'every one is at the disposure of his own will.'

Unfortunately, Locke seems to say the opposite in several other passages of the *Second Treatise*. In §211 he deals with 'what makes the community and brings men out of the loose state of nature into one politic society' and claims that the only act capable of giving birth to such a society 'is the agreement which every one has with the rest to incorporate and act as one body, and so be one distinct commonwealth.'[11] His point is that such a society remains intact when the government is dissolved from within and that it can be dissolved only by foreign conquest upon it. He adds that, when society is conquered, the government cannot exist as before. The reader should understand Locke's statement in the following way: the government cannot subsist when the society is dissolved and society can be dissolved only by external conquest; conversely, society can and must subsist when government is dissolved from within, that is through the alteration of the legislative by its legitimate incumbents or through the usurpation of this same legislative by those who have no authority or 'delegation' to exercise it. The consequence is that, when government is dissolved for any cause other than foreign conquest, men are not back in the state of nature; they are back to political society under the sovereign law of the majority as defined in chapter VIII (§§ 95–96)[12] and as described in chapter X (§132) under the name of a 'perfect democracy'.[13] Locke stresses that this political society is poles apart from the state of nature and that those entering it have an obligation which is entirely absent in the natural condition: 'an obligation to submit to the determination of the majority and to be concluded by it.'[14]

Locke speaks in the same key in the final paragraph of the *Second Treatise*: 'The power that every individual gave the society when he entered into it can never revert to the individuals again as long as the society lasts but will always remain in the community.' One notes that community and political society are used as equivalent terms, and also that this community is placed forever under the direction of its majority. Such a community can place the legislative and other functions of government in particular hands with or without time conditions. If, during the time conceded or at any time under an unlimited concession, those to whom this authority is entrusted forfeit their trust, their authority reverts to the society, and the people have a right to act as the legislative body themselves, or to erect a new

[11] ST §211.

[12] ST VIII, §§ 95–96: 'When any number of men have consented to make one community or government, they are thereby presently incorporated and make one body politic, wherein the majority have a right to act and conclude the rest. For, when any number of men have, by the consent of every individual, made a community, they have thereby made that community one body with a power to act as one body, which is only by the will and the determination of the majority.'

[13] ST §132: 'The majority having, as has been shewed, upon men's first uniting into society, the whole power of the community naturally in them, may employ all that power in making laws for the community from time to time, and executing these laws by officers of their own appointing; and then the form of government is a perfect democracy.'

[14] ST §97.

form, or keep the old form, but place it in new hands. No mention is made here of the state of nature nor of individuals being at the 'disposure' of their own will, since every one remains perpetually obligated to abide by what the majority of the community decides.

My conclusion is that it is not possible to dissolve these textual discrepancies in order to reduce them to a single coherent meaning. I suggest that they reveal some contradictory tendencies in Locke's political thought which may be vital in understanding the way he contributed to modern constitutionalism.

When Locke says that the body of the people is the supreme judge in its conflict with those to whom the legislative or executive powers have been entrusted, and when he says that, upon the dissolution of the government from within, political power reverts to the community acting through its majority, he is under the spell of a Hobbesian concept of sovereignty. His claim seems to be that, from the first moment of their association, men are absolutely subjected to the majoritarian decisions of the body of which they became members, so that this body is a kind of Hobbesian sovereign. If this were not the case, he argues, there would be no difference between civil society and the state of nature. Becoming a member of a political community would add no new obligations to those that men were submitted to in the state of nature. Locke writes:

> This original compact, whereby he with others incorporates into one society, would signify nothing, and be no compact, if he be left free, and under no other ties than he was before in the state of nature. For what appearance would there be of any compact, what new engagement if he were no farther tied by any decrees of the society than he himself thought fit and did actually consent to. This would be still as great a liberty as he himself had before his compact, or any one else in the state of nature has, who may submit himself and consent to any acts if he thinks fit.[15]

Several remarks should be added in order to complete this first interpretation.

First, separation of powers remains a possibility which could break or contain any tendency to absolutism. But the point is, as Hobbes suggests, that such a mixed political power is no less absolute or arbitrary than a unitary one when its various components act in agreement with one another, and that, when they cannot agree, such a disagreement makes it impossible to act. In the interpretation under review, Locke would have to say that separation of powers leads either to arbitrary power or to the absence of government.

Second, it might be suggested that in this interpretation, no Hobbesian sovereign is present in Locke's political theory, since Locke says that the power of the people is extinct or dormant while the government is acting conformably within the frame of its trust. The people would only exist on certain occasions, namely, when the government is dissolved. But this is a non-starter, for the people have to be alive and well in order to decide that the government has forfeited its trust, and so one cannot claim that the people as a sovereign body reappears after the government has been dissolved. Thus to say that the body of the people is dormant or inactive while the

[15] ST, § 97.

government functions is no remedy to the danger of arbitrary power in the majority of the people.

Third, there are some hints in Locke's text of the idea that popular sovereignty, or an unlimited sovereign power in the hands of the body of the people, is less dangerous, less noxious, and less prone to being arbitrary than that same kind of unlimited power in the hands of a king or an aristocracy. This suggests Locke's ideas are a forerunner to Rousseau's *volonté générale,* according to which the liberty of the subject depends on the idea that nobody can wish to hurt himself.[16] Such an equation of liberty with perfect democracy or popular sovereignty is not Locke's main idea, and he does not trust individual liberties and rights to the good will of the majority. Locke distances himself from any idea that the voice of the people should be taken as the voice of God when it comes to moral questions about rights and the content of the law of nature; to do so would be to cancel each person's moral responsibility to interpret the law of nature.

Fourth, even if Rousseau was yet to make his contribution, some political thinkers in the monarchomach tradition embraced the view that all governors were simply the officers of the people, that they could be dismissed or replaced at will, and that the body of the people remained always supreme and superior to them. There is a major difference between this monarchomach tradition and the concept of popular sovereignty we would have to attribute to Locke if we adopted this interpretation. In the monarchomach tradition, the people is a differentiated whole, placed under the direction of its wisest members (*sanior* or *valentior pars*), so that the decision of the people is not the arbitrary decision of a majoritarian will, but the informed and rational decision by some immanent wisdom lodged in that body and able to perceive what is just and reasonable and right. Nothing of the kind is to be found in Locke's writings, since one of his postulates is that every man has equal access to reason, so that any idea of natural subordination or natural direction of the less wise by the wisest is excluded. We still have to face, if we adopt this interpretation, a voluntarist view of the people's majoritarian decision. Locke will have no version of *major pars* as *sanior* or *valentior pars* since this is not compatible with the egalitarian premises from which he starts.

But the consequences of this interpretation are even worse than that. Suppose we claim that as soon as we have consented to be members of a political society, we are irremediably and forever placed under the sovereign will of the majority which can force us to act in a certain way. Suppose further that this majority-led body can delegate and reclaim powers at will, and that it has the capacity to decide at any moment that the government is betraying its trust and that it is thereby dissolved, with the power to act immediately reverting into the hands of that majority-led community or society. One of the inconveniences of such an interpretation is that

[16] For instance ST §57 where Locke seems to suggest a distinction between private and public will: the private will of another is of necessity an arbitrary will, whereas to live within the allowance of the law of the community would mean to be free of arbitrary power, the implication being that the law of the community can only be non-arbitrary or just. Henry Parker seems to have hinted at the idea that the people is unable to want its own wrong and that its collective will is thus necessarily innocuous (Henry Parker, *Observations upon some of His Majesties Late Answers and expresses* (London, 1642)).

the dissolution of the government would give birth to a form of government, namely 'pure' or 'perfect' democracy as Locke names it.[17] This is incoherent, at least from the point of view of vocabulary.

But there is more to come: such an interpretation is certainly compatible with constitutionalism in the sense of a democracy-preserving device, but it is clearly not compatible with constitutionalism as an individual rights-preserving device, for how could an individual be said to have such rights if he is obliged forever to submit to the decisions of the community acting through the voice of its majority? How can any individual be said to have moral rights against public authority if he is, as Locke says on several occasions, 'bound by his own consent to be concluded by the majority', or if he puts himself, by his own consent, 'under an obligation to every one of that society, to submit to the determination of the majority and be concluded by it'?[18] There is no personal freedom if the law can dispose as it pleases of our lives and liberties.

Moreover, such an interpretation is in conflict with one of the themes at the very heart of Locke's moral theory: that each man is placed under the authority of the moral law of nature and each man has to decide for himself and by himself whether some action is conformable or contrary to this law. This is the notion of personal moral responsibility which Locke emphasizes in his *Letter Concerning Toleration*: one cannot consent to be unconditionally led by the moral judgement of some other person, since, if this judgement is wrong, this person will not be able either to assume its consequences—we alone will have to bear them—or to compensate us for what we shall have lost in consequence of such a poor choice.[19] Since I will be the one who bears the consequence, I am the one to decide if this or that action is right or wrong.

For all these reasons, and despite the tendency to endorse the idea of the people as a kind of Hobbesian sovereign whose majority can conclude any individual member without any reservation as being present in the text of the *Second Treatise*, I suggest that this cannot be Locke's intention since it is incompatible with his vision of man as a moral being invested with the responsibility of his choices. If being a member of a political society implies that one can be unconditionally obliged to abide by a majoritarian decision of which one does not approve or which seems clearly to be morally wrong, there is incompatibility between being a citizen and being a moral creature of God. Besides, it would be impossible to think that the government is limited by a constitution stating the moral rights of individuals since the only thing that the constitution would guarantee would be that the collective will of the people will always be able to prevail upon the will of the government. But this is democracy, not liberal constitutionalism.

Is there an alternative solution? The answer is yes, but, as I suggest, it is not perfectly satisfactory since it forces us to bear some heavy theoretical casualties and to accept a drastic reformulation of what we are accustomed to place under the label of 'Locke's political thought'.

[17] Chapter X, ST §132. [18] ST §97. [19] ST §21.

The basis of this second interpretation is the alternative answer to our two questions: who shall be judge of whether another has put himself into a state of war with me? And what is the distinction between the dissolution of society and the dissolution of the government? On the first question, we have now to start from a different answer: the judge is not the body of the people acting through its majority, but 'each man for himself'; and on the question of the two dissolutions, the starting point is now that when the government is dissolved 'what is left is not perfect democracy but a kind of anarchy or state of nature' where every individual is at the disposal of his own will.

At first sight, this is impossible to swallow since this would simply erase any distinction between the natural and the civil condition, although Locke himself explicitly claims that making such a distinction is his major intellectual aim in writing the *Treatises*, and that 'inconveniences must certainly be great where men may be judges in their own case.'[20] In § 88, where he sets out to define civil or political society, Locke makes very clear that such a society is based on the fact that all private judgement is excluded:

> There and there only is political society, where every one of the members has quitted this natural power [to judge by himself whether the others have offended against the law of nature], resigned it up into the hands of the community in all cases that exclude him not from appealing for protection to the law established by it. And thus, all private judgement of every particular member being excluded, the community comes to be umpire by settled standing rules, indifferent and the same to all parties, and by men having authority from the community for the execution of those rules, decides all the differences that may happen between any members of that society concerning any matter of right.[21]

A few lines further on, Locke claims that it is very easy to discern those who are in a political society from those who are still in the state of nature: when political society exists no one is judge for himself because all have a common established law and judicature to appeal to with authority to decide controversies between them, but where the state of nature is still in existence, this means that there is no common appeal and that each man is both his own judge and executioner.

This text and others seem clear and appear to imply that no private judgement as to what is right or wrong can be allowed inside political society, and that all the members must consider as right what is defined as such by the public law of the community acting through the will of the majority. But, actually, no such conclusion can be drawn from Locke's text if we pay attention to its exact wording: private judgement is excluded, not in all cases, but only in 'cases that exclude not from appealing to the protection of the law'. This means that private judgement is in fact allowed where such an appeal is not available. But the problem is now whether it pertains to the private judgement to decide that such an appeal is not available. Would Locke's answer be that, at all times, the judgement of the legislature on such a question must be considered by each member as his own judgement? If so, he would then be a Hobbesian putting forth the concept of an arbitrary sovereignty in

[20] ST § 13. [21] ST § 88.

the hands of the community. Or, in others terms, he would say that there is no right of resistance and no moral responsibility attached to individual conscience either. But such is not Locke's thought. What he implies, on the contrary, is that it pertains to each individual conscience and reason to scrutinize the legislative's actions in order to decide whether they amount to the impartial judgement that all intended to procure for themselves when they entered civil society. In this sense, it is for each man individually to decide whether the impartial judge is still available or not. If any individual is convinced that such is not the case and that, instead of protecting the lives and properties of the citizens by impartial judgments, the legislative is leading them to servitude and thereby forfeiting its trust, it is each citizen's moral responsibility to appeal to the conscience of his fellow citizens and to invite them to join in his own judgements of the situation. If there was a quasi-unanimous non-formal agreement on this fundamental question of several individual persons judging in the same way and drawing the same conclusions, it would amount to that non-constituted or non-political society which is needed in order to launch constitutionalism as an intellectual project, since it opens the way to the possibility of a moral judgement which is common without being the judgement of an incorporated body.

Locke's view is thus that the government is monitored not by a political institution or by a settled or constituted body, as would be the case if it were monitored by the body of the people acting through the voice of its majority, but by a moral power lodged in a series of separate and independent moral consciences, which, on crucial occasions, can converge in their moral judgements. More precisely, the government is monitored by moral principles of right which are interpreted by these separate consciences.

Several comments are appropriate on this solution to our dilemma.

Locke did not invent such a solution, since it was available in two political tracts with which he was acquainted: George Lawson's *Politica Sacra et Civilis* and Philip Hunton's *A Treatise of Monarchy* (1644).[22] Another widely diffused text wherein such a quasi-anarchical position was defended and even heavily accentuated was Samuel Rutherford's *Lex, Rex*.[23]

III. Locke, Lawson, Hunton, and Rutherford

These three texts are based on a distinction between an association and a body politic properly constituted. When people associate together, they remain out of

[22] P. Hunton, *A Treatise of Monarchy containing two parts: 1. concerning monarchy in general; 2. concerning this particular Monarchy* (London, 1643); P. Hunton, *A vindication of the Treatise of Monarchy* (London, 1644); G. Lawson, *Politica Sacra and Civilis or a model of civil and ecclesiastical government*. Locke owned the works of these authors. Cf. J. Harrison and P. Laslett, *The Library of John Locke* (Oxford: Oxford University Press, 1971); on their influence on Locke's thought, see J. H. Franklin, *Locke and the Theory of Sovereignty* (Cambridge: Cambridge University Press, 1978).

[23] S. Rutherford, *Lex, Rex: The Law and the Prince* (London, 1644); on Samuel Rutherford, see J. Coffey, *Politics, Religion and the British Revolution* (Cambridge: Cambridge University Press, 1997).

the bonds of subjection to a politically constituted authority, which means that they are not subjects in the proper sense of the term and they have no obligation to any human power; it also means that no man is obliged to obey another or to submit his will to another will, whether individual or collective. This freedom from any obligation to any human power includes a freedom not to be bound by any majority decision and to remain outside the community, if one thinks that the means provided for the common preservation are not conformable to the law of nature as one interprets it. This association or community has nothing to do with what Locke calls perfect democracy.

On the other hand, what distinguishes such an association from a mere state of dispersion is firstly a resolution taken by each person to provide, together with the others and not each by himself, for their common preservation and to look together for the best means to realize such an aim. But, each member retains the right to disapprove of the moral quality of the means which are planned and to stay outside the plan if he thinks that to do this is the only way to submit to his own moral convictions. The second distinctive feature of this association is the capacity to achieve such aims and to establish a political power to which each of the participants will submit his will and which each of them would trust with the preservation of his life, property, and liberty. Such a community is a moral community where people remain equal in power and politically independent, but where they share and accept each for himself common moral principles of right and decency. We may define such a community as being made up of those who agree on such common principles, while those who disagree remain outside, with the result that the association is necessarily unanimous.

People so associated share a common moral aim but lack an agreement as to the best way to make their principles effective; they also lack an umpire capable of solving the potential disagreements which can arise about the application of such principles in particular cases. Since they have a capacity to decide on the best way to make sure that their common principles of right are respected and enforced, and since the establishment of a common political power is the best way to attain such an effect, one can say that they have in them a potential political power though they have no such power actually extant.

George Lawson's vocabulary to express this difference distinguishes between *civitas* (community) and *res publica* (commonwealth), and between *cives* (citizens) and *subdit* (subjects). The community of citizens, which is a community only by the virtue of the moral and non-political bonds between its various members, is not a *res publica* since it has no instituted political power to which it can resort in order to settle disagreements.[24] In such a community, men are equal from the point of view of power and none can be constrained to accept another will but his own as a rule for his conduct. The main point is that this community of equals is potentially political in the sense that it has a power to institute a political power. Once it is instituted as a *majestas personalis*, such political power is an instrument which the

[24] G. Lawson, *Politica sacra et civilis*, ed. C. Condren (Cambridge: Cambridge University Press, 1992), ch. 15, 218–20.

citizens of the pre-political community or *majestas realis* give to themselves for the preservation of their good and liberty. As far as the *majestas personalis* is an instrument, it is subordinated to the *majestas realis* and it stands only as long as its acts conform to the good of the community. As far as the *majestas realis* is not an actual but only a potential political power, the *majestas personalis* is really supreme in the *res publica* since it has no rival, no power which could limit or constrain it. *In nuce*, this is the solution to the Hobbesian dilemma: the limiting factor is not the same kind as the limited factor, so that its limiting faculty does not put it into the position of a new sovereign. The limiting factor is a moral community made of separate and equal free citizens, each placed under the sole direction of his own will and rationally agreeing on some moral principles of right and decency: the limited factor is a collective body, the members of which are subordinated to the supreme and unrivalled power of its majority. The community is supreme because it has a power to constitute power but it is not sovereign in the sense of a constituted power, and this is the concept of a constituent power as opposed to a constituted one. One consequence is that the constituted political entity (the *pars imperans*) has no power to reframe or change its own constitution or redefine its own trust, since such a power belongs exclusively to the community acting in its constituent capacity. Conversely, the constituent power has no power to make laws but only a power to establish a power to make laws. Nowhere in the Lawsonian political society can be found the Hobbesian unlimited sovereign, and the fragmentation of this sovereign in two different powers, constituent and constituted, opens the way to constitutionalism as a freedom-preserving device, since citizens have rights by way of the limits the constitution assigns to the *pars imperans*, while the power which defines those limits is itself devoid of any direct power to legislate for them.

What happens to the right of resistance in such a context? The answer is that there is no such right *inside* the constitution, and that no constituted body has any right to declare that the government is no longer in existence because it has betrayed its trust. No political entity has the right to deprive the government of its authority to legislate, but there is a moral community invested with the right to declare the fact that the government has forfeited its trust and is dissolved. The consequence of such a statement is not that the legislative power reverts to the hands of the community, because the community as such never had such power. The more accurate position is that the power to legislate disappears, that it vanishes with the institution in which it was invested. It may be re-established, either in the same form but in different hands or in another form. This has to be done by the community acting in its constituent capacity, in the same manner as it established a government for the first time.

One last point has to be added: when Lawson defines the community in *Politica Sacra et Civilis*, he makes a distinction between obligation and constraint. Citizens (as opposed to subjects) do have equal authority and no one can be constrained by another, but this does not mean that they are equal in wisdom, so that some of them, the less wise, who are simply *formaliter cives*, are morally obliged to follow the reason of the most wise who, according to Lawson, are *eminenter cives*.[25] So the community is devoid of relations of power, but not of subordination, hierarchy, and organisation since it is naturally led by its *sanior pars*. In his *Examination of the political part of Mr Hobbes* (1657), Lawson seems to abandon this theory and to replace it with a simpler idea: the community must now be defined not as an organism made of hierarchized reasons which would be naturally represented by the wisest, but as a collection of rational individuals who are as equal in wisdom as they are in power. This new definition stems from the fact that Lawson now contends that each person has to assume moral responsibility for his judgements, so that no one can be excused for having judged wrongly on the pretext that he followed another whom he considered wiser and more competent than himself.

Rutherford and Hunton also in turn resort to this distinction between community and commonwealth, but not without the individualistic premise which leads to the concept of the pre-political community as a collection of persons equal in their judgements, who have to assume separately and each for himself the consequences of their judgements.

Looking to Hunton in particular, we see that he is careful to say that the community is not a constituted body acting through its majority, and that in the case of a major conflict of interpretation about right and wrong between the government and the citizens, the community is not the constituted judge of the government's behaviour. To define the community in such a way would be to define it as a Hobbesian sovereign. But, as Hunton makes clear, no individual liberty is available under such a democratic sovereign and no individual rights could be protected against the will of the majority. This is what Hunton means when he says that 'the people is not judge in its own cause' implying that the people is not judge as a constituted body in accordance with a human law, but that the members of the people are judges as a collection of consciences in accordance with a natural and higher law. Their power is moral, not political—or, in other words, the people does not judge in accordance with the constitution, but in accordance with the moral principles the constitution is meant to embody.[26]

Again, Hunton is very clear on the fact that, in the community, there is no political power to constrain and no obligation to follow the wisest members either, and he stresses the principle of individual moral responsibility without any ambiguity: no man can trust the supposed wisdom of some other person when it comes to a decision as to what is right or wrong, but everyone has to judge by himself as an independent reasonable creature since everyone will have to bear the consequences of his decisions. If we trust some other person with the decision and if the decision is wrong, those who have misled us will not be able to compensate for the negative consequences we will have to bear, and this is why each of us must exercise personally his moral responsibilities.

Hunton also endorses the charge of anarchy: when the government is dissolved it is true to say that literally speaking there is no power and that we are in a state of

[25] Women and children are said in turn to be *diminute cives*.

[26] P. Hunton, *A Treatise of Monarchy*, Part I, chapter 2, section VII.

anarchy. This is not to accept Hobbes's idea that we are in a state of war of all against all. The state of nature is governed by a moral law of nature which each man has access to thanks to reason, so that this anarchical state which reappears when government disappears is less a state where there is no law than a state where there is no instituted power to interpret and enforce that law in particular cases.[27]

Now this seems to be what Locke wishes to say regarding the right of resistance and the dissolution of the government: no instituted political body inside the constitution has any right to judge that the government is leading towards servitude and that it has forfeited its trust; but in some cases violation of the principles of the law of nature are so clear and so evident that not a single citizen invested with a normally functioning reason can have any doubt about what is happening. In this case, each man, judging by himself, may appeal to the reason and conscience of his fellow citizens with a claim that government is effectively dissolved. This is not a formally constituted procedure but a moral appeal to individual judgements and, if there is enough of a wide convergence on such a judgement, then the citizens are freed from the bonds of subjection and free to reconstitute another government, either under the same form but in different hands, or under another form if they think it fit.

As John Simmons has rightly noticed,[28] this places Locke's political society on the edge of anarchy but, as with Hunton, the edge is not crossed, since Locke seems to suggest that rational or reasonable individuals do in fact agree on the broadest principles of right and decency they want their political association to be built around. This agreement is not a contract but the precondition of a contract: it is a pre-political agreement to which any contract giving birth to political institutions must conform in order to be legitimate. This requires us to correct our ordinary view of Locke's fundamental tenet: consent is not the basis of legitimacy and obligation, since only consent as it is conformable to those pre-political principles of right can be the basis of both legitimacy and moral obligation to abide by what is consented to. But this is precisely what liberal constitutionalism is about: no law, no institution can be legitimate, even with the greatest majority's consent, if it is in contradiction with some fundamental principles of right which are considered to be the basis of our association, or to be the principle of reciprocal behaviour for the protection of which our very association is supposed to have been founded. This means that all those who live or want to live in the territory where the constitution stating those principles is established are presumed to agree with those principles so that, at the basis of the political consent by which we govern ourselves, there is non-political moral convergence, which is not a formal consent, on the principles which our political agreements cannot violate without losing their legitimacy and their power to oblige us.

Admittedly, those very moral principles have to be interpreted, since claiming that all citizens have a right to the equal protection of the law leaves ample room for disagreement about who is qualified to be a citizen and what the equal protection of

[27] P. Hunton, *A Treatise of Monarchy*, Part I, chapter 2, section VII.

[28] J. A. Simmons, *On the Edge of Anarchy* (Princeton: Princeton University Press, 1993).

the law implies in particular cases. In the recent period, some fascinating works about the Constitution of the United States, for instance those of Akhil Reed Amar and Larry Kramer,[29] suggest that the original intention of the Framers was to give no decisive answer to the question of who, inside the constitution, must be the final and authorized interpreter of those principles. They suggest that the Congress and the Presidency, as well as the judiciary, were invested with this moral responsibility and that the debate between various institutions would be the ideal setting for citizens to exercise their moral responsibilities in deciding fundamental questions of political morality. The practice of the American government seems to have taken another direction, and to have trusted the Supreme Court with the final power to arbitrate on right and wrong in moral matters, but it is not quite sure that this is faithful to the intellectual tradition to which Locke was giving the final touch when he was writing the *Second Treatise* because it is not quite sure—Dworkin's claim to the contrary notwithstanding—that relying on the judiciary is the best way for the people, meaning each citizen considered individually, to exercise his moral responsibility.

[29] A. R. Amar, *The Bill of Rights, Creation and Reconstruction* (New Haven: Yale University Press, 1998); A. R. Amar *America's Constitution: A Biography* (New York: Random House, 2005); L. D. Kramer, *The People Themselves: Popular Constitutionalism and Judicial Review* (New York: Oxford University Press, 2004).

7

Narrative Constitutionalism and the Kinetics of James Harrington's *Oceana*

J. C. Davis

I

After Thomas Hobbes's *Leviathan* and John Locke's *Two Treatises of Government*, James Harrington's *Oceana* has been perhaps the most discussed political text from that most fertile period in the history of English political thought, the seventeenth century.[1] Yet, while the first two of these three works gave priority to issues of rights and obligations, the limits of authority or their absence, but had comparatively little to say about the detailed workings and machinery of government, Harrington's approach was the reverse of this.[2] He lavished attention on all of the civil, military, and religious processes and practices of every parish, hundred, and county, as well as those of the newly bound nation of Britain. The result is a level of detail and complexity, which, allied with his penchant for exotic names, has given Harrington's work, amongst both students and scholars, a reputation for inaccessibility if not incomprehensibility. Harrington was well aware of the problem and commented on it a number of times. As with the customs of his contemporaries, what perplexed were words and description, while deeds and practice should be clear to all. Harrington, the poet and lyricist,[3] knew the importance of literary form and style. In the four years after *Oceana*'s first publication (1656) he experimented with a number of genres, including dialogue and aphorism, to get a substantially consistent message across. But, for him, it was narrative which most effectively brought words and actions into convergence.[4] It is important then to recognize that a further contrast with *Leviathan* and the *Two Treatises* is that in *Oceana* Harrington deliberately chose a narrative mode. His aim in that work was, he said, 'a more

[1] My thanks for their comments and suggestions to Professors Glenn Burgess, Mark Knights, John Morrow, and Jonathan Scott.

[2] Although, if the attribution is correct, Locke followed the detailed Harringtonian model in his drafts for the Constitution of Carolina. For a convenient text see *John Locke: Political Writings*, ed. D. Wooton (London, 1993), 210–32.

[3] D. Norbrook, *Writing the English Republic: Poetry, Rhetoric and Politics* (Cambridge: Cambridge University Press, 1999), 362–4.

[4] Rhetoric was also a mode intended to link words and action via the direct energizing of the will. In part *Oceana* is a narrative of rhetorical performances, several of which also embrace narration.

full and perfect narrative of the whole' [72].[5] The contention of this essay is that, in underlining his deliberate choice of narrative, Harrington offered us a clue as to how we should read *Oceana.* Narrative was the form capable of giving expression to Harrington's belief that government was process or motion, a story as well as a set of rules or propositions. The veracity of the story might be reinforced by analysis but it could only be fully expressed by narrative rather than description.

Oceana's narrative intention was signalled in the concluding words of the epigraph from Horace which was prominently displayed on the title page: '*de te Fabula narratur*'. Hobbes had suggested that his teachings on the nature of man and on the requirements of civil society could be verified by the reader's introspection and a geometric rationality dependent on establishing the proper signification of words.[6] Harrington, by contrast, proposed that only by understanding our history, our story, could we grasp the forces which had brought us to our current condition and distinguish adequately between the means which would deepen our predicament and those which would help us to escape it. *Oceana* was substantially made up of four such histories the first a 'factual' one, the others fictional. These histories followed the First Preliminary of *Oceana,* which was substantially analytical (though supported by narrative case studies). It was, however, integral to the subsequent narratives in providing the keys to understanding the material, moral, and intellectual bases for thinking through contemporary political problems in their historical context and envisaging the practical means by which those problems might be permanently solved. The Second Preliminary provided the first history: an account of the fall from ancient into modern prudence, demonstrating how even the greatest exponents of the latter, Machiavelli and Hobbes, had failed to grapple with the consequences of the history of empire, or shifts in the balance of property ownership. In his second narrative, Harrington gave a heavily fictionalized account of a debate leading to a radically new style of commonwealth which alone could address the problems facing his fellow countrymen. Then came a more lightly fictionalized narration of the processes and sequence of actions by which a perfect and immortal commonwealth might be established, and thereby stability be restored, in England. Finally, Harrington told his story of the consequences of adopting such a commonwealth. This narrative framework embraced much analysis and rhetoric, and did so largely through subordinate narratives. The span of both narrative structure and its narrative underpinnings was truly impressive. It ran from the history of Israel, through Athens, Lacedaemon, Carthage, and Rome to Venice, Switzerland, and Holland, dealing with constitutional arrangements, and their material foundations and political ethos, as well as the actions of individuals and groups. The Second Part of the Preliminaries of *Oceana* was a history of post-Roman feudalism in England, leading on to the story of the collapse of that system in the sixteenth century and thence to an account of England's current troubles.

[5] Unless otherwise indicated references to both *Oceana* and *A System of Politics* will be to *Harrington: Oceana and a System of Politics*, ed. J. G. A. Pocock (Cambridge: Cambridge University Press, 1992). Page numbers will be given in square brackets in the text of my essay.

[6] See *Hobbes: Leviathan*, ed. R. Tuck (Cambridge: Cambridge University Press, 1991), 10.

This epic narration was well beyond anything in Locke or the historical exercises attempted by Hobbes in *Behemoth* or his translation of Thucydides.[7]

There were two underlying reasons for Harrington's choice of the narrative form. In the first place, he believed that experience, direct or vicarious, was the key to political understanding, both in identifying and operating an ideal political system: 'no man can be a politician, except he be first an historian or a traveller' [205]. Only they had the requisite experience of what had been or is possible and therefore could see what might be possible. But the appropriate form of expression for both historians and travellers was narrative. Second, Harrington's intention was not to delineate an inert model but to show the processes by which a viable commonwealth might be built and to witness it in operation. Words were one thing; action another. Description could leave the reader with a sense of alienation. Narrative was designed to make the reader a witness, to equip them with a vicarious experience of a new and unknown system in operation. Conveying action and motion was therefore vital [244–5] and the medium through which to do this was narrative. If the foundations of Hobbes's political philosophy in *Leviathan* lay in internal motion verified by introspection, those of Harrington were in external motion, a narrative tide of the social and institutional shaping of civic persona, behaviours, and political possibilities [72, 75]. Reading Harrington's experiment with, for example, aphorism in such works as *Aphorisms Political* (1659) or *A System of Politics* (written in 1661, published posthumously), one is immediately aware of greater economy, a pithiness which eschews complexity in favour of certainty, an allusiveness which abandons the ambition to show a system in detailed operation. The test for narrative in *Oceana* was whether stability, like disintegration and decline, could support a narrative mode. His answer lay in the dependence of political stability on the internal motions of the *polis*. His science (or *technê*) of politics came closer to that of Harvey's discovery of the heart's function as a circulatory pump [174] than to Hobbes's aspiration to Euclidian finality.

The ultimate question behind Harrington's choice of form was whether constitutions were better stabilized in words or deeds. Are they what we say or what we do? The enactment and maintenance of the Oceanic constitution was through an annual series of scripted performances. 'To philosophise further upon this art [of constitution-making], though there be nothing more rational, were not worth the while, because in writing it will be perplexed and the first practice of it gives the demonstration' [89–90]. Acting was, for this purpose, better than writing.[8] The best way of conveying such acting was through a narrative which functioned at three levels: an account of the kind of debate which would necessarily precede the establishment of the new commonwealth; a narrative of the commonwealth's first establishment or implementation; and the story of the annual rituals through which it was maintained. *Oceana* was very much about ritualized political performances staged within an appropriate political architecture and providing a kind of script for action: a story waiting to be turned into reality, or a piece of theatre waiting to be acted out.

[7] For an example of Harrington's emphasis on the structure of narrative binding *Oceana*, see [75].

[8] Significantly in *Oceana*, the Lord Archon is depicted as preferring action to writing [72].

II

The context of *Oceana*'s writing was itself a story—one of massive extra-constitutional civil violence, repeated national vulnerability and exposure, constitutional collapse, and the recurrent failure of attempts to reconstruct and stabilize the political order. That medium-term chronicle was set by Harrington in a longer-term history of social transformation wrought by property transfers on a scale sufficient to influence and unsettle the distribution of political power.

For the English, chronic instability had been manifest in three civil wars (1642–6, 1648, 1651); three invasions (1640, 1648, 1651); and, following the trial and execution of the king, the abolition of the monarchy and House of Lords. The Church of England had been dissolved by parliamentary ordinance earlier in the mid-1640s. These events underpin the claim that this, the 'English Revolution', was the first modern revolution. The reactions evoked and the expectations unleashed by them led to violent imperial expansion in Ireland and Scotland and, by 1656, the creation of something resembling a *British* state. Nevertheless, victory, revolution, and conquest brought neither stability nor security. In the seven years since 1649 and the declaration that England was a 'Free State' there had been five 'parliaments' and four parliamentary systems (by the Autumn of 1656, a fifth version was under consideration).[9] Meanwhile, a 'government in exile' sought to benefit from continuing uncertainty and economic distress exacerbated by high taxes.[10] Its supporters posed what was thought to be a considerable (and possibly exaggerated) security threat demonstrated as recently as 1655 in Penruddock's rising.

Difficulties in funding the standing military forces, their hostile treatment by some groups within parliaments, and their anxieties about the legal and secure provision for indemnity from prosecution for acts of war had led to the politicization of the military, a politicization verging on mutiny (1647) or resulting in *coups d'état* (Pride's Purge, December 1648; the expulsion of the Rump, April 1653). The situation oscillated unnervingly between military detachment (from early 1649 to April 1653; mid-1653; 1654) and military intervention (December 1648, April 1653, December 1653, August 1655–September 1656). The Instrument of Government, Britain's first written constitution, which was under consideration for revision in 1656, had been drawn up, approved, and imposed by the army in December 1653.[11] It made constitutional provision for the maintenance of a

[9] For Harrington's own estimate of the number of changes of government as eight see *Politicaster* (1659) in *The Political works of James Harrington*, ed. J. G. A. Pocock (Cambridge: Cambridge University Press, 1977), 709. This edition will be hereafter cited as *PWJH*.

[10] Principally to fund an unprecedented military establishment consequent upon the massive expansion of a professional ('mercenary') army and navy.

[11] The starting point for thinking about the Instrument of Government is now Blair Worden, 'Oliver Cromwell and the Instrument of Government', in S. Taylor and G. Tapsell (eds), *The Nature of the English Revolution Revisited: Essays in Honour of John Morrill* (Woodbridge: The Boydell Press, 2013), 123–50.

standing army of 30,000 men as a first charge upon the revenues of the state. In 1655 the country had been divided into ten (later eleven) regions, each to be overseen and in some respects administered by a Major-General supported by a contingent of professional troops. For obvious reasons, this had proven immensely unpopular amongst those used to being governed by their unpaid and unarmed neighbours, the constables, churchwardens, jurymen, overseers, muster masters, and Justices of the Peace to whom so much of the administrative burden, which amounted to governance for most people, had been devolved. This 'unacknowledged republic'[12] of self-governing communities had been under threat, and indeed had been frequently sidestepped, since the outbreak of hostilities in 1642 (if not before), but had not experienced anything as systematically menacing as the Major-Generals. Dismantling their apparatus required a new military settlement and we know that Harrington took a close interest in the Militia Ordinance being debated in parliament in the Autumn of 1656.

The victorious New Model Army, developed over the winter of 1644–5, was, as its name suggests, unprecedented: a professional standing army, officered by men chosen on merit, not aristocrats; a national force, recruited, officered, paid (when it was), and directed nationally, rather than a collection of locally raised and officered amateurs operating with considerable discretion. What had not developed was a 'New Model State', capable of sustaining the military revolution by satisfying its demand for new technologies, strategies, and more highly trained personnel, and consequently for a standing army and navy.[13] Unaddressed, as minimum requirements and in terms of constitutional continuity, were the continuing fiscal, administrative, and logistical necessities of such a force. What was left was a fragile interface between these demands and continued dependence on the unacknowledged republic whose normal expectations were that military activity would be temporary, costs limited, and that a good deal of the control of such activities would remain at the local level rather than being taken over by nationally focussed political groupings with little local knowledge or interest. Renewing that *republica anglorum*[14] itself faced considerable problems. Given the bitter factional divisions resulting from the protracted intra-communal violence associated with the civil wars, the proscription of the defeated (even when they retained substantial influence within their communities), and the record of spasmodic but frequently harsh central interference and coercion, that renewal was highly problematic. 'Healing and settling' or binding the wounds of those bruised communities was not a new project. Both prior to and throughout the civil wars, negotiation to find a

[12] M. Goldie, 'The unacknowledged republic: office holding in early modern England', in T. Harris (ed.), *The Politics of the Excluded c1500–1850* (Basingstoke: Palgrave, 2001), 153–94 provides an excellent summary of the literature on this.

[13] I. Gentles, *The New Model Army in England, Ireland and Scotland 1645–1653* (Oxford: Wiley-Blackwell, 1994); J. S. Wheeler, *The Making of a World Power: War and the Military Revolution in Seventeenth-Century England* (Stroud: Sutton, 1999).

[14] A phrase taken from Sir Thomas Smith's *De Republica Anglorum* and given new vitality in Patrick Collinson's seminal inaugural lecture *De Republica Anglorum: Or, History with the Politics Put Back* (Cambridge: Cambridge University Press, 1990). See also J. F. McDiarmid (ed.), *The Monarchical Republic of Early Modern England: Essays in Response to Patrick Collinson* (London: Ashgate, 2007).

settlement had been pursued. But, to the extent that negotiation had been war by other means, that process had left a good deal of mistrust and sense of betrayal. The wounds had again been re-opened with the introduction of a discriminatory tax on ex-royalists, the decimation tax, in association with the establishment of the Major-Generals system of regional oversight in late 1655.[15]

Before the outbreak of civil war, there had been a culture of faith in the 'ancient constitution' and its capacities as a 'pacificatory polity'.[16] The boast was that the constitution was so well balanced that it could resolve and contain any reasonable conflict of interests (and that the few unreasonable or extra-constitutional ones would be violently suppressed). Much of the negotiation and political discourse of the 1640s had been directed to restoring that balance. In one formulation (*The King's Answer to the XIX Propositions* of June 1642) the constitution was depicted as a balancing of classical forms—monarchy, aristocracy, and democracy—checking the tendency to corruption of any single form.[17] By the late 1640s this had worn thin in the minds of such diverse commentators as Robert Filmer, Henry Parker, the Levellers, and Thomas Hobbes. A mixed monarchy could be depicted as the problem rather than the solution. Nevertheless, many, perhaps a majority, yearned for something like the *status quo ante bellum* but there were enormous practical as well as theoretical obstacles to achieving that outcome—not least of which was the politicized New Model Army, which was not disposed to seeing the fruits of its victories surrendered. But, if not some form of restoration, what? The debate on the choice between constitutional revision or reversion to the ancient constitution was in part the dilemma of following the wishes of the conservative majority back to what could be seen as the bases of the original conflict or embarking on a more full-blown and theoretically considered constitutional revision of the types advocated by various minority groups, with all the risks of alienating the conservative majority which that entailed.[18]

Splits over religion and the fear of religious anarchy had been instrumental in enabling the king to gather sufficient support to fight what has been described as England's war of religion. Equally, on the parliamentary side, there was zeal for 'reforming the Reformation'. By 1646 the Church of England had been legally abolished and its forms of worship proscribed but, despite legislation to establish a Presbyterian church, in practice parochial self-determination in religious matters was the norm and the majority adhered to the observances of Prayer Book Anglicanism. The minority proliferation of sectarians was influential beyond their numbers because the army, in which they wielded considerable influence, favoured

[15] C. Durston, *Cromwell's Major-Generals: Godly Government during the English Revolution* (Manchester: Manchester University Press, 2001).

[16] For comment on the 'pacificatory polity' see D. Baumgold, *Hobbes's Political Theory* (Cambridge: Cambridge University Press, 1988), and G. Burgess, *Absolute Monarchy and the Stuart Constitution* (New Haven: Yale University Press, 1996). Also still useful in this regard is M. Judson, *The Crisis of the Constitution* (New York: Rutgers University Press, 1949).

[17] M. Mendle, *Dangerous Positions: Mixed Government, the Estates of the Realm and the Making of the Answer to the XIX Propositions* (Tuscaloosa: University of Alabama Press, 1985).

[18] For a general account see J. C. Davis, 'Political Thought 1640–1660' in B. Coward (ed.), *A Companion to Stuart Britain* (Oxford: Blackwell, 2003), 374–96.

liberty of conscience.[19] By 1656 tensions remained over whether a national church should be established and between the claims of those who sought to make the nation, willing or not, an instrument of God's will and of those believers in liberty of conscience who thought that to coerce others in matters of faith was to usurp God's authority.

The war had been fought between two minority coalitions and the problem of settlement was compounded by the bruising fragmentation of the victorious coalition.[20] Its disintegration into competing factions had begun with the conduct of the war (peace, war, and middle groups) and the question of the reformation of the church (Independents, Presbyterians, and a proliferation of mutually hostile sectarian groups). The 'Revolution' of 1648–9 underscored these divisions, splitting the political Independents and producing dependence on a very small minority of republicans, pragmatists, opportunists, and millenarians. The imposition of the Protectorate in December 1653 had further alienated republicans and many of the 'saints'. The coalition which had won the war was in ruins and Cromwell, whose long-term interests were civilian, remained critically dependent on the army. That coalition had had sufficient commonality of interest to wage war successfully. But as early as 1647 the divergence of the interests which it embraced had become so great as to prompt John Hall to compare it to a disassembled watch, a scattering of disparate pieces.[21] Settling the nation would require all the skills of a political watchmaker. Paralleling this fragmentation of political interests was a fragmentation of political discourse the emergence of a world of print and speech which appeared to have diminishing coherence, a 'public sphere' out of control.[22] Those who sought a settlement had to think through how to reverse this and achieve a convergence of interests and discursive meaning. For some, like Hobbes or Gerrard Winstanley, this might include the wholesale redefinition and 'fixing' of terms, establishing the proper signification of key words. But, for others, the disjunction between words and deeds had become intolerable.[23] For Harrington, the answer lay in skill both in political architecture, including the management of the spaces of the public sphere, and in the use of words to convey deeds, that is narrative.

The constitution imposed by the army in December 1653, the Instrument of Government, was a serious attempt to square the circle, appeal to all key interests

[19] J. Morrill, 'The Church in England, 1642–1649', in J. Morrill, *The Nature of the English Revolution* (Harlow: Longman, 1983); C. Durston and J. Maltby (eds.), *Religion in Revolutionary England* (Manchester: Manchester University Press, 2006).

[20] For a good general account of this phase see A. Woolrych, *Britain in Revolution 1625–1660* (Oxford: Oxford University Press, 2002); R. Ashton, *Counter-Revolution: The Second Civil War and Its Origins, 1646–1648* (New Haven: Yale University Press, 1994).

[21] J. Hall, *A True Account of the Character of the Times* (1647).

[22] D. Zaret, *The Origins of Democratic Culture: Printing, Petitioning and the Public Sphere in Early Modern England* (Princeton: Princeton University Press, 2000); J. Raymond, *Pamphlets and Pamphleteering in Early Modern Britain* (Cambridge: Cambridge University Press, 2003); J. Peacey, *Politicians and Pamphleteers: Propaganda During the English Civil Wars and Interregnum* (Aldershot: Ashgate, 2004).

[23] For one example amongst many see the writings of Winstanley in T. N. Corns, A. Hughes, and D. Loewenstein (eds), *The Complete Works of Gerrard Winstanley*, 2 vols (Oxford: Oxford University Press, 2009).

and establish a coordinated government of one person accountable to a council which was, in turn, accountable to a representative of the political nation. As a constitutional settlement, it had limped because for the civilians it was tainted by association with the army, for the republicans it was a betrayal, for the saints an apostasy, for royalist sympathizers a usurpation, and for radicals, with its narrowed franchise and single person, too much of a reversion to old forms. In 1654, its first parliament, faced with a considerable legislative programme, had to be substantially purged were it to have any hope of progress, and even so the hoped-for progress was not forthcoming. In 1656 the second parliament saw measures taken to prevent a substantial number of elected members from sitting.[24] The Instrument had failed and needed to be replaced. Debates about what to replace it with began in earnest in 1656 with the publication of Sir Henry Vane's *A Healing Question*, Marchamont Nedham's *The Excellency of a Free State*, Harrington's *Oceana*, and the introduction into parliament of The Humble Petition and Advice. The immediate context out of which Harrington's definitive work emerged was, then, one in which constitutional redesign had both assumed priority on the political agenda but also confronted a host of seemingly intractable problems.

III

James Harrington made extremely limited use of the language of 'constitution' and still less of that of 'constitutionalism'. In *Oceana* he referred to 'the constitution of the late monarchy of Oceana', but in the sense of the building up of that monarchy by the successive interventions of Romans, Saxons, Danes, and Normans [47]. In *A System of Politics* he pointed out that democracy could only be a stable system 'if rightly constituted' [281]. Elsewhere he referred to 'the constitution' as 'the motions of this commonwealth', which were spherical.[25] More often he wrote of the frame, or models of government, of form, institution, 'libration', polity, political architecture, and art. Ancient prudence, which he intended to follow, was 'an art whereby a civil society of men is instituted and preserved upon the foundations of common right or interest' [8]. It was the rule of laws, unlike modern prudence, which, since the fall of the Roman Empire, had been the rule of men pursuing private interests. The institution of a commonwealth should, therefore, mean the rule of laws (*ordini* or orders) rather than of men. Nevertheless, the art whereby governments were constituted was open to definition and exposition. 'Civil government is an art whereby a people rule themselves, or are ruled by others' [269].

[24] For a good recent survey of the problems, see the essays in P. Little (ed.), *The Cromwellian Protectorate* (Woodbridge: Boydell Press, 2007).

[25] He further refined this by arguing that 'spherical motions have their proper centre' and that 'The centre or basis of every government is no other than the fundamental laws of the same'. In *Oceana* these were the agrarian and the ballot [100].

That art was governed by two principles. First, 'All government is interest and the predominant interest gives the matter or foundation of government.' In another formulation, Harrington almost encapsulated the key principles behind his political architecture: 'I speak of a form supported by an interest sufficiently able to bear it, and of an interest contained under a form sufficiently able to secure it.'[26] Second, interest generated political will and was itself generated and sustained (or empowered) by property, by the distribution of the balance of property in land. Where one person owned the balance of land, the only sustainable form of government was absolute monarchy. Where the balance was owned by a few, aristocracy (or what Harrington called 'regulated monarchy') was the appropriate form. Where the many held the balance of land, then the basis existed for democratic rule or a commonwealth [272–3]. In England, since the reign of Henry VII and the expropriation of ecclesiastical property by his son, the balance of ownership in land had shifted from an aristocratic to a democratic basis. However, the superstructures of government had not been adjusted to changes in the foundations—to the balance of land ownership which embodied the social distribution of power. The Stuarts, especially Charles I, had attempted to rule with an aristocracy, which no longer possessed the balance of empire or land, instead of with the people, who did. The consequence of rule against the balance would eventually be violence and instability. But an even 'greater horror' [12], entailing perpetual civil war, arose where the balance of land ownership was equal between some combination of the one, the few, and the many. Even superstructures adjusted to the balance or overbalance of property ownership, as in the case of absolute monarchy or regulated monarchy, were inherently unstable. The former was vulnerable both to external threats, since, once the person of the single ruler was seized or removed, the state was rudderless, and to the threat of military coups against the single ruler. The latter suffered from endemic aristocratic factionalism. The only chance of enduring stability came when the balance was popular and an appropriate and well-regulated superstructure could be erected by those skilled in political architecture. It was in relation to the last of these, skill in political architecture, that Harrington came closest to fitting the brief of a constitutional thinker. The load-bearing elements of that political architecture were the *ordini* of the rightly instituted commonwealth, and Harrington provided thirty of these in *Oceana*.[27] It was, he observed elsewhere, not the people but the orders of the commonwealth which were to be trusted.[28] Building such a structure was then the 'art whereby a civil society of men is instituted and preserv'd upon the foundation of common right or interest ... it is the empire of laws and not men' [8].[29]

Harrington's political architecture builds, as the trope would suggest, from the bottom up (or from the periphery inwards). This may seem unusual by comparison with many written constitutions which begin with an identification of the system—monarchy, parliamentary, representative, and so on—and work from the top downward or the centre outwards. Two explanatory factors should be borne in

[26] *Valerius and Publicola* in *PWJH*, 797. [27] The number varied in other works.
[28] In the dialogue *Valerius and Publicola*. See *PWJH*, 795. [29] *PWJH*, 161.

mind. One is that, as has already been suggested, *Oceana* is first and foremost a narrative, an account of motion through time, rather than a description. Second, its primary narrative is the story of reinstating and then annually renewing a substantially devolved form of participatory government, acknowledging the unacknowledged republic, which it does through a sequence of elaborately conceived and timetabled ritual performances. First the actors (all male) divide themselves according to their allotted roles: servants and citizens; youth (18–30) and elders (over 30 years old); horse (those with incomes over £100 per annum) and foot (those with incomes under); and geographically into parishes, hundreds, and tribes (counties). On the first Monday in January every year the elders meet in the parish church and elect a fifth of their number as their deputies. The proposers who nominate candidates for election are chosen by lot. As well as choosing the elders, this parish assembly elects parish officeholders—overseers, a constable, and two churchwardens. It also confirms (or not) any new parish minister at the end of his first year in office. All those elected serve for a year and are then ineligible for election in the subsequent year. On the first Monday in February the deputies from ten parishes assemble for a meeting of the hundred and there elect a Justice of the Peace, a captain, an ensign, two jurymen (one of whom must be drawn from the foot), a coroner (again from the foot), and a high constable. On the first Monday in March all the deputies from twenty hundreds or 200 parishes meet as the assembly of the county (or tribe). Here they elect a sheriff, a Lord Lieutenant, a muster master, a quarter master, and two censors (who are responsible for order at the assembly and the monitoring of its observance of the political rites of the county). On the second day of the county assembly they elect a third of the senators who represent them for three years. Senators must be elected from the horse and serve for three years after which they must stand down for the same period. The deputies then elect a third of the members who will represent them in the popular assembly (or Prerogative Tribe) for the same period of service and vacation from office as the senators. Three of those elected could be from the horse and four must be from the foot, ensuring a majority representation in the assembly of the less affluent citizens. The officeholders of the county with the 20 JPs and 40 jurymen act as the council (or, in Harrington's terms, the 'phylarch') of the county, ensuring that the performance of these functions in the hundreds and parishes is in accordance with the rules, drafting petitions to parliament (each clause of which must be endorsed by a majority of the deputies), and, with the circuit judges, functioning as the quarter sessions. All commissions from parliament are mediated through the county council and all taxes apportioned by them to hundreds who in turn apportion them to parishes. Finally, for the civil part of the system, on the first Monday in April the senate and the popular assembly, with a third of their members newly elected at the county musters of the previous month, proceed to elect their officers and members of the executive councils.

These carefully scripted performances[30] amount to the recreation and thereafter the annual renewal of the parish, hundred, and county as political entities or civil

[30] For examples of the detail into which Harrington went in describing them see [78, 83–5, 245].

societies, conveying authority upwards through each tier and simultaneously appointing their own governing officers who would exercise considerable administrative discretion while remaining accountable to the deputies. The principles of rotation meant that all offices were held for fixed periods followed by a vacation from office. This all bore a close relationship to contemporary practice before the disruption of the civil wars commenced. Rates of participation in office-holding in early modern England were high and widely dispersed throughout the social ranks of heads of households. For example, in the small ward of Cornhill in London, 118 people were elected to public office each year out of 267 households or a total population of about 1800 persons. Approximately one in every three householders and one in every sixteen people was an office holder and such high rates of office-holding could be replicated in parishes, hundreds, and counties throughout the land.[31] Similarly, in a triennial cycle, over half the elders of Oceana would be called upon to hold office and there were severe penalties for refusal. What was different in Harrington's proposals was the anti-deferential device of ensuring that a number of offices and a majority of the seats in the popular assembly were reserved for the foot, the less substantial property owners.

The youth (men aged 18 to 30) went through a very similar series of timetabled processes (on the first Wednesdays of January, February, and March) to choose a military force culminating in a standing citizen militia 40,000 strong with a reserve amounting to 100,000. In emergency circumstances (the invasion of Oceana itself) the elders could also be mobilized [194].

Throughout, the use of annual assemblies or musters, lot, ballot, and rotation were the norm. Hobbes, like Cromwell, was not wedded and glued to forms of government but Harrington chose to elaborate a unique and imperative form, 'an institutionalised structure of action'.[32] But, like Hobbes, he believed that motion was the normal state of nature. 'For neither by reason nor by her experience is it impossible that a commonwealth should be immortal, seeing the people, being the materials, never dies, and the form *which is motion*, must without opposition be endless' [99, my emphasis]. This 'rapture of motion'[33] had led Harrington to devise a closed system where men could 'have no other motion than according to the order of their commonwealth'.[34] Rotation of office, a prime example of this civic motion, was 'a wheel which in the revolution of a few years turneth every hand that is fit, or fitteth every hand that it turns, unto the public work' [165]. *Oceana* might be stigmatized by some critics as 'a dumb show' but actions, motion, were more

[31] B. Coward, 'London and the English Civil War', *The Historian*, 99 (2008), 14; see also Goldie, 'The unacknowledged republic'.

[32] For naval provision, which is surprisingly brusquely treated in a work entitled *Oceana*, see *The Art of Lawgiving* in *PWJH*, 683. For further illuminating comment and context for Harrington's relative neglect of naval matters see J. Scott, *When the Waves Ruled Britannia; Geography and Political Identities, 1500–1800* (Cambridge: Cambridge University Press, 2011).

[33] J. Scott, 'The rapture of motion: James Harrington's republicanism', in N. Phillipson and Q. Skinner (eds), *Political Discourse in Early Modern Britain* (Cambridge: Cambridge University Press, 1993), 139–63.

[34] *A Discourse upon this saying* in *PWJH*, 568–9. See also J. C. Davis, *Utopia and the Ideal Society* (Cambridge: Cambridge University Press, 1981), 238.

important than words. It followed that the narration of actions would be the most appropriate form for conveying the constitution as a working system [204–5].

IV

For Harrington the reduction of the dynamics of instability to the kinetics of stability meant primarily the containment and channelling of motion. There were four preconditions or steps to such an achievement. The first was to recognize the historical process of the transmission and evolution of power as shaped by social change as a special and fundamental form of motion requiring appropriate attention. This involved recovering and narrating the story of the shifting social balance of the ownership of land. The ownership of property in land was critical for two reasons: first, well managed, it was inexhaustible, producing a new harvest every year; and, second, it produced food and all those who had to eat (that is, potentially everyone) became dependent on those who could feed them. In the most immediate sense, an army was a beast with a great belly and had to be fed. It was the capacity to achieve this which gave the ultimate power of command over it. Commercial property would not do the same job because it was exhaustible (once spent, it was gone) and because it was inherently unstable. It could, as we have all too visibly been recently reminded, disappear overnight. In a metaphor drawn from falconry, Harrington described commercial property as upon the wing while property in land was 'hooded and tied unto the perch'.[35] As we have seen, neither a balance of landed property in the one nor the few could produce an inherently stable politics. But a balance in the many, which Harrington believed to be the current situation, could only do so if political structures were erected which would appropriately manage social and political motion, including movements in the balance of property.

Accordingly, the second precondition was the establishment of the legitimacy or authority of such a structure as would give England (and Britain), with its popular balance of property in land, such managed motion. Since interest rather than passion shaped, or should shape, reason, the interest of the many, rather than of the one or the few, came closest to right reason. The preferred authority (especially where there was a popular balance of land ownership) was one which gave authority to the many and consequently privileged the common interest and right reason. However, the politics of party gave priority to sectional or private interest over the common interest and had therefore to be prevented. The corruption of popularly based commonwealths was most commonly a consequence of party or factional rule and arose in poorly constituted commonwealths, those where political architecture had failed [33]. A sound political architecture would eliminate party and, with it, partisan politics. In doing so, it would make reconciliation and inclusiveness possible.

[35] *The Prerogative of Popular Government* in *PWJH*, 404. See also [13].

The third precondition was then to seize the moment in which a popular balance could be perfected and immortalized by the adoption of the optimum in political architecture. This, in 1656, presumed a partnership between Oliver Cromwell, to whom *Oceana* was dedicated, and its author. In effect, Cromwell was invited to take part in a narrative pre-scripted and prescribed by Harrington. Cromwell would provide the political muscle to set in train the processes by which the Oceanic constitution would be adopted and implemented, and Harrington, the consummate political architect, would identify the right fit between empire (power) and authority (legitimacy).[36] So, the necessary features of that outcome were that the perfect and immortal commonwealth would contain the historical movement of the balance of property in land, maintain and embody its current popular balance, give full expression to the interest of the many, and ensure that while options might be identified by the wisdom of the few, final decisions would remain in the hands of the many from whom all power now emanated.[37]

To achieve the rule of common interest or right reason there had to be a reconciliation of interests and, since, by definition, parties represented sectional interests, the fourth precondition was an evaporation or elimination of party. Perfection of government for Harrington had been achieved when the system ensured that no one had either an interest in sedition or the power to engage successfully in the pursuit of it. A twofold reconciliation was involved in this. First, the reconciliation of power (or, in his terms, 'empire'), which flowed from the ownership of land, and authority, which was identified with the common interest as realized by the collective action of all the citizens. Second, 'wisdom', the capacity of the few to identify problems and potential solutions, had to be reconciled with the identification of the interest of all, which could only be approximated through the will of the many. Harrington believed that wisdom was attained by learning and the experience of different forms of society and government, which only study and travel could bring. The preconditions of both were leisure and resources, things only available to more substantial landowners [141]. Hence, the senate, which was the wisdom of the commonwealth and had the function of debate and proposal but not of decision, was elected exclusively from the more generously propertied horse. The popular assembly, which represented the interest of the commonwealth and

[36] In a number of places Blair Worden has argued that Harrington was so sceptical of Cromwell's intentions as to use *Oceana* to mock him rather than to persuade him. See, for example, Worden, '*Oceana*: Origins and Aftermath', in D. Wootton (ed.), *Republicanism, Liberty and Commercial Society* (Stanford: Stanford University Press, 1994), 120–4; Worden, *Literature and Politics in Cromwellian England* (Oxford: Oxford University Press, 2007), 109–10. For the contrary view see J. Scott, 'James Harrington's prescription for healing and settling', in M. J. Braddick and D. L. Smith (eds), *The Experience of Revolution in Stuart Britain and Ireland* (Cambridge: Cambridge University Press, 2011), 190–209; J. C. Davis, '*de te Fabula narratur;* the narrative constitutionalism of James Harrington's *Oceana*', in Taylor and Tapsell (eds), *The Nature of the English Revolution Revisited,* 151–73; J. C. Davis, 'The Prose Romance of the 1650s as a context for James Harrington's *Oceana*', in G. Mahlberg and D. Wiemann (eds), *Perspectives on English Revolutionary Republicanism* (Farnham: Ashgate, 2014), 65–83. Examples of what I would consider to be Harrington's seriousness in attempting to engage Cromwell can be found at [66, 67, 229, 233, 240–1, 253–4]. See also *PWJH*, 776 and Norbrook, *Writing the English Republic*, 367.

[37] *Valerius and Publicola* in *PWJH*, 783, 784.

had representatives from both horse and foot but with the majority from the latter, decided but had no power of proposal or debate. This bicameral specialization of function (replicated elsewhere in the system) ensured that nothing could be *proposed* against the interest of the more substantial landowners while nothing could be *decided* against the interest of the majority of landowners (which Harrington considered to be the closest approximation to the common interest). In his *Aphorisms Political* he summarized this as follows: 'A popular assembly without a senate cannot be wise. A senate without a popular assembly cannot be honest.'[38] For wisdom to operate in the system it was therefore important to preserve a class of substantial gentry and aristocrats without allowing them to overbalance, in terms of empire, the majority of the citizens, who embodied the communal interest. The separation of deliberation and decision minimized the influence of passion and left interest (which, as we have seen, Harrington tended to identify with reason) the dominant influence on the will [30–1]. But if interest moved the will, property both determined interest and conferred the independence to pursue it. The perennial constitutional question was whether to give predominance to the interest of one, the few, or the many. Given the existing popular balance of property ownership, stability and the pursuit of right reason could only be achieved by pursuing the interest of the many and investing final decision in them.[39] The dismembered interests of the disassembled watch of John Hall's *True Account* would thus be reabsorbed into a collective interest by ritual performance enacting, creating and renewing the community of the many in parish, hundred, county, and nation, and by a shared power of decision. Such performance, short of actual action, required narrative for its depiction.

Oceana also aimed to deprive religion of its partisan and destructive capacities. There would be a non-compulsive national church, since there had to be a 'national conscience'. Harrington believed that the majority of the population would follow such a national lead and, to ensure the quality of the clergy, provided that the income from church livings should be improved. But there would also be freedom for any Christian faith (excluding Roman Catholicism, which Harrington saw as having a foreign dependence) to congregate and practise their forms of worship provided they were not sacrilegious. To this extent, his proposals were not dissimilar to the arrangements for the Cromwellian church.[40] The rider was that no divine could interfere in politics and would be subject to severe punishments for attempting to do so. The clergy, like physicians, lawyers, bachelors, and wastrels were excluded from citizenship [203–4]. In addition, ministers of the national church would be accountable to their parishioners as, presumably, the ministers of voluntary religious associations would be to their congregations [81–2, 285].

A final objective was to achieve a commonwealth for expansion without dependence on mercenary arms and without disturbing the balance of property so as to undermine and corrupt the republic. A citizen militia and the obligation of all males between the ages of 18 and 30 to military service were intended to render

[38] *PWJH*, 771–2. [39] *PWJH*, 30–1.
[40] A. Hughes, 'Religion 1640–1660', in Coward (ed.), *Companion*, 350–75.

dependence on mercenary arms unnecessary. Without discharging these obligations, no man could become a citizen. To stabilize an imperial balance of property a suitably adapted Agrarian Law was extended to cover the provinces (Scotland, Ireland, and any further conquests). Such arrangements, Harrington believed, would create a military capacity not only for national defence but for vigorous expansion without jeopardizing the commonwealth. Being a citizen militia and generated from the parish upwards, the army would not be tempted to use its power to overawe the citizens.

V

Harrington knew that in the past republics had failed and therefore that Oceana's immunity to decay was unprecedented and required special explanation. The source, as he saw it, of Oceana's distinctive immunity to the corrosive forces of history was the unique combination of arrangements which also gave it the character of 'an equal commonwealth'.[41] Four features were essential to such a commonwealth. First, to restrain history's tendency to shift the balance of land ownership, an Agrarian Law was necessary. It was designed to prevent the balance of land ownership falling into the hands of less than 5,000 (the few) while preserving an aristocracy. The equality (or stability, which amounted to the same thing) of the commonwealth was identified with this balancing act. The Agrarian Law's design was driven by the consideration that, while wisdom may be in the few, the most reliable interest was in the many. The few must therefore be preserved without overbalancing the many.[42] Second, the secret ballot was to be used in all elections and decision-making. This was important to Harrington both in blocking the political workings of social deference and in preventing the formation of political parties. The third essential was a bicameral representation, with the functions of debate and decision divided between the two houses, plus a dependent number of executive councils and severe limitation on the public discussion of political issues outside of the senate [55]. Finally, rotation of office (limited terms followed by vacation from office) was a restriction applied to all officeholders from the parish upwards [33]. This, with the two previous provisions, was seen as preventing the formation of parties—a major step towards the elimination of partiality in politics.[43]

Beyond the provisions of the equal commonwealth there were a number of other features which should be seen as critically important. They included the following: a citizen militia; very high levels of citizen participation or office-holding, supplemented by representation (to be a community of self-ruling citizens the republic

[41] See, for example, *PWJH*, 180; J. C. Davis, 'Equality in an unequal commonwealth: James Harrington's republicanism and the meaning of equality', in I. Gentles, J. Morrill, and B. Worden (eds), *Soldiers, Writers and Statesmen of the English Revolution* (Cambridge: Cambridge University Press, 1998), 229–42.

[42] For an outline of Harrington's much-misunderstood Agrarian Law, see the appendix to this essay.

[43] *A Discourse Upon This Saying* in *PWJH*, 745.

had to provide for communal self-rule at all levels); assured representation of both the few and the many, for which it was necessary to prevent social deference having political effects and to ensure that the many had the preponderant voice in final decision-making; national religious provision with liberty of conscience; and controlled political discussion within and without the senate. Introducing political debate into a popular assembly was punished severely [94]. The importance of stopping public debate in London was given particular emphasis [187–8]. At the same time, a kind of public salon, The Academy of Provosts, would be open every week to members of the public who would be invited to air their views [128]. In this way, the promiscuous operation of the public sphere, witnessed since the collapse of censorship and the church courts in the early 1640s, would, Harrington thought, be brought under control. The balance of citizen activity would be shifted from words to deeds. All of these features were introduced as part of a double narrative: the staging and acting out of a debate hammering out the validity and practicality of these *ordini,* and the story, recounted as a process in specified times and places, of their implementation.

VI

What, then, was the place of the people in this perfect and immortal commonwealth? They were seen by Harrington as constitutive of the commonwealth not only in being the materials of it but also as the *actors* through whom it would be created and annually renewed. High levels of participation in the ritualistic processes through which this was achieved were matched by equally high expectations of participation in office-holding within the republic. The obligation to bear office was accordingly common to all citizens and refusal could be punished by servitude [195]. Provision was also made to ensure that the full participation of all independent citizens would not be hampered by deference: the secret ballot, salaried office, and allocated representation of the foot worked to that end. At the same time, anti-factional (or anti-party) measures—rotation of and vacation from office, bicameral division of function, controls on political discussion, and the exclusion of the dependent (children, women, servants)—were designed both to prevent the divisive, destabilizing effects of party and to ensure that the unmediated will of the people was decisive. Finally, the dispersal of power and authority, in civil, military, religious, and administrative matters, brought political control down to the grass roots of the parish. Oceana was, in terms of authorization, like an inverted pyramid with the people at the top. But, more particularly, it was like a hive swarming with activity, and narration was the appropriate vehicle for its depiction.

VII

It follows that looking for a sovereign authority (in the Bodinian or Hobbesian sense) in *Oceana* presents us with a problem. In some ways, the answer seems to be clear. The rule of 'King People' [98], or popular sovereignty, appears to prevail. Final authority, determinative will—legislatively, judicially, administratively, ecclesiastically, and militarily—is certainly not in the one (which, with the exception of the founding legislator, does not exist in Oceana) nor in the few. Decision is in the hands of ritualized popular assemblies at the national, county, hundred, and parish levels. Such authority as is invested upwards is always at the will of the generality of the citizens, is revocable by them and accountable to them. There is no appeal beyond the final authority of the popular assembly. So far, then, sovereign authority would appear to rest with this body. Yet the power of nomination, discussion, or proposal is withheld from it, and the attempt to introduce discussion into a popular assembly is punishable by servitude.

Characteristics of sovereign authority are often seen as including the devising of strategy or approving or rejecting, authorizing, implementing, and monitoring policy. Even if the detailed operation of these functions is delegated, we expect a Bodinian or Hobbesian sovereign to have ultimate control of all of them. But such a situation does not exist in Oceana. No body—personal or institutional—possesses authority over all of these functions. Is sovereignty so fragmented, brokered, and mediated by specialized and dispersed institutional functioning that no one and no single body fully possesses it? The notion of a 'balanced constitution', which was only optimally operational when its distinctive elements functioned in harmony, was a commonplace amongst both politicians and political thinkers before 1642.[44] This could be expressed in legal terms (the balance between prerogative and rights), institutional terms (the balance between king, lords, and commons), or socio-administrative terms (the balance between court and country). Balance in all of these senses had been swept away by civil war and its aftermath. Might it then be more appropriate to think of Harrington as a proponent of balanced or coordinated government rather than of the sovereignty so often associated by his contemporaries with absolutism? The closest Harrington came to conceding such an absolute authority was in his provision for emergency rule by a temporary body which he called 'the Dictator'. This was the senate's Council of War supplemented with an additional nine elected senators. Its term was three months and, during that period, it had full authority to levy men and money, make war and peace, and to enact laws which would be valid for only one year unless they were confirmed and extended by the senate and the popular assembly [129–30]. Its temporary powers, therefore, while conferring a kind of sovereignty upon it, should be set in the context of its limited term and the perpetual sitting of the senate and assembly. What distinguished Harrington from most contemporary advocates of a balanced constitution was his dynamic view of such a form of government. For them, the essence of balance was a state of rest in equilibrium. But a key feature of Harrington's equal commonwealth was in the kinetics of its rotation of office and its annual cycles of musters, assemblies, and ballots. In one of his rare references to the term 'constitution', as we have seen, he linked it to the 'motions of this commonwealth', which were

44 Judson, *Crisis of the Constitution*; G. Burgess, *The Politics of the Ancient Constitution* (Basingstoke: Palgrave Macmillan, 1992).

spherical [100]. Indeed, the immortality of his perfect commonwealth rested on these dynamics for 'the form which is motion, must without opposition, be endless' [99]. Locked in 'perpetual wheelings, marches and countermarches', 'sovereign powers' were, as Harrington saw it, both collected and dispersed and on this rested the commonwealth's safety [97, 99]. Perhaps, then, in looking for sovereignty in Oceana, we shall not find it in persons or institutions but in processes, motion, and ritual observances, and perhaps this is why Harrington preferred to convey its character by a 'full and perfect narrative' rather than by description [72].

VIII

There is a striking and dynamic fusion of legislative and executive in terms of election, rotation, and accountability. At any one time, about a quarter of the members of the senate would be holding office. Since the function of debate was exclusive to senators it was logical that the executive officers should be drawn from their ranks. At the same time they were directly accountable to the popular assembly and the legitimating of all their political actions depended on the endorsement of that body. It was also the case that, having no paid bureaucracy or dependent, standing army, the officers of the senate and the senate's four elected executive councils (of State, and for War, Religion, and Trade) were reliant for implementation and taxation on the elected officers of counties, hundreds, and parishes and ultimately on the citizens themselves. There was no executive in any modern sense and certainly not in any permanent form, which again underlines the difficulty of applying the modern concept of sovereignty to Oceana. The key thing about the Oceanic legislature and executive is, however, that they never stood still. Within a structural continuity, or architecture, rotation and annual elections constantly changed their composition. In human terms, description would have presupposed a fixity which did not exist. Historical narrative, even if it were a fictional one, was the only means of grasping its operation.

IX

Harrington was deliberately, possibly in a considered way, vague about the operation of the courts in Oceana. His assumption was that they would proceed 'according unto ancient custom' [94]. But the derivation and authorization of the courts was shifted radically from the crown to the popular will and, again, their membership constantly changed. The elders of the parishes elected parochial overseers, constables, and churchwardens who traditionally made presentations to the petty or quarter sessions (or in the case of the churchwardens to the ecclesiastical courts for which Harrington made no separate provision). This was the first tier of judicial discretion and was virtually identical with the arrangements most people would have been familiar with prior to the Civil War. The difference from the 1630s is in the absence of those instruments of central rule (the prerogative courts,

Star Chamber, and High Commission) which were capable of pressurizing these officers and their appointment. At the level of the hundred, the deputies elected a Justice of the Peace, two jurymen (one from the horse, one from the foot), a coroner, and a high constable. The phylarch of the county consisted of six elected officers (Lord High Sheriff, Lord Lieutenant, Custos Rotulorum, Conductor, and two censors). When joined by the twenty JPs and forty jurymen elected by the counties, they formed the Quarter Sessions and Assize Courts, which would operate in the traditional manner. The latter were to be presided over by itinerant judges. Harrington did not go into detail, but these were presumably the three Exchequer and three Equity judges elected by the senate (since these are the only judges mentioned in *Oceana*). Appeals were resolved by the popular assembly which was the highest court in the land [167]. The most striking features of this system are its dependence on election by bodies ranging from the parish assemblies to the senate, its subjection to rotation of office, and the absence of any dependence on trained and professional lawyers. Harrington, like other commentators of the period, saw the proliferation and complexity of the laws as a social evil, for which the professional lawyers, having a vested interest in its perpetuation, were largely responsible. Since they were ineligible for citizenship, lawyers could find no place in the structures of government. In *A System of Politics* (published posthumously), Harrington observed that, since every case was different, 'there must in every judicatory be some arbitrary power'. Two principles should be given operative force in mitigation of this reality. The first related to the drafting of law. 'That law which leaves the least arbitrary power to the judge or judicatory, is the most perfect law.' The second was that 'Arbitrary power, going upon the interest of the whole people, makes a just judicatory'. Oceana's attempt to address the two issues was expressed in its preference for short, simple laws and in its observance of a system in which, at each level of the discretionary operation of the judicial system (parish, hundred, county, and nation), the responsible officer would be elected by and accountable to the citizens or their representatives [288–90]. As we have seen, the final appellate authority was the popular assembly.

X

What appealed to many of Harrington's followers was his model's 'entireness'—its apparent ability to answer all questions and solve all problems. The price to be paid for this was complexity, and, like his readers since, Harrington was well aware of this. In acknowledging it, he pointed again to motion and ritual as key parts of the system, and suggested that it would be easier to understand in action rather than in writing. To those who still objected, he responded with a metaphor from navigation, itself a form of managed motion. The complexities may be many and difficult but, he asked:

> what seaman casts away his card because it hath four and twenty points of the compass? And yet those are very near as many and as difficult as the orders in the whole circumference of your commonwealth. Consider how we have been tossed with every wind of doctrine, lost

> by the glib tongues of your demagogues and grandees in our own havens! A company of fiddlers that have disturbed your rest for your groat; two to one, three thousand pounds a year to another, hath been nothing, and what for? Is there one of them that yet knows what a commonwealth is? And are you yet afraid of such a government in which these shall not dare to scrape, for fear of the statute? Themistocles could not fiddle, but could make of a small city a great commonwealth; these have fiddled, and for your money, till they have brought a great commonwealth to a small city [145–6].

The metaphor takes us back to motion and a preference for reliable and practical action over the vulnerability to manipulation of words.

Some of *Oceana*'s complexity is attributable to Harrington's own fascination (bordering, some would say, on obsession) with detail. But at the heart of the exercise was an attempt to reconcile contradictory forces and this was bound to involve some intricacy of design. The building that the political architect was called upon to re-establish in 1656 was falling apart, patched up—still tottering, but on the verge of collapse. It was a challenging project and required design skills beyond the ordinary. A central operating contradiction in Harrington's brief was his belief in establishing the rule of 'King People' [98] set against the necessity, as he saw it, to presume all men wicked and to have a system which would make evil men good. '[I]t is the duty of a legislator to presume all men to be wicked' [180]. The answer lay partly in the *ordini,* the political architecture of the commonwealth, partly in the relationship between the different parts of government, but also in the processes and rituals of self-government, which might only be fully grasped by experience or the attempt at the narration of that experience which *Oceana* embodied. 'Where the security is in the persons, the government makes good men evil; where the security is in the form, the government makes evil men good.' How could the people rule themselves if they were so deeply flawed? Only by setting behavioural constraints while maintaining the collective illusion of self-rule. The goal was not to be achieved by the balancing of forms—the one, the few, and the many—so typical of mixed-government advocates. That answer had been discredited by the persistence of civil conflict between the elements of such a constitution under both the late king and Cromwell. On the other hand, the problem of human wickedness which the designer of the constitution had to tackle was heightened by an insistence on potentially flawed citizens generating all tiers of government, which then remained accountable to them, and by Harrington's unusually inclusive criteria for citizenship. He, typically, excluded children, women, alms takers, and servants as dependent beings, incapable of self-rule. But for most of the groups trying to establish a legitimate and stable settlement after the war, the problem was addressed both by the republic and its critics by seeking to establish a subscriptional community in the sense that only those who had taken an oath of loyalty or, in the case of the Levellers, had endorsed the *Agreement of the People,* qualified as citizens. In extension of this, known enemies of the settlement, for example ex-royalists, were usually excluded from citizenship. Harrington provided for oaths of loyalty to the commonwealth but was perfectly happy to see ex-royalists granted full citizenship. Even if all the senators elected were royalists the republic would have nothing to fear.[45] Good laws and the constrained processes of participation embodied in them would make good men. The nature of citizen participation and the accompanying relationship between parts of the government were critical to this sense of security. The citizen participated in a set of rituals designed effectively to reduce his moral responsibility rather than enhance it. The bicameral division of debate and resolution, discussion and decision, for example, prevented any representative of the citizens being fully responsible for any decision or policy. Those who proposed might not decide and those who decided had no control over what they were called upon to decide. The secret ballot, rotation, and vacation from office, with the proscription of political debate outside of the senate only heightened this sense of the limited public relevance of private capacities. No citizen did anything in a fully moral sense and what he did do he didn't do for very long. Participation in Oceana consisted of the freedom to observe prescribed rituals and to accept predetermined limitations, the rejection of which would be folly, a self-destructive madness.[46]

The ambition of Harrington's project was in its attempt to reconcile arms and councils, force and legitimacy, power and authority, property and wisdom. At the start of his depiction of the process of establishing a perfect and immortal commonwealth, he gave warning of 'how unsafe a thing it is to follow fancy in the fabric of a commonwealth' [69]. Imagination must give way to an understanding of the processes of historical change and the intensive comparative study of the institutions of past commonwealths from Israel to Venice. In that sense, Harrington may, like Jean Bodin,[47] be seen as a precursor of the Enlightenment interest in comparative constitutionalism.

XI

Insofar as Harrington was simultaneously a constitutional and a utopian thinker, his historical observations, constitutional prescriptions, and utopian operational design were marked by an insistent sense of social and political dynamics, or by a kinetics which extended from context to operation. The paradox is that, nevertheless, all was contained within a stable framework. He began with a historical analysis, the narrative of which emphasized movements in the balance of property as a key determinant of persistent structural weaknesses in the polis and of the infrastructural sources of its repeated collapse. The story told here extended from ancient Greece to contemporary England. He wrote as from a fixed observational standpoint to meditate on a world of unceasing and dangerous mobility. Narrative was the appropriate, possibly the only, mode through which that fluidity could be

[45] Indeed to exclude royalists was anathema because it would create a party of government and a party of the excluded [62–3; see also 256–7].

[46] Davis, *Utopia and the Ideal Society*, 208–9.

[47] Harrington acknowledged the influence of Bodin in *The Prerogative of Popular Government*. See *PWJH*, 427.

conveyed. It was narrative, too, which was called upon to do the work of illuminating the transition from destructive to stabilizing motion. Secondly, therefore, he devised a constitution, a political architecture, intended to stabilize that dynamic in ways which he thought were not only apposite but which conferred immortality, the cessation of *structural* kinetics. But, thirdly, that structural stability (or immobility) was in part sustained by a never-ceasing internal motion. Oceana has a constitution grounded in socio-political performance. It is created, sustained, and perpetually renewed by the ritualized motion of its citizens through space and time—a social and political kinetics which ensure the interchangeability of the social and the political, itself the seal on immortality. There was thus a narrative of instability and one of stability. *Oceana*'s final ambition was to narrate the story of the process by which the one may be transformed into the other.

XI. Appendix: Harrington's Agrarian Law

Harrington had two statistical assumptions in mind:[48]

1. He believed that the total income from land was about £10,000,000 per annum.
2. He believed that, if the balance of land ownership fell into the hands of less than 5,000 proprietors, the balance would be moving from a popular to an aristocratic one.

It followed that some brake should be placed on the accumulation of estates worth more than £2,000 per annum.

- Accumulation by purchase was forbidden.
- Dowries were limited to a capital value of £1,500 (at contemporary rates of calculation the equivalent of £75 p.a.).
- Inheritance:
  - The law did not interfere where there was only one son and an estate worth over £2,000 p. a.
  - Where there was more than one son and a sufficiently large estate to provide for each an inheritance worth over £2,000 p.a., the estate must be divided equally between them.
  - Where there was more than one son and the estate was not large enough to provide each son with an inheritance worth over £2,000 p.a., the maximum that a single heir might inherit was £2,000 p.a.

Harrington thought that there were not more than 300 families with estates worth over £2,000 p.a. That meant that they controlled property worth in total something like £600,000 p.a. out of a total of £10,000,000 p.a. The objective was not to jeopardize *family* property but to preserve some very substantial estates while preventing a shift in the overall balance of property from a popular to an aristocratic basis.

[48] The text of the Agrarian Law, in slightly differing versions, can be found at [101] and *The Art of Lawgiving* in *PWJH*, 664–5.

8

David Hume

Constitution by Convention

John W. Adams

David Hume (1711–76), the philosopher of the Scottish Enlightenment, states in his *History of England* that the Glorious Revolution of 1688–9 put the English constitution 'beyond all controversy' and that, ever since, the English have enjoyed 'if not the best system of government, at least the most entire system of liberty, that ever has been known amongst mankind.'[1]

Hume has been credited, among other things, with being the 'most important philosopher ever to write in English', and with having a lasting and an important impact on political thinking, influencing particularly the drafters of the United States Constitution.[2] In order to take seriously his assertions regarding the English constitution, as well as his reputation as an important political philosopher, a number of issues must be addressed. On what basis does Hume support his assertions, and are they adequately supported by Hume and validated by history? And does the philosophy, especially as it relates to the nature of government and its constitution, have a more universal application? If government (and its constitution) is a matter of conventions and understandings developed within a community—as Hume argues it is—should the nature of government (and its constitution) vary from society to society?

To examine these issues requires understanding Hume as more than a political philosopher. Hume's political considerations are based on his observation of society and his historical insight, and his view of the nature of society as a product of psychological and economic influences.

David Hume is notable for his approach to understanding man and society, in general, and politics and the nature of government, in particular. He relied, in the first instance, on experience and observation to develop his philosophy, especially his political and social philosophy. '[T]is not, therefore, reason, which is the guide

[1] David Hume, *History of England: From the Invasion of Julius Caesar to the Revolution in 1688*, (first published 1754–63) 6 vols (Indianapolis: Liberty Classics, 1983) henceforth referred to as *'History'* or 'H'. H 6, 531.

[2] W. E. Morris and C. R. Brown, 'David Hume', in *The Stanford Encyclopedia of Philosophy*, Summer 2014 edition, edited by E. N. Zalta, http://plato.stanford.edu/archives/sum2014/entries/hume/.

of life, but custom.'[3] The nature of his search for political understanding casts him also as a philosophical historian. Hume believed that we may construct from history a rational process, not through speculation, but as the result of empirical investigation and the realities of fact.

Using Isaac Newton as a model, Hume sought to introduce the 'experimental' method to the study of human nature. Hume rejected religious enthusiasm as reliance on unknowable superstitions, discredited the philosophy of the ancients as speculative, and dismissed the a priori reasoning of Locke and the like for relying on the 'ought' rather than the 'is.'

> And tho' we must endeavour to render all our principles as universal as possible, by tracing up our experiments to the utmost, and explaining all effects from the simplest and fewest causes, 'tis still certain we cannot go beyond experience; and any hypothesis, that pretends to discover the ultimate original qualities of human nature, ought at first to be rejected as presumptuous and chimerical.[4]

While reliance on experience and observation has its limitations, Hume admitted, impressions and reflections based on observation of history and of society can lead to reasonable inference, probable conclusions, and effective planning. History, to Hume, deals with truth, and this truth is beyond reason. Examining experience—that is, history—is the most practical way to discover the inner principles of change and to discover patterns of change. Through his detailed examination of history and human thought, Hume sought to develop a secular, scientific account of the foundations of moral and social life. This was his 'science of man'.

Hume was a serious student of history. More than a pure empiricist, Hume analysed historical patterns and changes in social and political circumstances to develop broad-based political theories. Empirical analysis was only a part of his larger political theory. Studying both ancient and contemporary history, and with a realist's orientation to political conflict, he believed in a constancy of human nature. Hume believed that a variety of observations lead to a variety of maxims, but, in the end, will provide a degree of uniformity of principles.

Hume did not believe that all history represents progress, but did believe that it is evolutionary: an accumulation of conventions adapted by societies to deal with problems encountered in attempting a stable and orderly system of government. Hume aims to maintain a close correlation between his theorizing and his observation of history and its experience. An empirical study of history and regimes provides the basis through which he derives general theoretical conclusions about what kind of regimes best promote the happiness of those who live under them:

[3] David Hume, *A Treatise of Human Nature*, ed. D. F. Norton and M. J. Norton, (Oxford: Oxford University Press, 2007) (henceforth cited as T followed by book, part, section, and paragraph numbers), T 3.1.1.27.

[4] T Introduction 8.17.

These records of wars, intrigues, factions, and revolutions are so many collections of experiments by which the politician or moral philosopher fixes the principles of his science.[5]

The social and political changes of seventeenth-century England provided Hume with insights from which he formed—or confirmed—his more normative political philosophy. His analysis of this period of English history, both descriptive and causal, led him to a view of characteristics essential for good government. In a letter to Adam Smith, Hume explains why he chose to begin his *History of England* with the accession of the House of Stuart in 1603.

Twas under James [I] that the House of Commons began first to raise their Head, & then the Quarrel betwixt Privilege & Prerogative commenc'd. The Government, no longer opprest by the enormous Authority of the Crown, display'd its Genius; and the Factions, which then arose, having an Influence on our present Affairs, from the most curious, interesting, & instructive Part of our History . . .[6]

Hume viewed the seventeenth century in England as fitful progress towards a satisfactory, modern (although not perfect) form of government. He believed that legitimacy of government depends fundamentally on liberty, and this was not truly present in England, in his mind, until 1628 with the adoption by parliament, and acceptance by Charles I, James's son and successor, of the Petition of Right.

It may be affirmed, without exaggeration, that the king's assent to the petition of right, produced such a change in the government, as was almost equivalent to a revolution[.] . . . [I]t is ridiculous to consider the English constitution before that period as a regular plan of liberty. . . . [T]he incapacity of Buckingham encouraged the free spirit of the commons to establish in England a regular system of liberty.[7]

Hume believed that the Petition of Right was a turning point in the development of English government. The Magna Carta had singular importance,[8] but the Petition of Right represented acceptance by the crown of the civil liberties of the people and recognition of the requirement of the crown to work with parliament. The crown thereafter, from time to time, might choose to ignore the supremacy of law, and parliament over the course of the seventeenth century might overstep its position, but in Hume's mind these struggles led to a more effective government for the English: a balanced government and constitution providing an association of king, parliament, and the people.

The history of the English government in the seventeenth century, and Hume's reflections on that period as recorded in his *History,* sheds light on Hume's political philosophy and his sense of the nature of a more perfect constitution. Hume develops his themes of good government: a mixed government of balanced interests, the ultimate political importance of public opinion, and the rule of law and institutions of justice that form the constitution of a nation.

[5] David Hume, *Enquiries Concerning Human Understanding and Concerning the Principles of Morals*, ed. L. A. Selby-Bigge, 3rd edition by P. H. Nidditch (Oxford: Clarendon, 1985) (henceforth Enq), 83–4.

[6] HE 1, XIT.

[7] HE 5, 200.

[8] HE 5, 178: '. . . the GREAT CHARTER itself, the most sacred foundation of the laws and constitution.'

I. Hume's *History* and the Road to Parliamentary Constitutional Monarchy

The period from the coronation of James I (in 1603) to the English Civil War (in the 1640s) witnessed the erosion and then collapse of the Elizabethan constitution. The government under Charles I, in particular, was unstable and threatened by issues political, constitutional, and religious. Until the Long Parliament in November 1640, Charles followed the pattern of absolute kingship, which threatened the independence of the gentry and nobility. But war with Scotland forced Charles to go to parliament to raise taxes. This—and popular enthusiasm towards parliament—ensured ultimate political dominance by parliament. Parliament, spurred on by various factions hostile to the king, became intransigent in its dealings with the crown. Civil war ensued, and by early 1649, the king had lost his head. The monarchy was abolished.

> History, the great mistress of wisdom, furnishes examples of all kinds; and every prudential, as well as moral precept, may be authorized by those events which her enlarged mirror is able to present to us. From the memorable revolutions, which passed in England during this period, we may naturally deduce the same useful lesson, which Charles himself, in his later years, inferred; that it is dangerous for princes, even from the appearance of necessity, to assume more authority, than the laws have allowed them. But, it must be confessed, that these events furnish us with another instruction, no less natural, and no less useful, concerning the madness of the people, the furies of [religious] fanaticism, and the danger of mercenary armies.[9]

Hume, concerned with stability and security of the people, principally blames parliament for the military actions of the 1640s. Hume believed that parliament, with Charles acknowledging the limits of monarchy, should have taken the opportunity presented to establish a mixed constitution of parliament and king.

From the execution of Charles—and for the next eleven years—a different course was taken by the English, not that of a mixed constitution but towards a form of government that was intended to be a representative republic. It proved to be an unfortunate experience. England in the 1650s was marked by various forms of government and constitutional experiments, none of which proved satisfactory. The society of England, and its government, was influenced by religious fanaticism (Quakers, the Rangers, and others) and subjected to political factions and tyrannical leaders. These developments led to social and political instability. The country went from an ineffective Rump Parliament, which lasted until it was dismissed by Oliver Cromwell in 1653, to the imposition of an efficient but tyrannical Protectorate of Cromwell. While Hume believed that the government under Cromwell offered a sense of security to the people, the implications of his rule were dangerous. Security alone, without liberty, was not a satisfactory government according to

[9] HE 5, 545–6.

Hume. Cromwell's Protectorate confirmed Hume's belief that violence and injustice are inevitable where there is no restraint on the sovereign.

Hume also found unsatisfactory prescriptions offered by the then contemporary political philosophers. Of Hobbes, Hume wrote:

> Hobbes's politics are fitted only to promote tyranny, and his ethics to encourage licentiousness. Though an enemy to religion, he partakes nothing of the spirit of skepticism; but is positive and dogmatic as if human reason, and his reason in particular, could attain a thorough conviction in these subjects.[10]

And, as to Harrington:

> Harrington's Oceana was well adapted to that age, when the plains of imaginary republics were the daily subjects of debate and conversation, and even in our times it is justly admired as a work of genius and invention. The idea, however, of a perfect and immortal commonwealth will always be found as chimerical as that of a perfect and immortal man.[11]

For Hume, the ineffective attempt in the 1650s to establish a republic was an unfortunate interruption in the long-term development of the English constitution. The death of Cromwell in 1658 brought an end to any expected achievement of the Civil War. The experience had led to no workable vision of good government and no politically acceptable leadership. England was a kingdom missing a king, and restoration of the monarchy became inevitable.

The Restoration Settlement of 1659, negotiated between the Convention Parliament and agents of Charles II, returned the monarchy to the English government. Charles II assumed the crown in 1660. Although he assumed his monarchical role with few conditions imposed, the crown's position with parliament and the people was fundamentally different to how it had been before. As put by historian Mark Kishlansky:

> Parliament, church and king were now inextricably tied together. By withstanding attacks from the monarch and army, Parliament had made its claim to be the representative of the people, even if the concept of representation and the definition of the people remained elusive. If it had ever been an event, Parliament was now an institution . . . By surviving overthrow and exile, the monarchy laid claim to the hearts of the people . . . It was a system of government that the English people had self-consciously chosen when they had the choice: a system best able to provide security, stability and prosperity.[12]

From the Restoration and throughout the reign of Charles II, from 1660 until 1686, the monarchy gradually strengthened. Its relationship with parliament, while perhaps contentious, was at least tolerable: they needed each other. Charles focused on re-establishing the monarchical power rather than extending it. The government's fiscal situation was also relatively favourable, brought about through the combination of a conservative spending programme and increased tax revenue

[10] HE 6, 153. [11] HE 6, 153.

[12] Mark Kishlansky, *A Monarchy Transformed: Britain 1603–1714* (Penguin Books, 1997), 225–6.

derived from the growing commercial prosperity of the country. Thus the executive administration serving the monarchy was likewise developing into a more able and efficient part of government.

Notwithstanding the recognition of parliament as an independent political institution, the monarchy's effective administration, and the existence of a passable working relationship between these two elements of government, England in the early 1680s was a divided society. The division was in part related to the factional rivalry between Whigs and Tories. It was due also in part to the religious intolerance of the Church of England, which, working collaboratively with the king, pursued a programme of persecuting Catholics—still a substantial part of the population—as well as Protestant dissenters. This persecution of religious dissenters was supported by the Tory landed gentry, who considered religious dissent a threat to parliament.

Upon Charles's death, the accession of his brother, James II, was accepted, despite social unrest and the fact that James was a Catholic. Parliament and the people anticipated that James would follow the pattern of Charles II, who, when pressed, tended to compromise his monarchial rights. James, though, both in personality and beliefs, challenged expectations. First, he was a committed Catholic and moved to emancipate the followers of that religion. Second, he was a political reformer who sought boldly to strengthen and centralize the government under him. For example, he attempted to obtain from the English courts a common-law ruling affirming his power to dispense with the Acts of parliament, and dismissed judges who disagreed with his assertion of authority. In 1687, James attempted to pack parliament with his supporters, and he maintained a large standing army that employed Catholics of power within it.

The religious and political policies of James, pursued vigorously, cost him the support and confidence not only of the people, but of his natural allies as well. His position was further undermined by the birth of his son, who was baptized a Catholic. The male heir displaced in order of accession his daughter, Mary, a Protestant, and her Dutch husband, William, who was third in line through his mother, Mary Stuart. Tories, Whigs, and the Anglican Church deserted James, and encouraged William to invade England. James, rather than face the army of William, fled to France in late 1688. Parliament, after debate over the nature of James's action, determined that he had abdicated. Parliament replaced James with William III and Mary II. The Glorious Revolution had occurred without undue social or political turmoil.

What, then, led Hume to conclude that the English had enjoyed 'the best system of government, at least the most entire system of liberty, that ever was known amongst mankind?' In general, one can conclude from the final passages of his *History*, as well as from his political essays, that the accession of William and Mary and the political developments that followed brought to the English government relief from past political turmoil and strife. Hume believed that the English governments during the Stuart reign (from 1603 through to 1689) reflected a pattern of struggle over economic and political institutions. As English society during the course of the seventeenth century became centralized, social change, especially the development of prosperous and stable commercial markets, caused political influence to be distributed over a broader segment of the population. Yet political institutions, in Hume's mind, were slow to accommodate this political and social change. To Hume, the seventeenth century until 1689 reflected political instability caused by a constant quest for arbitrary power by, in turn, the king, parliament, and Cromwell. Hume believed that this political instability was exacerbated by the influence (especially in parliament) of political factions, religious fanatics, and parties that held their own interests closer to heart than those of their country.

Hume believed that the Glorious Revolution 'not only put an end to the hereditary succession, but resulted in a constitution changing the essential nature of the English government'. It was not so much that there was fundamental change ushered in by the Glorious Revolution, but rather that it advanced a fortuitous adjustment of existing institutions. To Hume there was no 'natural' arrangement for English government, one reliant on an ancient constitution or one based on some natural rights theory or divine representation. Hume developed a complex, historically based social and political philosophy. He concluded that good a government is one properly adapted to existing circumstances and that addressing public opinion is essential to all political authority.

The key to the development of English government, in Hume's mind, was an unplanned—but fortuitous—process during the reign of the Stuarts, which culminated in the crown and parliament being forced into a mutual dependency that limited the powers of each. To Hume, the key to this lay in the development of a mixed government, a division of power between the executive and legislative branches of government, an independent judiciary, and freedom of the press.

Much of the success of the Glorious Revolution was, to Hume, the product of the Bill of Rights of 1689, which was adopted by parliament and implicitly agreed to by William. The Bill of Rights, though vague, did establish central constitutional principles, including eliminating the crown's power to dispense with Acts of Parliament, levy taxes without the consent of parliament, and maintain a standing army without the consent of parliament. It included provisions that ensured free speech and the free election of parliament, and prevented debate in parliament from being impeachable or questioned by the crown. Furthermore, it was tacitly understood that if parliament had arranged to have a monarch removed, it certainly could do so again. But even without any specific constitutional agenda, William, perhaps distracted by conflict with France and in constant need of funds, did not pursue the power that had obsessed the Stuart kings.

From the revolution on, parliament more firmly determined state policy. Its influence was not only the product of political developments, but also the result of commercial expansion in England. Since members of parliament had significant investments in trade and industry, they had a strong incentive to enforce property rights. However, although parliament had the greater share of political power, the crown's patronages and influence in promoting the election of members to parliament tended to encourage members to act in concert with the crown, thereby maintaining the balance of the constitution.

In recognition of the changes realized in the reign of William and Mary, political institutions in England became increasingly pluralistic in nature. Parliament was subject to elections and, even though only 2 per cent of the English were entitled to vote, those who did felt empowered, not only for themselves but also as representatives of the community in general. The interests and responsiveness of parliament were reflected in changes to the economic institutions and government policies that would ultimately lead to the Industrial Revolution.

II. 'Moral Distinctions Not Deriv'd From Reason'

Hume's study of government and his political philosophy in general is the product of, and derived from, his insight into human nature. One cannot truly grasp Hume's political philosophy without some understanding of his reflections on human nature. To Hume, political maxims cannot be derived from a priori reason, but must be empirically grounded. Political ideas are dependent first on observing and then, and only then, reflecting on the nature of the individual and his social interaction. Hume does not, in contrast to Locke, look for a system of law based on some fundamental law of nature. Even if a grand design does exist, Hume believed, we are incapable of understanding it. Hume is a naturalist, observing and understanding the phenomena that may account for human beliefs and human institutions and practices. Political institutions are dependent on human nature and human experience.

Experience, which Hume sees as understanding derived from studied observation, is received only indirectly, through primary and secondary perceptions. Innate impressions, such as affection (love of virtue?) and other passions, originate in the heart. From these innate impressions we can derive ideas based on reflections, or secondary perceptions of external circumstances. But neither the senses nor reason, working with impressions and ideas, provide compelling proof of moral truth, because what is observed or experienced is just a phenomenon. Our perception of phenomena is merely a perception realized by our senses or actuated by our passions. History may represent truth, but our ability to understand it is coloured by our perceptions.

Passion can provide no incontrovertible path to reason—and no authoritative guide to conduct. We first form an impression through what we perceive and how we react to what we observe. Then, through the exercise of our reflection and reason, we can make moral judgments. When Hume speaks of 'moral' he refers to the psychology of what motivates people and to topics concerned with social theory. It is the science of human nature.[13] These moral judgements, to Hume, are universal but tentative, because they are conditioned or dependent on our perception of external phenomena. Reason is contingent and only probable as it is conditioned on our underlying emotions and perceptions based on our observations.

[13] T 3.1.1, also quoted in the title of this section.

Hume, though, is not discouraged by the limitations of reason. Through careful examination of experience and human life, we can attempt to construct a useful science of human nature. Experience can link cause and effect, and from this we can effectively plan.

If our reasoning permits us at best to reach only tentative judgements, why do we make moral judgements of ourselves and of others? Hume replies that it is in our nature and our self-interest to do so. 'In short, it may be establish'd as an undoubted maxim, that no action can be virtuous, or morally good, unless there be in human nature some motive to produce it, distinct from the sense of its morality.'[14] Through reasoning from our perceptions, impressions, and ideas, we determine what pleases us and what provides personal utility.

The sense of utility, explained by Hume as self-interest, provides the primary motivation in our relations with others. Adam Smith explains: 'It is not from the benevolence of the butcher, the brewer, or the baker, that we expect our dinner, but from regard to their own interest.'[15] Morality, then, is not a determination of 'right or wrong' or 'good or bad', but is a product of what we judge to be in our best interest. It is right if it serves us well. Morality is based on utility; it is a product of what we observe to work and what provides us benefit.

Individuals approach others, Hume said, with certain innate tools: moral sentiment, sympathy, and mirroring. Moral sentiment is one's judgement of what is acceptable behaviour, for both oneself and for others. Sympathy is our communication to others of our personal feelings about our own moral judgements, and our own recognition of what motivates others. We sympathize with others in the sentiments they entertain of us. We constantly reappraise ourselves, assessing right and wrong, by reflecting how others view us. By this, we maintain our sense of virtue. This sense of sentiment and sympathy promotes community with others. Observation is made, consciously, to verify common sentiment, an expectation. Hume goes further, providing a significant psychological means of analysis by describing the communication process he refers to as 'mirroring'. By mirroring, he explains, we subconsciously intuit what of ourselves pleases others, and we react accordingly. A person, often unknowingly, signals to us through a smile or a frown, for instance, whether or not our words or actions please him. We pick up these signals.

The understanding of how individuals come to mutually understood and agreed-upon moral judgements and sentiments leads Hume to the concepts of reciprocity and mutual advantage:

> I learn to do a service to another, without bearing him any real kindness; because I foresee, that he will return my service, in expectation of another of the same kind, and in order to maintain the same correspondence of good offices with me or with others.[16]

[14] T 3.2.1.7

[15] Adam Smith, [1776] 1976, *An Inquiry into the Nature and Causes of the Wealth of Nations* (Oxford: Oxford University Press; Indianapolis: Liberty Classics, 1981, reprint), 1.2.2, 26–7.

[16] T 3.2.5.9.

There develops from this a sense of reciprocity in our relationships to others. If I treat you fairly, then it is likely you will treat me well also. Mutual trust works to our mutual advantage. One might argue that keeping one's promise, then, is a normative virtue, a moral obligation leading to an 'ought'. Hume said this is not the case:

> In short, it may be establish'd as an undoubted maxim, that no action can be virtuous, or morally good, unless there be in human nature some motive to produce it, distinct from the sense of morality.

If you do not want to be perceived as being dishonest or untrustworthy, then you 'ought' to keep your promise. But if it suits you, you may break your promise. Hume refers to an act such as keeping your promise as an 'artificial virtue', as it is simply an understanding between individuals of agreed appropriate conduct under the circumstances. It is the understanding between or among individuals, a convention or an expectation, which creates the interpersonal sense of justice. A convention is useful to observe and it may be in our interest to do so, but it is not a compelling ideal.

The concept of 'convention' is important to understanding Hume and especially his political philosophy. For Hume, the idea promotes both individual and social utility:

> It has been asserted by some, that justice arises from Human Convention, and proceeds from the voluntary choice, consent, or combination of mankind. If by convention be meant a promise (which is the most usual sense of the word) nothing can be more absurd than this position. The observance of promises is itself one of the most considerable parts of justice, and we are not surely bound to keep our word because we have given our word to keep it. But if by convention be meant a sense of common interest; which sense each man feels in his breast, which he remarks to his fellow, and which carries him, in concurrence with others, into a general plan or system of actions, which tends to public utility; it must be owned that, in this sense, justice arises from human conventions.[17]

Convention to Hume, then, reflects a regular pattern of behaviour that gives rise to reliance, and a sense of common interest. He gives the example, in Appendix III of his *Enquiries*, of two men pulling oars. They do so together by common convention for common interest, without promise or contract.

If conventions and understandings promote a civil society, one in which people behave and conduct themselves spontaneously for the betterment of their personal and social interest, what then is the need for government? To Hume, the answer is the need for principles of justice. Justice, to Hume, delineates the rules that ensure basic order and structure for civil society, but, most particularly, the rules that specify rights related to property. Government is necessary for the conduct of foreign affairs, for instance, but is indispensable for the regulation of economic production and competition among members of civil society as they pursue their economic interests.

[17] Enq, App III, 306.

III. 'If not the best system of government, at least the most entire system of liberty'

Hume describes, principally in his *Treatise* and the *Enquiries*, the origin of societies and, through the evolution of custom and convention, the development of government. The 'art' of governing people in society, the elements necessary for good government, and his constitutional ideas are provided in Hume's *History* and his *Essays*. For Hume, there is no 'right' social arrangement inherent in history; government is contingent on accumulated principles arising over a period of time as social conventions adapt to changing circumstances. The coordinating nature of conventions establishes social order and structure. He rejects the idea that government is the product of an original contract, divine dispensation, or some natural rights thesis.

As society gradually emerged from its barbaric state, as Hume describes it, coordination among individuals beyond the immediate family became necessary to assure social order. Small societies can exist peacefully through the coordinating action of understanding and convention among the members of the community, where each monitors the behaviour of the others. Hume acknowledges that the likely first step towards government is the spontaneous leadership in defence of the community from forces outside it. But once the society becomes large, formal institutions must be provided to maintain order. Early society, to Hume, could exist without government, but as society grows in size and complexity, necessity and mutual advantage require conforming to conventions that have developed within the community.

Hume then introduces his understanding of the necessity of government. He rejects the principle that makes property rights arise prior to social order and government. He equally rejects the idea that property rights and commerce can exist only after government assures the protection of property rights. Hume reverses the usual sequence of government and commerce. In Hume's developing society, commerce precedes formal government. The introduction and development of commerce leads to the necessity of formal government and, with it, greater security and liberty of the people. From the sense of common interest and mutual advantage, emerging from custom and convention, developed the necessity of what to Hume is a system of justice. When Hume refers to 'justice' he is referring to the basic order and structure of civil society, and, in particular, to the principles and rules that specify the right to property. For Hume, there exists no notion of justice inferred entirely from reason or ideals. Justice is contingent on human nature and experience:

> It is only from the selfishness and confin'd generosity of man, along with the scanty provision nature has made for his wants, that justice derives its origin.... We may further confirm... that those impressions which give rise to this sense of justice, are not natural to the mind of man, but arise from artificial and human conventions.[18]

[18] T 3.2.2.18, 21.

These artificial and human conventions, necessary to justice, do not consist of collective social values, but to Hume are principally an aggregate of personal interests. Adherence to accepted conventions, or social rules of coordination, serve both personal and community needs:

> After men have found by experience, that their selfishness and confin'd generosity, acting at their liberty, totally incapacitated them from society; at the same time have observ'd, that society is necessary to the satisfaction of those very passions, they are naturally induc'd to lay themselves under the restraint of such rules, as may render their commerce more safe and commodious.[19]

Hume's principles of justice are based on the need for regulation of economic production and competition among members of civil society as they pursue their economic interests. Justice assures undisturbed private property, trade and exchanges (the market), and the performance of promise and contract. The institution of justice satisfies the principle of utility, that which furthers the common interests of both individuals and general society. Essentially, then, it is utility that determines the nature of justice.

Social rules—Hume's 'justice'—form the basis of conduct in extended groups and the obligations of individuals within the group. Hume weaves the evolution of commerce requiring cooperation among strangers into the institutionalism of a more formal legal system to enforce promises, the development of government to regulate action and provide security of property and stability in society, and, ultimately, the recognition of a constitution embodying the accumulated customs and conventions of the larger society.

The nature of government and the legal system necessary to promote commerce is depicted by Hume as the product of a 'virtuous cycle' of social progress and economic growth. As individuals become secure in the established conventions, re-enforced by law and regulated by government, there arises a need for increasingly sophisticated social institutions. Government, like the common law, is formed and developed for utilitarian, not ideal, purposes. It is not developed pursuant to some original social contract or grand design, but arises by the development of conventions accommodating the evolving needs of commerce and social order. The cycle was the product of iterative actions, cause and effect, unintended and unforeseen, over a long period of time. Tradition and custom bind together society and provide stability; yet as conventions change so too must its institutions. Indeed, the development of government can be seen as the product of the evolution of law.

These social rules—Hume's 'justice'—form the basis for conduct in extended groups, the basis for government, and the basis of allegiance to the government. People seek to protect those rules by the institution of government:

> When men have observ'd, that tho' the rules of justice be sufficient to maintain any society, yet 'tis impossible for them, of themselves, to observe those rules, in large and polish'd societies; they establish government, as a new invention to attain their ends, and preserve the old, or procure new advantages, by a more strict execution of justice.[20]

[19] T 3.2.2.24. [20] T 3.2.8.5.

Once the people seek the protection of government, Hume observes, they tend to submit to the government and resign their 'sentiments and passions to those of their rulers'. And although people first approach the rules of justice from the perspective of their personal interest, they gradually acquire and internalize, Hume believes, a sense of disinterested obligation to comply with the rules through the experience of living under them.

IV. 'Idea of a Perfect Commonwealth'

Hume, having examined the nature of man and society, as well as the origins of government, then proceeds, principally in his *History* and his essay 'Idea of a Perfect Commonwealth',[21] to examine the science of politics and the art of good government. His political thought is historically based rather than abstract, and he draws on his examination of English history, as well as the ancient political systems, as grounds for his political judgement. Hume is not interested in the moral quality of politics or the desire to form a virtuous society. He focuses instead on understanding the arrangements of political institutions necessary to ensure, in spite of man's nature, a secure and prosperous society.

A study of Hume's political judgement, and his concept of good government and constitutions, starts with his essay on the 'Idea of a Perfect Commonwealth'. There is a certain irony here, given Hume's comment about the 'chimerical' nature of the 'perfect commonwealth' presented by Harrington in his *Oceana*. One might conclude that Hume's essay is perhaps a satire of Harrington's efforts. That view sells short both philosophers. Hume states that, while *Oceana* is plainly 'imaginative' and therefore of little utility, Harrington presents the 'only valuable model of a commonwealth that has been offered'.

Hume dismisses as agreeable fantasies 'golden age' stories: the belief in the perfect nature of ancient governments. They are not helpful in putting realistic conditions on social life or useful as a guide to political objectives. Theorizing about ideas was popular in the mid-seventeenth century, but to Hume it is detrimental to political analysis. Like religious zealotry and political parties, in principle it tended to polarize and make for uncompromising political discussion.

A politician, Hume asserts, must take the world and people as they are, and as bad as they could turn out to be. There is small benefit in exploring 'imaginary, perfect governments' as the bulk of mankind prefer to be governed by authority, not reason. Why, or on what basis then, does Hume undertake this essay purporting to propose the nature of an ideal commonwealth? Hume attempts to escape the fallacy of idealist proposals by looking at eighteenth-century England as perhaps having an imperfect government, but one that served well the purposes of its society.

[21] David Hume, 'Idea of a Perfect Commonwealth', Essay Twenty-Seven, in *Hume: Political Essays*, ed. K. Haakonssen (Cambridge: Cambridge University Press, 2006), 221.

History represents truth, and it is Hume's aspiration, reflecting on both ancient and modern experience, as well as his belief in the constancy of human nature, to present empirically grounded principles of his science.

In any event, Hume indicates that a purpose in writing his 'perfect government' essay is that sometime in the future an opportunity might arise, either through the demise of a government or by men forming a new one in 'some distant part of the world,'[22] to put his political judgement into practice.

Bringing to bear his sense of realism and the lessons of history, and taking into account actual human motivations, Hume constructs a government based on a constitutional framework of competing and balanced institutions—those arrangements necessary to accommodate natural self-interest, parties and factions, and arbitrary power. His focus is on arrangements of political institutions. Hume regards self-interest in government as not only inevitable, but as morally permissible and even a desirable form of motivation in certain contexts. Self-interest creates a productive marketplace of ideas, so long as the rules of justice and the rights of others are not violated:

> Political writers have established it as a maxim, that, in contriving any system of government, and fixing the several checks and controls of the constitution, every man ought to be supposed a *knave* and to have no other end, in all his actions, but private interest. By this interest we must govern him, and, by means of it, make him cooperate to public good, notwithstanding his insatiable avarice and ambition.[23]

Hume similarly rejects the idea that factions should, or even could, be totally eliminated in a constitutional scheme. Even if there is no reason to oppose one another, factions nonetheless will arise, for humans are naturally fractious. Hume brings his economic model of competitive markets to politics:

> Governments too steady and uniform, as they are seldom free, so are they, in the judgement of some, attended with another sensitive inconvenience: They abate the active powers of men; depress courage, invention, and genius; and produce a universal lethargy of the people.[24]

Hume's idea is to incorporate the motivations of self-interest and factions within the constitutional framework, with the aim of providing an assembly of competition through opposition. His is a pluralistic constitution that allows for political competition.

Hume is also concerned with arbitrary power in any form and, for that reason, objects as well to the concept of majority rule. 'Every court or senate', when acting by majority rule, tends to allow the collective self-interest of the majority to dominate, to the detriment of other interests. His point, as in the 'knave' passage, is that there is a need for checks and controls—that is, political competition—to

[22] Hume, 'Idea of a Perfect Commonwealth', 222.

[23] David Hume, 'Of the Independency of parliament', Essay Five, in *Hume: Political Essays*, ed. Haakonssen, 24.

[24] H 6, 530.

restrain political behaviour. Hume envisions a mixed government checking and balancing the interests and influence of the legislature, the executive, and the courts, and forcing the constituent parts to work with one another. Hume went further, also advocating the institutional separation of executive and legislative powers.

To Hume, the constitutional history of the seventeenth century reflects a course of trial and error from which a mixed government, between king and parliament, emerged at the time of the Revolution. In large measure, this form of government balanced well the social and economic interests of the peerage, property-owning gentry, and merchants. For Hume, therefore, a good government could be in the form of a monarchy as well as a commonwealth. Hume, however, expressed some concern for the British form of government on the basis that it was a fragile mechanism too reliant on the uncertain ability of the crown. To that end, Hume proposed in his 'Idea of a Perfect Commonwealth' to provide for two 'councils'. The House of Commons, consisting of property-owners, would be the representatives of the people. And a House of Lords, with lifelong, non-hereditary office, would act as the senate. The senate would consist entirely of the men of good credit, ability, and interest in the nation.

> All free governments must consist of two councils, a less and a greater; or, in other words, of a senate and people. The people, as Harrington observes, want wisdom without the senate: The senate, without the people, would want honesty.[25]

Hume's conception of an acceptable constitutional arrangement of government provides for a normative commitment to law and a functional legal system. Law is for Hume a natural extension of his requirement of justice. It is essential for limiting and coordinating self-interest, factionalism, and arbitrary power; assuring security of property and person; and achieving liberty and promoting commerce.[26] The crucial feature dividing civilized and barbarous governments, he states, is that the former is a 'government of law, not men'. Barbarous governments are government of men. By the late seventeenth century in England, it was understood that the king was not above the law.

To Hume, there are three essential elements comprising the institution of law: the constitution; natural laws common to a society, which are the product of custom and courts; and civil law established by the legislature. The constitution is the fundamental law, establishing the offices of the state and defining and allocating the power and decision-making processes among the offices. It represents the effort of bringing legal order and regularity to the actions of government. The constitution, to Hume, is not derived from, nor does it have the characteristics of, a social contract. The idea of a constitution as a contractual arrangement is empirically false and conceptually confused. Instead, whether written or by custom, a constitution is the product of people seeking protection of the rules of justice through the institution of government. It is an iterative process of long-developed

[25] Hume, 'Idea of a Perfect Commonwealth', 228.
[26] David Hume, 'Of Civil Liberty', Essay Ten, in *Hume: Political Essays*, ed. Haakonssen, 56.

understandings and conventions, resulting in allegiance to a particular government. Opinion, the basis of authority, supports the institutions of the society.

Common law consists of general rules developed over time from early society, and is the result of custom and habit and dispute resolution by the common courts. Common-law principles that emerge as products of a court concern particular facts and issues unique to specific cases. Emanating from the aggregation of these rules are common-law principles fundamental to the rules of justice and the protection of property and person. People are motivated to follow these conventions because they provide mutual expectations and promote stability of property. Furthermore, the influence of common law provides a high degree of continuity within the institution of justice as required by a civil society.

Civil law, or positive law, is the product of the legislature. Civil law becomes necessary to coordinate behaviour of people when society becomes large. It exists to fulfill the same purpose as common law in situations too complex for natural law to provide definitive guidance. Acts of the legislature are framed to supply resolution to controversies general in nature, to provide universal and uniform principles, and to direct the procedure of judicial courts.

The power of the legislature to promulgate laws, however, is restricted by the opinion of people to see the law as being to their mutual advantage:

> A law, to have authority, must be derived from a legislature, which has right. And whence do all legislatures derive their right but from long custom and established practice? If a statute, contrary to public good, has, at any time, been rashly voted and assented to, either from violence of faction, or the inexperience of senates and princes; it cannot be more effectually abrogated, than by a train of contrary precedents, which prove, that, by common consent, it has been tacitly set aside, as inconvenient and impracticable.[27]

In his conception of a civilized government, Hume provides for the separation of legislative and judicial functions. General laws of the legislature are 'attended with inconveniences when applied to particular cases' and it is in the discretionary power of judges to interpret and apply general laws to specific cases. Judges must use discretion in deciding which laws to apply in particular cases, recognize their responsibilities and limitations, and act in good faith. Hume believes that this sense of responsibility is possible because a judge is likely not to have other than a remote personal interest in any specific case but does have an interest in promoting justice.

Hume states that opinion is the basis for authority. Institutions of government are the product of a marketplace of opinion, reflecting an aggregation of individual opinions and expectations as a coordinated process. A balanced government reflects a balancing of popular will as well as a balance of institutions. Once the people seek the protection of government, Hume observes, they tend to submit to the government and resign their 'sentiments and passions to those of their rulers'. Yet the continued allegiance to the now-established government is dependent on each person's perception that the general social opinion is that it is in the personal and mutual interest of individuals to remain in such a relationship with the government.

[27] H 5, 194.

When we enquire by what means this wonder is effected, we shall find, that as FORCE is always on the side of the governed, the governors have nothing to support them but opinion. It is therefore only that government is founded; and this maxim extends to the most despotic and most military governments, as well as the most free and most popular.[28]

To Hume, opinions are of two kinds: opinion of interest and opinion of right. Both kinds of opinions derive from the political beliefs and understandings of the people as formed through experience. The opinion of interest reflects the confidence that government can care for the public interest in maintaining a rule-bound institution of law, and that it can secure three kinds of property: internal satisfaction, external advantages of body, and enjoyment of possession. Opinion of right concerns who the people think should rule, who is most trusted to have the power, and who can best provide stability.

Hume, expressing the critical nature of opinion, considers the authority of government as being derived from the people. But the sense in which he defines 'the people' is limited. Hume views the people in the corporate sense, and it is the duty of the legislature—in England, the House of Commons—to represent the interest of the people. Hume's endorsement of mixed government in Britain, for instance, envisions a balance between the peerage and property-owning gentry and merchants, but no direct role in government for the poor:

The lower sort of people and small proprietors are good judges enough to one not very distant from them in rank or habitation; and therefore, in their parochial meetings, will probably choose the best, or nearly the best representative; but they are wholly unfit for country-meetings, and for electing into the higher offices of the republic. Their ignorance gives the grandees an opportunity of deceiving them.[29]

V. Concluding Comments

David Hume presents an empirically grounded understanding of the psychology of individuals, the development and implications of commercial markets, the nature and purpose of government, and the elements essential for effective political institutions. His political philosophy, closely related to his economic thought, is presented as a social science. Hume relies on the experience of history, especially English history, as a source and medium for his views.

Government and related political institutions, Hume contends, are not the product of some divine purpose, not based on natural rights, and not the result of an original contract. To Hume, the guide to understanding social organization, including the emergence of government, is to examine the customs and understandings of a community—those conventions ('artificial virtues'[30]) adopted to assure social order.

[28] David Hume, 'Of the First Principles of Government', Essay Three, in *Hume: Political Essays*, ed. Haakonssen, 16.

[29] Hume, 'Idea of a Perfect Commonwealth', 227–8.

[30] See especially: T 3.2.2.9–14.

This concept of conventions is critical to Hume. History reflects accumulation and evolution of social conventions necessary to provide a stable and orderly society. Phenomena such as security of property, justice, rule of law, and government are all the product of adopted conventions. Examination of the source and nature of these phenomena—not pure reason or divine inspiration—offers an understanding of political institutions.

Social order arises from rational decisions made by individuals in order to conform to conventions that serve their interest. Collectively this action—reliance on mutual advantage, and common interest—gives rise to justice, the security of property, and the development of an active commercial society. But as society becomes more complex, the requirements of mutual advantage necessitate coordination of understood, albeit diverse, conventions by a formal government and system of justice.

To Hume, the authority and legitimacy of government is derived from the power of conventions. Acquiescence and obedience to a regime is subject to the opinion of the people. A government cannot long exist by force, according to Hume, but is dependent on the opinion of the governed. A legitimate government, like an effective commercial market, is one that provides stability and order by coordinating diverse interests and managing conflict. It achieves this by adapting and sustaining conventions arising from interactions within society.

The constitution of a state—its fundamental law—settles the institutional structure and decision-making power to assure legal order and the regularity of government action. To acquiesce to a political regime, and its constitutional structure, the people must be of the opinion that it promotes their mutual interests and provides order and stability. Once this is observed by the people, there arises an accepted convention of obedience to the government. It serves people's interest to do so. This was the experience of England in the seventeenth century, Hume believed, and the lesson of the Glorious Revolution.

In his 'Idea of a Perfect Commonwealth', Hume suggests that his practical aims as a political theorist might contribute 'in some future age' to putting his theory into practice. There exists substantial evidence in the *Federalist Papers* of James Madison and Alexander Hamilton that Hume had a direct and significant effect on their explanation of the Constitution of the United States. James Madison, for example, in his *Federalist No. 10*, addresses the concerns involved in establishing a republican form of government in other than a small country, and was inspired by Hume and his essay regarding an ideal commonwealth. And, in his *Federalist No. 51*, Madison clearly had in mind Hume's 'knave' when he states, 'If men were angels, no government would be necessary. If angels were men, neither external nor internal controls on government would be necessary.'

Hume brought into his writings insight into the psychology of individuals, government, and political institutions. Yet still an issue lingers. Hume's political judgements are empirically based, and are largely reflective of the history of the English people he observed. He extrapolates those judgements onto his general philosophy. But Hume admits that there is no 'right' social arrangement, that government is contingent on accumulated principles, and that social conventions adapt to changing circumstances. The question remains whether, if the English constitution reflects the particular nature of the English people, as Hume posits, his observations and judgements reflect equally as well the nature of other societies? Do Hume's political judgements have universal application?

9

William Blackstone and the 'free Constitution of Britain'

Wilfrid Prest

I. Introduction

The 1753 Oxford broadsheet advertising a 'Course of Lectures on the Laws of England' by 'Dr Blackstone, of All-Souls College' was aimed not merely at 'such Gentlemen of the University, as are more immediately designed for the Profession of the Common Law', but 'such others also, as are desirous to be in some Degree acquainted with the Constitution and Polity of their own Country'.[1] Three years later, introducing an expanded syllabus of his lectures, Blackstone rephrased this latter passage to read 'desirous of some general Acquaintance with the Constitution and *legal* Polity of their native Country'.[2] Similarly the 'Discourse on the Study of the Law', delivered in October 1758 as the inaugural lecture of the foundation Vinerian Professor of the Laws of England in the University of Oxford, explained that the 'science thus committed to his charge, to be cultivated, methodized and explained in a course of academical lectures, is that of the laws and constitution' of England.[3] This same 'Discourse' was reprinted as a preface to the first of the four books of *Commentaries on the Laws of England*.[4] So although the word 'constitution' appears neither on the title page nor in the consolidated index of what were essentially Blackstone's Oxford lectures, intensively polished and reworked over more than a decade, their author had always been concerned with the institutions and practices of government (or as we might say, with constitutional and public law), as well as the rules and procedures of private law. A comprehensive, detailed, and systematic synthesis of political theory, history, and English law was not the least novel aspect of Blackstone's ambitious project.

[1] Dated 23 June 1753, the broadsheet is reproduced by D. A. Lockmiller, *Sir William Blackstone* (Chapel Hill NC: University of North Carolina Press, 1938), facing 48.

[2] W. Blackstone, *An Analysis of the Laws of England* (Oxford, 1756), iv (italics added).

[3] W. Blackstone, *A Discourse on the Study of the Law* (Oxford, 1758), 2.

[4] All references hereafter are to the 1979 University of Chicago Press facsimile of the first edition of the *Commentaries*; the quotation in this essay's title comes from W. Blackstone, *Commentaries on the Laws of England*, 4 vols (Oxford, 1765–9), i. 326.

Over the past two and a half centuries, the *Commentaries* have borne a decidedly mixed reputation. While contemporaries were immediately impressed by the work's broad scope, clarity, and elegance of expression, there was also criticism of its political and religious tendencies. Then his former pupil Jeremy Bentham's ferocious assault on Blackstone's alleged 'antipathy to reformation . . . universal inaccuracy and confusion' in the anonymously published *Fragment of Government* (1776) crystallized a range of objections and reservations which retain some residual force even today.[5] Over the course of the twentieth century, reappraisal of Blackstone's aims and achievements has gradually brought a more balanced appreciation of both. Yet towards its end, the *Commentaries* could still be characterized as both 'the most influential law book in Anglo-American history' and also 'a work that almost no one reads today and that is widely believed to rest on a silly, ponderous, formal, conceptual, outdated, deductive, mechanistic, naive and hopelessly unrealistic jurisprudence'.[6] In view of the now considerable body of interdisciplinary scholarship which tends to rehabilitate Blackstone's book from the charge of confused reactionary obscurantism, this was perhaps an excessively pessimistic judgement.[7] The following chapter draws both on that work and Blackstone's own writings in an effort to contextualize the formation and publication of his constitutional ideas, before discussing the general nature of Blackstone's constitutional thought, his depiction of the British constitution, and the long-term impact of his constitutional ideas.

II. Context

William Blackstone was born in 1723, just 35 years on from the Glorious Revolution and less than a decade after George Lewis, elector of Hanover, became King George I of Great Britain and Ireland. Those two events can now be seen to have sealed Britain's future as a Protestant constitutional monarchy, marking a decisive rejection of both Stuart absolutism and Roman Catholicism, or in contemporary parlance, arbitrary government and popery. But contemporaries could hardly know this was the case, especially so long as an exiled Catholic Stuart claimant to the British throne continued to draw material and moral support

[5] J. Bentham, *A Fragment on Government*, ed. J. H. Burn and H. L. A. Hart (Cambridge: Cambridge University Press, 1988), 4.

[6] A. A. Alschuler, 'Rediscovering Blackstone', *University of Pennsylvania Law Review*, 145 (1996), 2.

[7] Cf. W. S. Holdsworth, *A History of English Law*, 16 vols (London: Methuen, 1922–66), xii. 91–101, 702–37; R. Cross, 'Blackstone v. Bentham', *Law Quarterly Review*, 19 (1976), 516–27; R. A. Posner, 'Blackstone and Bentham', *Journal of Law and Economics*, 19 (1976), 569–606; S. F. Milsom, *The Nature of Blackstone's Achievement* (London: Selden Society, 1981); D. Lieberman, *The Province of Legislation Determined: Legal Theory in Eighteenth-Century Britain* (Cambridge: Cambridge University Press, 1989); P. O. Carrese, *The Cloaking of Power: Montesquieu, Blackstone and the Rise of Judicial Activism* (Chicago: University of Chicago Press, 2003); W. Prest (ed.), *Blackstone and his* Commentaries; *Biography, Law, History* (Oxford: Hart Publishing, 2009); H. L. Lubert, 'Sovereignty and Liberty in William Blackstone's *Commentaries on the Laws of England*', *Review of Politics*, 72 (2010), 271–97.

from co-religionists and sympathizers across the seas, not to mention their counterparts closer to home, in the Scottish highlands and the diverse ranks of England's Tory party. Whig politicians continued to play the Jacobite card against their demoralized and disunited opponents well into the second half of the century. Not until the accession of George III, two years after Blackstone's inaugural lecture as Vinerian Professor, did the venerable Whig and Tory labels lose any real operational significance in national politics. Their cultural, social, and symbolic connotations survived long after that.

So Blackstone grew up in a politically polarized world. The rhetoric of 'liberty and property', 'popery and wooden shoes', or conversely 'the king over the water', retained considerable resonance, with the previous century's conflicts between king and parliament far from forgotten. Georgian England remained a largely agrarian society in demographic and economic terms, while the upper ranks of the landed classes continued to dominate its politics and government. Yet the post-1689 expansion of banking, commerce, consumerism, finance, trade, urbanity, and urbanization raised concerns about the unsettling effects of new wealth drawn from non-traditional sources. There were also fears that loss by the established Church of England of its previous monopoly status had encouraged the proliferation of religious heterodoxy, materialism, scepticism, downright unbelief, and associated immorality—concerns not shared by those who agreed with Bernard Mandeville that private vices might well be public virtues. The burgeoning print media, which incorporated daily and weekly newspapers, journals, pamphlets, broadsheets, and satirical prints, no longer restrained by pre-publication censorship, thrived on such controversial issues. It also brought to its socially diverse readership every conceivable variety of useful knowledge and humane learning, besides a steady diet of political news, crime, scandal, accidents, and disasters (now as often attributed to natural as well as to supernatural causes).

While the mature Blackstone has been seen as a spokesman for the Tory country squires of Hanoverian England, his personal antecedents were in fact commercial and metropolitan.[8] His father, Charles, was a high-end London shopkeeper who had lived in considerable style on Cheapside near St Paul's Cathedral but died as a near-bankrupt five months before the birth of his youngest son in 1723. It is not without significance that William's widowed mother chose to christen her newborn son with the name of the Dutch prince and Whig hero of 1688. She herself came from a recently gentrified Wiltshire family of whiggish orientation. Plainly a person of energy and initiative, she took over her late husband's ailing silk drapery business in an effort to trade back to solvency; two of her brothers, a surgeon and a clergyman, helped bring up their orphaned Blackstone nephews and nieces; while a cousin prevailed upon Prime Minister Robert Walpole, one of the governors of the Charterhouse, to nominate William to a free place at that prestigious public school. The scholarship boy flourished, academically at least, topping the entire school before his fifteenth birthday, and receiving a silver medal donated by

[8] Biographical details here and below not otherwise referenced come from my *William Blackstone: Law and Letters in the Eighteenth Century* (Oxford: Oxford University Press, 2008, 2012).

another Whig politician for his verses (now lost) on the puritan republican poet John Milton.

These bourgeois, urban, and whiggish elements in Blackstone's family background and early life contrasted sharply with his Oxford University roles as undergraduate, fellow, professor, and head of house, not least in political terms. For at Oxford, Blackstone became prominent in the Tory 'Old Interest'. This academic faction championed the university's 'noble Independence' against any interference from the Whig ministries of the day, especially in matters of internal discipline and government (a stance he later characterized as 'inseparable from a Zeal for constitutional Liberty'[9]). Widely read in Anglican apologetics and sharing the orthodox distaste for both Wesleyan evangelicalism and Protestant nonconformity, his personal religious faith was seemingly firm, if undemonstrative. Yet, while his two elder brothers became clergymen, William's decision to undertake the Bachelor of Civil Laws degree, followed by his admission to the Middle Temple, pointed to other ambitions. These indeed prompted his best-known poem, 'The Lawyer's Farewell to His Muse', which provides a first glimpse of his legal philosophy. Here Blackstone's poetic persona resolves to seek out the fundamental principles of 'Justice', which had been preserved over the past millennium by that 'guardian of Britannia's law' and imbued with 'mighty [King] Alfred's piercing soul', despite an intervening 'thorny maze' of 'mystic, dark, discordant lore'.[10] Shortly after moving to London to read for the bar, he elaborated another figurative depiction of the common law, this time as an old house which once 'resembled a regular Edifice', but was subsequently 'swoln, shrunk, curtailed, enlarged, altered & mangled by various contradictory Statutes &c'.[11] Again, the approach is historicist and metaphorical, far removed from abstract theoretical analysis. Yet, within a year or so, the young barrister could confidently claim to have 'reduced [the law] to a system', just as he had previously digested and summarized the classical rules of architecture in two manuscript treatises. These juvenile essays can now be seen as trial attempts at synthesizing a large body of knowledge for heuristic purposes: dry runs for what eventually became the *Commentaries*.

Blackstone's first attempt to establish a practice at the London bar was unsuccessful, thanks largely to multiple Oxford distractions, including his successful role as campaign manager for the Tory candidate in a parliamentary by-election for the university constituency, and protracted litigation on behalf of All Souls College, where he had become a very active administrator after winning a prize fellowship in 1743. Ten years later, his decision to return full-time to Oxford was bound up with the prospect of presenting a lecture course on the common law for fee-paying students, thereby generating additional income to supplement his meagre fellowship stipend. Even if personal interests and involvements had not impelled him to

[9] William Blackstone to Roger Newdigate, 16 Feb. 1755, in *The Letters of Sir William Blackstone 1744–1780*, ed. W. R. Prest (London: Selden Society, 2006), 32.

[10] *William Blackstone*, 57–61. See also M. Mauger, '"Observe how parts with parts unite/In one harmonious rule of right": William Blackstone's Verses on the Laws of England', *Law and Humanities*, 6 (2012), 179–96.

[11] *The Letters of Sir William Blackstone*, 4.

include a substantial public law component, the viability of this truly pioneering venture depended on a syllabus which would appeal to the widest possible undergraduate audience, rather than a much smaller cohort of future lawyers, whose vocational interests might have been adequately served by a concentration on real property and other private law topics.[12]

As it turned out, enrolments fully justified Blackstone's gamble. Within a few years, he had replaced the single-page printed handouts that summarized each part of his course in tabular form with a text-book, the *Analysis of the Laws of England* (1756 and five subsequent editions), a work quarried by modern scholars as a prepublication epitome of the *Commentaries*. Less use has been made of some other minor writings, including his scholarly edition of Magna Carta (1759) and the slightly earlier *Considerations on Copyholders*, a brief for the (Tory) case against enfranchising copyholders in county elections, occasioned by the notoriously bitter Oxfordshire contest of 1754. Various sets of student notes transcribed from his lectures also survive; the lecturer's own manuscript has so far proved elusive. It was indeed the proliferation, circulation, and sale of such transcripts, 'in their nature imperfect, if not erroneous', that Blackstone cited as the main reason for the eventual publication of the *Commentaries,* 'as much the effect of necessity, as it is of choice'. But while the basic outline of that work, first printed in four volumes between 1765 and 1769, had been set in the early years of the previous decade, its author was an obsessive wordsmith who found it impossible to leave his text alone. The seven subsequent editions printed during his lifetime all incorporate authorial amendments, most merely stylistic, but some of real substance; the same seems true of the ninth and first posthumous edition of 1783.[13] Yet it is important to recognize that the *Commentaries* originated in the 1750s, just a few years after the Jacobite invasion of 1745 showed that the constitutional conflicts of the preceding century were still not quite safely put to bed.[14]

III. Constitutions

> 'SOCIETY is formed for the Protection of Individuals; and STATES, or Government, for the Preservation of Society.'[15]

In its first edition (1765), Book I of the *Commentaries* runs to 473 pages. Of these, 115 are taken up by the opening 'Introduction', which is divided into four sections. The first, 'Of the Study of the Law', reproduces the text of Blackstone's

[12] Cf. the contention that Blackstone was interested in law, not government, but perhaps felt 'an obligation as a scholar to say something about it': R. Harrison, introduction in *Fragment on Government*, ix–x.

[13] For a useful summary of these changes, see I. Doolittle, *William Blackstone: A Biography* (Haslemere: privately printed, 2001), 82–5.

[14] This point underlies I. Doolittle, 'Sir William Blackstone and his *Commentaries on the Laws of England* (1765–69): a biographical approach', *Oxford Journal of Legal Studies*, 3 (1983), 99–112.

[15] Blackstone, *An Analysis of the Laws of England*, 2.

introductory lecture as the foundation Vinerian Professor of the Laws of England in the University of Oxford, a post which he held from 1758 to 1766. The remaining three deal in turn with 'the nature of laws in general', the laws of England, and the jurisdictions where those English laws hold sway. It is in the two middle sections that we find most about the origins, purpose, and rationale of government broadly conceived, although relevant passages also occur later in Book I and in the other three volumes.

Blackstone's 'short enquiry concerning the nature of society and civil government' starts from a seemingly secular premise: 'the wants and fears of individuals' are the basis of all human society. He rejects as 'too wild to be seriously admitted' the notion of (unspecified) 'theoretical writers' that an original contract was formed by mutual agreement between a body of individuals living in 'an actually existing unconnected state of nature', who having 'met together in a large plain . . . chose the tallest man present to be their governor'. Yet his decisive objection has a religious, indeed scriptural basis, in 'the revealed accounts of the primitive origin of mankind, and their preservation some two thousand years afterwards: both which were effected by means of single families'. In other words, it was Adam and Eve, and Noah and his wife, who 'formed the first society'.[16] Then, as population increased and pastoralism gave way to agriculture ('which employs and can maintain a much greater number of hands'), formerly dispersed tribes 'reunited again; sometimes by compulsion and conquest, sometimes by accident, and sometimes perhaps by compact'. Here we may detect an element of Enlightenment stadial theory. The causal mechanism invoked is psychological: even if no formal 'convention of individuals' ever occurred as a matter of historical fact, 'it is the *sense* of their weakness and imperfection that *keeps* mankind together; that demonstrates the necessity of this union; and that therefore is the solid and natural foundation, as well as the cement, of society'.[17] And without the submission of all, 'it was impossible that protection could be extended to any'.

Thus, government 'results of course' from the formation of society, even if '[h]ow the several forms of government we now see actually in the world at first actually began, is matter of great uncertainty'. Brushing that question aside, Blackstone goes on to assert that in all states 'there is and must be . . . a supreme, irresistible, absolute, uncontrolled authority, in which the *jura summi imperii*, or the rights of sovereignty, reside'. Why exactly this should be so is not explicitly apparent (as Bentham and others pointed out). It seems possible that, consciously or not, Blackstone is making an argument from analogy: just as God ('the supreme being') created the universe and imposed upon it 'eternal, immutable laws of good and evil' binding upon the entire creation, so municipal or civil law, 'the rule by which particular districts, communities, or nations are governed' is 'prescribed by

[16] Cf. J. Locke, *Two Treatises of Government*, ed. P. Laslett (Cambridge: Cambridge University Press, 1960), 337: 'The *first Society* was between Man and Wife'. Blackstone occasionally refers explicitly to Locke, never to Hobbes or Hume.

[17] *Commentaries*, i. 47–8. Although Blackstone declined 'to meet the arguments of Hume that habit not consent was the basis of government', his account shares with Hume's a basis in human psychology: G. Jones, *The Sovereignty of the Law* (Toronto: University of Toronto Press, 1973), xli.

the supreme power in a state', that is to say, the legislature (which is the sovereign, since '[s]overeignty and legislature are indeed convertible terms').[18] But there is also a practical consideration. Because 'political communities are made up of many natural persons . . . these several wills cannot by any *natural* union be joined together, or tempered and disposed into a lasting harmony'. Thus a '*political* union' is necessary, 'by the consent of all persons to submit their own private wills to the will of one man, or of one or more assembly of men, to whom the supreme authority is entrusted'.[19] In the case of the British constitution at least, that consent is taken for granted, as 'an implied, original, and virtual allegiance, owing from every subject to his sovereign'.[20]

The next question which arises is 'in whose hands are the reins of government to be entrusted?' By analogy, those who possess the qualities 'which are among the attributes of him who is emphatically stiled the supreme being; the three grand requisites . . . of wisdom, of goodness, and of power . . . that ought to be found in every well constituted frame of government.'[21] Wisdom is needed to 'discern the real interest of the community', goodness to pursue that interest, and power to implement knowledge and intention. This general answer is, according to Blackstone, easy enough, although its application to specific cases 'has occasioned one half of those mischiefs which are apt to proceed from misguided political zeal.' But, rather than elaborating upon that throw-away line, he turns abruptly to another authority, the 'political writers of antiquity'. They are said to have recognized only three 'regular forms of government': democracy (where sovereignty is held by a participatory assembly comprising full members of an entire community); aristocracy (where all power resides in a council of 'select members'); and monarchy (where a single person is supreme). All other 'species of government' are variations on those three.[22]

Each form has its distinctive strengths and weaknesses. Democracy is characterized by 'public virtue, or goodness of intention', even if 'popular assemblies are frequently foolish in their contrivance and weak in their execution'. Aristocracy, being supposedly composed of the 'most experienced citizens', is wiser than the rest, but less public-spirited than democracy and weaker than monarchy. And while the prince who holds 'all the sinews of government' is most powerful, 'there is imminent danger of his employing that strength to improvident or oppressive purposes'. So, according to Cicero, the best government would combine all three elements. The reported dismissal of that opinion by Tacitus as 'a visionary whim' cues a paragraph extolling the distinctive virtues of 'the British Constitution', which

[18] *Commentaries*, i. 48–9, 38–40, 44, 46. Cf. *Fragment on Government*, chs. 1–2, and 92–3, 101.

[19] *Commentaries*, i. 52 (italics in the original). For Bentham's derisive treatment of this fictional 'consent', see *Fragment of Government*, 51–9.

[20] *Commentaries*, i. 356–7.

[21] *Commentaries*, i. 48. For Blackstone's debt here and elsewhere to the recently translated Swiss author J. J. Burlamaqui's treatise on natural law, see J. M. Finnis, 'Blackstone's Theoretical Intentions', *Natural Law Forum*, 12 (1967), 170–1.

[22] *Commentaries*, i. 49–50; cf. Aristotle, *Politics*, Bk. III, chs. 7–8; T. Hobbes, *Leviathan* (1651), Pt. 2, ch. 19.

is 'a standing exception to the truth of this observation', precisely because it does successfully combine all three types of government by incorporating the virtues of each.[23]

In a moment we shall look more closely at Blackstone's account of the balanced or mixed constitution of mid-eighteenth-century Britain. But meanwhile a causal question arises: how and why was this purportedly very fortunate outcome achieved? The answer is essentially historical, or historicist, in the sense of appealing to the past in order to explain the present, reflecting that 'consuming interest in the classical, British and Gothic past which gripped the upper classes of Britain and Ireland in the long eighteenth century.'[24] For first, 'by the intermixture of adventitious nations, the Romans, the Picts, the Saxons, the Danes, and the Normans', the unwritten laws of the ancient Britons gained 'the accumulated wisdom of divers particular countries'. Then King Alfred's '*dome-book* or *liber judicialis*' provided a 'code' for the entire Anglo-Saxon nation. Revived in the eleventh century after the Danish invasions by Edward the Confessor, this 'vigorously withstood the repeated attacks of the civil law' that in the twelfth century established 'a new Roman empire over most of the states on the continent: states that have lost, and perhaps upon that account, their political liberties; while the free constitution of England, perhaps upon the same account, has been rather improved than debased.'[25]

The same theme is further developed in the first chapter ('Of the Absolute Rights of Individuals') of Book I. Society's prime function is to protect the rights of its members, even when the 'natural liberty of mankind' is 'so far restrained by human laws (and no farther) as is necessary and expedient for the general advantage of the publick'.[26] For 'that constitution or frame of government, that system of laws, is alone calculated to maintain civil liberty, which leaves the subject entire master of his own conduct, except in those points wherein the public good requires some direction or restraint'—as was precisely the case in Britain.

The idea and practice of this political or civil liberty flourish in their highest vigour in these kingdoms, where it falls little short of perfection . . . Very different from the modern constitution of other states, on the continent of Europe, and from the genius of the imperial law; which in general are calculated to vest an arbitrary and despotic power of controlling the actions of the subject, in the prince, or in a few grandees. And this spirit of liberty is so deeply implanted in our constitution, and rooted even in our very soil, that a slave or a negro, the moment he lands in England, falls under the protection of the laws, and with regard to all natural rights becomes *eo instanti* a freeman.[27]

23 *Commentaries*, i. 50–52. Blackstone's dependence on Montesquieu for this and much else is elucidated in Carrese, *The Cloaking of Power*, 134 and chs. 5–7 *passim*.

24 A. Walsham, *The Reformation of the Landscape* (Oxford: Oxford University Press, 2011), 324.

25 *Commentaries*, i. 64–7. See also 231 (all 'Gothic systems of government' limited royal authority, but this principle had been 'overborne, by violence and chicane, in most of the kingdoms on the continent').

26 Blackstone distinguishes '*absolute* rights' (vested in all individuals 'by the immutable laws of nature') from'[s]uch rights as are social and *relative* result[ing] from . . . the formation of states and societies': *Commentaries*, i. 120–1 (italics in original).

27 *Commentaries*, i. 122–3. For subsequent authorial changes to the last sentence, and to Blackstone's position on slavery, see my *William Blackstone*, 250–3.

Yet, however organic or ancient ('coeval with our form of government'), the 'absolute rights of every Englishman' are 'subject at times to fluctuate and change: their establishment (excellent as it is) being still human'. So they have sometimes been 'depressed by overbearing and tyrannical princes', and at others flourished so luxuriantly 'as even to tend to anarchy' (although no examples of this latter state are cited). But eventually 'the vigour of our free constitution' reasserts itself, 'the convulsions consequent upon the struggle' subside, and 'the ballance of our rights and liberties' settles back to its 'proper level'. From the various medieval confirmations of Magna Carta to the 1701 Act of Settlement, this equilibrium state has been promoted by parliamentary enactments, which define:

> that *residuum* of natural liberty, which is not required by the laws of society to be sacrificed to public convenience; or else those civil privileges, which society hath engaged to provide, in lieu of the natural liberties so given up by individuals. These therefore were formerly, either by inheritance or purchase, the rights of all mankind; but, in most other countries of the world being now more less debased or destroyed, they at present may be said to remain, in a peculiar and emphatical manner, the rights of the people of England.[28]

Finally, at the end of Book IV, a more detailed and sustained chronological narrative concludes the whole text. This account 'Of the Rise, Progress, and Gradual Improvements, of the Laws of England' traces 'some rude outlines of a plan for the history of our laws and liberties' from ancient British and Saxon origins via Norman eclipse to 'the perfection they now enjoy'. Architectural metaphor is much in evidence: the 'mighty genius' of Alfred is credited with 'a most great and necessary work, which he is said to have executed in as masterly a manner. No less than to new-model the constitution; to rebuild it on a plan that should endure for ages; and, out of its old discordant materials, which were heaped upon each other in a vast and rude irregularity, to form one uniform and well-connected whole.' The closing peroration is also cast in architectural terms:

> Of a constitution, so wisely contrived, so strongly raised, and so highly finished, it is hard to speak with that praise, which is justly and severely its due—the thorough and attentive contemplation of it will furnish its best panegyric. It hath been the endeavour of these commentaries, however the execution may have succeeded, to examine its solid foundations, to mark its extensive plan, to explain the use and distribution of its parts, and from the harmonious concurrence of those several parts to demonstrate the elegant proportion of the whole. We have taken occasion to admire at every turn the noble monuments of ancient simplicity, and the more curious refinements of modern art. Nor have its faults been concealed from view; for faults it has, lest we should be tempted to think it of more than human structure: defects, chiefly arising from the decays of time, or the rage of unskilful improvement in later ages. To sustain, to repair, to beautify this noble pile, is a charge intrusted principally to the nobility, and such gentlemen of the kingdom, as are delegated by their country to parliament. The protection of THE LIBERTY OF BRITAIN is a duty they owe to themselves, who enjoy it; to their ancestors, who transmitted it down; and to

[28] *Commentaries*, i. 123–5.

their posterity, who will claim at their hands, this best birthright, and noblest inheritance of mankind.[29]

While the British constitution was no single written document, Blackstone clearly regarded this 'frame of government' as a coherent artefact of human devising, even if the liberty it so uniquely protected did originate with 'the supreme being [who] formed the universe'.[30]

IV. Institutions

Blackstone's account of how Hanoverian Britain was governed ('our excellent constitution') is largely contained in the first volume of the *Commentaries*. Book IV also deals with state power as exercised by the criminal law, while Books II and III contain relevant passages on other aspects of government, notably the judiciary and the courts. There is no separate treatment of 'the constitution' as such.[31] Because the prime aim is to map an already functioning system, rather than to present a series of ideal rules or abstract principles, much of the text is taken up with treatment, sometimes extensive, of the historical origins and contemporary rationale for specific constitutional institutions and measures.

Nevertheless, the whole work is carefully organized, proceeding by way of definition and division of its subject matter into component parts. Most subdivisions are binary (either/or), although three or four subdivisions sometimes appear. Printed student handouts presenting this material in tabular diagrammatic form summarized Blackstone's lecture syllabus, while similar tables are prefixed to the *Analysis of the Laws of England*.[32] Thus, both in the *Analysis* and the *Commentaries*, Book I addresses the rights (and duties) of persons. Persons are sequentially divided into natural and artificial (or corporate); the rights of natural persons are public or private; their public relations are those of magistrates or people; magistrates are supreme or subordinate—and so on. This mode of dissecting and sorting a complex body of knowledge for didactic purposes was originally applied to the common law by Sir Henry Finch (1558–1625), an English follower of the sixteenth-century French Huguenot dialectician Peter Ramus. Blackstone had earlier praised Finch's posthumously published *Law or a Discourse thereof* (1627) for its 'happy Progress in reducing the Elements of Law from their former Chaos to a regular methodical Science.'[33]

[29] *Commentaries*, iv. 435–6 (capitals in original). Cf. C. Matthews, 'A "Model of the Old House": Architecture in Blackstone's Life and *Commentaries*', in Prest (ed.), *Blackstone and his* Commentaries, 15–34.

[30] *Commentaries*, i. 122, 38. The same was also true of less-favoured constitutions, like those where Roman civil law had eroded natural liberty. Cf. B. Bailyn, *The Ideological Origins of the American Revolution* (Cambridge, MA: Harvard University Press, 1967), 68.

[31] For contemporary meanings of 'constitution', see D. Lieberman, 'The mixed constitution and the common law', in M. Goldie and R. Wokler (eds), *The Cambridge History of Eighteenth-Century Political Thought* (Cambridge: Cambridge University Press, 2006), 323.

[32] See my *William Blackstone*, plate 15 and 114, 143; *Analysis of the Laws*, sigs F–F2v.

[33] *Analysis*, vii; cf. my 'The Dialectical Origins of Finch's *Law*', *Cambridge Law Journal*, 36 (1977), 326–52.

Besides his use of architectural metaphors, Blackstone depicted the constitution 'in typical eighteenth-century fashion' as governed by Newton's laws of motion.[34] Thus the two houses of parliament and the crown, like 'three distinct powers in mechanics . . . jointly impel the machine of government in a direction different from what either, acting by themselves, would have done; but at the same time in a direction partaking of each, and formed out of all; a direction which constitutes the true line of the liberty and happiness of the community'.[35] This simile was peculiarly appropriate for what he elsewhere characterized as 'our free and active, and therefore compounded, constitution', its parts interacting through a complex system of checks and balances, so that 'every branch of our civil polity supports and is supported, regulates and is regulated, by the rest'.[36] As already seen, the purpose of this constitutional machine is to protect the rights, or liberties, of 'every Englishman', which were 'formerly, either by inheritance or purchase, the rights of all mankind', that is to say, 'the right of personal security, the right of personal liberty, and the right of private property'.[37]

In addition to those last three natural rights, which 'include the preservation of our civil immunities in their largest and most extensive sense', there were also 'auxiliary subordinate rights of the subject . . . barriers to protect and maintain inviolate the three great and primary rights'. For those latter would be 'in vain', were they merely 'declared, ascertained and protected by the dead letter of the law, if the constitution had provided no other method to secure their actual enjoyment'. The term 'subject' indicates that the specified auxiliary rights were not conferred on all humanity by the law of nature, but rather 'civil privileges' enjoyed by the fortunate denizens of the British Isles. They were five in number: the 'constitution, powers and privileges of parliament'; 'the limitation of the king's prerogative'; the right to seek justice in the courts; the right to petition the crown, or parliament, for redress of grievances; and the right 'of having arms for their defence, suitable to their condition and degree'.[38]

It has been suggested that, in Blackstone's view, this summed up the English constitution, as simply 'a body of rights belonging to the subject and vested in the subject'.[39] This concept of subject- or personhood was gendered, following mainstream contemporary assumptions and practice. True, it is nowhere explicitly stated or suggested that rights (natural or civil) belong only to males, and if Blackstone occasionally speaks of the rights of 'men' or 'every Englishman', he also uses gender-neutral terminology, such as 'persons', 'individuals', or 'people' in the same context. Nevertheless, females were evidently expected to play no formal

[34] Cf. E. N. Williams, *The Eighteenth Century Constitution 1688–1815* (Cambridge: Cambridge University Press, 1970), 1.

[35] *Commentaries*, i. 151, 153 ('emulation, or virtuous ambition . . . gives life and vigour to the community; it sets all the wheels of government in motion, which under a wise regulator, may be directed to any beneficial purpose').

[36] *Commentaries*, i. 239, 151.

[37] *Commentaries*, i. 125.

[38] *Commentaries*, i. 125, 136–9.

[39] E. Barker, 'Blackstone on the British Constitution', in Barker, *Essays on Government* (London: Oxford University Press, 1945), 142.

role in government or public life, despite a special exception for the queen of England, 'a public person'.[40] While gender or sex differences do not attract explicit attention in a constitutional context, rank and status distinctions feature prominently, as in the account of the membership of the two houses of parliament and the subsequent chapters on 'the people'. The latter are considered as alien and natural-born, clergy and laity, then divided into 'three distinct states: the civil, the military, and the maritime' (and only thereafter treated with regard to 'private oeconomical relations' as master and servant, husband and wife, parent and child, guardian and ward). A hierarchical, ordered, and formally unequal (indeed 'exclusionary') social structure is taken as given. Hence the axiomatic pronouncement that 'distinction of ranks and honours is necessary in every well-governed state' receives no further explanation or justification.[41]

The constitution's prime function is to preserve the subjects' rights and liberties, not to enhance the powers of the state. But having specified those rights in his first chapter, the following seven chapters (amounting to well over half of Book I) expound the composition, powers, and reciprocal relationships of parliament and the monarchy, the main organs of government. Blackstone's account updates the very well-established concept of England's mixed or balanced constitution (where, by virtue of their shared legislative authority, king, lords and commons kept each other in check). This was achieved by adding a new theme, evidently derived from Montesquieu's *The Spirit of the Laws* (first published in 1748, with an English translation in 1750), on the necessity of rigorously segregating parliament's legislative power from the executive power of the crown (since '[i]n all tyrannical governments . . . the right both of *making* and of *enforcing* the laws, is vested in one and the same man').[42] Yet parliament, 'the great corporation, or body politic, of the kingdom', both 'legislative power, and (of course) the supreme and absolute authority of the state', was itself a mixed body, comprising the king (sitting in the upper house 'in his royal political capacity') plus the Lords Spiritual and Temporal, and the House of Commons. Having justified this arrangement (invoking the royal veto power over legislation, last used in Queen Anne's reign, as a check against the legislature alone 'gradually assuming to itself the rights of the executive power'), Blackstone goes on to explain that a separate upper house was also required to prevent the nobility (those 'pillars, which are reared from among the people, more immediately to support the throne') from being 'borne down and overwhelmed by the popular torrent, which would effectually level all distinctions'.

The lower house (where Blackstone himself had sat since 1761) is said to consist of 'all such men *of any property* in the kingdom' (italics added) who were not peers; the formal property qualifications for MPs legislated in 1710 receive no mention.

40 *Commentaries*, i. 119, 121, 124, 212. Blackstone held the office of 'Solicitor General to Her Majesty' from 1763 to 1769.

41 *Commentaries*, i. 153, 410 & chs. 2, 10–17 *passim*. Cf. J. P. Greene (ed.), *Exclusionary Empire: English Liberty Overseas* (Cambridge: Cambridge University Press, 2010), 2–3.

42 *Commentaries*, i. 142. Carrese suggests that Blackstone's silence on the subjects of cabinet and ministerial responsibility may signify his disapproval of such merging of executive and legislative functions: *Cloaking of Power*, 136.

So the entire (male) population is said to enjoy 'a voice in parliament, either personally, or by his representatives', a venerable if plainly fictive concept of virtual representation.[43] Elections involved 'exercise of the democratical part of our constitution . . . the declaration of the people's will.' The franchise 'upon the true theory and genuine principles of liberty', should of course give 'every member of the community, however poor . . . a vote in electing those delegates, to whose charge is committed the disposal of his property, his liberty, and his life.' However 'persons of indigent fortunes, or such as are under the immediate domination of others' could not be expected to act independently; if they did have votes, 'they would be tempted to dispose of them under some undue influence or other'. Hence 'all popular states' had excluded from voting those 'suspected to have no will of their own', in order to set those 'whose wills be supposed independent, more thoroughly upon a level with each other'.[44]

This classical defence of a propertied franchise drew in part on a pamphlet Blackstone had drafted following the notoriously corrupt and bitterly fought Oxfordshire county election of 1754. Here it is suggested that if a 'new polity with respect to the qualifications of voters' for knights of the shire were to be established, it might reasonably enfranchise copyholders, tenants at will, and leaseholders, while the value of eligible freeholds 'should be greatly advanced above what is now required by law to entitle the holder to give his vote in country elections', presumably with a view to reducing electoral corruption.[45] This passage does not, however, appear in the *Commentaries*, although the danger of 'a great, an artful or a wealthy man' exercising 'a larger share in elections than is consistent with general liberty' is noted. Blackstone also makes the telling admission that his account represents 'the spirit of our constitution', which was in fact 'not quite so perfect as I have here endeavoured to describe it'. Indeed 'if any alteration might be wished or suggested in the present frame of parliaments, it should be in favour of a more complete representation of the people.'[46]

He goes on to outline the specific requirements for county and borough electors, the qualifications of candidates, and the manner of holding elections, especially those intended to prevent executive influence 'and the infamous practice of bribery and corruption'.[47] When these words first appeared in print, Blackstone was not only sitting as a member for the 'potwalloper' constituency of Hindon (thanks to the royal favourite and de facto prime minister Lord Bute, who had put up the necessary £2,000 for his election), but was simultaneously engaged in tightening the grip of his aristocratic client Lord Abingdon on the equally rotten borough of

[43] *Commentaries*, i. 143, 149–55. [44] *Commentaries*, i. 164–5.

[45] For *Considerations on the Question* (1758), see my *William Blackstone*, 127–9.

[46] *Commentaries*, i. 165, 166. In the 8th edition, which Blackstone revised after the publication of Bentham's *A Fragment on Government*, a footnote elaborates this point: 'the candid and intelligent reader' will observe that 'in many other parts of the work before him . . . the constitution is represented as nearly approaching perfection, without descending to the invidious task of pointing out such deviations and corruptions as length of time, and a loose state of national morals, have too great a tendency to produce': cf. Barker, 'Blackstone', 133.

[47] *Commentaries*, i. 166–73.

Westbury, to which seat he would himself transfer in the general election of 1767. (His text makes specific reference to Westbury, as the locus two hundred years before of 'the first instance that occurs of election bribery'.) If all this seems to smack of hypocrisy, self-deception, or both, his closing remarks on the subject suggest a reluctant recognition of the yawning gap between constitutional ideal and everyday reality: 'this practice [bribery] hath since taken much deeper and more universal root', hence the various 'wholesome' statutory provisions, 'to complete the efficacy of which, there is nothing wanting but resolution and integrity to put them in strict execution. Undue influence being thus (I wish the depravity of mankind would permit me to say effectually) guarded against'.[48]

In detailing the laws, customs, and privileges of parliament, both aggregate and for each separate house, Blackstone's assertion of its 'sovereign and uncontrolable authority... [to] do everything that is not naturally impossible... what they do, no authority on earth can undo' would prove highly contentious, both for contemporaries and later readers.[49] Apart from apparently conflicting with his earlier pronouncement that any human enactment infringing the law of nature or the revealed law of God must be invalid, such a conception of absolute parliamentary sovereignty explicitly denied (as its author freely admitted) the Lockean tenet of ultimate popular sovereignty, including 'devolution of power, to the people at large' if the legislature abused their trust.[50] However justified in theory, such a position (Blackstone argued) could not be incorporated or reconciled with 'any dispensation of government at present actually existing', precisely because it implied a wholesale return to the original state of nature, hence the end of both government and the constitution. If parliament should pass unjust or unreasonable laws, individuals were not morally obliged to obey them (although they must accept any consequent penal sanction). Furthermore, judicial interpretation offered another potent means to modify the impact of 'acts of parliament contrary to reason'.[51] But the final paragraph of this chapter reiterates the 'vast authority' attained by parliament after the Glorious Revolution, citing the Septennial Act (1716) whereby the 'very same house, that was chosen for three years, enacted its own continuance for seven'.[52]

This had been a leading grievance among opponents of the successive Whig juntas which came to power in 1714 and remained dominant until George III became king. Some trace of lingering Tory resentment may appear in Blackstone's

[48] *Commentaries*, i. 173. Cf. Bentham's criticism of the gulf between theory and reality in Blackstone's account of the supposed independence of the two branches of the legislature: *Fragment on Government*, 75–6.

[49] *Commentaries*, i. 156. Lieberman, 'Mixed constitution and the common law', 333; M. Lobban, 'Custom, Nature and Authority: the Roots of English Legal Positivism', in D. Lemmings (ed.), *The British and their Laws in the Eighteenth Century* (Woodbridge: Boydell and Brewer, 2005), 27–58.

[50] *Commentaries*, i. 156–7. While the rejection of Blackstone's conception of parliamentary sovereignty by James Burgh and John Cartwright has been attributed to their religious heterodoxy, it was not only dissenters and deists who found it unacceptable: cf. J. C. D. Clark, *The Language of Liberty 1660–1832* (Cambridge: Cambridge University Press, 1994), 119, 125 and S. J. Connolly, 'Precedent and Principle: The Patriots and their Critics', in S. J. Connolly (ed.), *Political Ideas in Eighteenth-Century Ireland* (Dublin: Four Courts Press, 2000), 147.

[51] *Commentaries*, i. 157, 56–7, 91. See also J. V. Orth, 'Blackstone's Rules on the Construction of Statutes', in *Blackstone and his* Commentaries, 82–90; Carrese, *Cloaking of Power*, 128–40.

[52] *Commentaries*, i. 182.

characterization of that measure as 'professedly' to prevent the expense of frequent elections and to maintain security following the 1715 Jacobite invasion. However, his subsequent six chapters on aspects of the monarchy as executive are more even-handed.[53] Thus while the Tory–Jacobite shibboleth of indefeasible hereditary divine-right monarchy is firmly refuted, the 'confusion, instability, and madness' which followed the trial of Charles I, 'told by those infamous judges, who pronounced his unparalleled sentence, that he was an elective prince' provides 'a standing argument in favour of hereditary monarchy'.[54] The crown's descent from the Saxon King Egbert to George I is recounted in detail, with the 1688 revolution presented as a fait accompli 'decided by the voice of the society itself', so now to be accepted by all those 'born under that establishment which was built upon this foundation, and obliged by every tie, religious as well as civil, to maintain it'. Blackstone further commends the prudence and moderation of the Convention Parliament, whose settlement ('however it might in some respects go beyond the letter of our antient laws') was nevertheless in 'the spirit of our constitution, and the rights of human nature'. Indeed, 1689 is said to have inaugurated a new era, when 'the bounds of prerogative and liberty have been better defined, the principles of government more thoroughly examined and understood, and the rights of the subject more explicitly guarded by legal provisions, than in any other period of the English history.'[55]

Moderation and balance are also prominent themes in the lengthy discussion 'Of the King's Prerogative'. While limitation of those powers is claimed to be 'one of the principal bulwarks of civil liberty, or (in other words) of the British constitution', when exercising his lawful prerogatives the king is 'so far absolute, that there is no legal authority that can either delay or restrain him'. Otherwise 'the power of the crown would indeed be but a name and a shadow, insufficient for the ends of government.'[56] Yet Blackstone disavows any advocacy of 'arbitrary power', since there always remain 'those *extraordinary* recourses to first principles, which are necessary when the contracts of society are in danger of dissolution, and the law proves too weak a defence against the violence of fraud or oppression'. Indeed he argues that failure to appreciate 'this obvious distinction' has been responsible for the 'doctrines, of absolute power in the prince and of national resistance by the people, to be much misunderstood and perverted by the advocates for slavery on the one hand, and the demagogues of faction on the other'. Proponents of passive obedience have gone to one extreme, 'over-zealous republicans' to the other, by 'fancifully (or sometimes factiously)' extending the right of resistance 'when the being of the state is endangered, and the public voice proclaims such resistance

[53] M. Francis and J. Morrow, 'After the Ancient Constitution: Political Theory and English Constitutional Writings, 1760–1832', in G. J. Schochet, P. E. Tatspaugh, and C. Brobeck (eds), *Empire and Revolutions* (Washington, DC: Folger Institute Center for the History of British Political Thought Proceedings, 6, 1993), 355.

[54] *Commentaries*, i. 182, 184, 188, 202–3.

[55] *Commentaries* i. 190–203, 205–6. Cf. J. C. D. Clark, *English Society 1688–1832* (Cambridge: Cambridge University Press, 1985), 204–7.

[56] *Commentaries*, i. 230–1, 243.

necessary', to 'every individual'—a 'doctrine productive of anarchy, and (in consequence) equally as fatal to civil liberty as tyranny itself'.[57] This seems to suggest that only parliament can sanction resistance, although it is earlier stated that *all* oppression, by either parliament or monarch, 'must necessarily be out of the reach of any *stated rule,* or *express legal provision*; but, if ever they unfortunately happen, the prudence of the times must provide new remedies upon new emergencies'[58]—as in 1688–9.

Finally, another long chapter, 'Of the King's Revenue', outlines the principles of public finance. Since most of the crown's original fiscal prerogatives were now 'in the hands of subjects', much to the general benefit in terms of civil liberties, the treatment of such matters as treasure trove and 'the right to *royal fish*' is appropriately antiquarian.[59] But the discussion of taxation also reflects Blackstone's broader experience and interests (as a former college bursar and current MP, among other things). Even if attainable, 'total abolition of taxes' would be undesirable, for 'the true idea of government' means that 'some few men are deputed by many others to preside over public affairs, so that individuals may the better be enabled to attend to their private concerns.' Hence it is necessary that the latter 'contribute a portion of their private gains, in order to support that government . . . which protects them in the enjoyment of their respective properties'. While the historical background to the land tax and customs and excise receives ample attention, current concerns and issues are also addressed. They include the danger of customs duties being 'a check and cramp upon trade', bearing excessively upon the ultimate consumer because of the profits extracted by every trader through whose hands a taxable commodity passes, and encouraging smuggling, the capital penalty for which put 'murderers upon an equal footing with such as are really guilty of no natural, but merely a positive offence'.[60] The post office, on the other hand, provides 'a manifest advantage to the public', besides yielding a steadily increased revenue to government; its protected monopoly of letter-carrying is 'absolutely necessary', as 'rival independent offices would only serve to ruin one another'. These various branches of the revenue are appropriated to pay interest on the national debt, which 'far exceeds all calculation of commercial benefit, and is productive of the greatest inconveniences', including excessive levels of consumption taxes. However, complaints of increased expenditure on the civil list are 'void of any rational foundation'; given the impact of price inflation, it is 'impossible to support that dignity, which a king of Great Britain should maintain, with an income in any degree less than what is now established by parliament'.[61]

An element of special pleading can hardly be ruled out at this point, given Blackstone's own status as a crown law officer in receipt of the 'modest emolument' of £180 p.a. from the civil list, and a personal relationship with George III dating back to the days when copies of his Oxford lectures were supplied to the then

[57] *Commentaries*, i. 243–4 (italics in original).
[58] *Commentaries*, i. 237–8 (italics in original).
[59] *Commentaries*, i. 271–2, 280, 285–6 (italics in original).
[60] *Commentaries*, i. 296–7, 306–7; cf. iv. 155–6.
[61] *Commentaries*, i. 311–12, 315–18, 321–2.

Prince of Wales. The same could be said of the 'short comparative review' of the royal prerogative past and present, with which, having 'chalked out all the principal outlines of this vast title of the law', the chapter concludes. Blackstone here points out that the crown's powers have apparently been 'greatly curtailed and diminished' since James I's reign, so that 'we may perhaps be led to think, that the ballance is enclined pretty strongly to the popular scale', leaving 'the executive magistrate... neither independence nor power' sufficient to 'form that check upon the lords and commons, which the founders of our constitution intended'. However, he goes on to point out that parliamentary revenues settled on the crown for life have restored the monarch's 'constitutional independence'. Moreover 'we may find perhaps that the hands of government are at least sufficiently strengthened', thanks to the increased national debt and taxes. This has 'given rise to such a multitude of new officers, created by and removeable at the royal pleasure, that they have extended the influence of government to every corner of the nation.'[62] There is also the advent of a standing army, 'raised by the crown, officered by the crown, commanded by the crown'. So 'whatever may have become of the *nominal*, the *real* power of the crown has not been too far weakened by any transactions in the last century'.[63] At some unspecified future date, when the national debt and taxes are reduced, and when 'a well planned and national militia... suffer[s] our formidable army to be thinned and regulated', this 'adventitious power of the crown will slowly and imperceptibly diminish'. Meanwhile 'good subjects and good Englishmen' were duty bound 'to reverence the crown, and yet to guard against corrupt and servile influence from those who are intrusted with its authority'—from, in other words, anything resembling the Whig administrations which had monopolized government both before and after Sir Robert Walpole's long ascendancy.[64]

Blackstone's readers are also exhorted to hope for the 'long, very long' reign of the young George III, who had not only 'manifested the highest veneration for the free constitution of Britain', but 'remarkably strengthened its outworks'. Whatever else this eulogistic reference pointed to, it certainly embraced the statutory provision enacted in 1761 'at the earnest recommendation of the king himself', whereby judges sitting in the superior courts retained office notwithstanding the death of the reigning monarch in whose name their commissions were made out.[65] The constitutional role of the judiciary is not the subject of a separate chapter or chapters in the *Commentaries*, and so might seem at first glance relatively minor, especially by contrast with those of parliament and monarchy. Yet there are grounds for thinking that Blackstone (influenced by and following Montesquieu, in this and other respects) regarded the judiciary as a vital third force, mediating between the legislative and executive powers. For although judges were appointed by the crown, the king was not the '*author* or *original*' of justice. Indeed the 'original power of judicature, by the fundamental principles of society, is lodged in

[62] *Commentaries*, i. 322–4. [63] *Commentaries*, i. 325 (italics in original).

[64] *Commentaries*, i. 326. On distrust of standing armies, see S. Skinner, 'Blackstone's Support for the Militia', *American Journal of Legal History*, 44 (2000), 1–18.

[65] *Commentaries*, i. 258.

the society at large'. The English constitution entrusted this power to the crown, which for practical reasons, 'by the long and uniform usage of many ages' had delegated it to the judges and the courts, 'the grand depositary of the fundamental laws'. These learned men were 'living oracles... bound by an oath to decide according to the law of the land'.[66] This 'distinct and separate existence of the judicial power, in a peculiar body of men', whom the crown nominated but could not remove, constituted 'one main preservative of the public liberty; which cannot subsist long in any state, unless the administration of common justice be in some degree separated both from the legislative and also from the executive power.'[67]

For if judges were part of the legislature, their arbitrary decisions would clearly threaten the subjects' rights, because they would not be constrained by the 'fundamental principles' which 'judges are bound to observe'. An equivalent problem would arise if they were not separated from the executive. Hence the abolition in 1641 not only of the court of Star Chamber, but also of the judicial powers of the Privy Council, lest it 'pronounce that for law which was most agreeable to the prince or his officers'.[68] This general consideration also explained why 'the absolute power, claimed and exercised' in France under Louis XV was 'more tolerable than that of the eastern empires'. Indeed the judicial power exercised by the French *parlements* offered the best hope of recovering that nation's former liberty; in Turkey, by contrast, 'where every thing is centered in the sultan or his ministers, despotic power is in its meridian, and wears a more dreadful aspect'.[69]

V. Conclusion

Blackstone's *Commentaries* were written less as a contribution to political theory than a general introduction to the structure and workings of English law and government. Besides relying on various fictions and unsubstantiated assertions, his account of the British constitution is in some respects incomplete, not least with regard to the practical operation of day-to-day politics. There are also seeming contradictions and internal inconsistencies, perhaps most notably in respect of the complex relationship between the untrammelled sovereign power of parliament and the rights and liberties of the 'polite and commercial people' which that power purportedly existed to protect. Nor were Blackstone's claims for the pre-eminent excellence of Britain's constitution wholly new. But there can be no doubt of the unrivalled contribution made by his work to the elaboration and dissemination of

[66] *Commentaries*, i. 257–8, 69.

[67] *Commentaries*, i. 257–9. Of course the separation was scarcely complete, so long as the Lord Chancellor presided over both the court of chancery and the House of Lords, or while chief justices (like Mansfield) also sat in cabinet.

[68] The Council retained jurisdiction only over appeals in admiralty and ecclesiastical cases, as well as those from British colonies: J. H. Baker, *An Introduction to English Legal History* (London: Butterworth, 2002) 141; *Commentaries*, i. 259–60.

[69] *Commentaries*, i. 260.

this 'constitutive story', one which 'functioned to tell people who they were, not simply to offer a version of the past'.[70] Despite the little-Englandism of its title, and various ambiguities and uncertainties about the relationship of non-English parts of the British Isles, not to mention colonies and plantations across the seas, to the forms and principles outlined in the *Commentaries*, Blackstone's work became the standard authority on the institutions and practices of government in the Westminster tradition, not only for Great Britain but throughout (and beyond) the Anglo-American common-law world.[71] Its influence in North America was and remains remarkable. 'Life, Liberty and the Pursuit of Happiness', that trio of 'unalienable' human rights which Thomas Jefferson embedded in the Declaration of Independence, has even been attributed to his reading of Blackstone (presumably with special reference to the claim made early in Book I that pursuit of happiness is the divinely sanctioned law of nature).[72] In recent years, American scholars have played a prominent role in reassessing the *Commentaries* 'as a comprehensive work of constitutionalism informed by a serious political philosophy'; in other words, as complex and subtle, rather than confused and contradictory.[73] In this task, they have built upon several earlier generations of rehabilitative scholarship by legal historians and historians of political thought.

No doubt the current revisionist project reflects a variety of agendas and positions. It may in part represent a reaction against the almost wholly negative assessments of radical critics such as Jerome Frank and Duncan Kennedy, as also an appreciation of the role Blackstone accorded natural law as a brake on excessive judicial and legislative ambition, coupled with respect for his generally cautious, incrementalist, moderate, and pragmatic outlook on public policy issues. Then there is the Blackstone Institute of Abilene, Texas, an organization avowedly committed to 'reviving the Constitution and its Blackstonian foundations', which latter being 'infused with Judeo-Christian principles', especially the Ten Commandments, are hailed as offering a clear pathway to national revival.[74]

[70] Cf. L. Colley, 'North and South', *London Review of Books*, 2 August 2012, 8.

[71] For Mirabeau, Blackstone, and the 1789 Declaration des Droits de l'Homme et du Citoyen, see J. Emerson, 'Did Blackstone get the Gallic Shrug?' in *Blackstone and his* Commentaries, 194–5. See also the essays by J. Cairns and M. Morin in W. Prest (ed.), *Reinterpreting Blackstone's* Commentaries: *A Seminal Text in National and International Contexts* (Oxford: Hart Publishing, 2014).

[72] *Commentaries*, i. 41–2; cf. J. Frank, 'A Sketch of an Influence', in P. Sayre (ed.), *Interpretations of Modern Legal Philosophies* (New York: Oxford University Press, 1947), 189; D. Armitage, 'The Declaration of Independence and International Law', *William and Mary Quarterly*, 59 (2002), 41.

[73] Carrese, *Cloaking of Power*, 8. Besides the work of Alschuler, Carrese, Lieberman, Lubert, and Posner cited in nn. 7–8 above, see H. Storing, 'William Blackstone', in L. Strauss and J. Cropsey (eds), *History of Political Philosophy* (Chicago: Chicago University Press, 1987); J. R. Stonor, *Common Law and Liberal Theory* (Lawrence: University Press of Kansas, 1992), ch. 10 ('Blackstone's Liberalized Common Law'); M. Franck, *Against the Imperial Judiciary: the Supreme Court vs. the Sovereignty of the People* (Lawrence: University Press of Kansas, 1996), 200–7; M. Zuckert, 'Social Compact, Common Law and the American Founding', in R. I. Pestritto and T. G. West (eds), *The American Founding and the Social Compact* (Lanham: Lexington Books, 2003), ch. 2.

[74] See <http://www.blackstoneinstitute.org/williamBlackstone.php>, accessed 13 July 2014. Cf. R. D. Stacey, *Sir William Blackstone and the Common Law: Blackstone's Legacy to America* (Eugene: ACW Press, 2003). The Liberty Fund Inc. has long had an interest in Blackstone: <http://oll.libertyfund.org/?option=com_staticxt&staticfile=show.php%3Fperson=4639&Itemid=28>.

But (pace Jeremy Bentham), Blackstone's legacy is not readily captured by any single ideological conviction or tendency. For while asserting that 'both public and private vices are subject to the vengeance of eternal justice', he also maintained that 'human laws can have no concern with any but social and relative duties; being intended only to regulate the conduct of man . . . as a member of civil society'.[75] Despite emphasizing the liberties or rights (not least to private property) of individual citizens, which enthusiasts for a free market and limited government find congenial, we have already seen that Blackstone placed considerable stress on the residual prerogatives of the crown as executive, and the absolute nature of king-in-parliament sovereignty. Thus the king is 'arbiter of commerce',[76] and his government remains entirely at liberty to regulate the economy and distort the market by imposing restrictions on the free flow of trade (such as the export of wool, and the internal carriage of letters) or consumer preferences, as with Charles II's statute prescribing woollen burial shrouds, 'a law consistent with public liberty, for it encourages the staple trade, on which in great measure depends the universal good of the nation'.[77] The conscription or 'pressing' of seamen for the Royal Navy, although a 'matter of some dispute, and submitted to with great reluctance', is nevertheless 'defensible from public security, to which all private considerations must give way'.[78]

Blackstone was also entirely comfortable with the provision of public welfare rather than 'private benevolence' to support the poor and to find 'employment for such as are able to work'. But he expressed his dislike of workhouses, as tending to 'destroy all domestic connexions (the only felicity of the honest and industrious labourer)', while putting 'the sober and diligent, upon a level, in point of their earnings, with those who are dissolute and idle'. And if the Elizabethan Poor Law of 1601 met with his approval, he strongly deprecated the various statutes passed after Charles II's restoration, which had given rise to 'the intricacy of our poor-laws', precisely because they departed too far from 'the foundation of the common law' (in this particular case, the administrative division of the country into shires, tithings, and hundreds).[79]

The good King Alfred had had much to do with that foundation, needless to say, although of course it went back long before even his time. Not that simple longevity—as distinct from functionality, humanity, and rationality, together with acceptance by 'common consent'—lent legitimacy to the constitution and the law.[80] For Blackstone was far from a wholly indiscriminate admirer of the

[75] *Commentaries*, iv. 41–2.

[76] *Commentaries*, i. 263. On the other hand, Blackstone pointed out that the law did not protect servants of the crown who committed 'injuries to the rights of *property*': *Commentaries*, iii. 255, as cited by H. W. Arndt, 'The Origin of Dicey's Concept of the "Rule of Law"', *Australian Law Journal*, 31 (1957), 119.

[77] *Commentaries*, i. 43, 122. See also an illuminating discussion by W. H. Greenleaf, 'Blackstone and the Office of Government', in R. Schnur (ed.), *Die Rolle der Juristen bei der Entstehung des Modernen Staates* (Berlin: Duncker and Humblot, 1986), 502–20.

[78] *Commentaries*, i. 405–7.

[79] *Commentaries*, i. 349–53.

[80] Cf. Zuckert, 'Social Compact, Common Law', 60; R. Willman, 'Blackstone and the "Theoretical Perfection" of English Law in the Reign of Charles II', *Historical Journal*, 26 (1983), 43–4, 46–7.

ancient constitution. Indeed he identified both 'too scrupulous an adherence to some rules of the antient common law, when the reasons have ceased upon which those rules were founded', and 'the not repealing such of the old penal laws as are either obsolete or absurd' as major causes of the criminal law's manifest failings (or rather, as he more delicately put it, 'some particulars, that seem to want revision and amendment').[81] He also thought that 'many modern judicial decisions' were superior in 'beauty and energy' to those of 'our ancestors'.[82] While 'often taken for a mere patriot or conservative, . . . he gives ample indication that neither his praise of what is English nor his devotion to what is old is to be taken simply at face value'.[83] Blackstone and his *Commentaries* continue to resist easy categorization. But their contribution to the expression and dissemination of modern constitutional ideas about human rights, the separation of powers, judicial independence, and the state's duty to its citizens remains undeniable.

[81] *Commentaries*, iv. 3–4.
[82] *Commentaries*, i. ii (Preface).
[83] Storing, 'Blackstone', 629.

10

Jeremy Bentham

Philip Schofield

I. Context

Jeremy Bentham (1748–1832), English philosopher and reformer, was hailed by one of his admirers, the Guatemalan statesman José del Valle, as 'legislator of the world'.[1] This phrase captures Bentham's central ambition in life, namely to draw up codes of law that were, for the most part, universally applicable, because founded upon the universal nature of man. His first attempt to produce a code was his projected 'Plan of a Penal Code', on which he worked from about 1776 to about 1788. His intention was that the first of the two projected books of the penal code would contain the provisions of the law in full (or *in terminis*, as Bentham himself expressed it), except where local circumstances might render this inappropriate, in which case, instructions would be issued to the legislator. The second book would contain the law of penal procedure. In both books, the relevant legal provisions would be accompanied with the reasons that justified them. The penal code would be completed with a series of Appendices, on such subjects as the promulgation of law, digestion (that is, the rendering of customary law into statute), and judicial interpretation.[2] The whole penal code would be preceded by an Introduction. The material printed in 1780 and then published in 1789 as *An Introduction to the Principles of Morals and Legislation*, consisting of sixteen chapters and the first two sections of the seventeenth chapter, had been written as the first part of this Introduction, and, in the event, was the only part of Bentham's 'magnum opus' that was published by Bentham himself.[3] Bentham's intention was that the material that came to constitute *An Introduction to the Principles of Morals and Legislation*, and hence the introduction to the penal code, should be continued

[1] See Jeremy Bentham, *'Legislator of the World': Writings on Codification, Law, and Education*, ed. P. Schofield and J. Harris (Oxford: Clarendon, 1998), 370–1, reproducing Del Valle's letter to Bentham, which the latter received in 1826. For Bentham's universalism see D. Armitage, 'Globalizing Jeremy Bentham', *History of Political Thought*, XXXII (2011), 63–82.

[2] See 'Plan of a Penal Code—Prospectus', in the hand of Jeremiah Bentham, Bentham's father, in the Bentham Papers, British Library Add. MS 33,556, fos. 139–42.

[3] The material was extensively drawn upon by Bentham's Genevan editor Étienne Dumont and appeared in French translation in *Traités de législation pénale et civile*, 3 vols (Paris: Bossange, Masson, et Besson, 1802). For Dumont's fascination with Bentham see R. Whatmore, *Against War and Empire: Geneva, Britain, and France in the Eighteenth Century* (New Haven: Yale, 2012), 273–89.

with the remainder of Chapter 17, which was entitled 'Of the Limits of the Penal Branch of Jurisprudence'. This chapter grew into a total of twenty-one sections, and constituted a book-length study in its own right.[4] Further chapters would deal with the subject of 'Indirect Legislation', that is measures to prevent offences by such means as did not involve direct prohibition,[5] and with 'Place and Time', that is the influence of local circumstances on legislation.[6] By the middle of 1782, Bentham had decided that he would devote separate books to each of these chapters, and a further volume would contain an 'Essay on Reward'.[7]

There was, in all this, very little discussion of constitutional law. Indeed, in a footnote added to the second edition of *An Introduction to the Principles of Morals and Legislation* in 1823, Bentham remarked: 'And the *constitutional* branch of law, what is become of it?' He went on to explain that, 'as far as recollection serves, that branch, notwithstanding its importance, and its capacity of being lodged separately from the other matter, had at that time scarcely presented itself to my view in the character of a distinct one: the thread of my enquiries had not as yet reached it.'[8] Even allowing for the fact that Bentham was not giving himself enough credit for the attention he had paid, albeit in passing, to constitutional law in the late 1770s and early 1780s, he had by 1823 come to have a very different view of the place of constitutional law. From around 1808, when he became interested in the reform of the Scottish legal system, Bentham had begun actively to tout his services as a codifier. The fact that he approached 'constituted authorities' as diverse as the President of the United States of America in 1811 and the Emperor of all the Russias in 1814 is significant. In both cases, he offered to draw up penal and civil codes.[9] He believed that utilitarian codes of penal and civil law could be introduced under any political regime. In or around 1818, however, he came to the conclusion that rulers would not introduce utilitarian legal reform under any form of government except under a representative democracy. Bentham had become a republican (he equated a representative democracy with a republic, meaning a political community without monarchy or aristocracy). The reasons for Bentham's transition to political radicalism, marked in 1809 by his beginning to work on the

[4] The work is now published as *Of the Limits of the Penal Branch of Jurisprudence*, ed. P. Schofield (Oxford: Clarendon, 2010).

[5] The essay was first published by Dumont in *Traités de législation*, iii, 1–207, and then in English translation in *The Works of Jeremy Bentham*, ed. John Bowring, 11 vols (Edinburgh: William Tait 1838–43) [hereafter Bowring], vol. i, 533–80.

[6] Bowring, vol. i, 168–94. The most recent version, based on the original manuscripts in the Bentham Papers, University College London Library, appears as 'Place and Time', ed. P. Schofield and S. G. Engelmann, in *Jeremy Bentham: Selected Writings*, ed. S. G. Engelmann, (New Haven: Yale, 2011), 152–219. For an analysis of the different versions of 'Place and Time', and for Bentham's remarkable lack of Eurocentric prejudice, see S. G. Engelmann and J. Pitts, 'Bentham's "Place and Time"', *The Tocqueville Review*, XXXII (2011), 43–66.

[7] Bentham to Lord Ashburton, 3 June 1782, *Correspondence of Jeremy Bentham*, ed. I. R. Christie vol. iii (London: Athlone, 1971), 123–30.

[8] Jeremy Bentham, *An Introduction to the Principles of Morals and Legislation*, ed. J. H. Burns and H. L. A. Hart (London: Athlone, 1970), 281.

[9] See Bentham, *'Legislator of the World'*, 5–35, 44–7.

material that would eventually be published in 1817 as *Plan of Parliamentary Reform*, have been extensively discussed.[10] The effective rejection of his panopticon prison scheme by the British government in 1803, and his subsequent discovery of systematic corruption throughout the political, legal, and ecclesiastical establishments, led Bentham to commit himself to 'democratic ascendancy'. However, the precise reasons for the timing of his later transition, that is from 'democratic ascendancy' to republicanism, remain obscure.

Whatever the case, when in April 1822 Bentham received, from the Portuguese Cortes, an acceptance of his offer to draw up penal, civil, and constitutional codes, he immediately began work on the constitutional code.[11] From a logical point of view, he always regarded the penal code as foundational; but from a political point of view, he recognized that without the prior establishment of a constitutional code enshrining some form of representative democracy, no progress in relation to the law elsewhere would be made. The point was that Bentham had realized that no other regime apart from a representative democracy was committed to promoting the greatest happiness of the greatest number. As the elderly Bentham, reflecting on his early career, remarked: 'I was . . . a great reformist; but never suspected that the people in power were against reform. I supposed they only wanted to know what was good in order to embrace it.'[12] Precisely 'what was good', according to Bentham, was legal reform based on the principle of utility. In the 1780s, he aimed to present enlightened sovereigns such as Catherine the Great with a plan for a rational penal code, and had hopes that she would enact it. In the 1790s, he aimed to present the British government with a plan for a model prison, and had hopes that he would be given the authority and the means to build it. In the 1800s, he had hopes that his plans for the reform of Scottish judicial procedure would be seized upon by a grateful government. None of his schemes came to fruition. The problem, Bentham came to believe, lay with the 'sinister interest' of rulers. The sole concern of rulers was to promote the greatest happiness of themselves, and only to the extent that prudence dictated did they pursue measures to promote the greatest happiness of the greatest number. Bentham, who began his career as the analyst of key terms in jurisprudence, ended it as a political activist—the self-confessed 'Leader of . . . the *Radicals*'.[13]

[10] See, for instance, J. R. Dinwiddy, 'Bentham's Transition to Political Radicalism', *Journal of the History of Ideas*, 35 (1975), 683–700; J. E. Crimmins, 'Bentham's Political Radicalism Reexamined', *Journal of the History of Ideas*, 54 (1994), 259–81; and P. Schofield, *Utility and Democracy: the Political Thought of Jeremy Bentham* (Oxford: Oxford University Press, 2006), 137–40.

[11] Jeremy Bentham, *First Principles Preparatory to Constitutional Code*, ed. P. Schofield (Oxford: Clarendon, 1989) Editorial Introduction, xx.

[12] Bowring, vol. x, 66.

[13] Bentham described himself as such in a letter of 1829 (quoted in Schofield, *Utility and Democracy*, 304–5). All italics, here and below, are in the original. The difference between the 'early' Bentham and the 'mature' Bentham is explored in J. H. Burns, 'Jeremy Bentham: From Radical Enlightenment to Philosophic Radicalism', *The Bentham Newsletter*, 8 (1984), 4–14.

II. The Meaning of a Constitution

For Bentham, a constitution should not consist of a set of fundamental articles, such as might be contained in a social contract or a declaration of rights, with the purpose of placing limits on government activity or regulating the relationship between government and governed. A constitution, for Bentham, was equivalent to the whole of the provisions enshrined in constitutional law, and which thereby included everything from determining the location of supreme power to specifying the duties of the lowliest official. Nor did he regard a constitution as something that should be considered to be unalterable or immutable, or only alterable according to some procedure that was more complex than that applied to other branches of the law. It was not that there was any logical difficulty involved in the notion of immutable laws—such laws were simply inexpedient, and to enact them was one of the grossest errors that could be made in legislation. Throughout his career, Bentham criticized severely any attempt to 'bind the hands' of future legislators. In 'Necessity of an Omnipotent Legislature', he objected to the clauses in the new French Constitution of 1791 that stipulated that any amendments to the constitution had to be approved by an Assembly of Revision, and only then after three successive legislatures had expressed a wish to see the proposed amendments implemented.

> If there were a proposition in government more self-evident than any other, one should think it would be that at every period there should be some one authority competent to do every thing that may require to be done by government, and that that authority should extend to every case whatsoever.[14]

To introduce immutability clauses into a constitution was to claim infallibility. It was absurd that the assembly of twelve hundred persons who had passed the constitution, and who, from the time of their election, had been 'doubting, disputing, changing, struggling, wrangling, sometimes one man's notions prevailing, sometimes another', should suddenly have 'worked itself up into infallibility'. And if they had become infallible, why did they restrict themselves to the constitutional code? Why did they not give to France an infallible penal code and an infallible civil code?[15] In the early 1820s, in 'Rid Yourselves of Ultramaria', Bentham similarly objected to an article in the restored Spanish Constitution, originally promulgated at Cadiz in 1812, which stipulated that there could be no amendments to the constitution for eight years.[16] Under Bentham's constitutional code, the legislature was to be 'omnicompetent'—no actions of men in the past were to bind the actions of men in the present. Furthermore, the constitutional

[14] Jeremy Bentham, *Rights, Representation, and Reform: Nonsense upon Stilts and other writings on the French Revolution*, ed. P. Schofield, C. Pease-Watkin, and C. Blamires (Oxford: Clarendon, 2002), 265.

[15] *Rights, Representation, and Reform*, 278–9.

[16] Jeremy Bentham, *Colonies, Commerce, and Constitutional Law: Rid Yourselves of Ultramaria and other writings on Spain and Spanish America*, ed. P. Schofield (Oxford: Clarendon, 1995) 182–4.

code was to be subject to amendment by the legislature in the same way as every other branch of law.[17]

The constitutional code would form one part of Bentham's pannomion, or complete code of laws. Bentham constructed his pannomion on the basis of his understanding of the various relationships he identified between the different branches of law. He made use of several distinctions, depending upon his purpose. He distinguished, for instance, between substantive law, consisting of the 'rule of action' itself, and adjective law, consisting of judicial procedure. The substantive law, therefore, included the civil, penal, and constitutional law. Another distinction he made was between private law and public law, the latter term being equivalent to constitutional law, 'in which individuals are regarded collectively and in some public capacity, with a view to the powers necessary to be exercised by some of them over others, for the good of the whole'. From this point of view, constitutional law was distinguished not by its form as such, but by the persons to whom it was addressed. A third distinction was between the civil law or distributive branch of law, which described the distribution of benefits and burdens, and the penal law, the purpose of which was to secure conformity to the civil law. From this point of view, constitutional law was made up of a combination of civil and penal law, in that it distributed the rights and duties of officials and announced measures to enforce compliance.[18]

III. The Point of the Constitution

Bentham's mature constitutional theory is contained in writings dating from 1822 onwards, following the acceptance by the Portuguese Cortes of his offer to draw up penal, civil, and constitutional codes. The result of this major endeavour of the final decade of Bentham's life was the virtual completion, and partial publication, of his constitutional code, a blueprint for representative democracy.[19] For Bentham, the point of the constitution was to replace the natural opposition of interests which existed between rulers and subjects with an artificial identification of interests. It is worth pausing here in order to explain Bentham's conception of the relationship

[17] Jeremy Bentham, *Constitutional Code*, vol. I, ed. F. Rosen and J. H. Burns (Oxford: Clarendon, 1983), 41–2, 44. For Bentham's attitude to infallibility in general see M. Schwartzberg, 'Jeremy Bentham on Fallibility and Infallibility', *Journal of the History of Ideas* LXVIII (2007), 563–85.

[18] Bentham, *'Legislator of the World'*, 191–2.

[19] Bentham printed the first volume of *Constitutional Code*, containing the first nine chapters, in 1827, and published it in 1830. The tenth chapter, dealing with the 'Defensive Force', was printed in 1830. Volume II was to consist of chapters ten and eleven, the latter dealing with 'Ministers Severally'. The eleventh chapter, together with the third volume, containing chapters twelve to thirty-two, and dealing mainly with the judicial establishment and local government, exists in manuscript in the Bentham Papers in University College London Library. The three volumes together were first published in Bowring, ix, under the confusing heading of Book II. In Bowring, Book I consists of a jumble of introductory material that Bentham composed for constitutional code itself, as well as some material on codification generally. For a detailed account of the constitutional code see F. Rosen, *Jeremy Bentham and Representative Democracy: A Study of the Constitutional Code* (Oxford: Clarendon, 1983).

between happiness and suffering, interest and sinister interest, and pain and pleasure. The notions were interconvertible. To say that a particular action or a state of affairs would promote the happiness of an individual was as much as to say that the individual in question had an interest in performing that action or in seeing that state of affairs brought into existence. Happiness was related to the sensations of pleasure and pain—it consisted in a balance on the side of pleasure over pain. Conversely, suffering or misery consisted in a balance on the side of pain over pleasure. It could similarly be said that an individual had an interest in any action or in any state of affairs in which he experienced pleasure or avoided pain.[20] Insofar as the happiness of rulers—the greatest happiness of the lesser number—came into competition with that of subjects—the greatest happiness of the greatest number—they possessed a 'sinister interest'. Bentham adopted the term 'sinister' on the grounds that, 'in the original physical sense', it was 'the opposite or reverse' of right. In other words, a sinister interest was any particular interest which was in opposition to the universal interest, that is, the aggregate interest of the members of the political community in question.[21]

In one of his preliminary writings intended to form an introduction to constitutional code, an essay entitled 'Constitutional Code Rationale', he laid out the fundamental purpose of constitutional law in the following, schematic way. He announced three positions or axioms. The first axiom was the greatest happiness principle, which stated that 'the right and proper end of government' was 'the greatest happiness of the greatest number': this was the principle of utility (he came to prefer to call it 'the greatest happiness principle').[22] The second axiom was the ruler's object-indicating principle, which stated that the actual end of government was the greatest happiness of those who exercised the powers of government. This occurred because 'self-regarding interest is predominant over all other interests put together'—that is to say each individual was, in general, primarily motivated by a desire to increase his own happiness, at whatever cost to the happiness of other individuals. This was not to say that some individuals might not be primarily motivated by a desire to increase the happiness of others, and that every individual might not at some time desire to increase the happiness of others. In legislation, however, it was not sensible to proceed on any other basis than on those features that were typical or characteristic. Rulers were no different from other individuals, and so it was prudent to assume that they would act to promote their own happiness, at whatever cost to the rest of the community. For proof of this 'general, indeed . . . all-comprehensive principle of human nature', one merely needed to study the actual practice of rulers 'as brought to view by the history of all nations'. If competition between the happiness of each individual and every other did not exist, there would be no difficulty. Yet, there often was competition, for instance in the

[20] Bentham, *An Introduction to the Principles of Morals and Legislation*, 12–13.

[21] See P. Schofield, 'Bentham on the Identification of Interests', *Utilitas* VIII (1996), 223–34; and G. J. Postema, 'Interests, Universal and Particular: Bentham's Utilitarian Theory', *Utilitas* XVIII (2006), 109–33.

[22] See Bentham, *An Introduction to the Principles of Morals and Legislation*, 11 n.

distribution of resources. It was for this reason that the right and proper end of government had to be expressed as the greatest happiness of the greatest number rather than as the greatest happiness of all.[23]

Given that the self-preference of rulers placed their interest in opposition to that of the political community as a whole, a third axiom was required, which Bentham termed the 'Means-prescribing, or Junction-of-interests prescribing, principle', the purpose of which was to bring 'the particular interest of rulers into accordance with the universal interest'. Bentham, therefore, began with what ought to be, proceeded to what is, and finished with the injunction to reconcile what ought to be with what is.[24] This strategy was a feature of Bentham's utilitarianism throughout his career. For instance, in his first major published work *A Fragment on Government*, which appeared in 1776, he had distinguished between 'expository jurisprudence', which described the law as it is, and 'censorial jurisprudence', which stated what the law ought to be. The former was characterized by an enquiry into facts, while the latter was characterized by the discussion of reasons. Under existing systems of law, stated Bentham, what is and what ought to be were divorced from each other (despite William Blackstone's claims to the contrary in relation to the laws of England).[25] Under the utilitarian, or 'natural', system of arrangement of law proposed by Bentham, what is would be properly reconciled with what ought to be: the leading terms of the law would be 'terms which if they can be said to belong to any science, belong rather to Ethics than to Jurisprudence'.[26] The phrase the 'junction of interests' first appeared two years later in 'A View of the Hard Labour Bill', where Bentham approved of the provision in the Penitentiary Bill of 1778 (enacted with amendments in 1779) that the salary of the governor of the proposed prison should depend on the quantity of labour performed by the inmates, whereupon it would 'become the *interest* as well as the *duty* of each governor to see that all persons under his custody be regularly and profitably employed'.[27] The principle, having migrated through the panopticon prison scheme,[28] and then the pauper panopticon scheme,[29] eventually found a central place in Bentham's constitutional theory.

[23] Bentham, *First Principles*, 232–5. For the history of the 'greatest happiness' phrase within Bentham's thought see J. H. Burns, 'Happiness and Utility: Jeremy Bentham's Equation', *Utilitas* XVII (2005), 46–61.

[24] Bentham, *First Principles*, 235.

[25] Blackstone had stated, in relation to the law of heresy, that 'Every thing is now as it should be': see *Commentaries on the Laws of England*, 4 vols (Oxford, 1765–9), vol. iv, 49. Bentham took this to be indicative of Blackstone's whole attitude towards English law.

[26] See Jeremy Bentham, 'A Fragment on Government', in *A Comment on the Commentaries and A Fragment on Government*, ed. J. H. Burns and H. L. A. Hart (London: Athlone, 1977), 397–8, 417–18.

[27] Bowring, vol. iv, 12.

[28] See J. E. Semple, *Bentham's Prison: A Study of the Panopticon Penitentiary* (Oxford: Clarendon, 1993), 149–52.

[29] The interest-and-duty-junction principle was one of the principles of management in Bentham's proposed pauper panopticons. The pecuniary profit reaped by the manager of each institution would be linked to the pecuniary profit reaped by the public. Bentham went on to say: 'To have compleated the junction between interest and duty in every line of human conduct would be neither more nor less than to have brought the science and art of government to perfection—to have established a perfect system of legislation.' See Jeremy Bentham, *Writings on the Poor Laws: Volume II*, ed. M. Quinn (Oxford: Clarendon, 2010), 115–16, 353.

The practical question, of course, was how to bring about the junction of interests between rulers and subjects? The answer was to destroy 'the influence and effect' of the sinister interest of rulers. This would leave them with their share in the universal interest. In other words, they would be so placed that they could only promote their own interest by promoting the universal interest, in which, like every other member of the community, they possessed a share. Given that an act took place when the desire and the power were combined, the sinister interest of the ruler might be overcome either by removing his desire to perform 'the sinister sacrifice', or by removing his power to do so. In a monarchy, where an individual—a monarch—had been granted supreme power by a constitution, that same constitution did not have the means to 'over-power' his sinister interest. Reward and punishment were the only means by which the interest of a person could be affected, but a monarch could have all the reward he wished for, and there was no one who could punish him. In a monarchy, then, the junction of interests was impossible.[30]

In order to bring about the junction of interests, in the first place the power of government—the supreme operative power as Bentham termed it—had to be distributed amongst a number of individuals. In the second place, a distinction had to be made between the supreme operative power, which was 'deputed' to individuals who would exercise it as trustees, and the supreme constitutive power, which would remain in the hands of those over whom the supreme operative power was exercised. The individual holding a share of supreme operative power, being appointed and subject to removal by the holders of constitutive power, was thereby made dependent on them, and insofar as the interest of the latter coincided with the universal interest, the interest of the holder of the share of supreme operative power was 'brought into accordance with the universal interest'. In the third place, the 'mass' of supreme operative power had to be minimized, since the less power that an official—or functionary in Bentham's terminology—possessed, the easier it was to keep his individual interest aligned with the universal interest. In the fourth place, supreme operative power had to be opposed or checked by the force of the moral or popular sanction, which was 'applied by the fictitious tribunal denominated the public opinion tribunal'. This counterforce was composed of 'the power of those whose interest composes the universal interest': in other words, it was the power of the possessors of the supreme constitutive power, but 'considered under a somewhat different point of view'. The sanction at the disposal of the public opinion tribunal was to punish rulers with 'dishonour' and to remove them from office. Hence, rulers would be treated by constitutional law in the same way that potential malefactors were treated by penal law. An individual who was motivated by sinister interest to contemplate the commission of a misdeed saw that the legislator had attached a punishment to the misdeed in question. The legal punishment, together with the force of the moral or popular sanction, overpowered the sinister interest, and prevented the misdeed. In the same way, the ruler who

[30] Bentham, *First Principles*, 235–7.

would otherwise have committed a misdeed would see that, because of the punishment he expected to receive at the hands of the moral or popular sanction, it was no longer worth his while to do so, and would modify his conduct accordingly.[31]

IV. The Place of the People

As noted above, from around 1818, Bentham was a republican. He had come to accept that only a representative democracy would promote the greatest happiness of the greatest number, for the junction of interest and duty could not be brought about under any other form of government. Underlying this commitment to democracy were the egalitarian implications of Bentham's utilitarianism itself. Happiness consisted in a balance on the side of pleasure over pain. The only thing that mattered was pleasure and pain. Hence, sentient beings mattered because they experienced pleasure and pain. Pleasure was the only good, and pain the only evil. The best action was that which produced the greatest quantity of pleasure or averted the greatest quantity of pain.[32] But no particular person's pleasure, quantity for quantity, counted for any more than anyone else's: 'Every individual in the country tells for one; no individual for more than one.'[33] Now, this did not in itself imply democratic government. Up until 1809 or thereabouts, Bentham was not a democrat, and in fact there is good evidence that, in the mid-1790s, when Britain was facing the threat of invasion from revolutionary France, he became, if anything, more hostile to democratic government.[34] The point was that an enlightened ruler, particularly if he or she was given appropriate advice, might know better than the people what their interests were, and promote them accordingly. It was Bentham's discovery and analysis of sinister interests, after the effective rejection of the panopticon prison scheme by the British administration in 1803, that led him to realize that, even if the ruler understood the interests of the people better than the people themselves, the ruler would not promote them. Having said that, there was a further egalitarian principle in Bentham's thought, namely that the best judge of an individual's interest was likely to be that individual himself. When the first principle, that each individual's interest was to possess the same value as that of everyone else, was combined with the second principle, that each individual was the best judge of his own interest, a rationale was provided for representative democracy. Each person's opinion, as expressed through the franchise, should carry equal weight.[35]

[31] Bentham, *First Principles*, 238–43. For a brief account of the sanctions, which were 'sources of pain and pleasure', see Bentham, *An Introduction to the Principles of Morals and Legislation*, 34–7.

[32] Bentham, *First Principles*, 11–13.

[33] *Rationale of Judicial Evidence, specially applied to English practice*, ed. J. S. Mill, 5 vols (London: Hunt and Clarke, 1827), vol. iv, 475 (Book VIII, Ch. XXIX) (reprinted in Bowring, vii. 334).

[34] P. Schofield, 'Jeremy Bentham and the British Intellectual Response to the French Revolution', XIII (2011) *The Journal of Bentham Studies*, 1–27, at <http://ojs.lib.ucl.ac.uk/index.php/jbs/article/view/72>.

[35] In late 1788 or early 1789, when he discussed these principles in an essay on the political situation in France, Bentham did not draw the conclusion that representative democracy was an appropriate form of government: see *Rights, Representation, and Reform*, 68–78. In 1817, when he once

Bentham's model for representative democracy was essentially a simple one. There would be no intermediate stages of election, no plural voting, no transferable vote, no second chamber—complication was an evil, and should be avoided unless some greater benefit ensued.[36] The electors, acting in their capacity of members of the supreme constitutive power, would appoint (locate, in Bentham's terminology) the members of the legislature—the deputies—who formed part of the supreme operative power. At the institution of Bentham's constitutional code, there would be universal manhood suffrage, subject to a literacy test. Bentham supported female suffrage in principle, but argued that any proposal to introduce it would, in the circumstances of the time, lead to the rejection of the whole scheme with a 'sneer'.[37] The political community would be divided into roughly equal electoral areas, and each election district would return one deputy by means of a first-past-the-post election. Elections would be held annually. In between elections, constituents would have the opportunity to remove (dislocate, in Bentham's terminology) their deputy by means of a petition of 25 per cent of the total electorate, followed by a majority vote. A vitally important element in the system was the secret ballot. The universal interest was the aggregate interest of all the particular interests of the individuals who belonged to the political community.[38] Each individual would vote for the candidate who most appealed to his particular interest. The candidate who appealed to the majority of the constituents in his electoral district would be elected. It was vital that each individual was able to vote in the way that would, as he saw it, best promote his own interest. If voting took place in public, this opened the way for influence, corruption, and bribery. A bribe would only be offered if the bribe-giver was certain that the bribe-taker would vote as instructed. Where there was public voting, the bribe-giver had that assurance; where the ballot was secret, he had no assurance whatsoever; in consequence, he had no incentive to offer a bribe. Government was a trust, and its operations would be conducted in public in order to secure responsibility. Voting, however, was not a trust: it was that part of the political process in which self-interest was to be given free rein—hence it would be conducted in secret.[39]

The people, as we have seen, not only had a role as members of the supreme constitutive power, but also as members of the public opinion tribunal. Unlike the suffrage, no one was excluded from the public opinion tribunal. Indeed, members of any other political community who took notice of any matter of relevance to the political community in question constituted part of the public opinion tribunal of that community. As members of the supreme constitutive power, the people exercised their will; as members of the public opinion tribunal, they exercised their judgment. Bentham went into great detail explaining the nature of public

again discussed these principles in *Plan of Parliamentary Reform*, he appealed to them to justify his call for 'democratic ascendancy': see Bowring, vol. iii, 452–4, 459.

36 Bentham, *First Principles*, 119–20 n.

37 Bentham, *First Principles*, 97–100; *'Legislator of the World'*, 305.

38 Bentham, *An Introduction to the Principles of Morals and Legislation*, 12.

39 Bowring, vol. iii, 547–8.

opinion, and the way in which it operated through the moral or popular sanction. Bentham believed that the moral or popular sanction was potentially very powerful, and its decisions constituted an informal 'system of law', analogous to the common law, in that there was 'no individually assignable form of words in and by which it stands expressed'. If all the persons who belonged to the political community in question were members of the public opinion tribunal, and if the aggregate interest of those members constituted the universal interest, then the opinions expressed by those members would be likely to reflect the universal interest. This was not always the case, but Bentham was optimistic that the 'dictates' of the public opinion tribunal 'coincide, on most points, with those of the *greatest happiness principle*', and that such 'deviations' as did exist were becoming 'less and less numerous, and less wide, and sooner or later they will cease to be discernible; aberration will vanish, coincidence will be complete.'[40]

In order for the public opinion tribunal to function effectively, its members needed relevant information, and they needed to be able to express opinions based on that information, and to communicate their opinions to other members. The most important instrument at the disposal of the tribunal was a newspaper, with the newspaper editor fulfilling a role of major importance:

> In a Representative Government, at any rate in a Representative Democracy, with the exception of the function of the principal Minister, greater is the importance [of] the function of this unofficial functionary than of any official one: more important, that is to say particularly to the great purpose here in question—that of making application of the power of the Public Opinion Tribunal in by far the most beneficial and highest character as a check upon misrule.[41]

A newspaper could receive and publish information on the issue in question, stimulate debate, announce its approval or disapproval of the conduct of those concerned, and produce changes in policy, or in personnel, or in both, as a result. Other aspects of the constitutional structure would ensure that the public opinion tribunal operated effectively. Hence government would be made as open and transparent as possible, with the activities of officials recorded in detail.[42] Because each decision or action would be taken by a single, identifiable functionary, each action or decision had a person who was responsible for it. Responsibility in this sense meant exposure not only to the rewards, but also and more pertinently to the punishments, at the disposal of the legal, including the political, sanction and the moral or popular sanction. The public could find out who had done what, and if they did not like what had been done, they could exert pressure, through the electoral system if necessary, to force the dismissal (dislocation) of the misbehaving official. Furthermore, the law of defamation would be adapted so that the truth of any accusation made in public would be regarded as a sufficient legal defence. Bentham

[40] Bentham, *Constitutional Code*, vol. I, 36.

[41] Jeremy Bentham, *Securities against Misrule and other Constitutional Writings for Tripoli and Greece*, ed. P. Schofield (Oxford: Clarendon, 1990), 45.

[42] The legal obligation imposed on functionaries to record their activities—to exercise the 'statistic function'—is regulated in minute detail in *Constitutional Code*, vol. I, 218–67.

had little sympathy for officials who, finding themselves accused of misbehaviour, resorted to the law to punish their accusers—he thought that they had sufficient means of publicity at their disposal to answer any criticisms that were directed at them.[43]

V. Sovereignty

The first volume of *Constitutional Code*, which was published in 1830, contains the first nine chapters of the code. As published in the new edition of *The Collected Works of Jeremy Bentham*, it runs to 457 pages of text. A whole chapter is devoted to the subject of sovereignty, but that chapter consists of just three short sentences:

> The sovereignty is in *the people*. It is reserved by and to them. It is exercised, by the exercise of the Constitutive authority, as per Ch. iv.[44]

The cross-reference is to a single Article in the following chapter, which states that the constitutive authority has the power to locate and dislocate the members of the legislature.[45] This, to state the obvious, is a cursory discussion of sovereignty, and even more extraordinary given Bentham's notorious prolixity. However, the constitutional code itself is not the place one should expect to find a discussion of sovereignty. The code contained the detailed provisions of constitutional law—the law *in terminis*. Another possible location for a discussion of sovereignty might be in the introductory material written for the civil code. He explained, in the 'Preface' to *Constitutional Code*, that he would there provide expositions of the 'words belonging to the vocabulary of *universal jurisprudence*', such as obligation, right, power, exemption, benefit, and trust.[46] The term 'sovereignty' is conspicuous by its absence. There is, however, a discussion of sovereignty in the introductory material that Bentham wrote for constitutional code, but again it is brief. Here, Bentham equated the sovereign with the authority that located the legislature, and through the legislature, the remainder of the operative power.

> By the sovereignty is meant the supreme constitutive authority: in virtue of which, immediately or unimmediately, the people exercise... the *locative*, and eventually the *dislocative* function, in relation to the possessors of all the several other authorities in the state.

[43] For the public opinion tribunal, and freedom of discussion more generally, see Jeremy Bentham, *On the Liberty of the Press, and Public Discussion and other Political and Legal Writings for Spain and Portugal*, ed. C. Pease-Watkin and P. Schofield (Oxford: Clarendon, 2012), 1–52; *First Principles*, 283–98; *Securities against Misrule*, 44–64; *Constitutional Code*, vol. I, 35–9.

[44] Bentham, *Constitutional Code*, vol. I, 25.

[45] Bentham, *Constitutional Code*, vol. I, 26. Bentham divided the constitutional code into chapters, sections, and articles. Each article carried one or more of five headings, which indicated its content: the 'enactive' contained the expression of the will of the legislator; the 'ratiocinative' contained the reasons in justification of those provisions; the 'expositive' contained explanations or definitions of terms; the 'instructional' contained instructions for the legislator; and the 'exemplificative' gave examples. This arrangement reflected the importance which Bentham attached to the 'form' in which the law appeared, that is the method by which the 'matter' or content of the law was presented. Both matter and form contributed to the utility of a code of law.

[46] Bentham, *Constitutional Code*, vol. I, 6.

Bentham went on to say that the term 'the people' referred to those persons who were 'admitted to act in the capacity of *electors*', while the persons qualified to act as electors were determined by the election code.[47] This appears to be circular. The people, in their capacity as electors, locate the legislature; the legislature enacts the election code, as part of the constitutional code; the election code determines who are to be electors. If the legislature determines who is to exercise the sovereign power, why is the legislature not the sovereign?

The most plausible answer, perhaps, begins with the observation that Bentham, when stating that the 'sovereignty is in *the people*', was not engaging in an exposition of the term 'sovereignty', but rather making a normative claim, namely that, according to the greatest happiness principle, the best disposition that could be made of the sovereign power was to give it to the people. Hence, he went on to argue that the people possessed a greater degree of appropriate aptitude (a term of art which will be discussed below) for the task of exercising sovereign power than a monarch or an aristocracy, or any combination of the three.[48] The implication of this is that, when Bentham used the term 'sovereignty', he did not mean to refer to a particular power, function, person, or class of persons, and that the 'sovereignty' might differ in those respects under different regimes. The sovereign power that was exercised, for instance, by an absolute monarch would not be the same sort of power as that exercised by the people in a representative democracy. In the former case, the monarch himself might constitute the legislature, whereas in the latter case, the people would not constitute the legislature. In other words, when Bentham said that, under his constitutional code, the sovereignty was in the people, and that as such they appointed the legislature, this was not a definition or an exposition of the term 'sovereignty', but rather described the particular form that sovereignty would take in that constitutional system.

In order to understand how Bentham understood 'sovereignty' in its most general sense,[49] it is necessary to note that he insisted that power on the one side was constituted by obedience on the other.[50] G. J. Postema has analysed the relationship between power and obedience in the context of Bentham's theory of sovereignty, and has shown that Bentham had in mind a dynamic, interactional relationship between rulers and subjects.[51] In other words, the extent of the authority of the rulers was dependent upon the extent to which their subjects

[47] Bowring, vol. ix, 96–7. [48] Bowring, vol. ix, 97.

[49] H. L. A. Hart, *Essays on Bentham* (Oxford: Clarendon, 1982), 242, did not think that the theory of sovereignty espoused in Bentham's early jurisprudential writings was the same as that espoused in his mature constitutional thought. In contrast, J. H. Burns, 'Bentham on Sovereignty: an Exploration', in M. H. James (ed.), *Bentham and Legal Theory* (Belfast: Northern Ireland Legal Quarterly, 1973), 133–50 argued that there was consistency, and it is Burns's approach that I adopt here.

[50] See, for instance, *Of the Limits of the Penal Branch of Jurisprudence*, 39, where Bentham refers to 'that disposition to submission and obedience [on the part of the people], by which the power of the sovereign, in point of fact, is constituted'; and *First Principles*, 154: 'Power on the one part is constituted by, correspondent and proportioned to obedience, active and passive, on the other.'

[51] G. J. Postema, *Bentham and the Common Law Tradition* (Oxford: Clarendon, 1986), 232–56. The subject is taken up in detail in O. Ben Dor, *Constitutional Limits and the Public Sphere: A Critical Study of Bentham's Constitutionalism* (Oxford: Hart, 2000).

were prepared to obey them. Moreover, the same person or group of persons could regard themselves as subject to more than one sovereign, as in the case of the Catholics of Great Britain who regarded themselves as subject to parliament, except in relation to religious matters, where they regarded themselves as subject to the Pope.[52] While in at least one prominent passage in his early writings Bentham equated the sovereign power with the legislature,[53] elsewhere he explicitly stated that a sovereign, as in the instance of a certain sort of absolute monarch, might rule through the exercise of 'autocratic power', or even by 'executive power'.[54] It seems that, for Bentham, the sovereign might exercise power through any of the different modes in which power might be exercised—that is legislative, executive, or judicial[55]—and by any person or group of persons—for instance a monarch, an aristocracy, or the people. The exact location of sovereignty would depend on the power–obedience relationships that, as a matter of social fact, existed within a particular society. The description of sovereignty given in constitutional code was not, therefore, circular, but rather assumed that the people had achieved such a degree of power as to be able to command the obedience of the other elements within society.

VI. Accountability of Officials

We have seen that, for Bentham, the purpose of constitutional law was to replace the natural opposition of interests between rulers and subjects with an artificial identification of interests. Another way of saying this is that the appointment of the right persons—or rather of persons possessing the right personal qualities—to official situations was the whole purpose of constitutional law:

> The goodness of the government will be as the aptitude of the portions of law enacted by it and the operations performed by it: their aptitude with relation to that same end.
>
> External circumstances the same, the aptitude of these same portions of law will be as the appropriate, or say relative, aptitude of the persons bearing part respectively in the enactment of them: the aptitude of the operations will be as the aptitude of the operators.[56]

If functionaries were endowed with the maximum of appropriate official aptitude, then government would be the best it could be. Bentham divided aptitude into three branches—moral, intellectual, and active. Moral aptitude was a 'negative quality', consisting in the absence of the 'propensity' to perform the sinister sacrifice. In other words, a functionary possessed moral aptitude when he had no desire to promote his own sinister interest at the expense of the general interest. This was not to say that he was left 'disinterested', and hence motiveless, but rather he was placed in such a situation that the only way in which he could promote his

[52] Bentham, *Of the Limits of the Penal Branch of Jurisprudence*, 42–3 n.
[53] Bentham, *Of the Limits of the Penal Branch of Jurisprudence*, 24–5.
[54] Bentham, *An Introduction to the Principles of Morals and Legislation*, 263–4.
[55] See Part VII of this chapter.
[56] Bentham, *First Principles*, 4.

own interest was by means of promoting the universal interest—his personal interest was identified with the universal interest. Rulers, for instance, might enjoy the pleasure of sympathy, that is the pleasure of seeing the people happy, or the pleasure of exercising power, or the pleasure derived from the possession of a good reputation, without any sacrifice of, but rather through the promotion of, the universal interest.

> By moral aptitude is therefore... meant but practical innoxiousness; and such innoxiousness not having any other cause than impotence, in the station of each functionary to establish this impotence, leaving him at the same time the necessary power—to render him unable to do wrong, yet sufficiently able to do right, is the great difficulty, and ought to be the constant object and endeavour of whatsoever labour is employed in the field of legislation.[57]

Hence, the general principle of the identification of interests would be applied to the situation of each and every functionary. In order to achieve the maximum of official aptitude, Bentham devised a number of 'securities' for the various branches of aptitude. For the securing of moral aptitude, Bentham recommended such measures as minimizing the quantity of power and money at the disposal of functionaries, making them responsible to the legal and moral sanctions, the exclusion of 'factitious dignity', and the minimization of their pay.[58]

Once the functionary, by means of the securities for moral aptitude, had been rendered 'innoxious', that is, given the appropriate motives to pursue the general interest, it was necessary to secure his intellectual aptitude. There was little point in a functionary having the desire to promote the greatest happiness, if he did not know what to do. Intellectual aptitude was itself divided into two branches, knowledge and judgement. Each and every functionary, with the exception of deputies in the legislature, would have to pass a public examination relevant to the business of their office.[59] Even if a functionary possessed moral and intellectual aptitude, this was still not enough: the third requisite was active aptitude, which referred to the physical performance of the relevant functions. The first security for active aptitude was attendance: if a functionary was not at his place of work, he could not perform his functions. Hence, pay would be linked to attendance: 'If no attendance, then no pay, such the rule for every day.' This rule applied to deputies in the legislature as well as to the most minor officials. The second security, related to the examination process, was the economical auction, or pecuniary competition. The point was to ascertain which candidates for office possessed 'relish for the function', that is the expectation of gaining pleasure from the exercise of the power associated with the office. Each candidate who was eligible, that is, each candidate who had passed the relevant examination, would make a sealed bid for the pay associated with the office. He could offer to take a smaller sum than the notional salary, or even offer a sum of money in return for appointment to the office.

[57] Bentham, *First Principles*, 13–15.

[58] For a discussion of aptitude see Schofield, *Utility and Democracy*, 272–303.

[59] Bentham, *First Principles*, 87–8.

Bentham argued that, all other things being equal, the more an individual was willing to pay for the office, the greater the pleasure he anticipated from exercising the functions of the office; and the greater the pleasure, the more likely that he would exercise them with greater skill. The public would also benefit from the reduction in the expense of government brought about by a reduction in the cost of official salaries. The patron, that is the senior official responsible for making the appointment, would have to make his decision on the basis of both the economical auction and the respective examination results of the candidates. He would not be constrained on either account, but since the results of both the auction and the examination would be made public, he would be responsible to the public opinion tribunal for his choice.[60]

VII. Character and Powers of the Legislature and Executive

Bentham's distinction between the various powers of government reflected his exposition of the term 'power'. This in turn reflected his views first, that the only thing on which existence could be predicated was 'substance', the stuff of which the physical world was made, and second, that for any abstract term to make sense, it had to be related to its 'real source' in the physical world. Power, then, was the capacity, either directly or indirectly, to change the condition of physical objects.[61] The powers of government were built up from the modes in which it was possible to exercise power, and hence the modes of changing the conditions of physical objects. In broad terms, power exercised over 'aggregates of persons or things' constituted legislative power; the application of the general rules to a particular person or thing was the exercise of executive power, and this itself was either administrative or judicial power depending upon whether there existed 'a contest between two or more parties in respect to the point of right'.[62] An important distinction, then, was between power concerned with types of actions (legislative) and power concerned with individual actions (executive). Judicial power was not a third type of power distinguished from legislative and executive power, but a branch of executive power.[63] We have already seen, in relation to the question of sovereignty, some of the implications of Bentham's theory of power. A further implication is that the fact that a certain institution was commonly referred to as a legislature, and another as an executive, did not in itself mean that the one exercised only legislative power and the other only executive power. It was quite possible, for instance, that the persons who normally exercised legislative power might on

[60] Bentham, *First Principles*, 87–94.

[61] Bentham Papers, box lxix, fo. 106 (*c.*1776).

[62] Bentham, *First Principles*, 6–7. Constitutive power was a type of 'investitive power': that is a power to vest another power in certain persons.

[63] I have ignored here a further distinction between supreme and subordinate power, which Bentham outlined in *An Introduction to the Principles of Morals and Legislation*, 263–4 n., and which remained an essential part of his theory of power in constitutional code. A regional legislature, for instance, exercised subordinate legislative power, insofar as its powers were given to it, and might be taken away, by a national legislature, which thereby exercised supreme legislative power.

occasion exercise executive power—the mere accident of who it was that happened to exercise the power did not alter 'the nature of the two Powers'.[64]

VIII. Courts and their Role in the Constitution

It would not be extravagant to argue that Bentham saw the courts (though he preferred the term 'judicatory' so as to avoid the monarchical associations of the word 'court') as the most important institution in the official establishment. This was where the law, which produced the security that was constitutive of civilized life, had a major impact on the lives of citizens. It was where, in terms of the happiness of the community, most was at stake. It was vital that the courts followed known and publicly accessible rules, and that everyone in the community, from the richest to the poorest, had equal access to them. Hence, Bentham argued that law should be cognoscible and justice accessible. Under the constitutional code, in order to render the courts accessible, there would be a court in every locality—an Immediate Judicatory—open every day of the year, with authority to deal with all cases, where the citizen could go directly to the judge to air his grievance or demand his right. Appeal from the decision of the Immediate Judicatory would be allowed, under certain circumstances, to an Appellate Judicatory. Judgments would be given by an individual judge. There would be no traditional jury giving a verdict, though there would be a three-member quasi-jury, representing the public opinion tribunal, who would be able to participate in the trial, and put their views on the record. Procedure would be summary, and therefore closer to inquisitorial than to adversarial procedure; trials would be characterized by oral evidence and cross-examination, rather than by written evidence (though that would have its place); and all evidence would be admissible, subject to the overarching principle of minimizing delay, vexation, and expense.[65] In order to render the law cognoscible, it had to be codified, enacted by a duly constituted legislature, and made available in 'bite-size' portions; so, as well as the penal, civil, and constitutional codes, the law would be divided into, for instance, the butcher's code, the master-and-servant's code, the husband-and-wife's code, and so on.[66] The common law, or any sort of judge-made law, would be abolished. Judge-made law could not provide the certainty in the law that was necessary to security. The role of judges was to enforce the pannomion, which had its source in the will of the legislature. Having said that, Bentham did work out a mechanism by which a judge, reflecting on the particular case before him, could suggest amendments to the pannomion. The suggested amendment would

[64] Bentham Papers, box lxix, fo. 110 (*c.*1776).

[65] See Bowring, vol. ix, 464–70, 473–4, 554–68. For a general account of Bentham's theory of judicial evidence see W. Twining, *Theories of Evidence: Bentham and Wigmore* (London: Weidenfeld & Nicolson, 1985).

[66] Bentham, '*Legislator of the World*', 8. The most convincing account of the role of judges under Bentham's constitutional code is F. Ferraro, 'Adjudication and Expectations: Bentham on the Role of Judges', *Utilitas* XXV (2013), 140–60.

be transmitted, through the Justice Minister, to the legislature, which would decide whether or not to adopt it.[67]

The judges themselves would be appointed by the Justice Minister, and through him would be rendered subordinate to the legislature (the Justice Minister was located by the legislature for life, but could be dislocated both by the legislature and by the constitutive authority on petition followed by majority vote), and through the legislature to the people.[68] Like all other officials, the judges would be subject to the securities for appropriate official aptitude, of which the most important would be publicity of procedure.[69]

IX. Relations between the Branches of Government

Bentham rejected the theory of the division of power, by which he meant both the theory of the balanced constitution (king, lords, and commons) and the theory of the separation of powers (legislative, executive, and judiciary). His argument was that, if the whole government operated in such a manner as to promote the greatest happiness of the greatest number, the existence of checks and balances was not only pointless, but pernicious. If the legislature, for instance, was so constituted that its interest was identified with that of the universal interest, any check it received from the executive or judiciary would, by definition, be counter to the universal interest. Bentham thought it much more likely that the division of power would lead to each element or branch of the constitution pursuing its own sinister interest. The result would be, and in the case of the British government had been, a confederacy of sinister interest, rather than any outcome which led to the promotion of the general interest.[70] Bentham opposed the division of the legislature into two or more chambers on the same grounds: if the first chamber was so constituted as to promote the universal interest, a second chamber either would agree with its measures, in which case it would be useless and the expense bestowed upon it sheer waste, or it would disagree, in which case it would be pernicious.[71]

Bentham's constitutional code was not, then, characterized by the division of power, but by chains of subordination. As we have seen, Bentham began by dividing all power into constitutive and operative power. The latter was the power by which the business was done, and the former was the power that determined the persons by whom it was exercised. The supreme constitutive power, vested in the people in their capacity as electors, was sovereign. The interest of the people, and hence the interest of the supreme constitutive power, was the universal interest. The supreme operative power was made subordinate to the supreme constitutive power, hence the interest of the holders of operative power was identified with the universal interest. More particularly, the supreme operative power was divided into the supreme legislative and the supreme executive power,

[67] Bowring, vol. ix, 435–7, 504–6.
[68] Bowring, vol. ix, 607, 610.
[69] Bowring, vol. ix, 535–7.
[70] Bentham, *Rights, Representation, and Reform*, 405–18.
[71] Bentham, *First Principles*, 101–12.

and the supreme executive power into the administrative and judicial powers. These powers did not, however, check and balance each other. Rather, the administrative and judicial branches of power, together constituting the supreme executive power, were rendered subordinate to the supreme legislative power. At the head of the administrative power was the Prime Minister, and at the head of the judicial power was the Justice Minister, both of whom were responsible to the legislature. Under the Prime Minister were thirteen ministers, and under them the functionaries in their respective subdepartments. Under the Justice Minister were the judges. Both administrative and judicial departments had responsibility for executing legislation, the former in those cases where there was no dispute, the latter in those cases, whether or not there was any dispute, over the question of right.[72]

X. Conclusion

There has perhaps not been any other major English philosopher so uncompromisingly committed to democracy as Jeremy Bentham. He began from the psychological insight that human beings had a desire for pleasure and an aversion to pain, and that they were predominantly, though not exclusively, driven by self-interest. The latent egalitarianism of the view that what mattered was pleasure and pain, and not the social status or any other personal attribute of the person experiencing the pleasure and pain, led, in a political context, to a radical vision of a democratic state. From a historical perspective, Bentham reached this conclusion when he combined the notion that every individual should count for one and no one for more than one, with the notion that the best judge of a person's interest was most probably, or was at least in most instances, that person himself. The key was to reconcile individual self-interest with the universal interest by creating a constitutional structure whereby rulers could best promote their self-interest by promoting the interest of the community as a whole. This entailed a legislature subordinate to the people, and an executive and judiciary subordinate, each in their turn, to the legislature. Bentham was perhaps unique in not only developing the general principles of moral, political, and legal philosophy that should underpin a constitution, but in drafting a constitutional code that he regarded as complete in its detailed provisions.[73]

[72] Bentham, *First Principles*, 6–7; *Constitutional Code*, vol. I, 171–2.

[73] For the continuing relevance of Bentham's constitutional thought see J. Elster, *Securities Against Misrule: Juries, Assemblies, Elections* (Cambridge: Cambridge University Press, 2013).

11

Montesquieu

Giovanni Grottanelli de'Santi

I. Introduction

The *Esprit des Lois* has been regularly cited in political science and constitutional texts throughout the two and a half centuries following its publication in 1748, thus belying Jeremy Bentham's portentous prediction that Montesquieu's fame would be short-lived.[1]

Charles Louis de Secondat (1689–1755), future Baron de Montesquieu, was born in Bordeaux in the same year in which William and Mary accepted the English throne in the aftermath of the Glorious Revolution. It was the same year in which the *Declaration of Rights* and the *Act of Toleration*, Locke's *Two Treatises of Government*, and the *Letter Concerning Tolerance* (already written in 1685) were published. France at this time was ruled by Louis XIV (1638–1715), the Sun King, considered in European history the epitome of royal absolutism, a form of government that would continue with Louis XV, after the Regency interlude, and therefore throughout Montesquieu's lifetime.

The end of the seventeenth century and the first half of the eighteenth have been described in European history as 'le temps des ouvertures',[2] that is a time of opening up and of change in the key sectors of knowledge; a time in which the *Political Treatise* by Baruch Spinoza (published posthumously in 1677) laid the foundations of liberalism, and in which a new and different idea of state and society took shape. It was a time when intellectual hegemony moved from southern to northern Europe, while France was fraught with particularly virulent Catholic and Protestant movements. The year 1685, mentioned above with regard to Locke's *Letter*, was also the date of the revocation in France of the *Édit de Nantes* and the consequent resumption of a policy of religious intolerance. A reaction to royal despotism develops towards a 'return' to the past (even though the intention is

[1] Quotations from *L'Esprit des Lois* in the text are to books in Roman numerals and chapters in Arabic numbers; the text referred to is the edition of R. Derathé: Montesquieu, *De l'Esprit des Lois, Tome I et II, Introduction, chronologie, bibliographie, relevé de variantes et notes par R. Derathé*, (Paris: Garnier, 1973). On Bentham's famously wrong prediction, see I. Berlin, 'Montesquieu', in *Against the Current* (Oxford: Oxford University Press, 1981), 130; see also J. N. Shklar, *Montesquieu* (Oxford: Oxford University Press, 1987), 120.

[2] D. Richet, *La France Moderne: l'Esprit des Institutions* (Paris: Flammarion, 1973), 142.

simply to alter the present) and a greater respect for private property.[3] Particularly during the first decades of the eighteenth century, intellectuals and reformers begin to form groups to discuss the subject of 'post-Louis XIV'. One of these stands out as having developed a form of liberalism imbued with the aristocratic ideal. Fénelon and Saint Simon, two particularly representative figures of the latter, felt the need to limit royal authority, envisaging a possible role to be assigned to the nobility.[4]

Rich, powerful, and prosperous, although troubled by many wars, Montesquieu's France was at the centre, and even according to some *was herself* the centre, of a new cultural awakening—the discovery of new horizons in both the scientific and literary fields together with a widespread promotion of studies in economics, all of which tended to improve the well-being and further the development of society in general. Throughout Montesquieu's lifetime and beyond, this atmosphere favoured the rise of the Enlightenment and it is difficult to imagine that, as well as a widespread sense of the crisis of the political and economic system, there was not also a feeling of being on the eve of great historical change. The press in France was subject to a rigid censorship, though this could vary with the times. The influence of the church and of the Jesuits in particular weighed heavily. Montesquieu was nineteen years old when, with the victory of the Jesuits, Port Royal was destroyed (1709) and the Jansenist community was ruthlessly suppressed. In 1724, an edict prohibited the meetings of heretics 'under penalty of sentence to perpetual galleys for men and life imprisonment for women', whilst Protestant preachers would be sentenced to death.[5] Notwithstanding this, we know that Montesquieu's wife was a practising Calvinist and remained so after their marriage.[6] The treatment of Protestants varied considerably according to the different areas of France. However, it is interesting to remember that in Montesquieu's Bordeaux the *parlement* ordered '46 persons to separate for concubinage, that is, for being married by Protestant rites, and declared their children illegitimate and incapable of inheriting their property.'[7]

Montesquieu received a lot from life. He was born into an aristocratic and clearly a wealthy family—'*noblesse de robe*' as recorded by all his biographers—and therefore to a high economic and social status—always a considerable asset, but at that time even more so. As well as being high-born and rich, he received an excellent classical education by the Oratorian Fathers, which was a sound basis for a career in law and parliament. At the age of 27, his parliamentary career reached a peak when he inherited from his uncle the presidency '*à mortier*' of his own *parlement* in Bordeaux. Although Montesquieu benefited much from privilege in birth and inheritance, he strove to put them to good purpose, cultivating a wide range of

[3] Richet, 144.

[4] See F. Diaz, *Filosofia e Politica nel Settecento francese* (Turin: Einaudi, 1962), 16 ff.

[5] A. Cobban, *A History of France* Vol. I (London: Pelican, 1957), 62.

[6] See Shklar, *Montesquieu*, 2: 'in spite of the real danger and disabilities that this involved'.

[7] Cobban, *A History*, Vol. I, 62.

scientific interests. He travelled to various European countries: of the three years (1728–31) dedicated to travel, he remained for one and a half in Britain.

Reading about his life we get the impression of a man who is showered with honours and consideration, yet who eschews opportunities for social and political success even though he is perfectly at ease with, and in fact deliberately spends time in, 'the corridors of power'.[8]

Montesquieu was afflicted with near blindness for many years and he also suffered several setbacks during his life; he was initially refused admission to the French Academy—though this was eventually granted in 1728. He was unable to prevent the great work of his life, *L'Esprit des Lois*, from being condemned by the church and included in the Index of Prohibited Books,[9] although he adopted a very conciliatory attitude which fell short of disavowal: the church's condemnation did not go so far as to number Montesquieu amongst the 'brazen flouters'[10] who would be refused funeral rites, and he was buried in the Church of Saint Sulpice. The book, though forbidden by the state censors, achieved such success as to compensate in large measure for the inevitable bitterness caused by the ban; the ban must have been expected, for the book was prudently printed in Geneva.

II. *L'Esprit des Lois*—Forms of Government and Social Structures

Many scholars of Montesquieu have tried to find some order in his great work and to explain the basic reasoning in his treatment and arrangement of the subject, but their several attempts have come up against so many difficulties that the inclusion of their various warnings, exceptions, and reservations have not done much to clarify the text. Given the character and relative brevity of these essays, it seems more useful to confine oneself to what appears to be the principal idea underlying Montesquieu's proposals for what he believes to be the best form of government. His descriptions do not always provide specific advice for the legislator and leave the reader with a considerable opportunity for interpretation. He presents his examination and analysis—every aspect, every institution in the different countries, the

[8] Montesquieu became an *habitué* at the most famous Parisian *'salons'* where that extraordinary political and cultural intertwining characteristic of French history in the eighteenth century was taking shape. When at the age of 36 Montesquieu sold his office of President at the Parlement of Bordeaux and established himself in Paris, the most notable of these salons was that held by Madame Tencin; see the *Préface* to Derathé, *Préface* to Montesquieu, L'Esprit. Madame Tencin was the sister of Cardinal Tencin, leader of the Ultramontane and anti-Jansenist party; in her salon gathered, among others, Crebillon, Fontenelle, and Voltaire. A quick and vivid account of the social and intellectual world of Paris in those years is in C. Larrère and C. Volpihac-Auger eds., *1748, l'année de l'Esprit des Lois* (Paris: Champion, 1999).

[9] By a decree dated 29 November 1751. Montesquieu's *Lettres Persanes* were condemned almost seven years after his death (10 February 1755), by a decree dated 24 May 1762.

[10] The moderate orientation of Benedict XIV is 'revealed in his publication of an improved edition of the Index (1758) preceded by a constitution (1753) prescribing fairer and more scholarly standards for the inclusion of books in it'. The same pope in a letter to the French bishops (October 1756, a year after Montesquieu's death) ruled that only the 'brazen flouters' of the Bull should be refused the last rites: see J. N. D. Kelly, *The Oxford Dictionary of Popes* (Oxford: Oxford University Press, 1986), 296–8.

different systems under consideration, and historical events in all their complexity—in a simple and concise manner. However, the reader of the *Esprit des Lois* should remain vigilant, for one can never be sure of immediately grasping the conclusions demonstrated by the sequence of propositions. The basic ideas, however, as with certain observations on human nature, stand out from the rest and emerge with a clarity which leaves no room for doubt.

The beginning is akin to the classic opening used in so many treatises on the subject of forms of government. The argument is: a society cannot survive without a government, and the force needed to govern may come from a single person or from many people (I, 3). Forces get together as a result of a union between diverse wills expressing human reason. The political and civil laws of every nation are indeed none other than particular cases where human reason is applied (I, 3).

Laws express the relationships and interconnections arising from the nature of things. They are conditioned by a considerable number of elements and also vary according to climate, earth quality, customs, religion, way of life and of governing, and many factors consolidated over a period of time; they also vary according to the degree of freedom compatible with the system.[11] The study and analysis of the interaction between these elements enables one to grasp 'the spirit' of the laws themselves. The political institutions that give life to the laws can be consistent with the various natural causes, although this is not so in every case.

The novelty of Montesquieu's analysis, and this point has been pressed by many writers, lies in his aim of reflecting on the link between political regimes and social structures. Hence the general recognition of Montesquieu as one of the founders of political sociology—a subject, as we well know in our time, destined to achieve great success in the future, but then, as now, not lacking a certain degree of vagueness. This kind of approach, tending towards a global evaluation, was obviously stimulated by the general optimism induced by the great scientific achievements in Europe at the time. The idea of a rational interdependence between human laws and the laws of nature was very exciting.

The range of natural and human causes studied by Montesquieu, and on which he bases his analysis, is very extensive and so it is often difficult to find a thread running through the whole work.

III. Constitutional Norms and Fundamental Laws—the Nature of Governments

Moving now to the more constitutional aspects, we should note that Montesquieu does not put forward a clear distinction between constitutional norms and ordinary norms,[12] but often uses the expression 'fundamental laws'. Sometimes, for example when referring to England, he speaks of the 'constitution of a state'. The only two

[11] '. . . elles doivent se rapporter au degré de liberté que la constitution peut souffrir', I, 3.
[12] See Derathé, Montesquieu, *L'Esprit*, 430.

fundamental laws considered 'fixed and unalterable' in France at that time were those concerning succession to the throne (Salic law) and the inalienability of the *'domaine royal'*.[13] All the others, the so-called *'lois du roi'*, could be freely abrogated by the king. Montesquieu is credited with the intention of including amongst the fundamental laws all the laws relating to the constitution of the realm; that is to say, all those that restrict *'la plénitude de la puissance législative'* of the king.[14] Certainly, when he condemns laws enacted solely by the sovereign because they would lead to impermanence,[15] he is attributing to fundamental norms a capacity for resistance which apparently other laws do not have. However, a clear distinction between constitutional or fundamental norms and ordinary norms was only proposed and then confirmed during the Revolution—with Sieyès, who, for the first time, introduced the concept of real and effective control of the constitutionality of laws.

For Montesquieu the first step was to assign a 'fundamental nature' to all those laws that derive from the *nature* of each government (II,1); therefore fundamental norms can be recognized as constitutional not by their inclusion in the document but by their content. For Montesquieu, 'nature' *is* the very identity of governments—it is the description of 'who governs'. Government may be entrusted to the entire population (democracy), or to a section of the population (aristocracy), or, finally, to one person (monarchy). The 'nature of government' is that which is understood by everybody, even by the uneducated. So we return to the very ancient distinction: government by the people, oligarchy, or monarchy.

At this point however, Montesquieu develops his description, shifting his attention to *how* to govern; he adds a new criterion because he moves on to a second classification concerning the *manner of governing*. This he calls 'the principle' (*le principe*) or rather 'the human passions' that activate the particular structure of government: this 'principle' is *virtue* in republics and in aristocratic systems (but with the support of *modération*) and it is *honour* in the case of monarchy (III, 1, 2, 3). At this point, we are faced with a significant change of direction: to the definition regarding monarchy he now adds the idea that a monarch can govern (1) according to the established laws (*selon des lois établies*) or (2) in a despotic manner.

In the course of his famous and, according to public opinion, most important chapter (XI, 6) Montesquieu shows clearly that he has no confidence in government either by the people alone or by the aristocracy alone. As to the abovementioned second kind of monarchy, his negative opinion of absolute government does not need comment: it is a *'despotique'* government, the ruler governing *'selon ses volontés et ses caprices'*. Obviously he has no confidence in government by only one person, not even if it is 'enlightened'; it is common knowledge that 'Enlightened Absolutism', father of a certain European reformism, contributed to the

[13] Derathé, Montesquieu, *L'Esprit*, 430, note 31.

[14] Derathé, Montesquieu, *L'Esprit*, 430, note 31.

[15] '. . . car, s'il n'y a dans l'État que la volonté momentanée et capricieuse d'un seul, *rien ne peut etre fixe et par consequént aucune loi fondamentale*' (II, 4) (italics added).

development of the modern state, and yet it remains, in his view, government by one person and therefore bound to degenerate.

The combination of these three forms of government (king, aristocracy, and the people) as it appears to him to exist in England, is the system he prefers,[16] because the components working together offer the best guarantee of freedom. Social classes are a fact; one could say that they exist 'in nature', and Montesquieu takes them for granted. He is not at all opposed to aristocracy, even though he is aware of its various flaws; in fact he even goes so far as to suggest that some of the aristocratic privileges should be preserved so that, as a social class, it could be put to better use within the system. In a democracy, furthermore, the need for virtue is vital because he who makes the laws knows that he must abide by them, whereas in a monarchy[17] the ruler has the feeling of being above the law (III, 3).

IV. Democracy and Education: Love for the Laws and for One's Native Country

About democratic education, Montesquieu appears as a convinced moralist and very perceptive pragmatist when he points out the importance of the link between education and virtue in a republican system. It also seems very meaningful in our time to find a consideration of this kind in a treatise on government. He writes that, in a republican government, virtue is even more necessary, but warns that political virtue is difficult to achieve because it involves the renunciation of self-interest (IV, 5).

According to Montesquieu, virtue is love of country and its laws, a love that requires preference for public interest as opposed to private interest. He sees this love as especially important in democracy because it is only in democracy that government is entrusted to each and every citizen; and it is clear that government is in no way different from anything else in this world: if you want to keep it you must love it. Consequently the most important mission in a republican government is to inspire the young with this love and nobody is better suited to this job than parents:

On est ordinairemet le maître de donner à ses enfants ses connaissances; on l'est encore plus de leur donner ses passions.

Si cela n'arrive pas, c'est que ce qui a été fait dans la maison paternelle est détruit par les impressions du dehors.

Ce n'est point le peuple naissant qui dégénère; il ne se perd que lorsque les hommes faits sont dejà corrompus (IV, 5).

[16] Montesquieu's 'mistakes' in the description of the constitution of England provide a frequent, almost regular, subject of debate; fairly recently, of considerable interest, see Laurence Claus, 'Montesquieu's Mistakes and the True Meaning of Separation', *Oxford Legal Studies* 25 (2005): 419; see also I. Stewart, 'Men of Class: Aristotle, Montesquieu and Dicey on "Separation of Powers" and the "Rule of Law"', in *Macquarie Law Journal* 4 (2004).

[17] Curiously, he does not add here that he speaks of monarchy of a despotic kind.

Moreover, Montesquieu holds that civic education and love of laws and country cannot be separated from the idea of consensus and the exercise of sovereignty. He considers this in relation to republican government and then again when he speaks of England:

Le peuple, dans la démocratie, est, à certains égards, le monarque; à certains autres, il est le sujet. Il ne peut etre monarque que par ses suffrages qui sont ses volontés. La volonté du souverain est le souverain lui même. Les lois qui établissent le droit de suffrage sont donc fondamentales dans ce gouvernement (II, 2).

The things that people cannot do for themselves have to go through its ministers, and ministers must be chosen by the people on the basis of trust. In addition, the people should elect judges, choosing them from their own ranks to ensure the necessary degree of confidence in their impartiality (XI, 6).

With regard to franchise, Montesquieu is very liberal in a modern sense. He thinks that in a free country all those that have a 'free soul' must govern themselves, so that people as a whole (*le peuple en corps*) have the power to legislate; although, in his view, an exception must be made for inferiors who may be deemed not to know their own will (XI, 6). The great advantage of having representatives is that they can discuss public affairs among themselves—the people, on the other hand, are not able to hold such discussions and this is one of the drawbacks of democracy (XI, 6).

Of the two election methods, by lot or by choice, Montesquieu believes that the best one for the people is election by lot, as it does not hurt anyone and gives everyone an equal chance to serve his country. The significant disadvantage in this system is that incompetent persons may happen to be elected, but this may be corrected by following the example of Solon who envisaged that, on the basis of certain criteria, some candidates would be disqualified from standing for election. People are capable of discerning merit and, according to Harrington,[18] tend to choose *'les élites naturelles'*. On the other hand, Montesquieu believes that people are incapable of reaching conclusive decisions.

V. The People and Intermediary Powers

The consensus, or, rather, the formation of the popular will, must be, according to Montesquieu, a matter for all. If the law is dependent on one person only, there cannot be fundamental laws (II, 4). Montesquieu always bears in mind the human tendency to abuse power, and in a monarchy this can degenerate into despotism. Therefore he outlines the great idea of the 'rule of law'—the idea that will develop extensively in Europe over the next two centuries; it has been given many different definitions but fundamentally it is simply the antithesis of arbitrary rule. Everybody, even the supreme authorities, must behave according to the law and no one can adopt different behaviour from that intended by the law.

[18] See B. Manin, *Principes du Gouvernement Representatif* (Paris: Calman Levy, 1995), 100.

To avoid degenerating into despotism the monarchy must govern according to the fundamental laws, and the channels through which the power flows (*coule la puissance*) will create checks on absolutism. Intermediary powers are also needed. The will of the monarch must be regulated, negotiated, filtered, because without these intermediary bodies, the will of the monarch would be unhindered and 'capricious'; were this the case, nothing could be regarded as fixed and permanent and no law could be regarded as 'fundamental' (II, 4). These channels of power—one is tempted to add 'not surprisingly'—are first of all constituted by the nobility. It is the nobility in fact that seems more suited to this intermediary role, because the nobility '*entre en quelque façon dans l'essence de la monarchie, dont la maxime fondamentale est: point de monarque, point de noblesse, point de noblesse, point de monarque: mais on a un despote*' (II, 4).[19] Other possible filters are the clergy, local governments, local '*parlements*'; all may have a role as intermediary bodies and can serve sometimes as a brake and sometimes as a channel for sovereign power. Without these intermediate channels as an alternative to despotic sovereignty, the people will install a popular state in which sovereign power will belong to everybody, and that means the establishment of a tyranny.

Montesquieu found that intermediate powers were already in existence and working in France in his time[20] even though their influence had been greatly reduced by the dominance of royal power. His great contribution is to have understood how, from the balance of these powers and from their mutual checks, the best conditions for freedom would be created.

With his usual brilliance, near the end of the chapter on despotism, Montesquieu wonders how it is that everybody claims to love freedom and hate violence and yet, when it comes to it, they succumb to a despotic government (V, 14).

A 'moderate government' on the other hand is a difficult masterpiece of legislation hardly ever produced by chance and seldom produced by prudence. In order to have a moderate government, '*il faut combiner les puissances, les régler, les tempérer, les faire agir; donner pour ainsi dire, un lest à l'une, pour la mettre en état de resister à une autre*' (V, 14).

VI. The Model of the English Constitution and the Three Separate Powers

Montesquieu found that this masterpiece of legislation already existed in the English constitution (XI, 6). In his opinion, England was different from all the other countries because the aim of her constitution was political freedom. One can notice a certain emphasis in his statement: why go to the trouble of looking around;

[19] A very evident reference to James I's 'no bishop no king' at the Hampton Court Conference; see C. R. Lovel, *English Constitutional and Legal History* (New York: Oxford University Press, 1962), 292.

[20] Amongst a very extensive literature see Bluche, *Louis XIV* (Paris: Fayard, 1986); Diaz, *Filosofia e Politica*, 13 ff., *passim*; A. Cambier, *Montesquieu et la Liberté* (Hermann 2010), 213 ff.

if the principles on which the constitution is based are good, freedom is bound to appear as the reflection of a mirror (XI, 5).[21]

Throughout the history of political and constitutional thought, Montesquieu's reference to England has been greatly praised,[22] discussed, and also much criticized. It has been said, and is still being said today, that powers in the English system of government, rather than being separate, are in fact confused.[23]

Montesquieu identifies three powers that correspond approximately to the powers we speak of today. First of all, the legislative power that consists of making new laws '*pour un temps ou pour toujours*' and correcting and repealing the old ones. The executive power is defined by indicating the matters it deals with: peace and war, diplomatic relations, security and prevention of invasions. Today these activities might be grouped under 'foreign affairs', 'defence', and perhaps 'public order'. Lastly, judicial power is enabled to punish crimes and to pass judgments on controversies between private parties.

It is worth noticing that Montesquieu does not describe legislative power using a definition of the essence of law as such, as would probably be done in a handbook today, especially in a civil-law country. For him, it is simply 'the power to make laws'. Today, however, this does not seem sufficient in the same way that it would not be sufficient to say that judicial power is 'the power to pass sentence'. In the course of the following centuries, and particularly in civil-law countries (as distinct from common-law countries), much has been written about how to define terms like 'power' and 'function' of the state. These are questions that, understandably, did not worry our great Author. As soon as there is mention of freedom, however, we realize how much it means to him and how important it is for the concept of government and for the desired relationship between state and citizen. The terms he uses to describe the evils opposing freedom (oppression, tyrannical enforcement of laws, arbitrary or capricious power) follow one another in a passionate style; one is tempted to say that all of a sudden Montesquieu abandons that distant sedate tone, that search for objective evaluation, weighing the positive and negative qualities of each institution and each system—a tone that has been noted by all his readers, starting with some of his illustrious contemporaries, and occasionally criticized.

According to Montesquieu, legislative power must be entrusted jointly to the aristocracy and to the people, but these two classes should meet in separate assemblies. In fact, the hereditary and privileged aristocracy being numerically inferior would be submerged by the people if they were to meet in a joint assembly. Furthermore, the assemblies must not have the power to convene themselves; this power, as well as the power of dissolution, should be assigned to the monarch

21 With the 'English model' Montesquieu adds in fact a *fourth* form of government to the three already numbered: see Cambier, *Montesquieu*, 18 ff.

22 A famous example is the enthusiastic praise of E. Burke in his *Appeal from the New and the Old Whigs*, in *The Works of the Right Hon. Edmund Burke* Vol. III (London: George Bell & Sons, 1891), 1 ff., 113.

23 See, e.g. J. E. K. Murkens, 'The Quest for Constitutionalism in UK Public Law Discourse', 29 *Oxford Journal of Legal Studies* (2009), 427 ff.

because he is in a better position to judge the appropriate time and duration of the meetings. The executive power should be accredited to the monarch, because it is a power that is better administered by one only, rather than by many (XI, 6).

If one or more of these three powers is exercised by one body only, for example the aristocracy, or the people, there would always be, according to Montesquieu's argument, the risk of loss of liberty and the subsequent danger of despotism. Nevertheless, the principle is not absolute, and the main purpose in allocating power to different bodies is to ensure that they can check on each other, although that does not mean that any of these bodies may participate in the exercise of a power not strictly its own. In this regard, the distinction between *faculté de statuer* (power to issue orders or to correct actions taken by others) and the *faculté d'empêcher* (power to annul resolutions adopted by another body) is of paramount importance. According to Madison's reading in *The Federalist No. 40*, the essence of the principle of separation seems to be that no one of these bodies can gather into itself all the powers of one of the other two. In fact, the flexibility of the principle of separation, as advocated by Montesquieu, prefaced the development of the doctrine of 'checks and balances' that was to become very important in the United States and in Western Europe. Thanks to the 'not strictly absolute' character of the principle of separation, the legislative power can check whether the laws it has passed have been executed correctly, and the monarch can take part in the legislative function by the exercise of the royal sanction or of a veto power.[24] Certainly the separation of the judicial power is stated with great insistence: if it were united either to the legislative or to the executive power then freedom would be lost because it is likely that the monarch himself or the senate itself might adopt tyrannical laws and execute them tyrannically (XI, 6). Judges have to be summoned in case of need and only for a limited period in the year. They should sit in court only for the time required for the trial; they should be chosen from among the people, for they must belong—as we have already seen—to the same class as the accused so that the accused may not feel he has fallen into the hands of those who wish him harm:

> *De cette façon la puissance de juger, si terrible parmi les hommes, n'étant attachée ni à un certain état, ni à une certaine profession, devient, pour ainsi dire, invisible et nulle. On n'a point continuellement des juges devant les yeux; et l'on craint la magistrature, et non pas les magistrats* (XI, 6).

For Montesquieu, the impartial judge is an accurate interpreter of the law:

> *Dans le gouvernement républicain il est de la nature de la constitution que les juges suivent la lettre de la loi* (VI, 3).

[24] The principle of separation has been regarded as necessarily flexible by various authors stressing how Montesquieu always speaks of *distribution* and uses the term '*séparé*' only with reference to judicial power: see Derathé, Montesquieu, *L'Esprit*, 474; see also Claus, 'Montesquieu's Mistakes', 445: 'When we call institutions "legislative", "executive" and "judicial", we identify a dominant characteristic of what each institution does, not an exclusive one.' Dicey's and Austin's critiques of the 'mistaken' analysis of the English constitution are discussed by Stewart, 'Men of Class'.

Essentially, this is the idea that the judge (*bouche de la loi*) communicates the will of the law exactly as it is according to a definition which has been widely accepted for centuries, deservedly or undeservedly. Montesquieu even considers 'these impartial judges' as inanimate beings (*inanimés*) as they 'cannot moderate either the force or the rigour of the law' to the point that in some cases it may be the task of the legislator rather than the judge to mitigate the rigour of the law. The kind of legislation without which moderate governments will not stand is rarely the product of chance and is hardly ever allowed to be produced by prudence (V, 14); powers have to be regulated, harmonized, made to work as 'ballast' so that they may balance each other, and the result should be perfect equilibrium, still and static, but 'as they are constrained to move by the necessary motion of things, they will be forced to move in concert' (XI, 6).

Significantly the verb '*tempérer*' reappears, indicating that element of *modération* that for Montesquieu is so necessary for the proper functioning of the preferred form of government.

The combination of the different social classes together with the delicate balance of different powers tends to create the best conditions for freedom to thrive. Freedom is the thread that connects every step in his analysis and, with it, the repeated condemnation of arbitrary or capricious behaviour, tyranny, and despotic power. With Montesquieu's decisive contribution, freedom in constitutional theory remains intrinsically bound to the form of government and can never be seen as a variable in the relationship between ruler and citizen, or as unnecessary at a constitutional level.

It is generally well known that the French Declaration of the Rights of Man and Citizen (26 August 1789) gave formal sanction to the principle of separation (art. 16); furthermore, reference to it has appeared in all French constitutional texts up to and including the one now in force (1958). At the end of the chapter (XI, 6), where he deals with the English constitution, Montesquieu distances himself from England and admits that he cannot say whether the English are in fact free, but it is enough for him to have made clear that freedom is established by the laws of that country.

VIII. The Meaning of Freedom

Freedom then appears as the result of the combination recommended; it is the goal to be reached by taking the English constitution as a model. One is led to think then that liberty itself is the principal aim of his work. Corruption and abuse of power, as well as the exercise of powers outside our jurisdiction, may always put freedom at risk. One may wonder, however, about the real meaning of 'freedom'; Montesquieu himself notes that no other word has been given so many meanings (*significations*), and he makes a list of examples that seems pertinent even in our time (XI, 2). In his writings, along with general definitions,[25] one has a feeling of

[25] E.g.:, '*La liberté, ce bien qui fait jouir des autres biens*' in *Mes Pensées*, in *Oeuvres Complètes de Montesquieu*, ed. Caillois (Paris: Gallimard, 1949–51), I, 1430. On the distinction between

realism, almost as if reference has been made to experienced situations; freedom is presented as the kind of tranquillity that comes from the feeling of safety and, for people to enjoy this sort of freedom, the government must ensure that no citizen is afraid of any other citizen. Moreover, Montesquieu does not limit himself to general statements: 'safety' means the feeling of being safe from either hindrance or interference by public or private forces except in those cases envisaged by the law. In fact, the citizen's freedom is essentially dependent on the criminal laws (XII, 4).

The citizen's freedom is lost when the innocent do not feel safe. So, Montesquieu insists that knowledge of the rules ensuring maximum safety in criminal proceedings is more important for mankind than anything else (XII, 4).

It has been pointed out that the fact that Montesquieu has been considered one of the founding fathers of liberalism is not due so much to his famous tribute to the English constitution but to his thinking on criminal law.[26] In this respect, we should say that his theories on the form of government and his ideas on criminal matters must not and cannot be seen separately. The security produced by the criminal law advocated by Montesquieu is consonant with the security to be achieved through the separation of powers. The reciprocal control exercised by the powers, as well as the balance pursued by the form of government he recommends and that he saw as being enjoyed by the English, makes sense only as long as there is a comprehensive vision of the freedom and dignity of the person. In fact, freedom and dignity of the person must be seen as the aim of both criminal laws and the laws that regulate trials. The result of this approach is a very broad view of what is allowed by the law or, conversely, a very restricted one of what is forbidden; above all, Montesquieu insists on the importance of a clear and unambiguous definition of what is regarded as a dangerous and punishable criminal offence. In addition we could remark on how the very structure of his recommended form of government is in itself a guarantee of a 'liberal' and not an overly harsh criminal legislation. In fact one can hardly imagine, except in times of crisis, that the different social classes represented in the two branches of parliament could agree to restrict the freedoms of the individual.

The search for a completely free and safe space for each individual in a France under an absolutist régime could easily be seen as revolutionary. The freedom envisaged by Montesquieu is that which enables individuals to act as they choose and do everything that is not forbidden by law:

pour jouir de la liberté il faut que chacun puisse dire ce qu'il pense... un citoyen dans cet État, dirait et écrirait tout ce que les lois ne lui ont pas défendu ***expressement*** *de dire ou d'écrire* (XIX, 27).[27]

Freedom in the modern sense, the freedom of our time, lies in that '*expressement*': the law must specify its prohibitions, its silence guarantees the citizen. This defines the sphere in which the state should not intervene; this is the freedom that seventy

political freedom and freedom of thought see G. Barrera, *Les Lois du Monde, Enquête sur le Dessein Politique de Montesquieu* (Paris: Gallimard, 2009) 99 ff.

[26] See J. N. Shklar, *Montesquieu*, 89 ff.

[27] Emphasis added.

years later Benjamin Constant would describe as separate and opposed to the classical concept of freedom, linked as it was, or—one might say—'restricted', to the exercise of political rights and citizens' participation in public life:[28]

Les paroles ne forment point un corps de délit; elles ne restent que dans l'idée. La plupart du temps, elles ne signifient point par elles-mêmes, mais par le ton dont on le dit... Quelquefois le silence exprime plus que tout les discours. Il n'y a rien de si équivoque que tout cela. Comment donc en faire un crime de lèse-majesté? Partout où cette loi est établie, non seulement la liberté n'est plus, mais son ombre même (XII, 12).

Whoever besmirches the glory of his prince with words should be punished lightly or not at all. Montesquieu takes the same attitude towards written words (XII, 13). His basic idea is that words constitute offence only if used in preparation for a crime proper or when they accompany or follow a crime, but they cannot in themselves constitute an offence:

Ce ne sont point les paroles que l'on punit; mais une action commise, dans laquelle on emploie les paroles... On renverse tout si l'on fait des paroles un crime capital, au lieu de les regarder comme le signe d'un crime capital (XII, 12).

Therefore, even in this case, if you really want to punish, a mere correction may well be adequate; he often advises either explicitly or implicitly a certain tolerance and indulgence.

With regard to slander, anonymous letters, magic, heresy, and crimes against nature, the penalty to be applied has to be in proportion to the offence; in fact all these offences arise out of ways of life and deeply rooted customs, and both ways of life and customs have a great impact on individual free will, greater than the one exercised by laws (XII ff.).

Montesquieu is eloquent when speaking about the need for complete separation between criminal law and religious matters, and outlines an approach that in time would become one of the fundamental principles of contemporary constitutionalism in the Western world.[29]

On the subject of criminal law and criminal procedure, his ideas and statements, including for example his rejection as unacceptable accusations based on the testimony of only one person, his total opposition to the use of torture, and his advocation of proportionality between the importance of the indictment and the

[28] Constant's speech at the Atheneum of Paris (1819) is rightly considered as a turning point in the history of political-constitutional thought: see B. Constant, *La libertà degli antichi paragonata a quella dei moderni*, ed. A. Zanfarino (Bologna: Il Mulino, 1962), 36 ff. Constant condemned Rousseau and Mably for their vision of popular sovereignty, which he regarded as very close to slavery, but he made an exception for Montesquieu; he blamed him for not having seen why the world, or rather the way of life of past generations, had changed; Montesquieu also, in the eyes of Constant, had thought that the cause of the change was to be found in the absence of virtue, in the importance given to luxury, industry, and the accumulation of wealth. Nevertheless it seems clear that in the *Esprit des Lois* there is already in a nutshell the profile of freedom of our time, or at least that side of it that prefers a negative (non-interventionist) role for the state.

[29] '*Il faut éviter les lois penales en fait de religion. Elles impriment de la crainte, il est vrai; mais comme la religion a ses lois penales aussi qui inspirent de la crainte, l'une est effacée par l'autre. Entre ces deux craintes différentes, les âmes deviennent atroces.*' (XXV, 12).

degree of evidence required, anticipate an ideal climate that makes one immediately think of Cesare Beccaria.

Montesquieu's contribution to the development of criminal law theory does not need any commentary; its importance, perhaps, may well appear belittled by his overwhelming impact on political and constitutional thought.

VII. Conclusion

As mentioned at the beginning of these notes, Montesquieu stands out among the most significant thinkers in the history of Western political thought as one who remains inextricably associated with a specific idea developed in the course of his major work.

Throughout the Western world, the great idea of the distribution of power and with it the theme of freedom have acquired a central role in the concept of the state. This has been Montesquieu's major contribution, regardless of what may have been the effect of the idea on the different constitutional systems. Indeed, the impact of the *Esprit des Lois* only a few decades before the two Revolutions of the late eighteenth century (1776 and 1789) was profound and swept rapidly throughout the Western world. This is proved by the fact that, in the two years following the first printing in Geneva, twenty-two editions of the *Esprit* were published in various parts of Europe.[30]

Democratic constitutional systems in the Western world are based on a set of principles that have acquired general recognition over the last two centuries; when we examine them, we have the impression that they stand by themselves, but on closer inspection we can easily see how tightly they are interwoven or how they even derive from the same idea, upon which the separation of powers is based. The independence of the judge, the due process of the law, the prohibition on retrospective legislation, the legality of state administrative action, and the rule against vagueness provide some of the examples which can be explained by, or at least connected to, the principle of separation.

It has been asserted that the principle has, at least to some extent, become essentially obsolete in states where there is a parliamentary system of government, at least inasmuch as the distinction between social classes has disappeared with the advent of universal suffrage, so that no safeguards should be needed once the power of the electorate is established and the executive needs the confidence of the majority of a democratically elected parliament. According to this idea only the judiciary should be kept separate and independent. Historical developments in Western Europe over the last two centuries point clearly in the opposite direction. Freely elected parliaments have on various occasions looked favourably on the establishment of dictatorships and the passage from a democratic to an autocratic form of government has been blessed at times by the formal approval of

[30] See Montesquieu's letter to the Duke of Nivernais, quoted by R. Derathé in his *Introduction*, p. XVI.

democratically elected majorities. Furthermore, it seems that we have to admit that independent judiciaries have hardly ever managed to obstruct dictatorships to any significant degree. Italy and Germany provide the best examples of this historical weakness of some post-World War I European democracies, if we limit ourselves to bigger countries in terms of size and population.

On the other hand, we have to point out that one of the first legislative reforms that usually follows the establishment of a dictatorship is the abolition of the separation of powers: the executive power takes full control of the law-making function, while the judiciary adds its stamp to whatever has been decided by the party in power. This course is particularly well-illustrated by the chain of the events in the last stages of the German Weimar Republic. The end of that post-World War I régime may well be dated to 1933 with the adoption of the 'Enabling Law' (Ermächtigungesetz) which gave Hitler full legislative power, adding it to his executive power as Chancellor. The judiciary in the Third Reich was kept nominally separate, but in 1942 the Reichstag gave Hitler power to remove judges when suspected of deciding cases too leniently or of not being sufficiently convinced of Nazi ideology. Promptly and aptly, some scholars of repute[31] praised the idea of 'unity of power' or 'Führergewalt' as opposed to the separation of powers that 'had been afflicting' the Weimar régime.

Along with the usual, unavoidable, reference to the separation of powers in every textbook, we could ask ourselves what Montesquieu has to offer now to young people who are studying law or political science and yet have no intention of becoming Montesquieu specialists. Reading his great work, we are faced with such a wealth of thoughts, theories, and information that any tentative selection, any attempt to establish some sort of priority is extremely arduous. His is no doubt a splendid example of how one can combine scholarly imagination with literary excellence in the best tradition of European Humanism. Montesquieu has the magic gift of stirring the reader's mind and of inviting him to take his thoughts further.[32]

It seems important to remember that Montesquieu was attacked for the *Esprit des Lois* from a double front: the Jesuits and the Jansenists. It was in the time of William Locke and Montesquieu—although not just because of them alone—that the idea developed, and became deeply rooted, that man could emancipate himself and that saving his soul was his and not his government's responsibility. Along with this latter thought—and less optimistically—Montesquieu warned us that man has a natural inclination to abuse his power. It is a warning that appears on almost every page of his work, and with it he insists on the vigilance necessary to forestall the danger of loss of freedom, a danger that especially in our time is so often masked by very seductive political ideologies; in fact, good and equitable laws are never sufficient to run a society without the daily active participation of every citizen.

[31] See E. R. Huber, *Verfassungsrecht des Grossdeutschen Reiches* 2nd ed. (Hamburg: Hanseatische Verlagsanstalt, 1939), 211 ff.; see also the very useful bibliographical survey of J. W. Hiden, *The Weimar Republic* (London: Longman, 1974).

[32] A good example of this is offered by Alexis de Tocqueville in Chapter IX of *L'Ancien Régime et la Revolution* (p.1003 of the édition Laffont, Paris, 1986) where the author develops into an articulate observation what had been expressed by Montesquieu as a mere feeling.

12

The General Will Constitution

Rousseau as a Constitutionalist

Ruzha Smilova

I. Introduction

The problem of political authority—how can the right of some to rule over the rest be justified?—is at the centre of Jean-Jacques Rousseau's manifold contributions to Western political thought. He offered a unique solution to it by declaring the people an absolute sovereign: people themselves wield the supreme authority over a territory. He thereby drew to its logical conclusion the assumption of social contract theory that men are by nature free, independent, and equal, naturally subordinate to no one. By endowing the popular sovereign with general will and pronouncing it the sole source of political authority, he radically solves the problem of political authority: no one has a right to rule over the rest. Rather, the people as a collective body rule themselves, preserving each member's freedom by submitting to the rule of the general will. Rousseau has thus arguably opened the door to a freedom-preserving political association, the association of the general will.

Following Rousseau's solution, popular sovereignty has become a defining mark of modern constitutionalism. Yet the attribute of absoluteness, of being unlimited, characterizing the sovereign, is in tension with another central feature of modern constitutionalism captured in the doctrine of limited government. Limited government is meant to safeguard personal liberty and rights against the threat of absolute government and of arbitrary rule. Both popular sovereignty and limited government thus try to solve basically the same problem: how to make political authority compatible with individual freedom. Yet the solutions they offer seem to be in tension. This tension is at the centre of the debates over constitutional democracy as possibly 'a paradoxical union of contradictory principles'.[1] In this text I shall look at the constitutional features of Rousseau's 'association of the general will' and shall address the issue of whether and how the tension between popular sovereignty and limited government is resolved. First, I provide an account of Rousseau's arguments for popular sovereignty and outline the main features of his 'association of the

[1] Jurgen Habermas, 'Constitutional Democracy: A Paradoxical Union of Contradictory Principles', *Political Theory* 29 (6) 2001.

general will'. It is an association where the rule of the general will does not deprive any of the associates of their freedom and the interests of each are equally well served. Then, I consider the issue of constitutional beginning: (1) how the sovereign is constituted: how a mere aggregate of individuals becomes an association of the general will with the above properties; and (2) how the general will is shaped. The godly Legislator as Rousseau's controversial solution to the problem of constitutional beginning is the focus of the second part. The last part is organized around the more strictly constitutional features of Rousseau's project. Here the issue is: What role does Rousseau envisage for constitutional safeguards of individual freedom within the association of the general will. I discuss in detail here his doctrine of limited government as involving supremacy and separation of the sovereign from government. Rousseau's account of the rule of law, as well as the related controversy over the limits on the general will, is next addressed. Rousseau's understanding of rights-protection, and his likely response to the charge of tyrannical majorities within the association of the general will, are the focus of the concluding section.

II. Rousseau's Popular Sovereign

A defining mark of modern constitutions is that they declare people the sole source of political authority. They are the sovereign enjoying supreme authority over a territory. Constitutions spell out the basic rules for the exercise of authority, defining the system of government and the main principles, and setting the scope and limits of governmental institutions. Constitutions normally enumerate the rights of citizens and provide institutional guarantees, protecting them against the state and other citizens.

The principle of popular sovereignty is linked to the social contract theories of the seventeenth and eighteenth centuries. The basis for political authority at that time was the consent of the governed. Starting from the assumption of the natural equality of men, authors in this tradition denied that there is a natural right of the few to rule over the many: the right to rule, rather, is conditional on the consent of each of the ruled. Despite this broad agreement, there are differences that directly bear on the issue of popular sovereignty. For Thomas Hobbes, for example, the source of political authority is the mutual consent of individuals to leave the state of nature by giving up their natural rights and to establish a sovereign authority necessary to protect them against each other. To be up to this task, the sovereign authority needs to be absolute and must be distinct from and not dependent on the people who establish it. The absoluteness of the sovereign places limits on the rights of individuals: only those recognized by the sovereign are valid rights. Being absolute, the sovereign no longer needs the consent of the governed: the fact that he provides protection is all that is needed to justify his rule. The only limit to his authority is his failure to provide the necessary protection, so that when the subjects' lives are endangered they are not bound to obey. Sovereignty as the mark of political authority is divorced from its source in the consent of the people.

John Locke grounded state authority on the mutual consent of the people who delegate the right to rule to a government as their trustee. Consent is conditional on governments respecting citizens' pre-contractual rights to their person, liberty, and property. The government as a trustee of the people is limited through its respect for their natural rights, which are reserved intact in their new condition as citizens. Some have concluded that, in Locke, natural law and natural rights rather than explicit consent are the source of political authority.[2] Whichever it is, for Locke the people retain their sovereignty: they have a right to resist and a right to reclaim their authority, if trust in government is lost. In a dispute between the people and government, the people are usually the judge of whether their natural rights have been violated. However, what people may decide is limited by their natural rights. Ultimately, it is not the people themselves, nor any other human authority, but God ('the appeal then lies nowhere but to heaven'[3]) who resolves conflicts between the government and the people. The people are sovereign but not an absolute sovereign here because they may not go against their natural rights. It is telling that Locke does not use the concept of sovereignty (which is associated with absoluteness) in referring to the people. Indeed, the concept rarely appears in his *Second Treatise of Government.*

Rousseau is the first to declare the people an absolute, unlimited sovereign: people hold supreme authority over a territory. This draws to its logical conclusion the claim that men are by nature independent, free, and equal, and naturally subordinate to no one. The Rousseauean solution adds to the modern voluntarist insight, which grounds political authority exclusively on individual consent and the ancient republican idea of the common good of a free people.[4] The result of this novel combination is the idea of a popular sovereign with the general will as the source of political authority, so that no one has a right to rule over the rest. The people as a collective body rule themselves, fully preserving each member's freedom.

Is this a convincing solution to the problem of justifying the right to rule? The answer is not straightforward and the account Rousseau gives is complex. The preliminaries are set out in *Discourse on the Origins of Inequality* (DI).[5] He starts off with the usual contractarian notion that men are born free, independent, and equal, having a natural concern for their own well-being (*amour de soi*) yet also having compassion (*pitié*) for the pain of others. During the course of human history, however, leaving behind their blissful natural state and entering civil society with its cultural advancement, men found themselves mutually dependent, unfree and unequal, riven by divisive *amour propre,* that is an inflamed concern for one's

[2] H. Pitkin, 'Obligation and Consent', *The American Political Science Review* 60 (1) (1966), 39–52.

[3] John Locke, *The Second Treatise of Civil Government* (1690), sec. 242.

[4] P. Riley, 'Rousseau's General Will', in P. Riley (ed.), *The Cambridge Companion to Rousseau* (Cambridge: Cambridge University Press, 2001).

[5] Jean-Jacques Rousseau, *Discourse on the Origins of Inequality* (1754) in *The Social Contract and the First and Second Discourses*, 'Rethinking the Western Tradition' series, ed. S. Dunn and G. May (New Haven and London: Yale University Press, 2002).

standing in the eyes of others.[6] Human life in the social state proved miserable and human nature is corrupted by civilization. Government is instituted but is itself a fraudulent conspiracy of the powerful (the rich) to subordinate the weak (the poor).

In *The Social Contract* (SC)[7] Rousseau finds a way out of this gloomy condition. It may be possible to regain men's freedom not by sending them back to their natural state, which is neither possible nor attractive. Rather, the solution is to transform society into

> a form of association that may defend and protect with the whole force of the community the person and property of every associate, and by means of which each, joining together with all, may nevertheless obey only himself, and remain as free as before.

Such is the fundamental problem of which the social contract provides the solution (SC I.6:163). If such an association could be established and sustained, it would rightly enjoy absolute sovereignty; it would have supreme authority with a right to demand absolute obedience from each associate, without at the same time depriving each of his full freedom. It is this promise of freedom-preserving political authority that inspired the founding fathers of modern constitutions to place popular sovereignty at their centre.

How does Rousseau see this freedom-preserving political association? His counter-intuitive answer is that this is an association where: each of us puts in common his person and all his power under the supreme direction of the general will; and in return each member becomes an indivisible part of the whole (SC I.6:164). It is counter-intuitive since individuals seem to dissolve in the collective body as its indivisible parts, losing their freedom along the way. However, as Rousseau explains, the act of consent, establishing the association, is reciprocal: each and every associate in entering civil society alienates not only his natural rights and freedoms, but his property and all other social advantages (the source of all dependency in the pre-contract state). Thereby he agrees to obey the general will alone. The result is: instead of losing one's freedom by becoming dependent on the will of another (an ever-present danger in the pre-contract state), all preserve their freedom by becoming dependent on their own general will only.

But is not obeying the general will a loss of freedom? For Rousseau it is not because the general will is the combined will of civic-minded citizens in a free and equal association, where dependency solely on one's own will is the hallmark of freedom. The change in the will from private to general in the transition from the natural into the social state requires a transformation of man from a self-loving noble savage into a moral being. It requires 'substituting a social and moral existence for the independent and physical existence which we have all received from nature' (SC II.7:181). This new social being would be able to act responsibly

[6] J. Cohen, *Rousseau: A Free Community of Equals* (Oxford: Oxford University Press, 2010), 101.

[7] Jean-Jacques Rousseau, *The Social Contract* (1762) in *The Social Contract and the First and Second Discourses*, 'Rethinking the Western Tradition' series, ed. S. Dunn and G. May (New Haven and London: Yale University Press, 2002).

for the common good of the collective body rather than his own narrow self-interest. The newborn citizen would thus have a general will and be able to control his private will.

An adequate answer to the question of how the transformation from natural to social being (known as the 'general will formation' problem) is to be achieved under conditions of widespread corruption of morals (which results from the domination in civilized men of *amour propre*) is crucial to Rousseau's thought. It is a test whether Rousseau's unique solution to the problem of freedom preserving-political authority (i.e. his project of 'association of the general will') could work.

III. Legitimacy between the Sovereign and its Author: the Constitutional Beginning Problem

The general will is the will of citizens with genuine solidarity towards their co-citizens, with strong civic spirit, always ready to put the common good before their private interests. These character traits, underpinning the general will in each associate, are usually the result of citizens being socialized and having lived in a well-ordered society, run by an effective general will. Yet they are themselves necessary for building a well-ordered society in the first place and should thus precede it. Without the presence of these traits, the presumably non-corruptible, non-malleable general will would be just the will of all, the sum of the self-interested private wills of the individuals (SC II.3:172). These private wills, driven by *amour propre*, are the source of all defects and dependencies of civilized societies, which deprive men of their freedom and prevent the emergence of a freedom-preserving political association.

I call the problem of building an association of the general will out of a mere aggregation of disparate individuals, transforming what Rousseau calls the 'will of all' into 'general will', the problem of constitutional beginning. Constitutional beginning is always problematic, even paradoxical, yet in Rousseau's project it is doubly so: it involves a need for a thorough break with and a radical transformation not only of political order but of men as well. For Rousseau the making and ratifying of regime-founding constitutions changes an individual from 'un animal stupide et borne' to 'un etre intelligent et un homme.'[8]

One of Rousseau's major contributions to moral and political philosophy is to destabilize the assumption that humans have a fixed, immutable nature. Rather, human nature is shaped by the social conditions under which humans live, and is amenable to change. For this change to happen, however, the social conditions should change first. Change of social conditions cannot happen by itself. An actor is needed, and this actor cannot be the men who are yet to be born and shaped by these changed conditions. Solving the problem of 'constitutional beginning', that is, of 'bringing into existence' a *citoyen* with civic virtue out of a private-minded

[8] S. Holmes, 'Precommitment and the Paradox of Democracy', in J. Elster and R. Slagstad (eds), *Constitutionalism and Democracy* (Cambridge: Cambridge University Press, 1988), 211.

bourgeois, is crucial for Rousseau's account. It requires an explanation as to 'how the effect may precede the cause'. Rousseau spells out the problem clearly:

> In order that a newly formed nation might approve sound maxims of politics and observe the fundamental rules of state-policy, it would be necessary that the effect should become the cause; that the social spirit, which should be the product of the institution, should preside over the institution itself, and that men should be, prior to the laws, what they ought to become by means of them (SC II.7:182).

He is aware that turning effect into cause amounts to a miracle and thus requires supra-natural powers.[9] Accordingly, he entrusts a supra-natural hero—a god-like Legislator—with the task of guiding a group of disparate individuals to become a sovereign people. To be up to the task, the Legislator must know the features of the group, their passions and aspirations, without experiencing and being dependent on them. This is important since, in addition to his *first task of constituting a specific body politic with a unique identity, he is also to draft its laws*, which the sovereign will only ratify. To be able to draft laws, i.e. general rules (general both in their object and content) for the life of the collective body, their author must be fully impartial. Impartiality is only attainable if the Legislator has no private interest in the laws he is drafting; he must be an outsider to the body politic:

> This office, which constitutes the republic, does not enter into its constitution; it is a special and superior office, having nothing in common with human jurisdiction; for, if he who rules men ought not to control legislation, he who controls legislation ought not to rule men; otherwise his laws, being ministers of his passions, would often serve only to perpetuate his acts of injustice; he would never be able to prevent private interests from corrupting the sacredness of his work (SC II.7:181).

Drafting the laws is also critical for the success of the project since 'the general will is always right, but the judgment which guides it is not always enlightened' (SC II.6:180). Hence 'the public must be taught to understand what they want' (SC II.6:180). The task of the Legislator is to bring 'Public enlightenment [which will] result [in] the union of understanding and will in the social body; and from that the close cooperation of the parts, and, lastly, the maximum power of the whole'(SC II.6:180). The Legislator cannot achieve his tasks by ordinary means; he 'cannot employ either force or reasoning, he must have recourse to an authority of a different order, which can compel without violence and persuade without convincing' (SC II.7:182).

The Legislator may not use violence because he would then be treating citizens as slaves, defeating his purpose of creating free, sovereign people. Nor can he use rational arguments since understanding is precisely what people lack and is the reason why they need the Legislator. What would this 'compelling' and 'persuading' amount to? The way for the Legislator to 'denature' men and turn them into

[9] '[Rousseau's] images of men of authority are so interesting because they are his answer to the question "how do we begin?" See Judith N. Shklar, 'Rousseau's Images of Authority', in Riley (ed.) *The Cambridge Companion to Rousseau*, 186.

citizens cooperating on equal terms is to use non-rational yet non-coercive means. What are these means?

In *Considerations on the Government of Poland* (henceforth referred to as *Poland*)[10] Rousseau, stepping into the shoes of the mythical Legislator, suggests that the Poles will only become a nation with a general will if the citizens, from an early age, are involved in national festivities, mass rituals, collective games, etc. These collective practices are designed by the Legislator to foster patriotic zeal and moral affection among compatriots, much needed for a community with general will. In the earlier *The Social Contract*, however, Rousseau is less explicit and suggests that the task of the Legislator is beyond the capacity of a human. Supra-natural authority is needed, to use effectively the resources of religion for the purposes of constituting a people and giving it laws. The origin of nations, concludes Rousseau, relies on religion.

The answer to the constitutional-beginning problem Rousseau gives—a god-like Legislator to start the process—is controversial. Some Rousseau scholars prefer to brush aside the issue of the general will formation and the uncomfortable role of the Legislator.[11] Rousseau's solution is unsatisfactory, however: even if the role of the Legislator is only to 'form [citizen] identity causally, [the Legislator] does not constitute it, it is not part of the meaning of what it is to be a citizen'.[12] One may understand what being a citizen of a sovereign people is without recourse to a Legislator, which only causally produces the citizen. Yet, while we understand the concept, this does not in itself show that, given certain relatively constant features of human nature (the temptation to succumb to *amour propre,* for example), citizens formed with 'supra-natural' external help would ever be able to exercise their sovereignty unaided (and this must be so if the association of the general will is to be freedom-preserving).

If the road to freedom is paved by the Legislator's manipulative compelling and persuading, the question remains whether the people are genuinely free, rather than dependent on the Legislator and the manipulative culture it designs for them. Further concern is raised by the question of whether the general will would genuinely legitimate the laws drafted by the Legislator if the sovereign lacks rational understanding, or if its understanding is entirely shaped by the Legislator through non-rational means. Patrick Riley presents the problem thus: 'Can the will be both an autonomous "moral cause" and be subject to the rationalizing, generalizing effect of educative authority?'[13] Presumably, the Legislator is a benevolent, disinterested teacher who would not use manipulation to further his own private interest, so the 'dangerous impracticality'[14] of Rousseau's

[10] *Considerations on the Government of Poland* (1772) at <http://www.constitution.org/jjr/poland.htm> (last visited 12 September 2012).

[11] Cohen, *Rousseau: A Free Community of Equals*, 35–36, 153.

[12] C. Bertram, *Routledge Philosophy Guidebook to Rousseau and the Social Contract* (Routledge, 2004), 145.

[13] Riley, 'Rousseau's General Will', 132.

[14] A. Bloom, 'Rousseau's Critique of Liberal Democracy', in Orwin and Tarcov (eds), *The Legacy of Rousseau* (Chicago and London: University of Chicago Press, 1997), 162.

solution may be the less serious concern. The threat, rather, is that to achieve his task, the Legislator uses freedom-compromising manipulation.[15] Doubts would linger over the independence of the sovereign—how free it is to reject the draft laws? If it rejects them, this may show that the Legislator still has work to do: the 'general will formation' is not yet complete, since the sovereign does not yet 'understand what it [really] wants'. If, on the other hand, the Legislator proposes the best laws only when the sovereign is ready to affirm them, it remains unclear which is the source of validity of those laws: the general will of the sovereign or the supra-natural powers of the Legislator, who makes sure (by continuing to educate and shape the general will) the rejection of those laws is not an option?

The question 'who is the sovereign, the source of legitimacy: the people themselves or its author, the Legislator?' naturally arises. It arises, since the Legislator works simultaneously from both ends. He builds the people, gives them *their* identity, their sense of shared being, their moral character, without which they are not sovereign people with general will. Yet he also gives the substance of their general will; he drafts the foundational laws to be ratified by the sovereign and to become its constitution. These ends meet if, and only if, the sovereign is ready to endorse the laws drafted by the Legislator. Only then is the job of the Legislator finished. The Legislator seems to be the author of the sovereign in a double sense: it gives it both its identity and the content of its general will.

Should we conclude, then, that state legitimacy depends on the Legislator, that it *is* the source of the authority of the sovereign? Not necessarily. A state is legitimate if the people do indeed exercise sovereignty through their general will. For this to be the case, a mere aggregation of disparate individuals should be transformed into a sustainable association of citizens with general will, able to control and suppress their partial wills. It is at this point that Rousseau's apparent paradox of 'forcing men to be free' dissolves. It does indeed make sense to insist that 'whoever refuses to obey the general will shall be constrained to do so by the whole body; which means nothing else than that he shall be forced to be free' (SC I.7:166), only when and on the condition that the sovereign is formed and has a clear, determinate and effective general will. Only then may it have a licence to use force against detractors 'so that the social pact not be a pointless device' (SC I.7:166). The work of the Legislator is only to form the communal identity necessary for this effective control over private wills. Once thus formed, the sovereign *is* the sole source of political authority in the mature state of the association of the general will.

Thus the next important question is: how does the mature association of the general will sustain itself without the help of a great Legislator? What would allow it to sustain itself without any external supervision of the body politic? What internal resources would keep the sovereign from the ever-present danger of degenerating into a disparate group of individuals, dominated by *amour propre*?

The answer, I argue, should be sought in the gift of the Legislator: the constitution he drafts for the people. It contains the fundamental laws and principles to

[15] Bertram, *Routledge Guidebook to Rousseau and the Social Contract*, 141.

govern the association of the general will sustainably. If this association proves to be self-sustaining, then Rousseau's unique solution to the legitimacy problem, that only a popular sovereign with a general will has the right to rule, would work. It would vindicate Rousseau's synthesis between the voluntarism of modern social contract theory and the morality of the common good of the ancients, compromised as it is at the start by the godly Legislator. Rousseau did not believe in original sin, nor did he believe that the beginnings of the community of the general will in its Legislator compromise it. Yet without an answer to the sustainability question, the promise of a freedom-preserving political authority, which has inspired the founding fathers of modern constitutions, remains only a promise.

IV. Constitution for an Association of the General Will

Is the general will equipped with strong enough constitutional safeguards to counteract the degeneration of its association into a mere aggregate of individuals? Is the association of the general will sustainable?

Constitutional safeguards can be grouped into two broad classes: institutional (or constitutional in the narrow sense) and cultural-educative. The character and scope of the institutional ones are well captured in the following statement: 'modern constitutionalism does impose certain definite broad requirements, such as, limited government, adherence to the rule of law, protection of fundamental interests and compliance with the demands of abstract equality'.[16] The cultural-educative safeguards to reach the same objective do not rely chiefly on the set-up and characteristics of the state structures and their relations, but on the socio-cultural framework, the system of mores and religious beliefs, and the predominant attitudes of the citizens, within which the state structures operate.

1. Cultural safeguards

In contrast to the institutionalist bent of most modern constitutional theorists, Rousseau is adamant in stressing the importance of the cultural-educative guarantees, defined in the previous paragraph:

> [it is] the most important of all, which is engraved neither on marble nor on bronze, but in the hearts of the citizens; a law which creates the *real constitution* of the State, which acquires new strength daily, which, when other laws grow obsolete or pass away, revives them or reinforces them, preserves a people in the spirit of their institutions, and imperceptibly substitutes the force of habit for that of authority. I speak of manners, customs, and above all of opinion—a province unknown to our politicians, but one on which the success of all the rest depends (SC II.12:191, emphasis added).

[16] Michel Rosenfeld, 'Modern Constitutionalism as Interplay between Identity and Diversity', in M. Rosenfeld (ed.), *Constitutionalism, identity, difference, and legitimacy: theoretical perspectives* (Durham and London: Duke University Press, 1994), 14.

To build these major constitutional safeguards, various mechanisms can be used: civic education, participation in civic rituals and collective games, distribution of public honours, etc. All of them help develop and sustain in citizens deep commitments to their civic culture of always putting the common good before their private interests. Thus socialized, citizens take their destiny in their own hands and presumably rule themselves unaided. I will not discuss in detail the various practices suggested by Rousseau for achieving this goal.

Culture and socialization undoubtedly play a significant role and may be particularly effective in sustaining the community of the general will. Yet, they involve serious drawbacks as well, which should not be brushed aside in discussing the effective safeguards for a self-sustaining community of the general will. The major concern has already been indicated: the procedures for bringing-up the associates of this community through inherently manipulative instruments may not allow them to develop their rational deliberative capacities. Without such capacities the sovereign could hardly be free, independent, and self-determining. Without repeating these critiques here, let me only point out that, despite his often-quoted reluctance to allow citizens communication during the vote (SC II.3) (motivated by his opposition to factions, which, he believed, distort the expression of the general will in voting), Rousseau constantly stresses the importance of public deliberation. Public deliberation is crucial, he argues, if the sovereign is to block effectively the usurpation of its power by abusive governments (I will expand on this below). The sovereign not only has 'the simple right of voting in every act of sovereignty [but also] the right of speaking, proposing, dividing and discussing, which the government is always very careful to leave to its members only' (SC IV.1:228), as Rousseau sarcastically notes. These deliberative capacities may indeed be compromised by the socializing practices that foster the necessary identity of the sovereign.

One may try to defend the socializing practices advocated by Rousseau by arguing that the deliberative capacities they are undermining are not necessary for the citizens of the association of the general will in its mature state. In mature and healthy republics, the general will finds *immediate* expression without the need for prior deliberation:

> the common good is everywhere *plainly clear and only good sense is required to perceive it.* A State thus governed needs very few laws; and in so far as it becomes necessary to promulgate new ones, this necessity is *universally recognized* (SC IV.1:227, emphases added).

Continuous deliberations are thus a mark of a declining state, and developing capacities for deliberation may indeed be viewed as counter-productive. But even if we agree that they are *not to be used* in the healthy association of the general will, deliberative capacities may still be necessary as a 'reserve tool', ready to use against the natural tendency of all governments to abuse their powers.

Since the socializing practices Rousseau is advocating (to foster citizens' commitment to the association of the general will) do adversely affect the development of capacities for rational deliberation, this remains a serious problem for Rousseau's project. In the rest of this text I cannot hope to do justice to this major issue; I will, instead, focus on the institutional safeguards for the association of the general will.

2. The association of the general will and democracy

What is the institutional framework of an association of the general will? It is often held that for Rousseau only direct democracy fits his mature state. Yet the Genevan is explicit that the government executing the general will of the sovereign may be democracy, aristocracy, or even monarchy, depending on a variety of contingent factors (SC III.8). The apparent discrepancy disappears once the sharp distinction Rousseau draws between *the sovereign* (the ultimate source of political authority) and its *government* is noted. The sovereign legislates through the general will directly: representative sovereignty, representing the general will is a contradiction in terms for him (SC III.14). When represented, what may have seemed a general will turns out to be just the partial will of a citizen or subclass of citizens (SC II.1:170). The government only executes the legislative decisions of the sovereign, applying, interpreting, and enforcing the laws. Government for Rousseau not only may, but must be representative in its form (I will come back to the roles and the form of government in the next section). The requirement that the general will be expressed directly by all is captured by Rousseau's claim that sovereignty is inalienable (SC II.1) and indivisible (SC II.2). These two characteristics are entwined. The moment an attempt is made to represent the general will of the sovereign through a part of it, the general will stops being general, dissolving into a particular will instead:

> Sovereignty cannot be represented for the same reason that it cannot be alienated; it consists essentially in the general will, and the will cannot be represented; it is itself or it is something else; there is no middle ground (SC III.15:221).

The argument against representation of sovereignty moves us closer to the issue of constitutional safeguards. It runs as follows: if the sovereign were to be represented by a citizen or a subgroup of citizens, an opportunity would open for one part of the body politic to dominate the rest. This would ultimately destroy the sovereign, which is a community of equals, a collective body created for the sole purpose of always aiming at the equal good of all. Only such a community of equals preserves the freedom of its associates. The only legitimate states (states with freedom-preserving political authority), concludes Rousseau, are those where the sovereign, the people as a whole, directly legislates. These legitimate states and only them Rousseau calls 'republics', irrespective of their specific form of government (even monarchies are 'republics' in his peculiar sense, if the popular sovereign directly legislates there).

Rousseau admits, however, that in larger modern states (such as Poland, or England) legislative power may need to be exercised by representatives rather than directly. Representation, however, opens it to corruption and endangers citizen freedom. This has been the fate of

> the English nation [which] thinks that it is free, but is greatly mistaken, for it is so only during the election of members of Parliament; as soon as they are elected, it is enslaved and counts for nothing. The use it makes of the brief moments of freedom renders the loss of liberty well-deserved (SC III.15:221).

The system of representation, coupled with parliamentary sovereignty and the lack of accountability of the MPs in Britain, has destroyed the freedom of citizens. The best guarantee for their freedom is the direct involvement of the whole body politic in the legislative power, since 'the whole citizen body is impossible to corrupt'. It cannot by its very nature allow domination of a part over the whole. Rousseau does not deny that the legislature, comprising the whole body politic, is easily manipulated by demagogues, yet this is for him a lesser evil than the corruption associated with representation: 'it is possible to enlighten someone who is mistaken; but how can you restrain someone who is for sale?' (*Poland*, VII).

To forestall this overtaking of sovereignty by representatives, Rousseau urges that they should be elected by local assemblies with all citizens present, given strict imperative mandates with no right of independent judgement and should always consult their constituents when a new issue arises. The terms of office should be short and re-election limited, and periodic activity reports should be presented to constituents, etc. (*Poland*, VII). It is true that these measures cannot fully counteract the adverse effects of the unfortunate fact of a large republic, yet for Rousseau they may mitigate and slow down the inevitable process of decline.

The problem of representing sovereignty affects even smaller republics, such as Rousseau's native Geneva. He notices a drive there towards delegating the legislative power to representatives, a drive coming from a passive, self-interested, self-indulging citizenry, not willing to forego personal convenience and profit for the common good. The love of luxury softens their mores and as their *amour propre* corrupts them they grow indifferent to the sovereign assemblies, leaving them hostage to the manipulations of representatives (SC III.15). The general will is substituted by the particular will of representatives: the interests of this latter group are served at the expense of the common good. By representing sovereignty citizens only speed up the death of their republic: 'As soon as public service ceases to be the Citizens' principal business, and they prefer to serve with their purse rather than with their person, the State is already close to its ruin.' (SC III.15).

In sum, the constitutional framework for an association of the general will is a republic, where the sovereign self-legislates, directly expressing its will in the legislature. Scholars have long debated whether Rousseau's commitment to the democratic principle of self-legislation is adequately translated into his republic's institutional design, or, rather, the democratic principles and their institutional implementation are in tension.[17] It has been argued that the real distribution of powers between the sovereign and its government shows Rousseau's preference for an elite-dominated republic with popular assemblies having purely expressive

[17] R. Fralin, *Rousseau and Representation: A Study of the Development of His Concept of Political Institutions* (New York: Columbia University Press, 1978); J. N. Shklar, *Men and Citizens: A Study in Rousseau's Social Theory*, 2nd ed. (Cambridge: Cambridge University Press, 1985).

and educative functions (an issue to which I return below). But even if we take Rousseau's democratic commitments at their face value, one may still argue that it is less clear what form of direct democracy he advocates. The requirement that the sovereign directly expresses its general will is liable to two interpretations: it is compatible both with strong participatory democracy and with plebiscitary democracy. The balance towards the plebiscitary interpretation is tipped by the role of the Legislator in the initial general will formation and drafting of the constitution (discussed above), as well as by the agenda-setting role of governmental magistrates in the later stages of the legislative process. On this interpretation, the sovereign has only ratifying prerogatives and does not actively participate in the general will formation and law drafting process. Yet, Rousseau insists that the civic virtues, necessary for a sustainable sovereign, are fostered only when exercised in *active* service by the sovereign. This fostering of civic virtues requires active participation of all citizens in shaping the general will and finding its best expression in laws. This stress on the importance of exercising civic virtues lends strong support to the participatory interpretation instead.

My conclusion is that Rousseau oscillates between two forms of direct democracy, depending on whether he focuses on people as they currently are (i.e. inactive, self-indulgent, self-interested bourgeois)—for them plebiscitary democracy is all that is possible—or he focuses on people as they ought to be (i.e. active citizens with strong civic virtues)—to whom participatory democracy is best suited.

3. Institutional safeguards

i. The limited government principle

Moving to the more specific institutional safeguards of citizen freedom, I first address the relation of the sovereign to its government and the way the domination of the former over the latter is ensured. The answer is provided by Rousseau's interpretation of the idea of limited government. How government can be limited is a major issue for Rousseau, since he believed that the primary threat to citizen liberty came from the tyrannical and arbitrary character of the absolutist monarchies of his time and from their abusive governments. Even in his native Geneva, the elected magistrates (sitting on the *Small Council*) were trying to extend their rights at the expense of those of the *General Council*, whose sovereignty they continuously contested throughout the early eighteenth century. The magistrates attempted to usurp the sovereign power by claiming to have exclusive rights to decide, unchecked by the *General Council*, all important public matters. Rousseau sided with the bourgeoisie in their striving to re-establish the *General Council* as the exclusive site of sovereignty in the Genevan republic.[18]

[18] H. Rosenblatt, *Rousseau and Geneva: From the* First Discourse *to the* Social Contract, *1749–1762* (Cambridge: Cambridge University Press, 1997).

Limiting government is thus one of the central tenets of Rousseau's constitutional project. The interpretation of limited government he offered, however, is narrow and applies only to the government in his rather idiosyncratic sense, i.e. to executive power, and not to the legislation of the sovereign. It also relies, I argue, on a peculiar understanding of 'separation' between the executive and the legislature, which, while guaranteeing the control of the legislature over the executive, leaves the former entirely unchecked.

Rousseau's understanding of the principle of 'limited government' may be untangled in a series of interpretative steps. The first step is to identify the role Rousseau assigns to government in the institutional structure of his mature state. The task of government is primarily to execute the general will of the sovereign. The government is thus a mere employee of the sovereign, with no rights of its own against the sovereign:

> the act by which a people submits to its leaders is not a contract... It is absolutely nothing but a *commission*, an *employment*, in which, as simple officers of the sovereign, they exercise in its name the power of which it has made them depositaries, and which *it can limit, modify, and take back when it pleases* (SC III.1:194).

Governments in the Rousseauean republic are given the power to apply, interpret, and enforce the laws adopted by the sovereign. In the earlier *Discourse on Political Economy*,[19] Rousseau had argued that government attends to the execution of the laws and to other 'administrative and economic details' under the guidance of the general will expressed through law.[20] Rousseau is all too aware of the dangers these powers of government present to the supremacy of the sovereign. To forestall the usurpation of sovereign power by the magistrates, which is his primary concern in constitutional design, he maintains that the citizens should regularly assemble. These assemblies, called by general law and not by ad hoc governmental decrees, control the power of the government. The magistrates' work is checked and, if found satisfactory, they may be granted further right to govern, as long as and to the extent that this pleases the sovereign (SC III.18). A further check on the power of the magistrates is the right of the assembly to decide on taxes and the funds available to government itself.

Some scholars have argued that in his less democratic moods (in the *Dedication to the Republic of Geneva* and some parts of the *Letters Written from the Mountain* (LM), for example), Rousseau gives governments stronger than strictly executive prerogatives.[21] Magistrates are granted rights of legislative initiative, of drafting laws, of checking popular legislative initiatives, and powers to determine their own successors

[19] Jean-Jacques Rousseau *Discourse on Political Economy* (1755), at <http://www.constitution.org/jjr/polecon.htm> (last visited 12 September 2012).

[20] J. T. Scott, 'Rousseau's Anti-Agenda-Setting Agenda and Contemporary Democratic Theory', *The American Political Science Review* 99 (1) (2005), 137–44, at 139.

[21] Jean-Jacques Rousseau, *Letters Written from the Mountain* (1764), in *Letter to Beaumont, Letters Written from the Mountain, and Related Writings*, vol. 9 of *Collected Writings of Jean-Jacques Rousseau*, ed. C. Kelly and E. Grace (Hanover: University Press of New England, Dartmouth College 2001).

through control over the nomination procedure, etc. They all go well beyond the mere execution of what the general will had already decided. In this picture, the principal-agent relation between the sovereign and its government is reversed: it is the agent that has all the real power, while the principal, formally preserving its sovereignty, in reality exercises merely symbolic, expressive functions. The description of the real powers of the legislative assembly vis-à-vis government arguably shows that Rousseau in fact defends an elitist regime: expert elites rather than the citizens set the political agenda and monopolize the legislative process, thus actively forming the general will instead of being its mere executioners.[22] While it is hard to dispute that Rousseau gives magistrates strong prerogatives, scholars debate their precise character and the implications for Rousseau's democratic theory.[23] Whether it is an exclusive right of elected experts, or whether the sovereign may also initiate laws, and, whether this and related prerogatives compromise the supremacy of the sovereign, are central problems.

The textual evidence for settling these issues definitively is inconclusive. In the *Dedication*, Rousseau seems to grant the government the exclusive right of legislative initiative: 'in order to prevent self-interested and ill-designed projects . . . no person should be at liberty to propose new laws at pleasure: . . . this should be the exclusive privilege of the magistrates' (DI: 74). Citizens should 'be content with the privilege of giving sanction to their Laws'. Against this interpretation, it may be argued that, even in this strongest textual evidence for the exclusive magisterial right of legislative initiative, Rousseau does not abandon his position that the sovereign enjoys supremacy over its government. He continues the above sentence thus: the people (and not the magistrates) are those who 'decide in a Body according to the recommendations of their leaders, the most important public affairs' (DI: 75). Even in his less democratic moods, when Rousseau deprives the sovereign of legislative initiative, he still insists that it is the people (even if only on the recommendations of their leaders) who decide the most important public issues and ratify (or refuse to do so) the laws. The sovereign remains a 'gatekeeper', even if it is not the 'agenda-setter'.[24]

The two roles—agenda-setter v. gatekeeper—are implicitly distinguished in Letter seven of LM. This text contains Rousseau's most detailed account of the troubled relation between the sovereign and its government, at the concrete level of institutions and their dynamic relations, not at the abstract level of political principle. Recognizing that government always tries to expand its powers and is often able, by imperceptible gradual changes, to corrupt the constitution, Rousseau insists that citizens should be always vigilant to check such attempts actively. They must publicly discuss and veto governmental suggestions that extend magisterial

[22] Fralin, *Rousseau and Representation*; Shklar, *Men and Citizens*.

[23] E. Putterman, 'Rousseau on Agenda-Setting and Majority Rule' in *The American Political Science Review* 97 (3) (2003), 459–69; E. Putterman, 'Rousseau on the People as Legislative Gatekeepers, Not Framers', *The American Political Science Review* 99 (1) (2005), 146–51; Putterman, *Rousseau, Law and the Sovereignty of the People* (Cambridge: Cambridge University Press, 2010); Scott, 'Rousseau's Anti-Agenda-Setting Agenda'.

[24] Putterman, 'Rousseau on the People', 147.

powers and approve only those which, in their opinion, serve the public good. For the purposes of effective 'gate-keeping', periodic assemblies of the General Council are necessary. If the sovereign is not alert to the dangers of governmental usurpation and does not convene regularly to check government, and to discuss and ratify, or refuse to do so, the draft laws, it will soon be overtaken by the government which is always willing to extend its power. The sovereign will be 'enchained', signalling the death of the republic.

At the same time, Rousseau is unwilling to give full licence to popular legislative initiatives. He imposes restrictions on legislative innovations proposed directly by citizens 'at their fancy'. These need to be checked by the magistrates first: 'the Law has very wisely provided that the establishment and even the proposing of such innovations would not pass without the approval of the Councils' (LM: 264). Rousseau here seems to grant magistrates monopoly over legislation, which is arguably inconsistent with his commitment to democratic principles in the SC. However, a more charitable reading of Rousseau's intentions in restricting popular legislative initiatives is available. It starts with the observation that Rousseau urges Genevans (and citizens of mature republics more generally) to be cautious in frequently introducing innovations to the laws. Frequent innovations, he argues, deprive the laws of 'the great antiquity... which principally contributes to render them sacred and venerable' (DI: 74), encouraging citizens instead to 'despise' them.

Against this background, his opposition to popular initiatives is understandable: if such initiatives were unconditionally upheld, the likelihood of undesirable changes would grow. Introducing governmental checks may be a good filtering device against harmful, frequent innovations. The filter also may serve systemic functions. By slowing down the legislative process, subjecting it to cumbersome, time-consuming checks, citizens are encouraged to act on their considered judgements rather than on passing fancies, raising the quality of the democratic legislation as a result. At the same time, these checks do not entirely discourage popular initiatives: if the government is too often deaf to popular concerns, the popular assembly may withdraw its support and change the government. Such is, according to Joshua Cohen, Rousseau's response to the classical critiques of democracy as riven by passion and leading to an unstable regime. Checks on popular initiatives tame passions and bring in stability, without compromising the democratic credentials of Rousseau's institutional solutions. Checks are placed in the hands of both players—the government and its sovereign—yet the last word belongs to the latter. Thus, despite granting the right to legislative initiative to the expert magistrates and limiting popular initiatives, Rousseau preserves the supremacy of the sovereign over the executioner of its general will—the government.

The second step in clarifying Rousseau's doctrine of limited government concerns the form of government. Government in Rousseau's mature state should be representative. While the sovereign may not be represented by anybody except itself (only in this sense, as 'represented sovereignty', is representation strictly opposed), the will of the sovereign body must be executed through representatives, that is, through magistrates. Rousseau not only admits that representative government is the only workable type of government for modern large republics, but also gives principled reasons against the sovereign executing its laws directly.

> It is not correct that the person who makes the laws execute them, nor that the body of the people divert its attention from general considerations in order to bestow it on particular objects. Nothing is more dangerous than the influence of private interests on public affairs; and the abuse of the laws by the government is a lesser evil than the corruption of the legislator, which is the infallible result of the pursuit of private interests (SC III.4:201).

In order to prevent the corruption of the sovereign, inevitably resulting according to Rousseau from applying the general laws to particular objects, this task is to be delegated to representative executives. The latter's inevitable corruption in applying the laws may be checked by the vigilant sovereign, while there is no one to check the corruption of the sovereign itself. Governments not only 'may', but 'must' be representative.

The third step concerns the separation between the sovereign as principal and the executive, as its agent. In order to prevent private interest from corrupting the sovereign, argues Rousseau, there should be separation between those who legislate and those who execute the pronouncements of the general will. Can we conclude, following some contemporary scholars,[25] that Rousseau's solution to the problem of limited government is 'separation of powers'? It has long been argued that denial of separation of powers follows directly from Rousseau's view that sovereignty is indivisible.[26] Yet with precisely the same argument—preventing interest from displacing the general will of the sovereign—Rousseau supports both the thesis of the indivisibility of the sovereign and the position that the sovereign and its government should be separate. Is indivisibility of sovereignty compatible with separation of powers, then, and, is it separation of powers that Rousseau advocated as the solution to the problem of abusive, tyrannical governments?

To address these questions, we should notice, first, that in Rousseau's peculiar use of the term 'power', it is only government and not the sovereign, who has power (which is to be used in executing the laws). The sovereign, rather, has authority, expressed through its indivisible and inalienable will. The sovereign, through its authority, morally obligates the people to obey its laws, while the government, through all its power, may only oblige them, i.e. physically 'compel' them, to comply with its decrees. If government's decrees have authority at all, it entirely derives from the pronouncements of the sovereign, the general laws. Noting this conceptual peculiarity in Rousseau, where authority (general will) and power are not just distinct, but may not reside in one body, and also noting that all power in this Rousseauean sense is and must be concentrated in the government alone, one may conclude that Rousseau is not a proponent of the doctrine of separation of powers in any form.

[25] D. L. Williams, *Rousseau's Platonic Enlightenment* (University Park: Pennsylvania State University Press, 2007); M. Quortrup, *The Political Philosophy of Jean-Jacques Rousseau: The Impossibility of Reason* (Manchester: Manchester University Press, 2003).

[26] A. Bloom 'Jean-Jacques Rousseau', in L. Strauss and J. Cropsey (eds), *History of Political Philosophy* (London and Chicago: University of Chicago Press, 1963), 571.

Putting these conceptual issues aside, however, it must be noted that the difficulty in answering the question whether 'separation of powers' is Rousseau's solution to the problem of abusive government, stems from the fact that this doctrine has been developed and is liable to different interpretations. The American 'checks and balances' system interprets the powers of the legislature, the executive, and the judiciary as having equal standing, checking each other in order to prevent abuse by each, without interfering with each other's well-defined powers. One does not find such a system in Rousseau's mature state. The legislature is identified with the sovereign there, with the supreme bearer of political authority, and the government only executes the sovereign's will, without itself being a bearer of authority: legislature has supremacy over the executive. The sovereign-legislator is the principal, and the government, its agent, is to be closely monitored, checked, and controlled by the former to avoid the latter's inherent abuses. It is true that at times Rousseau grants the executive magistrates the right to check the legislative initiatives of the people to avoid introducing innovations 'at fancy', yet Rousseau is adamant that, ultimately, it is the sovereign (the General Council in Geneva, to take his preferred example) alone which decides important public matters and ratifies (even if previously checked by the magistrates for impermissible private influences) the laws.

One hardly finds separation of powers in Rousseau's project, however, even if a weaker interpretation of this doctrine is taken: as a minimum it stipulates that powers be more or less well-balanced and enjoy independence vis-à-vis each other. Independence is needed to avoid excessive concentration and abuse of power by dispersing it among different yet equally placed branches of government. Rousseau's position on the supremacy of the sovereign over its government blocks the requirement for relative independence of the branches of power, characteristic of even a minimal doctrine of separation of powers.

Indicative of the ambiguous standing of Rousseau's separation of powers doctrine is the fact that it has been attacked from the opposite direction as well. It is compromised, one may argue, since the sovereign cannot effectively control its executive and, instead of being its master (as the view of its supremacy assumes), is dominated by it. This is the thrust of the arguments we have discussed above: that magistrates enjoy an exclusive right of legislative initiative and, as sole agenda-setters in Rousseau's republic, may successfully manipulate the sovereign to their own advantage. Here the roles of principal and agent are reversed, with the active part played by the expert magistrates, dominating the passive citizenry. Thus, in Rousseau's state we do not have separation of powers, and this is not on account of his position on the legislative supremacy of the sovereign, but, instead, because it is the magistrates who enjoy supremacy, left entirely unchecked by the sovereign.

To conclude, Rousseau's idiosyncratic doctrine of separation of powers is best interpreted as a functional separation between the sovereign and its government. It has little in common with the modern constitutionalist interpretation of that doctrine: 'nowhere in his writings does he propose a constitutional separating or balancing in the traditional sense of dividing or sharing sovereignty in order to restrain it.'[27]

The fourth, and last, interpretative step concerns the above-mentioned supremacy of the legislator, the sovereign's agent. The legislature is the seat where all authority is concentrated and it is unlimited by anything outside the general will. The legislature is itself the ultimate guarantor of the unity of the state. The functional separation of the sovereign from the government in Rousseau does not deny this 'unity of state power'. It is from this perspective that one cannot attribute to Rousseau a doctrine of separation of powers in modern constitutionalism's sense of dispersing state power among equally placed branches. Rousseau's doctrine of limited government, in short, is a doctrine of legislative supremacy over an executive.

In Rousseau's well-ordered, mature republic, the supremacy of the legislature is effectively maintained by an active citizenry, which prevents the corruption of government by limiting it. The exercise of power by the executive is indeed strictly limited to the application and enforcement of the laws adopted by the sovereign as expressions of its general will. The limitations of government are guaranteed through a constant supervision by the sovereign, which starts each assembly by reviewing the work of the magistrates and considers whether the executive still pleases it. The sovereign is the source of law and ultimate guarantor that the government executes nothing but the law. Yet, in Rousseau's mature state, the sovereign itself is not limited by the separation between government and legislator. It is here one finds the limitation of Rousseau's account of limited government.

ii. Rule of law

The next safeguard against loss of freedom and degeneration into dependency, the rule of law, is central to constitutionalism. If we can speak of constitutionalism in Rousseau, we should be able to find a special place for the rule of law. The association of the general will, Rousseau argued, would have a system of laws that are general, both in their object—'the object of the laws is always general . . . the law considers subjects collectively, and actions as abstract, never a man as an individual nor a particular action' (SC II.6:178)—and in their form, as expressions of the general will: 'the law combines the universality of the will with the universality of the object' (SC II.6:179). Because laws are in essence acts of the general will, laws cannot be unjust 'since no one is unjust to himself'. Nor is anyone un-free because he is subject to the laws, 'since the laws are only registers of our wills.' Thus freedom is guaranteed by rule of law: by rule of the acts of general will.

It must be stressed that to the purely formal requirement of rule by law rather than man, Rousseau adds a substantive requirement: laws are general in their content, in their object and in their pedigree, they are genuine acts of the general will. They are opposed to mere decrees, which lack generality. Republics are the

[27] Putterman, *Rousseau, Law and the Sovereignty of the People*, 60.

only legitimate states for Rousseau because they alone are governed by laws meeting the above requirements. In republics, the rule of law characterizes the work of government: there are substantive limits to what magistrates may do in executing and interpreting the laws. The limits are substantive since decrees contradicting the laws in their content are invalid.

The interesting question, however, is whether the rule of law requirement puts limits upon the sovereign as legislator, not just upon its agent the government. Any meaningful sense of the rule of law should involve limits on the sovereign as well. The issue of the limits on the sovereign has attracted considerable scholarship, and since I cannot do justice to this complex debate here, I will limit my discussion to a few observations. One may argue that there are limits to the sovereign despite Rousseau's insistence that 'there is not, nor can there be, any kind of fundamental law that is binding upon the body of the people, not even the social contract' (SC I.6:165) and 'there is in the State no fundamental law which cannot be revoked, not even the social compact' (SC III.18:226). The limits are imposed by the requirement that laws must meet certain substantive criteria.[28] They must be general in their object and content to qualify as sovereign laws. Justice, which is served by requirements of substantive generality, thus seems to impose limits on what the sovereign may legislate.

However, the generality requirement does not put substantive limits on the general will itself. The general will, by its very nature general, since directed at the equal good of all associates, cannot pass any acts that are not general and do not meet the requirements of substantive justice. Were it to pass such non-general acts, it would mean it was not expressing the general will of the citizens, but the particular will of a private *bourgeois* or a group thereof. Such acts would signal that the 'general will' had degenerated into a mere 'will of all', passing not 'laws' but partial 'decrees'. Rousseau contends that

> the general will, to be truly such, should be so in its object as well as in its essence; that it ought to proceed from all in order to be applicable to all; and that it loses its natural rectitude when it tends to some individual and specific object, because in that case, judging what is unknown to us, we have no true principle of equity to guide us (SC II.4:174).

It is true by stipulation that any act of the sovereign expressing its general will is law, that is, it necessarily meets the generality requirements and is not constrained by them. The sovereign, as long as it has a well-defined general will, is not externally limited by this requirement, since it cannot violate it without losing its identity as a sovereign. Hence, the sovereign is not bound by any law, not even by fundamental law. As long as it adopts laws and not decrees, they are fully coextensive with its general will, which is thus not limited by anything outside of it, not even by its previous acts.

[28] S. Holmes, 'Precommitment and the Paradox of Democracy', in J. Elster and R. Slagstad (eds), *Constitutionalism and Democracy* (Cambridge: Cambridge University Press, 1988), 211, n. 54.

The argument that the sovereign is not bound by law overlooks an important distinction between the sovereign and its empirical embodiment in the people.[29] While law does not constrain the sovereign, it may indeed constrain its empirical embodiment: the people in their legislative deliberations. People often err in their deliberations (only the general will is always upright) (SC II.3), and when they try, under the guise of laws, to adopt partial decrees, the generality requirement of laws do constrain them. The distinction between a sovereign with a general will and its empirical embodiment in the people deliberating about its general will is pertinent in cases where a community disagrees on whether a draft law meets the generality requirements and would be an expression of the general will or not. In voting in plenary meetings, citizens express their opinions on what the general good requires in order to clarify which of the proposals do meet the generality requirements. They try to decide precisely that: the content of the general will, which is neither determinate nor known in advance. They sustain their opinion on the basis that since the proposal meets the generality requirements, it must be a true expression of the general will, and not the reverse: because their proposal is the expression of the general will it meets the generality requirements. The dispute is precisely whether or not a proposal expresses the general will. The way forward is to appeal to an external criterion, the generality requirement, which, if met, would testify that the decision does indeed express the general will. The external criterion sets limits as to what counts as general will.

My conclusion is that, under conditions of disagreement, which is a constant condition of modern pluralist societies, Rousseau's position that there are no constraints on the general will loses its plausibility. It is true that disagreement is often down-played by Rousseau as a clear sign of a degenerating community, as the mark of a growing preoccupation of citizens with their private interests. The socialization practices he advocates aim to eliminate the causes of disagreement, which stem from self-interest. Yet disagreement may, instead, stem from pluralism, which is a characteristic feature of modern societies. Rousseau views the elimination of pluralism by culturally homogenizing practices as the way to build the communal bond necessary for the community of the general will. In homogeneous, non-pluralist societies, the sovereign may have a determinate and generally recognized general will and so not need an external criterion to be identified. If elimination of pluralism as the source of disagreement is not an option, a community may need external criteria, such as the rule of law, to identify its general will and make it effective. The rule of law is here a safeguard, limiting and directing the empirical embodiment of the sovereign in the people in their search for the general will.

[29] B. Gregg and D. Williams, 'Review of *Rousseau and Law*, by Thom Brooks (ed.)', *Law and Politics Book Review* 16 (5) (2006), 372–83; commenting on the 'enabling model' of fundamental law in Rousseau, see M. Schwartzberg 'Rousseau on Fundamental Law', in *Political Studies* 51 2003, 387–403.

iii. Protecting individual interests and rights

One last safeguard of citizen freedom is the institutional protection of individual interests and rights. Here the suggestion is whether there is such a safeguard in the society of the general will. The answer is no. Rousseau does not provide a list of individual rights to be protected against the claims of society, nor does he envisage any institutional mechanisms for their exercise. This has prompted liberals, with their preference for constitutionally entrenched and institutionally protected (through judicial review of popular legislation, for instance) individual rights, to criticize the anti-liberal tendencies of Rousseau's thought. The individual arguably disappears in the community of the general will, described by critics as a 'totalitarian democracy'.[30] The sovereign, which is identified with the majority, controls and may abuse the dissenting minority. The charge of the tyrannical majority is the liberal critique most often levelled against Rousseau. Is it justified?

Rousseau has provided us with an ample choice of texts where he supports absolute power:

> by putting in common his person and all his power under the supreme direction of the general will . . . each member becomes an indivisible part of the whole (SC I.6:164).

> the social pact gives the body politic an absolute power over all its members; and it is this same power which, when controlled by the general will, bears . . . the name of sovereignty (SC II.4:174).

These and many other characterizations of the sovereign and its general will hardly show the liberal credentials of Rousseau. Liberals might be relieved to read: 'We agree that whatever part of his power, property, and liberty each person alienates by accepting the social compact is only what is useful and important to the community' (SC II.4:174). Yet the qualification that follows confirms their fears: 'but we must also agree that the sovereign alone is judge of what is important' (SCII.4.17).

We owe to Jeremy Waldron a defence of Rousseau against the charge of tyranny of the majority.[31] His argument starts by distinguishing two models of democratic decision-making: a Benthamite and a Rousseauean. In the first, voters are self-interested utility maximizers, expressing their preferences, aggregated by the decision-making process to determine their choice. The majority is right to impose its decision on the minority, since in this way social utility is best served and the utilitarian ideal of the greatest happiness of the greatest number is realized. In Rousseau's model, by contrast, voters express 'their personal beliefs about the best way to promote the general good' and not their self-regarding preferences.[32] The decision-making process here approximates an epistemic mechanism, identifying what is the general will on an issue. Rousseau's idea is captured by the famous Jury Theorem, formulated by the eighteenth-century liberal Marquis de Condorcet: given sufficient competence and independence of the voters, the greater the

[30] J. Talmon, *The Origins of Totalitarian Democracy* (London: Mercury Books, 1961).

[31] J. Waldron, 'Rights and Majorities: Rousseau Revisited' in J. W. Chapman and A. Wertheimer (eds), *Majorities and Minorities* (New York: New York University Press, 1990).

[32] Waldron, 'Rights and Majorities: Rousseau Revisited', 50.

majority with which the decision is taken, the greater the chance of this decision being correct. The difference between the two models of democratic voting is well-illustrated by Rousseau's distinction between the general will and the will of all: 'the general will studies only the common interest while the will of all studies private interest and is indeed no more than the sum of individual desires'.[33]

With regard to the Benthamite model, the charge of tyrannical majorities is well taken: minority's interests are threatened by the self-interested will of all and so protection external to the democratic process is needed. Constitutional entrenchment of individual rights, enforced by a body external to the democratic process and able to block it may be necessary to protect the interests and rights of the dissenting minority. Granting rights as vetoes would make the 'individuals dictators on the issues they cover'.[34]

In Rousseau's model, by contrast, citizens are supposed 'to turn their attention to the common good, that is, to the rules and practices that benefit everyone.' The decision reached is likely to identify what the general will on an issue is and hence the interests of all citizens are protected. The majority here is not tyrannical; it does not promote its own interests at the expense of the interests of the minority. Rather, it is just proven to be correct in its judgement as to which of the competing proposals best promotes the interests of all. There is, therefore, *no* need for a protection external to the democratic process of the interests of the minority; they are protected, even if the minority does not realize it. Their opinion has been found incorrect in the decision-making process. That one's opinion does not prevail does not necessarily mean one's interests have been disregarded or one's rights violated: 'Nothing tyrannical happens to me merely by virtue of the fact that my opinion is not acted on'.[35] Even if the dissenter thinks that his interests were not taken into account by the majority and are thus threatened, that will not necessarily be an adequate motive for dissent.

The crucial point, Waldron maintains, is that 'Even if the issue on which A, the minority, differs from B and C is the proper level of respect due A's interests, there is no reason to take A's views of the matter any more seriously or think it more likely to be correct than the opinion shared by B and C. The majority is not necessarily right, but on a matter concerning the rights of minorities it is not necessarily wrong either.'[36] Opinions are to be respected but as nothing more than opinions: since they are not themselves interests, they do not need the special protection afforded interests. Next, if we admit that concerning their rights and interests the minority may be wrong, and the majority right, this applies to a handful of rights-guardians as well. The judges entrusted to review legislation for constitutionality may be wrong, and the majority, right. If politics is about principle, about striking the right balance between interests and protecting the rights of each associate, as in Rousseau's society of the general will, constitutionally

[33] Waldron, 'Rights and Majorities: Rousseau Revisited', 52–3.
[34] Waldron, 'Rights and Majorities: Rousseau Revisited', 68.
[35] Waldron, 'Rights and Majorities: Rousseau Revisited', 64.
[36] Waldron, 'Rights and Majorities: Rousseau Revisited', 65.

entrenching rights and giving special authority to non-elected courts to enforce them against the majority becomes much less plausible, concludes Waldron.

Waldron is right to say that when the democratic decision-making correctly identifies the common good, the interests of each are well attended to and there is no further need for external constraints to additionally guarantee these interests. But the defence works only on the assumption that citizens, driven by their civic virtues, vote according to their disinterested opinions about the just balance of interests in society and never according to their self-interested preferences. In this case, where the ideal of the general will is perfectly realized, constitutional constraints are indeed not needed. However, constitutional constraints, such as entrenchment of rights and external rights-guardians, may be indispensable safeguards of citizen freedom in the more likely, pessimistic case, where the majority of citizens vote to use the collective decision-making process to promote their private interests. In this case, minorities and dissenters may lose more than the right to act on their own opinion: their fundamental interests may also be at stake. Protection external to the democratic process of these fundamental interests is then indispensable. Such constraints are necessary even where some of the citizens vote according to their preferences, and some, their opinions. Into this category falls the case where citizens are confused as to what they are voting on: in expressing their opinions, they may well be influenced by partial interests.

Unless Rousseau has provided us with reason to believe that the latter cases are unlikely to occur, or are less likely than the optimistic case, the charge of opening the doors to tyranny of the majority is well-founded. If the optimistic case cannot be guaranteed, Rousseau has to give a clear criterion for distinguishing cases where the majority decision does express the general will from cases where it expresses only the will of all. He has given us a rough sketch of such a criterion: if in a society disagreement, factions, and wide inequalities abound, majorities are likely to express only their private wills. An association of the general will, conversely, is characterized by homogeneity, agreement, and rough equality, where majority decision as a rule does express the general will. Yet, as we have noticed above, disagreement and faction may be due to pluralism rather than preoccupation with private interest, and often disagreement will not be eliminated. Even if disagreement and faction are eliminated, there is no guarantee that the majority decision does express the general will; it may express the will of the dominant cultural group to abuse the dissenting minority. The ever-possible divergence between the infallible sovereign and its empirical embodiment in the fallible majority prompts the need for special protection, external to the democratic decision-making process, of individual rights and interests. Such protection is absent from Rousseau's mature state and this is a serious drawback of his constitutional theory.

In this part of the text I have considered the constitutional safeguards of Rousseau's association of the general will, the aim of which is to stop it degenerating into a mere aggregate of self-interested wills. Participatory democracy at the level of legislation, strict separation between the sovereign and its executive, and constant monitoring of the latter by the former, as well as rule of law requirements both for the legislature and the government, were identified as safeguards. However, since

Rousseau has assumed too readily that these safeguards are sufficient to protect individual rights and interests against majority abuse, he has found no need for their protection through devices external to the democratic process. But because majority abuse is not altogether ruled out, the lack of protection of individual interests is a serious defect of Rousseau's theory.

V. Conclusion

Rousseau's association of the general will held out the promise of a freedom-preserving political authority. It inspired the founding fathers of modern constitutions to place the principle of popular sovereignty at their centre. Further safeguards of individual freedom against the abuse of absolute government were added to limit popular sovereignty and what it may do to its members. In considering the constitutional implications of Rousseau's approach, I have found the main problems to be whether the promise of a freedom-preserving community is kept and the role of constitutional elements within it.

There are serious problems with the first step in solving what I term the 'constitutional beginning' problem. This asks how to build a freedom-preserving association of the general will out of a group of self-interested persons. The central role of the god-like Legislator in constituting the sovereign and its general will compromises the sovereign's freedom and independence, thus threatening Rousseau's project. Despite this original sin, the project would still be redeemed, I have argued, if Rousseau had equipped his association of the general will with sufficient constitutional safeguards to stop it from degenerating into a mere aggregate of self-interested individuals. Participatory democracy at the level of legislation, strict separation between the sovereign and its executive, and constant monitoring of the latter by the former, as well as rule of law requirements both for the legislature and the government, were identified as safeguards. Rousseau has denied individual rights and interests special protection against majority abuse through devices external to the general will, too readily assuming that the other constitutional safeguards discussed above have already made irreversible the transformation of human nature, and that the association of the general will is stable and self-sustaining. Because of his narrow and idiosyncratic understanding of limited government and separation of powers, the ambiguous scope of the rule of law doctrine, and the unclear interpretation of direct democracy at the legislative level, Rousseau has failed in my opinion to convince us that majority abuse is ruled out in his mature state. If such abuse is possible, the lack of special protection to individual rights and interests is a serious shortcoming of Rousseau's project, spelling out the clear limits to his freedom-preserving political association of the general will.

13

L'Abbé de Sieyès

Champion of National Representation, Father of Constitutions

Raymond Kubben

I. Introduction

Few *Ancien Régime* intellectuals ever had the chance to see their views on their polity's best constitution materialize through active involvement in politics at a time fit for radical change. Among the few is the French clergyman Emmanuel Joseph Sieyès (1748–1836). He might not have been among the most important philosophers to whom the eighteenth century gave birth, but he rose to the occasion as political events provided an opportunity for reform. He might have been thinking of his own career when he wrote in 1788: '*On lui a dit: "Quels que soient tes services, quels que soient tes talens, tu iras jusque-là; tu ne passeras pas outre."*'[1]

With his career in the church halted by the glass ceiling that closed out those of non-noble birth, Sieyès belonged to the group of well-educated, fairly wealthy middle-class men who combined the grievances of hampered ambitions with the ideological, rational convictions of the new age: exactly the kind of men who, together with some liberal nobles, stepped forward when a severe financial and political crisis forced the royal government to yield to decades-long pleas for the convocation of the Estates General.[2] In the turbulent period of the elections, Sieyès,

[1] E. Sieyès, *Qu'est-ce que le tiers état?* (Paris orig. 1789), 61. For this chapter, use was made of the 1822 edition: E. J. Sieyès, *Qu'est-ce que le tiers état? Précédé de l'essai sur les privilèges*, ed. Abbé Morellet (Paris, 1822, hereafter *QTE*. Part of the text can be found in J. Godechot, *La pensée révolutionnaire en France et en Europe, 1780–1799* (Paris, 1964), 74–89. For a translation in English, see Sieyès, *What is the Third Estate?*, ed. S. Finer (London, 1963), or *Sieyès: Political Writings*, ed. M. Sonenscher (Indianapolis, 2003).

[2] On the political history of the French Revolution in general, see G. Lefebvre, *La Révolution française* (Paris, 1930); R. Palmer, *The Age of the Democratic Revolution: A Political History of Europe and America 1769–1800*, 2 vols (Princeton, 1959–64); S. Schama, *Citizens: A Chronicle of the French Revolution* (New York, 1989); F. Furet and M. Ozouf (eds), *The French Revolution and the Creation of Modern Political Culture*, 3 vols (Oxford, 1989–94); W. Doyle, *The Oxford History of the French Revolution* (Oxford, 1990); P. Dwyer and P. McPhee (eds), *The French Revolution and Napoleon: A Sourcebook* (London–New York, 2002); D. Sutherland, *The French Revolution and Empire: The Quest for a Civic Order* (Oxford, 2003).

at the time vicar-general of the bishopric of Chartres and representative of the clergy in the Estates of the Orléanais, came to the fore as one of the leading pamphleteers and politicians of the day. In the years before the revolution, Sieyès had been a fervent student of political economy in his spare time, writing down, but never publishing, his thoughts. In his revolutionary pamphlets and speeches, he built on the insights gained from these studies. He also adapted his views to the political reality of the struggle for the control of the Estates General, the subsequent constitution-making process, and the atrocities and instability of the Terror and *Directoire*. Sieyès made the revolution as much as the revolution made him.

Sieyès's pamphlet *Qu'est-ce que le tiers état?* belongs to the classics of the French Revolution. Together with his *Essai sur les privilèges* and his *Vues sur les moyens d'exécution dont les représentants de la France pourront disposer en 1789*, it is part of a series of pamphlets published by Sieyès in the winter of 1788–9. The pamphlets were issued as part of a debate on the composition and *modus operandi* of the Estates General, and responded to claims about traditional procedures that would have placed the high nobility in control of the assembly, as well as producing a debate on France's constitutional future. He dealt with arguments and views that were issued by others, discussed and assessed the demands and offers made, and, finally, stated the principles on which the political order should be based.

Sieyès posited himself as champion of the liberal Patriots advocating the kind of political and social reform neither the king nor the better part of the nobility were likely to endorse.[3] He warned that the majority's demands of doubling the number of members of the Third Estate and voting *per capita* in lieu of by order in the Estates General would be insufficient to make the necessary reforms attainable, as were the concessions the nobility was willing to make.[4] Although still quite radical at the time of publication, the pamphlet did foreshadow the creation of the National (Constituent) Assembly (17 June 1789), which Sieyès advocated in *Qu'est-ce que le tiers état?*,[5] and the Tennis Court Oath (20 June 1789) by which that assembly swore to establish a constitution for the kingdom.[6] On both occasions, Sieyès was among the members of the Estates General who took the initiative. In the months to come, being on the assembly's constitutional committee, he was closely involved in the process of drawing up the constitution that was proclaimed in the summer of 1791 and that established a constitutional monarchy.[7]

[3] M. Forsyth, *Reason and Revolution: The Political Thought of the Abbé Sieyès* (New York, 1987), 16–20.

[4] Sieyès, *QTE*, 83, 99, 125–6, and 136–7.

[5] Sieyès, *QTE*, 190 and 195.

[6] See <http://www.historyguide.org/intellect/tennis_oath.html>; consulted on 27 August 2013.

[7] On French constitutional history of the revolutionary period, see e.g. M. Deslandres, *Histoire constitutionnelle de la France de 1789 à 1870. Tome premier: de la fin de l'Ancien Régime à la chute de l'Empire* (Paris, 1932); J. Godechot, *Les Institutions de la France sous la Révolution et l'Empire* (Paris, 1968); J. Godechot, *Les Constitutions de la France Depuis 1789* (Paris, 1970); P. Hartmann, *Französische Verfassungsgeschichte der Neuzeit (1450–1980)* (Darmstadt, 1985). For the texts of the period's constitutions see <http://www.conseil-constitutionnel.fr>.

Having kept aloof from politics during the Terror, Sieyès returned to active life after the *Thermidor* coup (27–8 July 1794) that brought Robespierre (1758–94) down. For some months, he served as a member of the Committee of Public Safety, mainly being involved in diplomatic affairs. For instance, he negotiated a treaty of peace and alliance with the newly founded Batavian Republic.[8] As a member of the Committee of Public Safety, he could not serve on the new constitutional committee. His 1795 *Thermidor* speeches in the National Convention, in which he expounded his views on the new constitution, are his main contributions to the drafting process. He refused a seat in the French government (*Directoire*) once the new constitution had entered into force in October 1795. After a stay abroad as envoy to the King of Prussia, Sieyès returned to a France rife with factionalism. With annual elections and no constitutional arrangements to solve conflicts between the government and the legislative councils, combined with a prolonged crisis of state finances, severe opposition from the radical left and the royalist right, and military misfortunes, the *Directoire* had only just managed to survive through a series of coups. It was yet another coup that made Sieyès a director in the summer of 1799. Making use of that position, Sieyès, the leading Patriot of 1789, who had become shrewd through the imbroglio of ten years of revolutionary politics, staged a final coup, the *Brumaire* coup of 9–10 November 1799 that resulted in the *Consulat* and brought Napoleon Bonaparte (1769–1821) to power. Together with the general and some other accomplices, provisional Consul Sieyès drew up the 1799 Constitution.

Until Napoleon's fall, Sieyès was a member of the *Sénat*, a position that prohibited him from holding any other public office. He backed the *Sénat*'s call for the emperor to abdicate in 1814, but supported him again after his return from Elba. He ended his political career a hereditary member of the Chamber of Peers, but he had no influence on the 1814 Constitutional Charter or on the 1815 Additional Act.[9] In the wake of the Battle of Waterloo (18 June 1815), Sieyès was exiled and deprived of all his titles and offices. He had spent fourteen years in Brussels when the 1830 July Revolution enabled him to return to France. Until his death six years later, he was no longer actively involved in politics.

This essay will focus on Sieyès's constitutional views as they developed throughout his active involvement in revolutionary politics. The character of the constitution, and the role of the constitution within the operation of the state, as well as its place within the legal hierarchy, are at the core of contemporary debates and of Sieyès's arguments. Attention will be paid first to his views on the nature of the constitution and the relation of the constitution vis-à-vis the nation, the legislature, and the government, as well as the formation and revision of the constitution. What is a constitution? In what sense does the constitution constitute fundamental law and to whom? Can the constitution be altered and, if so, by whom? The 1789

[8] Treaty of The Hague (16 May 1795); C. Parry (ed.), *The Consolidated Treaty Series*, vol. 52 (Dobbs Ferry, 1961–86), 383–91. See R. Kubben, *Regeneration and Hegemony: Franco–Batavian Relations in the Revolutionary Era 1795–1803* (Leiden: Brill Publishers, 2011).

[9] See e.g. P. Pilbeam, *The Constitutional Monarchy in France 1814–48* (Harlow, 2000).

pamphlets are the most coherent discussion of the nature and function of the constitution. A full discussion of how Sieyès's constitutional views evolved throughout the following decade, of the intellectual roots of these views, or of his more detailed views on government, would take more than the pages allowed here, and the interested reader is referred to numerous works on Sieyès's thought.[10] Three notions do merit further and separate elaboration, because they are paramount to Sieyès's political thought and were at the core of revolutionary discourse: the nation, citizenship, and representative government. Sieyès's understanding of the nation will be discussed and contextualized in the second section below, which will consider how he conceived of the nation and how his definitions of the nation relate to political debates at the time. The third section will delve into Sieyès's views on citizenship and representative government, including the role of the people in politics, and his view of representation. This section will include some observations on his views on the electoral system and the separation of powers.

II. The Constitution: Fundamental to Whom?

The constitution was of paramount significance to Sieyès. Its character and substance, as well as where the authority to make and revise it rests, were at stake at the time he published his three pamphlets. It is an essential concept in his thought to which all other aspects and ideas relate. Therefore, this section will focus on the ways he defined the constitution; his views on the character of the constitution; the role of the constitution within the operation of the state; and the place of the constitution within the legal hierarchy.

Sieyès adhered to a substantive definition of the constitution as the means by which a nation gives the body politic '*une organisation, des formes et des lois propres à lui faire remplir les fonctions auxquelles on a voulu le destiner*'.[11] Somewhat later, he defined constitutional laws as those laws that '*règlent l'organisation et les fonctions du corps législatif... déterminent l'organisation et les fonctions des différent corps actifs*'.[12] Designing the constitution means defining the institutions through which the common will can express itself and public functions can be performed.[13] The way in which the state is organized must serve liberty and guarantee that the government does not violate the rights it is obliged to protect. The constitution thus has a double function of both organizing the state and being a safeguard to ensure that government institutions act in conformity with their purposes. To keep the government purpose-bound, subjecting it to '*des formes certaines*' is necessary.

[10] J. Thompson, *Leaders of the French Revolution* (Oxford, 1929); G. van Deusen, *Sieyès: His Life and His Nationalism* (New York, 1932); Y. Koung, *Théorie Constitutionnelle de Siéyès* (Paris, 1934); P. Bastid, *Sieyès et sa Pensée* (Paris, 1970); Forsyth, *Reason and Revolution*; T. Hafen, *Staat, Gesellschaft und Bürger im Denken von Emmanuel Joseph Sieyès* (Stuttgart–Vienna, 1994); W. Sewell, *A Rhetoric of Bourgeois Revolution: The Abbé Sieyès and* What is the Third Estate? (Durham–London, 1994); A. Riklin, *Emmanuel Joseph Sieyès und die Französische Revolution* (Bern–Vienna, 2001); J. Guilhaumou, *Sieyès et l'Ordre de la Langue* (Paris, 2002).

[11] Sieyès, *QTE*, 158. [12] Sieyès, *QTE*, 160. [13] Sieyès, *QTE*, 158.

The government is to act pursuant to the constitution ('*formes constitutives*') for its actions to be legal.[14] This definition of the constitution is phrased almost *en passant* in *Qu'est-ce que le tiers état?* Sieyès then focused on the issue of who is entitled to alter the constitution and how the constitution relates to the nation and public institutions.

In dealing with these issues, Sieyès could, to a large extent, adopt pre-Revolutionary French constitutionalism. Decades before the outbreak of the French Revolution, conflict between the government and the supreme courts or *parlements* escalated, as the government sought to prolong wartime tax measures in the wake of the Seven Years' War (1756–63).[15] The judges took the lead in contesting the allegedly arbitrary use of royal power by insisting on due procedures and by exploiting their right to register royal legislation and to petition the king if they found objections to a decree offered for registration, the so-called '*remonstrances*.'[16] By making use of this instrument, the *parlements* had assumed the competence of judicial review, so to speak, based on the medieval notion of fundamental laws.[17] In reviving the notion of fundamental laws, they portrayed themselves as the guardians of the ancient constitution,[18] and introduced what Keith Baker calls a 'discourse of justice', posing lawful government against arbitrariness of the royal will.[19] In a 1763 remonstrance against tax measures, the *parlement* of Paris distinguished between '*ordonnances des rois*' and '*ordonnances du Royaume*', subsequently claiming the authority to assess whether the former complied with the latter.[20] The '*ordonnances du Royaume*' were said to be inviolable in the sense that the royal government was bound by them because the king's authority was based on those fundamental laws. As Alain Wijffels has already demonstrated, this distinction created room for an independent role of the *parlements* to review royal legislation in the light of the fundamental order of state and society.[21] Fundamental laws were invoked once more in 1788 to block government reform schemes, pushing the government to yield to calls for the Estates General.[22] Hence, the basic notion of constitutionalism, in the

[14] Sieyès, *QTE*, 158–9.

[15] J. Swann, *Politics and the Parlement of Paris Under Louis XV, 1754–1774* (Cambridge, 1995) 27–8, 122, 130–1, 157, 191, and 218–49; J. Shennan, *The Parlement of Paris* (Gloucestershire, 1998) 309–14; and D. Hudson, 'The Parlementary Crisis of 1763 in France and its Consequences', *Canadian Journal of History*, 7 (1972), 97–117.

[16] Hartmann, *Französische Verfassungsgeschichte*, 24; Swann, *Politics and the Parlement of Paris*, 2–3, 34–5, 56–8, 284, and 312; Shennan, *The Parlement of Paris*, 285–6, 289–90, 296–7, 307–9, and 313.

[17] E.g. Godechot, *Les Constitutions*, 25; J. Bredin, *Sieyès: La clé de la Révolution française* (Paris, 1988) 72–3; Swann, *Politics and the Parlement of Paris*, 34–5 and 290–1.

[18] A. Wijffels, 'De retoriek van het algemeen belang en van de rechtsstaat in absolutistisch Frankrijk. Achttiende-eeuwse remonstrantiebrieven van het Parlement van Parijs', in E. Broers and B. Jacobs (eds), *Interactie tussen wetgever en rechter vóór de Trias Politica* (The Hague, 2003) 85–107, at 89.

[19] K. Baker, 'Political languages of the French Revolution', in M. Goldie and R. Wokler (eds), *The Cambridge History of Eighteenth-Century Political Thought* (Cambridge: Cambridge University Press, 2006) 626–59, at 627.

[20] Reiterated in Wijffels, 'De retoriek van het algemeen belang', 102.

[21] Wijffels, 'De retoriek van het algemeen belang', 103.

[22] Bredin, *La clé de la Révolution*, 72–3.

sense of a government bound by fundamental law that the government cannot alter, was well known in France before the outbreak of the revolution.

In anticipation of the first meeting of the Estates General, the call for a written constitution after the American example became dominant in French public opinion.[23] To more conservative elements, the purpose of the constitution was to codify existing institutions, rights, and privileges.[24] The aristocracy, which had opposed government reform plans in the past and which was now convinced, considering the extreme financial and political crisis, that it had the government on its knees, saw that the time had come to consolidate its position. Patriots advocated a radical reform programme that was to be brought about by means of a written constitution.[25] It was essential for an unhindered implementation of this reform programme that conservative forces would be denied a position from which they would be able to block changes. Sieyès was adamant about preventing them from dominating the Estates General. Precisely this issue of who was entitled to alter the constitution was at stake in the clashing claims to national representation.

Political debate centred on how the Estates General were to vote. Traditionally, every Estate had one vote. Most Patriots demanded a doubling of the number of delegates from the Third Estate in combination with a *per capita* vote instead of voting by order.[26] The members of the Third Estate would equal those of the First and the Second combined and be able to secure a majority with the support of some liberal nobles and clergymen. Sieyès had set his mind on denying the First and Second Estates a separate voice altogether. In his view, the Third Estate either had to claim to be the sole representative of the entire nation or had to confine itself to demanding the election of a constituent assembly.[27] In response to the argument that the demands of doubling the Third Estate and voting *per capita* were unconstitutional as they infringed upon 'ancient forms' ('*anciennes formes*'), he asserted that the constitution should be based on 'true principles' ('*les vrais principes*').[28]

In *Qu'est-ce que le tiers état?*, Sieyès put aside the nobility as a faction that had alienated itself from the nation and was advocating party interests.[29] In this sense, *Qu'est-ce que le tiers état?* is said to be directed against the nobility in secondary literature,[30] but the political context provided Sieyès with a wider aim. The pamphlet was also to reject claims by the royal government to involvement in the process of constitution-making. Sieyès responded to those who asserted that the constitution

[23] Van Deusen, *Sieyès*, 31; Bastid, *Sieyès et sa Pensée*, 356; Godechot, *Les Constitutions*, 6; Forsyth, *Reason and Revolution*, 78; Hafen, *Staat, Gesellschaft und Bürger*, 169.

[24] D. Collofong, *Elemente einer Verfassungsgerichtsbarkeit in Frankreich von Sieyès zum Verfassungsrat der V. Republik* (Mainz, 1964) 22; Godechot, *Les Constitutions*, 6; Forsyth, *Reason and Revolution*, 18.

[25] Bastid, *Sieyès et sa Pensée*, 54–5, 157, and 356; Forsyth, *Reason and Revolution*, 18, and 98–9; Sewell, *A Rhetoric*, 4.

[26] Lefebvre, *La Révolution française*, 99–107; Bredin, *La clé de la Révolution*, 86.

[27] Sieyès, *QTE*, 189–202.

[28] Sieyès, *QTE*, 109–11 and 154.

[29] E.g. Sieyès, *QTE*, 64–5.

[30] Van Deusen, *Sieyès*, and 84–5; Koung, *Théorie Constitutionnelle*, 36–8; Forsyth, *Reason and Revolution*, 88–97; Bredin, *La clé de la Révolution*, 80 and 89–91; Sewell, *A Rhetoric*, 1, 5, and 54–5.

was to be a contract between king and people. The social contract, which features only marginally in Sieyès's thought and is in conflict with parts of it, is a contract that binds citizens in relation to each other, and is certainly not one between the people and the government. In Sieyès's theory, there is talk of a contract only in the sense of an agreement to form a nation between the associates, while the relation between the people and the government is not contractual.[31]

This aspect was not just a side-effect of the attack on the privileged orders, as Chimène Keitner presents it.[32] Repudiating the idea that the king had to consent to the new constitution was as essential as safeguarding a majority in the Estates General in favour of implementing the Patriots' radical reform programme.[33] Next to eliminating conservative forces within the Estates General by excluding the better part of the nobility and the clergy, Sieyès had to refute the assertion that the constitution is a contract between the people and the monarch.

To sustain his position that the reformed Estates General, or the constituent assembly convened in its wake, should design a constitution without involvement of the government, Sieyès set out to demonstrate four points: (i) the government is bound by the constitution; (ii) the constitution can be made and changed by man; (iii) the constituent power accrues to the nation exclusively; and (iv) the nation's constituent power can be represented. To prove the validity of these four propositions, Sieyès sketched a theory of state-formation in three stages.[34]

The first phase sees the genesis of the nation as a result of the joint expression of the will of a number of hitherto isolated individuals to form a political community. The nation as political community results from this act of association by which individuals ('*un nombre plus ou moins considérable d'individus isolés*') associate ('*se réunir*').[35] Although the association might result from a long-drawn-out process, Sieyès takes the voluntarist step by which the state of nature is left in favour of civil society. Sieyès is not a straightforward social contract theorist, but he does adhere to the idea of a pre-state situation that individuals choose to leave in order to form a state. The expression of this joint desire suffices to form the political body of the nation. According to Sieyès, the aim of entering into society is the protection of individual liberty understood as the equal enjoyment of civil rights, instead of the protection of particular privileges.[36] The individual does not entirely submit to the political community, nor does he lose his natural rights.[37] On the contrary, protecting and enhancing natural rights is the state's main aim and task.[38]

31 Sieyès, *QTE*, 121: '*Plus tôt ou plus tard, il faudra que toutes les classes se renferment dans les bornes du contrat social, contrat qui regarde et oblige tous les associés les uns envers les autres . . . On ne peut pas entendre autrement le contrat social: il lie les associés entre eux. C'est une idée fausse et dangereuse, que de supposer un contrat entre un peuple et son gouvernement. La nation ne contracte point avec ses mandataires, elle commet à l'exercice de ses pouvoirs.*' See also Godechot, *Les Constitutions*, 28; Bredin, *La clé de la Révolution*, 110; Hafen, *Staat, Gesellschaft und Bürger*, 52; Sewell, *A Rhetoric*, 55; Riklin, *Sieyès und die Französische Revolution*, 26; C. Keitner, *The Paradoxes of Nationalism: The French Revolution and Its Meaning for Contemporary Nation-Building* (Albany, 2007) 64.

32 Keitner, *Paradoxes of Nationalism*, 66.

33 Riklin, *Sieyès und die Französische Revolution*, 47.

34 Sieyès, *QTE*, 155–7.

35 Sieyès, *QTE*, 155.

36 Sieyès, *Essai*, 4 and 6, and *QTE*, 70.

37 Forsyth, *Reason and Revolution*, 125; Hafen, *Staat, Gesellschaft und Bürger*, 52.

38 Sieyès, *Essai*, 4 and 6.

In the second phase, it is the united will of the associates that defines public needs ('*besoins publics*') and introduces the instruments to meet those needs ('*des moyens d'y pouvoir*').[39] All members of the political body assemble and deliberate directly to form a common will.

Once this is no longer feasible, the step towards the third phase is taken. As the number of associates has become too large to define the common will directly, a representative government or government by proxy is established ('*un gouvernement exercé par procuration*').[40] At that instance, the nation, or the common will of the associates ('*la volonté commune*'), lays down a constitution to institutionalize the political community, that is to say, to establish and organize representative institutions and to invest them with powers. The creation of specialized institutions of government coincides with the transition to a third stage, since it is no longer a real common will that acts, but a represented one ('*une volonté commune représentative*'). However, the nation can preserve part of its powers and does not alienate its right to form a common will itself.[41] The representatives act on behalf of the nation, their powers have been granted by the nation, and they have no original powers of their own.[42] In the third phase, a representative government rules under the constitution to further the general interest.

1. The government is bound by the constitution

The first proposition was the least radical one. Here, Sieyès could simply follow in the footsteps of the *parlements* and France's anti-absolutist constitutional tradition. The position was a double-edged sword. Stating that the constitution is fundamental to the government upholds the view that there are legal limits to what the government is entitled to do, and excludes the government from the process of constitution-making. For in Sieyès's scheme of state-formation, the constitution precedes the government, or, in his words, 'constituted power' ('*pouvoir constitué*').[43] The constituted powers are established by the constitution. They derive their authority from the constitution. They do not exist but by the constitution. Their actions are legal only if within their constitutional powers. It would be contradictory to allow them a say in making or revising the constitution because the constitution itself is the basis of their existence and the source of their powers.[44] At this juncture, Sieyès adopted the distinction made by the *parlements* between '*ordonnances des roi*' and '*ordonnances du Royaume*', the latter being antecedent to the institutions established by them. Sieyès just called them '*lois positives*' and '*lois constitutionnelles*'.[45] The '*lois constitutionnelles*' are made in the second stage of state-formation, while in the third stage, where the constituted powers exist and function, they are inviolable. Here the constituted powers can make and alter only positive laws. The constituted powers, including the legislature, cannot change

[39] Sieyès, *QTE*, 155–6.
[40] Sieyès, *QTE*, 156.
[41] Sieyès, *QTE*, 157.
[42] Sieyès, *QTE*, 157–8.
[43] Sieyès, *QTE*, 160.
[44] Sieyès, *QTE*, 160.
[45] Sieyès, *QTE*, 159–60.

the constitution. In that sense, the constitution is fundamental.[46] To the constituted powers, the constitution is an inviolable fundamental law ('*Ces lois sont dites fondamentales*').[47]

2. and 3. The constitution is positive law, and the constituent power accrues to the nation

So, to the government, the constitution is an inviolable fundamental law, as the *parlements* had previously asserted. But Sieyès wanted to change the constitution, and to do so he had to demonstrate that the constitution, while fundamental to the government, can be altered. This meant having a power superior to the constitution and not bound by it, while excluding the ordinary institutions of government, including the legislature, from taking part.[48] These institutions cannot themselves change the basis of their authority, for otherwise Sieyès's argument of all representative institutions being bound by the constitution would be incoherent, and would fail to deliver. In other words, Sieyès had to reconcile the changeability of constitutional law and the binding force of that law vis-à-vis the government. And here the nation comes in. He introduced the distinction between the constituent power and the constituted powers as the first step in the separation of powers,[49] and thus included an understanding of the constitution as positive law into the *parlements*' constitutionalism.

Keith Baker states that Sieyès 'gave Revolutionary discourse its earliest form by dissolving claims for privilege and *parlementaire* constitutionalism in a rhetorical blending of a discourse of reason and a discourse of political will'.[50] This meant putting aside the *parlements*' so-called 'discourse of justice',[51] that is, a discourse that emphasizes government acting with respect for and according to traditional rights and due procedures, in favour of a 'discourse of will', in the sense that the constitution entirely depends on the will of the nation, which consequently has the right to change it, and a 'discourse of reason', in the sense that the national will is directed at a rational order consonant with natural law.[52] Sieyès did intend to say exactly this, but his argument did not stop there. It went on to state that the 'discourse of justice' is not absent. The discourses merely play at different levels of Sieyès's political theory. The order of state-formation implied that the government was bound by the constitution. The third stage in the process of state-formation is the realm of the *parlements*' 'discourse of justice', for in that stage a representative government exercises its powers in conformity with the constitution. Sieyès did not deal with that, but the other two discourses relate to the previous stages.

[46] Sieyès, *QTE*, 160: '*Aucune sorte de pouvoir délégué ne peut rien changer aux conditions de sa délégation.*'

[47] Sieyès, *QTE*, 159–60 and 162.

[48] Koung, *Théorie Constitutionnelle*, 84.

[49] Sieyès, *QTE*, 160: '*la constitution n'est pas l'ouvrage du pouvoir constitué, mais du pouvoir constituant.*'

[50] Baker, 'Political languages', 630.

[51] Baker, 'Political languages', 629–30.

[52] Baker, 'Political languages', 628, and 630.

The three stages in the formation of the state correspond to a triple sequence of law: natural right, constitutional law(s), and positive law(s).[53] The last are the ones made by established legislators to protect citizens and to further common interests.[54] Constitutional laws are made to settle the organization and functions of the legislative body and of the active parts of government. These laws are made by the nation or by special representatives.[55]

Finally, the origin of the nation is a fully political moment within the framework set by natural right. The nation, and hence the constituent power, is only preceded by and subordinated to natural right: '*La nation existe avant tout, elle est l'origine de tout.*' Consequently, '*sa volonté est toujours légale, elle est la loi elle-même. Avant elle et au-dessus d'elle il n'y a que le droit naturel.*'[56] This refers to the natural rights of man, which any political association serves to protect,[57] but also to some basic principles that are to be elaborated for particular societies.[58]

Natural right precedes the first step of state-formation and hence the nation, but the nation stands above any constitutional and positive law. The nation is thus not bound by or dependent on any positive law, constitutional laws included: '*La nation se forme par le seul droit naturel. Le gouvernement, au contraire, ne peut appartenir qu'au droit positif.*'[59] In the second stage of state-formation, the constitution can be changed and there the constituent power accrues to the nation. Since the nation is created in the first phase, it precedes the constitution and is thus '*indépendante de toutes formes civiles*'.[60] It would be ridiculous, in Sieyès's words, to assume that the nation itself would be bound by the constitution it makes to organize and limit government.[61] If the nation were bound by the constitution, there would be no power to settle constitutional disputes.[62] And last but not least, it is a matter of principle. The national will is free and independent, and the nation cannot and should not surrender or alienate its right to form its will freely. To do so would be to lose its liberty.[63]

Since constitutional laws, like ordinary positive ones, are only made within civil society, stages (ii) and (iii) are the process of state-formation: (i) the nation exists before constitutional laws; (ii) the nation makes constitutional laws and hence has the power to change them at will; and (iii) the government is established by the constitutional laws and hence is bound by them. Therefore, the fundamental nature of constitutional law does not mean that it cannot be changed, only that the ordinary government institutions cannot alter them.[64] The nation may change the constitution freely. The second stage is that of the 'discourse of will', and

[53] Sieyès, *QTE*, 159–60. [54] Sieyès, *QTE*, 161.
[55] Sieyès, *QTE*, 159–60. [56] Sieyès, *QTE*, 159.
[57] See Koung, *Théorie Constitutionnelle*, 64; Bastid, *Sieyès et sa Pensée*, 390; Forsyth, *Reason and Revolution*, 106; Hafen, *Staat, Gesellschaft und Bürger*, 97, 101, and 109–10; Riklin, *Sieyès und die Französische Revolution*, 40–1 and 209.
[58] Sieyès, *Essai*, 5. [59] Sieyès, *QTE*, 161–2. [60] Sieyès, *QTE*, 164–5.
[61] Sieyès, *QTE*, 161. [62] Sieyès, *QTE*, 165. [63] Sieyès, *QTE*, 162–4.
[64] Sieyès, *QTE*, 160: '*fondamentales, non pas en ce sens, qu'elles puissent devenir indépendantes de la volonté nationale, mais parce que les corps qui existent et agissent par elles, ne peuvent point y toucher.*'

Sieyès thus turned the constitution into man-made positive law as an intermediate step between natural right and the association of free individuals on one hand and government and positive law on the other. This law can be made and altered in a single instance on the basis of rational and abstract ('true') principles instead of evolving gradually through time. Edmund Burke reproached him for this in his *Reflections on the Revolution in France*,[65] while Thomas Paine defended Sieyès against Burke and in support of the nation's authority to alter the constitution at will.[66]

The nation's right to change the constitution was not entirely new. It was already part of the *parlements*' rhetoric. The changeability of the constitution had arisen within the framework of social contract theory, in which the constitution is deliberately made by the people but is also identified with the social contract, assuming that the genesis of the nation and the institution of government coincide in time. For someone wishing to establish or to alter the constitution of a centuries-old kingdom, this was not a welcome message. Sieyès had to emphasise the freedom of the nation in constitutional matters in order to counter the above-mentioned claim that France already had a constitution, albeit one based on a separation of society into orders, each with an equal say in determining the national will, and by which the nation would be bound to the ancient forms, according to which the Estates General was to be organized and to operate.[67] Sieyès's major innovation was to part company with this eighteenth-century mainstream thought by adding a second stage of state-formation that allowed him to distinguish the constitution from the moment of the formation of the political community itself.[68] The constitution is made by the nation when the nation as a political association already exists. This allowed him to claim that '*la nation est toujours maîtresse de réformer sa constitution*'.[69]

4. The nation's constituent power can be represented

Sieyès argued that the government is bound by the constitution, while the nation has the right to change it. But he went further yet. Unlike Rousseau, Sieyès was a man with the practical aim of sustaining the claim that the Third Estate and, later, the National Assembly would act on behalf of the nation in giving France a constitution. He had set out to present the reform party as the true representative of this nation, which later would exercise the constituent power on its behalf. So the next step was to assert that the constituent power could be represented too.[70] This was the claim Sieyès would make with the motion he introduced on 15 June 1789, arguing that the Third Estate represented the entire nation and was entitled to

65 E. Burke, *Reflections on the Revolution in France* (orig. 1790; Oxford, 1993), 32 and 60–1.

66 T. Paine, *Rights of Man*, in T. Paine, *Rights of Man, Common Sense, and Other Political Writings* (orig. 1791–2; Oxford, 1995), 99.

67 Sieyès, *QTE*, 174.

68 See Koung, *Théorie Constitutionnelle*, 69; Bastid, *Sieyès et sa Pensée*, 378 and 394.

69 Sieyès, *QTE*, 172–3.

70 Bredin, *La clé de la Révolution*, 88–9.

'interpret' the nation's will.[71] But Sieyès's theoretical claims in *Qu'est-ce que le tiers état?* already included the idea of a special constituent assembly representing the nation's constituent power.[72] The nation's constituent power could not be represented by the government or the legislative assembly since that would again blur the distinction between the constituent and constituted powers. To cope with the problem, he introduced the distinction between ordinary and extraordinary representatives ('*représentants ordinaires*' and '*représentants extraordinaires*').[73] The ordinary representatives are charged with the daily business of executing the common will within the limits of the constitution, whereas the extraordinary representatives meet in exceptional circumstances calling for constitutional change.[74] Sieyès asserted that extraordinary representatives replace the nation in its independence of the constitution ('*il remplace la nation dans son* indépendance *de toutes formes constitutionnelles*') and exercise the constituent power on its behalf.[75] Unlike the legislative assembly, this constituent assembly has to be convened on an ad hoc basis and be in session only temporarily.[76] The Constitutions of 1791, 1793, and 1795 all provided for distinct assemblies of revision convened on the initiative of the legislative body. However, the introduction of new constitutions often took place in an extraconstitutional way. The 1799 Constitution, drafted after the *Brumaire* coup, no longer contained any provisions on constitutional revision.

By 1795, Sieyès was advocating a new kind of institution in a speech in the National Convention entitled *Opinion sur les attributions et l'organisation du jury constitutionnaire.*[77] After a long period of revolutionary agitation, and having witnessed work on a new constitution three times in six years, Sieyès concluded that a constitution had to contain the means of its own completion and modification. A constitution had to be a living institution capable of adjusting to changed circumstances in a constitutional way, and to allow for partial revisions.[78] The constitution had to be dynamic in the sense that it had to be able to adjust to changed political circumstances. This dynamic quality, however, is essentially conservative because the increased changeability or reduced rigidity is intended to prevent the kind of full revision that had been initiated in France in 1793 and 1795. Sieyès was looking for a *via media* between a rigid constitution and permanent possibility of revision. He clung to the notion of an assembly of extraordinary

[71] Van Deusen, *Sieyès*, 37–8; Koung, *Théorie Constitutionnelle*, 12; Riklin, *Sieyès und die Französische Revolution*, 10–11; Forsyth, *Reason and Revolution*, 101; Sewell, *A Rhetoric*, 6 and 17.

[72] Sieyès, *QTE*, 179, 190, and 195.

[73] Sieyès, *QTE*, 167.

[74] Sieyès, *QTE*, 167.

[75] Sieyès, *QTE*, 168; Koung, *Théorie Constitutionnelle*, 55–6; Bastid, *Sieyès et sa Pensée*, 374 and 589; Sewell, *A Rhetoric*, 50–1.

[76] Sieyès, *QTE*, 168.

[77] Van Deusen, *Sieyès*, 61; Koung, *Théorie Constitutionnelle*, 22–3, 99, 102–3, 120, 140, and 144–50; Forsyth, *Reason and Revolution*, 187–94; Bredin, *La clé de la Révolution*, 366–67; Riklin, *Sieyès und die Französische Revolution*, 214–19. The full text of Sieyès's speech to the Convention can be found in P. Bastid, *Les discours de Sieyès dans les débats constitutionnels de l'an III (2 et 18 thermidor)* (Paris, 1939) 31–47.

[78] Riklin, *Sieyès und die Französische Revolution*, 217.

representatives. The jury would be a permanent representative assembly. The 108 jurors would initially be nominated by the National Convention, and one third of them would be renewed annually. The jury would nominate new members from the outgoing members of the legislature, rendering it a plainly political institution. Sieyès deemed judges unsuitable to serve on the jury since its work did not belong to the sphere of adjudication but to the exercise of the constituent power. The jury would have the power to review laws and acts of government and, if necessary, declare them void if deemed to violate the constitution. The power to initiate review lay with the legislative councils or the primary assemblies. The jury would also have the exclusive power to complete and modify the constitution, proposing revisions every ten years and thus excluding the need to rely on individual persons initiating revision.[79] In this way, the jury would both test the constitutionality of legislative and administrative acts and be in control of proposed revisions to be presented to the people in a referendum.[80] The constituent power and the supremacy of the constitution over the constituted powers would be institutionalized, and, as Paul Bastid put it, be 'disciplined'.[81]

Sieyès's proposal for a jury had been rejected in 1795, but was successful in 1799, when he was more in control as one of the instigators of the *Brumaire* coup.[82] By then he called the jury '*collège des conservateurs*' to be charged with maintaining the constitution and with its gradual improvement '*par les améliorations successives que les progrès des Lumières et les besoins de l'Etat pourraient solliciter*.'[83] The Council would have a hundred members appointed for life by way of co-optation,[84] and like the 1795 jury, it would have the authority to review legislative and administrative acts and the exclusive right to initiate constitutional reform, thus holding the key to the constituent power.[85] The institution Sieyès had envisaged was called the Conservative Senate, and Sieyès became its first president.

III. The Nation is Everything

The nation is one of the core concepts in Sieyès's thought and it was the catchword of the day in revolutionary France. This section examines how Sieyès defined 'the nation' and what he meant by it.

[79] Koung, *Théorie Constitutionnelle*, 144–50; Collofong, *Elemente einer Verfassungsgerichtsbarkeit*, 27–30; Bastid, *Sieyès et sa Pensée*, 170–1, 393, and 429–35; Forsyth, *Reason and Revolution*, 187–8; Bredin, *La clé de la Révolution*, 366; Hafen, *Staat, Gesellschaft und Bürger*, 200–5 and 216–19.

[80] Forsyth, *Reason and Revolution*, 187; Riklin, *Sieyès und die Französische Revolution*, 218.

[81] Collofong, *Elemente einer Verfassungsgerichtsbarkeit*, 28; Bastid, *Sieyès et sa Pensée*, 429–30; Hafen, *Staat, Gesellschaft und Bürger*, 88 and 98–9; Sewell, *A Rhetoric*, 19.

[82] Riklin, *Sieyès und die Französische Revolution*, 248–50.

[83] Riklin, *Sieyès und die Französische Revolution*, 250.

[84] Koung, *Théorie Constitutionnelle*, 129–30 and 149; Collofong, *Elemente einer Verfassungsgerichtsbarkeit*, 32–4; Forsyth, *Reason and Revolution*, 190–2; Bredin, *La clé de la Révolution*, 472; Hafen, *Staat, Gesellschaft und Bürger*, 240–2.

[85] Collofong, *Elemente einer Verfassungsgerichtsbarkeit*, 33.

The nation had already entered political discourse some decades before the revolution, as the *parlements*[86] had come to refer to the French nation in their opposition to royal absolutism, either to claim that changes in fundamental laws required the nation's consent or to present themselves as the nation's representatives.[87] The nation enabled the *parlement* to refer to an entity distinct from the person of the king and suitable for use as an abstract, primordial source of authority and legitimacy to counteract a more or less self-referential royal authority.[88] The concept of the nation was kept rather vague, paving the way for revolutionary discourse and providing Patriots like Sieyès with an empty box to be filled according to their needs. The nation served for Sieyès as the point of departure and the basis for his political theory. The vagueness with which the concept had been used to date allowed him to redefine the nation in a way that provided the best arguments to further his political aims. The definition of the nation in the political and social context in the months before the meeting of the Estates General is a significant merit of Sieyès's pamphlets.

Sieyès's view of political community, as discussed above, implies a political definition of the nation; indeed, the paramount definition in *Qu'est-ce que le tiers état?* is inherently political. The nation is defined by the political decision to associate and by the law and representative institutions that result from that association. It is the man-made political community of citizens, the '*universalité des citoyens*', '*l'ensemble des associés*', or '*la généralité des citoyens*'.[89] This association of citizens, as Sieyès understood the resulting community, lives on as '*un corps d'associés vivant sous une loi* commune, *et représentés par la même législature, etc*',[90] '*une loi commune et une représentation commune voilà ce qui fait une nation.*'[91] Equality before the law and representation as a whole is what defines the nation. The definition called for equality to replace differences based on privilege, for the nation is a single community of people living under the same law and represented by a single representative body. The implications of this definition are at least threefold. First, at the basis and origin of the nation as political community stands the self-determining individual.[92] Second, the nation represents political unity and equality before the law for all associates and thus serves as starting point for severe criticism of existing inequalities.[93] Legal equality is the quintessence of the nation, as the sphere within which equality before the law holds sway.[94] Third, through the act of association and the constitution, the nation becomes a single community that has one will, acts as one, and has the capacity to will and act through representation

[86] On the *parlements*, see e.g. J. Egret, *Louis XV et l'opposition parlementaire, 1715–1774* (Paris, 1970); J. Rogister, *Louis XV and the Parlement of Paris 1737–1755* (Cambridge, 1995); Swann, *Politics and the Parlement of Paris*; Shennan, *The Parlement of Paris*.

[87] For references to this notion by the *parlements*, see e.g. Bredin, *Sieyès*, 72; Hartmann, *Französische Verfassungsgeschichte*, 27; Keitner, *Paradoxes of Nationalism*, 17 and 53.

[88] Keitner, *Paradoxes of Nationalism*, 17, 23–4, and 36–7; Baker, 'Political languages', 627.

[89] E.g. Sieyès, *QTE*, 72 and 174, and *Essai*, 8–9.

[90] Sieyès, *QTE*, 67 (emphasis added).

[91] Sieyès, *QTE*, 72.

[92] Forsyth, *Reason and Revolution*, 72; Sewell, *A Rhetoric*, 146.

[93] Sieyès, *QTE*, 127–33.

[94] Sieyès, *Essai*, 4 and 7.

directed at common interests.[95] Privilege is eschewed because it enables particular interests to become paramount.[96]

Sieyès's conceptualization of the nation does not stop here; he defined the nation in at least three complementary ways. In the first place, the nation in a juridical sense is the bearer of supreme authority, the source of legitimacy, and the main power vis-à-vis public order.[97] It has the final say in constitutional disputes: '*seul juge compétent dans tous les différends qui touchent à la constitution*'.[98] This means that, according to Sieyès, supreme power is not located within the institutional framework of governance. At first, Sieyès attributed primacy to the legislature, but in the third stage all institutions of government are subordinated to the nation and all of them wield only derivative powers. The nation thus serves two essential functions:

> On the one hand, supreme authority is moved from the political system to a place outside of and transcending it, to a place that, due to the abstract character of the nation, is essentially empty. Supreme authority is not invested in the monarch or parliament, but in the community of citizens to which the monarch and the parliament must refer as source of their authority and the origin of all powers. On the other hand, the nation as a unified actor stands above the functionally-divided political system; it is the union that precedes the separation of power, thus keeping the entire system together.[99]

Sieyès also defined the nation in a socio-economic sense. Contrary to the *physiocrats*, Sieyès deemed labour and not land the main source of affluence.[100] The central tenet of the nation is the redefinition of society from being a hierarchical corporate entity to one encompassing a single system of production in which all functions necessary to sustain society are fulfilled.[101] Sieyès's account of man and inter-human relations begins, from an economic perspective, with human beings as creatures seeking the fulfilment of needs.[102] In the state of nature, the degree to which individuals succeed in this is limited, due to their restricted capacities. While the population increases, everyone's struggle for the fulfilment of needs causes tensions, insecurity, and enmity.[103] Individuals associate to counter increasing insecurity, but association allows a division of labour that enhances a society's affluence thus increasing the means to satisfy needs.[104] The act of association does not equal a radical break between the state of nature and civil society.[105] The selfish nature of man does not change upon entering into society and remains the basis of social interactions.[106]

95 Van Deusen, *Sieyès*, 77 and 80. 96 Sieyès, *QTE*, 68, and *Essai*, 18.

97 Van Deusen, *Sieyès*, 76; Hafen, *Staat, Gesellschaft und Bürger*, 74; Guilhaumou, *Ordre de la Langue*, 87; Keitner, *Paradoxes of Nationalism*, 46.

98 Sieyès, *QTE*, 153 and 199–200.

99 Bastid, *Sieyès et sa Pensée*, 398; Sewell, *A Rhetoric*, 46.

100 Forsyth, *Reason and Revolution*, 52; Sewell, *A Rhetoric*, 76 and 80–1.

101 Sieyès, *Essai*, 36, and *QTE*, 59–60.

102 Sieyès, *QTE*, 59. See also Bastid, *Sieyès et sa Pensée*, 378; Hafen, *Staat, Gesellschaft und Bürger*, 35.

103 Hafen, *Staat, Gesellschaft und Bürger*, 36.

104 Hafen, *Staat, Gesellschaft und Bürger*, 47–8.

105 Hafen, *Staat, Gesellschaft und Bürger*, 48.

106 Hafen, *Staat, Gesellschaft und Bürger*, 43–5.

Society achieves greater complexity by dynamic interaction of exchange and specialization.[107] The nation comes into being in a more gradual way than the instant creation of a single social contract, for society is shaped by a multiplicity of contracts, sustaining the process of specialization.[108] The nation amounts to a complete system of division of labour and consists of all who contribute to the joint affluence through labour.[109] In these studies Sieyès adopted an empirical, sociological approach. The account is descriptive of society and its evolution; it is then used for prescriptive purposes.

An alternative definition of the nation is paramount in Sieyès's 1788–9 pamphlets in which he compares the nation to the Third Estate.[110] As he had it, the Third Estate was '*tout*' and '*une nation complète*,'[111] thus excluding the members of the privileged orders. Individual nobles or clergymen could rejoin their countrymen by giving up their privileges,[112] but as long as they had not done so, they did not belong to the French nation, with all the consequences for political participation and a voice in upcoming reforms that were implied by Sieyès's wider political theory. The struggle for control of the Estates General and the constitution-making process was waged by defining the Third Estate in this way. As he feared the nobility would dominate the Estates General and use its position either to block reform or to direct reform towards a new order in which the nobility would maintain or improve its position as a distinct group (for example by introducing a House of Lords, that '*monument de superstition gothique*' that Anglophiles contemplated imitating[113]), the nobility was to be denied a say altogether.

The equation of nation and Third Estate was endorsed both by the political and the economic definition of the nation. The emphasis of the political definition on unity and equality opposed the notion of distinct estates as well as the existence of privileges and separate institutions. The nation was based on individualism and unity, as one association of individuals was opposed to the stratification of French society in estates and corporations with their own laws, customs, institutions, and privileges. Since the first and second estates, or 'the privileged orders' ('*les ordres privilégiés*'),[114] had their own representatives and were exempted from the common law due to their privileges, they essentially formed separate nations; '*un peuple à part*'.[115] The economic definition posited productive labour against the parasitic presence of idle nobles as well as the monopolization of public offices by nobles, thus blocking free competition for offices.[116] Since members of the Third Estate could and did fulfil all private and public functions involving real work, as Sieyès

107 Baker, 'Political languages', 639.

108 Forsyth, *Reason and Revolution*, 73; Bastid, *Sieyès et sa Pensée*, 361.

109 Forsyth, *Reason and Revolution*, 55; Hafen, *Staat, Gesellschaft und Bürger*, 72; Sewell, *A Rhetoric*, 80.

110 Bastid, *Sieyès et sa Pensée*, 55.

111 Sieyès, *QTE*, 57–9.

112 Sieyès, *QTE*, 223.

113 Sieyès, *QTE*, 146.

114 E.g. Sieyès, *QTE*, 64 and *Essai*, 40.

115 Sieyès, *QTE*, 67, 72, and 76 and *Essai*, 19 and 36.

116 Sieyès, *QTE*, 64–5, 67, and *Essai*, 38, 40, and 48.

maintained, the commons formed a comprehensive system of division of labour and thus the complete nation.[117]

IV. Active Citizens and Representative Government

A final aspect of Sieyès's thought that deserves elaboration concerns his views on the role of the people in government and on representation or representative government.

Judging from the emphasis Sieyès placed on equality, one is easily led to believe that his political theory was 'democratic' in the sense of championing universal suffrage. This would be a misrepresentation of his thought, for he was not that kind of egalitarian. Rather, he championed a sphere of equal opportunities in which talent would determine differences, as expressed in the first article of the 1789 *Déclaration des droits de l'homme et du citoyen*. In his 1789 pamphlets, he argued for equality of political rights for all citizens.[118] However, during the work on the 1791 Constitution and with an eye to the practical difficulties of designing a feasible and well-functioning political system, Sieyès introduced a distinction between active and passive citizens.[119] The distinction coincided with that between natural and civil rights (passive rights) on one hand and political rights (active rights) on the other.[120] Natural and civil rights accrue to everyone; active rights accrue solely to active citizens. Active citizens form the electorate. Due to Sieyès's preference for representative government, active rights—that is, the people's actual role in politics—amount to little more than the right to vote.[121]

In this distinction, the implications of the labour-based, economic definition of the nation become manifest. Sieyès did not advocate a tax-based franchise and, although a minor, voluntary payment appeared among his criteria for active citizenship, this was too small to exclude anyone but those disinterested in politics. The significant qualities were a person's intellectual and moral capacities and his contribution to society by means of labour.[122] Active citizens are essentially all men who work. Vagabonds, beggars, the homeless, and house servants are excluded from active citizenship, as are women, children, and foreigners.[123] The same goes for most nobles who, due to their idleness, are equated with vagabonds and beggars. In the true spirit of the Enlightenment, Sieyès expected the number of active citizens to increase, for passive citizens could become active. It was for

[117] Sieyès, *QTE*, 63–5. [118] Sieyès, *QTE*, 99.

[119] Van Deusen, *Sieyès*, 81. See Titre III, Section II, 1791 Constitution, <http://www.conseil-constitutionnel.fr/conseil-constitutionnel/francais/la-constitution/les-constitutions-de-la-france/constitution-de-1791.5082.html>.

[120] Bastid, *Sieyès et sa Pensée*, 363; Hafen, *Staat, Gesellschaft und Bürger*, 88; Riklin, *Sieyès und die Französische Revolution*, 65.

[121] Riklin, *Sieyès und die Französische Revolution*, 94. On Sieyès views on the electoral system, see Bastid, *Sieyès et sa Pensée*, 404–18; Sewell, *A Rhetoric*, 166–7; Riklin, *Sieyès und die Französische Revolution*, 101–3.

[122] Bastid, *Sieyès et sa Pensée*, 364 and 405; Sewell, *A Rhetoric*, 145.

[123] Sewell, *A Rhetoric*, 149.

government to improve the level of education and development in order to include more among the active citizenry.[124] Sieyès even criticized the exclusion of women, and considered it mere prejudice.[125] He acknowledged that their exclusion was inevitable for the time being, given '*l'état présent des mœurs*,'[126] but hoped and foresaw that women too, in time, would be deemed capable to vote.

Representation is central to Sieyès's political theory. He regarded representative government, which in his view does not equal democracy,[127] as the only legitimate way to organize a modern society. Representation, here, means acting on behalf of others, defending their interests, exercising their rights instead of one's own, or exercising delegated powers.[128] 'Others' can be the nation as a whole, or fellow citizens individually, although in the political sphere, representation of the nation as a whole holds sway. Representation also implies a proportional reflection of society in representative institutions, so a majority of the people, albeit it indirectly, determines outcomes instead of a minority having disproportionate influence.[129] For this proportional representation it is essential that people are represented by their peers; this implied that nobles or clergymen could not serve as representatives of the commons for there to be, in Sieyès's words, '*véritable procuration du peuple*'.[130] Only if these conditions were met would the general interest prevail and the representation be truly national in the sense that the representative assembly would represent the nation as community of citizens as a whole.[131] The Estates General, being based on a distinction of three orders, did not meet these conditions, in Sieyès's view.[132]

Sieyès's stress on representation in 1789 can be explained by his efforts to gain control of French politics for the Patriots. The equation of the Third Estate with the nation in *Qu'est-ce que le tiers état?* raised the position of the Third Estate's delegates in the Estates General. The pamphlet primarily contains a claim to the exclusive representation of the nation by the Third Estate.[133] The minority with disproportionate influence were the privileged orders of the first and second estates. However, tracing Sieyès's views on representation back entirely to the 1789 political context would not do him justice. The core of his theory on representation had already been developed years before the revolution.[134]

In his earlier work on political economy, Sieyès contended that representation is both a pragmatic necessity and the morally preferable option.[135] Political representation is not second best after impractical direct democracy, but is the system that best protects and enhances liberty.[136] Sieyès restated the familiar argument

[124] Van Deusen, *Sieyès*, 83; Bastid, *Sieyès et sa Pensée*, 364 and 406; Sewell, *A Rhetoric*, 147.
[125] Sewell, *A Rhetoric*, 147.
[126] Reiterated in Bastid, *Sieyès et sa Pensée*, 405; Sewell, *A Rhetoric*, 147.
[127] '*des représentants ne sont point des démocrates*'; Sieyès, *QTE*, 188.
[128] E.g. Sieyès, *QTE*, 81–2, 157.
[129] Sieyès, *QTE*, 101–5, 176–7.
[130] Sieyès, *QTE*, 73–5, 78, 87–9, 192, 206.
[131] Sieyès, *QTE*, 98 and 206–7.
[132] Sieyès, *QTE*, 192–3.
[133] Keitner, *Paradoxes of Nationalism*, 46.
[134] Bastid, *Sieyès et sa Pensée*, 376; Forsyth, *Reason and Revolution*, 147.
[135] Koung, *Théorie Constitutionnelle*, 67–9; Hafen, *Staat, Gesellschaft und Bürger*, 57–9.
[136] Sewell, *A Rhetoric*, 105.

that the nation consists of too many people to assemble and decide. Yet this is not enough to justify representative government, although it had led Rousseau to argue in favour of small communities as the only ones in which the people could really be sovereign.[137]

Sieyès managed to circumvent Rousseau by connecting political representation to political economy and thus turned Rousseau's rejection of representation around. For representation, to Sieyès, is essentially a matter of division of labour.[138] Division of labour allows for society to function in a more advanced and sophisticated way.[139] Instead of doing every task necessary to maintain oneself and improve one's situation, one agrees to concentrate on and specialize in the job one is most capable of doing and exchange the products of one's labour.[140] Everyone works on behalf of everyone else and is, in this sense, a representative of all other members of society. All depend on others to produce the necessities of life for them. All are representatives of others and are represented by others, since they act on behalf of them and simultaneously have them act on their behalf. In modern society everyone is a representative of and represented by all of his fellow citizens: '*Tout est représentation dans l'état social*'.[141]

Sieyès argued that representation is better at protecting and enhancing liberty. He based his theories on a dual concept of liberty. Liberty as independence, or negative liberty, meant being free to lead one's life unhampered in accordance with one's own will. The dominant form that creates and sustains the division of labour is the contract, so that in concluding contracts, people voluntarily nominate representatives.[142] In the political sphere, this takes place through elections.[143] The division of labour leads to such an extent of mutual dependence that despotism by one or a few is excluded. If everyone depends on everyone else, no one is capable of dominance.[144] Note that political participation is not included in this definition of liberty. The second kind of liberty Sieyès distinguished is liberty as capability or active liberty,[145] which means removing the causes that render people incapable of leading the life they want to lead. Liberty in this active sense is enhanced by living

[137] J. Rousseau, *Du contrat social* (Paris, 2001; orig. 1762), 65–6 (II.1); Bastid, *Sieyès et sa Pensée*, 578; Forsyth, *Reason and Revolution*, 60; Sewell, *A Rhetoric*, 47–9.

[138] Forsyth, *Reason and Revolution*, 19, 52–7, and 63; Koung, *Théorie Constitutionnelle*, 76–7; Bastid, *Sieyès et sa Pensée*, 369–70; Hafen, *Staat, Gesellschaft und Bürger*, 54–61; Sewell, *A Rhetoric*, 67 and 90; Riklin, *Sieyès und die Französische Revolution*, 31–2. See also Forsyth, *Reason and Revolution*, 129; Sewell, *A Rhetoric*, 68; Keitner, *Paradoxes of Nationalism*, 62.

[139] Baker, 'Political languages', 630.

[140] This line of reasoning is reminiscent of Adam Smith, but Sieyès had already expounded his views on representation and the division of labour two years before Smith published *The Wealth of Nations* (1776). See Forsyth, *Reason and Revolution*, 141; Sewell, *A Rhetoric*, 69 and 79.

[141] Sieyès, 2 *Thermidor* speech; reiterated in Hafen, *Staat, Gesellschaft und Bürger*, 55; Riklin, *Sieyès und die Französische Revolution*, 207.

[142] Forsyth, *Reason and Revolution*, 122–3; Sewell, *A Rhetoric*, 103.

[143] Forsyth, *Reason and Revolution*, 130; Riklin, *Sieyès und die Französische Revolution*, 32.

[144] Forsyth, *Reason and Revolution*, 120–1; Hafen, *Staat, Gesellschaft und Bürger*, 120–2; Sewell, *A Rhetoric*, 78, 91–4, and 100–2; Baker, 'Political languages', 640.

[145] Forsyth, *Reason and Revolution*, 120–1; Hafen, *Staat, Gesellschaft und Bürger*, 121–2; Riklin, *Sieyès und die Französische Revolution*, 174.

in a society based on a division of labour, exactly because it is the basis of increasing affluence due to gains in efficiency and rationality.[146] Specialization increases wealth, which allows people to improve themselves.

Political representation is part and parcel of the functional differentiation within society. Besides the private functions of agriculture, industry, commerce, and services, Sieyès distinguished four public functions: the army ('*l'épée*'), the judges ('*la robe*'), the church, and the administration.[147] The last includes a wide range of activities. They are essential to the advancement of liberty and affluence.[148] The government is limited to this aim and to its public functions.[149] In conforming to the general purpose of specialization, these public functions of governance are to be attributed to specialized institutions or at least to part of the citizenry enabled to specialize in them.[150] The constitution serves a pivotal end in Sieyès's notion of political representation, as part of the division of labour in a society. The constitution is the instrument by which the representative institutions are established and authority is attributed to them. Hence, the constitution creates and legitimizes the division of labour in the public sphere.

Within the sphere of politics, representation is a wide notion. Sieyès rejected the idea that only the legislative assembly represents the nation.[151] He considered all government institutions, the executive included, to be representative in the sense that they are all the nation's agents, that is to say, that they act and speak on behalf of the nation and exercise only delegated powers.[152] Therefore, representation both empowers and confines government institutions. This implies that the monarch is also the nation's representative,[153] as the 1791 Constitution would state.[154] In attributing this character to the monarch, Sieyès meant to stress that royal authority depends on the nation. The monarch is not instituted by God to rule over the people, but a public official deriving his authority from the nation.[155] Conversely, Sieyès did deem (constitutional) monarchy to be the best form of government, a preference he even held on to once the king became increasingly suspect. This brought him into conflict both with the Jacobins in Paris and with one of his British admirers, Thomas Paine, a well-known adversary to monarchical

[146] Hafen, *Staat, Gesellschaft und Bürger*, 57; Sewell, *A Rhetoric*, 77.

[147] Sieyès, *QTE*, 59–60.

[148] Bastid, *Sieyès et sa Pensée*, 363; Sewell, *A Rhetoric*, 77–8; Riklin, *Sieyès und die Französische Revolution*, 44.

[149] Hafen, *Staat, Gesellschaft und Bürger*, 54 and 62.

[150] Koung, *Théorie Constitutionnelle*, 77; Forsyth, *Reason and Revolution*, 129 and 147; Sewell, *A Rhetoric*, 88–91.

[151] Riklin, *Sieyès und die Französische Revolution*, 207–8; Baker, 'Political languages', 630.

[152] Koung, *Théorie Constitutionnelle*, 43, 57, 63, 81, and 132; Bastid, *Sieyès et sa Pensée*, 371 and 373; Forsyth, *Reason and Revolution*, 129 and 144; Hafen, *Staat, Gesellschaft und Bürger*, 55, 73, 179, and 185–92; Collofong, *Elemente einer Verfassungsgerichtsbarkeit*, 22–3.

[153] Koung, *Théorie Constitutionnelle*, 73 and 79–81; Forsyth, *Reason and Revolution*, 89 and 176; Hafen, *Staat, Gesellschaft und Bürger*, 94–5.

[154] Titre III, Article 2 1791 Constitution; <http://www.conseil-constitutionnel.fr/conseil-constitutionnel/francais/la-constitution/les-constitutions-de-la-france/constitution-de-1791.5082.html> (17 June 2010).

[155] See Hartmann, *Französische Verfassungsgeschichte*, 48; Forsyth, *Reason and Revolution*, 89 and 173.

government. Sieyès's response to Paine's call for a republic after Louis XVI's flight from Paris and arrest at Varennes (20–21 June 1791) testifies to his continued support of the monarchy.[156] Although he endorsed Paine's rejection of hereditary succession in principle, Sieyès the pragmatist claimed that there was no workable alternative[157] and repudiated the view that equated republican and representative government.[158]

This sense of representation also sustained the argument that the representatives were not to serve particular interests and were not to be bound to observe strict mandates from their leaders, since all institutions represent the nation as a whole rather than a particular constituency.[159] This meant that the delegates in Paris were no longer expected to further their leaders' or regions' interests. In *Qu'est-ce que le tiers état?* Sieyès held a brief for a strong connection between representative and represented in order to deny noblemen or clergymen the right to serve as representatives of the commons.[160] Some months later, he actually argued for an extension of the freedom of the deputies to the Estates General by repudiating the notion that they acted under mandate. In the summer of 1789, it was argued that members of the National Assembly were acting beyond the mandate they had received from their voters and therefore illegally. Sieyès responded that the nation's representatives were to be given a free hand. The division of labour among specialized agencies delivers the best outcomes if the work is left to those specialized in it. The National Assembly could freely express the national will, as it emerged from deliberation, on the basis of a free competition of views and opinions. Any other approach would paralyse legislation and hinder those best capable of acting on behalf of the nation.[161]

According to Sieyès, the separation of powers, is to be understood in terms of specialization and functional differentiation. The object of separation is not so much to provide checks and balances to enable the various institutions to act as countervailing powers vis-à-vis each other; that would hamper the efficacy of government and mix up various functions. Separation at the institutional level is an expression of the division of labour at the level of public functions.[162] The separation of powers is not just about separating the legislative, executive, and

[156] T. Paine, 'Public letter to M. Emanuel Syeyes', 8 July 1791, and Sieyès, 'Explanatory Note in Answer to the Letter of Mr. Paine and to Several Other Provocations of the Same Sort', in Sonenscher, *Sieyès: Political Writings*, 163–73. See also Paine, *Rights of Man*, 223–5.

[157] Sonenscher, *Sieyès: Political Writings*, 170.

[158] Sonenscher, *Sieyès: Political Writings*, 168.

[159] Sieyès, *QTE*, 98. See also Baker, 'Political languages', 382–3, 355, and 630; Riklin, *Sieyès und die Französische Revolution*, 94; Keitner, *Paradoxes of Nationalism*, 63.

[160] '*Un procureur fondé ne peut lier que ses commettans; un représentant n'a droit de porter la parole que pour ses représentés*': Sieyès, *QTE*, 192.

[161] See Bastid, *Sieyès et sa Pensée*, 384; Forsyth, *Reason and Revolution*, 131 and 170; Hafen, *Staat, Gesellschaft und Bürger*, 64; Riklin, *Sieyès und die Französische Revolution*, 37; Baker, 'Political languages', 636.

[162] See Bastid, *Sieyès et sa Pensée*, 399; Forsyth, *Reason and Revolution*, 45, 167, and 183; Bredin, *La clé de la Révolution*, 365; Hafen, *Staat, Gesellschaft und Bürger*, 201–3; Riklin, *Sieyès und die Französische Revolution*, 39 and 209–210.

judicial powers.[163] Sieyès sustained the separation of powers by a distinction between will and action, and by giving legislation a central position within the functional system.[164] The division of labour, however, continues within each branch of government.[165] For instance, while in *Qu'est-ce que le tiers état?* he advocated a unicameral legislature as part of his rejection of a division within the legislature based on social orders, he repudiated that a multi-cameral legislature based on distinct functions would be possible.[166] From 1795 onwards, in reaction to the abuse of power by the National Convention throughout the Terror, Sieyès advocated an institutional separation within the legislative power between proposing new legislation, and discussing and passing a bill.[167] This functional separation of power is to prevent despotism by way of the concentration of power, but would also make the work of government more rational and efficient.

V. Conclusion

Sieyès developed his constitutional views on the eve of and throughout the revolutionary period in France. His views are clearly connected to his critique of *Ancien Régime* society, the Patriot reform programme, and the political situation of 1789 and the 1790s. At the core of his views stands the nation acting through representation. He defined the nation in various complementary ways. Both his definition of the nation and his justification of representation rest on an economic theory of specialization and division of labour, which affected his attitude to the separation of powers. In respect to the nature of the constitution and the position of the constitution within and vis-à-vis the political system, Sieyès presented a theory that combines the changeability of the constitution with the rule of law as far as the government is concerned. This circle was squared by introducing the separation between constituent and constituted powers and by attributing the exercise of the constituent power to extraordinary representatives. Throughout the 1790s, this element of extraordinary representation evolved into a permanent institution charged with reviewing and revising the constitution. Despite the great degree of contingency, these tenets in Sieyès's writings still provide interesting insights to current debates on democracy and constitutionalism.

163 Initially Sieyès followed Locke's division of the legislative, executive, and federative powers; adjudication being part of the executive power. By the time of his revolutionary pamphlets he had adopted the now classical stance that distinguishes between administration and adjudication. See Riklin, *Sieyès und die Französische Revolution*, 42–3.

164 Bastid, *Sieyès et sa Pensée*, 397–8, 421, and 447–8.

165 Bastid, *Sieyès et sa Pensée*, 400.

166 Sieyès, *QTE*, 145 and 195, and his *Views of the Executive Means*, in Sonenscher, *Sieyès: Political Writings*, 38 and 46.

167 Koung, *Théorie Constitutionnelle*, vii–viii; Bastid, *Sieyès et sa Pensée*, 170, 424, and 446; Forsyth, *Reason and Revolution*, 181; Bredin, *La clé de la Révolution*, 365; Hafen, *Staat, Gesellschaft und Bürger*, 206, and 210; Sewell, *A Rhetoric*, 19; Riklin, *Sieyès und die Französische Revolution*, 42, 210–11, and 213.

14

'Perfection in Imperfection'

Joseph de Maistre and the Limitations of Constitutional Design

*Mila Versteeg**

I. Introduction

Few modern-day constitutional theorists would list Joseph de Maistre's works among 'the classics' in constitutional thought. A defender of the crumbling *Ancien Régime*, de Maistre despised most of the ideals embodied in modern constitutions.[1] Instead, he has been depicted as an enemy of liberty,[2] as 'a blind traditionalist and reactionary, as dogmatic, intransigent, absolute and violent as possible,'[3] and as 'an apostle of darkness'[4] whose ideas appeal to modern fascists.[5] Indeed, de Maistre discussed the virtues of the Spanish Inquisition, the genius of the feudal system, and the social value of the guillotine. His world vision, on the whole, seems dark and violent. Perhaps, then, it would be best to let de Maistre linger in obscurity.

Yet de Maistre was more than an ultra-conservative and religious defender of the *Ancien Régime*. In this essay, my aim is to show that de Maistre offers a unique but

* I would like to thank Kevin Cope, Denis Galligan, Raymond Kubben, and David Robertson, as well as participants at the Oxford Workshop on *Constitutions and the Classics* (June 2010) for helpful comments and suggestions. I thank Trevor Moore for excellent research assistance.

[1] I. Berlin, 'Two Enemies of Enlightenment: The Second Onslaught, Joseph de Maistre and Open Obscurantism' (Wolfson College Virtual Library, 2005), 22: <http://berlin.wolf.ox.ac.uk/lists/nachlass/maistre.pdf> accessed 5 September 2013.

[2] I. Berlin, 'Introduction', in H. Hardin (ed.), *Freedom and Its Betrayal: Six Enemies of Human Liberty* (Princeton: Princeton University Press, 2002), 5.

[3] O. Bradley, *A Modern Maistre: The Social and Political Thought of Joseph de Maistre* (Lincoln: University of Nebraska Press, 1999), ix.

[4] G. Gerrard, 'I. Berlin's Joseph de Maistre', in J. Mali and R. Worker (eds), *I. Berlin's Counter-Enlightenment* (Philadelphia: American Philosophical Society, 2003), 118.

[5] I. Berlin, 'The Counter-Enlightenment', in H. Hardin (ed.), *Against the Current* (Princeton: Princeton University Press, 1980) (noting that '[t]hese gloomy doctrines ... inspired nationalism, imperialism, and finally, in their most violent and pathological form, Fascist and totalitarian doctrines') 32; I. Berlin, 'Joseph de Maistre and the Origins of Fascism', in H. Hardy (ed.), *The Crooked Timber of Humanity: Chapters in the History of Ideas* (New York: Knopf, 1990). Cf. Bradley, (n. 3) (challenging Berlin's account by noting that de Maistre analysed violence and self-destruction, but never actually propagated it), xvi.

often overlooked perspective on constitutions, which sounds surprisingly modern today. It is a constitutional theory that emphasizes the limitations of rational constitutional design, the close connection of constitutions to society, the symbolic power of constitutions, and the inherent irrationality of stable constitutional systems.

Joseph de Maistre's constitutional theory has been woefully under-analysed. In political theory, attention to de Maistre has been scant and overwhelmingly negative.[6] Where de Maistre appears on the scholarly radar, he is portrayed as the 'enemy of liberty', or worse. One notable and recent exception is the work of Owen Bradley, who characterizes de Maistre as a modern, even postmodern, thinker. My reading of de Maistre builds on Bradley's,[7] as well as the literature that links early counter-enlightenment thinkers to today's postmodernists.[8] My focus, however, is exclusively on de Maistre as a constitutional scholar. I will not cover his writings on papal authority, his cross-cultural theory of sacrifice,[9] or his dark vision of human nature.[10] This focus, of course, affects the picture that I paint. De Maistre's approach to constitutions was more sociological than his approach to other topics, which he often considered from a chiefly theological angle. De Maistre also routinely contradicts himself, and his writings contain numerous inconsistencies.[11] Nonetheless, de Maistre offers a fairly consistent theory on constitutions. It is this theory that I will expound in this essay.

I will focus on three overarching themes that run through de Maistre's constitutional writings. First, a nation's true constitution is *indigenous* and particular to the nation. It is neither universal nor rational, but grows from each nation's past and best remains unwritten. Second, well-functioning and enduring constitutional rules are often *irrational*. They do not fit the philosopher's canon of logic. Instead, they come about by chance, with a strong element of randomness, and they develop in unexpected directions. Such perfection in imperfection is impossible to design. Third, constitutional power has a strong *symbolic* element. It is symbols and rituals that

[6] Bradley (n. 3) (noting that, as of 1999, there was 'no comprehensive account of Joseph de Maistre's social and political philosophy', existing accounts being either 'entirely biographical' or ideological in nature 'treating him as a mouthpiece of the forces of reaction') vii. The various ideological accounts include those by Isaiah Berlin as well as Stephen Holmes: S. Holmes, *The Anatomy of Anti-Liberalism* (Cambridge, MA: Harvard University Press, 1993) (deeming de Maistre significant because he is one of the first well-articulated, sophisticated, voices of the anti-liberal tradition), 14.

[7] I agree with Bradley that de Maistre 'is of value to the extent that his criticism is founded on a critical analysis of irrational social forces too often left unanalysed by critics working within liberal horizons.' Bradley (n. 3). I also built on Bradley when pointing out both the dangers of de Maistre's work and the dangers of ignoring it altogether.

[8] J. Habermas, 'Modernity vs. Post-Modernity', *New German Critique*, 22 (1981), 3, 7–11 (noting that modernity entails an extension of the rational norms of Enlightenment, and that rejecting the Enlightenment premises entails a rejection of modernity).

[9] Bradley uses de Maistre's theory on sacrifice as the main organizing principle to understand all his work. Bradley, (n. 3), vii.

[10] Berlin (n. 1).

[11] J. Lively, 'Introduction', in *The Works of Joseph de Maistre*, ed. J. Lively (New York: Schocken Books, 1971) (noting that these contradictions explain why there exist so many different depictions of de Maistre in the literature, ranging from de Maistre as a modern social scientist, to a dogmatic defender of religious authority, to the forefather of modern fascism), 3.

explain why constitutions are respected. Once people expose constitutions to reason and write them down, however, constitutions lose their sacred source of power.

Constitutional scholars may be sceptical of an attempt to uncover the 'enemy of liberty's' view of the rules whose first and foremost purpose is to protect liberty. Indeed, emphasis on indigenous constitutions can be an easy excuse for repressive regimes to circumvent rights in the name of tradition. Emphasis on the imperfection and irrationality of constitutional rules may legitimize inferior, even harmful, constitutional practice, and inhibit progress. Emphasis on the symbolic value of constitutional rules may undermine the potential of institutional constraints on government power. An emphasis on a constitution's limited capacity to induce societal change may prevent constitutional change altogether and transform the constitution into a mirror of the past. It is important to keep in mind these caveats when reading de Maistre.

On the other hand, ignoring de Maistre's work altogether may also be dangerous. Nineteenth- and twentieth-century constitution-makers have done almost everything de Maistre argued against. Since de Maistre's day, the world has witnessed a proliferation of constitution-writing, informed by a 'science' of constitutional design.[12] Constitutions are often written to erase the past and imagine a new future, and commonly conform to standardized international models. Against this backdrop, de Maistre's theory might be valuable for its emphasis on each nation's unique history, on historical happenstance, and on unintended consequences. What is more, this theory strikes a chord with contemporary notions of constitution-making. While it stands at odds with rationalist and universalist premises of constitutional design, it resonates with a number of recent themes in the constitutional literature. Indeed, de Maistre's constitutional theory can be viewed as simultaneously pre-modern and postmodern.[13]

The remainder of this brief essay unfolds as follows. Section II places de Maistre in his historical context. Sections III, IV, and V set out de Maistre's constitutional claims, namely that constitutions are respectively *indigenous*, *irrational*, and *symbolic* in nature. Section VI concludes by linking de Maistre's writing to the contemporary constitutional literature.

II. Context: Revolution and Reason

1. Situating de Maistre

No event has impacted on de Maistre's writing more than the French Revolution, which changed the course of his life.[14] Born and raised as a member of the upper

[12] On constitutional design, see D. S. Lutz, *Principles of Constitutional Design* (Cambridge: Cambridge University Press, 2006); R. Hirschl, 'The "Design Sciences" and Constitutional "Success"', *Texas Law Review* 87 (2009), 1339.

[13] Cf. Bradley (n. 3) (describing postmodernism in political theory and highlighting parallels between postmodern thought and early conservative thinkers like de Maistre in the counter-Enlightenment movement), xiii.

[14] R. A. Lebrun, *Joseph de Maistre: An Intellectual Militant* (Kingston: McGill-Queen's University Press, 1988).

classes, he left his home in 1792, leaving his family behind. It was in the following years abroad, while living in Lausanne and St. Petersburg, that he did most of his political writing. Scholars have suggested that these events turned de Maistre into an 'angry man.'[15] The ousting of the *Ancien Régime*, followed by the Reign of Terror, and a prolific law-making in the new republic (by de Maistre's count, fifteen thousand pieces of legislation adopted in less than five years[16]), all led de Maistre to conclude that things had gone very wrong. Indeed, much of de Maistre's writing is directed against the French Revolution and its underlying premises.[17]

The main evil behind the revolution, according to de Maistre, was the Enlightenment ideal of reason.[18] It is because of reason that the Enlightenment *philosophes* could constantly re-invent society and change the existing political order, and that one regime could overthrow the other. De Maistre's 'revolt against reason' has been well documented in the existing literature.[19]

It is noteworthy that, in his attack on reason, de Maistre relies primarily on empirical, especially historical and comparative, analysis. The main premises of Enlightenment thought, according to de Maistre, simply lacked empirical basis and ignored the lessons of history. Philosophy, in his view, was a false science that was irrelevant to understanding real-world politics and contemporary social life. Building a government upon such theories was therefore a gross mistake to him, as the events surrounding the revolution so neatly illustrated.[20]

History, not philosophy, was 'the only teacher in politics'.[21] Indeed, history informs most of de Maistre's analysis.[22] To illustrate, when de Maistre defends monarchy against democracy, he does so based on empirical observation. History reveals that monarchy is the natural mode of government;[23] 'If it was said to us that a dice, thrown [a] hundred million times, always showed only the five numbers, 1, 2, 3, 4 and 5, could we believe that there was a 6 on one of its faces?' de Maistre asks.[24] The dice of history always shows monarchy, the form of government that is

[15] Berlin (n. 1), 1; Bradley (n. 3) (noting that all existing accounts of de Maistre start with his negative response to the revolution, 'deducing therefrom the reactionary character of his thought as a whole'), vii.

[16] Joseph de Maistre, 'Considerations on France' (first published 1796), in *The Works of Joseph de Maistre*, ed. J. Lively (New York: Schocken Books, 1971) (hereinafter, de Maistre, 'Considerations'), 81.

[17] R. Nisbet, 'Foreword: A Note on Conservatism', in *The Works of Joseph de Maistre*, ed. J. Lively (New York: Schocken Books, 1971), xi.

[18] Lively (n. 11), 4. [19] Lively (n. 11), 4. [20] Lively (n. 11), 4.

[21] De Maistre, 'Study on Sovereignty' (first published 1884), in *The Works of Joseph de Maistre* (New York: Schocken Books, 1971) (hereinafter, de Maistre, 'Sovereignty') ('History is experimental politics; and just as, in the physical sciences, a hundred books of speculative theories disappear before a single experiment, in the same way in political science no theory can be allowed if it is not the more or less probable corollary of well-attested facts'), 114.

[22] With similar tools, de Maistre assesses political systems. 'In astronomy in particular we always talk of *average distance* and *average time*. To judge the merit of a government, the same method should be used': De Maistre, 'Sovereignty', 127. To evaluate the French monarchy, 'a sum of the virtues and vices of all the French kings should be made, and divided by sixty-six: the result is an average king; and the same is true of other monarchies': De Maistre, 'Sovereignty', 127.

[23] De Maistre, 'Considerations' (n. 16), 65–6.

[24] De Maistre, 'Considerations' (n. 16), 65–6.

'most ancient and the most universal'.[25] Republics, by contrast, have only 'sometimes been known'[26] and democracy has had just 'one brilliant moment' in the days of Athens.[27] Even though de Maistre acknowledges that many kings were fools, he concludes that monarchy represents the natural, and even divine, order of things.[28] A similar empirical assessment leads de Maistre to conclude that the French Revolution was irrevocable. No matter how much he dislikes the revolution's consequences, going back to the pre-revolutionary status was like 'trying to exhaust the lake of Geneva by collecting its water in bottles'.[29]

Notably, as a student of history, de Maistre finds very little optimism for mankind. Looking at history, he observes that people are 'dark, violent, and eager to sacrifice'.[30] De Maistre sees chaos, violence, and warfare, which would come to the fore when removing people's ancient constraints and building a political system upon reason.[31] Some have attributed remarkable foresight to his world vision. George Steiner wrote that de Maistre's vision 'may well be the principal feat of precise foresight in the history of modern political . . . theory'. According to Steiner, de Maistre's prophecy 'makes the futurology of Rousseau, of Hegel and Marx look utterly shallow', because '[t]he age of the Gulag and of Auschwitz, of famine and ubiquitous torture, of Idi Amin, Pol Pot and of Ceausescu is *exactly* that which de Maistre announced.'[32]

2. Situating de Maistre's constitutional thought

The French Revolution also had a profound impact on de Maistre's *constitutional* thought. Over the course of its first five years, the new republic adopted three separate constitutions. To de Maistre, this fickleness reveals both the instability of the new regime and the dangers of building a nation on reason. Written constitutions epitomize the very Enlightenment ideals that de Maistre despises, which is why a substantial portion of his writing concerns constitutions.

To understand the baseline from which de Maistre attacks constitutions based on Enlightenment ideas, it is helpful to review the constitutional ideas and ideals that prevailed before the Enlightenment. These 'ancient' constitutions have their roots in the ancient world, where the notion of constitution was essentially synonymous with organized political structure.[33] The ancient Greeks used the term *politeia*[34] to describe the state as it actually is.[35] Aristotle, for example,

[25] De Maistre, 'Sovereignty' (n. 20), 113.
[26] De Maistre, 'Considerations' (n. 16), 65–6.
[27] De Maistre, 'Sovereignty' (n. 20), 127.
[28] De Maistre's historicism often takes a religious turn. He was a Whig historian, drawing lines from one big event to another, and looking for overarching patterns or historical change. He did so not merely to study the world around him, but to look for a divine order, and to discover the revealed teachings of religion. For de Maistre, history could provide insight into the divine order, the way in which God had meant the world to function. Lively (n. 11), 31–45.
[29] Berlin (n. 1), 2–3.
[30] Bradley (n. 3), xi.
[31] Bradley (n. 3), xi.
[32] Bradley (n. 3) (quoting George Steiner), xi.
[33] C. H. McIlwain, *Constitutionalism: Ancient and Modern* (Ithaca: Cornell University Press, 1947) 3.
[34] McIlwain, *Constitutionalism*, 24.
[35] McIlwain, *Constitutionalism* (quoting Isocrates, *Panathenaicus*, ¶138) 26.

described the constitution as the way of life of the citizens,[36] while Plato regarded it as 'a "representation" of the finest and noblest life'.[37] The same ideals prevailed in the Roman Republic.[38] As Cicero wrote in *De Res Publica*, 'the constitution of the republic is the work of no single time or of no single man.'[39]

The ideals of ancient constitutionalism persisted throughout the middle ages.[40] Law-making at this time was fundamentally backward-looking and precedent had to be found in the nation's past, and especially the models of the Ancient Greeks and the Roman Republic.[41] Through the force of their example, the Greek and Roman constitutional ideals therefore endured until de Maistre's day. Indeed, de Maistre quotes from Plato when defining a constitution as an amalgam of 'population, customs, religion, geographical situation, political relations, wealth, [and] good and bad qualities' of a nation, whose purpose is to 'find the laws that suit it'.[42]

In de Maistre's day, modernity forecast a new type of constitution: a constitution written by a popular assembly, based on a social contract, and designed to reshape the existing social and political order. At this time, a world vision based on wisdom from the past was replaced by one that was forward-looking and based on scientific discovery. According to Enlightenment *philosophes*, the whole world was governed by natural laws, which were to be uncovered only through human reason.[43] What is more, the notion of 'being "modern" by looking back to the ancients' was replaced by a belief that people could continuously improve themselves and the world around them.[44] Law no longer had to be found in history but could be created.[45] Constitutions, perhaps more than any other law, could reshape and reconstruct society.[46] As Thomas Paine put it, '[a] constitution is a thing antecedent to a government, and a government is only the creature of a constitution.'[47] With human reason—i.e. 'intelligent men coming together for deliberation about how

[36] Aristotle, *The Politics* (first published *c.*350 B.C.E.), ed. and tr. T. A. Sinclair and T. J. Saunders (New York: Penguin Books, 1982), 266.

[37] Plato, *The Laws* (first published *c.*360 B.C.E.), tr. T. J. Saunders (New York: Penguin Books, 1982), 310.

[38] S. Gordon, *Controlling the State: Constitutionalism from Ancient Athens to Today* (Cambridge, MA: Harvard University Press, 1999), 86–115.

[39] McIlwain (n. 31) (quoting Cicero), 24.

[40] McIlwain (n. 31) (quoting Cicero), 24.

[41] F. A. Hayek, *The Constitution of Liberty* (Chicago: University of Chicago Press, 2011) (noting that '[f]or centuries it was recognized doctrine that kings or any other human authority could only declare or find the existing law, or modify abuses that crept in, and not create law'), 235; Habermas (n. 8) (noting for centuries to come, the constitutions of ancient Athens and Rome would serve as important models 'to be recovered through some kind of imitation'), 4.

[42] Bradley (n. 3) (pointing out de Maistre's reliance on Plato), 95.

[43] R. Lesaffer, *European Legal History: A Cultural and Political Perspective* (Cambridge: Cambridge University Press, 2009), 372–84.

[44] Habermas (n. 8), 4.

[45] Hayek (n. 39) (noting that '[o]nly gradually, during the later Middle Ages, did the conception of deliberate creation of new law . . . come to be accepted' and was legislation used 'for the first time as an instrument of deliberate policy'), 235–6.

[46] G. A. Billias, *American Constitutionalism Heard Around the World 1776–1989: A Global Perspective* (New York: New York University Press, 2010), 56–7.

[47] Thomas Paine, *Rights of Man, Common Sense, and Other Political Writings* (first published 1791), ed. M. Philip (Oxford: Oxford University Press, 1995), 122.

to make the world anew'—people could *create* liberty.[48] The famous words '[t]he past is a foreign country' squarely describe the Enlightenment tradition.[49]

It is at this critical juncture of history—when the old meets the new—that de Maistre develops his ideas. His starting point is clearly that of the ancient constitution. As he often notes, the true constitution of France is 'written in the hearts of Frenchmen.'[50] But what makes de Maistre's writing so interesting is that his views on ancient constitutionalism intersect with the events of the French Revolution. He struggles with the questions of whether constitutions can be written, whether people can enter into a social contract with their government, and how political institutions endure.

Rather than simply attacking the new in the name of the old, he resorts to empirical methods, looking at real-world examples across both space and time. De Maistre was a comparativist, frequently using examples from other countries. He examines constitutions in France, Britain, Poland, Turkey, and China and develops a constitutional theory more sociological than normative. 'Looking scrupulously at the patterns of change which it presents to us,' de Maistre 's[aw] nothing that favours this chimerical system of deliberation and political engineering through previous reasoning.'[51] De Maistre therefore concludes that the social contract is nothing but a fairy tale, and that the writings of Rousseau and other social contract thinkers are merely 'a novel'.[52] In the remainder of this essay, I describe what, according to de Maistre, history and comparative analysis teaches us about constitutions and constitution-writing.

III. The Indigenous Constitution

A first and recurring theme in de Maistre's constitutional writing is that constitutions are neither universal nor rational, and best remain unwritten. For de Maistre, a constitution is indigenous to the nation and a reflection of the nation's identity. The 'true' constitution of France is 'what you feel when you are in France'. It is 'the mixture of liberty and authority, law and opinion that made the foreign traveler in France believe that he was living under a government different from his own'.[53] A constitution is thus an amalgam of the nation's distinct history, its culture, and its traditions.

If a constitution is a uniquely national product, it follows that there exist no universal principles for constitutional design. As de Maistre put it:

48 Hayek (n. 40), 112–13.

49 This famous phrase comes from L. P. Hartley, *The Go Between* (London: Hamish Hamilton, 1953), 9.

50 Joseph de Maistre, 'Essay on Generative Principles' (first published 1809), in *The Works of Joseph de Maistre* (New York: Schocken Books, 1971) (hereinafter, de Maistre 'Generative Principles'), 147.

51 De Maistre, 'Considerations' (n. 16), 84.

52 Bradley (n. 3) (quoting from de Maistre's personal notes), 99.

53 De Maistre, 'Considerations' (n. 16), 85.

> The 1795 constitution, like its predecessors, was made for man. But there is no such thing as man in the world. During my life, I have seen Frenchmen, Italians, Russians, and so on; thanks to Montesquieu, I even know that one can be *Persian*; but I must say, as for man, I have never come across him anywhere; if he exists, he is completely unknown to me.[54]

Universal constitutional rules, therefore, only exist in the minds of philosophers: '[a] constitution that is made for all nations is a constitution that is made for none.' Such a constitution, de Maistre argues, is 'a pure abstraction, an academic exercise of the mind, according to some hypothetical ideal, that should be addressed to *man,* in whatever imaginary realm he inhabits'.[55] He therefore concludes that '[e]ach people should be assigned a particular institutional system, which is the best, not perhaps in itself, but for the state for which it was intended.'[56]

The same rejection of universalism can be found in the work of some of his French and European predecessors and contemporaries. Montesquieu, for example, notes that 'laws should be so appropriate to the people for whom they are made that it is very unlikely that the laws of one nation can suit another.'[57] The Genevan philosopher Rousseau likewise emphasizes the particularistic nature of constitutions.[58] These same assertions characterize the older constitutional tradition that predates Enlightenment thought.

De Maistre, however, goes further than these other thinkers, rejecting not only the Enlightenment's universalism, but also its rationalism. Unlike Montesquieu or Rousseau, he does not regard the constitution as a tool to shape society. He insists that written constitutions are merely declarations of pre-existing rights: 'popular rights are never written' but 'always only declaratory statements of anterior rights, of which nothing can be said other than they exist because they exist'.[59] For that reason, 'no nation has ever succeeded in developing, by written constitutional laws, rights other than those present in its natural constitution.'[60] De Maistre notes that the English would never have written the Great Charter (Magna Carta) 'if these rights had not existed before the Charter'.[61] A constitution should not just be tailor-made for a nation, but should be grown from that nation's past.

De Maistre's theory, then, seems to restrict each nation to its past and to inhibit change. Indeed, he notes that liberty, 'since it will not grow under every climate, is not open to every nation'.[62] Therefore, '[n]o one should ask what the best form of

[54] De Maistre, 'Considerations' (n. 16), 80.

[55] De Maistre, 'Considerations' (n. 16), 80.

[56] De Maistre, 'Sovereignty' (n. 20), 100.

[57] Lesaffer (n. 41) (citing Montesquieu), 420.

[58] Lively (n. 11) (noting that de Maistre quoted Rousseau with approval on this subject), 4. De Maistre points out the inconsistencies in Rousseau's contextualism: '[I]f there are as many different governments as there are different peoples . . . it is no longer permissible to talk of a *compact*'; 'If a man himself worked out these unshakable principles in a book designed to establish that "it is always necessary to go back to a convention" [quoting Rousseau]; if he writes in one chapter that "man was born free" [quoting Rousseau]; and in another that "liberty, since it will not grow under every climate, is not open to every nation" [quoting Rousseau], his utter folly could not be contested.' De Maistre, 'Sovereignty' (n. 20), 100–1.

[59] De Maistre, 'Considerations' (n. 16), 77.

[60] De Maistre, 'Considerations' (n. 16), 78.

[61] De Maistre, 'Generative Principles' (n. 48), 154–5.

[62] De Maistre, 'Sovereignty' (n. 20) (quoting Rousseau). 101.

government is in general, since none is suitable for every nation.'[63] Instead, each nation 'has its own, as it has its own language and character, and this government is the best for it'.[64] De Maistre therefore dismissed the social contract: '[s]ince none of the varying circumstances depend on men, it follows that the consent of the people plays no part in the formation of government.'[65]

But if liberty cannot be created, can an 'unfree' nation ever be free? For de Maistre, the answer to this question is both 'yes' and 'no'. The answer is 'no' because a nation cannot give itself liberty by drawing up a written document that proclaims that all men are free: 'No nation can give itself liberty if it has not it already.'[66] But the answer is also 'yes', because a constitution *can* change when society changes. Where a tradition of liberty grows, constitutional change will follow. Every important institution, according to de Maistre, is 'formed of itself by the occurrence of a thousand agents' and as a result of their unconscious acts, the institution they created 'vegetates intensely over the ages'.[67] In other words, constitutional growth tracks the growth in society. If liberty matures, so does the constitution. Constitutional change can come about through incremental change and evolution, but not revolution.

De Maistre not only insists that constitutions are neither universal nor rational, he also suggests that they best remain unwritten. He ridicules the *philosophes* who

> believe that an assembly can constitute a nation, that a constitution . . . is an artefact like any other, requiring only intelligence, knowledge, and practice, that the job of constitution-making can be learned, and that, the moment they think about it, men can say to other men *make us a government*, as a workman is told *make us a fire engine or a loom*.[68]

In other words, constitutional documents that aim to design society based on theory, but are disconnected from the existing social order, are doomed to fail. De Maistre characterizes as 'profound stupidity' the notion that 'legislators are men, that laws are pieces of paper and that nations may be created *by ink*.'[69]

His rejection of written constitutions is even more general. He rejects even those that accurately reflect the existing social order. In this sense, he distinguishes himself from other conservative theorists such as Edmund Burke, with whom de Maistre shares many views in common. While Burke also emphasizes the indigenous nature of constitutions and organic constitutional growth, Burke thinks that constitutional rules would become stronger when written down.[70] De Maistre, by contrast, believes that written constitutions are a sign of frailty and instability. It is when existing practices come under attack and the existing order is challenged from

[63] De Maistre, 'Sovereignty' (n. 20) (quoting Rousseau), 126.

[64] De Maistre, 'Sovereignty' (n. 20) (quoting Rousseau), 126.

[65] De Maistre, 'Sovereignty' (n. 20) (quoting Rousseau), 126.

[66] De Maistre, 'Considerations' (n. 16), 78.

[67] De Maistre, 'Considerations' (n. 16), 81–2.

[68] De Maistre, 'Considerations' (n. 16), 81–2.

[69] De Maistre, 'Generative Principles' (n. 48), 157.

[70] Edmund Burke, 'Speech to the House of Commons', in *Parliamentary History of England from the Earliest Period*, (1783) ('If these natural rights are further affirmed and declared by express covenants, if they are clearly defined and secured against chicane, against power and authority, by written instruments and positive engagements, they are still in a better condition'), 1315.

the outside that they are written down. De Maistre observes, for example, that it was only because existing rights were violated that the Magna Carta was written. Written constitutions represent a constitutional order in decline. As he puts it, because '[l]aws are only declarations of rights, and rights are not declared except when they are attacked', 'a multiplicity of written constitutional law shows only the multiplicity of conflicts and the danger of destruction'.[71] As a result, 'the weakness or fragility of a constitution is in direct relationship to the number of written constitutional articles.'[72]

IV. The Irrational Constitution

A second theme in de Maistre's writing is that well-functioning constitutional rules are often irrational. A nation's true constitution does not make sense from a philosopher's viewpoint; it does not conform to the canons of reason. Instead, it is a set of irrational, if not random, rules that manage to withstand the tides of change and which successfully govern the nation. Such irrational rules, according to de Maistre, are impossible to design.

De Maistre provides numerous examples of irrational constitutional rules that have demonstrated remarkable longevity. One is the monarchy. 'What is more irrational or absurd than that the son of a king, even a good king, should succeed him because he is his son?'[73] de Maistre wonders. 'A wise king may have a stupid son, a good king may have an abominable son.'[74] A more rational system, he points out, is that of Poland, in which nobles elected their king. 'But what has actually happened?' he asks. 'France was governed by sixty-six kings, some good, some bad, but mostly efficient, mostly capable . . . whereas Poland with its rational system is plunged into constant turbulence and has collapsed.'[75] The constitution of England was another irrational system which de Maistre much admired. That system 'works only by not working'.[76] He notes, for example, that '[h]abeas corpus . . . has been suspended so often and for such long periods that it could be argued that the exception has become the rule.'[77]

De Maistre's view was that the complex harmony of irrational rules is impossible to design. For example, the Habeas Corpus Act, which maintains itself through exception, could never have been designed this way: '[s]uppose for a moment that the authors of this famous Act had attempted to lay down the cases when it could be suspended, they would by that deed have destroyed it.'[78] The notion that an entire constitutional system can be designed from scratch is even more foolish, according to de Maistre. '[N]o assembly, a small number of men in relation to the

[71] De Maistre, 'Considerations' (n. 16), 78.
[72] De Maistre, 'Generative Principles' (n. 48), 151.
[73] Berlin (n. 1) (citing de Maistre), 7.
[74] Berlin (n. 1) (citing de Maistre), 7.
[75] Berlin (n. 1) (citing de Maistre), 7.
[76] De Maistre, 'Generative Principles' (n. 48), 151.
[77] De Maistre, 'Generative Principles' (n. 48), 149.
[78] De Maistre, 'Generative Principles' (n. 48), 149.

total population can ever carry through such a task.'[79] He asks '[w]hat eye is capable of comprehending all the circumstances that must fit a nation to a particular constitution?' and concludes that '[u]nless they refuse to see the truth, they must agree that this is impossible.'[80]

Such irrational rules, he argued, cannot be designed, but emerge unconsciously, or simply by accident: '[n]othing great has great beginnings.'[81] Even democracy, the form of government that the Enlightenment *philosophes* aimed to design, had accidental origins. De Maistre observes that in England, national representation 'was not a product of deliberation or the result of an action of the people making use of its ancient rights' but the result of the actions of 'an ambitious soldier' who, 'to satisfy his own designs, created the balance of the three powers after the Battle of Lewes, without knowing what he was doing.'[82] Likewise, democracy organically emerged from the feudal system. 'Having formed the local communities, the royal authority called them to the national assemblies; they could appear there only through deputies, and from this arose the representative system.'[83] De Maistre again points out that '[o]ne would have to have very little insight into what Bacon called *interiora rerum* to believe that men could have achieved such institutions by an anterior process of reasoning and that such institutions could be the product of deliberation.'[84] Thus, whenever democracy has succeeded in the past, it did so because of historical accident, not grand design.

De Maistre thus draws our attention to an element of randomness in constitution-making. Constitutional rules emerge unconsciously, through random acts that have unforeseen consequences. They develop through the acts of 'a thousand agents', who are mostly unconscious of what they are doing. De Maistre draws on the British experience when he notes that '[n]ever have statesmen gathered together and said: *Let us create three powers [and] balance them in such and such a manner.*'[85] Instead, the British constitution was the work of a finite number of unconscious acts: '[r]oman, ecclesiastic, and feudal law, Saxon, Norman and Danish customs, every kind of class privilege, prejudice and ambition, wars, revolts, revolutions, conquests and crusades, all the virtues, vices, sciences, errors and passions' all acted together to produce 'the most complex unity and the most delicate equilibrium of political forces the world has ever known'.[86]

These complex and irrational rules may be far from perfect. '[E]very political constitution has its essential faults which spring from its nature and which cannot be separated from it.'[87] Yet de Maistre believes that it is a mistake to think that such flaws can simply be removed, through an act of rational (re-)design. 'Social harmony is subject to the law of temperament, as is harmony properly speaking

[79] De Maistre, 'Considerations' (n. 16), 107.
[80] De Maistre, 'Considerations' (n. 16), 107.
[81] De Maistre, 'Generative Principles' (n. 48), 158.
[82] De Maistre, 'Considerations' (n. 16), 66–7.
[83] De Maistre, 'Considerations' (n. 16), 66.
[84] De Maistre, 'Considerations' (n. 16), 66.
[85] De Maistre, 'Generative Principles' (n. 48), 152.
[86] De Maistre, 'Generative Principles' (n. 48), 152.
[87] De Maistre, 'Generative Principles' (n. 48), 167.

in the musical scale.'[88] When one tries to '[g]et the fifths carefully in tune[,] the octaves will clash, and vice versa'. Discord therefore is 'inevitable', an intrinsic part of the divine order of constitutions.[89]

The irrational elements of constitutions ensure their stability. If we acknowledge that constitutions are irrational and can neither be designed nor perfected, political systems will be stable. By contrast, when constitutions are based on reason, the political system will be inherently unstable: what one man considers reasonable may be challenged and destroyed by another. Only where constitutions have irrational, deep historical foundations, with 'neither author nor date', will they produce stable government and withstand the tides of time. For de Maistre, therefore, there was perfection in imperfection.

V. The Symbolic Constitution

A third theme running through de Maistre's work is that constitutions succeed because of their symbolic nature. Constitutional rules remain unchallenged and upheld because of their symbolic value and their connection to something mystical. These symbolic and mystical elements both shape constitutions and make them work in practice. As discussed in the previous section, de Maistre rejects the very notion of constitutional design. A constitutional assembly may write a constitution, but it will be meaningless if it does not reflect the nation's true constitution. Even if it does reflect the nation's character, it still signals a constitutional order that is being challenged and therefore in decline. What is more, not all can be written. 'Although written laws are always only declarations of anterior rights, yet it is very far from true that everything that can be written is written; there is even in every constitution always something that cannot be written and that must be left behind a dark and impenetrable cloud on pain of overturning the state.'[90] De Maistre explains: 'as there is something in music that is impossible to annotate, there is something in all governments that is impossible to write.'[91]

What is impossible to write are the constitution's origins, which have 'neither author nor date'.[92] Constitutions have unknown roots, covered in a 'dark impenetrable cloud'. At times, de Maistre conceptualizes these origins in the religious realm and attributes them to God: 'since every constitution is divine in its origin, it follows that man cannot do anything unless he relies on God'.[93] At other times, de Maistre conceptualizes these mystical origins in a more sociological fashion and attributes them to the nation's history. It was the acts of a thousand agents, unconscious of what they were doing, that produced the constitution with 'neither author nor date'.[94]

88 De Maistre, 'Generative Principles' (n. 48), 167.
89 De Maistre, 'Generative Principles' (n. 48), 167.
90 De Maistre, 'Considerations' (n. 16), 77–8.
91 Bradley (n. 3) (citing de Maistre), 96.
92 De Maistre, 'Considerations' (n. 16), 77.
93 De Maistre, 'Generative Principles' (n. 48), 162.
94 Overall, in De Maistre, 'Generative Principles' (n. 48), de Maistre takes a more religious turn than in De Maistre, 'Considerations' (n. 16), which is more sociological.

It is this part that cannot be written, those mystical origins, that makes the constitution work in practice and endows governments with authority. Governments may try to obtain power through coercion—and many do—but the real source of power is symbolic, based on something sacred. This sacred source of power can be found in mythology, language, literature, tradition, and the hearts of all people.[95] All power, de Maistre argues, rests upon prejudices, or on 'opinions of some kind adopted prior to all examination'.[96] De Maistre's concept of prejudice is important here. He urges us not to 'take this word in bad part' because '[i]t does not necessarily signify false ideas, but only, in the strict sense of the word, any opinions adopted without examination.'[97] Such prejudices, according to de Maistre 'are essential to man; they are the real basis of his happiness and the palladium of empires' and '[w]ithout them, there can be neither religion, morality, nor government.'[98] Thus, according to de Maistre, it is the rules that are followed unthinkingly, and out of habit, that give government power.

Constitutions' sacred origins give them force. If something feels sacred, people will not touch it. By contrast, when people write down what is supposed to remain unwritten, governments lose their true source of power. De Maistre states that '[m]en never respect what they have made.'[99] As he explains, '[t]hat is why an elective king never possesses the moral force of a hereditary sovereign because he is not sufficiently *noble,* that is to say, he does not pose the kind of grandeur independent of men which is the work of time.'[100] In the end, people 'submit to sovereignty because they feel that is it something sacred that they can neither create nor destroy'.[101] This, according to de Maistre, is the real secret of power.

Prejudices and the mystics of government can be cultivated through symbols. De Maistre often compares government to religion: '[g]overnment is a true religion; it has its dogmas, its mysteries, its priests; to submit it to individual discussion is to destroy it; it has life only through the national mind, that is to say, political faith, which is a creed.'[102] The coronation of kings, for example, serves this purpose. It is a ritual of government, which enhances its sacred nature and its legitimacy.[103] Thus, like religion, government needs its symbols and dogmas to ensure the faith of its subjects.

In focusing on the symbolic nature of constitutions, de Maistre effectively excludes 'the people' from the constitution-making process.[104] While people may take part in the growth of constitutions, they should do so in unintentional ways, as constitutions remain insulated from the sphere of conscious decision. Constitutional power lies in the realm of prejudice, and ought to be taken for granted and followed unthinkingly. When a constitution has sacred origins, people cannot simply change it. Or, as de Maistre puts it, 'supposing that a law of this importance exists because it is written,

[95] Bradley (n. 3), 96. [96] De Maistre, 'Sovereignty' (n. 20), 108.
[97] De Maistre, 'Sovereignty' (n. 20), 108. [98] De Maistre, 'Sovereignty' (n. 20), 108.
[99] De Maistre, 'Sovereignty' (n. 20), 104. [100] De Maistre, 'Sovereignty' (n. 20), 104.
[101] De Maistre, 'Sovereignty' (n. 20), 104. [102] De Maistre, 'Sovereignty' (n. 20), 108–9.
[103] De Maistre, 'Generative Principles' (n. 48), 162.
[104] De Maistre, 'Sovereignty' (n. 20) ('of all monarchies, the hardest, most despotic, and the most intolerable is King *People*'), 127–8.

it is certain that whatever authority has written it will have the right to annul it... The essence of a fundamental law is that no-one has the right to abolish it: but how is it beyond human power if it has been made by someone?'[105]

De Maistre believes that the sacred and symbolic element of constitutions constrains even absolute monarchs. Even though written constitutions do not offer constraints, the symbolic and sacred dimensions of constitutions do: 'it is far from true that the will of the king does everything in a monarchy... Religion, laws, customs, opinion, class, and corporate privileges restrict the sovereign and prevent him from abusing his power; it is striking that kings have even been much more often accused of lacking will than of overexerting it.'[106] De Maistre's ideal government is thus a moderate monarch who is constrained by custom, habit, and prejudice.[107] He believes that only those ancient constraints can keep mankind's violent nature at bay.

VI. Conclusion: A Postmodern de Maistre?

Modern constitution-making is a product of Enlightenment thought.[108] Today, constitutions are always written, mostly rational, and often conform to global templates. The nineteenth and twentieth centuries brought the full force of modernity to bear on constitution-writing, and witnessed all those things that were so forcefully condemned by de Maistre.

While modern constitution-making is undoubtedly a product of Enlightenment thought, recent decades have seen an emerging attention to de Maistre's conception of a constitution. First, constitutional scholarship recognizes that there do not exist universal templates for constitutional design, and that constitutions need to be tailor-made for each nation. To illustrate, in a 1994 edited book volume on constitutionalism and identity, scholars including Jon Elster, Fred Schauer, and Cass Sunstein agree that '[m]odern constitutionalism cannot be reduced to any particular form or any specific identity or difference' and that 'cross-cultural transplantation of constitutional provisions is always dangerous, as an unreflected generalization from experience in a single culture is always likely to be wrong'.[109] Even international financial institutions such as the IMF and World Bank, which are well known for their focus on best practices and uniform policy prescriptions around the world, are increasingly touting the importance of tailor-made institutions.[110]

105 De Maistre, 'Generative Principles' (n. 48), 147.

106 De Maistre, 'Sovereignty' (n. 20), 115.

107 Bradley (n. 3), ix.

108 Hayek (n. 39), 108.

109 M. Rosenfeld, 'Modern Constitutionalism as Interplay Between Identity and Diversity', in M. Rosenfeld (ed.), *Constitutionalism, Identity, Difference and Legitimacy: Theoretical Perspectives* (Durham: Duke University Press, 1994), 35.

110 D. M. Trubek, 'The Rule of Law in Development Assistance: Past, Present and Future', in D. M. Trubek and A. Santos (eds), *The New Law and Economic Development* (Cambridge: Cambridge University Press, 2006), 74.

Second, like de Maistre, some modern scholars have challenged the notion that constitutional rules should be rational. Development economist Dani Rodrik, in a 2008 article in the *American Economic Review,* propagates a 'second-best mindset' in institutional design, which focuses on 'second-best institutions', which may actually be preferable to all others because of a nation's existing practices and culture.[111] Third, ever since Robert Merton popularized the idea,[112] attention has been paid to the accidental origins of constitutions as well as the unintended consequences that flow from constitutional design.[113] In a recent volume on *The Social and Political Foundations of Constitutions*, several scholars observe that important constitutional rules and practices have emerged by accident. In New Zealand, for instance, proportional representation was put on the agenda because the Prime Minister misread his note on national television.[114]

Finally, even the notion of constitutions as symbolic and sacred, probably the most controversial one among de Maistre's constitutional theories, has a surprisingly modern ring. Jack Balkin, in his 2011 book *Constitutional Redemption*, argued that the US Constitution is upheld because people have faith in it, much like they have faith in God. 'A well-designed constitution can fall apart in months without public attachment and support; an imperfect constitution can last for centuries', Balkin notes, because what ultimately matters is whether the people have faith in their constitution.[115] Like de Maistre, Balkin argues that 'constitutional traditions have much in common with religious traditions', and draws on the religious metaphor extensively to explain why the American Constitution is legitimate and complied with in practice.[116] What matters is not how well the constitution is designed, but whether it manages to capture popular imagination, and whether it gains a sacrosanct status.

All of these contemporary themes are arguably postmodernist in nature: they reject the excessive rationalism and universalism of modernity and instead emphasize 'human finitude, imperfection', 'limits', and 'irrationality'.[117] Indeed, it has been noted that these contemporary postmodern themes are essentially an extension of the counter-enlightenment tradition found in the writings of not only de Maistre, but also Burke, Vico, and Von Savigny, to name but a few. Both the counter-enlightenment thinkers of de Maistre's day and the postmodernist of today focus on the indigenous, the irrational, and the symbolic aspects of constitutions. These similarities suggest that there may still be a place for de Maistre in twenty-first-century constitutional thought.

[111] D. Rodrik, 'Second Best Institutions', *American Economic Review* 98 (2008), 100.

[112] R. K. Merton, 'The Unanticipated Consequences of Purposive Social Action', *American Sociological Review* 1 (1936), 894.

[113] D. J. Galligan and M. Versteeg, 'Theoretical Perspectives on the Social and Political Foundations of Constitutions', in D. Galligan and M. Versteeg (eds), *The Social and Political Foundations of Constitutions* (New York: Cambridge University Press, 2014), 23.

[114] D. Erdos, 'New Zealand: Abandoning Westminister?', in Galligan and Versteeg (eds), *The Social and Political Foundations of Constitutions*, 338.

[115] J. M. Balkin, *Constitutional Redemption: Political Faith in an Unjust World* (Cambridge, MA: Harvard University Press, 2011), 6.

[116] Balkin, *Constitutional Redemption*, 7.

[117] Bradley (n. 3), xiii; Habermas (n. 8), 7–11; Nisbet (n. 17), xvi.

15

James Madison's Republican Constitutionalism

Mark A. Graber

I. Introduction

James Madison's writings during the late eighteenth century made much of the distinction between a democracy and a republic.[1] Both were species of popular government. Democracy, Madison believed, had been tried and failed. History demonstrated that democratic governments were too unstable and too prone to violating rights. *The Federalist No. 14* admitted that the classical criticisms of popular government were correct when applied to democracy.[2] Four papers earlier, Madison asserted, 'a pure democracy . . . can admit no cure for the mischief of factions.'[3] This disease had fatally weakened all previous regimes whose power was derived solely from the general populace. Republican governments, Madison believed, promised to treat this deadly democratic failing. Aided by the new science of politics, republicanism was the last best hope for friends of popular government.[4]

Contemporary constitutionalists make much less of the distinction between a democracy and a republic. Consider the republican revival that took place in American constitutional law scholarship during the 1970s and 1980s. Bernard Bailyn and Gordon Wood had previously detailed how such civil republican thinkers as Thomas Gordon and John Trenchard, as well as prominent participants in the Scottish enlightenment, influenced American revolutionary and constitutional thought during the late eighteenth century.[5] Frank Michelman, Cass Sunstein, and others sought to translate this new-found republican heritage into constitutional doctrine. '[C]ontemporary American constitutional understanding and

[1] See especially, A. Hamilton, J. Madison, and J. Jay, *The Federalist Papers* (New York: New American Press, 1961), 82.

[2] Hamilton, Madison, and Jay, *The Federalist Papers*, 100.

[3] Hamilton, Madison, and Jay, *The Federalist Papers*, 81.

[4] See G. S. Wood, *The Creation of the American Republic, 1776–1787* (Chapel Hill: University of North Carolina Press, 1969).

[5] See G. S. Wood, *The Creation of the American Republic, 1776–1787* (Chapel Hill: University of North Carolina Press, 1969); B. Bailyn, *The Ideological Origins of the American Revolution* (Cambridge, MA: Harvard University Press, 1967).

analysis might benefit', Michelman wrote in 1988, 'from serious and sympathetic (but not uncritical) reflection upon the civic–republican strain in political thought that has been identified, traced, and analyzed in much recent writing on history, social and political theory, and American constitutionalism.'[6] The target of this republican revival was the classical liberalism represented by John Locke and Adam Smith rather than the proto-democratic commitments of some anti-Federalists. Sunstein asserted, '[i]t is no longer possible to see a Lockean consensus in the founding period, or to treat the Framers as modern pluralists believing that self-interest is the inevitable motivating force behind political behavior.'[7] Republicans, revisionists claim, are democrats. Michelman, Sunstein, and others insisted that infusing contemporary American constitutionalism with classical republican values would make the political system more democratic. Suzanna Sherry declared, '[a] republican polity . . . would recognize the importance of instilling in children the values and virtues necessary for life in that democratic society.'[8] Sunstein emphasized the republican commitment to political equality. 'Political equality, in republican terms', he stated, 'is understood as a requirement that all individuals and groups have access to the political process; large disparities in political influence are disfavored.'[9]

Contemporary democratic theorists similarly conflate republics and democracies. Robert Dahl, the pre-eminent American democratic theorist of the late twentieth century, rejects any strong distinction between these forms of popular government. Dahl declares 'mistaken' the 'not uncommon belief among Americans . . . that the United States is not a democracy but a republic'.[10] This mistaken belief, Dahl complains, has unfortunate consequences. Convinced that the constitution rejects democracy, some citizens blithely tolerate such undemocratic constitutional practices as the Electoral College or state equality in the Senate.[11]

Madison's analysis in the *Federalist Papers* is one source of this widespread error. The crucial passage in *The Federalist No. 10* insisted:

> [T]he two great points of difference between a democracy and a republic are: first, the delegation of the government, in the latter, to a small number of citizens elected by the rest; secondly, the greater number of citizens, and sphere of country, over which the latter may be extended.[12]

This eighteenth-century distinction between 'a democracy and a republic', Dahl points out, corresponds to the contemporary distinction between 'direct democracy' and 'representative democracy'.[13] Nowhere in the *Federalist Papers* does

[6] F. Michelman, 'Law's Republic', *Yale Law Journal* 97 (1988), 1493.

[7] C. R. Sunstein, 'Beyond the Republican revival', *Yale Law Journal* 97 (1988), 1539, 1540.

[8] S. Sherry, 'Speaking of Virtue: A Republican Approach to University Regulation of Hate Speech', *Minnesota Law Review* 75 (1991), 933, 942.

[9] Sunstein, 'Republican Revival,' 1552.

[10] R. A. Dahl, *How Democratic is the American Constitution?* (New Haven: Yale University Press, 2002), 5.

[11] See generally, Dahl, *How Democratic is the American Constitution?*, 4–6.

[12] Hamilton, Madison, and Jay, *The Federalist Papers*, 82.

[13] Dahl, *How Democratic is the American Constitution?*, 160.

Madison distinguish between majority rule and some other grounds popular governments might employ when making official decisions. Terminology aside, little difference apparently exists between what Madison thought was a republic and what contemporary citizens think is a representative democracy. Michelman, Sunstein, and Sherry seem right when they insist that better republican practices are better democratic practices.

Madison bears some responsibility for this contemporary terminological confusion. His writings, and those of many contemporaries, fail to define consistently 'democracy' and 'republic.' Many eighteenth-century constitutionalists commonly spoke of 'democracy' and 'republic' when describing similar governing arrangements. Dahl and others observe how the terms were 'used rather interchangeably in both common and philosophical usage'.[14] Madison did not even consistently adhere throughout the rest of the *Federalist Papers* to the distinction he made in *The Federalist No. 10* between 'a republic and a democracy.' *The Federalist No. 39* states:

> [W]e may define a republic to be a . . . a government which derives all its powers directly or indirectly from the great body of the people, and is administered by persons holding their offices during pleasure, for a limited period, or during good behavior.[15]

If this is the definition of a republic, then both representative and some direct democracies are republics. Any direct democracy which entrusts implementation to particular individuals is a republic. Certainly this definition of a republic does not distinguish a republic from a polity committed to majority rule. More precise and rigorously followed terminology might be useful. Nevertheless, if our concern is with majority rule, Dahl is correct to observe that Madison's distinction between democracies and republics does little work at present and was not followed consistently even at a time when direct democracy might have seemed a viable form of government.

Dahl recognizes some differences between Madison's understanding of popular government and contemporary democratic constitutionalism. Classical republicanism, he writes:

> both in theory and in practice leaned somewhat more toward aristocracy, limited suffrage, concern for property rights, and fear of the populace than toward a broadly based popular government more dependent on 'the will of the people.'[16]

Dahl treats these practices as deficiencies in early democratic theory. The Framers appeared rather early in the democratic evolutionary chain. Their understandings of popular government were immature. The democratic deficits in the Constitution of 1789 are consequences of the political inexperience and naivety of its drafters. Under the heading 'What the Framers Couldn't Know', Dahl states, '[w]ise as the

[14] Dahl, *How Democratic is the American Constitution?*, 160.
[15] Hamilton, Madison, and Jay, *The Federalist Papers*, 241.
[16] Dahl, *How Democratic is the American Constitution?*, 160.

framers were, they were necessarily limited by their profound ignorance.'[17] Dahl points out that 'ideas and beliefs about what democracy requires, and thus what a democratic republic requires, would continue to evolve down to the present day'.[18] This developmental process would take popular government 'far beyond the conceptions of the Framers and would even transcend the views of such early democrats as Jefferson and Madison'.[19] So understood, Madison's republicanism emerges as an inferior conception of constitutional democracy rather than an as alternative governing arrangement.

This paper takes Madison's distinction between a republic and a democracy more seriously than do many contemporary scholars. Eighteenth-century republicans championed governing arrangements that they perceived were quite different from democratic orders. They understood both republics and democracies as forms of popular government in which all government power is derived from the people through regular elections or appointments by officials who are regularly elected. Nevertheless, the 'telos' of these forms of popular government differs. Classical republicans saw representation primarily as a means for promoting the common good and protecting minority rights. Popular government is superior to a monarchy, an aristocracy, or a balanced regime, from the republican perspective, because a system in which popular majorities exercise the ultimate control over public policy is more likely to promote the common good and protect minority rights than a balanced regime or a regime that excludes popular participation completely. Contemporary democrats see representation as a means, often a necessary evil, for ensuring that government is responsive to public opinion. Popular government is superior to a monarchy, an aristocracy, or a balanced regime, from the democratic perspective, because a system in which popular majorities exercise the ultimate control over public policy is more likely than a regime in which political power is inherited to promote a society of equal power holders in which all persons and interests are treated with equal concern and respect.

Madison was a republican constitutionalist. He and most of his contemporaries rejected the foundational egalitarian commitments of contemporary democratic constitutionalism. Madison rejected equality as the foundational value of popular government. He believed that the purpose of popular government, republican government in particular, was to secure the common good and protect individual rights. Republican institutions in the United States were designed to secure the same ends as balanced government in Great Britain. Both were means for promoting a prosperous, secure society that respected property and religious freedom. Republican government was superior to both balanced government and democratic government because republican means were more likely to achieve the ambitions of

[17] Dahl, *How Democratic is the American Consttution?*, 7. See also S. Levinson, *Our Undemocratic Constitution: Where the Constitution Goes Wrong (and How We the People Can Correct It)* (New York: Oxford University Press, 2006), 15.

[18] Dahl, *How Democratic is the American Constitution?*, 10.

[19] Dahl, *How Democratic is the American Constitution?*, 10.

those regimes. Madison rejected the contemporary democratic aspiration to a society of equal power holders. He believed that republican political institutions should be designed in ways that privileged the election of a virtuous elite likely to secure the common good and protect individual rights. Public opinion, in his view, checked government tendencies towards oppression, but was not the proper guide for official decision-making. To the extent that deviations from universal suffrage contributed to the instrumental goals of republican governance, Madison had no difficulty abandoning the democratic commitment to political equality. He rejected government neutrality towards the good, believing that a common good existed that was independent of what popular majorities might think at any time. Republican institutions were designed to identify and secure that common good, not to identify and satisfy popular interests or preferences. Rights were closely connected with public and private virtues. People had rights to freely practise their religion, because voluntary devotion to God was more virtuous than coerced obedience.

Nothing in this essay hinges on the precise distinction between 'democratic' and 'republican'. Both political theory and politics defy attempts to standardize the terms of political discourse. Madison did not always use the terms consistently, and neither did his contemporaries.[20] The founders of the Republican Party insisted that Jacksonians who called themselves 'Democrats' were actually part of a coalition dominated by a slave-power bent on violating the right of white majorities to rule.[21] Contemporary members of the Republican Party in the United States are no more republican (or democratic) than contemporary members of the Democratic Party. The republican revival, both in American history and American constitutional law, treats republicanism as an alternative to liberalism rather than to democracy. Lest this confusion seem insufficient, Stephen Feldman has recently published a history of free speech and democracy in the United States that relies on a different distinction between a republic and a democracy than found in the following pages.[22] In short, no politician or scholar has good title to 'democracy' or 'republicanism'. The crucial point is that what Madison classified as a 'republican' regime had different foundational principles than what many contemporaries classify as a 'democratic' regime.

Madison's distinction between a republic and a democracy was rooted in an appreciation of important differences in the forms of popular regimes or constitutions. Madison championed popular government for republican reasons. He believed that well-designed popular governments were the best means for securing the common good and protecting substantive liberties. Regarding elections primarily as a means to these ends, he sought to design constitutional orders that would enable particularly virtuous persons to hold public office. The Madisonian commitment to the existence of a common good, a virtuous elite, and particularly

[20] Dahl, *How Democratic is the Constitution?*, 179–84.

[21] See E. Foner, *Free Soil, Free Labor, Free Men: The Ideology of the Republican Party Before the Civil War* (New York: Oxford University Press, 1970).

[22] S. M. Feldman, *Free Expression and Democracy in America: A History* (Chicago: University of Chicago Press, 2008).

desirable life plans was grounded in the principles that he thought best justified popular government. Contemporary democrats who reject these commitments do so because they believe popular government serves very different ends, not because two hundred years of experience led them to conclude that Madisonian ends are best served by non-Madisonian means.

Madison's republican constitutionalism is quite different from contemporary democratic constitutionalism, even when we recognize that few contemporary democrats endorse direct democracy. Contrary to Robert Bork, Madison did not believe that 'in wide areas of life majorities are entitled to rule... simply because they are majorities'.[23] Contrary to Cass Sunstein, Madison did not believe that constitutions should foster deliberation about politics among ordinary citizens.[24] More generally, what now passes for Madisonian constitutionalism has everything to do with New Deal understandings of constitutional democracy, and very little in common with most eighteenth-century thinkers.[25] Madisonian republicanism was rooted in notions about the common good, a virtuous class of potential political leaders, and a theory of the human good. Few contemporary democrats hold these values. Rather, contemporary democratic thought is rooted in far more relativistic and egalitarian principles. This essay does not referee the contest between eighteenth-century republicanism and turn-of-the-twenty-first-century democracy. Contemporary democrats may well be right that Madisonian commitments mask an undemocratic elitism. Still, given that Madisonian commitments are far too aristocratic for the taste of any contemporary constitutional theorist, those thinkers should acknowledge the contemporary roots of their constitutional thinking and not pretend that they are merely elaborating themes announced in *The Federalist Nos 10* and *51*.

II. Madison as Republican

Madison was a 'faint-hearted' majoritarian,[26] but not an egalitarian. Proponents of republican government, in his view, were committed to majority rule. His 'Vices of the Political System of the United States' declared that 'the fundamental principle of republican government' is that 'the majority who rule in such governments are the safest guardians both of public good and private rights.'[27] This commitment to

[23] R. H. Bork, *The Tempting of America: The Political Seduction of the Law* (New York: Free Press, 1989), 139.

[24] See C. R. Sunstein, *The Partial Constitution* (Cambridge, MA: Harvard University Press, 1998).

[25] The best account of the transformation of democracy during the New Deal is E. A. Purcell, *The Crisis of Democratic Theory: Scientific Naturalism and the Problem of Value* (Lexington: University of Kentucky Press, 1973).

[26] See generally, A. Scalia, 'Originalism: The Lesser Evil', *University of Cincinnati Law Review* 57 (1989), 849, 863–4 (claiming to be a 'faint-hearted originalist').

[27] J. Madison, 'Diagnosis of the American Confederacy: A Critical Case', *The Mind of the Founder: Sources of the Political Thought of James Madison*, ed. M. Meyers (Hanover: University Press of New England, 1981), 62.

majority rule did not, however, entail commitments to a political system in which all persons have an equal influence on public policy or a political system in which the policy preferred by the most persons is always chosen. Madison rejected the contemporary democratic principle that whatever majorities in a properly constructed electoral system prefer constitutes the best conception of the 'public good and private rights'. He favoured popular republican government because he believed popular republican government was the best means for achieving desirable political ends. The 'Father of the American Constitution' thought public good and private rights had an existence independent from public opinion. Madison and other republican proponents of popular government claimed that well-designed republican institutions could better secure the public good and private rights than balanced government, aristocracy, or monarchy. Significantly, this proposition was empirical not normative. Madison believed the connection between republicanism and the public good required the test of experience, not an axiom which identified the public good with whatever majorities might want.

The Federalist No. 10 articulated the instrumental nature of republican government. That essay first expressed concern with the 'instability, injustice, and confusion introduced into the public councils' by popular government in the United States.[28] Madison then stated that these failings have had serious consequences:

> Complaints are everywhere heard from our most considerate and virtuous citizens . . . that our governments are too unstable, that the public good is disregarded in the conflicts of rival parties, and that measures are too often decided, not according to the rules of justice and the rights of the minor party, but by the superior force of an interested and overbearing majority.[29]

These problems were caused by the political factions that form in political regimes committed to popular sovereignty. 'By a faction', Madison declared:

> I understand a number of citizens, whether amounting to a majority or minority of the whole, who are united and actuated by some common impulse of passion, or of interest, adverse to the rights of other citizens, or to the permanent and aggregate interests of the community.[30]

Democracies cannot resolve the problems that factions cause. Madison maintained:

> [t]he smaller the society, the fewer probably will be the distinctive parties and interests composing it; the fewer the distinct parties and interests, the more frequently will a majority be found of the same party; and the smaller the number of individuals composing a majority, and the smaller the compass within which they are placed, the more easily will they concert and execute their plans of oppression.[31]

Republican governments, by comparison, deliver the goods. *The Federalist No. 10* pointed to two distinctions between a republic and a democracy that make republics

[28] Hamilton, Madison, and Jay, *The Federalist Papers*, 77.
[29] Hamilton, Madison, and Jay, *The Federalist Papers*, 77.
[30] Hamilton, Madison, and Jay, *The Federalist Papers*, 78.
[31] Hamilton, Madison, and Jay, *The Federalist Papers*, 83.

far more likely than democracies to secure the public good and private rights. The first advantage of republicanism 'consist[s] in the substitution of representatives whose enlightened views and virtuous sentiments render them superior to local prejudices and to schemes of injustice'.[32] The second advantage of republicanism was 'the greater security afforded by a greater variety of parties, against the event of any one party being able to outnumber and oppress the rest'.[33]

Madison judged republicanism by results, not by procedures. Unlike Dahl or Rawls, Madison insisted that popular government was justified primarily as a means to distinctive ends. The end of government is the public good and the protection of individual rights: '[t]o secure the public good and private rights against the danger of such a faction, and at the same time to preserve the spirit and the form of popular government, is then the great object to which our inquiries are directed', *The Federalist No. 10* asserted.[34] For Madison, a perfect system of political equality constitutes good government only to the extent that political equality secures those ends.

In the *Federalist Papers*, in the 'Vices', and in other writings, Madison claims that popular government is on trial. He wrote, 'The friend of popular governments never finds himself so much alarmed for their character and fate, as when he contemplates their propensity to [faction].'[35] Republicans need to prove that they can construct a popular government that performs better than the British constitution. Should experience demonstrate that a hereditary aristocracy performs better than the people's elected representatives, that experience would justify rule by the traditional nobility.

Madison's dispute with Hamilton over the structure of the executive branch provides an even clearer example of the former's distinctive republican commitments. Hamilton believed that the chief executive should be elected for life, and may even have favoured British-style balanced government with a hereditary monarchy.[36] Hamilton favoured these arrangements because he believed every elected official who had to curry favour with popular majorities would neglect the permanent interests of the community. At the framing convention, the New Yorker asserted:

> The English model was the only good one on this subject. The hereditary interest of the king was so interwoven with that of the nation, and his personal emoluments so great, that he was placed above the danger of being corrupted from abroad, and at the same time, was both sufficiently independent and sufficiently controlled to answer the purpose of the institution at home.[37]

[32] Hamilton, Madison, and Jay, *The Federalist Papers*, 83–4.

[33] Hamilton, Madison, and Jay, *The Federalist Papers*, 83.

[34] Hamilton, Madison, and Jay, *The Federalist Papers*, 80.

[35] Hamilton, Madison, and Jay, *The Federalist Papers*, 77.

[36] I am indebted to Michael Evans for this point, and more generally, for the analysis in this paragraph. See M. C. Evans, *The Republic and Its Problems: Alexander Hamilton And James Madison On The 18th Century Critique Of Republics* (PhD dissertation, University of Maryland, 2009).

[37] James Madison, 'Journal of the Constitutional Convention', in *The Writings of James Madison: Comprising His Public Papers and His Private Correspondence* (Vol IV), ed. G. Hunt (New York: G. P. Putnam's Sons, 1902), 191.

Madison disagreed. He strongly favoured an elected executive. He did so, however, because he believed an elected executive and the prospect for re-election would more likely encourage office holders to pursue the public good. Consider Madison's analysis of executive removals. He began with the premise that a simple removal process was vital to republican government. 'The danger to liberty, the danger of mal-administration, has not yet been found to lie so much in the facility of introducing improper persons into office', he informed Congress in 1789, 'as in the difficulty of displacing those who are unworthy of the public trust.'[38] Madison then emphasized that republican virtue would best be maintained by giving an elected president the sole right to determine whether a cabinet official be removed. He stated:

> Vest this power in the Senate jointly with the President, and you abolish at once that great principle of unity and responsibility in the Executive department, which was intended for the security of liberty and the public good. If the President should possess alone the power of removal from office, those who are employed in the execution of the law will be in their proper situation, and the chain of dependence be preserved; the lowest officers, the middle grade, and the highest, will depend, as they ought, on the President, and the President on the community. The chain of dependence therefore terminates in the supreme body, namely, in the people, who will possess, besides, in aid of their original power, the decisive engine of impeachment.[39]

At no point did Madison suggest that elections had intrinsic virtues or that Hamilton was wrong to worry about elections being popularity contests. Madison was for an elected executive only because he believed that, properly checked and with a sufficient term of office, an elected executive would have more incentive to pursue the public good than a hereditary monarch.

Having different governing officials check each other, as Gordon Wood points out, revised inherited understandings about how the separation of powers would promote the common good and protect rights. The traditional understanding, from Aristotle to John Adams, was that the common good and private rights were best secured when different governing institutions represented different interests. Dividing government between the one (hereditary monarch), the few (the aristocracy), and the many (the people) empowered the populace to prevent government tyranny while placing power in the hands of those most attached to and best able to discern the permanent interests of the community. Madison thought the same ends would be achieved more efficiently if different government institutions representing the same constituency checked each other. The necessary diversity would be a consequence of the different manner in which government officials in each branch of government were selected, their different terms of office, and their different powers. 'In the compound republic of America', Madison wrote:

> the power surrendered by the people is first divided between two distinct governments, and then the portion allotted to each subdivided among distinct and separate departments.

[38] *Annals of Congress*, 1st Cong., 1st sess., 515.

[39] *Annals of Congress*, 1st Cong., 1st sess., 496, 499.

> Hence a double security arises to the rights of the people. The different governments will control each other, at the same time that each will be controlled by itself.[40]

In keeping with the inherited republican suspicion of popular rule, Madison insisted that the legislature—the most democratic branch of the national government—was the national governing institution whose power required the most checks. *The Federalist No. 51* maintained that the more politically accountable the branch of government, the more the branch needed to be weakened. Madison declared:

> In republican government, the legislative authority necessarily predominates. The remedy for this inconvenience is to divide the legislature into different branches; and to render them, by different modes of election and different principles of action, as little connected with each other as the nature of their common functions and their common dependence will admit ... As the weight of the legislative authority requires that it should be thus divided, the weakness of the executive may require, on the other hand, that it should be fortified. An absolute negative on the legislature appears, at first view, to be the natural defense with which the executive magistrate should be armed. But perhaps it would be neither altogether safe nor alone sufficient ... May not this defect of an absolute negative be supplied by some qualified connection between this weaker department and the weaker branch of the stronger department [the Senate], by which the latter may be led to support the constitutional rights of the former, without being too much detached from the rights of its own department?[41]

The goal of democratic representation is to increase the influence of public opinion on public policy. As Madison's analysis of the separation of powers suggests, republican constitutionalism seeks to combine frequent elections with a governing structure that minimizes the influence of public opinion on public policy.

Madison's instrumental defence of popular government explains why he was far less concerned with voting rights than contemporary democratic theorists. Both Madison and contemporary democratic theorists believe that government is more likely to advance the common good only if the great body of people votes. Madison in *The Federalist No. 52* insisted, '[t]he definition of the right of suffrage is very justly regarded as a fundamental article of republican government.'[42] He did not, however, insist on universal (male) suffrage or that the constitution adopt the principle of one person/one vote. Madison in *The Federalist No. 52* seemed content with the constitutional provision that gave persons a right to vote in federal elections if they had a right to vote for a member of the most numerous branch of the state legislature.[43] Neither during the constitutional convention nor in the Virginia state legislature did Madison lead the fight for removing restrictions on suffrage. When deviations from one person/one vote might promote the common good, Madison was willing to deviate. With respect to both real property and slavery, he insisted that who cast ballots should depend on what electorate would be most likely to pursue the public good, not on the intrinsic value of the right to vote.

[40] Hamilton, Madison, and Jay, *The Federalist Papers*, 323.
[41] Hamilton, Madison, and Jay, *The Federalist Papers*, 322–3.
[42] Hamilton, Madison, and Jay, *The Federalist Papers*, 326.
[43] Hamilton, Madison, and Jay, *The Federalist Papers*, 326.

Madison opposed universal suffrage on the grounds that 'the rights of property or the claims of justice may be overruled by a majority without property, or interested in measures of injustice'.[44]

When defending the three-fifths clause—the clause which counts slaves as three-fifths of a person for purposes of apportioning representatives to the lower house of the national legislature—Madison declared:

> Government is instituted no less for protection of the property, than of the persons, of individuals. The one as well as the other, therefore, may be considered as represented by those who are charged with the government.[45]

The Federalist No. 54 recognizes that the three-fifths clause was one of the 'compromising expedients'[46] of the constitution. Nevertheless, Madison supported that compromise. He would not have the president elected by a popular vote, because that would deny southerners representation 'on the score of their Negroes'.[47]

Madison the republican constitutional thinker was as concerned with the character of the representatives as with the character of the electorate. When preparing for the constitutional convention in 1787, he came to the conclusion that the fundamental flaw in the constitutional governments of the United States was that unqualified persons were being elected. Democratic elections were rewarding popularity rather than virtue. Under the Articles of Confederation, Madison bemoaned, politicians successfully gained power by 'veiling [their] selfish views under the professions of public good, and varnishing [their] sophistical arguments with the glowing colors of popular eloquence'.[48] The large republic remedied this democratic failing by promoting virtuous rather than popular representation. *The Federalist No. 10* asserts that one consequence of expanding the sphere of government will be:

> to refine and enlarge the public views, by passing them through the medium of a chosen body of citizens, whose wisdom may best discern the true interest of their country, and whose patriotism and love of justice will be least likely to sacrifice it to temporary or partial considerations.[49]

Madison insisted this system of republican representation would yield public policy far better than would be the case if an unmediated public opinion were permitted to reign. '[T]he public voice, pronounced by the representatives of the people, will be more consonant to the public good', he wrote, 'than if pronounced by the people themselves, convened for the purpose.'[50]

[44] Madison, 'Property and Suffrage: Second Thoughts on the Constitutional Convention', in *The Mind of the Founder*, 395.

[45] Hamilton, Madison, and Jay, *The Federalist Papers*, 332.

[46] Hamilton, Madison, and Jay, *The Federalist Papers*, 339.

[47] *The Records of the Federal Convention of 1787*, ed. M. Farrand (New Haven: Yale University Press, 1937), 57.

[48] Madison, 'Diagnosis of the American Confederacy', in *The Mind of the Founder*, 62.

[49] Hamilton, Madison, and Jay, *The Federalist Papers*, 82.

[50] Hamilton, Madison, and Jay, *The Federalist Papers*, 82.

The precise role virtuous statespersons play in Madisonian thought is not entirely clear. When detailing the merits of a large republic, *The Federalist No. 10* acknowledges that voters would not always elect the most qualified governing officials. 'It is in vain to say that enlightened statesmen will be able to adjust . . . clashing interests and render them all subservient to the public good', Madison wrote. In his famous view, '[e]nlightened statesmen will not always be at the helm.'[51] Institutional arrangements were necessary to compensate for the deficit of virtue. Madison thought the large republic and the separation of powers would hinder interest representation in part by placing difficult barriers against elected officials who had some penchant for factional behaviour. One advantage of extending the sphere of government, he wrote, 'consist[s] in the greater obstacles opposed to the concert and accomplishment of the secret wishes of an unjust and interested majority'.[52]

Still, the Madisonian system required that voters more often than not elect candidates capable of discerning the public good and protecting private rights. Madison believed that Americans in the early 1780s were experiencing a failing political regime because government practices were generating elected officials without the requisite capacities for governing. He complained about 'interest' and 'ambition' motivating more government officials than the 'public good'. 'How frequently', Madison wrote, 'will the honest but unenlightened representative be the dupe of a favorite leader?'[53] The Constitution of the United States promised two solutions to this problem. The first was a large republic which would 'substitut[e] . . . representatives whose enlightened views and virtuous sentiments render them superior to local prejudices and schemes of injustice'.[54] The second was:

> such a process of elections as will most certainly extract from the mass of the Society the purest and noblest characters which it contains; such as will at once feel most strongly the proper motives to pursue the end of their appointment, and be most capable to devise the proper means of attaining it.[55]

When the *Federalist Papers* mention the virtues of republican constitutionalism, the first merit is that responsible representatives are more likely to be elected in more populous election districts and the second is that the large republic will force representatives to act virtuously. *The Federalist No. 57* insists that:

> [t]he aim of every political constitution is, or ought to be, first to obtain for rulers men who possess most wisdom to discern, and most virtue to pursue, the common good of the society; and in the next place, to take the most effectual precautions for keeping them virtuous whilst they continue to hold their public trust.[56]

Such practices as the separation of powers and the large republic are designed to force representatives to pursue the common good rather than the interests of their

[51] Hamilton, Madison and Jay, *The Federalist Papers*, 80.
[52] Hamilton, Madison and Jay, *The Federalist Papers*, 84.
[53] Madison, 'Diagnosis of the American Confederacy', 62.
[54] Hamilton, Madison, and Jay, *The Federalist Papers*, 83–4.
[55] Madison, 'Diagnosis of the American Confederacy', 65.
[56] Hamilton, Madison and Jay, *The Federalist Papers*, 350.

constituents. Madison's republican constitutionalism, in short, established a popular government that privileged the election of the virtuous and established a political process that facilitated the creation of virtuous republican representatives.

Prominent late-eighteenth-century proponents of republican government shared Madison's commitment to virtuous representation. Gordon Wood points out that many American Revolutionaries believed '[i]f the political rulers were men of merit and talent and governed only in the public interest, they would naturally command the affection and respect of the people'.[57] Most Framers may not have understood or endorsed Madison's argument in *The Federalist No. 10* that large republics generate a political process that better promotes the public good.[58] Nevertheless, proponents of ratification in the late 1780s consistently celebrated the constitution for establishing procedures for staffing the federal government that privileged the selection of particularly qualified representatives. Ratification, John Jay declared, would guarantee that 'the best men in the country will not only consent to serve, but also will generally be appointed to manage [the polity]'.[59] 'The process of election affords a moral certainty', Hamilton wrote, 'that the office of President will never fall to the lot of any man who is not in an eminent degree endowed with the requisite qualifications.' In his republican view, '[i]t will not be too strong to say, that there will be a constant probability of seeing the station filled by characters pre-eminent for ability and virtue'.[60]

Madisonian republicanism and contemporary democratic theory reject simple voting systems, but they do so for different reasons.[61] Madison endorsed complex forms of government in order to prevent public opinion from having too much influence on public policy. The point of the large republic and long terms of office are to loosen the bond between elected officials and citizens, thereby reducing the problem of faction. Elections are necessary to ensure that governing officials procure the public good, but they should not be structured in ways that promote too close a connection between social interests and public policy. Representation, Madison thought, was a means 'to refine and enlarge the public views by passing them through the medium of a chosen body of citizens, whose wisdom may best discern the true interest of their country'. '[I]t may well happen', he declared, 'that the public voice, pronounced by the representatives of the people, will be more consonant to the public good than if pronounced by the people themselves.'[62] Many contemporary democratic theorists reject simple majority rule because that system weakens the influence of public opinion on public policy. They propose voting schemes designed to increase the number of people who influence

57 G. S. Wood, *The Radicalism of the American Revolution* (New York: Alfred A. Knopf, 1992), 189.

58 See L. D. Kramer, 'Madison's Audience', *Harvard Law Review* 112 (1999), 611.

59 Hamilton, Madison, and Jay, *The Federalist Papers*, 3.

60 Hamilton, Madison, and Jay, *The Federalist Papers*, 414.

61 For a longer version of the argument in this paragraph, see M. A. Graber, 'Conflicting Representations: Lani Guinier and James Madison on Electoral Systems', *Constitutional Commentary* 13 (1996), 291.

62 Hamilton, Madison, and Jay, *The Federalist Papers*, 82.

governmental decisions, maximize representation, or fine-tune the extent to which every interest is treated with equal concern and respect. Douglas Amy maintains that proportional representation will 'minimize wasted votes, give minor parties fair representation in our legislatures, improve the quality of campaigns, increase the number of women and racial minority officeholders, encourage more voter participation, and increase the responsiveness and legitimacy of government'.[63] Lani Guinier believes that cumulative voting enables significant political minorities to 'assert their most salient interests and to hold their elected officials accountable for advocating those interests'.[64] Madison had little interest in such electoral schemes, with the crucial exception of those aimed at balancing the political powers of the free and the enslaved.[65] His representatives were supposed to be virtuous, not representative.

III. The Common Good

Madison's notion of the common good partly blurs the sharp line this paper draws between republican and democratic constitutionalism. Professor Steven Elkin observes that 'Madison . . . said surprisingly little about the content of the permanent interests of the community'.[66] Most of what he said suggests that all forms of popular government share common purposes. The first seventeen papers of *The Federalist* identify the public good with such ends as commercial prosperity, domestic peace, and national security. These political goals are shared by virtually all democratic citizens. Sociopaths and the bloodthirsty might disagree with the above ends, but most democratic theorists do not treat the interests of such persons with equal concern and respect.[67]

American constitutional purposes seem to have survived intact the transition from republic to democracy. Rogers Smith suggests that both liberal republicans of the late eighteenth century and liberal democrats of the late twentieth century are committed to such values as preserving the peace, promoting the capacity of individuals to control their lives, security, and prosperity.[68] A good case can be made that Madison would endorse the main objectives of both the Bush II and Obama administrations, even if he might have favoured different means to achieve

[63] D. J. Amy, *Real Choices/New Voices: The Case for Proportional Representation Elections in the United States* (New York: Columbia University Press, 1993), 115.

[64] Lani Guinier, '[E]racing Democracy: The Voting Rights Cases,' *Harvard Law Review* 108, (1994), 133 n. 141.

[65] See Farrand, *Records* (Vol. 2), 9–10, 57, 81. See generally, M. A. Graber, *Dred Scott and the Problem of Constitutional Evil* (New York: Cambridge University Press, 2006), 101–6.

[66] S. L. Elkin, *Reconstructing the Commercial Republic: Constitutional Design After Madison* (Chicago: University of Chicago Press, 2006), 30.

[67] Whether democratic theorists can do so consistently with their premises is a separate issue.

[68] R. M. Smith, *Liberalism and American Constitutional Law* (Cambridge, MA: Harvard University Press, 1980), 198–225.

those goals. Contemporary American democrats who think that the constitution is outdated remain enthusiastic about the commitments laid out in the Preamble.[69]

Eighteenth-century republicans identified American regime aspirations with more universal ambitions. Hector Crevecoeur captured the essence of this aspect of American national identity when he asked, 'What then is the American, this new man?'

> He is either a European, or the descendant of a European, hence that strange mixture of blood, which you will find in no other country. I could point out to you a family whose grandfather was an Englishman, whose wife was Dutch, whose son married a French woman, and whose present four sons have now four wives of different nations. *He* is an American, who leaving behind him all his ancient prejudices and manners, receives new ones from the new mode of life he has embraced, the new government he obeys, and the new rank he holds.[70]

Thomas Jefferson believed Americans to be united by a common commitment to universal human rights. The second paragraph of the Declaration of Independence states, 'We hold these truths to be self-evident, that all men are created equal, that they are endowed by their Creator with certain unalienable Rights, that among these are Life, Liberty and the pursuit of Happiness.'[71]

Madison apparently shared this understanding of the American character, although he wrote very little on the subject. At no point did his famous writings indicate that the common good for Americans might be different to the common good for the British, French, or other 'civilized nations'. The purposes set out in the Preamble, Madison seems to have thought, represent the ends of any decent government.[72] His writings do not endorse manifest destiny or even special white-man's burdens. Madison favoured the Louisiana Purchase because he believed the acquisition of more territory would promote commercial prosperity and national security.[73] Expansion was not an end in itself.

Madison's republican constitutionalism for the most part endorsed the contemporary democratic antipathy towards aggressive state attempts to fashion virtuous citizens. His writings break from a long tradition in political thought, dating from at least Aristotle, which insists that a crucial regime function is to shape preferences in ways that make the interests and capacities of most citizens compatible with the constitutional order. Social institutions, Aristotelians claim, should '[mould] the characters and tastes of citizens' so that cultural and political life are mutually reinforcing:

[69] Levinson, *Our Undemocratic Constitution*, 12.

[70] J. Hector St. John Crevecoeur, *Letters from an American Farmer* (New York: Fox, Duffield & Company, 1904), 54.

[71] T. Jefferson, 'Declaration of Independence', in *American Constitutionalism* (Vol II: Rights and Liberties) ed. H. Gillman, M. A. Graber, and K. E. Whittington (New York: Oxford University Press, 2013), 105.

[72] With the exception of the analysis of slavery and the three-fifths compromise, Madison's essays in *The Federalist* rarely refer to distinctive conditions in the United States.

[73] *The Mind of the Founder*, 277–87.

Guided by a 'higher-law' standard of natural right that prescribes *virtue* as man's natural end, ancient constitutionalism turns the classification of regimes into an exercise in moral choice, a problem of choosing the regime best suited to make men virtuous—to make them courageous, moderate, just, and prudent.[74]

The Federalist No. 10 rejects this means for maintaining regime stability. Madison noted that the problem of faction could be solved in theory if all persons were socialized to have common interests. He then rejected this method as both impractical and inconsistent with a commitment to liberty. Madison thought government was incapable of fashioning a homogeneous citizenry. 'The latent causes of faction', he observed, 'are . . . sown in the nature of man.'

As long as the reason of man continues to be fallible, and he is at liberty to exercise it, different opinions will be formed. As long as the connection subsists between his reason and self-love, his opinions and his passions will have a reciprocal influence on each other; and the former will be the objects to which the latter will attach themselves.[75]

Madison more importantly maintained that a homogeneous society is undesirable. A well-functioning republican constitutionalism, by guaranteeing persons the right to use their unequal capacities to develop different economic interests, would facilitate rather than inhibit the social diversity that fostered factions. He wrote:

From the protection of different and unequal faculties of acquiring property, the possession of different degrees and kinds of property immediately results; and from the influence of these on the sentiments and views of the respective proprietors, ensues a division of the society into different interests and parties.[76]

When Madison endorsed government policies that he thought might shape public preferences, the preferences he sought to forge were democratic. His speech introducing the Bill of Rights to Congress in 1789 emphasized how textual commitments might help fashion citizens who internalized such liberal and republican values as a commitment to free speech and the liberty of conscience. Constitutional provisions protecting various rights, Madison declared, 'have a tendency to impress some degree of respect for them, to establish the public opinion in their favor, and rouse the attention of the whole community'.[77] This position is consistent with much contemporary democratic theory. Dahl points out how democracies are likely to thrive only when most political elites have internalized democratic values: 'A country is very likely to develop and sustain the institutions of polyarchy', he contends, only 'if it possesses a political culture and beliefs, particularly among political activists, that support the institutions of polyarchy.'[78]

[74] R. P. Kraynak, 'Tocqueville's Constitutionalism', *American Political Science Review* 87 (1987), 1175, 1177.

[75] Hamilton, Madison, and Jay, *The Federalist Papers*, 78.

[76] Hamilton, Madison, and Jay, *The Federalist Papers*, 78.

[77] *Annals of Congress*, 1st Cong., 1st Sess., 455.

[78] R. A. Dahl, *Democracy and Its Critics* (New Haven: Yale University Press, 1989), 264.

Nevertheless, Madison's devotion to the common good clearly distinguishes his republican constitutionalism from contemporary democratic theory. Eighteenth-century republican constitutionalists understood the common good as ascertainable and existing independently from individual preferences. *The Federalist No. 45* asserts, 'the public good, the real welfare of the great body of the people, is the supreme object to be pursued, and ... no form of government whatever has any other value than as it may be fitted for the attainment of this object.'[79] *The Federalist No. 10* insists that in a society of multiple, diverse interests, public policy will reflect the common good, not the interests of a majority of the affected interests: '[e]xtend the sphere and you take in a greater variety of parties and interests: you make it less probable that a majority of the whole will have a common motive to invade the rights of other citizens.'[80]

Madison opposed the logrolling politics that characterize contemporary democracy. He would have found bizarre Dahl's assertion that 'in a pluralistic country with even a moderately complex society, ... it is difficult to specify "the common good" precisely enough to guide collective decisions'.[81] The purpose of the large republic was to ensure that legislation reflected the public good. Elkin observes that Madison was 'no pluralist—at least not in the sense that he thought that law should arise from the clash of multiple interests'.[82] 'The great desideratum in Government', Madison stated, 'is such a modification of the Sovereignty as will render it sufficiently neutral between the different interests and factions.'[83] Well-designed government institutions in heterogeneous regimes ensure government officials pursue the public interest and do not logroll. Madison stated:

> In the extended republic of the United States, and among the great variety of interests, parties, and sects which it embraces, a coalition of a majority of the whole society could seldom take place on any other principles other than those of justice and the general good.[84]

Madison's commitment to government promotion of education and the arts suggests that his republican notion of the common good entailed political and controversial policies not designed simply to satisfy the preferences of most citizens. During the convention debates, Madison proposed that government be granted power to create a national university and support 'the advancement of useful knowledge and discoveries'.[85] Many early American elites shared Madison's enthusiasm for these more aristocratic ends. George Washington's first State of the Union message urged Congress to consider establishing a national university.[86] John Quincy Adams, the last president of the republican generation, called for legislation

[79] Hamilton, Madison, and Jay, *The Federalist Papers*, 289.
[80] Hamilton, Madison, and Jay, *The Federalist Papers*, 83.
[81] Dahl, *Democracy and its Critics*, 303. [82] Elkin, *Commercial Republic*, 30.
[83] Madison, 'Diagnosis of the American Confederacy', 64.
[84] Hamilton, Madison, and Jay, *The Federalist Papers*, 325.
[85] Farrand, *Records* 2, 325.
[86] See George Washington, 'First Annual Address', in *A Compilation of the Messages and Papers of the Presidents, 1789–1897*, ed. J. D. Richardson (Washington: Government Printing Office, 1897), 66.

promoting exploration and education.[87] These measures were not understood merely as means for facilitating broadly shared commitments to commercial prosperity and related consensual ends. Rakove points out that Madison and other Enlightenment thinkers thought that 'the promotion of wisdom and culture were legitimate responsibilities of government'.[88] '[M]oral, political, intellectual improvement', John Quincy Adams asserted, 'are duties assigned by the Author of Our Existence to social no less than to individual man.'[89] Not everyone in the United States agreed, as demonstrated by the failure of early American national legislators to establish a national university. Madison's commitment to a national university, in this light, suggests that he believed that virtuous representatives should have both special knowledge about how to achieve the consensual ends of government and be experts on the nature of those ends.

IV. Republican Rights

Republican rights differ from democratic rights. Democratic rights promote equality. People have rights to equal influence on government policy, they have the right to be treated the same as other similarly situated people, and government must treat their interests with equal concern and respect. Republican rights promote classical virtues. Rights are vehicles that enable human beings to live more noble lives rather than simply means that enable people to follow whatever life plan they think best. People have rights to employ their facilities productively, to fulfil religious duties, and to satisfy their public duties as republican citizens. The common republican distinction between liberty and licence rejects the contemporary constitutional indifference to the nature of the good life. Madison's conception of property rights, free speech rights, and rights to religious freedom were all derived from his beliefs about proper human behaviour. Freedom allowed human beings to exhibit public and private virtues. Actions that did not demonstrate those virtues could be regulated. When Madison insisted on state neutrality between competing notions of the good, as was the case for religious liberty, that neutrality was rooted in a positive, Christian notion about how people should behave.

1. Property

Madison's analysis of property consistently drew close connections between what he believed were virtuous activities and private rights. Many Framers maintained that only property holders had the virtues necessary to exercise the franchise. John Adams declared that '[m]en . . . who are wholly destitute of Property, are also too

[87] J. Q. Adams, 'First Annual Message', in *American Constitutionalism* (Vol. I: Structures of Government), ed. H. Gillman, M. A. Graber, and K. E. Whittington, 192–3.

[88] J. N. Rakove, *James Madison and the Creation of the American Republic* (Glenview: Scott, Foresman and Company, 1990), 66.

[89] Adams, 'First Annual Message', 192.

little acquainted with public Affairs to form a Right Judgment, and too dependent upon other Men to have a Will of their own'.[90] Madison agreed. During the debates over suffrage requirements in the constitutional convention, Madison insisted that '[t]he freeholders of the Country would be the safest depositories of Republican liberty'.[91] Unlike many classical republican theories, Madison tied protections for property to the virtues involved in acquiring property. In his view, the more virtuous the means by which certain property was acquired, the greater the degree of protection that property warranted.

Madison's earliest published essays, written during the first half of the 1780s, tied the rights of government bondholders to be repaid in full to the reasons bondholders had loaned money to the American cause. Persons who provided financial support for American freedom had special rights to have their claims honoured by the national government. 'A wise nation', Madison stated, 'will never permit those who relieve the wants of their country, or who rely most on its faith, its firmness, and its resources, when either of them is distrusted, to suffer by the event.'[92] Soldiers who were owed money by the federal government were the other class of creditors who had acquired rights through meritorious behaviour. Madison, when describing the government obligation to veterans, described soldiers as 'that illustrious and patriotic band of fellow-citizens, whose blood and bravery have defended the liberties of their country, who have patiently borne . . . the privation of their stipends'.[93] Military virtue, not the mere fact of a debt, created obligations for repayment.

Bondholders whose motives were less noble did not enjoy the same rights to full repayment. During the early 1790s, Madison opposed Hamilton's proposal to have the national government assume and pay off the debts states had acquired to private persons during the Revolutionary War. Most bondholders by that time, he believed, were speculators seeking to make a profit on the distress of their country and their fellow citizens. They were not the noble patriots of the previous decade, helping the cause of the nation. Speculators, Madison insisted, had no right to be paid the full value of the bonds. Jack Rakove notes:

> Through the long years of national bankruptcy, many of these securities—notes promising payment to Continental soldiers, loan certificates subscribed by patriotic citizens—had been purchased by speculators at a fraction of their original value. Madison accordingly called for a plan of discrimination that would give original holders full value but pay speculators less.[94]

As Madison in 1790 informed Congress:

[90] 'John Adams to James Sullivan, May 26, 1776', *The Papers of John Adams* (Vol. I), ed. R. Taylor, M. Kline, G. L. Lint, and C. Walker (Cambridge, MA: Harvard University Press, 1977), 395.

[91] Farrand, *Records* 2, 203–4.

[92] Madison, 'Public Credit and the Republican Cause', *The Mind of the Founder*, 25.

[93] Madison, 'Public Credit and the Republican Cause', *The Mind of the Founder*, 24.

[94] Rakove, *Madison*, 89.

He must renounce every sentiment which he had hitherto cherished, before his complaisance could admit that America ought to erect the monuments of her gratitude, not to those who saved her liberties, but to those who had enriched themselves in her funds.[95]

One's republican property rights against the United States depended on whether one had patriotic or pecuniary reasons for obtaining American securities.

Madison's analysis of property in *The Federalist* and his 1792 essay on property asserted similar connections between rights and socially desirable behaviour. Persons acquired rights to property through the exercise of private virtues. Madison in 1788 assumed that differences in wealth reflected the different capacities of human beings. '[T]he rights of property originate', he stated in 1788, from 'the diversity in the faculties of men.'[96] Economic inequality was a consequence of the 'different and unequal facilities of acquiring property'.[97] Some persons had more property than others because they were more productive. Free governments ensured their citizens opportunities to gain property through productive action and protected property so gained. Madison's essay 'Property' asserted:

That is not a just government, nor is property secure under it, where arbitrary restrictions, exemptions, and monopolies deny to part of its citizens that free use of their faculties, and free choice of their occupations, which not only constitute their property in the general sense of the word; but are the means of acquiring property strictly so called.[98]

Madison was far less enthusiastic about the need to protect property when considering inheritance, the means by which persons acquire property without the 'free use of their faculties, and free choice of their occupations'.[99] He joined Jefferson's crusade to abolish primogeniture, a practice they believed would quickly ensure that the distribution of property after a generation would reflect merit rather than ancestry.[100] Both promoted the 1776 Virginia statute that put an end to fee tail, a common means of preserving large family estates. The Preamble to that statute made a tight connection between republican virtue and property rights. '[T]he perpetuation of property in certain families, by means of gifts made to them in fee taille', Madison and his legislative allies stated, 'is contrary to good policy, tends to deceive good traders . . . , discourages the holder thereof from taking care and improving the same, and sometimes does injury to the morals of youth, by rendering them independent of and disobedient to their parents.'[101] Laws abolishing fee tail, Madison later informed Jefferson, facilitate 'a greater simplicity of manners, consequently a less consumption of manufactured superfluities, and a less

95 *Annals of Congress*, 1st Cong., 2nd Sess., 1308.

96 Hamilton, Madison, and Jay, *The Federalist Papers*, 78.

97 Hamilton, Madison, and Jay, *The Federalist Papers*, 78.

98 J. Madison, 'Property', in *The Writings of James Madison* (Vol. IV), ed. G. Hunt (New York: G. P. Putnam's Sons, 1906), 102.

99 Madison, 'Property', *The Writings of James Madison*, 102.

100 For a more detailed discussion of the subject of this paragraph, see J. F. Hart, '"A Less Proportion of Idle Proprietors": Madison, Property Rights, and the Abolition of Fee Tail', *Washington and Lee Law Review* 58 (2001), 167.

101 Hart, 'Madison', 167 (quoting Act of Oct. 1776, ch. XXVI).

proportion of idle proprietors and domestics'.[102] A good republican thinker, Madison believed 'inculcating virtue in the citizenry could... justify taking away property rights'.[103] 'Inherited entailed property was such a socially undesirable way of acquiring property', John Hart notes, that Madison thought 'it was appropriate for the legislature to abolish this form of land tenure.'[104]

The distinctions Madison made between bondholders and his antipathy to inheritance illustrate some differences between republican and libertarian regimes concerning property rights. Madison was not a proponent of laissez-faire, free trade, or the Hamiltonian attempt to make the speculative class the crucial economic backbone of the country. He opposed redistribution, but believed that government could regulate economic activity when doing so promoted the public good.[105] Government could constitutionally impose protective tariffs because those duties were legitimate means of raising revenue and promoting the domestic economy.[106] Government could not expropriate ordinary farmland because farming enabled persons to develop agrarian virtues. Agriculture was more virtuous than industrial labour, both Madison and Jefferson believed, because the farmer was not dependent on the beneficence of others. Madison spoke of 'the independent situation and manly sentiments of American citizens, who live on their soil'.[107] When criticizing the mercantile interests likely to benefit from Hamilton's economic programme, Madison declared that '[t]he greater the proportion of [farmers] to the whole society, the more free, the more independent, and the more happy must be the society itself'.[108] Those who tilled the soil and bought bonds at their original value acquired property rights because their behaviour satisfied republican standards. Speculators and heirs who gained property without exhibiting the same republican virtues did not acquire the same republican rights.

2. Religion

Religion was another matter on which Madison yoked a theory of private virtue to the allocation of public rights. Madison's defence of a strict separation between church and state was grounded in an understanding of proper Christian behaviour. His goal, when protesting state establishments, was to promote Christianity. When justifying state neutrality between religions, and between religion and non-religion, Madison never declared that atheism or non-Christian faiths merited constitutional protection for their own sake. Establishments, he believed, weakened Christianity, properly understood and practised.

102 'James Madison to Thomas Jefferson, June 19, 1786', in *The Writings of James Madison* (Vol. II) ed. G. Hunt (New York: G. P. Putnam's Sons, 1901), 248.

103 Hart, 'Madison', 191. 104 Hart, 'Madison', 191.

105 See Hart, 'Madison', 189–91.

106 'James Madison to Joseph C. Cabell, September 18, 1828', in *Letters and Other Writings of James Madison* (Vol. III) (New York: R. Worthington, 1884), 636–47; 'James Madison to Joseph C. Cabell, October 30, 1828,' *Letters*, 648–54.

107 Rakove, *Madison*, 101.

108 James Madison, 'Republican Distribution of Citizens', in *The Writings of James Madison* (Vol. VI), 99.

The 'Memorial and Remonstrance Against Religious Assessments' relied heavily on explicitly religious and Christian reasons for disestablishing the church and promoting the free exercise of religion. The first substantive paragraph of that tract repeatedly emphasized that state laws compelling religious worship interfered with religious virtues. Madison contended that 'we hold it for a fundamental and undeniable truth, "that religion or the duty which we owe to our Creator and the manner of discharging it, can be directed only by reason and conviction, not by force or violence."' In his view, '[i]t is the duty of every man to render to the Creator such homage and such only as he believes to be acceptable to him', Religious freedom was rooted in the principle that '[b]efore any man can be considered as a member of Civil Society, he must be considered as a subject of the Governour of the Universe'.[109] Government could not compel persons to practise or contribute to religion, because such practices were inconsistent with Madison's Christian understanding of the human good. State establishments mistakenly imply that religious service is a duty owned to government, not God. Madison maintained that '[i]f this freedom be abused, it is an offence against God, not against man: To God, therefore, not to man, must an account of it be rendered'.[110]

Madison was particularly concerned that state promotion would foster religious vice rather than religious virtues. Government coercion made religious leaders lazy and corrupt, by substituting state power for the power of the Lord's word. The proposed assessment for religious teaching that inspired the Remonstrance, Madison claimed, 'implies either that the Civil Magistrate is a competent Judge of Religious Truth; or that he may employ Religion as an engine of Civil policy. The first is an arrogant pretension falsified by the contradictory opinions of Rulers in all ages, and throughout the world: the second an unhallowed perversion of the means of salvation.'[111] Worse, he continued, religious establishments would corrupt Christianity. Patrick Henry's proposal to use the taxing power to support Christianity 'at once discourages those who are strangers to the light of revelation from coming into the Region of it; and countenances by example the nations who continue in darkness, in shutting out those who might convey it to them'. Madison complained, 'Instead of Levelling as far as possible, every obstacle to the victorious progress of Truth, the Bill with an ignoble and unchristian timidity would circumscribe it with a wall of defence against the encroachments of error.'[112]

The Remonstrance read in full suggests a sharp difference between state and constitutional neutrality. Madison believed that states should be neutral between religions, as well as between religion and non-religion. Government had no business being involved in any religious affair. When president, Madison insisted that official prayers by presidents, which did not coerce anyone, were inconsistent

[109] J. Madison, 'Freedom of Conscience: Memorial and Remonstrance', in *The Mind of the Founder*, 7.

[110] Madison, 'Memorial and Remonstrance', 8–9.

[111] Madison, 'Memorial and Remonstrance', 9.

[112] Madison, 'Memorial and Remonstrance', 11–12.

with the constitutional separation between church and state.[113] The constitution, however, was not as neutral as the government. State neutrality, in Madison's view, was the best constitutional means for promoting sound religious doctrines and ensuring citizens correctly fulfilled their religious duties. Establishment would 'weaken in those who profess [Christian] Religion a pious confidence in its innate excellence' and 'foster in those who still reject it, a suspicion that its friends are too conscious of its fallacies, to trust it to its own merits'.[114] Unlike Jefferson, Madison never declared indifference to his neighbours' religious beliefs.[115] Persons had rights to free exercise of religion only because religious virtue was contingent upon the existence of these rights and the lack of a state establishment.

3. Free speech

Madison's defence of free speech during the controversy over the Alien and Sedition Acts provides a third example of how republicans connected private right with public virtue. As Gordon Wood notes, political elites in Madison's generation believed that 'a citizen... achieved his greatest moral fulfillment by participating in a self-governing republic'. In their view, '[a]ll men of genius and leisure, all gentlemen, had an obligation to serve the state'.[116] Free-speech rights in such a polity permitted persons to exercise public virtue. Madison in 1799 asserted that 'it is the duty, as well as the right, of intelligent and faithful citizens to discuss and promulgate' criticisms of public officials.[117] The state had to be neutral (to some degree) on the merits of political criticism only because the Constitution of the United States was rooted in a republican vision of the good life which proclaimed politics as the highest calling of the natural elite. Persons could exercise their obligation to participate in a republican regime only if they had rights to express their ideas.[118]

Free speech rights were a republican means for maintaining the virtue of elected officials. Madison insisted that 'the right of freely examining public characters and measures... has been justly deemed the only effectual guardian of every other right'.[119] Bans on political dissent, he believed, promoted political corruption.

113 J. Madison, 'Monopolies, Perpetuities, Corporations, Ecclesiastical Endowments', reprinted in G. Hunt (ed.), 'Aspects of Monopoly One Hundred Years Ago', *Harper's Magazine* 128 (1914), 489.

114 Madison, 'Memorial and Remonstrance', 9.

115 T. Jefferson, *Notes on the State of Virginia* (London: Burlington-House, Piccadilly, 1787), 265 ('it does me no injury for my neighbour to say there are twenty gods or no god. It neither picks my pocket nor breaks my leg').

116 Wood, *The Radicalism of the American Revolution*, 104.

117 James Madison, 'Republican Manifesto: The Virginia Report', in *The Mind of the Founder*, 264.

118 As Saul Cornell has demonstrated, late-eighteenth-century republicans held a similar conception of the right to bear arms. Citizens had duties to participate in the militia. This duty could be fulfilled only if citizens could possess weapons. Hence, the right to bear arms gave eligible persons the capacity to fulfil their civic duties. See Saul Cornell, *A Well-Regulated Militia: The Founding Fathers and the Origins of Gun Control in America* (New York: Oxford University Press, 2006).

119 James Madison, 'Republican Manifesto: The Virginia Report', in *The Mind of the Founder*, 263.

The Virginia Report asserted that the Alien and Sedition Acts were 'equivalent to a protection of those who administer the government, if they should any time deserve the contempt or hatred of the people'. '[I]f those in public trust be shielded by penal laws from such strictures of the press as may expose them to contempt, disrepute, or hatred, where they may deserve it', Madison continued, 'in exact proportion as they may deserve to be exposed, will be the certainty and criminality of the intent to expose them.' The end result would be the collapse of republican virtue. Corruption would reign when criticism was suppressed. Madison concluded, 'a government thus intrenched in penal statutes, against the just and natural effects of a culpable administration, will easily evade the responsibility, which is essential to a faithful discharge of its duty'.[120]

What Madison thought about the many free-speech ideas that occupy contemporary democratic thinkers is difficult to discern. He was a political activist, not a legal treatise writer. Madison wrote about free-speech issues that were politically salient at the turn of the nineteenth century. The Alien and Sedition Acts inspired a sophisticated defence of the right to criticize public officials. No analogous controversy took place in the early republic that might have inspired Madison to pen remarks on the status of non-political speech in a constitutional republic.

Still, broader republican practice provides some hints on how Madison might have approached various First Amendment problems. Few antebellum Americans had any constitutional difficulties limiting commercial speech and obscenity.[121] The persons responsible for the constitution and the Bill of Rights spoke only of political commentary when discussing free speech. One of the first articles to defend constitutional protections for advertising asserts, 'One searches in vain for an indication from any of the people involved with the drafting or ratifying of the first amendment that they were concerned with anything besides politically oriented speech.'[122] Given that no one had a republican duty to produce speech for commercial purposes and such speech did not promote virtue, republican political theory provided no grounds for a republican right to advertise and produce material that was not designed to persuade people about matters of public interest. The Framers were more explicit about sexual expression. Madison's contemporaries restricted such speech in the name of public virtue. 'That actions of public indecency were always indictable as tending to corrupt the public morals', Chief Justice Tilghman of the Supreme Court of Pennsylvania declared in 1815, 'I can have no doubt.'[123]

[120] J. Madison, 'Republican Manifesto: The Virginia Report', *The Mind of the Founder*, 266.

[121] See D. I. Dennis, 'Obscenity Law and the Conditions of Freedom in the Nineteenth-Century United States', *Law and Social Inquiry* 27 (2002), 369, 382–5; A. Kozinski and S. Banner, 'Who's Afraid of Commercial Speech?', *Virginia Law Review* 76 (1990), 627, 631–3.

[122] Kozinski and Banner, 'Commercial Speech', 632.

[123] *Commonwealth v Sharpless*, 2 Serg. & Rawle 91, 100–1 (Pa., 1815).

V. Madison, Republicanism, and Contemporary Democratic Constitutionalism

Far more often than Jefferson, Hamilton, Adams, Washington, or other notables of that era, Americans read Madison to learn about the general principles of the constitution ratified in 1789 and amended in 1791. That Jefferson thought all constitutions expired after a short period of time[124] and Adams continued favouring some version of English balanced government[125] are of little constitutional significance for Americans. These principles were not incorporated into the Constitution of the United States. Madisonian scholarship has more political bite. Even though some practices Madison thought fundamental to the constitutional order were rejected by the drafting convention,[126] most studies of the constitution treat the principles Madison articulated in the *Federalist Papers* and his other writings of that time as the fundamental principles underlying the constitution. For this reason, Madison the republican thinker is a particularly important object of examination.

Studies of Madison more concerned with understanding the original constitutional order than the peculiarities of a particular individual's thought should focus on the distinction between democracies and republics, rather than on the extended republic. Madison's analysis of faction in the extended republic was his distinctive contribution to political thought. Nevertheless, little evidence exists that most Framers or ratifiers believed that extending the sphere of a republic would mitigate the problem of faction.[127] For that matter, little evidence exists that Madison's analysis was correct. Certainly as a means for inhibiting two-party politics, the proposals laid out in *The Federalist No. 10* were dismal failures. If anything, political parties proved necessary to navigate the complex system of checks and balances Madison endorsed.[128] Far more constitutional thinkers of the late eighteenth century endorsed the Madisonian distinction between a republic and a democracy, even if the precise terminology was somewhat fluid. Madison and many crucial Framers believed that popular government was the best means for securing the common good and protecting private rights. They had similar notions of what constituted the public good and made close connections between private rights and conceptions of the good life. Madison and his peers were republican on all matters in which republican values conflicted with democratic equality. The public good, in their view, could best be achieved if suffrage was limited, the political equality of all voters was rejected, and electoral systems designed so that particularly virtuous

124 'Thomas Jefferson to James Madison, September 6, 1789', *The Papers of Thomas Jefferson* (Vol. 15) ed. J. P. Boyd (Princeton: Princeton University Press, 1958), 395–6.

125 See C. Bradley Thompson, *John Adams and the Spirit of Liberty* (Lawrence: University of Kansas Press, 1998).

126 See Rakove, *Original Meanings*, 81–2.

127 See L. Kramer, 'Madison's Audience', *Harvard Law Review* 112 (1999), 611.

128 See S. M. Milkis, *Political Parties and Constitutional Government: Remaking American Democracy* (Baltimore: Johns Hopkins University Press, 1999).

persons would gain office. Rights facilitated public and private virtues, neither of which trumped the public good nor were grounded in a state obligation to be neutral between conceptions of the good. Virtue and the common good were often not precisely defined, but Madison and his contemporaries thought, to paraphrase Justice Stewart's famous observation on pornography, they 'would know it when they saw it'.[129]

Madison's republicanism looked backward as much as forward. Eighteenth-century republicans had no quarrel with the ends of the balanced English constitution. Gordon Wood notes that many republicans before the American Revolution believed that republican 'ideals . . . could exist in a monarchy'.[130] Madison and others broke from the classical republican tradition by claiming that having all government officials either elected or appointed by elected officials was the best means for protecting the common good and private rights. Popular government, in their view, delivered the aristocratic goods better than those forms of government in which political power was inherited.

History played a practical joke on the American founders. The combination of popular government as a means and aristocratic virtues as an end proved unstable during the nineteenth century. When commitments to equality and virtue clashed, Americans in the Jacksonian era either chose equality or insisted that the first virtue was a commitment to equality. Wood observes how '[a] new generation of democratic Americans was no longer interested in the revolutionaries' dream of building a classical republic of elitist virtue out of the inherited materials of the Old World'.[131] The end result of this historical process is a constitution that is democratic in both means and ends. The contemporary commitment to democratic equality provides both the standard for evaluating political processes and the output of those political processes.

History plays a similar practical joke on contemporary constitutional theorists. Numerous contemporary constitutional commentators with very different democratic agendas presently pose as Madison. Robert Bork is Madison.[132] Cass Sunstein is Madison.[133] Lani Guinier is Madison.[134] In fact, Madison rejected the foundational principles of contemporary constitutionalism. He was not a democrat who believed that all persons should have an equal share of political power. He was not an egalitarian who believed that all interests should be treated with equal concern and respect. He was not a liberal who believed the primary function of

[129] *Jaconellis v State of Ohio* 378 U.S. (1964) 184, 197 (Stewart, J., concurring) ('I shall not today attempt further to define the kinds of material I understand to be embraced within that shorthand description; and perhaps I could never succeed in intelligibly doing so. But I know it when I see it').

[130] Wood, *The Radicalism of the American Revolution*, 96.

[131] Wood, *The Radicalism of the American Revolution*, 369.

[132] See R. H. Bork, 'Neutral Principles and Some First Amendment Problems', *Indiana Law Review* 47 (1971), 1, 2–3.

[133] See C. R. Sunstein, *The Partial Constitution* (Cambridge, MA: Harvard University Press, 1993), 19–22.

[134] See L. Guinier, *The Tyranny of the Majority: Fundamental Fairness in Representative Democracy* (New York: Free Press, 1994), 3–5.

government was to enable people to pursue their idiosyncratic notion of the good life. Madison was an eighteenth-century republican whose constitutional vision provides grounds for neither the contemporary left nor right in the contemporary United States.

The eighteenth century does not provide standards for interpreting the constitution of 2015. An originalism based on the political thought of James Madison will ultimately founder on republican premises, which Americans at the turn of the twenty-first century believe incorrect, incoherent, and ultimately incomprehensible. Americans no longer believe in a political elite with a particular capacity for governing. We no longer believe in rights that facilitate virtuous behaviour. Most importantly, contemporary citizens do not believe the function of government is to promote aristocratic notions of the good life. When thinkers as diverse as Robert Bork and Lani Guinier claim that the Constitution of the United States is committed to liberal, democratic equality, they are interpreting the living protean constitution inherited from the New Deal, and not reviving the regime Madison sought to establish in 1789.

16

The Constitutional Thought of Alexander Hamilton

M. N. S. Sellers

I. Introduction

Alexander Hamilton's influence on modern constitutionalism arises primarily from his pre-eminence in promoting and interpreting the Constitution of the United States to Americans and to the world, but he also played a central role in creating and protecting the document itself. Hamilton fought for American Union throughout his life, and believed, with reason, that 'perhaps no man in the United States has sacrificed or done more for the present Constitution than myself.'[1] He made this observation at the end of his career when his political enemies were ascendant, Hamilton was excluded from government, and the judgement of the people had made it clear (as even Hamilton understood) that 'this American world was not made for me'.[2] Hamilton's ultimate defeat marks the true measure of his contribution to the Constitution of the United States and to constitutionalism more broadly. After the election of Thomas Jefferson to the presidency (secured in part by Hamilton's intervention), Hamilton delivered his political opponents a strong, stable, functioning constitutional republic. Alexander Hamilton so well established the 'frail and worthless fabric'[3] of the United States Constitution that men of his stature would not be needed (or seen) again in the politics of the American republic.[4]

[1] Alexander Hamilton to Gouverneur Morris, 29 February 1802. This letter and a well selected collection of the most important writings of Alexander Hamilton are conveniently collected in A. Hamilton, *Writings*, ed. J. B. Freeman (New York: The Library of America, 2001), 986. The most complete collection of Hamilton's papers is A. Hamilton, *The Papers of Alexander Hamilton*, ed. H. C. Syrett (New York: Columbia University Press, 1961–1979).

[2] Hamilton to Morris, 29 February 1802.

[3] Hamilton to Morris, 29 February 1802.

[4] Recent volumes on Alexander Hamilton and the United States Constitution include M. Meyerson, *Liberty's Blueprint: How Madison and Hamilton Wrote the Federalist Papers, Defined the Constitution, and made Democracy Safe for the World* (New York: Basic Books, 2008); H. Flaumenhaft, *The Effective Republic: Administration and Constitution in the Thought of Alexander Hamilton* (Durham, NC: Duke University Press, 1992); M. J. Frisch, *Alexander Hamilton and the Political Order: An Interpretation of His Political Thought and Practice* (Lanham: University Press of America, 1991); G. Stourzh, *Alexander Hamilton and the Idea of Republican Government* (Stanford: Stanford University Press, 1970); C. L. Rossiter, *Alexander Hamilton and the Constitution* (New York: Harcourt Brace, 1970).

Hamilton was, with George Washington, the most tireless proponent of American federalism. He was, with James Madison, the most persuasive advocate of the United States Constitution. He was decisive in securing constitutional ratification in recalcitrant New York. As a member of Washington's cabinet, he was the primary architect of the constitution's actual application to government. But, like his friend Gouverneur Morris, Hamilton always remained 'an exotic' in North America.[5] Born on the Caribbean island of Nevis in unfavourable and somewhat louche circumstances, and raised on anarchic St. Croix, he escaped to New York as a teenager on the strength of his pen and his wit.[6] Hamilton's influence, reputation, and political career began in 1774 when he offered a 'Full Vindication of the Measures of the Congress, from the Calumnies of their Enemies'.[7] He was not yet twenty years old.[8] He followed with 'A more Impartial Comprehensive View of the Dispute between Great Britain and the Colonies'[9]—and so it would continue for the rest of his life. Hamilton found himself, grew up, and triumphed with the United States of America, and the nation's constitutional project was his too, from the beginning.

When Alexander Hamilton embraced as a youth 'the cause of virtue and mankind',[10] he adopted the programme, attitudes, and vocabulary of a current of thought present in Britain and her empire for generations,[11] and in European political culture for centuries before.[12] The innovation of the American revolutionaries was not in their principles, which they borrowed from English commonwealth ideology[13] and from republican Rome,[14] but in their attention to the details

5 Hamilton to Morris, 29 February 1802, in Hamilton, *Writings*, 986.

6 For an entertaining account of Hamilton's childhood and youth, see J. T. Flexner, *The Young Hamilton: A Biography* (Boston: Little Brown, 1978).

7 A Friend to America [Alexander Hamilton], *A Full Vindication of the Measures of the Congress, from the Calumnies of their Enemies* (James Rivington, 1774); also found in Hamilton, *Writings*, 10 ff.

8 The year of Alexander Hamilton's birth has been disputed. His own account of 1757 has been called into question. Perhaps it was as early as 1755.

9 A Friend to America [Alexander Hamilton], *The Farmer Refuted: or A more Impartial and Comprehensive View of the Dispute Between Great Britain and the Colonies* (James Rivington, 1775).

10 *The Farmer Refuted*, 43.

11 I have set out the nature and origins of American constitutionalism at length in M. N. S. Sellers, *American Republicanism: Roman Ideology in the United States Constitution* (Basingstoke: Macmillan, 1994); cf. B. Bailyn, *The Ideological Origins of the American Revolution* (Cambridge, MA: Harvard University Press, 1967); J. Adams, *Defence of the Constitutions of Government of the United States of America* (London: Dilly, 1787–8).

12 For more detail on the origin of these ideas and their history, see M. N. S. Sellers, *The Sacred Fire of Liberty: Republicanism, Liberalism and the Law* (Basingstoke: Macmillan, 1998); cf. M. van Gelderen and Q. Skinner (eds), *Republicanism: A Shared European Heritage* (Cambridge: Cambridge University Press, 2009).

13 In addition to the works cited above (n. 12), see C. Robbins, *The Eighteenth-Century Commonwealthman: Studies in the Transmission, Development and Circumstance of English Liberal Thought from the Restoration of Charles II until the War with the Thirteen Colonies* (Cambridge, MA: Harvard University Press, 1959); Z. S. Fink, *The Classical Republicans: An Essay in the Recovery of a Pattern of Thought in Seventeenth-Century England*, 2nd ed. (Evanston: Northwestern University Press, 1962).

14 In addition to the works cited above (nn. 12–13), see D. J. Bederman, *The Classical Foundations of the American Constitution* (Cambridge: Cambridge University Press, 2008); J. C. Richard, *The Founders and the Classics: Greece, Rome and the American Enlightenment* (Cambridge, MA: Harvard University Press, 1994).

of constitutional reform, and their willingness to attempt republican government on a continental scale—something not considered possible in Europe, and only ever applied before on the most restricted geographical basis.[15] Americans sought to apply 'reason' and 'experience' to the 'science of politics',[16] 'establishing good government by reflection and choice',[17] to secure the 'liberty', the 'dignity', and the 'happiness' of the people.[18]

II. Continentalism

Alexander Hamilton began his adult life as an officer in the Continental Army, abandoning his studies in 1776 to serve as a captain in the artillery and then, when his heroism and literary ability came to the attention of George Washington, as aide-de-camp and principal drafter of letters, orders, and all manner of reports for the commander-in-chief. More than five years' service in this cosmopolitan setting, among the men of all colonies who suffered most to establish American independence, confirmed for Hamilton (as for most continental officers) his impatience with localism, his dissatisfaction with the weakness of existing federal institutions, and his strong desire to improve the power and the credit of the United States. This latter point is particularly important, because it determined the partisan divide that would create and then challenge the United States Constitution. Almost all participants in the Revolution shared a commitment to what they called 'republican principles' in general and to the republican form of government in particular, including the separation of powers, an elected executive, a bicameral legislature, independent judges, and fundamental human rights.[19] The patriots differed among themselves primarily on whether the dominant locus of republican government should be in the federal government or in the states. Hamilton took the 'federalist' side in this debate from the beginning.[20]

Alexander Hamilton began his fight for a stronger federal constitution by writing six essays in 1781 as the 'Continentalist', in which he sought to counter the 'extreme jealousy of power' that is 'attendant upon all popular revolutions' by

[15] On the impossibility of large republics, see Montesquieu, C. de Secondat, baron de la Brède et de, *De L'Esprit des Lois* (1748), I. viii.16; J. Rousseau, *Du Contrat Social* (1762), III.1;16.

[16] See 'Publius' [Alexander Hamilton], *The Federalist No. 9* in *The Independent Journal* (November 21, 1787), republished in T. Ball (ed.), *The Federalist, with Letters of Brutus* (Cambridge: Cambridge University Press, 2003), 36.

[17] 'Publius' [Hamilton], *The Federalist No. 1* in *The Independent Journal* (27 October 1787) in Ball, *The Federalist*, 1.

[18] *Federalist No. 1*, at 3.

[19] For a detailed discussion of this widely shared republican ideology, see Sellers, *American Republicanism*.

[20] For a good discussion of Hamilton's political career, see F. McDonald, *Alexander Hamilton: A Biography* (New York: W. W. Norton, 1979).

vastly extending the authority of the Federal Congress.[21] The government as constituted by the Articles of Confederation was incapable, Hamilton argued, either of a vigorous prosecution of war, or the preservation of the Union in peace.[22] The United States needed enough authority 'to make and execute the laws with vigour'.[23] Hamilton applied 'experience and reason'[24] to the problems of the confederation, to illustrate the dangers of ceding too much authority to the separate states.[25] *The Continentalist* regretted that Congress, charged with the administration of public affairs, lacked the 'means necessary to fulfil that responsibility'.[26] Hamilton proposed that the federal government should be given powers of direct taxation and the regulation of trade.[27] This would provide the Union with sufficient credit to raise funds as needed for the prosecution of the war and other necessary responsibilities of government.[28]

Hamilton left active service after the American victory at Yorktown, returned to New York, and set out immediately to secure a general convention to strengthen the Articles of Confederation that had governed the United States throughout the war. There was 'something noble and magnificent', he believed, 'in the perspective of a great Federal Republic, closely linked in the pursuit of a common interest, tranquil and prosperous at home, respectable abroad', and there is 'something proportionably diminutive and contemptible in the prospect of a number of petty states, with the appearance only of union, jarring, jealous and perverse, without any determined direction, fluctuating and unhappy at home, weak and insignificant by their dissentions, in the eyes of other nations'.[29] Hamilton had identified the central element in the future success of the United States, and the greatest difference for the next two centuries between the United States and other constitutional republics. As a federation, the United States would need sufficient power to control and regulate its constituent states, or none of them would long succeed in a hostile world.[30]

The argument for continentalism began with the commonwealths of Greece, whose failure to unite raised 'pain and disgust' in Hamilton, contemplating the excesses of their 'usurping demagogues' and tyrants.[31] When Hamilton and his fellow Continental Army officers united after the war to preserve 'those exalted rights and liberties of human nature for which they... fought and bled', they

[21] A. Hamilton, *The Continentalist No. I*, in *The New-York Packet, and the American Advertiser* (12 July 1781), in Hamilton, *Writings*, 99.

[22] *The Continentalist No. I*, 99.

[23] *The Continentalist No. I*, 100.

[24] *The Continentalist No. I*, 100.

[25] A. Hamilton, *The Continentalist No. III*, in *The New-York Packet, and the American Advertiser* (9 August 1781), in Hamilton, *Writings*, 104.

[26] *The Continentalist No. III*, 104.

[27] A. Hamilton, *The Continentalist No. IV*, in *The New-York Packet, and the American Advertiser* (30 August 1781), in Hamilton, *Writings*, 107.

[28] *The Continentalist No. IV*, 108.

[29] A. Hamilton, *The Continentalist No. VI*, in *The New-York Packet, and the American Advertiser* (4 July 1782), in Hamilton, *Writings*, 118.

[30] *The Continentalist No. III*, 101 ff.

[31] *The Continentalist No. I*, 100.

looked to Rome for their model in the character of Lucius Quinctius Cincinnatus, who left his plough to serve the republic, and then returned to his farm—but not before securing the death of the Roman demagogue Spurius Maelius, who had courted popularity at the expense of the common good.[32] The 'Cincinnati' (as they called themselves) pledged, with Alexander Hamilton in the chair, to preserve their 'unalterable determination to promote and cherish, between the respective states, that Union ... so essentially necessary to their happiness, and the future dignity of the American empire'.[33]

III. Constitutionalism

Hamilton himself, writing as 'Phocion', appealed to the people of New York to defend the true 'spirit of Whiggism'—or 'legal liberty'—against 'arbitrary acts of the legislature' and 'the lawless combinations of unauthorized individuals'.[34] The Athenian Phocion had been an old soldier, famous for his personal austerity, who faced down the demagogues of Athens, and eventually paid for this probity with his life.[35] Hamilton wrote (as he explained) to protect the Constitution of New York and 'the most solemn obligations' of the peace treaty with Britain against the 'violence of rash and unprincipled men'.[36] The principle that Hamilton sought to preserve was the ancient common-law doctrine that no person should be 'disfranchised or defrauded of any ... rights or privileges under the Constitution, except by the law of the land or the judgment of his peers'.[37]

The Constitution of New York, as interpreted by Hamilton, in explicitly guaranteeing trial by the 'law of the land', thereby also implicitly secured the 'due process of law' described by Sir Edward Coke in his commentary on Magna Carta.[38] Hamilton's claim of 'Whiggism', his citation of Coke, and his reference to Magna Carta all illustrate the extent to which the Roman tradition that Hamilton claimed as a 'Cincinnatus' and the Greek probity that he claimed as 'Phocion' both supplemented an English constitutional tradition long cherished in the British colonies. But Hamilton knew that even 'English Whigs'[39] were subject to the 'heat and violence' of 'momentary passions'.[40] The 'barriers of the constitution' and 'solemn engagements of the United States' should restrict the tendency towards 'usurpation' and 'corruption'.[41] Hamilton insisted that liberty requires

[32] *Institution of the Society of the Cincinnati* (10 May 1783).

[33] *Institution of the Society of the Cincinnati.*

[34] A. Hamilton, *A Letter from Phocion to the Considerate Citizens of New-York on the Politics of the Day* (January 1784), in Hamilton, *Writings*, 127.

[35] L. Mestrius Plutarchus, *Phocion*, trans. J. Dryden, in *The Lives of Noble Grecians and Romans.* Hamilton took detailed notes from Plutarch in the pay book he kept as a Captain of Artillery: *Alexander Hamilton's Pay Book* (1777), ed. E. P. Panagopoulos (Detroit: Wayne State, 1961).

[36] *Letter from Phocion*, 127.

[37] *Letter from Phocion*, 128.

[38] *Letter from Phocion*, citing Edward Coke.

[39] *Letter from Phocion*, 129.

[40] *Letter from Phocion*, 128.

[41] *Letter from Phocion*, 129.

equal rights and privileges for all[42] and a constant respect for the '*fundamentals* of the constitutions', including the constitution of the Federation itself.[43] This remained the primary weakness in the post-war United States—not so much imbalances in the constitutions of the states themselves, although these certainly existed, as in their collective federal institutions, which Hamilton thought too weak to fulfil their basic obligations to Americans (in any of the states), or to the world.[44]

Alexander Hamilton took the lead, as a New York commissioner at a meeting of state delegates at Annapolis in 1786, in calling for a new convention, with 'more enlarged powers' to be held in Philadelphia the following May.[45] The 'Address of the Annapolis Convention', as drafted by Hamilton, and circulated to the states, requested a 'general meeting of the States' to 'devise such further provisions as shall appear to them necessary to render the constitution of the Federal Government adequate to the exigencies of the Union'.[46] Hamilton himself would become a New York delegate to this 'Constitutional Convention' in the summer of 1787. As the representative of a lightly settled and politically divided state, Hamilton did not play a prominent role in the proceedings, but he did make a long and detailed speech to the convention on 18 June, in which he set out his own proposals for reforming the federal government. The debates in the convention were kept secret, but records maintained by James Madison and Robert Yates give a good sense of Hamilton's views on the Federal Constitution, as frankly expressed to his colleagues.[47]

Hamilton had no illusion in the Constitutional Convention that he could significantly influence the deliberations, nor did he expect his remarks to be made public, so they were extraordinarily frank, and give a clearer sense of Hamilton's personal views than some of his more public remarks. His first and most important desire, as always, was to strengthen the federal government at the expense of the states,[48] in order to check the 'ambitions of demagogues'.[49] Hamilton believed that a certain measure of military force would always be necessary to protect national unity (as demonstrated by contemporary insurrections in Massachusetts) and gave the usual examples of Greece and Germany to illustrate the costs of disunion.[50] He would have been perfectly happy to reduce the states to provinces, to save the expense of their separate governments.[51] Hamilton wanted federal institutions to replicate the excellence of the mixed and balanced constitution of English liberty (already established in most of the states), rather than to preserve the parochial sovereignties of the separate states themselves.[52] Hamilton

[42] *Letter from Phocion*, 130. [43] *Letter from Phocion*, 132.
[44] *Letter from Phocion*.
[45] *Address of the Annapolis Convention* (17 September 1786), in Hamilton, *Writings*, 144.
[46] *Address of the Annapolis Convention*, 144.
[47] James Madison's and Robert Yates's accounts were not released for more than fifty years after they were written, but are now available online and in Hamilton, *Writings*, 151 ff. (Madison) and 159 ff. (Yates).
[48] *Writings*, 151. [49] *Writings*, 152. [50] *Writings*, 153.
[51] *Writings*, 155. [52] *Writings*, 156.

remained an enthusiastic 'republican', like other Americans of his era, but also (like his contemporaries) 'as loud as any in declaiming against the vices of democracy'.[53]

The virtue of the British constitution, as Hamilton and many of his contemporaries understood it, was its ability to unite 'public strength' with 'individual security'.[54] Hamilton wanted similar 'checks' in the American Constitution to control the 'violence and turbulence' of the 'democratic spirit'. This made Hamilton a strong advocate of a bicameral legislature, with a powerful senate, serving for extremely long terms in office, perhaps for life, and for an elected executive, also serving for life.[55] Hamilton believed that such stable republican governments, electing senators and executive officers for life, or 'during good behaviour', could guard against the 'popular passions' that 'spread like wild fire' and 'become irresistible'.[56] Hamilton well understood the impossibility of creating such long terms of office at the federal level, given the state of contemporary public opinion, but made his point anyway, in a spirit of resigned detachment.[57] In his bicameralism, desire for an executive veto, and commitment to checks and balances in government, Hamilton simply endorsed the enlightened consensus of his era.[58]

IV. Federalism

The United States Constitution, when it emerged from Philadelphia, differed in many ways from Hamilton's ideals, as he expressed them in the Convention; nor did it correspond with New York public opinion, from which Hamilton in any case remained estranged. But he embraced the constitution immediately and worked tirelessly to secure its ratification, because it strengthened the federal government with new powers over commerce, foreign affairs, and above all taxation, to fulfil the purposes and obligations of the Union. Hamilton took it upon himself to organize the ratification movement in New York, and, as 'Publius', with the help of John Jay and James Madison, wrote *The Federalist*, a series of essays explaining and defending the constitution against its critics—essays which have had a vast and continuing influence on public understanding of the document. Written to persuade his sceptical contemporaries, *The Federalist* gives clear insights into what Hamilton and other eighteenth-century Americans thought important in constitutional government, and how the United States Constitution sought to secure these purposes.[59]

The first number of *The Federalist* appeared on October 27, 1787, in New York's *Independent Journal*, at a time when the fate of the Federal Constitution remained very much in doubt. The Confederation Congress had transmitted the proposed constitution to the states in September, with a call for state conventions to consider ratification, but none had yet done so. Hamilton wrote in the character

53 *Writings*, 156. 54 *Writings*, quoting Jacques Necker. 55 *Writings*, 157.
56 *Writings*, 157. 57 *Writings*, 158–9. 58 *Writings*, 165.

59 James Madison considered *The Federalist* 'the most authentic exposition of the text of the Federal Constitution, as understood by the Body which prepared and the authority which accepted it'. James Madison to Thomas Jefferson, 8 February 1825, in *Writings of James Madison*, ed. G. Hunt (New York: G. P. Putnam's Sons, 1900–10), vol. IX, 218.

of 'Publius', co-founder with Brutus of the Roman republic, and champion of the '*imperium populi*' or 'sovereignty of the people'.[60] The declared purpose of *The Federalist* was fourfold: *first*, to demonstrate that 'societies of men are really capable . . . of establishing good government from reflection and choice';[61] *second*, to expose the errors and 'ambition' of local politicians opposed to a closer union;[62] *third*, to show that 'vigour of government is essential to the security of liberty';[63] and *fourth*, to demonstrate 'the conformity of the proposed constitution to the true principles of republican government'.[64] Hamilton's great rival, Thomas Jefferson, would recognize *The Federalist* as 'the best commentary on the principles of government which was ever written'.[65]

The argument for Union, as repeated in *The Federalist*, began with the likelihood of 'domestic factions' and 'convulsions' within and between the states themselves.[66] Here, as before, the negative examples were Greek,[67] supplemented by England, France, and now the recent experience of Massachusetts and the rebellion of Daniel Shays.[68] Given the histories of Sparta, Athens, Rome, and Carthage,[69] Hamilton denied that the 'genius of republics' was necessarily pacific or that 'perpetual peace' between neighbours would prevail without a strong federation to support it.[70] Hamilton understood that Americans, like the rest of the world, were 'yet remote from the happy empire of perfect wisdom and perfect virtue'.[71] He quoted the Abbé de Mably to support his contention that the neighbouring states would be natural enemies, without a 'confederate republic' and federal constitution to extinguish the 'secret jealousy' that 'disposes all States to aggrandize themselves at the expense of their neighbours'.[72]

Hamilton's reference to Mably's proposal for a public law of Europe illustrates the extent to which his first concern, as 'Publius', was already the project of substituting public law for international relations, at least on the North American continent. Territorial conflicts between Pennsylvania and Connecticut,[73] New York

60 See T. Livius, *Ab urbe condita*, II.7.7. Cf. L Mestrius Plutarchus, *Publicola*. On 'Publius' and similar pseudonyms, see M. N. S. Sellers, *American Republicanism: Roman Ideology in the United States Constitution* (Basingstoke: Macmillan, 1994), 8–10.

61 *The Federalist No. 1* in *The Independent Journal* (27 October 1787), in Ball, *The Federalist*, 1.

62 *The Federalist No. 1*, 2.

63 *The Federalist No. 1*, 3.

64 *The Federalist No. 1*, 4, where these purposes are listed in somewhat starker form, along with their necessary corollaries.

65 Thomas Jefferson to James Madison, 18 November 1788 in *Papers of Thomas Jefferson*, ed. J. P. Boyd, C. T. Cullen, and J. Catanzariti (Princeton: Princeton University Press, 1950) vol. XIV, 188.

66 *The Federalist No. 6*, in *The Independent Journal* (14 November 1787), in Ball, *The Federalist*, 19.

67 *The Federalist No. 6*, 20.

68 *The Federalist No. 6*, 21.

69 *The Federalist No. 6*, 22.

70 *The Federalist No. 6*, 21.

71 *The Federalist No. 6*, 24.

72 *The Federalist No. 6*, 25, citing G. B. deMably, *Principes des Négociations pour servir d'introduction au Droit Public de l'Europe* (Amsterdam, 1757).

73 *The Federalist No. 7* in *The Independent Journal* (17 November 1787), in Ball, *The Federalist*, 26.

and Vermont, and others had already led to bloodshed,[74] as might future commercial disagreements,[75] and some states' recent repudiations of their public debt.[76] Hamilton warned of 'war',[77] 'plunder', and 'devastation'[78] in the absence of a Continental Union, since only federation could protect separate states from the 'ambition' and 'jealousy' of their neighbours.[79] Hamilton's desire here was not to overcome or deny ambition through the agency of a federal government, but rather to harness it to make the vigilance of the collected states in the Union a barrier against 'domestic faction' or 'insurrection' in any of their members.[80]

Hamilton's federal constitutionalism rested on his settled conviction that 'a Firm Union' would be of 'utmost moment to the peace and liberty of the States'.[81] The history of the 'petty Republics of Greece and Italy' excited his 'horror and disgust' at their 'rapid succession of revolutions', their 'extremes of tyranny' and their 'tempestuous waves of sedition and anarchy'. In contrast (the reference is to Rome), 'stupendous fabrics reared on the basis of liberty' have 'flourished for ages',[82] through 'ENLARGEMENT of the ORBIT within which such systems ... revolve either in respect to the dimensions of a single State, or to the consolidation of several smaller States into one great confederacy'.[83] Hamilton cited the Baron de Montesquieu to support his claim that the institution of a 'confederate republic' could secure the primary advantages of monarchy, by 'extending the sphere of popular government'.[84] A 'confederate Republic', as Hamilton understood the term, signified the association of several states into one larger and more powerful Union.[85] Hamilton claimed that this arrangement could prevent the encroachment of any single member against the rest, while quelling 'popular insurrections' that might arise in any of the constituent republics.[86]

V. Republicanism

The Federalist set out to demonstrate 'the conformity of the proposed constitution to the true principles of republican government'.[87] The term 'republic' was synonymous, for Hamilton, as for all Americans of his age,[88] with 'civil liberty'

[74] *The Federalist No. 7*, 27. [75] *The Federalist No. 7*, 28.
[76] *The Federalist No. 7*, 30.
[77] *The Federalist No. 8*, in *The New-York Packet* (20 November 1787), in Ball, *The Federalist*, 30.
[78] *The Federalist No. 8*, 31. [79] *The Federalist No. 8*, 34.
[80] *The Federalist No. 9* in *The Independent Journal* (21 November 1787), in Ball, *The Federalist*, 35.
[81] *The Federalist No. 9*, 35. [82] *The Federalist No. 9*, 35.
[83] *The Federalist No. 9*, 36. [84] *The Federalist No. 9*, 37.
[85] *The Federalist No. 9*, 39.
[86] 'Publius' [Alexander Hamilton] *The Federalist No. 9*, 30, quoting at length from Montesquieu, Charles Louis de Secondat, baron de la Brède et de, *De L'Esprit des lois* (1748), Book VIII, chapter 16.
[87] 'Publius' [Alexander Hamilton], *The Federalist No. 4*.
[88] Cf. George Washington, 'The First Inaugural Speech' (30 April 1789), in *George Washington: A Collection*, ed. W. B. Allen (Indianapolis: Liberty Fund, 1988), 460 ff.

and 'free government'.[89] This required elections, of course, as Hamilton had recognized at the Constitutional Convention,[90] but also further guarantees, to be discovered by applying 'the science of politics' to the circumstances of the North American states.[91] Hamilton identified several useful principles of constitutional government now known to 'the enlightened friends of liberty' that 'were either not known at all, or imperfectly known to the ancients'. These included 'The regular distribution of power into distinct departments—the introduction of legislative balances and checks—the institution of courts composed of judges holding their offices during good behaviour—[and] the representation of the people in the legislature by deputies of their own election'.[92]

Hamilton's list of 'new discoveries' and political ideas that 'have made their principal progress towards perfection in modern times'[93] provided republicans (Hamilton believed) with the 'means, and powerful means' through which 'the excellencies of republican government may be retained and its imperfections lessened or avoided'.[94] Hamilton's originality lay not so much in this list, which corresponded very closely to a similar list provided by John Adams in his *Defence of the Constitutions of Government of the United States of America*,[95] as it did in his addition of federalism to the basic protections of republican government.[96] Hamilton promoted 'the utility of confederacy' not only 'to suppress faction', but also 'to guard the internal tranquility of states', and 'to increase their external force' against others.[97] A 'vigorous executive' in a republican confederation would provide a constant protection against the assaults 'of ambition, of faction, and of anarchy'.[98]

The American model for successful republican government was Rome, but Rome itself had succumbed to 'absolute power', the 'tyranny' of 'ambitious individuals', and the 'seditions of whole classes of the community'.[99] Even in its republican days, as Hamilton well understood, 'Rome was never sated of carnage and conquest'.[100] How, then, to improve upon the ancient model, but by 'reason and good sense'?[101] Free trade among the states would make them all richer, stronger, and more creditable to foreigners,[102] more amenable to taxation,[103] and economically prosperous,[104] provided that the federal government took authority to rule directly over individuals, not indirectly, as when acting through the states.[105]

[89] *The Federalist No. 9*, 35.

[90] See Madison's notes on Hamilton's remarks at the Constitutional Convention, in Hamilton, *Writings*, 157.

[91] *The Federalist No. 9*, 36.

[92] *The Federalist No. 9*, 36.

[93] *The Federalist No. 9*, 36.

[94] *The Federalist No. 9*, 36.

[95] Adams, *Defence of the Constitutions of Government*, i.

[96] *The Federalist No. 9*, 36.

[97] *The Federalist No. 9*, 36.

[98] *The Federalist No. 70* in *The Independent Journal* (15 March 1788), in Ball, *The Federalist*, 341.

[99] *The Federalist No. 70*, 341.

[100] *The Federalist No. 6*, 22.

[101] *The Federalist No. 70*, 343.

[102] *The Federalist No. 11*, 51.

[103] *The Federalist No. 12*, 53.

[104] *The Federalist No. 13*, 57.

[105] *The Federalist No. 15*, 67.

Hamilton's desire to strengthen the federal government carried with it the necessary corollary that federal institutions should also be protected by all the republican checks and balances against arbitrary power already being applied in the states.[106] If the federal government were to act directly on individuals, as Hamilton desired that it should, with the ability to apply sanctions through its laws,[107] then it ought also be subject to independent courts,[108] and rest in all the branches of government, and in its own ratification, ultimately on the 'consent of the people', which Hamilton considered to be the 'pure original fountain of all legitimate authority'.[109]

Alexander Hamilton understood the United States of America, as established under the Constitution of 1787, to be a 'republic', but specifically a 'confederate' republic,[110] existing primarily for certain purposes, including 'the common defence of the members—the preservation of the public peace as well against internal convulsions as external attacks—the regulation of commerce with other nations and between the States—[and] the superintendence of... intercourse, political and commercial, with foreign countries'.[111] As to these purposes, the federal republic would need 'all the powers, which a free people *ought to delegate to any government*'.[112] Hamilton supposed it likely, in any case, that the federal government would enjoy better administration than the governments of the states, because it would have a 'greater knowledge' and 'more extensive information' to draw on.[113] The government of the United States would be 'less apt to be tainted by the spirit of faction, and more out of the reach of those occasional ill humors or temporary prejudices... which in smaller societies frequently contaminate the public councils' or 'beget injustice and oppression'.[114]

VI. The Rule of Law

Alexander Hamilton praised the new Constitution of the United States as the 'supreme law of the land', superior to the laws and constitutions of all the several states in the Union.[115] The legislatures, courts, and magistrates of all member States were to be 'incorporated into the operations of the national government' as auxiliaries in the enforcement of its laws,[116] overseen by federal judges serving '*during good behaviour*'—'one of the most valuable of the modern improvements in the practice of government'.[117] Tenure during good behaviour (secured in England by the Act of Settlement in 1701) had proved under monarchy to be 'an excellent barrier to the despotism of a prince'. Hamilton suggested that in a republic it would

[106] *The Federalist No. 71*, 350. [107] *The Federalist No. 21*, 94.
[108] *The Federalist No. 22*, 104. [109] *The Federalist No. 22*, 104.
[110] *The Federalist No. 9*, 38. [111] *The Federalist No. 23*, 106.
[112] *The Federalist No. 23*, 109 (emphasis in original).
[113] *The Federalist No. 27*, 125. [114] *The Federalist No. 27*, 125.
[115] *The Federalist No. 27*, 127. [116] *The Federalist No. 27*, 127.
[117] *The Federalist No. 78*, 377.

be 'no less excellent' as a 'barrier to the encroachments and oppressions of the representative body'.[118]

Hamilton praised judicial independence as 'the best expedient which can be devised in any government, to secure a steady, upright and impartial administration of the laws'.[119] Supporting, as he did, a general separation between the legislative, executive, and judicial branches of government[120] and a constitutional system of checks and balances to control them all, Hamilton identified judges as the 'least dangerous' of the constitutional powers.[121] The judiciary has no power over the sword (controlled by the executive), or the purse (controlled by the legislature). Judges have (he explained) 'neither force nor will, but merely judgment' and will need 'permanency in office' to protect the 'freedom and independence' of their judgments against coordinate branches of government.[122] Hamilton suggested that independent judges best protect 'the citadel of public justice and the public security' and insisted that 'complete independence of the courts of justice' is 'peculiarly essential' for a limited constitutional government.[123]

Limited constitutions can persist in practice, Hamilton believed, and control the excesses of legislative authority only through the courts of justice, 'whose duty it must be to declare all acts contrary to the manifest tenor of the constitution void'. Without this 'all the reservations of particular rights' would amount to nothing.[124] Hamilton insisted that judges must have the power to pronounce legislative acts 'void', because otherwise legislators would become sole arbiters of their own constitutional powers, with licence to surpass constitutional limitations at will. 'A constitution is in fact, and must be regarded by the judges as a fundamental law.' This made interpretation 'the proper and peculiar province' of courts. Hamilton as 'Publius' repeated that judges alone should settle the meaning of the constitution, and all laws made pursuant to its authority.[125] '[W]here the will of the legislature, declared in its statutes, stands in opposition to that of the people declared in the Constitution . . . [then] judges ought to regulate their decisions by the fundamental laws, rather than by those which are not fundamental.'[126]

Hamilton's commitment to judicial independence as the primary protection of the rule of law reflects centuries of English history (and French philosophy), but also his own experience of American justice. Only the 'permanent tenure' of judges could secure the 'bulwark' of the constitution against legislative 'encroachments'.[127] Hamilton considered the independence of judges 'equally requisite' to protect the rights of individuals against 'designing men' and 'serious oppressions'.[128] 'Until the people have by solemn and authoritative act annulled or changed the established

[118] *The Federalist No. 78*, 377. [119] *The Federalist No. 78*, 377.
[120] *The Federalist No. 78*, 378, quoting Montesquieu, Book XI, chapter 6.
[121] *The Federalist No. 78*, 378. [122] *The Federalist No. 78*, 378.
[123] *The Federalist No. 78*, 378. [124] *The Federalist No. 78*, 379.
[125] *The Federalist No. 78*, 379. [126] *The Federalist No. 78*, 380.
[127] *The Federalist No. 78*, 381. [128] *The Federalist No. 78*, 381.

form, [the Constitution] is binding upon them collectively, as well as individually, and no presumption, or even knowledge of their sentiments, can warrant their representatives in a departure from it.'[129] No such protection could be expected, Hamilton believed, without independent judges, secure in their tenure of office,[130] and well enough paid to justify the renunciation of ordinary legal practice.[131]

Alexander Hamilton's 78th letter as *The Federalist* offered a paean to judges, judicial independence, and constitutionalism, which has had an enormous influence in strengthening the resolution of judges in the United States and elsewhere to maintain the rule of law against legislative enthusiasm. The practice of judicial review of legislation, perpetuated by United States Supreme Court Chief Justice John Marshall in the famous case of *Marbury v Madison*, closely followed the reasoning of *The Federalist*.[132] *The Federalist* also reinforced the prohibition of *ex post facto* laws and sanctity of the writ of *habeas corpus* as essential 'securities' to 'liberty' and 'republicanism' against 'arbitrary government'.[133] 'The establishment of a constitution,' Hamilton asserted, 'by the voluntary consent of the whole people, is a PRODIGY, to the completion of which I look forward with trembling anxiety.'[134] For Hamilton, the primary virtues of the Constitution of the United States were the unity, energy, justice, and legality that federal republican institutions would bring to government, throughout the Union.

VII. Conclusion

The systematic exposition of Hamilton's constitutional thought ended with the entry into force of the United States Constitution, and the election of George Washington as President of the United States, with Hamilton as his Secretary of the Treasury and *de facto* chief of staff. Henceforth, Hamilton's primary concerns would be the practical problems of consolidating a federal republic from what had been a loose society of states. Hamilton's *Report on Public Credit* established the necessity of a sound public debt.[135] His *Report on a National Bank* secured the finances of the United States.[136] Both required constitutional support, but only as related to their relationship with the states, and Hamilton had no difficulty getting the best of that argument.[137] His *Report on the Subject of Manufactures* laid the groundwork for the subsequent prosperity of the Union,[138] and his tenacity in the newspapers defeated the most persistent opponents of the federal project.[139]

129 *The Federalist No. 78*, 381–2.

130 *The Federalist No. 78*, 382.

131 *The Federalist No. 79*, 384.

132 *Marbury v Madison*, 5 U.S. 137 (1803).

133 *The Federalist No. 84*, 418.

134 *The Federalist No. 85*, 431.

135 Alexander Hamilton, *Report on Public Credit* (9 January 1790).

136 *Report on a National Bank* (13 December 1790).

137 Alexander Hamilton, *Opinion on the Constitutionality of a National Bank* (23 February 1791), in Hamilton, *Writings*, 759.

138 Alexander Hamilton, *Report on the Subject of Manufactures* (5 December 1791).

139 See his response as 'An American' to the machinations of 'State-power' against 'National Authority' in 'An American' [Alexander Hamilton], *For the Gazette of the United States* (4 August 1792).

Hamilton would continue, both in and out of office, to take to the lists as 'Pacificus',[140] 'Tully',[141] 'Titus Manlius',[142] and so forth, in defence of 'an inviolable respect for the Constitution and the laws' as the 'greatest source of security in a Republic'.[143] As his carefully chosen Roman pseudonyms attest, Hamilton kept faith with the old Roman conception of balanced republican government against democratic and self-interested 'anarchy', (towards which 'contempt of the laws is the high road').[144] Hamilton distinguished a 'government of FORCE' or 'despotism' from a 'government of LAWS', or 'liberty', and insisted on the 'obvious truth' that 'a sacred respect for the constitutional law is the vital principle' of a 'free government'.[145]

'How long, ye Catilines,' Hamilton demanded as 'Tully', 'will you abuse our patience!'[146] Hamilton saw constitutional government in the United States beset by his enemies, and pursued them in print with philippics, to the point that they conspired at his downfall, and eventual death, like his Roman alter ego.[147] Throughout his career, Hamilton acted on the principle that although the people 'commonly intend the public good', they 'do not always reason right about the means of promoting it'.[148] The 'republican principle demands', he asserted, that the '*deliberate* sense of the community' should govern their affairs, not 'every sudden breeze of passion' or 'every transient impulse which the people may receive from the arts of men'. The beauty of constitutional government lay in its ability to distinguish mere 'inclinations' from true 'interests' of the people.[149]

Alexander Hamilton shared the republican constitutional principles of his contemporaries, including their commitment to bicameral legislatures, elected executives, the separation of powers, checks and balances in government, and representative (rather than direct) democracy. He differed somewhat in his much stronger commitment to federalism, to executive power, and to judges, as the 'bulwark' of constitutional liberty. Hamilton became as 'Publius' (with Madison) in *The Federalist* the foremost advocate and interpreter of constitutional government as it would ultimately be implemented in the United States. All these principles, widely accepted in theory by 'enlightened' political writers of Hamilton's era, were made real in the American state constitutions, and the Federal Constitution of 1787, from which they have extended across the globe. Continentalist, federalist, republican, and devotee of the rule of law, it was as a constitutionalist that Hamilton left his greatest legacy. Great modern federations, such as

[140] 'Pacificus' [Alexander Hamilton], *Pacificus No. I*, in *Gazette of the United States* (29 June 1793), defending Washington's proclamation of neutrality.

[141] *Tully No. I* in *Dunlap and Claypoole's American Daily Advertiser* (23 August 1794), against attempts in Western Pennsylvania to defy the constitution's authority.

[142] *The Stand* in the *New York Commercial Advertiser* (10 March 1798).

[143] *Tully No. III* in *Dunlap and Claypoole's American Daily Advertiser* (28 August 1794).

[144] *Tully No. III.* [145] *Tully No. III.*

[146] *Tully No. III.*

[147] See e.g. letter from Aaron Burr, 22 June 1804, in Hamilton, *Writings*, 1014–15.

[148] *The Federalist No. 71*, 349.

[149] *The Federalist No. 71*, 349 (emphasis added).

the European Union, the Federal Republic of Germany, and even nominally monarchical Australia take their ambition and primary example from the American Federalists' creation of that 'stupendous fabric' of government, reared 'on the basis of liberty', that has 'flourished for ages' to the amazement and inspiration of the world.[150]

[150] Cf. 'Publius' [Alexander Hamilton], *The Federalist No. 9* in *The Independent Journal* (21 November 1787), republished in Ball, *The Federalist*, 35.

17

Jefferson's Constitutions

Gerald Leonard

I. Introduction

The story of the writing of the American Constitution is a familiar one. A little less familiar is the story of Thomas Jefferson's pivotal role in altering the operative meaning of the constitution between 1787 and the Jacksonian ascendancy of the late 1820s and 1830s. To explain this aspect of Jefferson's career serves to explain many of Jefferson's constitutional convictions and the ways in which they did and did not change with changing circumstances.

The drafters of the 1787 Constitution designed the new national government to gather more power at the centre, while resisting democracy, and neutralizing parties and factions. Large districts for House members, long terms for senators, an executive veto, and judicial review, among other structural devices, were designed to promote the election of eminent men, to encourage deliberation, and to frustrate attempts to organize a dominant party or faction. Enhanced powers at the centre and new limitations on state powers would insulate government from excessively direct control of the people and limit the states' capacities to violate rights of property and the like.[1]

By the time of Jackson's presidency, enabled by the mastermind of the Democratic party, Martin Van Buren, much of this understanding had changed. Speaking for the ascendant Democratic party, Van Buren articulated a radically democratic theory of the Constitution in which the will of the people as expressed through the party became the authoritative word on both policy and constitutional meaning. He celebrated the 'exclusive and towering supremacy'[2] that the party had achieved under Jefferson's leadership, and made clear his expectation that the party would continue to be the organ of the people as a whole, not just one of two or more parties dividing the people. The only principle as important as the party's

[1] See, among many others, G. S. Wood, *The Creation of the American Republic, 1776–1787* (Chapel Hill: University of North Carolina Press, 1969); J. Rakove, *Original Meanings: Politics and Ideas in the Making of the Constitution* (New York: A. A. Knopf, 1996); J. Nedelsky, *Private Property and the Limits of American Constitutionalism: The Madisonian Framework and Its Legacy* (Chicago: University of Chicago Press, 1990).

[2] M. Van Buren, *The Autobiography of Martin Van Buren*, ed. J. C. Fitzpatrick (New York: Da Capo Press, 1973), 303.

right to dictate to the officeholders—functionally overriding all the structural checks designed by the Framers—was the principle of states' rights.[3] By the 1820s, the Democrats' radical states' rights positions were dominant, and Van Buren and the Democrats hoped that a firm states' rights position would help them solve the problem of slavery. Stipulating, in effect, that slave states were nevertheless republican states, they organized the democracy nationally on the basis that each state's domestic arrangements were off limits to the national government. Experience, however, would show, as Jefferson had always feared, that the challenge of slavery to the republican experiment could never be so easily finessed.

If the big story between the 1780s and the 1830s was the democratization of the constitution, largely by the device of party organization, as well as the tugging of the constitution in the direction of states' rights and the entrenchment of slavery, then Thomas Jefferson was at the centre of the story in all these aspects. He was the most democratic of the prominent men of the founding generation, yet he stopped short of the radical democracy that became dominant under Jackson and Van Buren. Instead, he insisted on the centrality of law to republican government and hesitated to assume that the people could always be trusted to respect the essential restraints of reason and legal tradition. He adhered to a radical states' rights position from the earliest days of his public life to the last. And, all his life, he struggled intellectually with the challenges that slavery presented to the states' allegedly republican experiments, never doubting the deep wrongness of the institution but always defending the autonomy of the states, even as that came to mean the ever-deeper entrenchment of slavery. Van Buren and Jackson would ultimately leave Jefferson behind in their embrace of party-based democracy, but, however inadvertently, Jefferson laid out much of the road to that destination, including its doomed method for dealing with slavery, over the course of his long public career.

This essay will elucidate Jefferson's constitutional thought across half a century of constitutional development. Given space constraints, it will be highly selective. It will first discuss his revolutionary tract, the *Summary View*, a foundational document of American federalism. Then, it will turn to his one book, *Notes on the State of Virginia*, which, among other matters, explored the internal constitution of a republic (as opposed to the larger confederation of republics). Remarkably democratic for its time, it nevertheless elevated law and constitutional structures, such as the separation of powers, above democracy and the 'sovereign' people. The *Notes* also tried to face up to some of the powerfully anti-republican effects of slavery, though it offered no solutions. Finally, this essay will discuss some political events of the 1790s and 1800s that are particularly useful in illuminating Jefferson's reluctant movement, as well as the limits on that movement, in the direction of democracy and party organization. The essential themes, then, in this account of Jefferson's constitutional thought are democratization and its relation to the rule of law, the emergence of party, federalism (states' rights), and slavery.

[3] On Van Buren and the Democratic party, see G. Leonard, *The Invention of Party Politics: Federalism, Popular Sovereignty, and Constitutional Development in Jacksonian Illinois* (Chapel Hill: University of North Carolina Press, 2002).

II. Jefferson's *Summary View* and the Origins of American Federalism

Jefferson's commitment to federalism appeared even before the revolution. As the imperial crisis reached boiling point in the mid-1770s, Jefferson wrote *A Summary View of the Rights of British America*, which was published as a pamphlet to promote resistance to British pretensions. The essay does not lack for the vindications of natural rights that one might expect from a revolutionary pamphlet. For example, Jefferson identifies 'a right which nature has given to all men, of departing from the country in which chance, not choice, has placed them, of going in quest of new habitations, and of there establishing new societies', as well as those 'rights of human nature, deeply wounded by [the] infamous practice' of slavery.[4]

Nevertheless, as Peter Onuf argues, the pamphlet's essential argument is not a defence of a natural right to self-government alone. It is a defence of republican *federalism* as a theory of the British Empire. Written as a propaganda piece, it perhaps aimed less for descriptive, historical accuracy, since few people before 1774 would have had the temerity to suggest that the British Empire was simply a league of equal states, than at integrating the colonists' emergent republicanism with their continued commitment (as of 1774) to the British Empire. But, as much as it was a creature of its moment, the *Summary View* adumbrated the essentials of the confederal structure that Jefferson would advocate for the rest of his life, not only reading them into the imperial structure of 1774 but finding them in the constitution's embrace of federalism in 1787 as well.[5]

Jefferson's opening paragraph characterized the colonies not as George's 'colonies' but as 'his states';[6] this, two years before the colonies declared independence. Claiming that Britain had never assisted the emigrants to America in the settlement of their new lands, he insisted that British Americans' continuing bond with Britain was strictly limited and a matter of choice: 'settlements having been thus effected in the wilds of America, the emigrants thought proper to adopt that system of laws under which they had hitherto lived in the mother country, and to continue their union with her by submitting themselves to the same common sovereign, who was thereby made the central link connecting the several parts of the empire'.[7]

Americans voluntarily chose to hold onto the monarchy as the essential link in a federal system, in which each local legislature, including the parliament in London, rightly legislated only for its own domestic constituency. Jefferson did not hesitate to catalogue the alleged substantive injustices of parliament's American legislation, which purported to subordinate American interests and rights to British. But he emphasized that the American claim was *not* a claim to substantively fair treatment by parliament but a constitutional claim to complete independence from parliament:

[4] Thomas Jefferson, *A Summary View of the Rights of British America* (Williamsburg: 1774).

[5] P. S. Onuf, 'Thomas Jefferson, Federalist', in *The Mind of Thomas Jefferson* (Charlottesville: University of Virginia Press, 2007).

[6] Jefferson, *Summary View*, 5. [7] Jefferson, *Summary View*, 7.

> [W]e do not point out to his majesty the injustice of these acts, with intent to rest on that principle the cause of their nullity; but to shew that experience confirms the propriety of those political principles which exempt us from the jurisdiction of the British parliament. The true ground on which we declare these acts void is, that the British parliament has no right to exercise authority over us.
> ...Can any one reason be assigned why 160,000 electors in the island of Great Britain should give law to four millions in the states of America...?[8]

The British Empire was not a metropolitan empire with authority concentrated at the centre, but a network of equal and independent republics—a confederation—linked only by the monarchy.

And so the *Summary View* looked to the monarchy to rectify the wrongs attempted by parliament. But why did Jefferson accept a constitutional role for the king at all in a rapidly republicanizing America? Because republicanism *required* federalism, and federalism required a federal head. Jefferson's theory of republicanism held that the freedom and prosperity of each political community depended on the existence of a central authority, empowered to preserve peace and commerce among otherwise independent states. Thus, 'we do earnestly entreat his majesty, as yet the only mediatory power between the several states of the British empire, to recommend to his parliament of Great Britain the total revocation of these acts, which, however nugatory they be, may yet prove the cause of further discontents and jealousies among us',[9] and he endorsed the king's constitutional authority to employ the veto to prevent such unequal laws.

But, in fact, George had already exposed his unwillingness to serve as an impartial functionary of the empire. Jefferson argued that George had already abused the veto power in rejecting American laws 'of the most salutary tendency'.[10] Moreover, these were not minor ordinances but included vital efforts, so Jefferson claimed, to rid the colonies of slavery. That institution, he insisted, was already a burden in 1774 (and of course would become the ever more salient curse of the American experiment across the remaining decades of Jefferson's life): 'The abolition of domestic slavery is the great object of desire in those colonies,...yet our repeated attempts to effect this by prohibitions, and by imposing duties which might amount to a prohibition, have been hitherto defeated by his majesty's negative.' Thus had the king abdicated his responsibility to treat the empire's component states impartially, instead 'preferring the immediate advantages of a few African corsairs to the lasting interests of the American states, and to the rights of human nature, deeply wounded by this infamous practice'.[11] Further examples—the dissolving of American assemblies, the landing of troops in American states without local consent, etc—filled out the indictment, even as Jefferson purported to plead with George to resume his proper role in a confederal empire: 'Let no act be passed by any one legislature which may infringe on the rights and liberties of another. This is the important

[8] Jefferson, *Summary View,* 10–12. [9] Jefferson, *Summary View,* 16.
[10] Jefferson, *Summary View,* 16. [11] Jefferson, *Summary View,* 16–17.

post in which fortune has placed you, holding the balance of a great, if a well poised empire.'[12]

This embrace of an 'empire' of equal states, insisting that a 'great' empire should be a 'balanced' and 'well poised' empire, would continue to inform Jefferson's thought under the United States Constitution a generation later. Separation from the British Empire would not lead Jefferson to leave the notion of empire behind but instead to conceive of America as just the sort of empire outlined in the *Summary View*. In the new Constitution of 1787, he saw the blueprint of an 'empire for liberty', in which the national government would hold the balance of an expanding empire of republics. But that national government would remain strictly limited to that role, never interfering in the internal affairs of the component republics and never engrossing any more power than what was granted to it by the states. As Peter Onuf describes Jefferson's later thought, Jefferson ultimately extended this model ever downward, imagining a pyramid of republics: 'ward' republics at the foundation, county republics built on that base, republican states poised above, and the national government at the apex. But being higher in the pyramid entailed only those powers necessary to maintain peace and equal justice among the component 'republics' just below. Such restrictions on power ultimately conduced to the preservation of individual liberties in the communities at the bottom.[13]

Note that in the *Summary View* Jefferson primarily developed the theory and practice of an empire of self-governing republics, and had little occasion to develop ideas about the sort of constitution that might make a state republican in the first place. He was prepared to accept, or at least chose not to deny, that Britain with its '160,000 electors' was sufficiently republican to join with the 'four millions in the states of America' in composing an empire of peace and mutual advantage. He addressed the scourge of slavery but said nothing about the relationship of that institution to the republican (or not) character of the states where it existed in large numbers. He eagerly expounded self-government and the natural equality of all men, whether American or British, but he did not elaborate on the proper conditions of a republican constitution. Still, Jefferson's theory of federalism was essential to his theory of republican constitutionalism, because he believed that no single republic could long sustain itself without a larger federal structure.[14]

III. Jefferson's *Notes on the State of Virginia* and the Ingredients of a Republican Constitution

First drafted during the continuance of the revolution (1781, with substantial revisions through 1784), *Notes on the State of Virginia* had little to say about

[12] Jefferson, *Summary View*, 23.

[13] P. S. Onuf, *Jefferson's Empire: The Language of American Nationhood* (Charlottesville: University Press of Virginia, 2000), 117–21.

[14] Onuf, *Jefferson's Empire*, 8, 120.

federalism and much more to say, although somewhat haphazardly, about the internal constitution of a republic and specifically the republic of Virginia. For his time and his generation, and his social position as a planter and large slaveholder, Jefferson took surprisingly democratic and emancipationist positions. For an icon of democratic revolution and the natural right to liberty and equality, however, he proved notably stuck in his slaveholding, pre-democratic time and place. While *Notes* was hardly a constitutional tract—it was something of a miscellaneous commentary on Virginia—it contained much material pertinent to Virginia's constitution. In particular, Jefferson devoted substantial space to considerations of the character that must be fostered in a sovereign people, of the nature of leadership in a republic, of the challenge of slavery to republicanism, and of the preeminence of law, even over the will of the people, in rendering a society republican. Moreover, the ideas developed here remained largely stable over the course of Jefferson's life, although some significant development will be discussed in the next section.

If the people were to be sovereign and their will always to be obeyed, Jefferson nevertheless implied that that will must be just to be truly republican and that, to be just, that will must emanate from a people whose character had been properly fostered. He claimed, first, that only husbandry cultivated the sort of virtue necessary to maintenance of a republican constitution:

> Those who labour in the earth are the chosen people of God, if ever he had a chosen people, whose breasts he has made his peculiar deposit for substantial and genuine virtue. . . . [L]et our workshops remain in Europe. . . . It is the manners and spirit of a people which preserve a republic in vigour. A degeneracy in these is a canker which soon eats to the heart of its laws and constitution.[15]

Once a sufficient portion of the people had abandoned husbandry and adopted habits of 'subservience and venality', the natural habits of those who laboured for others or who depended on customers for their living, the way would open for those with 'designs of ambition' to extinguish republican government.

But mere engagement in husbandry, it turns out, was not the whole story. Rather, Jefferson sought wide education with the goal of 'rendering the people the safe, as they are the ultimate, guardians of their own liberty'. The people must be educated to spy 'corruption and degeneracy' in government from afar because: 'Every government degenerates when trusted to the rulers of the people alone. The people themselves therefore are its only safe depositories. And to render even them safe their minds must be improved to a certain degree.'[16]

Moreover, even an educated population of husbandmen might not be enough, thanks to slavery. In the *Notes*, Jefferson did not directly confront, but implicitly acknowledged, the tension between his celebration of the husbandman's virtue and his description of the effects of slavery, not to mention the latter's manifest

[15] Thomas Jefferson, *Notes on the State of Virginia*, ed. W. Peden (Chapel Hill: University of North Carolina Press, 1955), 165.
[16] Jefferson, *Notes*, 148.

injustice. He described Virginia slavery as a statewide training ground for despotism and indolence on the part of white Virginians and subservience on the part of black Virginians, hardly consistent with the popular character he had deemed essential to republicanism and likely, in fact, to lead eventually to full-scale insurrection:

> There must doubtless be an unhappy influence on the manners of our people produced by the existence of slavery among us. The whole commerce between master and slave is a perpetual exercise of the most boisterous passions, the most unremitting despotism on the one part, and degrading submissions on the other... The man must be a prodigy who can retain his manners and morals undepraved by such circumstances... With the morals of the people, their industry also is destroyed. For in a warm climate, no man will labour for himself who can make another labour for him... [We can only hope somehow] for a total emancipation, and that this is disposed, in the order of events, to be with the consent of the masters, rather than by their extirpation.[17]

Jefferson's hopes were bolstered somewhat by Virginia's ban on slave importation, a first step to undermining 'this great political and moral evil, while the minds of our citizens may be ripening for a complete emancipation of human nature'.[18] But he always insisted that emancipation be gradual and accompanied by colonization because of his deeply racist conviction that free blacks and free whites could not live together without entering into a war that would end in the 'extermination of the one or the other race'.[19]

In sum, the Jefferson of the 1780s wrote frankly about the already visible and dire threats to the republican revolution. Jefferson seemed to acknowledge that all depended on the rooting out of slavery and ignorance. On the question of slavery, he joined many in the founding generation, many of them slaveholders themselves, who looked forward to abolition. Yet forty years later, as slavery became more entrenched and as the dream of emancipation faded from view, Jefferson would find himself travelling the same road as his state: he still personally possessed something like 175 slaves; he supported the entry of new slave states into the Union; and he stoutly defended the principle of state equality that was by then the principal defence of the slave states. Yet he never retracted his early characterization of slavery as productive of just the sort of 'degeneracy' that would '[eat] to the heart of [a republic's] laws and constitution.'[20]

As he pressed past the challenges of slavery, Jefferson took remarkably democratic positions in the *Notes*. He made very clear that sovereignty lay in the people as a whole, that the moral virtue of the people was an essential element of defence against anti-republican usurpations, and that much wider suffrage than commonly obtained in the states ought to be guaranteed. Still, he neglected to provide any careful analysis of the role the people would actually play in a republican constitution. Almost thirty years later, he would develop the notion of 'ward republics': small geographical units in which each white man would play an active role in

[17] Jefferson, *Notes*, 162–3. [18] Jefferson, *Notes*, 87.
[19] Jefferson, *Notes*, 138. [20] Jefferson, *Notes*, 165.

governance.[21] But the *Notes* failed to offer any detail about the role of the people in republican governance, indicating that this original animator of American democracy remained significantly less democratic in his thinking than is sometimes supposed.

Jefferson's discussion of education suggests the same point. Jefferson advocated a constitutional mandate for a programme of public education, and the particular scheme that he advocated had clearly constitutional goals on two dimensions. I have already noted his claim that wide education would equip the people to identify the seeds of tyranny before they grew. But, just as importantly, he sought to identify the most talented young Virginians, the state's natural aristocracy if properly cultivated, thus hoping 'to avail the state of those talents which nature has sown as liberally among the poor as the rich'.[22] Sovereignty and a kind of watchdog suffrage, extending as far as a right of revolution, lay in the people, but he intimated that the people could not expect to play a role any more active than that. He had no thought of competitive elections turning on issues of public policy, nor of popular parties instructing their representatives, nor of candidates chosen for their fealty to popular opinion rather than their manifest talents. In the words of Gordon Wood, Jefferson 'was not a modern democrat, assuming as he did that a natural aristocracy would lead the country, [but] he had a confidence in the capacity and virtue of the people to elect that aristocracy that was unmatched by any of the other founders'.[23]

If this most democratic of American Founders harboured such elements of elitism, he also seemed to consider established principles of law more important than the will of the people. Jefferson's reverence for law is manifest in his discussion of the defects in the first Virginia Constitution. Here, he emphasized that the constitution must not simply guarantee the supremacy of popular will but must supply a mechanism by which law would hem in the legislature and by which law would guide and structure the people's will.

In particular, he objected to the constitution's failure adequately to separate powers and thus to equip each branch of government to enforce the legal limits on the other branches' authority: 'All the powers of government, legislative, executive, and judiciary, result to the legislative body. The concentrating these in the same hands is precisely the definition of despotic government.' Without proper, functional separation, the government was not limited by law: 'An *elective despotism* was not the government we fought for; but one . . . in which the powers of government should be so divided and balanced among several bodies of magistracy, as that no one could transcend their legal limits, without being effectually checked by the others.'[24] In fact, Jefferson noted that Virginia's 'ordinance of government',

[21] See the discussions in R. K. Matthews, *The Radical Politics of Thomas Jefferson: A Revisionist View* (Lawrence: University Press of Kansas, 1984); and G. W. Sheldon, *The Political Philosophy of Thomas Jefferson* (Baltimore: Johns Hopkins University Press, 1991).

[22] Jefferson, *Notes*, 148.

[23] G. S. Wood, *Revolutionary Characters: What Made the Founders Different* (New York: Penguin Press, 2006), 107.

[24] Jefferson, *Notes*, 120.

which he was not willing to call a 'constitution', nominally adopted just such a separation of powers but left executive and judicial salaries and tenure in the hands of the legislature. It thus undermined the other branches' capacities to defend the law against legislative incursions.

He thought the constitution a mere 'ordinance' not only because it failed to impose legal limits on government but because of its method of adoption. Jefferson claimed that the provisional, ad hoc legislature elected in April 1776, which produced the ordinance/constitution, was never elected for the special purpose of forming a constitution. At the time of the election, no voter contemplated such a thing because Virginia's independence had not yet been declared nor decided upon in the public mind. For Jefferson, the absence of specific authorization from the voters to form a constitution deprived that body's emergency enactment of the legal status of a constitution, notwithstanding its being 'entitled a Constitution or Form of Government'.[25] Instead, every newly elected legislature had power to alter the constitution, and sometimes had done so, rather than feeling itself constrained by a constitution imposed from without.

I am not much concerned with whether Jefferson got his history right on this question, but his argument nicely demonstrates his view of how a constitution might accrue authority. Something of a law-and-society scholar, he implied that sociological and historical evidence of popular acceptance would be enough to authorize a document or practice to place legal limits on government actors and especially legislatures. Thus the employment of a constitutional convention rather than a legislature might be enough, even though each body derived its power from the same electorate, since the people's purposes were presumably different in the two cases. Neither such a convention nor popular ratification was essential, but some such evidence of wide acceptance was indispensable. Thus, in trying to de-legitimate the Virginia Constitution of 1776, Jefferson chose to attack the evidence of popular acceptance offered by defenders of the constitution, rather than assert that some formal legal procedure had been omitted. In the event, the law of prevailing practice went against Jefferson, and Virginia's 1776 Constitution remained in place and fully functioning until the constitutional revision of 1830.

Had Jefferson been a real democrat of the Jacksonian sort, he would have proposed constitutional reforms for giving the people at large an ever more active and close control over their officeholders. But, for Jefferson, problems with the content of the constitution and its mode of adoption demonstrated not inadequate popular control but an inadequate legal structure to bind the government:

> Our situation is indeed perilous, and I hope my countrymen . . . will apply, at a proper season, the proper remedy; which is a convention to fix the constitution, to amend its defects, to bind up the several branches of government by certain laws, which when they transgress their acts shall become nullities; to render unnecessary an appeal to the people, or in other words, a rebellion, on every infraction of their rights . . .[26]

[25] Jefferson, *Notes*, 122. [26] Jefferson, *Notes*, 129.

In this very pre-Jacksonian quotation, he seeks to avoid appeals to the people, which he equates with 'rebellion,' and looks instead to the discipline of clear law.

This preoccupation with law, of course, necessarily implied a concern with enforcement mechanisms. In the quotation just above, Jefferson seemed implicitly to look to the judiciary to render legislative transgressions 'nullities'. In principle, he referred to the obligation of each branch to control the other two where possible. But the most salient mechanism would be the specifically judicial refusal to implement unconstitutional statutes, a power that he again embraced just a few years later when advocating the inclusion of a bill of rights in the federal constitution.

Concomitantly, he revealed a scepticism that the people at large could or would (or should) do much to roll back usurpations by this or that branch of government. They might be roused to demand a constitutional convention and might (rarely) rebel against a long train of oppressions, but they wouldn't be much good at resisting the slow accumulation of unconstitutional power in the government.[27] For that, reliance had to be placed on well-designed legal mechanisms—'bind[ing] up the several branches of government by certain laws'—that would empower each branch to defend its own prerogatives.

I will not discuss Jefferson's passionate defences of freedom of religion, but it was at the end of one such defence in the *Notes* that he eloquently summed up the practical relationship between the people's severely limited constitutional capacities and those of the constitution itself as a specifically legal document:

> It can never be too often repeated, that the time for fixing every essential right on a legal basis is while our rulers are honest, and ourselves united. From the conclusion of this war we shall be going down hill. It will not then be necessary to resort every moment to the people for support. They will be forgotten, therefore, and their rights disregarded. They will forget themselves, but in the sole faculty of making money, and will never think of uniting to effect a due respect for their rights. The shackles, therefore, which shall not be knocked off at the conclusion of this war will remain on us long, will be made heavier and heavier, till our rights shall revive or expire in a convulsion.[28]

In short, the people might be sovereign, but only clear foundational law—not the suffrage and not a right of rebellion—would ensure an adequate regard for their rights.

* * *

The essential themes established by a look at Jefferson's early work, then, are as follow. Notwithstanding his belief that only the people at large could and should be entrusted with the ultimate defence of their liberties, he expected his state and the nation to be ruled in the normal course less by the people than by a natural aristocracy, an elite of talents and merit, he hoped, rather than one of hereditary

[27] A similar argument was made about the same time by soon-to-be Supreme Court Justice James Iredell. See G. Leonard, 'Iredell Reclaimed: Farewell to Snowiss's History of Judicial Review', *Chicago-Kent Law Review* 81 (2006), 867, 874–6.

[28] Jefferson, *Notes*, 161.

right or demagogic skills. He recognized, however, the unlikelihood that virtue would always characterize the republic's leadership. So he emphasized the necessity of clear foundational law to discipline the rulers of the moment, by way of the separation of powers, equipping some officeholders (e.g. judges) to resist the transgressions of others. But clear constitutional law would also supply the people with clear criteria for identifying the approach of tyranny. Jefferson did not seem to expect regular activity from the people, but he deemed indispensable both broad suffrage and the popular right to rebel on the basis of clear law. Still, Jefferson's failure to imagine any actual mechanisms by which the suffrage would be effectively deployed against usurpers—he had little concept of party or political organization short of rebellion—suggests again that he expected little of the people until a long series of abuses might bring them to the point of rebellion. After all, his own experience with popular resistance to misrule came in the American Revolution; the alternative of peaceful resistance to usurpation through the ballot box was little more than an imagined abstraction in this pre-party and anti-party era.

Although Jefferson anticipated only limited popular action, he nevertheless emphasized the centrality of the character of the people. Republican character required that husbandry remain the dominant economic pursuit of the people. Otherwise, the ceaseless efforts of the ambitious to render the people dependent must eventually triumph. At the same time, he recognized the profound threat of slavery to the character of the people and to the spirit of law, and he never tired of making futile pronouncements as to the necessity of emancipation.

Finally, as I turn to Jefferson's experience under the Federal Constitution, it is important to re-emphasize Jefferson's federalism. He believed that the durability of republican government required that each republic lay within a confederation even as it retained its own sovereignty on all internal matters. The central, linking authority of the confederal structure—once the King of England but later the 'general government' of the US—would limit the constituent republics' independence only insofar as it was necessary to preserve peaceful interstate and international relations.

IV. Jefferson and the Democratization of the Federal Constitution

From the moment of the nation's rebirth under a new national constitution in 1787–9, Jefferson played a major role in the constitutional development of the United States. As an officeholder, politician, and central figure in most of the constitutional controversies of the nation's first twenty years, he held consistently to most of the positions outlined above. But he also found himself advancing both the democratization of the constitution and the injection of party into the constitution in unexpected and sometimes unintended ways.

When the Constitutional Convention met in the summer of 1787, Jefferson resided in Paris, serving as the American minister to France. He returned to the States only in late 1789 and took up the position of Secretary of State under the new constitution. In the meantime, his role in the Founding was limited mostly to an exchange of letters with his close friend, James Madison.

These letters seem to confirm that Jefferson was less concerned with ensuring the democratic quality of the constitution than ensuring adequate legal checks on the exercise of power. First, in spite of his wariness of centralized power, he readily supported this effort to strengthen the national government within its limited sphere. Despite some reservations,[29] he did not go in with the Antifederalists, a motley but nearly victorious group of oppositionists who generally shared his confederal principles.[30] Rather, he firmly supported a constitution that his friend Madison and the other delegates had designed as a mechanism not for enhancing popular power but for maximizing the chances that public-spirited gentlemen would be placed in power and, once there, that they would be suitably policed by other officeholders and by structural checks.[31]

As readily as he endorsed this not-so-democratic constitution, he did express some limited objections. Most importantly, he joined with the Antifederalist opponents of the constitution in pressing for a bill of rights. Madison was sceptical. Madison considered the constitution less a source of law than a machine, an institutional arrangement that might frustrate faction while empowering statesmanship. Like Jefferson, he recognized that a declaration of rights might establish explicit principles against which the people and the state governments could test exertions of national power and on which they might found a resistance when necessary. But he doubted that the 'parchment barriers' of a bill of rights would really make much difference.[32] Jefferson disagreed, however, famously educating his friend on the importance of judicial review, a legal mechanism of constitutional enforcement that Madison had neglected: 'In the arguments in favor of a declaration of rights, you omit one which has great weight with me; the legal check which it puts into the hands of the judiciary.'[33] Celebrating the 'learning and integrity' that he thought would characterize any independent judiciary, he easily imagined the judges regularly and effectively standing in the way of usurpation—something he could not easily imagine of the people themselves. But to do that in the normal course, the judges (like the state legislatures) needed clear legal texts in the form of a written constitution and bill of rights.

[29] D. N. Mayer, *The Constitutional Thought of Thomas Jefferson* (Charlottesville: University Press of Virginia, 1994), 95–9, describes Jefferson's hesitations but addresses mainly his fully fledged endorsement of the constitution on virtually all counts but the omission of a bill of rights.

[30] S. Cornell, *The Other Founders: Anti-Federalism and the Dissenting Tradition in America, 1788–1828* (Chapel Hill: University of North Carolina Press, 1999).

[31] On the designs of Madison and the Framers to blunt popular will and empower those with supposedly clearer access to principles of public good, see Nedelsky, *Private Property*, ch. 2 on Madison, and Rakove, *Original Meanings*, ch. 8 on representation in the constitution. Also, see Madison's famous argument in *The Federalist* No. 10 as to the importance of a constitutional mechanism for ensuring that federal representatives would be statesmen of enlarged views rather than mere delegates from an inevitably factious people.

[32] See Mayer, *Constitutional Thought*, 150–3, on Madison. And see James Madison to Thomas Jefferson, 17 October 1788, in *The Republic of Letters: The Correspondence between Thomas Jefferson and James Madison 1776–1826*, ed. J. N. Smith (New York: Norton, 1995), vol. I, 564.

[33] Thomas Jefferson to James Madison, 15 March 1789, in *The Republic of Letters*, vol. I, 587.

With Madison ultimately on board, the amendments that we now call the Bill of Rights were soon added to the constitution, but I want to emphasize that they were not seen simply as guarantees of individual rights. They were just as much understood as protections for the states against overreaching by the national government. As Gordon Wood has argued, 'the Antifederalists in their demand for amendments and a bill of rights had actually been more concerned with weakening the power of the federal government in its relation to the states in matters such as taxation than with protecting "personal liberty alone"'.[34] Once the government actually went into operation, the same could be said of the Jeffersonian opposition to Alexander Hamilton and his centralizing Federalists.

In the 1790s, Hamilton's economic programme of a national bank, national assumption of state debts, and the national imposition of excise taxes directly on the people provoked heated resistance from defenders of state autonomy. Jefferson and Madison organized newspaper campaigns against the Bank of the United States and other Hamiltonian policies. Scattered Democratic–Republican Societies, precursors of Jeffersonian party organization, emerged briefly to organize opposition to the pro-British Jay Treaty among other things, but disappeared rapidly under the onslaught of condemnations for party activity. Rebels in western Pennsylvania resisted the Federalist excise tax on whisky by resort to violence and threats before being scattered by a show of federal force.

Finally, in an episode I want to develop more fully, Jefferson and Madison turned to the state legislatures themselves to resist the Alien and Sedition Acts of 1798. The Federalist judiciary was not an option for enforcing the legal rights of the states against a Federalist Congress, as things had turned out. And, for all his apparently partisan activity in the 1790s, Jefferson had not yet imagined a resort to organized, popular resistance, that is, mass party activity rather than rebellion, as a proper course. That left the state legislatures as the principal remaining institutions that the pair had originally imagined as enforcers of constitutional limits. Jefferson's resolutions of 1798, drafted for the Kentucky legislature, and Madison's resolutions for the Virginia legislature sought to test the capacity of the state legislatures to fulfil this role.

Among the most controversial aspects of the Alien and Sedition Acts was the provision that federalized the common law offence of seditious libel. Although the federal statute embraced doctrines that were actually more liberal than the established common law offence, Jefferson objected that the constitution nowhere authorized the national government, as opposed to the state governments, to criminalize speech. In other words, he claimed that direct regulation of speech was a matter that belonged exclusively to the individual state republics, not the sort of interstate matter that belonged to the federal government. Thus the constitution had granted the national government no power over speech, and the First Amendment had made explicit that the national government was not to have this power. Jefferson's resolutions on behalf of Kentucky made his case in a distinctly legalistic

[34] Wood, *Creation*, 543.

way that was reminiscent of a court's exercise of judicial review. Citing the First and Tenth Amendments as well as the general theory of the constitution, he declared the seditious libel provisions 'altogether void and of no force', and he found that 'the power to create, define, & punish such other crimes is reserved, and of right appurtains solely and exclusively to the respective States, each within it's own territory'.[35] The Sedition Act was an unconstitutional assertion of Federalist consolidationism and a demonstration of the close linkage between states' rights and individual liberties.[36] The Kentucky legislature adopted most of Jefferson's draft intact, including his legal argument for the nullity of the federal law as well as clear affirmations of the compact theory of the Union. But the ultimate question of enforcement remained: could a state legislature simply declare a federal statute unconstitutional?

Mimicking the confederalism of the *Summary View*, Jefferson's draft defended this state power. He declared it obvious that the constitution was a 'compact' among the sovereign, independent states, which created 'a general government for special purposes, delegated to that government certain definite powers, reserving, each state to itself, the residuary mass of right to their own self-government'.[37] The draft inferred from this premise a state's right to nullify certain federal laws. While Jefferson's opponents denied that any state could unilaterally nullify a federal act, Jefferson insisted that the general government was a mere 'creature'[38] of a compact among the states, such that its alleged usurpations could be judged only by the parties to the compact, the states themselves. He oddly accepted that an '*abuse* of the delegated powers' (emphasis added) would call only for a judgement by the people at the next election: 'a change by the people would be the constitutional remedy.'[39] But an assumption of altogether undelegated powers justified resort to nullification:

> where powers are assumed which have not been delegated a nullification of the act is the rightful remedy: that every state has a natural right, in cases not within the compact... to nullify of their own authority all assumptions of power by others within their limits: that without this right, they would be under the dominion, absolute and unlimited, of whosoever might exercise this right of judgment for them.[40]

Moreover, he expected that 'the co-states... will concur in declaring these acts void & of no force & will each take measures of it's own for providing that... these acts... shall [not] be exercised within their respective territories'.[41]

Jefferson thus eagerly followed the logic of sovereignty from the *Summary View* to its natural conclusion. Still, enchanting as his logic was, Jefferson could see that it

[35] 'Jefferson's Draft', in *The Papers of Thomas Jefferson*, ed. B. B. Oberg (Princeton: Princeton University Press, 2003), 30: 536.
[36] Cornell, *Other Founders*, 240–2, 230–45; Onuf, *Jefferson's Empire*, 93–8.
[37] 'Jefferson's Draft', *Papers* (ed. Oberg), 30: 536.
[38] 'Jefferson's Draft', *Papers* (ed. Oberg), 30: 539.
[39] 'Jefferson's Draft', *Papers* (ed. Oberg), 30: 539.
[40] 'Jefferson's Draft', *Papers* (ed. Oberg), 30: 539.
[41] 'Jefferson's Draft', *Papers* (ed. Oberg), 30: 541.

might lead all the way to disunion, and ultimately pulled back from the precipice. Loosening his grip on rigid confederalist principle, he called for the prudent, though not legally required, step of consultation among the 'parties to the compact' to produce a collective remedy for federal illegalities.[42]

In some ways, these resolutions were stillborn. Kentucky, for its part, adopted Jefferson's legal logic but excised the argument for nullification, merely requesting that Congress repeal the statute and calling on the states to correspond on the issue. Worse, no other legislature joined Kentucky and Virginia in any of their resolutions. The 'co-states', the 'parties to the compact', seemed to have forgotten the *Summary View*.

Yet, in other ways, the resolutions proved of major importance. They turned out to be a critical step in the development of American constitutional dynamics. They neither established the constitutional authority of state legislatures nor a doctrine of nullification (although that doctrine would make a notorious, slavery-defending comeback in the 1830s). But they did play an important role, largely unintended though it was, in advancing democratic politics and party organization. In the words of Koch and Ammon, 'As political propaganda ... the Resolutions were tremendously effective, frightening the Federalist ranks, and uniting, as Hamilton feared they might, the Republicans into a determined party with "body and solidity".'[43] Jefferson and Madison may have completely failed in their predictions of 1788–9, anticipating a partyless future in which the state governments would defend the limits on the federal government. Further, they may have completely failed in their efforts of 1798–9 to vindicate the constitutional prerogatives of the state legislatures. But within two years, party organization would succeed where the state legislatures had failed—and with Jefferson, of all people, leading the way.

In 1800, the idea of popular sovereignty became real and active in an unprecedented way. For the first time, a majority of the electorate seized on the tools of party organization to peacefully defy and turn out those in possession of the national government. Jeffersonian newspapers sprang up. Campaign committees were formed. A party ticket of Jefferson and Aaron Burr was nominated by the Republican congressional caucus. In politically advanced areas like New York City, the Republicans under Burr even conducted a comprehensive get-out-the-vote operation.[44]

Jeffersonian squeamishness about party was assuaged not only by the failure of all other methods of opposition but also by the knowledge that traditional antipartyism did seem to make room for an exception. Just as the people might come together to effect their right of revolution (as they did in 1776), they might likewise

[42] 'Jefferson's Draft', *Papers* (ed. Oberg), 30: 539.

[43] A. Koch and H. Ammon, 'The Virginia and Kentucky Resolutions: An Episode in Jefferson's and Madison's Defense of Civil Liberties', *The William and Mary Quarterly*, Third Series, Vol. 5, No. 2 (April 1948), 145–76, 147. See also S. Elkins and E. McKitrick, *The Age of Federalism* (New York: Oxford University Press, 1993), 721–6, which neatly describes the centrality of this episode in the Republicans' transition from loosely joined, party-wary oppositionists to an organized party of 'principle'.

[44] S. Dunn, *Jeffersons's Second Revolution* (Boston: Houghton Mifflin, 2004), 179–80.

organize a temporary party of the constitution to attempt salvation by peaceful, political means when the constitution was in danger of usurpation. Such a party would not count as a deviation from traditional anti-party values as long as it limited itself to an ad hoc defence of a fundamental constitutional principle, here the reserved rights of the states.[45]

A committed antipartyist,[46] Jefferson learned in the campaign of 1800 to appreciate the necessity of party and the effectiveness of the sophisticated techniques of campaign organization at work in some parts of the United States. While keeping himself out of any public role in the campaign, he nevertheless served in effect as a national party leader in the election that he came to refer to as the 'Revolution of 1800'. We often now look back on this election as a founding moment of the American two-party system, legitimating organized opposition to the government and peaceful transitions between equally legitimate parties. But that is not how Jefferson saw it. He accepted party organization, mobilization of the people at large, only in emergency conditions and as a peaceful alternative to the right of revolution. In ordinary times, he expected that party would melt away, its disciplinary function to be served simply by the quiet operations of the law.

Jefferson's abiding antipartyism, moreover, was vindicated in the vexing denouement of the campaign. Because of the quirks of a constitution that was not made to accommodate party tickets, the election results nearly led to civil violence. When Jefferson and his running mate, Burr, received the same number of electoral votes from an overly disciplined collection of Republican electors, the breaking of the tie fell, in effect, to Federalist members of the lame-duck Congress. Believing Jefferson a genuine revolutionary, and lacking all experience with regularized party competition, the Federalists in Congress could not in good conscience give up any tool that might keep Jefferson out of office. Predictably enough, this shameless disregard for the will of the people only cemented the Jeffersonian view of the Federalists as monarchists and aristocrats. In this crisis, the prospect of a resort to arms was a real one until a small crack in the ranks of the Federalists opened the door to Jefferson's peaceful installation.[47]

The following passage from Jefferson's first inaugural address reflects both the severity of the political contest and Jefferson's determination to overcome rather than institutionalize the party conflict. It nicely summarizes his desire for unity rather than party division, his principled deference to popular will, but also his commitment to law as perhaps the only thing more fundamental to republican government than was the authority of the people:

[45] R. Ketcham, *Presidents Above Party: The First American Presidency 1789–1829* (Chapel Hill: University of North Carolina Press, 1984), 100–13; R. Hofstadter, *The Idea of a Party System* (Berkeley: University of California Press, 1969), 123–8.

[46] Hofstadter, *Idea*, 122–8; P. S. Onuf, *Jefferson's Empire: The Language of American Nationhood* (Charlottesville: University Press of Virginia, 2000), 85–8.

[47] B. Ackerman, *The Failure of the Founding Fathers* (Cambridge: Belknap Press of Harvard University Press, 2005), 89–92.

During the contest of opinion through which we have past, the animation of discusions and of exertions has sometimes worn an aspect which might impose on strangers unused to think freely, and to speak and to write what they think; but this being now decided by the voice of the nation, announced according to the rules of the constitution, all will of course arrange themselves under the will of the law, and unite in common efforts for the common good.

All too will bear in mind this sacred principle, that though the will of the majority is in all cases to prevail, that will, to be rightful, must be reasonable; that the minority possess their equal rights, which equal laws must protect, and to violate would be oppression. . . . And let us reflect that having banished from our land that religious intolerance under which mankind so long bled and suffered, we have yet gained little if we countenance a political intolerance, as despotic, as wicked, and capable of as bitter and bloody persecutions.[48]

Jefferson never accepted the idea that party organization might be a permanent feature of republican government. Rather, he hoped to overcome party division and cement a mode of governance in which all recognized that, as he continued in his First Inaugural, 'We are all republicans: we are all federalists'; that is, that virtually all Americans shared the republican principle of representative government and the federalist principle of states' rights within a strong union. For him, the constitution was sufficiently clear about these principles that there could be no room for ongoing party conflict if all would simply demonstrate a due regard for law.

During his presidency, moreover, he again manifested a special regard for clear constitutional law as essential to a republican constitution. Again in his First Inaugural, he not only emphasized the necessity of 'equal laws' as a condition on the raw power of majority will, but he also pointed to a popular regard for law as the quality that made the American government 'the strongest Government on earth. I believe it the only one, where every man, at the call of the law, would fly to the standard of the law, and would meet invasions of the public order as his own personal concern.' Further, Jefferson emphasized that public law must be clear and readily enforceable so that it might genuinely discipline officeholders rather than just providing occasions for sophistical interpretation. This attitude can be seen in his most important act as president, the acquisition of the Louisiana Territory. While few doubted the constitutional power of the president and senate to add territory to the nation by way of treaty, Jefferson could not satisfy himself that anything in the constitution actually authorized the acquisition with sufficient clarity. Jefferson insisted that

When an instrument admits two constructions, the one safe, the other dangerous, the one precise, the other indefinite, I prefer that which is safe & precise. I had rather ask an enlargement of power from the nation, where it is found necessary, than to assume it by a construction which would make our powers boundless. Our peculiar security is in the possession of a written Constitution. Let us not make it a blank paper by construction.[49]

[48] See <http://www.princeton.edu/~tjpapers/inaugural/infinal.html>, which reprints Jefferson's First Inaugural as it appears in *The Papers of Thomas Jefferson, Volume 33: 17 February to 30 April 1801* (Princeton: Princeton University Press, 2006), 148–52.

[49] Jefferson to Wilson Carey Nicholas, 7 September 1803, quoted in J. D. Bailey, *Thomas Jefferson and Executive Power* (Cambridge: Cambridge University Press, 2007), 182.

In the end, he allowed himself to be convinced that the acquisition was so important to the future of republican government that he should put aside his scruples. But those scruples nicely demonstrate that he deemed law at least as fundamental as popular sovereignty.

I cannot conclude this account of Jefferson's constitutional thought without returning to the question of slavery. As indicated above, Jefferson understood from the beginning that slavery would be the curse of the American experiment in republican government. If he recognized the moral indefensibility of slave-owning, and at least made gestures towards a programme of emancipation in his early years, he ultimately did precious little even to ameliorate the conditions of the enslaved, let alone to advance emancipation. Rather, he pressed forward, mostly ignoring the issue as he led the cheers for the alleged triumph of liberty and self-government in America. In his old age, the Missouri Crisis of 1819–21 forced the issue to his attention once more and compelled him to articulate the choice he had made over the course of decades. As Northern politicians resisted the addition to the Union of another slave state, offering the nation a chance to confine slavery geographically and move it that little bit towards eventual abolition, Jefferson remained securely on the Southern train to self-destruction. Over time, he had more and more clearly elevated his foundational principle of state sovereignty over the equal principle of anti-slavery, sometimes for the very purpose of protecting slave-state prerogatives. So in the Missouri Crisis he attacked the Northern politicians for betraying the revolution, blaming them for what he took to be the near prospect of secession and thus the failure of the American experiment in self-government: 'If they would but dispassionately weigh the blessings they will throw away against an abstract principle [anti-slavery] more likely to be effected by union than by scission, they would pause before they would perpetrate this act of suicide on themselves and of treason against the hopes of the world.'[50] This argument, predicated on the fantasy that 'diffusion' of slavery would advance the prospects of emancipation and that state autonomy regarding slavery was an essential and fixed doctrine of the constitution, had a certain logic in the abstract. But in reality it only served to defer a reckoning with America's fatal contradiction and entrench slavery ever deeper, causing the Democrats of the next two generations to extend and extend Jefferson's futile approach until a bloodbath, akin to that feared by Jefferson all along, finally began the necessary work.

V. Conclusion

Unlike Jefferson himself, the new generation of Republicans that came of age in 1800 betrayed much less concern for law than for popular sovereignty and states' rights. Chief among these young Republicans was the 18-year-old Martin Van

[50] Jefferson to John Holmes, 22 April 1820, quoted in R. B. Bernstein, *Thomas Jefferson* (New York: Oxford University Press, 2003), 186.

Buren, eventually to be the eighth president, destined to convert his worship of Jefferson into a life devoted to the construction and maintenance of the Democratic party. He and his kind concluded that party organization must be a permanent feature of republican constitutionalism because aristocracy (under the name of federalism or otherwise) would remain a permanent threat. Thus, the Democratic party, often known as 'the democracy' to distinguish itself from 'the aristocracy', had to be more than a kind of political militia, reserved for rare constitutional emergencies. Instead, it had to become the chief governing agency of the nation, even more fundamental and constitutional than the particular government institutions mandated by the constitutional text itself. The party, as the immediate tool of the people, would be the source of nominees for public office as well as the source of policy positions and instructions for ensuring that officeholders did precisely the will of the people. In this vision, there was no room for Madison's filtration and refinement of popular opinion and enabling of statesmen, nor for Jefferson's similar ideal of rule by a natural aristocracy, even one chosen directly by the people. Rather, the people were themselves to rule as directly as possible. Officeholders were to be chosen for their fidelity to the party and rotated out of office regularly, thus vindicating the postulate that ability was less important than was close identification with the desires of the people.[51]

Jefferson, in contrast, for all his sincere declarations of the supremacy of the people's will, had had no thought of creating an institution that might allow the people to articulate their will with regularity and clarity. Only in 1810 did he begin to imagine an extension of his pyramid of republics down to the ward level, contemplating the active involvement of every white man in governance.[52] This extension added a bit more democracy to his federalist pyramid: a national government, resting on state governments, resting on county governments. But it was Van Buren, not Jefferson, who adapted this model for Democratic party organization (in which ward meetings would instruct county conventions, which would instruct state conventions, which would instruct national conventions). Where Van Buren used that model to show how every white man might exercise his equal share of control over every action of his representatives, Jefferson used it only to show that every white man might participate in governance at a level of government appropriate to his abilities.

Jefferson was probably the most democratic figure among the eminent men of his generation, but his inherited opposition to party and his lawyerly preoccupation with clear and equal law proved especially salient principles of his republicanism. And these principles conditioned his democratic inclinations in ways that separated him from his radical successors. He was also the greatest champion of states' rights in his generation and a pretty radical champion at that, never really giving up on the confederal model built in the *Summary View*. Unfortunately, his

[51] See generally Leonard, *Invention of Party Politics*.

[52] See Matthews, *Radical Politics*, 81–9, and Sheldon, *Political Philosophy*, 67–72, 143–5, both of which suggest that Jefferson embraced this notion of ward democracy and an actively self-governing people from his earliest days in public life but which cite evidence only beginning in 1810.

commitment to states' rights came to have its most dramatic effect in preserving slavery. In the slave states, even avowed opponents of slavery like Jefferson mostly proved incapable of turning against their own self-interest to eliminate it. Meanwhile, the doctrines born from the *Summary View* proved decisive for as many northerners as southerners, blunting all anti-slavery efforts from outside the South and leaving another generation to bear the awful cost of beginning the republican experiment anew.

18

John Adams, Constitution Monger

David Thomas Konig

I. Introduction

At the end of the summer of 1790, John Adams returned to the new nation's temporary capital of New York from Philadelphia, to where he had travelled to arrange lodgings in anticipation of the relocation of the government later that year. With few duties as vice-president, Adams began a correspondence with his old revolutionary ally and second cousin, Samuel Adams, then serving as Lieutenant-Governor of Massachusetts. 'What, my old friend, is this world about to become?' he asked. Reflecting on the force of political change at work in the United States, he looked to the accelerating revolution in France. 'Every thing will be pulled down. So much seems certain. But what will be built up? Are there any principles of political architecture? What are they?'[1] This was, of course, a rhetorical question, posed so that he could revisit and reiterate the republican constitutional principles that he had been developing and elaborating for decades. By the time he wrote to his cousin in 1790, his constitutional principles had been matured, shaped and then tested by the tumultuous events he had seen since his earliest revolutionary writings. When he asked 'What are they?' of constitutional principles, he had secured his place in the history of constitutional thought by comprehensively articulating three core elements of electoral democracy: a meaningful way of implementing the sovereignty of the people; a functional separation of governmental powers; and the articulation of written and binding governmental limitations. Adams might have been exaggerating his role in the history of constitution-making when he boasted in 1807 that 'I made a Constitution for Massachusetts, which finally made the Constitution of the United States',[2] but his contributions were creative and profound. As his crowning achievement, he almost single-handedly wrote the Massachusetts Constitution of 1780, the first to be drafted by a popularly elected convention and then ratified by the people, and which remains to this day

[1] Adams to Samuel Adams, 12 September 1790, *The Works of John Adams, Second President of the United States: With a Life of the Author, Notes and Illustrations*, ed. C. F. Adams, 10 vols (Boston: Little, Brown and Co., 1850–6), vol. 6, 411–12 (hereinafter, *Works*).

[2] A. H. Bullock, *The Centennial of the Massachusetts Constitution* (Worcester: C. Hamilton, 1881), 18.

the oldest written constitution in continuous use anywhere in the world. Though serving as minister to Great Britain and not in attendance at the drafting of the Federal Constitution in Philadelphia in 1787, his recently published three-volume *Defence of the Constitutions of Government of the United States of America*[3] led Benjamin Rush to remark, 'Our illustrious Minister in this gift to his country has done us more service than if he had obtained alliances for us with all the nations of Europe.' Rush, a signer of the Declaration of Independence, was at the time urging ratification of the new Federal Constitution and the drafting of a new and more moderate constitution for Pennsylvania to replace that state's radical 1776 document. Adams's 'excellent principles' provided potent support for both efforts.[4]

A self-described 'Constitution monger',[5] Adams devoted his public life to creating and advancing republican government in North America and, he hoped, in Europe as well. As he confronted that task in his *Thoughts on Government* in 1776, he conceded that Britain had offered a model, but one that was republican only 'as long as it is bound by fixed laws, which the people have a voice in making, and a right to defend'. Aristotle, Livy, and Harrington had provided the true meaning of a republic: 'They define a republic to be a *government of laws, and not of men.*'[6] Seeking a constitutional framework for republican government to satisfy that definition became his life's work. Fundamentally a conservative, seeking continuity with what he found best in the tradition of English government, he moved—reluctantly though forcefully—to accept and incorporate emerging principles of popular sovereignty into a constitution. 'Adams', writes Peter Shaw, 'was a radical in spite of himself.'[7]

Reflecting a quarter of a century's immersion in political upheaval, reform, and nation-building, Adams's correspondence with his cousin reveals a process of responding to the provocations of events that challenged or confirmed his ideas—what Bernard Bailyn has called Adams's practice of drawing 'his ideas as much from his feelings, from his sensitive reactions to the human realities about him, as he did from the great array of writings, ancient and modern, that he had mastered'.[8] The lieutenant-governor had replied politely to his cousin John's invitation by stating, 'The best formed constitutions that have yet been formed by the wit of man, have, and will come to an end; because the kingdoms of the earth have not been governed by reason.' Appealing for education and the elevation of 'reason' as the guide to government and as the proper method of restraining the 'turbulent passions of men', he identified the importance of 'educating their *little*

[3] *Defence of the Constitutions of Government of the United States of America, against the Attack of M. Turgot, in his Letter to Dr. Price, 22 March 1778* (1787).

[4] Rush to Richard Price, 18 May 1787, cited in C. Warren, *The Making of the Constitution* (Boston: Little, Brown and Co., 1928), 157.

[5] Adams to Benjamin Rush, 4 November 1779, *The Papers of John Adams*, ed. Robert J. Taylor, et al., 17 vols to date (Cambridge, MA: Harvard University Press, 1977–), vol. 8, 279 (hereinafter, *Papers*).

[6] Adams, *Works*, vol. 4, 106–7.

[7] P. Shaw, *The Character of John Adams* (Chapel Hill: University of North Carolina Press, 1976), 88.

[8] B. Bailyn, 'Butterfield's Adams: Notes for a Sketch', in *William and Mary Quarterly*, 3rd ser., 19 (1962), 253.

boys and *girls*'. The lieutenant-governor looked to a day 'when the wolf shall dwell with the lamb, and the leopard lie down with the kid... none shall then hurt or destroy, for the earth shall be full of the knowledge of the Lord.'[9]

This answer did not satisfy the vice-president, who launched into an unguarded attack on the inadequacy of 'the universal, or at least more general prevalence of knowledge and benevolence'. Unlike himself, he wrote, 'Philosophers, ancient and modern, do not appear to have studied nature', by which he explained he meant 'human nature'. The vice-president explicitly addressed the fallacy of his cousin's reasoning by quoting him: '"The love of liberty," you say, "is interwoven in the soul of man." So it is, according to La Fontaine, in that of the wolf....'[10]

John cautioned that man's 'rational, generous, or social' capacities do not inhere in any one person more than in another:

> The numbers of men in all ages have preferred ease, slumber, and good cheer to liberty, when they have been in competition. We must not then depend alone upon the love of liberty in the soul of man for its preservation. Some political institutions must be prepared, to assist this love against its enemies.[11]

Although leadership would always have to come from 'the nobility', Adams had no illusions about the reliability of the 'few'. 'Let us be impartial, then, and speak the whole truth. Till we do, we shall never discover all the true principles that are necessary. The multitude, therefore, as well as the nobles, must have a check. This is one principle.'[12]

The vice-president's honesty in expressing his sceptical opinions has not been questioned, though some at the time found in them reason to question his wisdom and even his sanity. When Adams embarked on his ill-fated campaign for adopting titles of office in 1789, Thomas Jefferson described it to James Madison as 'the most superlatively ridiculous thing I ever heard of' and commented that the new vice-president was '[a]lways an honest man, often a great one, but sometimes absolutely mad'.[13] Jefferson never gave up his suspicions about Adams's true political beliefs, and as late as 1825 he wondered, 'Can any one read Mr. Adams' defence of the American constitutions without seeing he was a monarchist?'[14] The

9 Samuel Adams to John Adams, 4 October 1790, *Works*, vol. 6, 413–14. (Emphasis in original.)

10 John Adams to Samuel Adams, 18 October 1790, *Works*, vol. 6, 416, 417.

11 John Adams to Samuel Adams, 18 October 1790, *Works*, vol. 6, 418.

12 John Adams to Samuel Adams, 18 October 1790, *Works*, vol. 6, 418.

13 Jefferson to James Madison, 29 July 1789, *The Papers of Thomas Jefferson*, 40 vols to date (Princeton: Princeton University Press, 1950–), vol. 15, 315–16. In using this description, Jefferson was following Benjamin Franklin's remark of 1783, made after enduring complaints about Adams from French diplomats, that his colleague 'means well for his Country, is always an honest Man, often a wise one, but sometimes, and in some things, absolutely out of his senses'. In making this observation, Franklin confided that he had done so 'believing it my duty, tho' I know that I hazard by it a mortal Enmity'. Franklin to Robert Livingston, 22 July 1783, *The Writings of Benjamin Franklin: Collected and Edited with a Life and Introduction*, ed. A. H. Smyth, 10 vols (New York: Macmillan, 1907), vol. 9, 62.

14 Jefferson to William Short, 8 January 1825, *The Writings of Thomas Jefferson*, ed. Paul Leicester Ford, 10 vols (New York: G. P. Putnam's Sons, 1892–9), vol. 10, 332. Jefferson was referring specifically to Adams's *Defence of the Constitutions.*

point to be made about them is that Adams's constitutional principles reveal a reluctance to abandon completely the basic foundations of English mixed government, which he succeeded in incorporating into a republicanized government of separated powers and balanced government.

Such ideas came naturally to Adams from his experience in Massachusetts before and during the revolution, which, for him, was *not* an entirely 'revolutionary' act but rather a republicanizing of British forms. Contemporaries who identified in him tendencies that they found monarchical or aristocratic were not concocting political smears of the sort that did, in fact, beset the era. Deeply suspicious of innovation in language as well as in politics,[15] Adams couched his innovative notions of mixed government in a language of traditional politics, and as a result, Bradley Thompson explains, he 'was constantly misunderstood because he used these old concepts representatively rather than literally, without making clear the difference'.[16] While his readers and correspondents accurately perceived his lingering conservatism and sympathy for the class-based nature of British mixed government, they often underestimated his commitment to popular sovereignty and overlooked his nuanced fusion of traditional Whig mixed government with that of modern balanced government and the separation of powers.

II. Puritans and Patriots: the Backgrounds of Adams's Constitutionalism

To understand the crucial nexus within which this took place—Adams's ideas about human nature and politics—one must begin with his own beginnings, in eastern Massachusetts. Only such a biographical approach can reveal what historians must understand about Adams and his crucial role in the development of modern constitutional thought, and enable us to

> see more clearly than ever before the fundamental pattern of Adams's character and motivation, to observe both the basic continuity and critical transitions in his development, and, above all, to perceive, to some degree at least, the intensely personal roots of his ideas and beliefs which this leading Revolutionary statesman introduced into the most creative debate in modern history.[17]

Adams entered Harvard College with plans to pursue a career in the ministry, and the legacy of growing up in a society whose puritanism had only recently been secularized was only the first of many collisions of past and present in his life. Upon the outbreak of open political conflict between parliament and the colonies, the founding of Massachusetts Bay a century and a half earlier became an example of

[15] See, for example, his sneering dismissal of neologisms in his letter to Thomas Jefferson, 16 December 1816, in *The Adams-Jefferson Letters: The Complete Correspondence Between Thomas Jefferson and Abigail and John Adams*, ed. L. J. Cappon (Chapel Hill, [1959] 1988), 500–1.

[16] C. Bradley Thompson, *John Adams and the Spirit of Liberty* (Lawrence: University Press of Kansas, 1998), 259.

[17] Bailyn, 'Butterfield's Adams', 243.

the challenge to the Stuarts' political and ecclesiastical tyranny, and thus a useful trope for Adams, who repeatedly used it to justify his own generation's resistance. Invoking the founders by writing pseudonymously as 'Governor Winthrop' to 'Governor Bradford',[18] he wrote, 'it was the unwearied endeavor of our lives to establish a society on English, humane, and Christian principles.'[19] Such efforts fused religion with a secularized appreciation of human nature, and his remarks to this effect can be seen clearly in his first extended political work. On that point he is worth quoting in full:

> To render the popular power in their new government as great and wise as their principles of theory, that is, as human nature and the Christian religion require it should be, they endeavored to remove from it as many of the feudal inequalities as could be spared, consistently with the preservation of a mild limited monarchy. And in this they discovered the depth of their wisdom and the warmth of their friendship to human nature. But the first place is due to religion.[20]

This passage is noteworthy not to argue a powerfully religious foundation for the constitutions he would be evaluating and writing. Rather, it serves to bring to the fore his view of the correspondence between the traditional puritan view of fallen human nature, the political view of corruption that dominated contemporary English reform politics, and the need to base a constitution on 'the popular power'. It also draws the parallel between Adams's understanding of puritanism as a purge of medieval ecclesiastical corruptions and his belief in the way that the British constitution had to be reformed of its abuses but retained in its substance.[21]

Adams's Massachusetts, and especially Boston, once he began his law practice there, opened his eyes to the urban ferment that the town shared with its metropolitan capital in England. Urban protest demonstrated to him the power of the lower orders when roused to action in defence of their rights as they saw them. He learned many lessons from watching the riots that accompanied the Stamp Act and the collective action of the Boston Tea Party, as well as from his being thrust into the role of defending the British soldiers on trial for the Boston Massacre. He realized that he could not ignore the fact that no effective resistance would have been possible without the crowd. As much as he had misgivings about unleashed popular action, he nonetheless recognized in it the conservative principles and a moral economy that he shared. British actions against the government of Massachusetts he regarded as unacceptable '[i]nnovations . . . introduced, to the Injury of our Constitution of civil Government'.[22] Protection of traditional charter privileges

[18] The first governors of Massachusetts Bay (John Winthrop) and Plymouth (William Bradford).

[19] John Adams as 'Governor [John] Winthrop', 26 January 1767, in *The Revolutionary Writings of John Adams*, ed. C. Bradley Thompson (Indianapolis: Liberty Fund, 2000), 57.

[20] John Adams, 'A Dissertation on the Canon and Feudal Law' (1765), in *Works*, vol. 3, 453.

[21] On the enduring force of the puritan colony's origins in his political thinking, see T. H. Breen, 'John Adams' Fight Against Innovation in the New England Constitution: 1776', *New England Quarterly* 40 (1967), 501–20.

[22] *The Diary and Autobiography of John Adams*, ed. L. H. Butterfield, 3 vols (Cambridge, MA: Harvard University Press, 1961), vol. 2, 3, cited by Breen, 'Innovation', 506. As Edward Countryman notes, such efforts at the outset of the conflict were 'the act of people who wanted to restore or protect

had powerfully motivated those who had taken up arms in the 1770s. It was a cause that he had celebrated in his 'Novanglus' essays after the Stamp Act agitation of 1765, and one that Levi Preston, a minuteman who had had fought at Concord in 1775, continued to remind Americans of long after the revolution when, as a ninety-one-year-old, he was interviewed by a young Massachusetts schoolteacher who asked him, 'what did you mean in going to the fight?' The veteran frustrated the interviewer's attempts to uncover any articulated ideological impulses behind it. Denying any knowledge of Harrington, Sidney, or Locke, the veteran said of the events of 1775, 'Young man, what we meant in going for those red-coats was this: we always had governed ourselves, and we always meant to. They didn't mean we should.'[23] Adams, to be sure, knew those writers well, and what he learned from them certainly had informed his own thoughts and actions. But behind that reading lay a deep commitment to a legacy he wished to preserve and, ultimately, adapt for the future.

Boston's own 'Loyal Nine' (soon to be known as 'Sons of Liberty') held a tenuous control over the mob there, relying on the efforts of shoemaker Ebenezer Mackintosh to mobilize the populace to enforce what Governor Thomas Hutchinson called their own 'model of government'. Describing the horror of the scene to former Governor Thomas Pownall, Hutchinson noted its hierarchical structure: 'I will begin with the lowest branch partly legislative partly executive. This consists of the rabble of the town of Boston headed by one Mackintosh who I imagine you never heard of. He is a bold fellow.' Mackintosh took his direction from the Loyal Nine, but he remained nonetheless 'as likely a Massienello as you can well conceive'. Boston thus had a 'government' by which the crowd 'are somewhat controuled by a superior set consisting of the master-masons carpenters &c of the town. . . . When anything of more importance is to be determined as opening the custom house or any matters of trade these are under the direction of a committee of merchants.'[24]

At the same time, Adams saw the potential for such violence to get out of hand. He was not alone in that. Benjamin Franklin's wife, Deborah, keeping the home fires burning while he served as colonial agent in London, wrote him of her terrified night during a riot against the Stamp Act in Philadelphia, describing the way she had asked her 'Brother to Cume and bring his gun' to join her in barricading a room as a 'sorte of defens upstairs'.[25] As in Boston, such upheavals were instigated and led by local elites, but their control was tenuous and their authority to lead,

something good, not of people who were driven by a vision of change': Edward Countryman, *The American Revolution* (New York: Hill and Wang, 1985), 75.

[23] Mellen Chamberlain relates his conversation with Captain Levi Preston in 'Remarks Before the Sons of the American Revolution' [1894], which he includes in his *John Adams, The Statesman of the American Revolution; with other Essays and Addresses, Historical and Literary* (Boston: Houghton, Mifflin, and Company, 1898), 248–9. I am indebted to R. B. Bernstein for this citation.

[24] E. S. Morgan and H. M. Morgan, *The Stamp Act Crisis: Prologue to Revolution* (rev. ed., New York: Collier Books, 1962), 234–5.

[25] Deborah Franklin to Benjamin Franklin, 22 September 1765, *The Papers of Benjamin Franklin*, ed. L. W. Labaree, et al., 37 vols to date (New Haven: Yale University Press, 1959–), vol. 12, 271.

fragile; violence might explode beyond the restraints they worked to impose. In Newport, Rhode Island, the Stamp Act rioting was led by an immigrant newly arrived from England, who had known the boisterous style of London crowd activity. Not accustomed to deferring to men of a higher station whom he did not know, he 'enjoyed a brief but terrifying rule as leader of the Newport mob'.[26]

Adams nevertheless retained an outward confidence in the legality and orderliness of the lower orders acting in crowds. The Stamp Act violence, he insisted, was 'an honourable and glorious action, not a riot'.[27] Publicly, he offered stronger justification. The Tea Party actions, he wrote, demonstrated 'great order, decency, and *perfect submission to government*'.[28] Indeed, he was following the orthodox Whig line expressed by a writer to the New York press in 1768, that 'Good Laws and good Rulers will always be obey'd and respected', and that 'Mobs and Tumults never happen but thro' Oppression and scandalous Abuses of Power'.[29] The urban lower orders, that is, were not roused to violence but by provocation. It was this line of argument that he employed in his defence of British soldiers on trial for the Boston Massacre in 1770. The myth of his 'rule of law' or 'right to counsel' commitment has been amply demolished by Hiller Zobel, who finds that Adams was put up to the defence by the Sons of Liberty in order to prevent his co-counsel from making the obvious and effective plea of self-defence. Adams's task was to prevent the introduction of the most forceful form of evidence in such a plea, namely, that of a concerted plot by the Sons to provoke a British overreaction that would have potent political effect in Boston, but would persuade the ministry to crack down on the town and its radical leaders. Adams's eloquent defence of the soldiers thus relied on the argument that the crowd in the streets of Boston that night were good and dutiful subjects of the Crown, acting only in rage against evil subaltern officials.[30]

As it had demonstrated elsewhere, however, the Stamp Act crisis also showed Adams an uglier side of the mob, with the brutal tarring and feathering of royal agents and the destruction of homes, including that of Governor Hutchinson. More privately, he confided to his diary his fear that crowd violence might become a commonplace tool of the dissatisfied. This 'dangerous Tendency and Consequence', he believed, must be replaced by more formal institutions of authority.[31] Ten years later, he recorded his encounter with a 'common Horse Jockey' whom he knew of from the man's brushes with the courts, who now crowed at the closing of the courts: 'Oh! Mr. Adams what great Things have you and your Colleagues done for us! We can never be gratefull enough to you. There are no Courts of Justice now

26 Morgan, *Stamp Act Crisis*, 245.

27 *Diary and Autobiography of John Adams*, ed. Butterfield, vol. 1, 259–61. See also Adams's comments writing as 'Novanglus', in *Works*, vol. 4, 74–5.

28 Adams, *Works*, vol. 9, 334. (Emphasis in original.)

29 Cited by P. Maier, *From Resistance to Revolution: Colonial Radicals and the Development of American Opposition to Britain, 1765–1776* (New York: Knopf, 1974), 22.

30 H. B. Zobel, *The Boston Massacre* (New York: W. W. Norton, 1970), 206–40.

31 Adams, *Diary and Autobiography*, vol. 1, 260 (15 August 1765).

in this Province, and I hope there never will be another!' Sourly, Adams noted in his diary:

> Is this the Object for which I have been contending? . . . I rode along without any Answer to this Wretch. . . . If the Power of the Country should get into such hands, and there is great danger that it will, to what purpose have We sacrificed our Time, health, and every Thing else? Surely we must guard against this Spirit and these Principles, or We shall repent of our Conduct.[32]

As action in the streets pushed Adams and other political leaders into ever more insistent protests against the British, it also exposed the tenuous hold of their authority.[33] To James Warren, Adams expressed his pleasure at 'the prospect of free and Popular Governments'. 'But', he confided, 'there is great Danger, that those Governments will not make us happy.' He feared that they would bring 'Noise not sense', 'Meanness, not Greatness', 'Ignorance not Learning', and 'that it will be impossible to convince and perswade People to establish wise Regulations'.[34] His solution merits full quotation, as emblematic of his political ideas responding to the issues of the times:

> There is one Thing, my dear Sir, that must be attempted and most sacredly observed or We are all undone. There must be a Decency, and Respect, and Veneration introduced for Persons in Authority, or every Rank, or we are undone. In a popular Government, this is the only way of supporting order.[35]

Adams had to take a public stand against looming anarchy as royal authority collapsed and events moved steadily towards independence, where order in Massachusetts would become a challenge for its own leaders. Anonymously, he had addressed the issue in 1774 in response to the Coercive Acts (referred to as 'Intolerable Acts' by the colonists), enacted in reaction to what parliament regarded as the lawlessness of Massachusetts in the Boston Tea Party. Among the provisions of the Acts, one limited the authority of the Boston town meeting (a major agent of authority and control of opposition activity) and another authorized the governor to remove political opponents to Britain for trial. In the summer of that year, Adams placed unsigned letters in the *Massachusetts Spy*, justifying what had transpired in the streets of the city: the popular protests were, he insisted, the frustrated reaction of a populace whose voice was not represented in parliament, not illegal actions taken against grievances for which legal, established means of redress existed. Popular disorder, he explained, might also result from 'Resentment for private Wrongs or in pursuance of private Prejudices and passions', which, he insisted, 'must be discountenanced'.[36] Using the pseudonym 'Novanglus'

32 Adams, *Diary and Autobiography*, vol. 3, 326 (August 1775).

33 For an extended argument on the force of popular insurgency on propelling the elite leadership of Massachusetts towards independence, see T. H. Breen, *American Insurgents, American Patriots: The Revolution of the People* (New York: Hill and Wang, 2010).

34 John Adams to James Warren, 22 April 1776, *Papers*, vol. 4, 137.

35 John Adams to James Warren, 22 April 1776, *Papers*, vol. 4, 137.

36 *Massachusetts Spy*, 11 August 1774, cited by Maier, *Resistance*, 274.

in 1774 he made the same vital distinction, contrasting anarchy and 'revolution-principles'.[37]

III. Coming to Terms with *'Popular Government'*

Adams learned other lessons from these experiences, lessons about human nature and social stratification that would shape his thinking about the role of the lower orders once republicanized institutions were established. For Adams, the acts of the crowd had demonstrated their slowness to mobilize without the leadership of the 'few', whose reading and learning had made them sensitive to the existence of plots before they took more obvious form in the overt public 'outrages' that the crowd would understand. The enthusiasm of the crowd waned after the repeal of the Stamp Act, despite the relentless movement towards tyranny that Adams and his social class had learned to look for. 'Calamities are the caustics and cathartics of the body politic', he wrote early in 1767. 'They arouse the soul. They restore original virtues. They reduce a constitution back to its first principles.' 'But how soon is this ardor extinguished!' he lamented. 'In the course of a few months they have cooled down into such a tame, torpid sense of indolence and inattention.'[38] The reason was obvious, and it had clear implications for acknowledging and balancing the differences of the few and the many in governmental forms: 'Though a few individuals may perceive the approaches of arbitrary power, and may truly publish their perceptions to the people, yet it is well known, the people are not persuaded without the utmost difficulty to attend to facts and evidence.'[39]

For Adams, the 1770s demonstrated the need for institutionalized mechanisms of leadership. He realized that leadership in Massachusetts had taken actual form in the creation of committees of correspondence, which controlled the flow of information and fanned the flames of resistance when needed. 'What an engine!' he later recalled of those committees; without them, independence might never have been achieved.[40] County assemblies had filled the gap in leadership and facilitated defence of public order when a power vacuum threatened, producing 'covenants' calling for peace.[41] Like the informal control exerted by the Sons of Liberty over the crowd, established lines of militia authority had been necessary to maintain a monopoly of violence. It was not a great leap for Adams to translate these reservations about the lower orders into a philosophy about popular rule.

'Popular government' or 'democracy' for Adams need not equate to rule *by* the people, however. He never yielded his belief that 'Laws and Government are founded on the Consent of the people', but popular consent need not mean popular control. He was not alone in agreeing with Hume's observation that

[37] 'Novanglus: or a History of the Dispute with America, from its Origin, in 1754, to the Present Time. Written in 1774', *Papers*, vol. 2, 230.

[38] Adams as 'Governor Winthrop', 26 January 1767, *Revolutionary Writings*, 59–60.

[39] Adams as 'Governor Winthrop', 9 and 16 February 1767, *Revolutionary Writings*, 62.

[40] Adams, *Works*, vol. 10, 196–7.

[41] Brown, *Committees*, 213–14.

'[n]othing is more surprizing to those, who consider human affairs with a philosophical eye, than to see the easiness with which the many are governed by the few; and to see the implicite submission with which men resign their own sentiments and passions to those of their rulers'.[42] Hume had identified 'opinion' as the reason; for Adams and most leaders of the independence movement the principle of the consent of the governed allowed political institutions to rest on the assent of the people at large even if the people did not control all the actual mechanisms of power. This is not to deny the genuinely democratizing effect of the revolution. 'There can be no free government', Adams wrote in the *A Defence of the Constitutions of Government of the United States of America*, 'without a democratical branch in the constitution.'[43] Rather, it is only to bring into the discussion his efforts to republicanize representation, to make popular sovereignty more meaningful than what he had seen in the British constitution and yet constrain such democratization within some framework of institutionalized order. 'It is certain in Theory, that the only moral Foundation of Government is the Consent of the People', he wrote in 1776. 'But to what Extent Shall We carry this Principle?'[44]

How, that is, could the sovereignty of the people be acknowledged and, simultaneously, institutionalized and channelled? Struggling with this problem, he remained unwilling to abandon the British forms and concepts with which he was most comfortable. Conservative socially and distrustful of the people out-of-doors, he turned naturally in his *Thoughts on Government* in 1776 to the balance of 'the monarchical splendor, the aristocratical independency, and the democratical freedom'; three qualities represented by three distinct social strata. This tripartite British model of mixed government continued to direct his plans. American society, though less stratified than Britain's, nevertheless continued to exhibit the few/many dichotomy. This belief shaped his widely circulated *Thoughts*, which he repeated and summarized in numerous letters to fellow writers of state constitutions. In composing his *Thoughts* as a guide to other newly independent states in 1776, therefore, Adams tried to understand the social structures of the different regions in order to identify the constitutional frameworks appropriate to each. As he wrote to Patrick Henry in the month before independence was declared, 'The usages, and genius, and manners of people must be consulted.' What he perceived as the greater social stratification of the South (producing 'the pride of the haughty', which, he confided to James Warren, 'must . . . come down a little') called for upper legislative branches elected for seven years, while a state like Massachusetts ought to have an upper house appointed by the lower, from among its own members or the voting public.[45]

But such plans were already falling behind the accelerating popular impulses of the times, as colonial political reform gained momentum in 1776. Ten years earlier

[42] D. Hume, 'Essay V. Of the First Principles of Government', in *Essays and Treatises on Several Subjects* (London, 1758), 20.

[43] Adams, *Works*, vol. 4, 289.

[44] Adams, *Papers*, vol. 4, 208.

[45] Adams to Patrick Henry, 8 June 1776, *Works*, vol. 9, 386; Adams to James Warren, 16 June 1776, *Works*, vol. 9, 398.

he had witnessed the force of grassroots insurgency. Witnessing popular mobilization against the Stamp Act, he had observed, 'The people, *even to the lowest ranks*, have become more attentive to their liberties, more inquisitive about them, and more determined to defend them, than they were ever before known or had occasion to be.'[46] By 1776 such a force could not be ignored; any government would have to acknowledge, incorporate, and constitutionalize it. Eight days after Congress voted for independence, he wrote to Abigail from Philadelphia: 'You will see in the Newspapers...with what Rapidity, the Colonies proceed in their political Maneuvres.' Popular sovereignty was expanding beyond the narrow confines he had written of, and even in the aristocratically inclined Southern colonies, the pace of democratization had exceeded his expectations: 'In constituting their new Governments, their plans are remarkably popular, more so than I could ever have imagined, even more popular than the "Thoughts on Government".' Regrettably, voters had rejected men who had enjoyed 'the Place of Fortune, Family, and every other Consideration, which used to have Weight with mankind'.[47] Even so, the course of events around him had demonstrated to him the undeniable reality of popular politics and the need to acknowledge it, if only as a matter of legitimacy in a society of increasingly assertive citizens. Yet his acceptance of popular politics was more than merely a grudging concession. Contemplating the task of achieving 'a Revolution of Government', he concluded, 'An Interprize of so much difficulty can never be planned and carried on without Abilities, and People cannot have confidence enough in each other.'[48]

IV. Preserving Popular Government: Bicameralism and the Separation of Powers

The practical and theoretical force of popular sovereignty led Adams inexorably by 1780 to revisit a concept to which he had given nominal attention before independence but which now took on a more prominent role in his maturing constitutional thinking: a separation of powers in which each branch—executive, legislative, and judicial—did not represent a specific social class but embodied the constituent authority of the people as a whole. In 1775 he had written to Richard Henry Lee of the basic structure:

A legislative, an executive, and a judicial power comprehend the whole of what is meant and understood by government. It is by balancing each of these powers against the other two,

[46] Adams as 'Earl of Clarendon' to William Pym, *Revolutionary Writings*, 50–1 (20 January 1766).

[47] Adams to Abigail Adams, 10 July 1776, *The Adams Family Correspondence*, ed. L. H. Butterfield, et al., 9 vols to date (Cambridge, MA: Harvard University Press, 1963–), vol. 2, 42–3.

[48] Quoted by J. R. Howe, Jr, *The Changing Political Thought of John Adams* (Princeton: Princeton University Press, 1966), 57. Howe comments in a footnote, 'A careful reading of Adams' correspondence further suggests that his confidence in the American people and his conviction of their abiding virtue increased as the Revolution progressed. One can find in his earliest letters considerably more skepticism than during the 1770s.'

that the efforts in human nature towards tyranny can alone be checked and restrained, and any degree of freedom preserved in the constitution.[49]

What had changed by 1780 was not the structure of functional separation, which had been a commonplace among American Loyalists and British court Whigs who pointed with pride to Montesquieu in order to praise British checks and balances.[50] What made it creative and distinct from other iterations of the idea was the constitutional theory behind it, by which it was seamlessly integrated into a coherent philosophy of constitutionalism based on the sovereignty of the people. To understand the process of change, we must examine Adams's central role in the creation of a new constitution for the Commonwealth of Massachusetts in 1779, and in his robust defence of that government written in 1787 while he was in France.[51] It is in that effort that we can see most clearly the emergence of a fully conceived system drawing on the past and acknowledging the present.

The very act of convening a popular convention whose product would be subjected to popular judgement has been called, justifiably, a 'turning point' in the development of constitutionalism.[52] If the constitution were to be truly the act of the sovereign people, it had to be drafted by the people, not the legislature, and be subject to the broadest electorate conceivable at the time. Ratification of the constitution he crafted, therefore, would require not a simple majority, but the approval of two-thirds of all free males aged twenty-one or older. This reasoning was only logical, given the transformation of ideas wrought by the years of political activity among conventions, committees of correspondence, and other ad hoc assemblies of the people designed to express popular will and legitimize their efforts as a mandate. By the time Adams, elected for the town of Braintree, met with other delegates to the Massachusetts constitutional convention in Cambridge in 1779, he had seen the movement for independence expand into one that more genuinely merits the term 'revolution'.[53] The crowd played a role that had evolved from its essentially conservative and restorationist impulses of the pre-revolutionary period into an agency of challenge and change. Edward Countryman notes that whatever their role at the outset of the crisis, 'we must also understand that in the Revolution crowds left that background behind. Beginning as a normal, almost functional part

[49] Adams to R. H. Lee, 15 November 1775, *Works*, vol. 4, 186.

[50] On this, see, for example, M. Hullung, *The Social Contract in America from the Revolution to the Present Age* (Lawrence: University of Kansas Press, 2007), 13.

[51] *A Defence of the Consitutions of Government of the United States of America.* (See Adams, *Works*, vol. 4, 289.)

[52] Hullung, *Social Contract*, 27.

[53] It had evolved, as in Carl Becker's classic description, from a struggle for 'home rule' into one over 'who should rule at home'. Becker wrote as one of the great 'Progressive' historians, who argued that the revolution represented a massive challenge to an old order. C. L. Becker, *The History of Political Parties in the Province of New York, 1760–1776* (Madison: University of Wisconsin, 1909), 22. Though eclipsed after World War II, their work has been taken up by historians who have widened the focus of study to include groups excluded from the master narrative, as well as to recover and bring into the discourse of revolutionary politics the threat of class upheaval by small farmers and urban mechanics and labourers. For a survey of more recent contributions to this question, see *Whose Revolution Was It? Historians Interpret the Founding*, ed. A. H. Young and G. H. Nobles (New York: New York University Press, 2011).

of the old order, they played a major part in bringing that order down.'[54] Richard Brown's study of the committees of correspondence reveals the same change: 'After six generations Massachusetts was turning away from the traditional idea of active leaders with passive followers towards the radical goal of an alert, engaged populace.'[55] Such a change, which destroyed the accustomed balance of rulers and ruled, shook the foundation of an order that Adams wanted to republicanize and purge of corruption, but not to reject.

The circumstances of the drafting suggest how Adams sought to acknowledge such change and to embody his constitutional philosophy in the new commonwealth constitution. 'I attended that convention of near four hundred members', he recalled thirty years later. There were actually only 312, but Adams's recollection of the much higher attendance, seen in the context of his next comment about it, suggests his lingering misgivings about unmediated rule by the many:

> Here I found such a chaos of absurd sentiments concerning government that I was obliged daily, before that grand assembly, and afterwards in the Grand Committee, to propose plans, and advocate doctrines, which were extremely unpopular with the greater number.[56]

For a man who saw government as a balance of social orders, the convention itself was a balancing act of popular and conservative interests.

The delegates meeting in Cambridge were not the first to attempt to draft a constitution for the new Commonwealth of Massachusetts. In 1778 the state legislature had met, produced a constitution, and submitted it to popular ratification, only to see it resoundingly defeated for being simultaneously too popular and too aristocratic: the popular vote was six to one against it. Popular forces had objected to its creation by the assembly, not by a popular convention, and in response the nation's first popular constitutional convention convened in 1779. But opposition also came from those who believed that the 1778 document had gone too far in democratizing the frame of government by proposing such innovations as an upper house elected directly by the people. Led by conservative easterners concentrated in the seaboard towns of Essex County, their 'Essex Result' listed numerous objections. It cited examples of inadequately separated powers, but its major thrust was the failure adequately to embody the 'established principles' of mixed government, which taught that

> we are to look further than to the bulk of the people, for the greatest wisdom, firmness, consistency, and perseverance. These qualities will most probably be found amongst men of education and fortune. From such men we are to expect genius cultivated by reading, and all the various advantages and assistances, which art, and a liberal education aided by wealth, can furnish.[57]

[54] Countryman, *Revolution*, 75.

[55] Brown, *Committees*, 246. Also pertinent is Breen, *American Insurgents.*

[56] John Adams to Benjamin Rush, 12 April 1809, *Works*, vol. 9, 618.

[57] *The Popular Sources of Political Authority: Documents on the Massachusetts Constitution of 1780*, ed. O. Handlin and M. F. Handlin (Cambridge, MA: Harvard University Press, 1966), 333–4. The full text is at 324–65. Theophilus Parsons, a leader of the conservative 'Essex Junto' opposing the proposed constitution, is generally considered its primary author. Wood, *Creation*, 217–19.

The writers of the 'Result', whose support Adams would seek the next year in Cambridge, saw government as a mixture of different virtues possessed by different orders of society. They acknowledged the inevitable exceptions among those of any rank; the 'Result' could not claim

> that the bulk of the people, the farmers, the merchants, the tradesmen, and labourers, are all honest and upright, with single views to the public good, or that they are not. In each of the classes there are undoubtedly exceptions, as the rules laid down are general. The proposition is only this. That among gentlemen of education, fortune and leisure, we shall find the largest number of men, possessed of wisdom, learning, and a firmness and consistency of character. That among the bulk of the people, we shall find the greatest share of political honesty, probity, and a regard to the interest of the whole, of which they compose the majority. That wisdom and firmness are not sufficient without good intentions, nor the latter without the former. The conclusion is, let the legislative body unite them all. The former are called the excellencies that result from an aristocracy; the latter, those that result from a democracy.[58]

Among the 'chaos of absurd sentiments concerning government' that Adams encountered there, he discovered to his dismay that even John Hancock and Samuel Adams supported a unicameral legislature of the sort advocated by Thomas Paine, which did not balance the few and the many.[59] Stiffening his resolve, he determined not to act, since he had derided Thomas Paine's motives in writing *Common Sense*, out of 'a mere desire to please the democratical Party'. The contents of that pamphlet, he sneered decades later, were a 'poor, ignorant, malicious, short-sighted, crapulous mass'.[60]

By winter, harsh weather had reduced attendance at the convention to fewer than three dozen, heavily dominated by the more conservative (and geographically closer) eastern delegates, a fact that did not fail to go unnoticed or without complaint. Thirty-two committees were formed, but seven of them consisted of a single delegate, and other subcommittees were dominated by a small number of men serving on several committees.[61] Adams, who believed that a constitution might be properly drawn by a single man, got his wish: 'I was by the Convention put upon the Committee—by the Committee upon the sub committee—and by the sub Commitee appointed a sub sub Committee —so that I had the honour to be the principal Engineer.'[62]

[58] Handlin and Handlin, *Popular Sources*, 334–5.

[59] Adams to Rush, 12 April 1809, *Works*, vol. 9, 618.

[60] Adams to Thomas Jefferson, 22 June 1819, *Works*, vol. 10, 380.

[61] R. J. Taylor, 'Construction of the Massachusetts Constitution', *American Antiquarian Society, Proceedings*, 90 (1980), 323–5, 329. Attendance dropped to fewer than ninety at times, as the *Massachusetts Spy* reported in January that 'For twenty years past the traveling has not been known to be worse than at present'. Cited by H. A. Cushing, *History of the Transition from Provincial to Commonwealth Government in Massachusetts* (New York: Columbia University Press, 1896), 238n. One irate critic charged, 'I do not see with what Justice such a part could be denominated *the* Convention'; Cushing, *Transition*, 240 (emphasis in original).

[62] Adams to Edmund Jenings, 7 June 1780, *Papers*, vol. 9, 388.

V. Lawmaking in '*an Empire of Laws, and Not Men*'

Drafting a constitution allowed Adams, a committee of one, to put into reality his thoughts on republican government, which he had defined in his *Thoughts on Government* in 1776 as 'an empire of laws, and not men.'[63] This famous remark, or its many variants that he used over the years, stands as his watchword on government, but its meaning bears scrutiny. In context, we find that he continues, 'As good government is an empire of laws, how shall your laws be made?' It was a difficult question, but it led him to assert that in creating a government based on the sovereignty of the people, an assembly 'should be in miniature an exact portrait of the people at large. It should think, feel, reason, and act like them.' Because a large nation could not practice direct democracy, Adams noted that representatives must be chosen. 'The first necessary step, then, is to depute power from the many to a few of the most wise and good.'[64] What he had called for in 1776 would become a reality in 1780. Writing as the proposed Massachusetts constitution was 'laid before the whole Body of the People in their Town Meetings, that every Man may have an opportunity, to express his Mind, and suggest his amendments,' Adams boasted,

> No Government was ever made so perfectly upon the Principle of the Peoples Right and Equality. It is Locke, Sidney, and Rousseau and De Mably reduced to Practice, in the first Instance.[65]

When he wrote his *Defence* of the American constitutions Adams was in England not only responding to the political instability of the newly independent state governments that he read of from afar (most notably, Daniel Shays's uprising in western Massachusetts), but also reacting to radical critics sceptical of the genuinely revolutionary nature of the new American states. Adams was especially nettled by the charge that his countrymen were merely replicating the British system of mixed government, particularly its bicameral parliament. So annoyed was he at such charges that his *Defence* took as its starting point a letter that the French physiocrat Turgot had sent to Richard Price in 1778. Doubting that the Americans will 'give to the world the example of a constitution wherein man may enjoy all his rights, exercise freely his whole faculties, and be governed by nature, reason, and by justice', Turgot had taken the Americans to task for their 'unreasonable imitation of the usages of England'. In establishing their bicameral legislatures, he argued, they were 'striving to prevent imaginary dangers'. How, he asked, 'could [they] be of any use in republics' that did not have the legal class distinctions of Britain?[66]

Adams's *Defence* offered his long-standing belief that a single-chamber legislature would begin as an aristocracy, but 'in a few days, or at least years' become an oligarchy, 'and then it will divide into two or three parties, who will soon have as many armies'. But the *Defence* did more than reiterate the balance of social orders that Turgot had seen and criticized. Though unapologetic about the need to balance social orders in a bicameral legislature, Adams argued that a unicameral

[63] Adams, *Works*, vol. 4, 194. [64] Adams, *Works*, vol. 4, 194–5.

[65] He added, 'These Principles ought to be spread in England at this time as much as possible.' John Adams to Edmund Jenings, 20 June 1780, Adams, *Papers*, vol. 9, 446–7.

[66] 'Extract of a Letter of M. Turgot to Dr. Richard Price,' 22 March 1778, in Adams, *Works*, vol. 4, 279.

assembly would defeat the sovereignty of the people: whether a single chamber then devolved into a dictatorship of a 'victorious general' or 'a government hereditary in a few families', it would 'in time exclude the people from all share even in elections'.[67] Although the hierarchy of society would be replicated in Adams's system of bicameralism, it did so within a constitutional framework that placed government more squarely within the control of the people whose consent had conferred sovereignty. 'We shall have reason to exult, if we make our comparison with England and the English constitution', he concluded. Britain's parliament and government by the one, the few, and the many provided only an imperfect republicanism by failing to complement mixed government with a balance of separated functional powers, all of which drew their authority from the sovereignty of all the people. 'Our people are undoubtedly sovereign', he continued. Among their other virtues, American constitutions allowed no 'hereditary titles, honors, offices, or distinctions.' In addition, 'the legislative, executive and judicial powers are carefully separated from each other; the powers of the one, the few, and the many are nicely balanced in the legislatures'.[68] Both houses of the 1780 Massachusetts Constitution embodied the sovereignty of the people and, moreover, were to be elected annually, as he carried into the constitution-building era his belief in annual elections as he had stated it in 1776: *'there is not in all science a maxim more infallible than this, where annual elections end, there slavery begins.'*[69]

The Massachusetts Senate was nonetheless distinguished from its House of Representatives in several ways. In the first place, the senate expressly represented property as well as people. Senatorial districts would be created from existing counties, with their representation apportioned according to the amount of taxes paid. The result was to place the weight of political power in the wealthier eastern counties of the state: Essex, Suffolk (Boston), Middlesex, and Worcester chose 23 of the 40 Senators.[70] Voters, Christian males of age twenty-one and above possessing a freehold of £3 or £60 'other real or personal estate' were to elect men of £300 freehold who had lived in Massachusetts (though not necessarily in their own district) for seven years. Wealthy absentees thus could serve, and, without a quorum requirement, any number of them might control the upper house.[71] Yet Adams had no illusions about any infallibility or trustworthiness in wealth. 'The rich, the well-born, and the able', his *Thoughts on Government* cautioned, 'acquire an influence among the people that will soon be too much for simple honesty and plain sense, in a house of representatives.' For that reason, a bicameral structure allowed for the insulation of the more propertied senators from the lower house in their own chamber: 'the most illustrious of them must, therefore, be separated from

[67] Adams, *Works*, vol. 4, 406. [68] Adams, *Works*, vol. 4, 382.

[69] Adams to John Penn, January 1776, Adams, *Works*, vol. 4, 203–5. (Emphasis in original.) Adams was responding to a request by the North Carolina delegates to Congress for advice in the event of independence. He gave the same advice to John Dickinson Sergeant, who had asked for advice in New Jersey's constitution-making process.

[70] Adams, 'Report', in *Revolutionary Writings*, 304–5.

[71] Adams, 'Report', in *Revolutionary Writings*, 305, 307.

the mass, and placed by themselves in a senate; this is, to all honest and useful intents, an ostracism.'[72]

Adams demonstrated the sincerity of his belief in government as resting on the sovereignty of the people in constituting the House of Representatives. Like Hume, he believed that only the 'opinion' of the people could legitimize government and effective rule by the few over the many. If the many were to concede constitutional control of government to the few, they had to do so through their consent as expressed in constitutionally created political channels. Adams therefore began by specifying that representation in the house be based on ratable polls (all males sixteen and older), a broader segment of the population than the voting population alone. Voters would have to meet the same requirements as senate voters, but property requirements were lower for representatives, whose threshold of eligibility was a £100 freehold. Representation in the house would be direct and actual, not virtual: a member of the house had to be a resident of the town that elected him, and would lose his seat 'on ceasing to be a freeholder within the same'. Unlike the upper house, which a small group of absentee senators might control if attendance was poor, Adams's report on the Convention set a quorum of sixty, out of a potential upper limit of two hundred members.[73]

Even so, Adams returned to the principle that he had stated in 1776, that of government by the 'most wise and good,' by including in the report a provision that 'members of the house of representatives shall be chosen . . . from among the wisest, most prudent, and virtuous of the freeholders.'[74] The report did not, by contrast, make such a specification for members of the senate, or upper house. Was Adams assuming that such men, of much higher social and economic rank, would by definition rank as 'the wisest, most prudent, and virtuous' of the commonwealth? When the convention convened and reviewed Adams's report, it made no such distinction and removed Adams's wording.[75] It also lowered the property qualifications for suffrage.

VI. Maintaining Balanced Government: the Executive

But it was on the executive office that the convention made its strongest objections to Adams's plan to create a powerful governor, an office that, to many, smacked of monarchy. The importance he attached to the executive office rested on his ideas about human nature and government, and, outwardly at least, points to the traditional monarchical background of the executive role. The governor, as proposed in the report, was to bear the title 'His Excellency', an honorific distinction of a sort used only by Georgia and New Hampshire.[76] Despite the derision such a title would elicit when he later proposed it for the President of the United States, Adams remained convinced of the practical necessity of such an appropriately

[72] Adams, *Works*, vol. 4, 290.

[73] Adams, 'The Report of a Constitution, or Form of Government, for the Commonwealth of Massachusetts', in *Revolutionary Writings*, 309.

[74] Adams, 'Report', in *Revolutionary Writings*, 309.

[75] Taylor, 'Construction', 341.

[76] Adams, 'Report', in *Revolutionary Writings*, 310.

dignified title. He viewed such titles as necessary to induce men of stature to accept high office and did not intend them as permanent; instead, they attached to the office, not the man.

Despite the outwardly regal implications of the title, Adams's thinking about the office of governor reveals a sharply different model than that of the monarch within the British constitution of mixed government. More significant than the social status of the governorship in a system of the one, the few, and the many was its functional purpose in a system of separated powers, not separated social orders. Misunderstanding of the reasons behind a strong executive office constantly exasperated him, especially when it came from friends who, he believed, ought to know better. Clarifying his position to Benjamin Rush in 1790, he wrote, 'My friend Dr. Rush will excuse me, if I caution him against a fraudulent use of the words *monarchy* and *republic.* I am a mortal and irreconcilable enemy to Monarchy. I am no friend of *hereditary limited* monarchy in America.' Adams explained that hereditary monarchy would require the counterweight of a hereditary senate, which he knew to be 'unattainable and impracticable', and which he would oppose. Emphatically, he continued:

> Do not, therefore, my friend, misunderstand me and misrepresent me to posterity. I am for a balance between the legislative and executive powers, and I am for enabling the executive to be at all times capable of maintaining the balance between the Senate and the House, or in other words, between the aristocratical and democratical interests.

Both chambers and the executive, he insisted, must be subject to the people through regular elections.[77]

The Massachusetts governor was the most powerful executive among any established in the first round of state constitutions, and behind that robust role stood a constitutional principle. Elected directly by the people (a procedure unique when proposed), the governor possessed the legitimacy of popular sovereignty necessary to counterbalance the legislature. The executive as proposed by Adams was to possess an absolute veto and to have full appointment powers of militia officers. To his 'Sorrow', he conceded, the convention removed both powers.[78] The militia authority drew on his recollection of the way that the Sons of Liberty in Massachusetts and other colonies had relied on their control of the militia during the tumultuous days of the decade before independence, and Adams was equally aware of the need to mobilize state militias in the future. He had sought to vest the choice of officers with the governor and his advisory council, but the more democratically inclined convention gave that power to the legislature instead.

Adams's governor was to be independent of the other branches, and he intended his provision that the governor be elected directly by the people to prevent legislative influence over executive action. The purpose of the veto, as provided in the report, was to confer on the governor 'the power to preserve the independence of the

[77] Adams to Benjamin Rush, 18 April 1790, *Works*, vol. 9, 566. (Emphasis in original.)
[78] Taylor, 'Construction', 316 n. 15.

executive and judicial departments'.[79] He considered the office of governor, in fact, to be a third branch of the legislature because of its role in controlling wayward legislation. 'I am clear for three Branches, in the Legislature', he wrote to Elbridge Gerry during the convention's deliberations. 'The Executive, which ought to be the Reservoir of Wisdom, as the Legislature is of Liberty, without this Weapon of Defence will be run down like a hare before the Hunters.'[80] Although the convention removed that power and replaced it with the more limited veto of the sort later included in the United States Constitution, Adams remained committed to the principle, which he understood to be based as much on the doctrine of separation of powers as on traditional mixed government. Philadelphia convention delegate Roger Sherman's objection to an absolute veto, Adams wrote barely three months into assuming the office of Vice-President, rested on a false logic. '[T]the rational objection here is, not that the executive is blended with the legislature, but that it is not blended enough; that it is incorporated with it, and made an essential part of it. If it were an integral part of it, it might negative a law without much noise, speculation, or confusion among the people.'[81] This executive-cum-legislator was even to have the authority to initiate the removal of judges with the approval of his advisory council, whose act would then be effected by a joint action of the two other legislative chambers.[82] Names did not matter. 'The monarchical and the aristocratical power in our [Federal] Constitution, it is true, are not hereditary; but this makes no difference in the nature of their power, in the nature of the balance, or in the name of the species of government', he explained to Sherman. The new system of separation of powers would be fused with that of mixed government, with its 'balance which is in the legislature – between the one, the few, and the many.'[83] Agreeing with the people of Wells, whose ratification report described the governor as the 'common Representative of the people', Adams never abandoned his view on the need for an executive whose authority came from the sovereign people,[84] and who could preserve republican government. As he wrote in the *Defence*,

> If there is one certain truth to be collected from the history of all ages, it is this; that the people's rights and liberties, and the democratical mixture in a constitution, can never be preserved without a strong executive, or, in other words, without separating the executive from the legislature.[85]

Traditional Whig politics of the mixed constitution would not suffice to answer what he called 'the great question': 'What combination of powers in society, or what form of government, will compel the formation, impartial execution, and faithful interpretation of good and equal laws, so that the citizens may constantly

[79] Adams, 'report', in *Revolutionary Writings*, 303. [80] Taylor, 'Construction', 336n.
[81] John Adams to Roger Sherman, 17 July 1789, *Works*, vol. 6, 432.
[82] Adams, 'Report', in *Revolutionary Writings*, 318.
[83] Adams to Sherman, 17 July 1789, *Works*, vol. 6, 429.
[84] On the validating force of popular consent required in the executive to resist legislative encroachment, see E. S. Morgan, *Inventing the People: The Rise of Popular Sovereignty in England and America* (New York: W. W. Norton and Co., 1988), 258–9. Quotation at 259.
[85] Adams, *Works*, vol. 4, 290.

enjoy the benefit of them, and may be sure of their continuance?'[86] Separation of powers was essential, and the Massachusetts Constitution began its 'Frame of Government' with an express command: 'In the government of the Commonwealth of Massachusetts, the legislative, executive, and judicial power shall be placed in separate departments, to the end that it might be a government of laws, and not of men.'[87]

VII. The Restraint of Power: A Bill of Rights

In commencing their work, however, the delegates had acknowledged that '[w]e may not expect to agree in a perfect System of Government'. To guide themselves, they opened their deliberations by stating a few political maxims, including the principle that 'a Power without *any* Restraint is Tyranny'. Before turning to the particulars of 'political Architecture',[88] therefore, the convention appointed Adams, his cousin Samuel, and James Bowdoin to be a subcommittee to draft a declaration that would restrain government. The other two, as John proudly recalled in 1812, 'insisted that I should prepare a plan in writing'. As a result, he said, 'The Declaration of Rights was drawn up by me.'[89]

The declaration made clear the constituent power that lay behind all branches of government:

> All power residing originally in the people, and being derived from them, the several magistrates and officers of government, vested with authority, whether legislative, executive, or judicial, are their substitutes and agents, and are at all times accountable to them.[90]

By thus recognizing the sovereign power of the people, the convention was establishing a body of fundamental constitutional law higher than the ordinary legislation that an elected legislature would produce, and superior to it in authority. The declaration, therefore, went beyond what previous state declarations had done. Its language was not simply admonitory. Although it provided, for example, that

[86] Adams, *Works*, vol. 4, 406.

[87] Massachusetts Constitution of 1780, Chapter II, 'The Frame of Government'. This provision was repeated and amplified in Article XXX.

[88] 'An Address to the Convention, for Framing a New Constitution of Government, for the State of Massachusetts-Bay, to their Constituents', in Handlin and Handlin, *Popular Sources,* 435–6.

[89] Adams to W. D. Williamson, 15 February 1812, Massachusetts Historical Society, *Proceedings*, 13 (1873–75), 300n–301n, cited by Robert A. Rutland, *The Birth of the Bill of Rights, 1776–1791* (Chapel Hill: University of North Carolina Press, 1955), 69. Adams later disclaimed any responsibility for Article III, which provided for public support of religion.

[90] Massachusetts Declaration of Rights, Article V. Accountability to the people explains both the good behaviour tenure of judges and their removability by the governor and council 'upon the address of both houses of the legislature', Article V, Chapter V, 'Judiciary Power'. Adams gave less systematic thought to the judiciary, but he regarded its independence as necessary and 'salutary' to balanced government. 'Letters to John Taylor of Caroline, Virginia, in Reply to His Strictures on Some Parts of the Defence of the American Constitutions'. *Works*, vol. 6, 488. As he explained further, 'the judiciary power is balanced against the house, the senate, the executive power, and the state governments.' *Works*, vol. 6, 467.

'Every subject of the commonwealth *ought* to obtain right and justice freely...'[91] it also included mandatory commands and prohibitions, among them, 'No subject *shall* be held to answer for any crimes or offence, until the same is fully and plainly, substantially and formally, described to him; or be compelled to accuse, or furnish, evidence against himself'.[92]

Leaving for France shortly after completing his work at the convention, Adams proudly took with him published copies of its report as it would be sent to the towns for ratification. He spoke no French and had to have his work translated, but on doing so he was pleased that it was 'exceedingly applauded' by the French and Spanish to whom he gave it, as well as by a select group of English sympathizers.[93] On his return to the United States a decade later, he could take pleasure in the adoption by other states of written constitutions with bills of rights guaranteeing popular sovereignty and providing for separation of governmental powers. A federal government along those same principles had been established, too. Though ever fearful for the fate of republican government, what he saw gave him confidence that 'Where all these circumstances take place, it is unnecessary to add that the laws alone can govern'.[94]

VIII. Conclusion: A *'Constitution of Human Nature'*

Adams was an active participant in the transatlantic Enlightenment project of constitution-making, and his carefully measured approach to reform produced a notably warm reception among moderate reformers attempting to stem the tide of more radical measures. He was praised in debate at the French Constituent Assembly when he was included in a list of worthies being invoked: in calling for a mixed and balanced government in the revolutionary summer of 1789, one delegate identified his own programme with 'Lycurgus and Polybius, with Cicero and Tacitus, with Montesquieu, Gibbon, De Lolme, Blackstone, [and] Adams'.[95] With his emphasis on balanced government in which power was expressly set out and limited in a written constitution with a mandatory bill of rights, Adams stood as a major figure in what has been identified as the 'Moderate Enlightenment' rather than part of its more radical manifestation in what he regarded as the 'democratical hurricane, inundation, earthquake, pestilence, call it what you will, [that] at last aroused and alarmed all the world, and produced a combination

[91] Massachusetts Declaration of Rights, Article XI. (Emphasis added.)

[92] Massachusetts Declaration of Rights, Article XII. (Emphasis added.)

[93] *Adams Family Correspondence*, vol. 3, 228n. Ironically, doubt continues to this day as to whether the required two-thirds majority necessary for ratification was achieved for every article. The closest study 'suggests that the Convention deliberately juggled the returns in order to make it appear' so for two of them. Samuel Eliot Morison, 'The Struggle over the Adoption of the Convention of Massachusetts, 1780', *Proceedings of the Massachusetts Historical Society* 50 (1916–17), 400.

[94] Adams, *Works*, vol. 4, 382.

[95] Thompson, *Adams*, 257.

unexampled, to prevent its further progress'.[96] His tenacious defence of a bicameral legislature in which power was divided between social classes and subject to an executive veto set him apart from more radical writers such as Thomas Paine, whose 'General Reform' would uproot and replace the existing hierarchies of social, religious, and political institutions.[97] For adherents of the Radical Enlightenment, reason alone would suffice as a guide to such reform and direct the actions of a single-chamber assembly. Adams had no use for either the theory or the political institution they championed. His political antagonists thus seized on his acceptance of inequality as an inevitable by-product of human nature and caricatured it as a call for official recognition and legal protection of an aristocracy. Speaking of himself in the third person in writing to Samuel Adams, he unashamedly admitted that 'he takes men as God has made them'. In this, he was returning to his belief that

> [b]y the law of nature, all men are men, and not angels – men, and not lions – men, and not whales – men, and not eagles – that is, they are all of the same species; and this is the most that the equality of nature amounts to. But man differs from man, almost as much as man from beast.[98]

It was such differences that separated men into different social orders, and which a government had to acknowledge. Indeed, when Adams discoursed on such ideas at length in his *Defence of the Constitutions* in 1787, he was prepared for the criticism it would receive. 'This Book', he predicted, 'will make me unpopular.'[99] Though widely influential—or, perhaps because of its wide popularity—it drew harsh criticism; although a series of newspaper essays he had published as a 'sequel' to it in 1790 attracted less attention, he nevertheless published them as its fourth volume in 1813. These *Discourses on Davila,* he would note in the margin of his personal copy, had 'powerfully destroyed his [Adams's] popularity. It was urged as full proof that he was an advocate for monarchy, and laboring to introduce a hereditary president in America.'[100] Such criticism of his four volumes, emerging out of the heated political partisanship of the era, polarized the discourse of politics and produced caricatures of serious writing. Adams, with his unfortunate use of terminology drawn from the lexicon of British political philosophy—he was, after all, writing for a transatlantic audience—gave his critics ample opportunity to lampoon his thoughts as monarchical, whether or not they had actually read his work.[101] As a candidate in the nation's first contested presidential election in 1796, his identification with the Federalist party and its opposition to the rising tide of

[96] Adams, *Works*, vol. 4, 485–6. On the Moderate and Radical Enlightenments, see Jonathan Israel, *A Revolution of the Mind: Radical Enlightenment and the Intellectual Origins of Modern Democracy* (Princeton: Princeton University Press, 2010), 32, 40.

[97] Israel, *A Revolution of the Mind*, 32, 40.

[98] Adams to Samuel Adams, 4 February 1794, *Works*, vol. 1, 462.

[99] Adams to James Warren, 9 January 1787, cited by Joseph Ellis, *Passionate Sage: The Character and Legacy of John Adams* (New York: W. W. Norton and Co., 1993), 147.

[100] The work, a series of essays he had written for the *Gazette of the United States* in 1790, was published in 1813 as *Discourses on Davila: A Series of Papers on Political History. By an American Citizen.* It can be found in *Works*, vol. 6, 223–403, with Adams's remarks at 227.

[101] For anecdotes of such attacks, see Thompson, *Adams*, 274–5.

Jeffersonian democracy made him fair game for further exaggeration and left his reputation so tarnished that there still exists what Bradley Thompson calls a 'common scholarly opinion that his political ideas became irrelevant by the 1790s'.[102] To the contrary, Adams had the depth of insight to recognize, as even many of his fellow conservatives failed to, what Edmund Morgan has shown to be a powerful truth about American politics, namely, 'that conservatism in America would have to be built on popular sovereignty'.[103]

Political assaults, and his responses to them over half a century, provide a coherent summary of his thinking and achievements as a 'constitution monger' in an age of vast upheaval. They also allow us to understand how his experiences and his ideas about human nature shaped his constitutional ideas.

Adams had endured such polemics for decades without making any public response, but in 1814 his patience was exhausted when the arch-republican John Taylor of Caroline took direct aim at him, identifying his *Defence* and the writings of 'Publius' in *The Federalist* as responsible for the nation's abandonment of agrarian democracy.[104] Charles Francis Adams, collecting his grandfather's writings in the 1850s, attributed Taylor's intemperate attack on the *Defence* to the 'violent party times' and the 'perversion and misrepresentation' of opponents' actions. Taylor's criticisms of Adams's writings were, he wrote, 'rather the result of violent inference than of his language'— a style that led Taylor to go so far as to compare Adams to Filmer.[105] In countering Taylor's 650-page polemic, the retired president took umbrage at the caricatures, but he also used the opportunity to reiterate the basic principles that had guided his constitution-making. He took particular pains to reject Taylor's charge that the *Defence* was a recombination of 'political skeletons', a mere 'elevation of the British form of government'.[106]

Adams was nearing eighty years of age when he responded to the publication of Taylor's *Inquiry* in 1814, and though his essay showed the influence of events subsequent to his active political life, its substance reflected the basic principles that had informed his constitution-mongering. As he had described them to Roger Sherman in 1789 he had sought to formulate a governmental framework that would accept and control 'the constitution of human nature, and the constant course of human affairs' that tended to subvert government.[107] Adams's reply to Taylor consisted of a long essay—actually, thirty-two separate letters that his grandson described as '[e]vidently intended as his last explanations of his meaning in the most disputed portions of his system'. Taylor's assault, wrote Charles Francis Adams, typified the 'tendency to metaphysical niceties' that characterized criticism

[102] Thompson, *Adams*, 251. [103] Morgan, *Inventing the People*, 260.

[104] John Taylor, *Inquiry into the Principles and Policy of the Government of the United States* (Fredericksburg: Green and Cady, 1814). Adams received an unsigned manuscript copy in 1813. On its publication in 1814 as *An Inquiry into the Principles and Policy of the Government of the United States*, see Ellis, *Passionate Sage*, 144–5.

[105] 'Editor's Preface', *Works*, vol. 6, 445–6. Taylor had opposed Adams ever since his Vice-Presidency, with an animus that grew in reaction to Adams's support of the Alien and Sedition Acts when president. Adams took special exception to being associated with Filmer, remarking that it "may excite a smile!": *Works*, 455.

[106] Taylor, *Inquiry*, v, vi. [107] Adams to Roger Sherman, 17 July 1789, *Works*, vol. 6, 432.

of his grandfather's constitutional ideas. By contrast, he wrote of the man who had written the *Defence*, 'He deals with the realities of life as he finds them in history and in his own experience.'[108] John Adams's reply to Taylor allowed him to reiterate a central theme: 'A "social order" there must be', he wrote, 'unless we would return to the forests'.[109] Social distinctions arose because men are not 'born of dispositions exactly alike . . . of equal weight; equal strength; equal length; equal delicacy of nerves; equal elasticity of muscles; equal complexions; equal figure, grace, or beauty'.[110] Such distinctions were created by God and could be neither prevented nor erased. Referring to himself in the third person, 'Mr. Adams' admitted that 'he takes men as God made them'.[111] He explained:

> That all men are born to equal rights is true . . . This is as indubitable as a moral government in the universe. But to teach that all men are born with equal powers and faculties, to equal influence in society, to equal property and advantages through life, is as gross a fraud, as glaring an imposition on the credulity of the people, as ever was practiced by monks, by Druids, by Brahmins, by priests of the immortal Lama, or by the self-styled philosophers of the French revolution. For honor's sake, Mr. Taylor, for truth and virtue's sake, let American philosophers and politicians despise it.[112]

It was fatuous, he argued, to try to end such inequality or the political inequality that allowed such an aristocracy, whether artificial or natural, to influence and control the votes of others. In this, he differed sharply from his rival Thomas Jefferson, who believed that it was the purpose of a constitution to create a 'system by which every fibre would be eradicated of antient or future aristocracy; and a foundation laid for a government truly republican'.[113] The steps necessary to bring that about, Adams warned, would likely 'produce greater inequalities than ever were seen in the world'.[114]

Adams believed that any civilized society would have to deal with the power of an aristocracy, which could appear in many different forms, reflecting the infinite variety of the human race. The 'aristocrat' possessed numerous ways of corrupting elections and gaining power:

> Whenever I use the word *aristocrat,* I mean a citizen who can command or govern two votes or more in society, whether by his virtues, his talents, his learning, his loquacity, his taciturnity, his frankness, his reserve, his face, figure, eloquence, grace, air, attitude, movements, wealth, birth, art, address, intrigue, good fellowship, drunkenness, debauchery, fraud, perjury, violence, treachery, pyrrhonism, deism, or atheism; for by every one of these instruments have votes been obtained and will be obtained.[115]

[108] Charles Francis Adams, 'Preface', *Works*, vol. 6, 446.

[109] Adams, 'Letters to John Taylor of Caroline, Virginia, in Reply to His Strictures on Several parts of the Defence of the American Constitutions', *Works*, vol. 6, 459.

[110] Adams, 'Letters to John Taylor', *Works*, vol. 6, 452.

[111] Adams, 'Letters to John Taylor', *Works*, vol. 6, 454.

[112] Adams, 'Letters to John Taylor', *Works*, vol. 6, 453–4.

[113] Thomas Jefferson, 'Autobiography', in *Jefferson: Writings*, ed. M. Peterson (New York: Library of America, 1984), 44.

[114] Adams, *Works*, vol. 6, 459.

[115] Adams, *Works*, vol. 6, 457.

Adams's constitutionalism acknowledged the inevitable influence of an aristocracy, which, he had conceded to Roger Sherman in 1789, was 'greater than either the monarchical or democratical. That will, therefore, swallow up the other two.'[116] Looking back on the history of the new republic in his 1814 reply to Taylor, he saw the sad truth of his prediction. Although the Federal Constitution had followed many of Adams's ideas in creating a government of separated powers with a written constitution and bill of rights, the senate, removed from popular control and possessing powers over the executive and judicial branches, had upset the delicate balance intended in Philadelphia. 'These few, these very few, thirty-four citizens only in seven or eight millions', he complained of senators, were not chosen by the people, but by state legislatures, and stood as an ominous 'resemblance of aristocracy in our government'.[117] Moreover, with the power to refuse to enact legislation passed by the house, to veto executive appointments, and to impeach judges, the senate had amassed 'powers in legislation, in execution, and in judicature', exceeding in power even 'the nobility in Prussia, Germany, Russia, France, or Spain'.[118] This allowed them to break the confines that Adams had provided in the Massachusetts Constitution, where their 'ostracism' would restrain their authority.[119]

Adams, excoriated for his supposedly aristocratic leanings, showed in his extensive constitutional writings that no sector of society was above suspicion, and that all must be 'controlled, checked, or balanced by constitutional energies'.[120] Coming of political age in the tumultuous political world of revolutionary Boston, he had cautioned against the excesses of the mob and for his efforts had been labelled an enemy of democracy. Looking back on half a century of political and constitutional development, however, he denied arguing that 'democracy is more pernicious than monarchy or aristocracy'.[121] In writing his 'Thoughts on Government' in 1776, he had been reacting to the turmoil in the streets of Boston and responding to the dangers of Paine's radical *Common Sense*. In that time and place, he explained, 'it was my duty to show that democracy was as unsteady, equally envious, ambitious, vain, proud, cruel, and bloody, as aristocracy or monarchy'.[122] In his eightieth year, he summed up the credo of his career: 'My opinion is, and always has been, that absolute power intoxicates alike despots, monarchs, aristocrats, and Jacobins, and *sans culottes*.'[123] Accepting that fact, he concluded, 'All that men can do, is to modify, organize, and arrange the powers of human society' to secure mankind's rights.[124]

116 Adams, *Works*, vol. 6, 431.
117 Adams, *Works*, vol. 6, 471.
118 Adams, *Works*, vol. 6, 471.
119 See text at note 72, above.
120 Adams, *Works*, vol. 6, 454.
121 Adams, *Works*, vol. 6, 477.
122 Adams, *Works*, vol. 6, 487.
123 Adams, *Works*, vol. 6, 477.
124 Adams, *Works*, vol. 6, 458.

19

Thomas Paine

Richard Whatmore

I

Thomas Paine has often been seen as the most radical thinker to have contributed to politics in Britain. For his views, he was condemned to death in his native England, narrowly escaped the guillotine in his adopted France, and was vilified in North America, the country to which he was most devoted despite always proclaiming himself a 'citizen of the world'. Paine was undoubtedly the most disparaged individual on two continents in his day, such was the vitriol directed against him, often by government authorities or their proxies. The radical printer Joseph Johnson at first refused to publish the first part of *The Rights of Man* in February 1791, so extreme was the book's content. As Horace Walpole put it, Paine's *Rights of Man*, in answer to Edmund Burke's *Reflections on the Revolution in France*, 'deserves a putrid fever. His doctrines go to the extremity of levelling.'[1] In Burke's view, Paine had contributed to the creation of 'a seductive liberty' by a 'revolution of doctrine and theoretick dogma'. Paine was deadly because he was plotting to create a universal republic by means of 'the abolition of monarchy, nobility, and church establishments . . . in each country'.[2]

Such bitter condemnation was echoed in hundreds of pamphlets. Paine's prosecution for sedition by the British government in June 1792 was based on the claim that he 'reviled what was most sacred in the Constitution, destroyed every principle of subordination and established nothing in their turn'.[3] Living at the time in Paris, Paine was informed that his image was being burned across England.[4] Yet he was also the most popular author of his day. Paine's works outsold every book, except

[1] Letters to Mary Berry, 3 April and 26 July, 1791, *Horace Walpole's Correspondence* (New Haven, CT: Yale University Press, 1937–83), 48 vols, vi, 239, 319.

[2] E. Burke, *Thoughts on French Affairs* [December, 1791], *Further Reflections on the Revolution in France*, ed. D. E. Ritchie (Indianapolis: Liberty Fund, 1992), 208–11.

[3] Paine, *Fifth edition of Paine's letters. Containing a letter to Mr Secretary Dundas, in answer to his speech on the late proclamation: together with two letters addressed to Lord Onslow, chairman of the meeting at Epsom, June 18, 1792, convened to address His Majesty on the late proclamation* (London: J. Parsons, 1792), 4.

[4] Gouverneur Morris, *The Diary and Letters of Gouverneur Morris, Minister of the United States to France, Member of the Constitutional Convention*, ed. A. C. Morris (London: Kegan Paul, Trench & Co., 1889), 2 vols, II, 8.

the Bible, across the Atlantic world between 1792 and 1802. When a thousand copies was deemed a good print run, the *Rights of Man* sold 500,000 in Britain in the decade after its publication in two parts in 1791–2. One Frenchman reported, on visiting England, that 'Paine's book works mightily'.[5] Paine himself claimed that, although the British government had 'honoured me with a thousand martyrdoms, by burning me in effigy in every town in that country', the *Rights of Man* 'had the greatest run of any work ever published in the English language'.[6]

Paine has always attracted considerable attention, both scholarly and more generally. Politicians of every rank continue to invoke his name. Commentators have associated Paine with a variety of political traditions, including liberalism and social democracy. More recently, scholars have credited Paine with fathering more radical contemporary political creeds, with founding the welfare state, and with being the source of the so-called contemporary secular enlightenment.[7] Whether considered famous or infamous, two problems have prevented a full understanding of why his contemporaries took Paine so seriously. The first is that we do not know enough about the origins of Paine's ideas. Paine insisted that he did not read any books at all except his own, all of which he knew by heart.[8] He presented his own ideas as altogether new and invariably rejected attempts to link them to other writers. As he put it in *The American Crisis*, 'what I write is pure nature.'[9] The consequent lack of clarity about Paine's intellectual lineage is tied to an uncertainty about what he was seeking to do in practice. Paine is commonly described as the source of modern ideas in general terms without precisely linking him to the reform philosophies of his own time. In consequence, Paine's writings have not been properly read in the context of the movements that speculated about international relations and the future of Europe, and which flourished in Britain, France, and

[5] Morris, *The Diary and Letters*, vol. I, 417.

[6] Paine, *Letters to the Citizens of the United States* (New York, 1802), Letter 1.

[7] E. Foner, *Tom Paine and Revolutionary America* (New York, Oxford: Oxford University Press, 1976); A. O. Aldridge, *Thomas Paine's American Ideology* (Delaware: University of Delaware Press, 1984); B. Vincent, *Thomas Paine, ou la religion de la liberté* (Paris: Aubier, 1987); D. A. Williams, *Paine and Cobbett: The Transatlantic Connection* (Kingston and Montreal: McGill-Queen's University Press, 1988); G. Claeys, *Thomas Paine: Social and Political Thought* (London: Unwin Hyman, 1989) and 'Republicanism and Commerce in Britain, 1796–1805', *Journal of Modern History* 66 (1994), 249–90; M. Philp, *Paine* (Oxford: Oxford University Press, 1989); J. R. Fruchtman, *Paine: Apostle of Freedom* (New York: Four Walls Eight Windows, 1994) and *The Political Philosophy of Thomas Paine* (Baltimore: Johns Hopkins University Press, 2009); D. Wootton, 'The Republican Tradition: from Commonwealth to Common Sense', in *Republicanism, Liberty and Commercial Society, 1649–1776* (Stanford: Stanford University Press, 1994), 1–44; J. Keane, *Tom Paine: A Political Life* (London: Bloomsbury, 1995); M. Ezran, *Thomas Paine: le combattant des deux révolutions, américaine et française* (Paris: l'Harmattan, 2004); E. Larkin, *Thomas Paine and the Literature of Revolution* (Cambridge: Cambridge University Press, 2005); H. J. Kaye, *Thomas Paine and the Promise of America* (New York: Hill and Wang, 2005); V. J. Vickers, *'My Pen and My Soul Have Ever Gone Together': Thomas Paine and the American Revolution* (New York: Routledge, 2005); C. Nelson, *Thomas Paine: Enlightenment, Revolutions, and the Birth of Modern Nations* (New York: Penguin Books, 2005); C. Hitchens, *Thomas Paine's 'Rights of Man': A Biography* (New York: Grove/Atlantic, 2007).

[8] E. Dumont, *Souvenirs sur Mirabeau*, ed. Jean Bénétruy (Paris: Presses Universitaires de France, 1950), 180.

[9] Paine, *The American Crisis*, 13 January 1777 (London: R. Carlile, 1819), 33.

across the Continent from the late 1770s into the mid-1790s. This is especially the case with his constitutional thought.

An illustration of the uncertain nature of Paine's constitutional ideas can be found in the comments of Paine's brilliant contemporary Emmanuel-Joseph Sieyès, who could not understand Paine's popularity because he believed that Paine's constitutional philosophy was altogether vague. Sieyès's perspective needs to be taken seriously because he was acknowledged by contemporaries to be the father of the French Revolution. It was Sieyès' three pamphlets, *Vues sur les moyens d'exécution dont les répresentants de la France pourront disposer en 1789*, *Essai sur les privilèges*, and *Qu'est-ce que le tiers état?*, published between November 1788 and May 1789, that convinced the members of the Estates General at Paris to embrace national sovereignty. Sieyès defined national sovereignty as a union of productive labourers within a specified territory. He was convinced that founding a political system upon such an idea would rapidly transform the international authority of France. This view of national sovereignty, or what Sieyès called 'the constituting power of a state', was incompatible with aristocracy as traditionally conceived. It was equally incompatible with an independent role for the church in politics separately from the state. National sovereignty entailed an end to absolute monarchical sovereignty, and could not be squared with the sovereignty of a monarch in parliament. Defining the nation as the locus of sovereignty further required the affirmation of 'Frenchness' against regional diversity. The revolution in France was accordingly defined by the transformation of monarchy, aristocracy, church, and national identity. Sieyès expected to create happy citizens by restoring France to greatness and by thoroughly modernizing the state. Sieyès called his new science of societal improvement a 'social art', 'social science', or 'social mechanics' for moderns.

Sieyès's reputation and achievement in the early 1790s, before the failures of the republican constitutions and the tarnishing of his name through his involvement with Bonaparte, make his comments on Paine all the more significant. The controversy between them was conducted in July 1791 in the pages of the newspaper *Le Moniteur*, an English version appearing the following month in the *European Magazine and London Review*. Louis XVI had fled from Paris on 21 June 1791, only to be captured and returned by troops four days later from the town of Varennes near the north-east border with Austrian-held Belgium. One response was to call for the replacement of the monarchy by a republic. Paine was in the vanguard with an article in a new daily newspaper *Le Républicain*. Sieyès defended monarchy in *Le Moniteur* on 6 July and Paine replied on 8 July, stating that he had declared war 'against the whole hell of Monarchy'. Paine pointed out that, by republicanism, he did not mean 'that which bears the name in Holland or in some Italian States' but rather 'simply as a Government by representation; a Government founded upon the principles of the "Declaration of Rights"', which were 'but one and the same thing in principles, and almost in expressions', in the American and the French cases.[10]

[10] Sieyès, *Gazette Nationale, ou Le Moniteur*, 6 July 1791, 46–7; Paine, *Le Moniteur* of 16 July, 137–9.

Sieyès responded in turn that he could not understand why Paine confounded 'two notions so distinct as those of a representative system and republicanism.' France had, Sieyès claimed, since 1789 established the 'purest and best' representative system 'which has hitherto appeared in the world'. This was the case despite having a monarch as head of the executive power of the state. Sieyès defined republics as states in which executive power lay 'in a Council of Execution appointed by the people or by the National Assembly'. By contrast, monarchy found 'an individual of superior rank, in whom is represented the stable unity of Government, or, what is the same, of National Monarchy', select and dismiss the heads of ministerial departments in the name of the people. Sieyès argued that government by a republican committee could not be seen *de jure* to be superior to government by a monarch. It could never be said that on point of principle the rule of a collective body in the name of the people was superior to the rule of a single figure also ruling in the name of the people. Paine's thought could be boiled down to a defence of what Sieyès termed polyarchy. The problem was that in opposing an ill-defined republican system to the present rule of the National Assembly there was no evidence that a new dawn for France would be established. Indeed, Sieyès feared that in removing the unity of action that characterized monarchical government, Paine's republic would experience faction, inaction, and inefficiency. Sieyès could not understand the force of Paine's definition of a republican constitution, because it amounted to nothing more than government by a multitude of committees.[11]

There is no evidence of Paine's rejoinder to Sieyès but it can easily be found in his subsequent writings. The foundation of Paine's constitutional ideas was the equality of rights. All men were equal and compacted together to create a government (Paine does not mention women with regard to the exercise of political rights). At the same time, the first political act had to be the establishment of a constitution and a declaration of the rights that guided actors in political life. These documents had to be adhered to, and were expected to be read by everyone in every home in the land and to be a constant political reference point. In large states, representation was necessary and the people delegated the exercise of their decisions as legislators to their representatives. Government offices equally had to be drawn from the people, to which the individual would return once his term of office was concluded. All offices were of limited duration and there was no sense, as there is in the thought of many of Paine's contemporaries such as James Madison, of the superiority of the political officeholder or of the legislator. Paine's constitutional thought was egalitarian and he increasingly opposed any association between representation and property. As he put it in the *Dissertation on First Principles of Government* (1795), 'wealth is often the presumptive evidence of dishonesty; and poverty the negative evidence of innocence.' As a consequence, all men had a right to vote. To take away such a right 'is to reduce man to slavery, for slavery consists in being subject to the will of another, and he that has not a vote in the election of representatives is in this case.' Paine did not believe that any person ought to be a

[11] Sieyès, *Political Writings*, ed. Michael Sonenscher (Indianapolis: Hackett, 2003), 163–73.

slave. The most fundamental violation of the equality of rights was to treat people as a form of property. What was most distinctive in Paine's thought was the concern that first principles needed to be periodically revisited. The constitution was an evolving document and needed to be revised by future generations in accordance with the principle of equal rights. Paine summarized this notion in stating that 'we frequently refresh our patriotism by reference to first principles'.

Sieyès noticed that Paine was not interested in constitutional detail. Paine was full of praise in *The Rights of Man* and other works for the Constitution of Pennsylvania of 1776, which was among the most democratic of state constitutions. Paine described the careful process, overseen by Benjamin Franklin, by which the people selected their representatives and established a constitution, and then ratified it and chose their government. Paine had an overwhelming faith in the people. Paine presented events in North America, for most of his life, as proof that his ideas were both practical and proven. Accordingly, Sieyès was overly harsh in condemning Paine as a political theorist who committed elementary mistakes. Paine made sure in the *Dissertation on First Principles of Government* to distinguish between principle and opinion, and argued that particular forms of government, including decisions about bicameral or unicameral legislatures, were dependent upon circumstance. He preferred a constant division of power, and precise rules about the making of laws and their execution, but he did not feel that it was necessary to be prescriptive. The key was to get the fundamental laws right. It was the neglect of adherence to equality of rights that had allowed what Paine termed 'aristocrats' such as Robespierre to ruin the early years of the French Revolution. As a constitutional theorist, Paine was most interested in the means of transforming existing societies from corruption to peace and liberty, and, in most of his works, focused on the transition mechanism that would do exactly this. In consequence, he put forward a vision of an altogether transformed world of peaceful republics existing for the good of their citizens and enjoying the benefits of developing and moralized forms of trade. Traditionally, republicans and radicals had associated commerce with effeminacy and the collapse of republican virtues. Paine, by contrast, held that his republic would support commerce and all the moral virtues. The only free state, whether small or large in size, was a republic without king or aristocracy. Paine associated his commercial republic with the moral transformation of the populace. Moral transformation occurred in the very process of making the people free, when the people took control of their lives through involvement in the process of choosing and evaluating legislators and governments. Paine was certain that the establishment of state constitutions had done exactly this in North America. The regular return to first principles, by means of periodic constitutional conventions, was the surest means of maintaining the moral calibre of the populace and, in consequence, their liberty. The republic Paine envisaged would institute in consequence what he called 'a gigantic manliness', which to Paine meant adherence to a republican culture of openness, honesty, and self-sacrifice in every mode of living, both public and private, for the good of the community. Such virtues were to be adhered to by the entire population of adult males, who were Paine's citizens.[12] So great was the patriotic virtue of the citizenry that Paine's republic had nothing to fear from war. Only defensive wars would occur because Paine's republic renounced empire and was entirely pacific, recognizing that peace aided trade. Paine believed that he was part of a radical enlightenment characterized by the institution of revolutionary governments, validated by republican constitutions, and supported by writers who fostered the egalitarian and libertarian political cultures necessary to sustaining republics in the modern world. Commerce and perpetual peace was a possible future for the world for the first time in history, and Paine struggled ardently to make his vision a reality. This chapter reveals the extent to which Paine's alternative future for lovers of liberty relied upon different transition mechanisms through which liberty would be established and secured. Paine altered his ideas about the means to establish a republican constitution in the 1780s and 1790s, before ultimately returning to the perspective he outlined when he came to fame as a republican constitutionalist in 1776.

II

Eighteenth-century politics was characterized by a profound uncertainty about the likely future of Europe's states. A central reason was the rise of Britain and the remarkable capacity of the British to wage war successfully, despite such an achievement being rarely associated in history with mixed or constitutional governance. From the perspective of the majority of commentators, the eighteenth century ought to have seen a conclusion to a seventeenth-century trend: the rise across Europe of the power of France, and the movement of France to a position akin to that of Rome in ancient times, being a hegemonic state for the Continent. The France of Louis XIV was the most sophisticated and populous state in Europe, the most united in terms of the commitment of the populace to Gallican Catholicism, the most adept in war, and the closest to universal monarchy, whether through union with the Spanish Bourbons, by imperial endeavour, or growing economic dominion. Traditionally, the capacity of burgeoning empires to extend themselves might have been limited by small groups of patriots infused with the courage and manliness that exemplified ancient republican virtue. Either through singular feats in battle illustrated by the history of the Swiss, the Dutch, and other republics such as Venice or Genoa, or through the capacity of a city to withstand a siege, the multitude of small states and federated republics that made up so much of early modern Europe had managed to survive against their larger neighbours. Such capacities were increasingly distant memories by the end of the seventeenth century. The first fact of modern politics was that small states could no longer stand against their larger neighbours. Either through the revolution in military technology carried forward by the great French engineer Sébastien Le Prestre,

[12] R. Whatmore, 'A gigantic manliness: Thomas Paine's republicanism in the 1790s', in S. Collini, R. Whatmore, and B. Young (eds), *Economy, Polity and Society: Essays in British Intellectual History, 1750–1850* (Cambridge: Cambridge University Press, 2000), 135–57.

Marquis de Vauban and others, or through the revolution in public credit that allowed large states to put gargantuan armies in the field, smaller powers considered their independence to be increasingly under threat from Europe's greatest state.

This situation changed because of the rise of Britain after the Dutch-supported Glorious Revolution and the union of England with Scotland less than a decade later. Britain's success in war against Louis XIV was initially ascribed to fleeting factors, such as the genius of Marlborough or the rare unity among Protestant powers in the first decade of the eighteenth century. But as Britain's economy strengthened, allowing public credit to support the expansion of the navy and imperial missions across the globe, a sense developed of Britain being a genuine challenge to French supremacy, despite the lack of political focus and the faction and corruption characteristic of Britain as an archetypal mixed monarchy. Britain's success on mainland Europe, and across the empire against France in the Seven Year's War, at once underlined the association between Britain and military victory and also between Britain and an uncertain future. Britain had triumphed but was close to bankruptcy. The end of the war brought the veneration of Pitt and hysterical prophecies of imminent national decline exemplified by John Brown's *Estimate of Manners* (1757/8) identifying 'a crisis so important and alarming'. For Brown, as for so many authors contributing to the literature of jeremiad, Britain was too small to defeat France, too indebted, too corrupt, and too backward in terms of its capacity to maintain a military as well as a commercial supremacy over Europe's natural overlord. As Brown put it, an excess of trade and wealth had brought on a 'national debility' characterized by 'effeminate manners' and 'loss of principle'.[13] A more general view became commonplace of a Europe on the brink of a precipice—because commerce might so easily decline, because national bankruptcy was so close at hand for warring commercial monarchies, and because corruption was endemic in political systems that fostered the fake forms of politeness and effeminacy that thrived in modern capitals. For many observers, Europe was reliving the history of Rome and would be brought down by barbarian invaders from the east, by internal collapse and civil war, and by overreliance upon the unstable force of commerce. Such themes explained the popularity of the writings of Jean-Jacques Rousseau, who predicted 'a century of revolutions' by which 'the great become small, the rich become poor, and monarchs become subjects'.[14]

The general sense of crisis was most acute in Europe's republics. One of the most important facts about eighteenth-century thought, which too many historians have ignored, is that republican doctrines were seen to be backward and largely irrelevant by the 1760s. The survival strategies for maintaining states associated with republics were no longer deemed to be functional. Dreams of republican empire inspired

[13] John Brown, *Estimate of the Manners and Principles of the Times*, 7th ed. (London: Davis & Reymers, 1758), 108.

[14] Jean-Jacques Rousseau, *Du Contrat social, ou Principes du droit politique* (Amsterdam: Marc Michel Rey, 1762), Book II, ch. 8, 62. *Émile; ou, De l'éducation* 2 vols (Frankfurt: Marc Michel Rey, 1762), Book III, 59–60.

by Machiavelli, or renascent classical republics founded on envisaged modern counterparts of the ancient slave economies, were impractical because of reduced means of self-defence, and in consequence had ceased to be direct models for statesmen and projectors.[15] Accordingly, republican states were everywhere in decline. Even cases where republics had been thriving within living memory, such as the Dutch republic, were recognized to be rare meteors that fell as soon as they reached their zenith. All republics appeared to be doomed to decline and collapse. Commerce made republican government increasingly problematic because of the incapacity of such states to defend themselves against larger rivals resourced by public credit and mercantile power, with extensive agricultural and commercial sectors sustaining them. Republics could not, it was argued, cope with luxury, could not defend themselves against larger states, and had been in terminal decline for two centuries through their intestinal corruption and divisions. Like other small states, they would fall to predatory enterprises, as appeared to be happening across Europe by the 1760s. The marquis de Chastellux in *De la félicité publique* (1772) had contemporary republics in mind when he wrote that 'nothing can be more deplorable, and at the same time more contemptible than republics in their decline . . . The love of glory is extinguished, and in its place, appear an empty ostentation, and a mean presumption, which render these vices, thus odious in themselves, so particularly ridiculous.'[16] The sense of a crisis for republics was usefully captured by Adam Ferguson, the Professor of Moral Philosophy at the University of Edinburgh, in *An Essay on the History of Civil Society* (1767) where he explained that small republics were no longer masters of their own destiny. Vocally refusing to give up their precarious liberty, they pretended to be independent at the same time as their prospects were ever more uncertain, while their capacity for self-defence was minimal. They found themselves in the unenviable position of having little influence over their own future while forever fighting against the slavery that had become their actual condition. Republics in the modern world were 'like shrubs, under the shade of a taller wood, choked by the neighbourhood of more powerful states'.[17] Ferguson saw modern Europe as being infested by 'a contagion of monarchical manners'.

Paine's perspective upon Britain outlined in his early writings, and exemplified by *Common Sense* and *The American Crisis*, was a continuation of the jeremiad literature that was so prominent in England. Britain had declined and now faced acute problems. Britain's government was unstable, tyrannical, and despotic, altogether unsuited to a populace claiming to be free-born. Even among critics of Britain's government and pessimists about Britain's future, Paine was distinctive in the vitriol he directed against the balance of the constitution and its monarchical element. Mixed government, Paine argued, was a contradiction in terms because

[15] J. G. A. Pocock, *Barbarism and Religion*, vol. 3: *The First Decline and Fall* (Cambridge: Cambridge University Press, 2003).

[16] François-Jean de Chastellux, *De la félicité publique, ou considérations sur le sort des homes. Dans les différentes Epoques de l'hiftoire* 2 vols (Amsterdam: Marc Michel Ray, 1772), vol. I, 115.

[17] Adam Ferguson, *An Essay on the History of Civil Society* (Edinburgh: A. Millar & T. Caddel, 1767), 91.

'the power which has most weight will govern'. In 1688/9 the English might have 'been wise enough to shut and lock a door against absolute monarchy', but at the same time they 'have been foolish enough to put the crown in possession of the key'. Britain's monarchy was absurd and ridiculous. 'Fools, madmen, knaves and tyrants' were conducting British policy.[18] The parricides of the constitution were only to be found in Britain.[19] Paine's advice to Americans was that Britain was neither as strong nor as united as might be presumed from prior military exploits. The greatness of Britain was a thing of the past. Americans had nothing to lose from separation. Indeed, independence amounted to the severing of a corrupt limb that if left would infect the existing colonies with the same cancer that had weakened Britain. Remaining connected to Britain would embroil America in European wars; Americans should look to 'the miseries of Hanover' for confirmation. America needed to 'steer clear of European contentions'.[20] Continued union with Britain would also infect America with British modes of life and above all the corrupt forms of commerce that Paine saw to be the currency of politics in the mother country.

Paine frequently stated that his ideas were all of a piece, and in later writings constantly referred back to *Common Sense*, which he perceived to be his political testament.[21] Particular themes do span the first and the final writings, including the critique of monarchy and mixed government, and the veneration of moderate wealth. But there was a clear limit to Paine's vision in the 1770s. If *Common Sense* and *The American Crisis* are compared with Paine's writings from his *Letter to the Abbé Raynal* (1782) onwards, a significant difference becomes evident. *Common Sense* praised 'the republican . . . part of the constitution of England', which was identified with 'the liberty of choosing a house of commons'.[22] Georgian monarchs were blamed for poisoning this republican element. The crown had 'engrossed the commons'. Paine's point when writing in the 1770s was that Britain was sickly and in consequence was both weak and corrupt. Paine was not seeking to foment revolution in Britain. Another form of government being embraced by the British was inconceivable because of the extent of the corruption of the populace. Europe, too, could remain as it was, mired in corruption and not offering anything to republicans. Monarchy and hereditary succession were the sources of the ills of states, as the history of Europe proved. Europe was of course overwhelmingly monarchical. War, ignorance, and corruption were the consequence of their dominion. Monarchy in modern times had become 'the popery of government'.[23] Paine too wanted to avoid the example of 'the states of Holland'. In this republic divided into individual states, 'their disjointed condition exposes them to numerous intrigues, losses, calamities and enemies'. In consequence, decisions were delayed, and decisions taken rarely acted upon. The best state in Europe, according to Paine, was France, whose 'exemplary greatness and universal liberality' ought to be lauded

[18] Thomas Paine, *Common Sense; addressed to the inhabitants of America* (Philadelphia: R. Bell, 1776), 14–16.

[19] Paine, *The American Crisis*, 9 August 1775 (London: R. Carlile, 1819), 2, 10.

[20] Paine, *Common Sense*, 39.

[21] Paine, *Letters to the citizens of the United States* (New York: s. n., 1802), Letter 1.

[22] Paine, *Common Sense*, 31.

[23] Paine, *Common Sense*, 23.

everywhere.[24] The alliance between the absolute monarchy of France and the American republics was the foundation of the latters' continued liberty.

Things were altogether different in America. Only a state beyond Europe could hope to be a republic. By contrast with the pitiful state of Europe's republics, in America the unity of the entire confederation was 'the great palladium of our liberty and safety'.[25] Excessive commerce was equally dangerous. In *Common Sense*, Paine declared that in North America 'our plan is commerce', claiming that liberty of trade would 'secure us the peace and friendship of all Europe'. Yet in the final section of the pamphlet, 'Of the Present Ability of America', he modified his tone. Commerce made for powerful states, but it was also a corrupting force in republics because it generated luxury and inequality. Commerce was everywhere the enemy of aggressive patriotism. The fact that America was a largely non-commercial nation therefore increased rather than diminished her military capabilities. A spirit of patriotism derived from yearning for independence made the American soldier more than a match for his British counterpart because the latter's addiction to luxury-based commerce 'diminishes the spirit both of patriotism and military defence'.[26]

Paine's verdict on Britain in the 1770s was at one with the opponents of the existing mixed monarchy in Britain, all of whom agreed that despite the evils that corrupted the politics of the state, Britain could never be transformed into a republic.[27] Britain might be reformed, but the model that had to be followed could not be the same as that pursued in the former colonies. North America was a unique experiment. Its distance from Europe meant that it did not need to invest in large armies for defence. As such, it did not require an extensive national debt. Such factors made the republics in North America immune to the politics of luxury and empire that was destroying Europe. America was subsequently lauded as the land of liberty. The revolution was described as the greatest event in modern times. Authors in Europe called for Europe to follow the North American example. Diderot famously did this with respect to the abolition of ranks and the creation of general assemblies in his contributions to the abbé Raynal's *Histoire philosophique des deux Indes* of the early 1780s and in his *Vie de Senèque* (1782). But Diderot did not describe how Europeans might become more like Americans in practice.[28] Equally, when the Physiocrats praised North America as *the* modern state in which land ownership could most easily be made the foundation of citizenship, there was

[24] Paine, *The American Crisis*, 19 April 1783, 191.

[25] Paine, *The American Crisis*, 19 April 1783, 192.

[26] *Common Sense*, 35; also, 'Thoughts on the Peace', in *Letter to the Earl*, 3 vols *of Shelburne* 9th ed. (London: D. Jordan, 1792), 23–5.

[27] C. Macaulay, *The History of England from the Accession of James I to that of the Brunswick Line*, 8 vols (London: J. Nourse, 1763–83), vol. iv, 355. n; J. Burgh, *Political Disquisitions*, 3 vols (London: E. and C. Dilly, 1774–5), vol. iii, 297–9; R. Price, *The Evidence for a Future Period of Improvement in the State of Mankind* (London: H. Goldney for T. Cadell, 1787), in *Political Writings*, ed. D. O. Thomas (Cambridge: Cambridge University Press, 1991), 164–5.

[28] Diderot (1875) *Essai sur les règnes de Claude et de Néron, et sur les mœurs et les écrits de Sénèque pour servir d'introduction à la lecture de ce philosophe, Œuvres complètes de Diderot* (ed.) J. Assézat, 12 vols (Paris: Garnier), vol. III, 48, 71, 321–4.

no sense that the conditions to be found in America, meaning abundant land and a small population, could be mapped onto European life.[29] All of the physiocratic admirers of the new republic acknowledged the different worlds to be found on either side of the Atlantic, with North America allowing a contrast to be drawn with the Machiavellianism of European polities. As Paine put it, America had been established as a place of religious liberty and freedom from the horrors of religious intolerance across Europe. Since then 'every spot of the old world is over-run with oppression'. Freedom, 'hunted round the globe', no longer existed in Asia or Africa, and in Europe it had become rare. Britain had 'given her warning to depart'. It was for America to 'receive the fugitive and prepare an asylum for mankind'.[30] Until the mid-1780s Paine continued to call America 'this last asylum of expatiated liberty'.[31] In short, he believed he was writing for Americans and those interested in taking the journey from Europe to America just as he had done. The journey from despotism to liberty could only be taken by abandoning the old world. Paine, in the 1770s, was no advocate of general rebellion and no exponent of a general theory of reform or revolution. As such, his ideas were close to the critics of Britain's government and politics, for whom, like Paine, liberty could only thrive in particular circumstances, such as those uniquely to be found in North America.

III

Paine changed his perspective during the 1780s. He came to the view that Europe, too, could be reformed and that America might play a role as a model polity within a globe characterized by commerce and peace. Undoubtedly this change of opinion was stimulated by his return to Europe. Paine travelled as part of a diplomatic visit to France and to the Dutch Republic while the war with Britain was ongoing, between February and June 1781. He was part of a group including Benjamin Franklin and John Laurens, negotiating a transfer of funds from France to the new republic, funds that he later claimed did more than Washington's military activities to win the war against the British.[32] During this time, he made contacts with *philosophes* in Paris, such as André Morellet, who was part of the French diplomatic effort. Paine returned for a longer period to France and thence to Britain in 1787, in order to find buyers for his iron bridge. Arriving in France in May 1787, his friendship with Thomas Jefferson, then American minister at Paris, led him to make further contacts among the reforming groups associated with Marie Jean Antoine Nicolas de Caritat, marquis de Condorcet and Morellet, both of whom enjoyed good relations with Jefferson.

[29] Marie Jean Antoine Nicolas de Caritat, marquis de Condorcet, *The life of M. Turgot* (London: J. Johnson, 1787), 321–2.

[30] Paine, *Common Sense*, 58.

[31] Paine, article in *Worcester Magazine*, 1 November 1786, published in Paine, *A Collection of Unknown Writings*, ed. H. Burgess (London: Palgrave Macmillan, 2010), 54–5.

[32] Paine, *Thomas Paine's Letter to the Late General George Washington, When President of the United States: Dated, Paris, June 30, 1795* (New-York: R.D. Taylor, 1803).

When Paine travelled on to Britain, arriving on 3 September 1787, the now-famous author of *Common Sense* was welcomed in circles that had supported the American cause. Some radical groups within Britain were speculating about the prospect of establishing commerce and perpetual peace and a world without war or empire. It was particularly to such circles that Paine was drawn. One of the most important circles was that of William Petty, 2nd Earl of Shelburne. Morellet may have advised Paine to make contact with Shelburne on his return to England; Morellet considered Shelburne the most enlightened of public figures and engaged in a long-term correspondence with him to promote reform on both sides of the Channel.[33] Paine and Shelburne shared other friends also, including Benjamin Franklin and Benjamin Vaughan. Paine made contact with Shelburne after his arrival in England, expressing the view in a letter that 'I wish that this infamous business of perpetual wrangling between England and France might end', and adding that 'peace might be easily preferred were proper persons in the management of affairs'.[34] Paine was greatly impressed by certain members of Shelburne's entourage. One of Shelburne's closest friends was the dissenting minister and philosopher Richard Price, whom Paine later called 'one of the best-hearted men that exists', and also 'a friend and republican'.[35] Shelburne's circle was equally known for its veneration of the writings of Adam Smith. Paine was to claim Smith for his radical cause in *The Rights of Man*, against the 'disorderly cast of [Burke's] genius'.[36] Paine's description of republican government as natural to man, and the American and French Revolutions as 'a renovation of the natural order of things . . . combining moral with political happiness and national prosperity', owed a great deal to Smith's idea of 'natural liberty'.[37] Aside from such comments and personal connections, there is evidence of Paine's involvement in the campaigns of the Shelburne circle in his writings of the 1780s.

Shelburne shared with Paine the view that Britain was in decline. War in North America, in worsening the debt and in damaging trade, accentuated the sense of crisis. As prime minister, for a short period from July 1782 to April 1783,

[33] E. Fitzmaurice, *Life of William, Earl of Shelburne*, 2 vols (London: Macmillan & Co, 1912), vol. I, 429–33; André Morellet to Shelburne, 8 January 1772 (Letter 676), *Correspondance générale d'Helvétius: Volume III: 1761–1774/Lettres 465–720*, ed. D. Smith, A. Dainard, M. Inguenaud, J. Orsini, and P. Allan (Toronto: University of Toronto Press; Oxford: Voltaire Foundation, 1991), 386–7; André Morellet to Shelburne, 18 February 1777 (Letter 727), *Correspondance générale d'Helvétius: Volume IV: 1774–1800/Lettres 721–855, suivies de lettres relevant des périodes des trois premiers volumes et découvertes depuis leur parution*, ed. D. Smith, J. Orsini, M. Inguenaud, P. Allan, and A. Dainard (Toronto: University of Toronto Press; Oxford: Voltaire Foundation, 1998), 13–17.

[34] Paine to Shelburne, 20 November 1787, published in Paine, *A Collection of Unknown Writings*, 59.

[35] Paine, *Rights of Man: Being an Answer to Mr Burke's Attack on the French Revolution*, 7th ed. (London: J. S. Jordan, 1791), 8; 'Lettre à MM. Chabroud et Chapelier', *Le Républicain, ou le défenseur du gouvernement représentatif, par une société des républicains*, no. 2 (July, 1791), 31.

[36] *Rights of Man*, 63.

[37] *Rights of Man*, 117, 167–71; *Rights of Man. Part the Second. Combining principle and practice* (London, 1792), 65, 82. See further D. Winch, *Riches and Poverty: An Intellectual History of Political Economy in Britain 1750–1834* (Cambridge: Cambridge University Press, 1996), 100–3, 128–31, 150–6.

Shelburne negotiated the Peace of Paris, and fell from office in consequence. Shelburne, with Morellet and others, was responsible for ensuring that a clause of the Treaty of Paris stated that a commercial treaty between Britain and France would be signed within three years.[38] This was to become the Eden/Rayneval Treaty of 1786. Shelburne's belief was that commercial ties between nations could be relied upon to prevent future wars. Peaceful mercantile links between states could be relied upon to be a voice for peace.[39] Commercial alliances allowed politicians to see directly the benefits of trade and the negative consequences of war for trade. Shelburne pushed such arguments by a variety of means. All of the members of his circle were involved in propaganda to promote treaties of commerce with the aim of reducing duties and preventing war. Shelburne's circle was active in Britain, France, and North America, with popular works being authored by Richard Price, the dissenting minister Andrew Kippis, Benjamin Vaughan, Morellet, and the physiocrat Pierre-Samuel Dupont de Nemours.[40] Their view, inspired by Adam Smith and by Anne-Robert-Jacques Turgot, was that Europe could be moved towards a growth path based on the natural progress of opulence.[41] Peace was deadly to the mercantile system. Trading systems could be reformed by fostering free trade and by the eradication of commercial corruption wherever it was identified. The reform of commerce was the necessary first step towards constitutional reform, which was anticipated in both France and Britain.

Paine's commitment to the arguments of the Shelburne circle can be seen as early as his *Letter to the Abbé Raynal* in 1782. Here, Paine identified 'a new cast to the mind of man' through the progress of science and of commerce. He argued that 'the mind once enlightened cannot again become dark', and that such enlightenment could be seen to be developing in France in the main because of the alliance with the American republics. War had become irrational and war for profit particularly so. This was one of the lessons of the events in America. While Britain was in decline, requiring 'a total reformation', the movement for peace across the world

[38] Fitzmaurice, *Life of William, Earl of Shelburne*, II, 264, Morellet, *Mémoires inédits de l'abbé Morellet... sur le dix-huitième siècle et sur la révolution*, 2nd ed., 2 vols (Paris: Ladvocat, 1822), vol. I, 27.

[39] Shelburne to Richard Price, 22 November 1786, *Correspondence of Richard Price, Volume III: February 1786–February 1791*, ed. W. B. Peach (Durham NC: Duke University Press, 1994), 86–7. See further R. Whatmore, 'Shelburne and Perpetual Peace: Small States, Commerce and International Relations within the Bowood Circle', in N. Aston and C. Campbell Orr (eds), *An Enlightenment Statesman in Whig Britain: Lord Shelburne (1737–1805) in Context* (London: Boydell & Brewer, 2011), 249–73.

[40] André Morellet, *Lettres de l'abbé Morellet de l'Académie française à Lord Shelburne, depuis marquis de Lansdowne, 1772–1803*, ed. E. Fitzmaurice (Paris: Librairie Plon, 1898), Morellet to Shelburne, 12 March 1776, 102; 30 December 1777, 130–5; Richard Price, *Observations on the nature of civil liberty, the principles of government, and the justice and policy of the war with America* (Dublin: J. Exshaw, 1776), 98; Andrew Kippis, *Considerations upon the provisional peace treaty with America and the preliminary articles of peace with France and Spain*, 2nd ed. (London: J. Stockdale, 1783), 5, 79–81; Dupont de Nemours, *Lettre à la chambre du commerce de Normandie, Sur le Mémoire qu'elle a publié relativement au Traité de Commerce avec l'Angleterre* (Rouen and Paris: Moutard, 1788), 74–5; Benjamin Vaughan, *New and old principles of trade compared; or a Treatise on the Principles of Commerce between Nations* (London: J. Johnson and J. Debrett, 1788).

[41] William Petty, Lord Lansdowne, to Dugald Stewart, 1795 in *The Collected Works of Dugald Stewart* (Edinburgh: T. Constable and Co., 1858), ed. Sir William Hamilton, 10 vols, X, 95.

proceeded apace. A new politics was being established on the basis of the recognition that 'the idea of conquering countries, like the Greeks and the Romans, does not now exist'.[42] Such sentiments dovetailed with the opinions of the Shelburne circle. In restoring peace between France and Britain, the Treaty of Paris put an end to the post-1763 era of crisis. In underlining the costs and dangers of an expansive empire, it reminded the British that it was better to rely on trade rather than arms to sustain the state, and represented a warning against future colonization. Above all, it was a chance for Europe to return to the natural progress of opulence, by dealing a heavy blow against the mercantile system of controlled trade. Shelburne in the House of Lords identified 'the era of Protestantism in trade', the argument being that the new principle of commercial liberty was better suited to Protestant states, and that the progress of trade would partner the progress of religion. Free commerce with North America was the best future for Britain: 'All Europe appear enlightened, and eager to throw off the vile shackles of oppressive ignorant monopoly, of that unmanly and illiberal principle, which is at once ungenerous and deceitful.'[43] Reforming the constitution to create a fairer representative system, to limit the power of the crown, and to establish civil and political liberty for Protestant dissenters and Catholics was expected to follow.

When Paine returned to Britain in 1787, he sent Shelburne a copy of his latest pamphlet, *Prospects on the Rubicon*. Paine here once again praised the French and damned the British. The French, he claimed, 'are beginning to think for themselves'. By contrast, the people of England were 'resigning up the prerogative of thinking'. The British press, according to Paine, promoted 'the most barefaced perfidiousness', in public life; in print, 'the most abandoned principles are daily propagated' and 'scarcely any thing is to be seen, but mean abuse and low scurrility'.[44] The foolishness of British politics was exemplified by William Pitt's arming of the state in preparation for a potential war against France over the condition of the Dutch Republic, which was internally divided into a Patriot party, supported by France, and the party of the ruling Stadtholder, favoured by Britain. Prussia invaded the republic in support of the Stadtholder just as Paine was completing the pamphlet, and Pitt warned France that war would be the consequence of intervention against Prussia. Paine was sickened by the fact that what he called 'the disposition to peace', which had been evident in international relations in recent times, had not been taken advantage of. Rather, Britain was once again on the verge of war. Such a stance was stupid because France had become as commercial as Britain and was much better prepared for armed conflict. Pitt was about to destroy 'the harmony that appeared to be growing up between the two nations; to lessen, if not totally destroy, the advantages of the Commercial Treaty, and to lay the seeds of future wars, when there was a prospect

[42] Paine, *Letter to the Abbé Raynal* (London, 1782).

[43] Shelburne, *The Speech of the Right Honourable the earl of Shelburne, in the House of Lords, on Monday, February 13, 1783, on the Articles of Peace* (Ipswich: Charles Punchard, 1783), 4.

[44] Paine, *Prospects on the Rubicon: or an investigation into the causes and consequences of the politics to be agitated at the next meeting of parliament* (London: W.T. Sherwin, [1787] 1817), 30.

of a long and uninterrupted peace.' Paine anticipated upheaval within Britain because of the extent of the national debt.

The warning message of *Prospects on the Rubicon* was at one with that which Shelburne and his associates were propagating in British and in French circles. International peace needed to be maintained to provide time for the commercial alliances to do their work. Going to war at such a point in time would upset all of the labours of the past decade. Warnings were issued to Pitt in a variety of forms. As Benjamin Vaughan wrote to Franklin, 'These late struggles have unhappily shown however, how little any of these people [Pitt, Fox, and Sheridan] are capable of grand political ideas or plans. They understand faction, and even that often but ill, but seem to know nothing of the new systems of general politics.'[45] Jeremy Bentham, another friend of Shelburne's, attacked 'Pitt's Machiavellian System'.[46] Although general European war was avoided in the Dutch case, the era of relative international harmony was over; war between Britain and France was again anticipated. In such circumstances, the old question marks about Britain's constitution once again came to the fore. In the context of the Regency crisis of 1788/9, and the ongoing debt problems of the state, the future of Britain appeared ever more uncertain.

Shelburne and his circle became increasingly pessimistic about Britain's future at this time. For them, Britain's constitution supported a politics that was irrational and corrupt in its addiction to monopolistic commerce and to war. In looking towards France, they envisaged a Gallican revolution akin to that of England 1688/9. Their great hope was that a reformed version of Britain's constitution would be created in France, and that commercial and other kinds of alliance would flourish once this was the case. Reform in France might be a means of reforming Britain's constitution and dealing with the national debt.[47] Paine wholeheartedly embraced particular elements of the Shelburne programme. The latter had particularly emphasized the relationship between corrupt commerce and aristocracies in trade. Aristocracies could easily pollute political life and exactly this had happened in Britain, where the patronage of the monarch and the excessive wealth of particular individuals led to indefensible examples of corrupt commerce, which in turn fuelled Britain's lust for empire. Paine followed this argument and began to emphasize in all of his political writings that both monarchy and aristocracy were responsible for the ills of European states. The aristocracies of Europe were degenerate stock and co-responsible for national decline. Paine called aristocrats parasites and identified them as 'a kind of fungus'. He claimed that the example of the Jews confirmed 'that the human species has a tendency to degenerate, in any small number of persons, when separated from the general stock of society'.[48] Paine

[45] Benjamin Vaughan to Benjamin Franklin, 4 March 1789, The Papers of Benjamin Franklin Online, <http://franklinpapers.org/franklin/framedVolumes.jsp>.

[46] S. Conway, 'Bentham versus Pitt: Jeremy Bentham and British Foreign Policy 1789', *Historical Journal* 30 (1987), 791–809.

[47] R. Whatmore, 'Etienne Dumont, the British Constitution, and the French Revolution', *Historical Journal* 50/1 (2007), 23–47.

[48] Paine, *Rights of Man*, 73–7, 106–8.

was also different. Where Shelburne, Price, and others believed that economic reform would improve domestic politics, and ensure that a reformed version of the mixed constitution would survive, Paine stated the intention 'to exterminate the monster Aristocracy, root and branch'. Paine's simple message was that unless Britain became a republic it could not be described as a free state. Only republican constitutions were capable of sustaining liberty and good morals in the modern world.

IV

Paine's *Rights of Man* made the most radical argument in eighteenth-century constitutional thought. Britain could and ought to be transformed into a republic. Paine had not made the argument before, believing either that reform was possible, or that Europeans should abandon their continent to experience true liberty in America. But in 1791 and after, Paine became convinced that a general theory of revolution could be developed for European states like Britain and France. He saw his writings as paving the way for putting theory into practice. Paine defined republican government as 'no other than government established and conducted for the interest of the public, as well individually as collectively'. The key to the establishment of such a government was the election of all political officers by all adult males. Exclusion from the franchise only occurred 'as a punishment for a certain time upon those who should propose to take away that right from others'.[49] The political representation of all men was the great discovery of the moderns. Paine was certain that open and free elections would ensure that individuals were elected who were enlightened and as such genuine servants of the public. Commitment to the liberties that came with representation meant that a homogeneous political culture developed. It also created a fierce patriotism that made representative republics impregnable in self-defence:

> So powerful is the Representative System; first, by combining and consolidating all the parts of a country together, however great the extent; and secondly, by admitting of none but men properly qualified into the government, or dismissing them if they prove to be otherwise, that America was enabled thereby totally to defeat and overthrow all the schemes and projects of the Hereditary Government of England against her.[50]

Paine recognized that he was overturning the hitherto uncontested claim that republics could only survive in small states. The complexity of politics in large states demanded executive action, and this was incompatible with republican politics as traditionally conceived. Paine claimed in response that commerce was already eroding ranks and creating similar cultures across the globe. Politics was going to become simpler, and government less necessary, as countries began to

[49] Paine, *Dissertation on First Principles of Government* (London: The proprietors, 1795), 21.
[50] Paine, *Fifth edition of Paine's letters: containing a letter to Mr Secretary Dundas, in answer to his speech on the late proclamation* (London: J. Parsons, 1792), 2–3.

share cultures, and as they recognized that war, empire, monarchs, and nobles were feudal vestiges and detrimental to commerce and enlightenment. As Paine wrote, if monarchy was anywhere to be justified it was in a small state where issues were so basic as to be within the capacity of a single individual. Large states had to be republics because 'when it is attempted to extend this individual [monarch's] knowledge to the affairs of a great country, the capacity of knowing bears no longer any proportion to the extent or multiplicity of the objects which ought to be known, and the Government inevitably falls from ignorance into tyranny'.[51]

The first step towards the creation of a republic was a national convention of the representatives of the nation. This could only take place once ranks had been abolished. The term rank had to signify an occupation rather than status. Paine called 'equality of Rights . . . the true and only basis of representative government', meaning that rights were incompatible with the existence of aristocracy and monarchy.[52] The problems of 'the old governments of Europe' could be traced to 'distortedly exalting some men, so that others are debased, till the whole is out of nature'.[53] In future there would be no courtiers and no patronage. The term 'commons', which in earlier times Paine had praised, he now damned as degrading. He said it was 'unknown in free Countries'.[54] The consequences of the removal of ranks Paine was sure would be momentous. In future, there would be 'no riots, tumults, and disorders'. Furthermore, conditions would improve for all to the extent that an end would be seen to the 'class of poor and wretched people who are so numerously dispersed all over England'.[55] The only way to address the problem of poverty was to remove monarchs and noblemen. The latter explained the fact that the majority of European subjects found themselves 'far below the condition of an Indian'.[56]

Paine took a step beyond the Shelburne circle when he argued that the only means of abolishing war in the modern world, and of establishing perpetual peace, was to remove the causes of international conflict, which could be found in the ambition of kings, princes, and nobles for glory, lucre, and land. War was a consequence of the need for revenue within monarchical polities: 'Man is not the enemy of man, but through the medium of a false system of Government.' War was productive for politicians because 'it easily furnishes the pretence of necessity for taxes and appointments to places and offices'. War was 'a principal part of the system of old Governments' and a core element of established monarchical constitutionalism. By contrast, republics were pacific 'because the nature of their Government does not admit of an interest distinct from that of the Nation'.[57] In the second part of the *Rights of Man*, Paine repeated the argument that wars could be blamed on the forms of government that had an interest in maintaining them.

[51] Paine, *Lettre aux auteurs du Républicain, Le Républicain*, no. 2 (July 1791), 9.

[52] Paine, *Dissertation on First Principles of Government*, 18.

[53] Paine, *Rights of Man*, 37.

[54] Paine, *Letter Addressed to the Addressers on the Late Proclamation* (London: H. D. Symonds, and Thomas Clio Rickman, 1792), 28–30, 51–8.

[55] Paine, *Fifth edition of Paine's letters*, 8.

[56] Paine, *Rights of Man. Part the second*, 79.

[57] Paine, *Rights of Man*, 169–70.

Europe in recent decades was characterized by 'a perpetual system of war and expense... [which] drains the country and defeats the general felicity of which civilization is capable'. Paine stated that '[a]ll the monarchical governments are military. War is their trade, plunder and revenue their objects'.[58] He followed this with the argument that commerce in its natural form tended to peace, and would ultimately establish peace between nations, once the corrupt forms of politics had been eradicated, as had happened in France. He praised the new French republic as the ideal state founded upon anti-monarchical constitutionalism.

Paine had hopes at this point that the British might follow the French in rising up against their government, and establish sister republics that would create a new world order.[59] Paine's script for republican revolution declared the identity of the rebellions in America and in France. The *Rights of Man* sought 'the happiness of seeing the New World regenerate the Old', concluding that 'better times are in prospect... the insulted German and the enslaved Spaniard, the Russ and the Pole, are beginning to think', inspired by a generation in North America living as 'the Adam of a new world'.[60] Paine's goal was a globe of pacific and commercial republics, protected by constitutions that enshrined the principles of representation. That France was following North America was the foundational argument in favour of Britain joining the republics in a union sufficiently powerful to challenge the barbarisms of absolute monarchy and institutionalized Christianity, and inaugurate an age of reason in politics, religion, and morals. Nothing in British traditions of political argument foreshadowed such a vision. By contrast, the most radical of domestic anti-Burke tracts, James Mackintosh's *Vindiciæ Gallicæ,* defended the 'manly' legacy of 1688 and the 'senatorial nobility' then established, concluding that 'nothing can be more absurd than to assert that all who admire wish to imitate the French Revolution'.[61] Paineite republicans within Britain, such as John Thelwall, began to describe themselves as part of an international cosmopolitan movement, and as contributors to a new science of politics with global applicability.[62] The language of constitutional life had become universal, couched in terms of the rights of all men, rather than the particular interests of nations, communities, or corporations.

Paine was stung by Sieyès's criticisms of July 1791 and made clear why a republic was incompatible with any kind of monarchy in the second part of the *Rights of Man*. Here he underlined over and over again his claim that, if war was to be avoided, republican constitutions without monarchs either hereditary or elected had to be established. Monarchy was part of the old world and not part of the new. Aristocracy of any form was equally seen to be incompatible with a republican constitution. Paine was therefore fuller in his description of a republic, adding

[58] Paine, *Rights of Man, Part the second,* 4, 16–17, 19, 71.

[59] Paine, *Rights of Man, Part the second,* 79–84.

[60] Paine, *Rights of Man,* dedication to George Washington.

[61] J. Mackintosh, *Vindiciæ Gallicæ* 2nd ed. (London: G.G.J. and J. Robinson, 1791), 18, 63–7, 250–60, 293–302, 351.

[62] J. Thelwall, *The Tribune: a periodical publication, consisting chiefly of the political lectures of J. Thelwall* (London: printed for the author, 1795), 111.

measures intended to maintain the material equality of the citizenry. The establishment of moderate wealth became a fundamental element of his political strategy, to prevent merchants, legislators, judges, or landowners from becoming noblemen. A policy of pensions, annuities, a progressive income tax, and a civic education were all to be included in a constitutional document enshrining the principles of political equality and equal rights. Revolution in France was great because it was the first upheaval in Europe to recognize the importance of ending social hierarchies. Men had become 'of one degree'. There were 'no more titles, no nobility or aristocracy... the peer is exalted into the *man*'. The French would be rewarded with a society where 'the poor are not oppressed, the rich are not privileged. Industry is not mortified by the splendid extravagance of a court rioting at its expense.'[63] Low taxes would allow commerce to thrive while the nation would be better and more justly governed. It was a historical fact that 'the greatest characters the world has known rose on the democratic floor'. Paine's aim was to regenerate humanity by reconstructing the social order. Ranks would not be associated with political or civil inequalities, and moderate wealth would protect this social constitution.

Paine's universal constitutionalism rested on the success in the first instance of the North American Republic. In all of his writings about Europe, Paine returned to the example of the revolution in America and the remarkable transformation of political culture that had followed the institution of political representation, political equality, and civil and religious liberty. Paine's point was that, if a nation committed itself to the rights of everyone, politics would become more open and less factious. The public good became more obvious and the interest of the whole both more transparent and more realizable. When Paine was converted to the view that a similar process could be initiated in Europe, the test case was of course France. Paine was impressed by the constitution created by the National Assembly and defended it in the first part of the *Rights of Man*. But once he realized that the transformation of France into a republic was a possibility, his advocacy was ceaseless. Gouverneur Morris recalled that after the flight to Varennes, Paine was 'inflated to the eyes and big with a litter of revolutions'.[64] Once more Paine expected the creation of a republican constitution to bring stability and calm to politics, and the benefits of republican life to be both obvious and self-sustaining, as a culture of republican virtue permeated the populace. The people, Paine was sure, had a passionate interest in maintaining a republican constitution, because it protected their interests as no alternative could, and accordingly it was the people as a body who would defend the republic against domestic and external enemies.

Proof of the reality of Paine's vision lay above all else in the condition of Britain; Britain had to collapse if Paine's analysis of the injustice and instability of the old constitution was accurate. Furthermore, Britain had to be defeated by France in war, because of the weakness of Britain Paine had identified since 1776, because of the military superiority of France he had claimed throughout the 1780s, and above

63 Paine, *Rights of Man, Part the second*, 13.
64 Gouverneur Morris, *The diary and letters*, July 4 1791, I, 429.

all because of the superiority of France's republican government and the republican valour of its populace. War came on 1 February 1793, supported by Paine and his friends and colleagues in the Girondin governments. They were led by Jean-Marie Roland and included the philosopher Condorcet and the merchant Etienne Clavière, both associates of Paine from the late 1780s and supporters like him of the initiatives of the Shelburne circle.[65] They were now agreed that as domestic revolution in Britain had yet to occur, a war against Britain was necessary, to collapse the constitution that represented the greatest threat to the establishment of a global republic and a pacific world founded on cosmopolitan principles. Paine may well have been pushing for war with Britain since 1790, having reputedly written a paper for Lafayette recommending 'an attack in the Channel by the combined fleets'.[66]

V

That Paine had doubts about the republican constitutionalism he had so stridently and confidently advocated in the *Rights of Man*, was suggested in a letter to Thomas Jefferson on 20 April 1793. As the war between France and the First Coalition appeared to be in stalemate, Paine noted that France was disordered internally and that he was thinking of returning home: 'Had this revolution been conducted consistently with its principles, there was once a good prospect of extending liberty through the greatest part of Europe; but I now relinquish that hope.'[67] Military victory by France, Paine said, would of course alter things. But despite French successes in arms over the following months, events did not follow Paine's predictions. The greatest blow was the outbreak of the Terror, which underscored the extent to which Paine's reputedly united republic was internally riven and murderous. The state based on rights violated them in a fashion shocking to every observer. The damage to Paine was direct because he was imprisoned by Robespierre as an enemy of the state in December 1793, and only escaped the guillotine by quirk of fortune. Paine spent almost a year in the Luxembourg prison at Paris, released only after ministrations by the American ambassador James Monroe succeeded in November 1794. Paine later claimed he should be considered, along with Sieyès, almost the sole survivor 'of those who began the revolution, and that through a thousand dangers'.[68]

The additional tragedy for Paine was that while in prison, and just as he was living through the failure of the equality of rights in France by losing his liberty, he began to doubt the republican experiment in America. The reason was highly

[65] R. Whatmore, *Against War and Empire: Geneva, Britain and France in the Eighteenth Century* (New Haven: Yale University Press, 2012), 243–8.

[66] Gouverneur Morris, *The diary and letters*, entry for 15 August, 1790, I, 341.

[67] Paine to Jefferson, 20 April 1793, The Papers of Thomas Jefferson Digital Edition, ed. B. B. Oberg and J. Jefferson Looney (Charlottesville: University of Virginia Press, Rotunda, 2008).

[68] Paine, *Letters to the citizens of the United States* (New York: Printed for the purchasers, 1802), Letter 1.

personal. Paine had almost two decades before renounced Britain and considered himself a citizen of the United States of America. He had been awarded and accepted additionally citizenship in France. Gouverneur Morris, the American ambassador to Paris until April 1794, refused to intervene to help secure Paine's release from prison on the grounds of his citizenship. Morris detested Paine, whom he considered conceited and mad; they met regularly in Paris to provide Paine with information about American affairs.[69] But Paine blamed George Washington for failing to restore his freedom rather than Morris. Paine became convinced not only that Washington was a monarchist, whom he accused of wanting members of his family to inherit the presidency, but also that a Washington-led faction that was antagonistic to republican principles was growing stronger in America. This faction, led by John Adams, was corrupting the country by introducing ideas from the old world, including aristocracy, a standing army, irregular elections, luxury, and controls over trade, and even the aspiration to empire.[70]

Adams was the living embodiment of an alternative vision to Paine's own. Both claimed to be articulating republican ideas for the modern world, but Paine refused to acknowledge that Adams was in any sense a republican, despite the success of the *A defence of the Constitutions of the United States* (1787). Adams had always admired the British constitution and believed that it could be used as a model for modern republican constitutions. Stronger commercial links between the countries was a natural consequence, and Paine attacked Adams's activities to this end, seeing all that he did as an attempt to restore British political traditions in North America.[71] Paine claimed that this led to the definition of a republic as an 'empire of laws and not men'.[72] Adams's mistake, according to Paine, was that bad laws could turn such an empire into 'the worst of all tyrannies'.[73] Such an opposed perspective made Adams a target of Paine's vitriol in his final writings. Adams was equally antagonistic, calling Paine a 'disastrous meteor' and Paine's writings 'profligate and impious'.[74] Looking back from 1805, Adams stated Paine's influence over thirty years had been prodigious. The consequence was that, rather than experiencing an 'age of reason', the 'age of Paine' was accompanied by 'folly, vice, frenzy [and] brutality'.[75] Like so many contemporaries, Adams had from the first found Paine's principles to be excessively democratic and reliant upon popular virtues that could not actually be found. On reading *Common Sense*, Adams noted that he 'dreaded

69 Gouverneur Morris, *The diary and letters*, I, 400, 403, 515.

70 Paine, *A letter from Thomas Paine to George Washington, President of the United States of America* (Philadelphia: Benj. Franklin Bache, 1796), 7–11.

71 Paine, *A letter to George Washington, on the subject of the late treaty concluded between Great-Britain and the United States of America, including other matters* (London: T. Williams, 1797), 17–34.

72 John Adams, *Defense of the constitutions of government of the United States of America* (Boston: T. Williams, 1988), 96–100.

73 Paine, *Letters to the citizens of the United States*, Letter 1.

74 John Adams autobiography, part 1, 'John Adams', through 1776, sheets 9 and 23 of 53 [electronic edition]. *Adams Family Papers: An Electronic Archive.* Massachusetts Historical Society. <http://www.masshist.org/digitaladams/>.

75 John Adams to Benjamin Waterhouse, 29 October 1805, *Statesman and Friend: Correspondence of John Adams with Benjamin Waterhouse, 1784-1822*, ed. W. C. Ford (Boston: Little, Brown, and Co, 1927), 31.

the effect so popular a pamphlet might have, among the People'.[76] Years later he was afraid that Paine's rejection of ranks was tantamount to the destruction of social order and that Paine's zeal for an ill-defined democratic republic would always lead to anarchy and violence.

Paine's response to the double challenge of the rise of the Federalist Party in America and the Jacobins in France was to blame old mores for new corruption. As he put it in 1795, 'All the disorders that have arisen in France during the progress of the Revolution have had their origin, not in the *principle of equal rights*, but in the violation of that principle'.[77] Had a republic been established at the outset of the revolution in France, the later violence would have been avoided because of the greater bond of union between the citizens. At the same time, Paine recognized that measures had to be taken to restore the pacific and cosmopolitan character essential to republican citizenship. The establishment of a republican constitution was no longer sufficient, because priestcraft continued to infect societies whether republican or monarchical. Paine advocated a rational religion founded on the equality of men, teaching the duties of 'justice, loving mercy, and endeavouring to make our fellow-creatures happy'. Arguing that 'my mind is my own church', Paine demanded the closure of all churches on the grounds that they were 'human inventions set up to terrify and enslave mankind and monopolize power and profit'. Paine attacked Christianity as a cause of the ills of the present times, for having inaugurated the 'age of ignorance'. His preference was a form of deism teaching a morality derived from nature, which he associated with the Quakers. Such ideas, appearing in the *Age of Reason*, published on Paine's emergence from the Luxembourg Prison, sought to instil in citizens patriotism capable of distinguishing between enthusiasm and fanaticism, protective of civil liberty and immune to the lust for wealth or fame.[78] Rather than promoting republican constitutionalism, the *Age of Reason* tarnished Paine's name and his politics, as his criticisms of Revelation, the person of Jesus, the Bible, and what he termed the influence of 'dead languages', brought a storm of condemnation.[79]

Paine continued to recognize, however, that his prophetic republicanism was tied directly to the fate of the First French Republic. He continued to predict the imminent demise of Britain in the significant pamphlets *The Decline and fall of the English system of finance* (1796) and *Agrarian justice* (1797). The latter pamphlet was dedicated to the French Directory and noted that 'the present constitution of

[76] John Adams autobiography, part 1, sheet 23, *Adams Family Papers* <http://www.masshist.org/digitaladams/>. Adams commented further: 'The Arguments in favour of Independence I liked very well: but one third of the Book was filled with Arguments from the old Testiment, to prove the Unlawfulness of Monarchy, and another Third, in planning a form of Government, for the seperate States in One Assembly, and for the United States, in a Congress. His Arguments from the old Testiment, were ridiculous, but whether they proceeded from honest Ignorance, and or foolish [Superstition] on one hand, or from wilful Sophistry and knavish Hypocrisy on the other I know not.'

[77] Paine, *Dissertation on First Principles of Government*, 33 (italics in original).

[78] Paine, *The Age of Reason, being an investigation of true and fabulous theology* (London: B. D. Cousins, 1794), 2–4, 73–82, 101–3.

[79] Jack R. Fruchtman, *Thomas Paine and the Religion of Nature* (Baltimore: Johns Hopkins University Press, 1993), 150–63.

the French Republic [is] the *best organised system* the human mind has yet produced' (italics in original). Paine's only criticism was that the Constitution of 1795 violated 'the equality of the right of suffrage' and in doing so diminished 'the enthusiasm that right is capable of inspiring'. Only universal manhood suffrage would create a stable and united polity. Paine continued to be involved in the Directory's plans for the invasion of England from 1798 and argued that France would defeat Britain in war because of the tyrannical nature of Britain's government and the superiority of the French Republic.[80]

The popularity of Paine's political writings, and more especially the *Rights of Man*, which was regularly reprinted into the 1840s, did more to resuscitate republican constitutionalism than any other work. By a republic Paine meant universal manhood suffrage, a constitution in which all powers were limited and subject to the choice of the people, and regular elections. But as significant was what had to be abolished in Paine's republic, including monarchy, aristocracy, national churches, luxury, and excessive wealth. Paine claimed consistency, but in fact the context in which he believed his republic could survive altered radically. In the 1770s he believed that only America, because of its unique position, could support republican government. In the 1780s he believed that European states could be reformed, but not by revolution or domestic upheaval. Only the commencement of the French Revolution and its early turbulence led him to formulate a plan for the transformation of all states into pacific and cosmopolitan republics. Revolution to inaugurate a republican constitution was the means to the higher end of developing commerce and perpetual peace.

As successive revolutions failed, Paine added greatly to his constitutional thought, demanding the institution of measures for the prevention of luxury and for establishing moderate wealth, and for putting an end to what he saw to be the corruption inherent in contemporary religious belief. Above all, Paine began to blame Britain for sustaining anti-republican ideas and non-republican states. War upon Britain became the surest means to make Paine's republican vision a reality. Paine was disheartened by the fact that people in North America and in France had not adhered to the declarations of rights and constitutions that had been established. He dreamt of a world in which politicians and legislators were forever being scrutinized by the people, and evaluated by reference to foundational national documents, which would themselves be periodically revised by the people. But as he saw the zeal for liberty decline or become tarnished he became more interested in other means of making people free, and it might be said that he broadened the very nature of constitutional theorizing in consequence. Without a transition mechanism to establish a free state and clear measures to maintain it constitutional thought was bankrupt. This was the problem with Sieyès's thought, which had given too much authority to the revolutionary legislators themselves, thereby introducing the risk of Terror as political actors became corrupted by power and refused to maintain the equality of rights.

[80] Paine, *A letter to the English people, on the invasion of England* (London: W. T. Sherwin, [May 1804] 1817), 7–10.

Paine believed he had provided a diagnosis of what was wrong with contemporary society and a clear explanation of why the revolutionary experiments of the final decades of the eighteenth century were unstable. Others felt that Paine, being a political actor himself and an author of the revolutions, failed himself. He had become an arch-critic of North American politics by the turn of the century and the state he was more associated with than any other, republican France, experienced crisis after crisis. When he returned to America, many treated him with contempt because of his unorthodox religious views, but more particularly because his politics had been so unsuccessful in Europe. Bonaparte, despite personal praise for Paine and his work, could not be represented as the culmination of Paine's republican vision before or after he had proclaimed himself Emperor of the French. Paine then turned his back on Europe. He returned to the argument of *Common Sense*, attacking federalism in America and arguing that Thomas Jefferson's politics and philosophy was the only hope for republican liberty. Europe was once again a lost continent. Future generations of radicals who continued to espouse a Paineite vision of republican government—in which the people were directly involved in politics, where elections were regular, and where the transition mechanism to such a state was a constitutional refounding, abolishing monarchy and aristocracy—had to work out why his democratic ideas had come to nothing and what might be done to make them effective. Paine's immediate legacy was the association of his republican philosophy with mob violence, civil and international war, religious and civil disunity, and political turbulence.

Index

accountability of officials
  Bentham 244–6
Adams, J. W. 24, 191–209
Adams, John 32, 42, 43, 48–50, 335, 363, 389–413, 412–13, 434–5
  background 389–92
  chapter 389–413
  constitution 403–5, 409
  constitutionalism 392–7, 400
  democracy, version of 389 *see also* people
  executive 405–8
  people
    government by 397–402
    preserving popular government 399–403
  republicanism 390–1
  rights, bill of 408–9
  sovereignty 398ff, 405
Adams, John Quincy 343–4
agreement of the people 147–151
Aquinas, Thomas 10
arbitrariness 136–40, 204

Bailey, Bernard 327
Baker, Keith 298
Balkin, Jack 326
Bentham, Jeremy 7, 28–30, 231–49
  accountability of officials 244–6
  background 231–3
  branches of government, relations among 248–9
  chapter on 231–49
  constitution
    meaning of 234
    purpose of 236–9
  courts 247–8
  legislative and executive power 246–7
  people 239–42
  public opinion tribunal 240–2
  representative democracy 233, 240
  sovereignty 242–4
  sinister interests of rulers 236–9
Blackstone, William 23, 25–7, 35, 36, 41, 209–30
  background 210–4
  chapter on 210–30
  constitution
    balanced 224–5
    nature of 214–19
    rights, protection of 220–2
  courts 226–7
  English constitution, origins and evolution 215–19
  institutions of government 219–27
  parliament, sovereignty of 223–4
  prerogative power 224–5
  public finance 225–6
  rights, protection of 220–2
Bork, Robert 332, 352
Bradley, Owen 313
Burke, Edmund 27–8, 31, 41

Coke, Edward 18–20, 86–107, 358
  accountability 96–8
  career 87–9
  English constitution, view of 94–6
  institutions of government 96–8
  judicial independence 102–5
  parliament 98–102
  political thought 92–4
  writings 89–92
common good
  Madison on 340–4
Constant, Benjamin 37
constituent power
  Sieyès 300ff
Constitution
  Adams on 403–9
  ancient constitution 69–71
  Bentham on 231–49
  Blackstone on 214–19
  Coke on 94–5
  de Maistre on 313ff
  English
    de Maistre on 322
    Hamilton on 360
    Montesquieu on 257–8
  Jefferson 377ff
  Levellers' notion of 136–44
  Montesquieu on 253–8
  nature of 1–2, 152–4
  Rousseau on 271–5
  Sieyès on 293–7
  symbol, as 323–5
constitutionalism
  Adams on 392–7, 400
  democratic 327–8
  Hamilton on 358–60, 366–8
  Madison on 327–8, 340ff
  meaning 152–4
  Paine on 432–3, 436
  republican 340ff

conventions
  Hume on 200
courts
  Bentham on 247–8
  Blackstone on 226–7
  Harrington on 186–7
Crevecoeur, Hector 341

Dahl, Robert 328–9, 342–3
de Maistre 31, 41–2, 312–26
  background 310–14
  chapter on 310–26
  constitutions
    design of 320–1
    indigenous 313, 318–21
    irrational nature of 321–3
    symbol, as 323–5
    universal nature, against 319–20
    constitutional ideas, origins 316–8
    people, no role in constitution-making 324–5
Davis, Colin 22, 169–90
democracy
  Adams 389
  Montesquieu 255–6
  Rousseau 275–7

Elkin, Stephen 340
Elster, Jon 325
English constitution
  Coke on 94–6
Executive power *see* legislative power
  Adams 408

federalism 360–2
  Jefferson 371–3
Federalist, The Federalist Papers 43, 327ff, 360–2
Ferguson, Adam 27
Fortescue, John 10–11, 51–85
  background to views 56–9
  English dominium 62–7
  King 74–81
  law 67–74
  main works 52, 59
  politicum dominium 51–85
  views 51–85
French Revolution 434ff

Galligan, D. J. 122–51
general will
  Rousseau 265–87, 289
  Sieyès on 40
government
  limited, Rousseau on 277–83
Graber, Mark 44, 327–53
Grottanelli de'Santi, Giovanni 33, 250–64
Guinier, Lani 352

Hamilton, Alexander 32, 42, 43, 45–6, 335, 347, 354–68
  background 354–8
  British constitution 360
  chapter on 354–68
  constitutionalism 358–60, 366–8
  continentalism 356–8
  federal government 359–60
  federalism 360–62
  Federalist, writings in 360–62
  judicial independence 365–6
  republicanism 362–4
  rule of law 364–6
Hardin, Russell 35
Harrington, James 17, 22–3, 169–90
  background 169–76
  chapter on 169–90
  complexity of 187–9
  constitution, nature of 176–80
  courts 186–7
  legislative and executive 186
  main writings 169–70
  motion, centrality of 180ff
  Oceana, republic of 169–90
  participatory government 178ff
  people, place of 180ff
  property, critical role of 180ff
  sovereignty 184–6
  success of a republic, conditions of 183–4
Hart, John 347
Henry, Patrick 348
Hobbes, Thomas 6, 7, 14–15, 36, 107–21, 154–5
  Aristotle, critique of 108–9, 117–21
  chapter on 108–21
  constitutions, writings on 111–14
  government, purpose of 110–11
  science of politics 117–121
  sovereignty 113–7
Hooker, Richard 12–13
Hunton, Philip 166–7
Hume, David 7, 23–5, 31, 35, 41
  background 191–8
  chapter on 191–209
  common law 206
  conventions 200, 202–3, 208
  human nature, centrality to constitutions 198–200
  law, importance of 205
  mixed constitution 205
  perfect commonwealth, idea of 203
  utility, importance of 199–200

Jay, John 360
Jefferson, Thomas 25, 31, 42, 43, 46–7, 347,354, 369–88, 433

background 369–70
chapter on 369–88
constitution 377
education 376
federalism 371–3
law 376–8, 380
people 377–9, 387 *see also* sovereignty of the people
political parties 384–5, 387
republicanism 373–9
rights, protection of 380–1
separation of powers 376
slavery 373–9, 386
sovereignty, of the people 374–5, 383–4

John of Salisbury 10
Judicial independence
Coke on 102–5
Hamilton on 365–6

Kelly, M. R. L. L. 11–12, 51–85
king
Fortescue, on 74–81
Konig, David 48, 389–413
Kubben, Raymond 38, 290–311

law
fundamental law 138–40
Hume on 205
importance of in the constitution 136–40
Jefferson 376–8, 380
Levellers 136ff
Paine 418
rule of law
Rousseau 283ff

Lawson, George 164–5
legislative and executive powers
Bentham 247–8
Madison 336
Montesquieu 258–9
Rousseau 279ff
Sieyès 309

Leonard, Gerald 46, 369–88
Levellers
agreement of the people 147–51
arbitrariness 136–40
background 122–4, 126–8
chapter on 122–51
constitution
competing conceptions 133–6
nature and purpose of 129–33
constitutional context 128–9
law
fundamental law 138–40
place of 136–40
people 140–51
relevance of 124–6
representation 142–7

Liberty
two views 38
Lilburne, John 21
Locke, John 7, 15–18, 36, 152–68, 267
chapter on 152–68
consent 167
limiting government 155–63
people, place of 159–62
political society 163–8
right of resistance 165–8

Mably, Abbe de 361
Machiavelli, Nicolo' 421
Madison, James 6, 17, 31, 42, 43–4, 327–53
background 327–32
chapter on 327–53
common good 340–4
constitutionalism
democratic version 351–2
republican 330–2, 343, 351–3
democracy, nature of 327–32, 343
faction, problem of 342
legislative power 336
popular government 336–7
representation
virtuous 339–40
representative government
preferable form of government 337–8
representatives, character of 337
republic
nature of 327–32, 332, 351–3
utility of 333–5
republicanism *see* republic
rights
bondholders, rights of 345–6
free speech 349–50
property 344–7
religion 347–9
republican 344–51
separation of powers 335–6

Marsilius of Padua 10
Merton, Robert 326
Michelman, Frank 32–77
Monroe, John 433
Montesquieu 26, 32–3, 248–64
background 250–3
chapter on 250–264
constitutions
English constitution 257–8
nature of 253–5
democracy and self-government 255–6
freedom, liberty 260–3
L'Esprit des Lois 252–3
governments, nature of 253–5
legislative power 258–9
people 256–7
separation of powers 257–60

Montesquieu (*cont.*)
virtue, necessity for republican government 255–6
More, Thomas 12

nation
concept of 39
Sieyès on 39, 296ff

Overton, Richard 21

Paine, Thomas 7, 32, 49–50, 152, 414–37
background 414–29
chapter 414–37
constitutionalism 432–3, 436
law 418
monarchy 430
republicanism 420–1, 423–5, 429–30, 435–6
rights, equality of 418
Rights of Man 429ff
Sieyès, debate with 416ff, 431
Palmer, Claire 1–50
Parliament
Blackstone on 223–4
Coke on 98–102
sovereignty of 28, 223–4
people *see* ruling, self-rule
Adams 397–403
Bentham on 239–42
de Maistre 324–5
Fortescue 51–85
idealist approach 5–10
Harrington, view of 180ff
Jefferson 377–9, 380
Locke, view of 159–64
Madison 336
Montesquieu 256–7
participation, Harrington's views 178ff
pragmatic approach 5–10
sovereignty of 160
Perry, William, Earl of Shelburne 425–8
political parties
Jefferson 384–5, 387
popular government *see* people
pragmatic approach to constitutions 5–10, 35
Prest, Wilfrid 26, 210–30
Price, Richard 425
public opinion tribunal
Bentham on 242–4

Rainsborough, Thomas 149
Rakove, Jack 345
Representation *see also* representative government
Bentham on 233, 240
Levellers' approach to 142–7
Rousseau 280ff
Sieyès on 39–40, 307ff
representative government
Madison 337ff
Rousseau on 280–3
Sieyès on 306
republic
Hamilton on 362–4
Madison on 327ff
republicanism *see* republic
Adams 390ff
Jefferson 373–5
Madison 327ff
rights
Adams 408–9
Blackstone 220–2
free speech 349–50
Jefferson 380–1
Madison 344ff
Paine 418ff
property 344–7
republican 344–51
religion 347–9
Rousseau 286ff
Robespierre 433
Rodrik, Danny 326
Rousseau, Jean-Jacques 31, 34–8, 160, 265–89
chapter on 265–89
constitution
association of the general will, constitution for 273–5
creation of 271
culture, importance of 273–5
democracy
association of the general will, relation to 275–7
executive power 281
general will 265, 268–9
institutions, safeguards, as 277–83
legislator
constitution, relation to 271–2
nature of 270–2
legislative power 279
limited government 277–83
popular sovereignty 265–9
representation
representative government 280–3
sovereignty, relation to 275–6
rights, protection of 286–9
rule of law
Hamilton on 364–6
place of 283–5
sovereignty, in relation to 285
separation of powers 282
social contract 265–8
sovereignty
absolute 267
government, relation to 275–7
identity 272
Jefferson 376
popular 265–9

ruling
  ruling and being ruled 4–10
  self-rule 5–10
rule of law
  Rousseau 286ff

sinister interests of rulers 236–9
Schauer, Fred 325
Schofeld, Philip 30, 231–49
Sellers, Mortimer 42, 354–68
Self-rule 5–10
separation of powers
  Madison 335–6
  Montesquieu on 257–60
  Rousseau 282ff
  Sieyès 310
Sexby, Richard 21
Sieyès, Emmanuel 3, 38–4, 289–311
  background 289–93
  chapter on 289–311
  constituent power 300ff
    representation of 300–2
  constitution
    nature of 293–7
  legislative power 309
  nation
    constitution, relation to 299
    formation of 296ff
    nature of 302
    Third Estate, relation to 305
  Paine, controversy with 416–18, 431
  representation 300ff
    centrality of 307–11
    constituent power, representation of 300–2
    extraordinary 301–2
    liberty, relation to 308ff
  representative government
    people, relation to 306
  separation of powers 310–11
Sieyès, Emmanuel 3, 38–4, 289–311
Simmons, John 167
Slavery, Jefferson on 373–9, 386
Smilove, Ruzha 36, 265–89
Smith, Adam 7, 41, 425
Smith, Rogers 340
Smith, Thomas 12
social contract
  Rousseau 265ff
Sorell, Tom 14, 108–21
sovereignty
  Adams 398ff
  Bentham on 242–4
  Harrington, view of 184–6
  Jefferson 374–5, 383–4
  parliamentary 28
  people, sovereignty of 9–10, 242–4, 374–55, 383–4
  popular
    Locke on 160
    Rousseau 265–9
  Rousseau 37, 267ff
Spitz, Jean-Fabien 14, 152–68
St Germain, Christopher 12
Stuart, Charles: King Charles I 8, 31
Sunstein, Cass 325, 327, 332, 352
Sydney, Algernon 18

Trenchard, John 327

utility
  Hume on 199–200

Vaughan, Benjamin 428
Versteeg, Mila 41, 312–26
Vico, Giambattista 7, 41
virtue, republican
  Montesquieu 255–6

Waldron, Jeremy 286–8
Walwyn, William 21
Washington, George 355, 366
Whatmore, Richard 49, 414–38
Wildma, John 21
William of Ockham 10
Williams, Ian 18, 86–107
Wood, Gordon 327, 335, 349, 352

Yates, Robert 359

The manufacturer's authorised representative in the EU for product safety is Oxford University Press España S.A. of el Parque Empresarial San Fernando de Henares, Avenida de Castilla, 2 – 28830 Madrid (www.oup.es/en or product.safety@oup.com). OUP España S.A. also acts as importer into Spain of products made by the manufacturer.

www.ingramcontent.com/pod-product-compliance
Lightning Source LLC
LaVergne TN
LVHW011903200926
848484LV00002B/508

9780198714989

